The Word Book II

The Word Book II

BASED ON THE *NEW* AMERICAN HERITAGE DICTIONARY

compiled by
Kaethe Ellis

Houghton Mifflin Company · Boston

All correspondence and inquiries
should be directed to
Reference Division
Houghton Mifflin Company
One Beacon Street, Boston, MA 02108

Library of Congress Cataloging in Publication Data

Ellis, Kaethe, 1943–
  The word book II.

  1. Spellers. 2. English language—Pronunciation.
3. English language—Syllabication. I. Title.

PE1146.E43 1983   428.1   83-8501
ISBN 0-395-34028-4

Contents

Houghton Mifflin Company
Reference Division

Margery S. Berube
Director of Editorial Operations

Mark H. Boyer	Kaethe Ellis	Diane J. Neely
Project Editor	**Revision Editor**	**Traffic Coordinator**

Editorial Assistants   **Proofreading**

Caroline L. Becker   Judith L. Drummond
Laura A. Tweedale   Deborah Karacozian

Art Director
Geoffrey Hodgkinson

How to Use This Book

The Word Book II presents basic information about the most commonly used words in the English language: how to spell a word, how to divide a word into syllables, and which syllables are stressed when a word is pronounced. The list of more than 40,000 words contained in this new edition is drawn from *The American Heritage Dictionary: Second College Edition*. Word selection is based on the latest computer frequency studies developed by Houghton Mifflin Company, a leader in dictionary publishing and a pioneer in the creation of computer software for spelling verification and correction.

Obsolete, rare, and archaic forms have not been included in *The Word Book II*. Many colloquial words and technical and scientific terms, particularly those in common use, have been entered. Proper names and nouns have been omitted unless they appear as part of another, frequently used compound.

Normally, one-syllable words have not been entered, unless they present spelling difficulties, may be confused with another word, have irregular inflected forms, or do not appear elsewhere in the book as part of a compound form.

The Word Book II also has special features that will save you time and effort: a guide to the formation of plurals, an explanation of the Seven Basic Rules of Spelling, a Sound Map that will aid you in finding words that you know how to pronounce but are not sure how to spell. In addition, there is other useful information: an alphabetical list of the most commonly used abbreviations, an explanation of proofreading symbols, a table of weights and measures, and a guide to the often-confusing metric system.

Although *The Word Book II* is simple to use, the following guide will help you make the maximum utilization of its special benefits and features.

DIVISION OF WORDS

The Word Book II clearly shows how a word may be divided into syllables. Such divisions are indicated by a centered dot, by an accent mark, or by a hyphen:

ce·ment'   e·vap'o·ra'tion   top'sy-tur'vy

Note: Whenever a hyphen is indicated in an entry word, that hyphen is part of the word, and must be retained when the word is used.

At the end of a line of type, a word may be broken wherever a syllable division is indicated. However, it is good English practice to observe these exceptions:

a. A syllable consisting of a single letter should not be separated from the rest of the word, as in:

a·bide'   stealth'y

(Many typesetters also consider it bad practice to separate initial or final syllables of two letters, such as the prefix *un-* or the suffix *-er*. If possible, it is better to avoid such divisions.)

b. A hyphenated word should be divided only at the hyphen.

A MATTER OF STRESS

The Word Book II indicates whenever a syllable is stressed in pronunciation. Two different stress marks are used. The first, a boldface stress, indicates the syllable that receives the primary stress in the word:

cen'ter   le'gal

Normally, only one syllable in a word receives primary stress. However, certain compound words may have more than one primary stress. *The Word Book II* will aid you in such cases.

The second mark, a lighter stress, indicates syllables that are not as strong as the one marked with a primary stress, but are still stronger than unmarked syllables:

def′i·ni′tion   re·gen′er·a′tion

At times, syllable stress depends on how a word is used; for example:

rec′ord (noun)   pre·fix′ (verb)
re·cord′ (verb)   pre′fix′ (noun)

The Word Book II indicates when such a shift in stress occurs; it also indicates whenever a plural form has an added stress or a shift in stress:

for′mu·la *pl.*
-las *or* -lae′

INFLECTED FORMS

In *The Word Book II* all irregular inflected forms have been included at the main entry for that word. These irregular inflected forms include noun plurals; the past tense, past participle, and present participle of verbs; and comparative and superlative forms of adjectives whenever the syllabic division of such a word changes. Such irregular forms—except, of course, in the case of one-syllable entries or forms—have been "clipped," or shortened, to save space:

ac′ti·vate′, -vat′ed,
  -vat′ing
brave, brav′er,
  brav′est
bring, brought,
  bring′ing

ce′cum *pl.* -ca
fly, flew, flown,
  fly′ing
po′di·um *pl.* -di·a
  or -di·ums

swim, swam,
  swum, swim′ming
wake, woke,
  waked *or* woke
  or wok′en,
  wak′ing

In the above examples, you will notice that verbs may have two or three added inflected forms. If only two forms are given, the first is both the past tense and the past participle (e.g., *brought*); if three forms are given, the first is the past tense, the second the past participle (e.g., *swam*—past tense; *swum*—past participle). If there are alternate forms for inflected forms, these are also shown (e.g., the alternate plurals *-dia* or *-diums* for *podium*; the alternate past participles *waked* or *woke* or *woken* for *wake*).

Note: Words chosen for inclusion in *The Word Book II* show the most complicated forms of that particular word. Consequently words such as *package* appear as a verb:

pack'age, -aged, -ag·ing

However, *package* is also a noun, and may be used as a modifier, or adjective. In such cases, *The Word Book II* includes only the part of speech that has irregular inflected forms, unless the stress pattern or word division changes.

WORDS LIKELY TO BE CONFUSED OR MISUSED

In *The Word Book II*, glosses, or short identifying definition, are given for all pairs or sets of words that are likely to be confused. If the words are separated alphabetically, cross-references to the other words are included.

Such words fall into three categories:

a. Homophones, or words that are pronounced precisely the same, but are spelled differently:

yew *(tree)*   Yule *(Christmas)*
   ◆ *ewe, you*   ◆ *you'll*

(**Note:** many such sets of homophones are given even though one of the words does not have a separate entry.)

b. Words that are likely to be confused because they are closely related in spelling or pronunciation:

ac·cept *(to receive)*
  ◆ *except*

a·dopt' *(to choose)*
  ◆ *adapt, adept*

c. Troublesome words whose meanings are likely to be misused:

bi·week'ly *(once
  in two weeks)*
  ◆ *semiweekly*

sem'i·week'ly
  (twice a week)
  ◆ *biweekly*

Should such words fall in regular alphabetical order, only the gloss is shown:

co'co *(palm tree)*
co'coa *(beverage)*

toil *(labor)*
toile *(fabric)*

These glosses will help you quickly identify and locate the work you want. For further information on the usage of words, a dictionary should be consulted.

VARIANTS

The Word Book II includes variant spellings of words whenever these different spellings are in common use in English. Such variant spellings appear only at the main entry for that word. If the variants are used almost equally, they appear as follows:

clay'ey *or* clay'ish

For most words, however, one form is preferred over the other:

out'size' *also*
  out'sized'

o'ver·all' *also*
  o'ver-all'

As noted above in the section on inflected forms, all variant verb forms and plurals are also indicated.

PREFIXES

Many words that have prefixes like *self-* and *un-* have been included in *The Word Book II*, but it is impossible to include all such words. However, most prefixes follow regular rules when they are combined with other words. The following is a brief guide to the most commonly used prefixes.

Prefix	*Compounds are usually formed:*
anti- non- pre- pro- semi- un-	Without a hyphen, unless the prefix is followed by a capital letter.
out- over-	Without a hyphen.
re-	Without a hyphen, unless a distinction must be made between a word in which the prefix means "again" or "anew" and a word that has a special meaning: *re-creation* and *recreation*.
self-	With a hyphen.

A

aard'vark'
a·back'
ab'a·cus pl. -cus·es or
  -ci'
a·baft'
ab'a·lo'ne
a·ban'don
a·ban'doned
a·base', a·based',
  a·bas'ing
a·bash'
a·bate', a·bat'ed,
  a·bat'ing
ab'at·toir'
ab'ba·cy pl. -cies
ab'bé
ab'bess
ab'bey pl. -beys
ab'bot
ab·bre'vi·ate', -at'ed,
  -at'ing
ab·bre'vi·a'tion
ab·bre'vi·a'tor
ab'di·cate', -cat'ed,
  -cat'ing
ab'di·ca'tion
ab'di·ca'tor
ab'do·men
ab·dom'i·nal
ab·duct'
ab·duc'tion
ab·duc'tor
a·beam'
a·be·ce·dar'i·an

a·bed'
ab·er'rant
ab'er·ra'tion
a·bet', a·bet'ted, a·bet'-
  ting
a·bet'tor also a·bet'ter
a·bey'ance
ab·hor', -horred',
  -hor'ring
ab·hor'rence
ab·hor'rent
a·bide', a·bode' or
  a·bid'ed, a·bid'ing
a·bil'i·ty
ab'ject'
ab·jec'tion
ab·jure' (to renounce),
  -jured', -jur'ing
  ♦adjure
ab·la'tion
ab'la·tive
a·blaze'
a'ble
a'ble-bod'ied
a·bloom'
ab·lu'tion
ab'ne·gate', -gat'ed,
  -gat'ing
ab'ne·ga'tion
ab·nor'mal
ab'nor·mal'i·ty
a·board'
a·bode'
a·bol'ish
ab'o·li'tion
ab'o·li'tion·ar'y
ab'o·li'tion·ism

ab'o·li'tion·ist
A'-bomb'
a·bom'i·na·ble
a·bom'i·nate', -nat'ed,
  -nat'ing
a·bom'i·na'tion
a·bom'i·na'tor
ab'o·rig'i·nal
ab'o·rig'i·ne'
a·bort'
a·bor'tion
a·bor'tion·ist
a·bor'tive
a·bound'
a·bout'
a·bout'-face'
a·bove'
a·bove'board'
a·bove'ground'
ab'ra·ca·dab'ra
a·brade', a·brad'ed,
  a·brad'ing
a·bra'sion
a·bra'sive
a·breast'
a·bridge', a·bridged',
  a·bridg'ing
a·bridg'er
a·bridg'ment also
  a·bridge'ment
a·broad'
ab'ro·gate', -gat'ed,
  -gat'ing
ab'ro·ga'tion
a·brupt'
ab'scess'

ab·scise′, -scised′,
 -scis′ing
ab·scis′sa *pl.* -sas *or*
 -sae
ab·scis′sion
ab·scond′
ab′sence
ab′sent
ab′sen·tee′
ab′sen·tee′ism
ab′sent-mind′ed
ab′sinthe
ab′so·lute′
ab′so·lute′ly
ab′so·lu′tion
ab′so·lut′ism
ab′so·lut′ist
ab′so·lu·tis′tic
ab·solv′a·ble
ab·solve′, -solved′,
 -solv′ing
ab·solv′er
ab·sorb′ *(to take in)*
 ♦adsorb
ab·sorb′en·cy
ab·sorb′ent
ab·sorp′tion
ab·sorp′tive
ab·stain′
ab·ste′mi·ous
ab·sten′tion
ab′sti·nence
ab′sti·nent
ab′stract′ *adj.*
ab′stract′ *n.*
ab·stract′ *(to remove)*

ab′stract′ *(to summa-
 rize)*
ab·stract′ed
ab·strac′tion
ab·strac′tion·ism
ab·strac′tion·ist
ab·struse′
ab·surd′
ab·surd′i·ty
a·bun′dance
a·bun′dant
a·buse′, a·bused′,
 a·bus′ing
a·bus′er
a·bu′sive
a·but′, a·but′ted,
 a·but′ting
a·but′ment
a·but′ter
a·bysm′
a·bys′mal *(unfathoma-
 ble, extreme)*
 ♦abyssal
a·byss′
a·bys′sal *(unfathoma-
 ble, of oceanic
 depths)*
 ♦abysmal
a·ca′cia
ac′a·deme′
ac′a·de′mi·a
ac′a·dem′ic
ac′a·de·mi′cian
ac′a·dem′i·cism *also*
 a·cad′e·mism
a·cad′e·my

a·can′thus *pl.* -thus·es
 or -thi′
a′ cap·pel′la
ac·cede′ *(to agree)*,
 -ced′ed, -ced′ing
 ♦exceed
ac·ced′ence
ac·ced′er
ac·cel′er·ate′, -at′ed,
 -at′ing
ac·cel′er·a′tion
ac·cel′er·a′tive
ac·cel′er·a′tor
ac·cel′er·om′e·ter
ac′cent′
ac·cen′tu·al
ac·cen′tu·ate′, -at′ed,
 -at′ing
ac·cen′tu·a′tion
ac·cept′ *(to receive)*
 ♦except
ac·cept′a·bil′i·ty
ac·cept′a·ble
ac·cep′tance
ac′cep·ta′tion
ac·cess′ *(entrance)*
 ♦excess
ac·ces′si·bil′i·ty
ac·ces′si·ble
ac·ces′sion
ac′ces·so′ri·al
ac′ces·so·ry
ac′ci·dence
ac′ci·dent
ac′ci·den′tal
ac′ci·dent-prone′
ac·claim′

ac·cla·ma'tion *(praise)*
  ♦*acclimation*
ac·clam'a·to'ry
ac·cli'mate', -mat'ed,
  -mat'ing
ac·cli·ma'tion *(adaptation)*
  ♦*acclamation*
ac·cli'ma·ti·za'tion
ac·cli'ma·tize', -tized',
  -tiz'ing
ac·cliv'i·ty
ac'co·lade'
ac·com'mo·date',
  -dat'ed, -dat'ing
ac·com'mo·da'tion
ac·com'mo·da'tive
ac·com'pa·ni·ment
ac·com'pa·nist
ac·com'pa·ny, -nied,
  -ny'ing
ac·com'plice
ac·com'plish
ac·com'plish·ment
ac·cord'
ac·cor'dance
ac·cord'ing·ly
ac·cor'di·on
ac·cor'di·on·ist
ac·cost'
ac·count'
ac·count'a·bil'i·ty
ac·count'a·ble
ac·count'ant
ac·count'ing
ac·cou'ter
ac·cou'ter·ment

ac·cred'it
ac·cred'i·ta'tion
ac·cre'tion
ac·cru'al
ac·crue', -crued', -cru'-
  ing
ac·cul'tur·ate', -at'ed,
  -at'ing
ac·cul'tur·a'tion
ac·cu'mu·late', -lat'ed,
  -lat'ing
ac·cu'mu·la'tion
ac·cu'mu·la'tive
ac·cu'mu·la'tor
ac'cu·ra·cy
ac'cu·rate
ac·curs'ed *also* ac·
  curst'
ac'cu·sa'tion
ac·cu'sa·tive
ac·cu'sa·to'ri·al
ac·cuse', -cused', -cus'-
  ing
ac·cus'er
ac·cus'tom
ace
a·cerb'
ac'er·bate', -bat'ed,
  -bat'ing
a·cer'bic
a·cer'bi·ty
ac'et·al'de·hyde'
ac'e·tate'
a·ce'tic *(of acetic acid)*
  ♦*ascetic*
ac'e·tone'
a·ce'tyl

a·cet'y·lene'
a·ce'tyl·sal'i·cyl'ic
  acid
ache, ached, ach'ing
a·chieve', a·chieved',
  a·chiev'ing
a·chieve'ment
a·chiev'er
A·chil'les
ach'ro·mat'ic
ac'id
a·cid'ic
a·cid'i·fi·ca'tion
a·cid'i·fy', -fied', -fy'-
  ing
a·cid'i·ty
ac'i·do'sis
a·cid'u·late', -lat'ed,
  -lat'ing
a·cid'u·la'tion
a·cid'u·lous
ac·knowl'edge,
  -edged, -edg·ing
ac·knowl'edge·a·ble
ac·knowl'edg·ment
  also ac·knowl'edge·
  ment
ac'me
ac'ne
ac'o·lyte'
ac'o·nite'
a'corn'
a·cous'tic *also* a·cous'-
  ti·cal
a·cous'tics
ac·quaint'
ac·quain'tance

ac·quaint'ed
ac'qui·esce', -esced',
  -esc'ing
ac'qui·es'cence
ac'qui·es'cent
ac·quir'a·ble
ac·quire', -quired',
  -quir'ing
ac'qui·si'tion
ac·quis'i·tive
ac·quit', -quit'ted,
  -quit'ting
ac·quit'tal
ac·quit'tance
a'cre
a'cre·age
a'cre-foot'
ac'rid
a·crid'i·ty
ac'ri·mo'ni·ous
ac'ri·mo'ny
ac'ro·bat'
ac'ro·bat'ic
ac'ro·bat'ics
ac'ro·nym'
ac'ro·pho'bi·a
a·crop'o·lis
a·cross'
a·cross'-the-board'
a·cros'tic
a·cryl'ic acid
ACTH
ac'tin
act'ing
ac·tin'ic
ac'ti·nide'
ac·tin'i·um

ac'tion
ac'tion·a·ble
ac'ti·vate', -vat'-
  ed,-vat'ing
ac'ti·va'tion
ac'ti·va'tor
ac'tive
ac'tiv·ism
ac'tiv·ist
ac·tiv'i·ty
ac'tor
ac'tress
ac'tu·al
ac'tu·al'i·ty
ac'tu·ar'y
ac'tu·ate', -at'ed, -at'-
  ing
ac'tu·a'tion
ac'tu·a'tor
a·cu'i·ty
a·cu'men
ac'u·punc'ture
a·cute'
ad (advertisement)
  ♦add
ad'age
a·da'gio pl. -gios
ad'a·mant
ad'a·man'tine'
a·dapt' (to adjust)
  ♦adept, adopt
a·dapt'a·bil'i·ty
a·dapt'a·ble
ad'ap·ta'tion
a·dapt'er also a·dap'-
  tor
a·dap'tive

add (to total)
  ♦ad
ad'dax'
ad'dend'
ad·den'dum pl. -da
add'er (one that adds)
ad'der (snake)
ad'der's-tongue'
ad·dict' v.
ad'dict n.
ad·dic'tion
ad·dic'tive
add'ing machine
ad·di'tion (increase)
  ♦edition
ad'di·tive
ad'dle, -dled, -dling
ad·dress'
ad'dress·ee'
ad·dress'er also ad·
  dres'sor
ad·duce', -duced',
  -duc'ing
ad·duct'
ad·duc'tion
ad'e·nine'
ad'e·noid'
ad'e·noi'dal
a·den'o·sine'
a·dept' (skillful)
  ♦adapt, adopt
ad·ept' (expert)
ad'e·qua·cy
ad'e·quate
ad·here' (to stick),
  -hered', -her'ing
  ♦cohere

ad•her′ence
ad•her′ent
ad•he′sion
ad•he′sive
ad hoc′
ad ho′mi•nem
ad′i•a•bat′ic
a•di′das® *also* A•di′-
  das
a•dieu′ *(good-by), pl.*
  a•dieus′ *or* a•dieux′
  ♦*ado*
ad in•fi′ni•tum
a′di•os′
ad′i•pose′
ad•ja′cen•cy
ad•ja′cent
ad•jec•ti′val
ad′jec•tive
ad•join′
ad•join′ing
ad•journ′
ad•journ′ment
ad•judge′, -judged′,
  -judg′ing
ad•ju′di•cate′, -cat′ed,
  -cat′ing
ad•ju′di•ca′tion
ad•ju′di•ca′tive
ad•ju′di•ca′tor
ad′junct′
ad•junc′tive
ad′ju•ra′tion
ad•jure′ *(to entreat),*
  -jured′, -jur′ing
  ♦*abjure*
ad•just′

ad•just′a•ble
ad•just′er *also* ad•jus′-
  tor
ad•just′ment
ad′ju•tant
ad-lib′, -libbed′, -lib′-
  bing
ad-lib′ber
ad′man′
ad•min′is•ter
ad•min′is•tra′tion
ad•min′is•tra′tive
ad•min′is•tra′tor
ad′mi•ra•ble
ad′mi•ral
ad′mi•ral•ty
ad′mi•ra′tion
ad•mire′, -mired′,
  -mir′ing
ad•mir′er
ad•mis′si•ble
ad•mis′sion
ad•mit′, -mit′ted,
  -mit′ting
ad•mit′tance
ad•mit′ted•ly
ad•mix′
ad•mix′ture
ad•mon′ish
ad•mon′ish•ment
ad′mo•ni′tion
ad•mon′i•to′ry
ad nau′se•am
a•do′ *(fuss)*
  ♦*adieu*
a•do′be
ad′o•les′cence

ad′o•les′cent
A•don′is
a•dopt′ *(to take as
  one's own)*
  ♦*adapt, adept*
a•dop′tion
a•dop′tive
a•dor′a•ble
ad′o•ra′tion
a•dore′, a•dored′,
  a•dor′ing
a•dor′er
a•dorn′
ad•re′nal
a•dren′a•line
a•drift′
a•droit′
ad•sorb′ *(to hold on a
  surface)*
  ♦*absorb*
ad•sorp′tion
ad′u•late′, -lat′ed,
  -lat′ing
ad′u•la′tion
ad′u•la′tor
ad′u•la•to′ry
a•dult′
a•dul′ter•ant
a•dul′ter•ate′, -at′ed,
  -at′ing
a•dul′ter•a′tion
a•dul′ter•er
a•dul′ter•ous
a•dul′ter•y
a•dult′hood′
ad•um′brate′, -brat′-
  ed, -brat′ing

ad'um·bra'tion

ad·vance', -vanced',
-vanc'ing

ad·vance'ment

ad·vanc'er

ad·van'tage, -taged,
-tag·ing

ad'van·ta'geous

ad'vent

Ad'vent'ist

ad'ven·ti'tious

ad·ven'ture, -tured,
-tur·ing

ad·ven'tur·er

ad·ven'tur·ous

ad'verb'

ad·ver'bi·al

ad'ver·sar'y

ad·verse' (hostile, op-
posed)
♦averse

ad·ver'si·ty

ad·vert'

ad'ver·tise', -tised',
-tis'ing

ad'ver·tise'ment

ad'ver·tis'er

ad·vice' (guidance)
♦advise

ad·vis'a·bil'i·ty

ad·vis'a·ble

ad·vise' (to offer coun-
sel), -vised', -vis'ing
♦advice

ad·vis'ed·ly

ad·vise'ment

ad·vis'er also ad·vi'sor

ad·vi'so·ry

ad'vo·ca·cy

ad'vo·cate', -cat'ed,
-cat'ing

adz or adze

ae'gis also e'gis

aer'ate', -at'ed, -at'ing

aer·a'tion

aer·a'tor

aer'i·al

aer'i·al·ist

aer'ie (nest)
♦airy, eerie

aer'o·bat'ics

aer·obe'

aer·o'bic

aer·o'bics

aer'o·dy·nam'ics

aer·ol'o·gy

aer'o·me·chan'ics

aer'o·naut'

aer'o·nau'tic also aer'-
o·nau'ti·cal

aer'o·nau'tics

aer'o·pause'

aer'o·sol'

aer'o·space'

aer'o·stat'

aer'o·stat'ics

aes'thete' or es'thete'

aes·thet'ic or es·thet'ic

aes'the·ti'cian or es'-
the·ti'cian

aes·thet'i·cism or es·
thet'i·cism

aes·thet'ics or es·thet'-
ics

ad·vi'so·ry

af'fa·bil'i·ty

af'fa·ble

af·fair'

af·fect' (to influence,
imitate)
♦effect

af'fec·ta'tion

af·fect'ed

af·fec'tion

af·fec'tion·ate

af·fec'tive

af'fer·ent

af·fi'ance, -anced,
-anc·ing

af·fi·da'vit

af·fil'i·ate', -at'ed, -at'-
ing

af·fil'i·a'tion

af·fin'i·ty

af·firm'

af'fir·ma'tion

af·fir'ma·tive

af·fix'

af·fla'tus

af·flict'

af·flic'tion

af·flu·ence

af·flu·ent

af·ford'

af·ford'a·ble

af·fray'

af·front'
Af'ghan' *(person, dog)*
af'ghan' *(blanket)*
a·fi'ci·o·na'do *pl.* -dos
a·field'
a·fire'
a·flame'
a·float'
a·flut'ter
a·foot'
a·fore'
a·fore'men'tioned
a·fore'said'
a·fore'thought'
a for'ti·o'ri
a·foul'
a·fraid'
a·fresh'
Af'ri·can
Af'ri·kaans'
Af'ri·kan'er
Af'ro' *pl.* -ros'
Af'ro-A·mer'i·can
aft
af'ter
af'ter·birth'
af'ter·burn'er
af'ter·care'
af'ter·deck'
af'ter·ef·fect'
af'ter·glow'
af'ter·im'age
af'ter·life'
af'ter·math'
af'ter·noon'
af'ter·taste'
af'ter·thought'

af'ter·ward *also* af'ter·
    wards
af'ter·world'
a·gain'
a·gainst'
a·gape'
a'gar *also* a'gar'-a'gar'
ag'ate
a·ga've
age, aged, ag'ing
aged *(of the age of)*
a'ged *(elderly)*
age'ism'
age'less
age'-long'
a'gen·cy
a·gen'da
a·gen'dum *pl.* -da *or*
    -dums
a'gent
age'-old'
ag'er·a'tum
ag·glom'er·ate', -at'-
    ed, -at'ing
ag·glom'er·a'tion
ag·glu'ti·nate', -nat'-
    ed, -nat'ing
ag·glu'ti·na'tion
ag·glu'ti·na'tive
ag·glu'ti·nin
ag·gran·dize', -dized',
    -diz'ing
ag·gran'dize·ment
ag·gran'diz·er
ag'gra·vate', -vat'ed,
    -vat'ing
ag'gra·va'tion

ag'gra·va'tor
ag'gre·gate', -gat'ed,
    -gat'ing
ag'gre·ga'tion
ag'gre·ga'tor
ag·gres'sion
ag·gres'sive
ag·gres'sor
ag·grieve', -grieved',
    -griev'ing
a·ghast'
ag'ile
a·gil'i·ty
ag'i·tate', -tat'ed, -tat'-
    ing
ag'i·ta'tion
ag'i·ta'tor
a·gleam'
a·gley'
a·glim'mer
a·glit'ter
a·glow'
ag·nos'tic
ag·nos'ti·cism
a·go'
a·gog'
a·gon'ic
ag'o·nize', -nized',
    -niz'ing
ag'o·ny
a·go'ra *pl.* -rae' *or* -ras
ag'o·ra·pho'bi·a
ag'o·ra·pho'bic
a·gou'ti *pl.* -tis *or* -ties
a·grar'i·an
a·grar'i·an·ism

a·gree′, a·greed′,
  a·gree′ing
a·gree′a·ble
a·gree′ment
ag′ri·busi′ness
ag′ri·cul′tur·al
ag′ri·cul′ture
ag′ri·cul′tur·ist
ag′ro·chem′i·cal
ag′ro·nom′ic *also* ag′-
  ro·nom′i·cal
a·gron′o·mist
a·gron′o·my
a·ground′
a′gue
a·head′
a·hoy′
aid *(to help)*
aide *(assistant)*
aide′-de-camp′ *pl.*
  aides′-de-camp′
ai·grette′ *or* ai·gret′
ail *(to feel ill)*
  ♦*ale*
ai·lan′thus
ai′le·ron′
ail′ing
ail′ment
aim′less
air *(atmosphere)*
  ♦*are (metric unit),*
  e′er, ere, heir
air′borne′
air′brush′
air′bus′
air′-con·di′tion *v.*
air′-cool′

air′craft′ *pl.* -craft′
air′drome′
air′drop′
Aire′dale′
air′field′
air′flow′
air′foil′
air′glow′
air′i·ness
air′less
air′lift′
air′line′
air′lin′er
air′mail′ *v. & adj.*
air′man
air′plane′
air′port′
air′ship′
air′sick′
air′sick′ness
air′space′
air′strip′
air′tight′
air′-to-air′ missile
air′-to-sur′face mis-
  sile
air′waves′
air′way′
air′wor′thy
air′y *(breezy)*
  ♦*aerie*
aisle *(passageway)*
  ♦*I'll, isle*
a·jar′
a·kim′bo
a·kin′

Al′a·bam′i·an *also*
  Al′a·bam′an
al′a·bas′ter
à′ la carte′
a·lac′ri·ty
A·lad′din
à′ la king′
à′ la mode′
a·larm′
a·larm′ist
a·las′
A·las′kan
alb
al′ba·core′
Al·ba′ni·an
al′ba·tross′
al·be′do *pl.* -dos
al·be′it
Al·ber′tan
al′bi·nism′
al·bi′no *pl.* -nos
al′bum
al·bu′men *(egg white)*
al·bu′min *(protein)*
al·caz′ar
al·chem′i·cal *or* al′
  chem′ic
al′che·mist
al′che·my
al′co·hol′
al′co·hol′ic
al′co·hol·ism′
al′cove′
al′de·hyde′
al den′te
al′der
al′der·man

al'der·man·cy
ale *(beverage)*
♦*ail*
a·lee'
ale'house'
a·lem'bic
a·lert'
ale'wife'
a·lex'i·a
al·fal'fa
al·fres'co
al'gae *sing.* -ga
al'gal
al'ge·bra
al'ge·bra'ic
al'ge·bra'ist
Al·ge'ri·an
al'gid
AL'GOL'
al'go·rithm'
a'li·as
a'li·bi' *pl.* -bis'
a'li·en
al'ien·a·ble
al'ien·ate', -at'ed, -at'-
ing
al'ien·a'tion
al'ien·a'tor
al'ien·ist
a·light', a·light'ed *or*
a·lit', a·light'ing
a·lign' *also* a·line',
a·lined', a·lin'ing
a·lign'ment *also*
a·line'ment
a·like'
al'i·ment

al'i·men'ta·ry
al'i·men·ta'tion
al'i·mo'ny
al'i·phat'ic
al'i·quant'
al'i·quot'
a·live'
al'ka·li' *pl.* -lis' *or* -lies'
al'ka·line'
al'ka·lin'i·ty
al'ka·li·za'tion
al'ka·lize', -lized', -liz'-
ing, *also* al'ka·lin·
ize', -ized', iz'ing
al'ka·loid'
al'ka·lo'sis
al'kyd
al'kyl
all *(total)*
♦*awl*
Al'lah
all'-A·mer'i·can
al·lan'to·is *pl.* -i·des
al·lay'
al'le·ga'tion
al·lege', -leged', -leg'-
ing
al·leg'ed·ly
al·le'giance
al'le·gor'ic *also* al'le·
gor'i·cal
al'le·go'rist
al'le·go'ry
al·le'gro *pl.* -gros
al·lele'
al·le'lic
al'le·lu'ia

al'le·mande'
al'ler·gen
al'ler·gen'ic
al·ler'gic
al'ler·gist
al'ler·gy
al·le'vi·ate', -at'ed,
-at'ing
al·le'vi·a'tion
al·le'vi·a'tor
al'ley *(passageway)*
♦*ally*
al'ley·way'
al·li'ance
al·lied'
al'li·ga'tor
all'-im·por'tant *adj.*
al·lit'er·ate', -at'ed,
-at'ing
al·lit'er·a'tion
al·lit'er·a'tive
al'lo·cate', -cat'ed,
-cat'ing
al'lo·ca'tion
al'lo·morph'
al'lo·mor'phic
al'lo·nym'
al'lo·path'ic
al·lop'a·thy
al'lo·phone'
al'lo·phon'ic
al·lot', -lot'ted, -lot'-
ting
al·lot'ment
al'lo·trope'
al'lo·trop'ic *also* al'lo·
trop'i·cal

al·lot′ro·py
all′-out′ adj.
all′-o′ver adj.
al·low′
al·low′a·ble
al·low′ance
al·low′ed·ly
al·loy′ n.
al·loy′ v.
all′-pur′pose adj.
all read′y (completely
    prepared)
    ♦already
all right
all′-round′ adj., also
    all′-a·round′
all′spice′
all′-star′ adj. & n.
all′-time′ adj.
all to·geth′er (collec-
    tively)
    ♦altogether
al·lude′ (to refer to),
    -lud′ed, -lud′ing
    ♦elude
al·lure′, -lured′, -lur′-
    ing
al·lu′sion (reference)
    ♦illusion
al·lu′sive (suggestive)
    ♦elusive, illusive
al·lu′vi·al
al·lu′vi·um pl. -vi·ums
    or -vi·a
al·ly′, -lied′, -ly′ing
al′ly′ (friend)
    ♦alley

al′ma ma′ter or Al′ma
    Ma′ter
al′ma·nac′
al·might′y
al′mond
al′mo·ner
al′most′
alms′giv′er
al·ni′co′ pl. -cos′
al′oe
a·loft′
a·lo′ha′
a·lone′
a·long′
a·long′shore′
a·long′side′
a·loof′
a·loud′ (audibly)
    ♦allowed
al·pac′a
al′pen·horn′
al′pen·stock′
al′pha
al′pha·bet′
al′pha·bet′i·cal also
    al′pha·bet′ic
al′pha·bet·ize′, -ized′,
    -iz′ing
al′pha·nu·mer′ic also
    al′pha·mer′ic
al′pine′ (of high moun-
    tains)
Al′pine′ (of the Alps)
al·read′y (previously)
    ♦all ready
al′so
al′so-ran′

al′tar (religious table)
    ♦alter
al′tar·piece′
al′ter (to change)
    ♦altar
al′ter·a′tion
al′ter·a′tive
al′ter·cate′, -cat′ed,
    -cat′ing
al′ter·ca′tion
al′ter·nate (happening
    in turn)
    ♦alternative
al′ter·nate′ (to occur in
    turn), -nat′ed, -nat′-
    ing
al′ter·na′tion
al·ter′na·tive (allowing
    a choice)
    ♦alternate
al′ter·na′tor
al·the′a also al·thae′a
alt′horn′
al·though′ also al·tho′
al·tim′e·ter
al′ti·tude′
al·ti·tu′di·nal
al′to pl. -tos
al·to·cu′mu·lus
al·to·geth′er (com-
    pletely)
    ♦all together
al′to·stra′tus
al′tru·ism
al′tru·ist
al′tru·is′tic
al′um

a·lu'mi·na
a·lu'min·ize', -ized',
　-iz'ing
a·lu'mi·nous
a·lu'mi·num
a·lum'na *pl.* -nae'
a·lum'nus *pl.* -ni'
al·ve'o·lar
al·ve'o·lus *pl.* -li'
al'ways
a·lys'sum
a·main'
a·mal'gam
a·mal'ga·mate', -mat'-
　ed, -mat'ing
a·mal'ga·ma'tion
a·mal'ga·ma'tor
am'a·ni'ta
a·man'u·en'sis *pl.* -ses
am'a·ranth'
am'a·ran'thine
am'a·ryl'lis
a·mass'
am'a·teur'
am'a·teur'ish
am'a·teur'ism
am'a·to'ry
a·maze', a·mazed', a·
　maz'ing
a·maze'ment
Am'a·zon' *also* am'a·
　zon
Am'a·zo'ni·an *also*
　am'a·zo'ni·an
am·bas'sa·dor
am·bas'sa·do'ri·al
am'ber

am'ber·gris'
am'bi·ance *also* am'bi·
　ence
am'bi·dex·ter'i·ty
am'bi·dex'trous
am'bi·ent
am'bi·gu'i·ty
am·big'u·ous
am·bi'tion
am·bi'tious
am·biv'a·lence
am·biv'a·lent
am'ble, -bled, -bling
am·bro'sia
am·bro'sial
am'bu·lance
am'bu·la·to'ry
am'bus·cade'
am'bush'
a·me'lio·rate', -rat'ed,
　-rat'ing
a·me'lio·ra'tion
a·me'lio·ra'tive
a·me'lio·ra'tor
a·men'
a·me'na·bil'i·ty
a·me'na·ble
a·mend' *(to alter)*
　◆emend
a·men'da·to'ry
a·mend'ment
a·mends'
a·men'i·ty
a·merce', a·merced',
　a·merc'ing
A·mer'i·can
A·mer'i·ca'na

A·mer'i·can·ism
A·mer'i·can·i·za'tion
A·mer'i·can·ize',
　-ized', -iz'ing
am'er·i'ci·um
am'e·thyst
a'mi·a·bil'i·ty
a'mi·a·ble
am'i·ca·bil'i·ty
am'i·ca·ble
am'ice
a·mid' *also* a·midst'
a·mide'
a·mid'ships'
a·mi'go *pl.* -gos
a·mine'
a·mi'no acid
A'mish
a·miss'
a·mi·to'sis
a·mi·tot'ic
am'i·ty
am'me'ter
am'mo
am·mo'nia
am'mon·ite'
am·mo'ni·um
am'mu·ni'tion
am·ne'sia
am·ne'si·ac'
am'nes·ty
am'ni·o·cen·te'sis *pl.*
　-ses'
am'ni·on
a·moe'ba *or* a·me'ba
　pl. -bas *or* -bae
a·moe'bic *or* a·me'bic

a·mong' *also*
  a·mongst'
a·mon'til·la'do *pl.*
  -dos
a·mor'al
a'mo·ral'i·ty
am'o·rous
a·mor'phous
am'or·ti·za'tion
am'or·tize', -tized',
  -tiz'ing
a·mount'
a·mour'
a·mour'-pro'pre
am'per·age
am'pere'
am'per·sand'
am·phet'a·mine'
am·phib'i·an
am·phib'i·ous
am'phi·bole'
am'phi·the'a·ter
am·pho'ra *pl.* -rae' *or*
  -ras
am'ple
am'pli·fi·ca'tion
am'pli·fi'er
am'pli·fy', -fied', -fy'-
  ing
am'pli·tude'
am'ply
am'poule *or* am'pule
am'pu·tate', -tat'ed,
  -tat'ing
am'pu·ta'tion
am'pu·ta'tor
am'pu·tee'

Am'trak'
a·muck' *also* a·mok'
am'u·let
a·muse', a·mused',
  a·mus'ing
a·muse'ment
am'yl
am'y·lase'
am'y·lop'sin
An'a·bap'tist
an'a·bol'ic
a·nab'o·lism'
a·nach'ro·nism
a·nach'ro·nis'tic
an'a·con'da
an'aer·obe'
an'aer·o'bic
an'a·gram'
a'nal
an'al·ge'si·a
an'al·ge'sic
an'a·log' computer
a·nal'o·gous
an'a·logue' *also* an'a·
  log'
a·nal'o·gy
a·nal'y·sis *pl.* -ses'
an'a·lyst *(one who ana-
  lyzes)*
  ◆annalist
an'a·lyt'ic *also* an'a·
  lyt'i·cal
an'a·lyze', -lyzed',
  -lyz'ing
an'a·pest' *also* an'a·
  paest'
an'a·phase'

an'a·phy·lac'tic
an'a·phy·lax'is
an·ar'chic *or* an·ar'chi·
  cal
an'ar·chism
an'ar·chist
an'ar·chis'tic
an'ar·chy
an·as'tig·mat'ic
a·nath'e·ma *pl.* -mas
a·nath'e·ma·tize',
  -tized', -tiz'ing
an'a·tom'i·cal *also*
  an'a·tom'ic
a·nat'o·mist
a·nat'o·mize', -mized',
  -miz'ing
a·nat'o·my
an'ces·tor
an·ces'tral
an'ces'try
an'chor
an'chor·age
an'cho·rite'
an'cho·rit'ic
an'chor·man'
an'chor·wom'an
an'cho'vy
an'cient
an'cil·lar'y
an·dan'te
an·dan·ti'no *pl.* -nos
and'i'ron
and/or
an'dro·gen
an'dro·gen'ic
an·drog'y·nous

an·drog′y·ny
an′droid′
an′ec·do′tal
an′ec·dote′
a·ne′mi·a also a·nae′-
mi·a
a·ne′mic also a·nae′-
mic
an′e·mom′e·ter
a·nem′o·ne
a·nent′
an′er·oid′ barometer
an′es·the′sia also an′-
aes·the′sia
an′es·the′si·ol′o·gist
also an′aes·the′si·ol′-
o·gist
an′es·the′si·ol′o·gy
also an′aes·the′si·ol′-
o·gy
an′es·thet′ic also an′-
aes·thet′ic
an·es′the·tist also an·
aes′the·tist
an·es′the·ti·za′tion
also an·aes′the·ti·za′-
tion
an·es′the·tize′, -tized′,
-tiz′ing, also an·aes′-
the·tize′
an′eu·rysm also an′eu·
rism
a·new′
an′gel
an′gel·fish′ pl. -fish′ or
-fish′es

an·gel′ic also an·gel′i·
cal
an·gel′i·ca
an′ger
an·gi′na pec′to·ris
an′gi·o·sperm′
an′gle, -gled, -gling
an′gler
an′gler·fish′ pl. -fish′
or -fish′es
an′gle·worm′
An′gli·can
An′gli·can·ism
An′gli·cism
An′gli·ci·za′tion
An′gli·cize′, -cized′,
-ciz′ing
an′gling
An′glo-A·mer′i·can
An′glo·phone′
An′glo-Sax′on
an·go′ra (yarn)
An·go′ra (cat, goat,
rabbit)
an′gos·tu′ra
an′gry
angst
ang′strom or ång′-
ström
an′guish
an′gu·lar
an′gu·lar′i·ty
an·hy′dride′
an·hy′drite′
an·hy′drous
an′i·line also an′i·lin
an′i·mad·ver′sion

an′i·mad·vert′
an′i·mal
an′i·mal′cule
an′i·mal·ism
an′i·mal·is′tic
an′i·mate′, -mat′ed,
-mat′ing
an′i·ma′tion
an′i·ma′tor also an′i·
mat′er
an′i·mism
an′i·mist
an′i·mis′tic
an′i·mos′i·ty
an′i·mus
an′i·on
an′i·on′ic
an′ise
an′i·seed′
an′i·sette′
an′kle
an′kle·bone′
an′klet
an′nal·ist (chronicler)
♦analyst
an′nals
an·neal′
an·ne·lid
an·nex′ v.
an′nex′ n.
an′nex·a′tion
an·ni′hi·late′, -lat′ed,
-lat′ing
an·ni′hi·la′tion
an·ni′hi·la′tor
an′ni·ver′sa·ry
an′no Dom′i·ni′

an'no•tate', -tat'ed,
-tat'ing
an'no•ta'tion
an'no•ta'tive
an'no•ta'tor
an•nounce',
-nounced', -nounc'-
ing
an•nounce'ment
an•nounc'er
an•noy'
an•noy'ance
an'nu•al
an•nu'i•tant
an•nu'i•ty
an•nul', -nulled', -nul'-
ling
an•nu•lar
an•nul'ment
an'nu•lus pl. -lus•es or
-li'
an•nun'ci•ate', -at'ed,
-at'ing
an•nun'ci•a'tion
an•nun'ci•a'tor
an'ode'
an'o•dize', -dized',
-diz'ing
an'o•dyne'
a•noint'
a•nom'a•lous
a•nom'a•ly
an'o•mie or an'o•my
a•non'
an'o•nym'i•ty
a•non'y•mous
a•noph'e•les'

an'o•rec'tic or an'o•
ret'ic, also an'o•rex'ic
an'o•rex'ia nerv•o'sa
an•oth'er
an•ox'i•a
an•ox'ic
an'swer
an'swer•a•ble
ant (insect)
♦aunt
ant•ac'id
an•tag'o•nism
an•tag'o•nist
an•tag'o•nis'tic
an•tag'o•nize', -nized',
-niz'ing
Ant•arc'tic
an'te, -ted or -teed, -te•
ing
ant'eat'er
an'te•bel'lum
an'te•ce'dence
an'te•ce'dent
an'te•cham'ber
an'te•date', -dat'ed,
-dat'ing
an'te•di•lu'vi•an
an'te•lope' pl. -lope' or
-lopes'
an'te me•rid'i•em
an•ten'na pl. -nae or
-nas
an'te•pe'nult
an'te•pe•nul'ti•mate
an•te'ri•or
an'te•room'
an'them

an'ther
ant'hill'
an•thol'o•gist
an•thol'o•gize',
-gized', -giz'ing
an•thol'o•gy
an'tho•zo'an
an'thra•cene'
an'thra•cite'
an'thrax'
an'thro•po•cen'tric
an'thro•poid'
an'thro•po•log'ic also
an'thro•po•log'i•cal
an'thro•pol'o•gist
an'thro•pol'o•gy
an'thro•po•mor'phic
an'thro•po•mor'-
phism
an'ti' pl. -tis'
an'ti•a•bor'tion
an'ti•air'craft'
an'ti•bal•lis'tic mis-
sile
an'ti•bi•o'sis
an'ti•bi•ot'ic
an'ti•bod'y
an'tic
an'ti•christ'
an•tic'i•pate', -pat'ed,
-pat'ing
an•tic'i•pa'tion
an•tic'i•pa'tor
an•tic'i•pa•to'ry
an'ti•cler'i•cal
an'ti•cli•mac'tic
an'ti•cli'max

an·ti·cline'
an·ti·co·ag'u·lant
an·ti·cy'clone
an·ti·de·pres'sant
an·ti·dot'al
an·ti·dote'
an·ti·freeze'
an·ti·gen' *also* an·ti·
    gene
an·ti·gen'ic
an·ti·he'ro *pl.* -roes
an·ti·his'ta·mine'
an·ti·knock'
an·ti·log'a·rithm'
an·ti·ma·cas'sar
an·ti·mag·net'ic
an·ti·mat'ter
an·ti·mis'sile missile
an·ti·mo'ny
an·ti·neu·tri'no *pl.*
    -nos
an·ti·neu'tron
an·ti·ox'i·dant
an·ti·par'ti·cle
an·ti·pas'to *pl.* -tos
an·ti·pa·thet'ic *also*
    an·tip·a·thet'i·cal
an·tip'a·thy
an·ti·per'son·nel'
an·ti·per'spi·rant
an·ti·phon'
an·tiph·o'nal
an·tiph'o·ny
an·tip'o·dal
an·tip'o·pode'
an·tip'o·des'
an·ti·pov'er·ty

an·ti·pro'ton
an·ti·py·ret'ic
an·ti·quar'i·an
an·ti·quar'y
an·ti·quate', -quat'ed,
    -quat'ing
an·ti·qua'tion
an·tique', -tiqued',
    -tiqu'ing
an·tiq'ui·ty
an·ti-Sem'ite'
an·ti-Se·mit'ic
an·ti-Sem'i·tism
an·ti·sep'sis
an·ti·sep'tic
an·ti·slav'er·y
an·ti·smog'
an·ti·so'cial
an·ti·spas·mod'ic
an·ti·sub'ma·rine'
an·ti·tank'
an·tith'e·sis *pl.* -ses'
an·ti·thet'i·cal *also*
    an'ti·thet'ic
an·ti·tox'ic
an·ti·tox'in
an·ti·trades'
an·ti·trust'
an·ti·ven'in
ant'ler
ant'lered
an'to·nym'
an·ton'y·mous
a'nus *pl.* a'nus·es
an'vil
anx·i'e·ty
anx'ious

an'y
an'y·bod'y
an'y·how'
an'y·more'
an'y·one'
an'y·place'
an'y·thing'
an'y·time'
an'y·way'
an'y·where'
an'y·wise'
A'-O·K' *also* A'-O·
    kay' *adj. & adv.*
A'-one'
a·or'ta *pl.* -tas *or* -tae'
a·or'tal *or* a·or'tic
a'ou·dad'
a·pace'
a·part'
a·part'heid'
a·part'ment
ap'a·thet'ic
ap'a·thy
ape, aped, ap'ing
a·pé'ri·tif'
ap'er·ture
a'pex' *pl.* a'pex·es *or*
    a'pi·ces'
a·pha'sia
a·pha'si·ac'
a·pha'sic
a·phe'li·on *pl.* -li·a
a'phid
aph'o·rism
aph'o·ris'tic
aph'ro·dis'i·ac'
a'pi·a·rist

a'pi·ar'y
ap'i·cal
a'pi·cul'ture
a·piece'
ap'ish
a·plomb'
a·poc'a·lypse'
a·poc'a·lyp'tic *also*
   a·poc'a·lyp'ti·cal
A·poc'ry·pha
a·poc'ry·phal
ap'o·gee'
a'po·lit'i·cal
A·pol'lo
a·pol'o·get'ic
ap'o·lo'gi·a
a·pol'o·gist
a·pol'o·gize', -gized',
   -giz'ing
a·pol'o·giz'er
a·pol'o·gy
ap'o·plec'tic
ap'o·plex'y
a·pos'ta·sy
a·pos'tate'
a pos'te·ri·o'ri
a·pos'tle
ap'os·tol'ic
a·pos'tro·phe
a·pos'tro·phize',
   -phized', -phiz'ing
a·poth'e·car'ies'
   measure
a·poth'e·car'y
ap'o·thegm' *(maxim)*
ap'o·them' *(geometric
   distance)*

a·poth'e·o'sis *pl.* -ses'
Ap'pa·la'chi·an
ap·pall'
ap'pa·loo'sa
ap'pa·nage *also* ap'a·
   nage
ap'pa·ra'tus *pl.* -tus *or*
   -tus·es
ap·par'el, -eled *or*
   -elled, -el·ing *or* -el·
   ling
ap·par'ent
ap'pa·ri'tion
ap·peal'
ap·pear'
ap·pear'ance
ap·pease', -peased',
   -peas'ing
ap·pease'ment
ap·peas'er
ap·pel'lant
ap·pel'late
ap'pel·la'tion
ap'pel·lee'
ap·pend'
ap·pend'age
ap·pen·dec'to·my
ap'pen·di·ci'tis
ap·pen'dix *pl.* -dix·es
   or -di·ces'
ap'per·ceive', -ceived',
   -ceiv'ing
ap'per·cep'tion
ap'per·tain'
ap'pe·tite'
ap'pe·tiz'er
ap'pe·tiz'ing

ap·plaud'
ap·plause'
ap'ple
ap'ple·jack'
ap'ple·sauce'
ap·pli'ance
ap'pli·ca·bil'i·ty
ap'pli·ca·ble
ap'pli·cant
ap'pli·ca'tion
ap'pli·ca'tor
ap·plied'
ap'pli·qué', -quéd',
   -qué'ing
ap·ply', -plied', -ply'-
   ing
ap·point'
ap·point'ee'
ap·point'ive
ap·point'ment
ap·por'tion
ap·por'tion·ment
ap·pose' *(to arrange
   side by side)*, -posed',
   -pos'ing
   ♦oppose
ap'po·site *(appropri-
   ate)*
   ♦opposite
ap'po·si'tion
ap·pos'i·tive
ap·prais'al
ap·praise' *(to evalu-
   ate)*, -praised',
   -prais'ing
   ♦apprise
ap·prais'er

ap·pre′cia·ble
ap·pre′ci·ate′, -at′ed,
 -at′ing
ap·pre′ci·a′tion
ap·pre′cia·tive
ap·pre′ci·a′tor
ap′pre·hend′
ap′pre·hen′sion
ap′pre·hen′sive
ap·pren′tice, -ticed,
 -tic·ing
ap·pren′tice·ship′
ap·prise′ (to inform),
 -prised′, -pris′ing
 ♦appraise
ap·proach′
ap·proach′a·bil′i·ty
ap·proach′a·ble
ap′pro·ba′tion
ap·pro′pri·ate′, -at′ed,
 -at′ing
ap·pro′pri·a′tion
ap·pro′pri·a′tor
ap·prov′al
ap·prove′, -proved′,
 -prov′ing
ap·prox′i·mate′,
 -mat′ed, -mat′ing.
ap·prox′i·ma′tion
ap·pur′te·nance
a′pri·cot′
A′pril
a pri·o′ri
a′pron
ap′ro·pos′
apse
ap′ti·tude′

apt′ly
aq′ua
aq′ua·ma·rine′
aq′ua·naut′
aq′ua·plane′, -planed′,
 -plan′ing
a·quar′i·um pl. -i·ums
 or -i·a
A·quar′i·us
a·quat′ic
aq′ua·tint′
aq′ue·duct′
a′que·ous
aq′ui·fer
aq′ui·line′
Ar′ab
ar′a·besque′
A·ra′bi·an
Ar′a·bic
ar′a·ble
a·rach′nid
a·rag′o·nite′
Ar′au·ca′ni·an
ar′bi·ter
ar·bit′ra·ment
ar′bi·trar′y
ar′bi·trate′, -trat′ed,
 -trat′ing
ar′bi·tra′tion
ar′bi·tra′tor
ar′bor
ar·bo′re·al
ar′bo·re′tum pl. -tums
 or -ta
ar′bor·vi′tae
ar·bu′tus pl. -tus·es
arc (to curve), arced or

arcked, arc′ing or
 arck′ing
 ♦ark
ar·cade′
ar·cane′
arch
ar′chae·o·log′i·cal or
 ar′chae·o·log′ic, also
 ar′che·o·log′i·cal or
 ar′che·o·log′ic
ar′chae·ol′o·gist or
 ar′che·ol′o·gist
ar′chae·ol′o·gy or ar′-
 che·ol′o·gy
ar′chae·op′ter·yx
ar·cha′ic
ar′cha·ism
ar′cha·is′tic
arch·an′gel
arch·bish′op
arch·dea′con
arch·di·oc′e·san
arch·di′o·cese
arch·du′cal
arch·duch′ess
arch·duke′
arch·en′e·my
arch′er
arch′er·y
ar′che·typ′al also ar′-
 che·typ′ic, ar′che·
 typ′i·cal
ar′che·type′
arch·fiend′
ar·chi·e·pis′co·pal
ar′chi·pel′a·go′ pl.
 -goes′ or -gos′

ar'chi·tect'

ar'chi·tec·ton'ic *also*
  ar'chi·tec·ton'i·cal

ar'chi·tec·ton'ics

ar'chi·tec'tur·al

ar'chi·tec'ture

ar'chi·trave'

ar'chives'

ar'chi·vist'

arch'ly

arch'way'

arc'tic

ar'den·cy

ar'dent

ar'dor

ar'du·ous

are *(metric unit)*
  ♦*air, e'er, ere, heir*

are *v.*

ar'e·a *(space)*
  ♦*aria*

Area Code *also* area
  code

ar'e·a·way'

a·re'na

aren't

Ar'es

ar'gent

Ar'gen·tine' *also* Ar·
  gen·tin'e·an

ar'gon'

ar'go·sy

ar'got

ar'gu·a·ble

ar'gue, -gued, -gu·ing

ar'gu·ment

ar'gu·men·ta'tion

ar'gu·men·ta·tive

ar'gyle' *also* ar'gyll'

a·ri·a *(melody)*
  ♦*area*

ar'id

a·rid'i·ty

Ar'ies

a·right'

ar'il

a·rise', a·rose', a·ris'en,
  a·ris'ing

ar'is·toc'ra·cy

a·ris'to·crat'

a·ris'to·crat'ic

Ar'is·to·te'li·an *also*
  Ar'is·to·te'le·an

a·rith'me·tic *n.*

ar'ith·met'ic *adj.,* also
  ar'ith·met'i·cal

Ar'i·zo'nan

ark *(boat)*
  ♦*arc*

Ar·kan'san

ar'ma'da

ar'ma·dil'lo *pl.* -los

ar'ma·ment

ar'ma·ture'

arm'band'

arm'chair'

arm'ful' *pl.* -fuls'

arm'hole'

ar'mi·stice

arm'let

ar·moire'

ar'mor

ar'mored

ar·mo'ri·al

ar'mor·y

arm'pit'

arm'rest'

arms

ar'my

ar'ni·ca

a·ro'ma

ar'o·mat'ic

a·round'

a·rouse', a·roused',
  a·rous'ing

ar·peg'gi·o *pl.* -os'

ar·raign'

ar·raign'ment

ar·range', -ranged',
  -rang'ing

ar·range'ment

ar·rang'er

ar'rant

ar'ras

ar·ray'

ar·rears'

ar·rest'

ar·ri'val

ar·rive', -rived', -riv-
  ing

ar'ro·gance

ar'ro·gant

ar'ro·gate', -gat·ed,
  -gat'ing

ar'ro·ga'tion

ar'ro·ga'tive

ar'ro·ga'tor

ar'row

ar'row·head'

ar'row·root'

ar·roy'o *pl.* -os

ar′se·nal
ar′se·nate
ar′se·nic
ar′son
ar′son·ist
art′ dec′o
ar·te′ri·al
ar·te′ri·ole′
ar·te′ri·o·scle·ro′sis
ar·te′ri·o·scle·rot′ic
ar′ter·y
ar·te′sian well
art′ful
ar·thrit′ic
ar·thri′tis
ar′thro·pod′
ar′ti·choke′
ar′ti·cle
ar·tic′u·lar
ar·tic′u·late′, -lat′ed,
    -lat′ing
ar·tic′u·la′tion
ar·tic′u·la′tor
ar′ti·fact′ *also* ar′te·
    fact′
ar′ti·fice
ar′ti·fi′cial
ar′ti·fi′ci·al′i·ty
ar·til′ler·y
ar′ti·san
art′ist
ar·tis′tic
art′ist·ry
art′less
art′ nou·veau′
art′work′
art′y

ar′um
as′a·fet′i·da
as·bes′tos *also* as·bes′-
    tus
as·cend′
as·cen′dan·cy *also* as·
    cen′den·cy, as·cen′-
    dance, as·cen′dence
as·cen′dant *also* as·
    cen′dent
as·cen′sion
as·cent′ *(upward slope)*
    ♦*assent*
as′cer·tain′
as·cet′ic *(austere)*
    ♦*acetic*
as·cet′i·cism
a·scor′bic acid
ɑ3′cot
as·cribe′, -cribed′,
    -crib′ing
as·crip′tion
a·sep′sis
a·sep′tic
a·sex′u·al
a·shamed′
ash′en
a·shore′
ash′tray′
A′sian
A′si·at′ic
a·side′
as′i·nine′
as′i·nin′i·ty
ask
a·skance′
a·skew′

a·slant′
a·sleep′
a·so′cial
asp
as·par′a·gus
as′pect′
as′pen
as·per′i·ty
as·perse′, -persed′,
    -pers′ing
as·per′sion
as′phalt′
as′pho·del′
as·phyx′i·a
as·phyx′i·ate′, -at′ed,
    -at′ing
as·phyx′i·a′tion
as·phyx′i·a′tor
as′pic
as′pi·dis′tra
as′pi·rant
as′pi·rate′, -rat′ed,
    -rat′ing
as′pi·ra′tion
as′pi·ra′tor
as·pire′, -pired′, -pir′-
    ing
as′pi·rin
as′sa·gai′ *or* as′se·gai
as·sail′
as·sail′a·ble
as·sail′ant
as·sas′sin
as·sas′si·nate′, -nat′-
    ed, -nat′ing
as·sas′si·na′tion
as·sault′

as•say' *n.*

as•say' *(to analyze)*
♦*essay*

as•sem'blage

as•sem'ble, -bled,
-bling

as•sem'bly

as•sent' *(agreement)*
♦*ascent*

as•sert'

as•ser'tion

as•ser'tive

as•sess'

as•sess'a•ble

as•sess'ment

as•ses'sor

as•set'

as•sev'er•ate', -at'ed,
-at'ing

as•si•du'i•ty

as•sid'u•ous

as•sign'

as•sig•na'tion

as•sign•ee'

as•sign'ment

as•sim'i•la•ble

as•sim'i•late', -lat'ed,
-lat'ing

as•sim'i•la'tion

as•sim'i•la'tive *also*
as•sim'i•la•to'ry

as•sist'

as•sis'tance

as•sis'tant

as•size'

as•so'ci•ate', -at'ed,
-at'ing

as•so'ci•a'tion

as•so'ci•a'tive

as'so•nance

as'so•nant

as•sort'

as•sort'ed

as•sort'ment

as•suage', -suaged',
-suag'ing

as•sume' *(to take on),*
-sumed', -sum'ing
♦*presume*

as•sump'tion

as•sur'ance

as•sure' *(to declare,
make secure or cer-
tain),* -sured', -sur'-
ing
♦*ensure, insure*

as•sur'ed•ly

as'ta•tine'

as'ter

as'ter•isk'

as'ter•ism

a•stern'

as'ter•oid'

as•the'ni•a

asth'ma

asth•mat'ic

as•tig•mat'ic

a•stig'ma•tism

a•stir'

a•ston'ish

a•ston'ish•ment

a•stound'

a•strad'dle

as'tra•khan'

as'tral

a•stray'

a•stride'

as•trin'gen•cy

as•trin'gent

as'tro•dome'

as'tro•labe'

as•trol'o•ger

as•tro•log'ic *also* as'-
tro•log'i•cal

as•trol'o•gy

as'tro•naut'

as'tro•nau'tic *also* as'-
tro•nau'ti•cal

as'tro•nau'tics

as•tron'o•mer

as•tro•nom'i•cal *also*
as•tro•nom'ic

as•tron'o•my

as'tro•phys'i•cal

as'tro•phys'i•cist

as'tro•phys'ics

As'tro•Turf'®

as•tute'

a•sun'der

a•sy'lum

a•sym•met'ric *also*
a'sym•met'ri•cal

a•sym'me•try

as'ymp•tote'

as'ymp•tot'ic *also* as'-
ymp•tot'i•cal

at'a•rac'tic *also* at'a•
rax'ic

at'a•vism

at'a•vis'tic

a•tax'i•a *also* a•tax'y

a·tax′ic
at′el·ier′
a′the·ism
a′the·ist
a′the·is′tic *also* a′the·
　is′ti·cal
ath′e·nae′um *also*
　ath′e·ne′um
A·the′ni·an
a·thirst′
ath′lete′
ath′lete's foot′
ath·let′ic
ath·let′ics
a·thwart′
a·tilt′
At·lan′tic
At·lan′tis
at′las *(maps)*
At′las *(giant, missile)*
at′mos·phere′
at′mos·pher′ic *also*
　at′mos·pher′i·cal
at′mos·pher′ics
a′toll′
at′om
a·tom′ic
at′om·i·za′tion
at′om·ize′, -ized′, -iz′-
　ing
at′om·iz′er
a·to′nal
a′to·nal′i·ty
a·tone′, a·toned′,
　a·ton′ing
a·tone′ment
a·top′

a′tri·um *pl.* a′tri·a *or*
　a′tri·ums
a·tro′cious
a·troc′i·ty
a·troph′ic
at′ro·phy, -phied,
　-phy·ing
at′ro·pine′ *also* at′ro·
　pin
at·tach′
at′ta·ché′
at·tach′ment
at·tack′
at·tain′
at·tain′a·ble
at·tain′der
at·tain′ment
at·taint′
at′tar
at·tempt′
at·tend′
at·ten′dance
at·ten′dant
at·ten′tion
at·ten′tive
at·ten′u·ate′, -at′ed,
　-at′ing
at·test′
at′tic
at·tire′, -tired′, -tir′ing
at′ti·tude′
at′ti·tu′di·nal
at′ti·tu′di·nize′,
　-nized′, -niz′ing
at·tor′ney *pl.* -neys
attorney general *pl.*
　attorneys general

at·tract′
at·trac′tion
at·trac′tive
at·trac′tor *or* at·tract′-
　er
at·trib′ut·a·ble
at·trib′ute, -ut·ed, -ut·
　ing
at′tri·bute′ *n.*
at′tri·bu′tion
at·trib′u·tive
at·tri′tion
at·tune′, -tuned′, -tun′-
　ing
a·twit′ter
a·typ′i·cal
au′burn
au cou·rant′
auc′tion
auc′tion·eer′
auc·to′ri·al
au·da′cious
au·dac′i·ty
au′di·bil′i·ty
au′di·ble
au′di·ence
au′di·o′ *pl.* -os′
au′di·om′e·ter
au′di·o·phile′
au′di·o·vis′u·al *adj.*
au′di·o·vis′u·als *n.*
au′dit
au·di′tion
au′di·tor
au′di·to′ri·um *pl.* -ri·
　ums *or* -ri·a
au′di·to′ry

auf Wie′der•seh′en
au′ger *(tool)*
　♦*augur*
aught *(all, at all), also*
　ought
aught *(zero), also* ought
aug•ment′
aug′men•ta′tion
aug′men•ta′tive
au gra′tin
au′gur *(to predict)*
　♦*auger*
au′gu•ry
au•gust′ *(majestic)*
Au′gust *(month)*
auk
auld lang syne′
aunt *(relative)*
　♦*ant*
au′ra *pl.* -ras *or* rae
au′ral *(of the ear)*
　♦*oral*
au′re•ate
au′re•ole′ *also* au•re′o•
　la
au re•voir′
au′ri•cle *(ear part)*
　♦*oracle*
au•ric′u•lar
au•rif′er•ous
au′rochs′
au•ro′ra
aurora aus•tra′lis
aurora bo′re•al′is
aus•cul•ta′tion
aus′pice *pl.* -pi•ces′
aus•pi′cious

aus•tere′
aus•ter′i•ty
aus′tral
Aus•tra′lian
aus•tra′lo•pith′e•cine′
Aus′tri•an
au•teur′
au•then′tic
au•then′ti•cate′, -cat′-
　ed, -cat′ing
au•then′ti•ca′tion
au•then′ti•ca′tor
au′then•tic′i•ty
au′thor
au•thor′i•tar′i•an
au•thor′i•tar′i•an•ism
au•thor′i•ta′tive
au•thor′i•ty
au′thor•i•za′tion
au′thor•ize′, -ized′,
　-iz′ing
au′thor•ship′
au′tism
au•tis′tic
au′to *pl.* -tos
au′to•bahn′
au′to•bi•og′ra•pher
au′to•bi′o•graph′i•cal
　also au′to•bi′o•
　graph′ic
au′to•bi•og′ra•phy
au′to•clave′
au•toc′ra•cy
au′to•crat′
au′to•crat′ic
au′to•graph′
au′to•harp′

au′to•mat′
au′to•mate′, -mat′ed,
　-mat′ing
au′to•mat′ic
au′to•ma′tion
au•tom′a•ton
au′to•mo•bile′
au′to•mo•bil′ist
au′to•mo′tive
au′to•nom′ic
au•ton′o•mous
au•ton′o•my
au′top′sy
au′to•sug•ges′tion
au′tumn
au•tum′nal
aux•il′ia•ry
aux′in
a•vail′
a•vail′a•bil′i•ty
a•vail′a•ble
av′a•lanche′
a′vant-garde′
av′a•rice
av′a•ri′cious
a•vast′
av′a•tar′
a•venge′, a•venged′,
　a′veng•ing
av′e•nue′
a•ver′, a•verred′, a•ver′-
　ring
av′er•age, -aged, -ag•
　ing
a•verse′ *(reluctant)*
　♦*adverse*

a•ver'sion
a•vert'
a'vi•an
a'vi•a•rist
a'vi•ar'y
a'vi•a'tion
a'vi•a'tor
a'vi•a'trix
av'id
a•vid'i•ty
a'vi•on'ics
av'o•ca'do pl. -dos
av'o•ca'tion
av'o•cet'
a•void'
a•void'a•ble
a•void'ance
av'oir•du•pois'
a•vouch'
a•vow'
a•vow'al
a•vowed'
a•vow'ed•ly
a•vun'cu•lar
aw interj.
    ♦awe
a•wait'
a•wake', a•woke',
    a•waked', a•wak'ing
a•wak'en
a•wak'en•ing
a•ward'
a•ward•ee'
a•ware'
a•wash'
a•way' (absent)
    ♦aweigh

awe (to fill with won-
    der), awed, aw'ing
    ♦aw
a•weigh' (clear of the
    bottom)
    ♦away
awe'some
awe'-struck' or awe'-
    struck'en also awe'-
    strick'en
aw'ful
aw'ful•ly
a•while'
awk'ward
awl (tool)
    ♦all
awn'ing
a•wry'
ax or axe, axed, ax'ing
ax'i•al
ax'i•om
ax'i•o•mat'ic also ax'i•
    o•mat'i•cal
ax'is pl. ax'es
ax'le
ax'le•tree'
ax'o•lotl'
ax'on' also ax'one'
aye (affirmative), also
    ay
    ♦eye, I
a•zal'ea
az'i•muth
Az'tec' also Az'tec'an
az'ure
az'u•rite'

B

baa, baaed, baa'ing
bab'ble, -bled, -bling
babe
ba'bel
ba•boon'
ba•bush'ka
ba'by, -bied, -by•ing
Bab'y•lo'ni•an
ba'by's-breath' or
    ba'bies'-breath'
ba'by-sit', -sat', -sit'-
    ting
bac'ca•lau're•ate
bac'ca•rat'
bac'cha•nal'
bac'cha•na'lian
bach'e•lor
ba•h'e•lor's-but'ton
bac'il•lar'y also ba•cil'-
    lar
ba•cil'lus pl. -li'
back'ache'
back'bite', -bit', -bit'-
    ten, -bit'ing
back'bit'er
back'board'
back'bone'
back'break'ing
back'drop'
back'er
back'field'
back'fire', -fired',
    -fir'ing
back'-for•ma'tion

back'gam'mon
back'ground'
back'hand'
back'hand'ed
back'ing
back'lash'
back'log'
back'pack'
back'rest'
back'side'
back'slap'per
back'slide', -slid',
  -slid' or -slid'den,
  -slid'ing
back'space', -spaced',
  -spac'ing
back'spin'
back'stage'
back'stairs'
back'stitch'
back'stop'
back'stretch'
back'stroke'
back'track'
back'-up' *n. & adj.*
back'ward *also* back'-
  wards
back'wash'
back'wa'ter
back'woods'
ba'con
bac•te'ri•a *sing.* -ri•um
bac•te'ri•al
bac•te'ri•cid'al
bac•te'ri•cide'
bac•te'ri•o•log'ic *also*
  bac•te'ri•o•log'i•cal

bac•te'ri•ol'o•gist
bac•te'ri•ol'o•gy
bad *(not good)*, worse,
  worst
  ♦*bade*
badge
badg'er
bad'i•nage'
bad'lands'
bad'min'ton
bad'mouth' *also* bad'-
  mouth'
baf'fle, -fled, -fling
bag, bagged, bag'ging
bag•a•telle'
ba'gel
bag'gage
bag'gy
bag'pipe'
bag'pip'er
ba•guette'
Ba•ha'mi•an
bail *(money)*
  ♦*bale*
bail *(to empty)*
  ♦*bale*
bail'iff
bail'i•wick'
bail'out'
bairn
bait *(lure)*
  ♦*bate*
baize
bake, baked, bak'ing
Ba'ke•lite'®
bak'er's dozen
bak'er•y

ba'kla•va'
bal'a•lai•ka
bal'ance, -anced, -anc•
  ing
bal•brig'gan
bal'co•ny
bal'da•chin *also* bal'-
  da•chi'no *pl.* -nos.
bal'der•dash'
bald'-faced'
bald'head'ed
bald'ing
bald'pate'
bal'dric
bale *(to bundle)*, baled,
  bal'ing
  ♦*bail*
ba•leen'
bale'ful
bal'er
Ba•li•nese'
Bal'kan
balk'y
ball *(round object,
  dance)*
  ♦*bawl*
bal'lad
bal'lad•eer'
bal'lad•ry
bal'last
bal•le•ri'na
bal•let'
bal•let'o•mane'
bal•let'o•ma'ni•a
bal•lis'tic
bal'lis•ti'cian
bal•lis'tics

bal·loon'
bal·loon'ist
bal'lot
ball'park'
ball'play'er
ball'-point' pen
ball'room'
bal'ly·hoo' pl. -hoos'
bal'ly·hoo', -hooed',
-hoo'ing
balm'y
ba·lo'ney (nonsense)
  pl. -neys, also bo·lo'-
  ney
  ♦bologna
bal'sa
bal'sam
Bal'tic
Bal'ti·mo're·an
bal'us·ter
bal'us·trade'
bam·bi'no pl. -nos or
  -ni
bam·boo' pl. -boos'
bam·boo'zle, -zled,
  -zling
ban, banned, ban'ning
ba·nal'
ba·nal'i·ty
ba·nan'a
band (strip, group)
  ♦banned
band'age, -aged, -ag·
  ing
Band'-Aid'®
ban·dan'na or ban·
  dan'a

band'box'
ban·deau' pl. -deaux'
  or -deaus'
ban'de·role' or ban'-
  de·rol'
ban'di·coot'
ban'dit
ban'dit·ry
band'mas'ter
ban'do·leer' or ban'-
  do·lier'
band'stand'
band'wag'on
ban'dy, -died, -dy·ing
ban'dy-leg'ged
bane'ful
ban'gle
bang'-up' adj.
ban'ish
ban'ish·ment
ban'is·ter also ban'nis·
  ter
ban'jo pl. -jos or -joes
ban'jo·ist
bank'book'
bank'er
bank'ing
bank'roll'
bank'rupt'
bank'rupt·cy
ban'ner
banns
ban'quet (feast)
ban·quette' (bench)
ban'shee
ban'tam
ban'tam·weight'

ban'ter
ban'yan
ba'o·bab'
bap'tism
bap·tis'mal
Bap'tist
bap·tis·ter·y also bap'-
  tis·try
bap·tize', -tized', -tiz'-
  ing
bar, barred, bar'ring
barb
bar·bar'i·an
bar·bar'ic
bar'ba·rism
bar·bar'i·ty
bar'ba·rous
bar'be·cue', -cued',
  -cu'ing
barbed
bar'bel (feeder)
bar'bell' (weight)
bar'ber
bar'ber'ry
bar'ber·shop'
bar'bi·can
bar'bi·tal'
bar·bi'tu·rate
bar·bi'tu'ric acid
bar'ca·role' also bar'-
  ca·rolle'
bard (poet)
  ♦barred
bare (naked), bar'er,
  bar'est
  ♦bear

bare (to uncover),
   bared, bar'ing
   ♦*bear*

bare'back' *also* bare'-
   backed'

bare'faced'

bare'foot' *also* bare'-
   foot'ed

bare'hand'ed

bare'head'ed

bare'leg'ged

bare'ly

bar'gain

barge, barged, barg'ing

bar•gel'lo *pl.* -los

bar•ite'

bar'i•tone'

bar'i•um

bark (sound, outer cov-
   ering, ship)
   ♦*barque*

bar'keep'er

bar'ken•tine' *also*
   bar'quen•tine'

bark'er

bar'ley

bar'ley•corn'

bar'maid'

bar'man

bar mitz'vah

bar'na•cle

barn'storm'

barn'yard'

bar'o•graph'

ba•rom'e•ter

bar'o•met'ric *also*
   bar'o•met'ri•cal

ba•rom'e•try

bar'on (nobleman)
   ♦*barren*

bar'on•ess

bar'on•et

ba•ro'ni•al

bar'o•ny

ba•roque'

ba•rouche'

barque (ship)
   ♦*bark*

bar'racks

bar•ra•cu'da *pl.* -da *or*
   -das

bar'rage (dam)

bar•rage' (to direct fire
   at), -raged', -rag'ing

bar'ra•try

bar'rel, -reled *or*
   -relled, -rel•ing *or*
   -rel•ling

bar'rel•house'

bar'ren (sterile)
   ♦*baron*

bar•rette'

bar'ri•cade', -cad'ed,
   -cad'ing

bar'ri•er

bar'ri•o *pl.* -os

bar'ris•ter

bar'room'

bar'row

bar'tend'er

bar'ter

Bart'lett pear

bar'y•on'

bas'al

ba•salt'

ba•sal'tic

base (bad), bas'er, bas'-
   est
   ♦*bass (voice)*

base (to support),
   based, bas'ing
   ♦*bass (voice)*

base'ball'

base'board'

base'born'

base'man

base'ment

ba•sen'ji *pl.* -jis

bash

bash'ful

ba'sic (fundamental)

BA'SIC (computer lan-
   guage)

ba'si•cal•ly

bas'il

bas'i•lar *also* bas'i•lar'y

ba•sil'i•ca

bas'i•lisk'

ba'sin

ba'sis *pl.* -ses'

bask (to take pleasure)
   ♦*basque, Basque*

bas'ket

bas'ket•ball'

bas'ket•ry

basque (bodice)
   ♦*bask*

Basque (people)
   ♦*bask*

bas'-re•lief'

bass *(fish)*, *pl.* bass *or*
  bass'es
bass *(voice)*
  ♦*base*
bas'set
bas'si•net'
bas'so *pl.* -sos *or* -si
bas•soon'
bas•soon'ist
basso pro•fun'do *pl.*
  basso pro•fun'dos *or*
  bassi pro•fun'di
bass'wood'
bast
bas'tard•ize', -ized',
  -iz'ing
baste, bast'ed, bast'ing
bas•tille' *also* bas•tile'
bas'ti•na'do *pl.* -does,
  also bas'ti•nade'
bas'tion
bat, bat'ted, bat'ting
batch
bate *(to lessen)*, bat'ed,
  bat'ing
  ♦*bait*
ba•teau' *pl.* -teaux'
bath *n.*
bathe, bathed, bath'-
  ing
bath'er
ba•thet'ic
bath'house'
bath'o•lith'
ba'thos'
bath'robe'
bath'room'

bath'tub'
bath'y•scaph' *also*
  bath'y•scaphe'
bath'y•sphere'
ba•tik'
ba•tiste'
ba•ton'
bats'man
bat•tal'ion
bat'ten
bat'ter
bat'ter•ing-ram'
bat'ter•y
bat'ting
bat'tle, -tled, -tling
bat'tle-ax' *or* bat'tle-
  axe'
bat'tle•dore'
bat'tle•field'
bat'tle•front'
bat'tle•ground'
bat'tle•ment'
bat'tle•ship'
bat'ty
bau'ble
baud *(unit of speed)*
  ♦*bawd*
baux'ite'
bawd *(prostitute)*
  ♦*baud*
bawd'y
bawl *(to cry)*
  ♦*ball*
bay *(water, recess, red-
  dish-brown color,
  barking, laurel tree)*
  ♦*bey*

bay'ber'ry
bay'o•net', -net•ed *or*
  -net•ted, -net•ing *or*
  -net•ting
bay'ou *pl.* -ous
ba•zaar' *(market)*, *also*
  ba•zar'
  ♦*bizarre*
ba•zoo'ka
be *(to exist)*, *present
  tense* am, are *or ar-
  chaic* art, is, *pl.* are,
  are, are; *present par-
  ticiple* be'ing; *present
  subjunctive* be; *past
  tense* was, were *or
  archaic* wast *or* wert,
  was, *pl.* were, were,
  were; *past participle*
  been; *past subjunc-
  tive* were
  ♦*bee*
beach *(shore)*
  ♦*beech*
beach'comb'er
beach'head'
bea'con
bead'ing
bea'dle
bead'work'
bead'y
bea'gle
beak
beak'er
beam
bean'bag'
bean'ie

bean′pole′
bean′stalk′
bear *(animal)*
 ♦*bare*
bear *(to support)*, bore,
 borne *or* born, bear-
 ing
 ♦*bare*
bear′a·ble
beard′ed
bear′er
bear′ing *(mien)*
 ♦*baring*
bear′ish
bé′ar·naise′ sauce
bear′skin′
beast′ly
beat *(to hit)*, beat,
 beat′en *or* beat,
 beat′ing
 ♦*beet*
be·a·tif′ic
be·at′i·fi·ca′tion
be·at′i·fy′, -fied′, -fy′-
 ing
be·at′i·tude′
beat′nik
beau *(suitor)*, *pl.* beaus
 or beaux
 ♦*bow (weapon)*
beaut
beau′te·ous
beau·ti′cian
beau·ti·fi·ca′tion
beau′ti·ful
beau·ti·fy′, -fied′, -fy′-
 ing

beau′ty
beaux-arts′
bea′ver
be·calm′
be·cause′
beck′on
be·cloud′
be·come′, -came′,
 -come′, -com′ing
bed, bed′ded, bed′ding
be·daub′
be·daz′zle, -zled,
 -zling
bed′bug′
bed′cham′ber
bed′clothes′
bed′ding
be·deck′
be·dev′il
be·dew′
bed′fel′low
be·di′zen
bed′lam
bed′pan′
bed′post′
be·drag′gle, -glad,
 -gling
bed′rid′den
bed′rock′
bed′roll′
bed′room′
bed′side′
bed′sore′
bed′spread′
bed′spring′
bed′stead′
bed′time′

bee *(insect, gathering)*
 ♦*be*
beech *(tree)*
 ♦*beach*
beech′nut′
beef *pl.* beeves *or* beefs
beef′steak′
beef′y
bee′hive′
bee′keep′er
bee′line′
beer *(beverage)*
 ♦*bier*
bees′wax′
beet *(plant)*
 ♦*beat*
bee′tle *(insect, mallet)*
 ♦*betel*
be·fall′, -fell′, -fall′en,
 -fall′ing
be·fit′, -fit′ted, -fit′ting
be·fog′, -fogged′, -fog′-
 ging
be·fore′
be·fore′hand′
be·foul′
be·friend′
be·fud′dle, -dled,
 -dling
beg, begged, beg′ging
be·get′, -got′, -got′ten
 or -got′, -get′ting
be·get′ter
beg′gar
be·gin′, -gan′, -gun′,
 -gin′ning
be·gin′ner

be•go′nia
be•grime′, -grimed′,
  -grim′ing
be•grudge′, -grudged′,
  -grudg′ing
be•guile′, -guiled′,
  -guil′ing
be•guil′er
be•guine′
be•half′
be•have′, -haved′,
  -hav′ing
be•hav′ior
be•hav′ior•al
be•hav′ior•ism
be•hav′ior•ist
be•head′
be•he′moth
be•hest′
be•hind′
be•hind′hand′
be•hold′, -held′,
  -hold′ing
be•hold′en
be•hoove′, -hooved′,
  -hoov′ing
beige
be′ing
be•la′bor
be•lat′ed
be•lay′
bel can′to
belch′er
bel′dam *also* bel′dame
be•lea′guer
bel′fry
Bel′gian

be•lie′, -lied′, -ly′ing
be•lief′
be•li′er
be•liev′a•ble
be•lieve′, -lieved′,
  -liev′ing
be•liev′er
be•lit′tle, -tled, -tling
Be•liz′e•an *or* Be•liz′i•
  an
bell (*instrument*)
  ♦belle
bel′la•don′na
bell′-bot′tom
bell′-bot′toms
bell′boy′
belle (*woman*)
  ♦bell
belles-let′tres
bell′flow′er
bell′hop′
bel′li•cose′
bel′li•cos′i•ty
bel•lig′er•ence
bel•lig′er•en•cy
bel•lig′er•ent
bel′low
bel′lows
bell′weth′er
bel′ly, -lied, -ly•ing
bel′ly•ache′, -ached′,
  -ach′ing
bel′ly•but′ton
be•long′
be•lov′ed
be•low′
belt′ing

be•lu′ga
bel′ve•dere′
be′ma *pl.* -ma•ta
be•mire′, -mired′,
  -mir′ing
be•moan′
be•muse′, -mused′,
  -mus′ing
bench
bend, bent, bend′ing
be•neath′
ben′e•dic′tion
ben′e•fac′tion
ben′e•fac′tor
ben′e•fice
be•nef′i•cence
be•nef′i•cent
ben′e•fi′cial
ben′e•fi′ci•ar•y
ben′e•fit
be•nev′o•lence
be•nev′o•lent
be•night′ed
be•nign′
be•nig′nant
be•nig′ni•ty
Be•nin•ese′ *pl.* -ese′
ben′i•son
ben′ny
bent
ben′thic
ben′thos′
be•numb′
Ben′ze•drine′®
ben′zene′
ben′zine′ *also* ben′zin
ben′zo•ate′

ben·zo′ic acid
ben′zol′
be·queath′
be·quest′
be·rate′, -rat′ed, -rat′-
  ing
ber·ceuse′
be·reave′, -reaved′ or
  -reft′, -reav′ing
be·reave′ment
be·ret′
ber′ga·mot′
ber·i·ber′i
ber·ke′li·um
Ber·mu′da shorts
Ber·noul′li's effect
ber′ry (fruit)
  ♦bury
ber·serk′
berth (bed)
  ♦birth
ber′tha
ber′yl
be·ryl′li·um
be·seech′, -sought′ or
  -seeched′, -seech′ing
be·seem′
be·set′, -set′, -set′ting
be·side′ (next to)
be·sides′ (in addition)
be·siege′, -sieged′,
  -sieg′ing
be·smear′
be·smirch′
be·sot′, -sot′ted, -sot′-
  ting

be·span′gle, -gled,
  -gling
be·spat′ter
be·speak′, -spoke′,
  -spok′en or -spoke′,
  -speak′ing
be·spec′ta·cled
be·spread′, -spread′,
  -spread′ing
be·sprin′kle, -kled,
  -kling
best
bes′tial
bes·ti·al′i·ty
bes′ti·ar′y
be·stir′, -stirred′, -stir′-
  ring
be·stow′
be·strew′, -strewed′,
  -strewed′ or -strewn′,
  -strew′ing
be·stride′, -strode′,
  -strid′den, -strid′ing
best′-sell′ing
bet, bet, bet′ting
be′ta
be·take′, -took′, -tak′-
  en, -tak′ing
be′ta·tron′
be′tel (plant)
  ♦beetle
bête noire′
be·think′, -thought′,
  -think′ing
be·tide′, -tid′ed, -tid′-
  ing
be·times′

be·to′ken
be·tray′
be·troth′
be·troth′al
be·trothed′
bet′ter (greater)
  ♦bettor
bet′ter·ment
bet′tor (one who bets)
  ♦better
be·tween′
be·twixt′
bev′a·tron′
bev′el, -eled or -elled,
  -el·ing or -el·ling
bev′er·age
bev′y
be·wail′
be·ware′, -wared′,
  -war′ing
be·wil′der
be·witch′
bey (governor)
  ♦bay
be·yond′
bez′el
be·zique′
Bhu·tan·ese′ pl. -ese′
bi·a′ly pl. -lys
bi·an·nu·al (twice a
  year)
  ♦biennial, semiannual
bi′as, -ased or -assed,
  -as·ing or -as·sing
bi·ath′lon
bi·ax′i·al
bib, bibbed, bib′bing

bi·be·lot
Bi'ble
Bib'li·cal *also* bib'li·cal
bib'li·og'ra·pher
bib'li·o·graph'i·cal
    also bib'li·o·graph'ic
bib'li·og'ra·phy
bib'li·o·ma'ni·a
bib'li·o·ma'ni·ac'
bib'li·o·phile'
bib'u·lous
bi·cam'er·al
bi·car'bon·ate'
bi·cen·ten'a·ry
bi·cen·ten'ni·al
bi'ceps' *pl.* -ceps' *or*
    -ceps'es
bi·chlo'ride
bick'er
bi'col·or *also* bi·col'-
    ored
bi·con·cave'
bi·con·vex'
bi·cus'pid
bi'cy·cle, -cled, -cling
bi'cy·clist
bid *(to order, invite),*
    bade, bid'den *or* bid,
    bid'ding
bid *(to strive, offer),*
    bid, bid'ding
bid'der
bid'ding
bid'dy
bide, bid'ed *or* bode,
    bid'ed, bid'ing
bi·den'tate'

bi·det'
bi·en'ni·al *(once in two*
    years)
    ♦*biannual, semian-*
    nual
bier *(coffin stand)*
    ♦*beer*
bi·fo'cal
bi'fur·cate', -cat'ed,
    -cat'ing
bi'fur·ca'tion
big, big'ger, big'gest
big'a·mist
big'a·mous
big'a·my
Big Dip'per
big'-heart'ed
big'horn'
bight *(loop, bay)*
    ♦*bite, byte*
big'ot
big'ot·ed
big'ot·ry
big'wig'
bi'jou' *pl.* -joux'
bike, biked, bik'ing
bike'way'
bi·ki'ni
bi·lat'er·al
bile
bilge, bilged, bilg'ing
bi·lin'gual
bil'ious
bilk'er
bill'board'
bil'let

bil'let-doux' *pl.* bil'-
    lets-doux'
bill'fold'
bill'hook'
bil'liard
bil'liards
bill'ing
bil'lings·gate'
bil'lion
bil'lion·aire'
bil'lionth
bil'low
bil'ly
bi'me·tal'lic
bi·met'al·lism
bi·met'al·list
bi·month'ly *(once in*
    two months)
    ♦*semimonthly*
bin *(container)*
    ♦*been*
bi'na·ry
bin·au'ral
bind, bound, bind'ing
bind'er
bind'er·y
bind'weed'
binge
bin'go
bin'na·cle
bin·oc'u·lar
bi·no'mi·al
bi'o·as'say'
bi'o·as'tro·nau'tics
bi'o·chem'i·cal *also*
    bi'o·chem'ic
bi'o·chem'ist

bi·o·chem'is·try
bi·o·de·grad'a·ble
bi·o·en'gi·neer'ing
bi·o·feed'back'
bi·o·gen'e·sis
bi·o·ge·o·graph'ic *also*
   bi·o·ge·o·graph'i·cal
bi·o·ge·og'ra·phy
bi·og'ra·pher
bi·o·graph'i·cal *also*
   bi·o·graph'ic
bi·og'ra·phy
bi·o·log'i·cal *also* bi·o·
   log'ic
bi·ol'o·gist
bi·ol'o·gy
bi·o·lu'mi·nes'cence
bi·o·lu'mi·nes'cent
bi'ome'
bi·o·med'i·cine
bi·o·met'rics
bi·on'ics
bi·o·phys'i·cist
bi·o·phys'ics
bi·op'sic
bi·op'sy
bi·o·rhythm'
bi·o·rhyth'mic
bi·os'co·py *pl.* -pies
bi·o·sphere'
bi·o·syn'the·sis
bi·o·syn·thet'ic
bi·o'ta
bi·ot'ic
bi'o·tin
bi·par'ti·san
bi·par'ti·san·ism

bi·par'tite'
bi·par·ti'tion
bi'ped'
bi'plane'
bi·po'lar
bi·ra'cial
bi·ra'cial·ism
birch
bird'bath'
bird'brain'
bird'cage'
bird'call'
bird'house'
bird'ie
bird'lime'
bird'seed'
bird's'-eye'
bi·ret'ta
birr *(whirring sound)*
   ♦bur, burr
birth *(beginning)*
   ♦berth
birth'day'
birth'mark'
birth'place'
birth'rate'
birth'right'
birth'stone'
bis'cuit
bi'sect'
bi·sec'tion
bi·sec'tor
bi·sex'u·al
bish'op
bish'op·ric
bis'muth
bi'son

bisque
bis'tro *pl.* -tros
bi·sul'fate'
bit
bite *(to cut or tear)*, bit,
   bit'ten *or* bit, bit'ing
   ♦bight, byte
bit'ter
bit'tern
bit'ter·root'
bit'ters
bit'ter·sweet'
bi·tu'men
bi·tu'mi·nous
bi·va'lent
bi'valve'
biv'ou·ac, -acked,
   -ack·ing
bi·week'ly *(once in two*
   weeks)
   ♦semiweekly
bi·year'ly *(once in two*
   years)
   ♦semiyearly
bi·zarre' *(odd)*
   ♦bazaar
blab, blabbed, blab'-
   bing
blab'ber
blab'ber·mouth'
blab'by
black'-and-blue' *adj.*
black'ball'
black'ber'ry
black'bird'
black'board'
black'bod'y

black'cap'
black'damp'
black'en
black'-eyed' pea
black'-eyed' Su'san
black'guard
black'head'
black'ing
black'jack'
black'list'
black'mail'
black'-mar'ket v.
black'out' n.
black'smith'
black'snake'
black'thorn'
black'top', -topped',
  -top'ping
blad'der
blade
blad'ed
blah
blain
blam'a•ble also
  blame'a•ble
blame, blamed, blam'-
  ing
blame'less
blam'er
blame'wor'thy
blanch (to whiten), also
  blench
blanc•mange'
bland
blan'dish
bland'ly
blan'ket

blank'ly
blare, blared, blar'ing
blar'ney
bla•sé'
blas•phemc',
  -phemed', -phem'ing
blas'phe•mous
blas'phe•my
blast'off' n., also
  blast'-off'
blas'tu•la pl. -las or
  -lae'
bla'tan•cy
bla'tant
blath'er
blath'er•skite'
blaze, blazed, blaz'ing
blaz'er
bla'zon
bleach
bleach'ers
bleak'ly
blear'y
blear'y-eyed'
bleat'er
bleed, bled, bleed'ing
bleed'er
bleed'ing-heart'
bleep
blem'ish
blench (to shy away)
  ♦blanch
blend'er
bless, blessed or blest,
  bless'ing
bless'ed adj.
blight

blimp
blind'ers
blind'fold'
blink'er
blintz also blin'tze
blip'
bliss'ful
blis'ter
blithe, blith'er, blith'-
  est
blitz
blitz'krieg'
bliz'zard
bloat
blob
bloc (group)
block (solid substance)
block•ade', -ad'ed,
  -ad'ing
block•ade'-run'ner
block'age
block'bust'er
block'head'
block'house'
bloke
blond fem. blonde
blood'cur'dling
blood'ed
blood'hound'
blood'less
blood'let'ting
blood'line'
blood'mo•bile'
blood'root'
blood'shed'
blood'shot'
blood'stain'

blood'stone'

blood stream *also*
  blood'stream'

blood'suck'er

blood'thirst'y

blood'y, -ied, -y·ing

bloom'er

bloop'er

blos'som

blot, blot'ted, blot'ting

blotch

blot'ter

blouse, bloused,
  blous'ing

blow, blew, blown,
  blow'ing

blow'-dry', -dried',
  -dry'ing

blow'er

blow'fish' *pl.* -fish' *or*
  -fish'es

blow'gun'

blow'hard'

blow'hole'

blow'out' *n.*

blow'pipe'

blow'torch'

blow'up' *n.*

blow'zy *also* blow'sy

blub'ber

bludg'eon

blue *(of the color blue),*
  blu'er, blu'est
  ♦*blew*

blue *(to color),* blued,
  blu'ing
  ♦*blew*

blue'bell'

blue'ber'ry

blue'bird'

blue'bon'net

blue book *also* blue'-
  book'

blue'bot'tle

blue'-chip' *adj.*

blue'-col'lar *adj.*

blue'fish' *pl.* -fish' *or*
  -fish'es

blue'grass'

blue'jack'et

blue'nose'

blue'-pen'cil, -ciled *or*
  -cilled, -cil·ing *or*
  -cil·ling

blue'print'

blue'-rib'bon *adj.*

blues

blue'stock'ing

blu'ets

bluff'er

blu'ing *also* blue'ing

blu'ish *also* blue'ish

blun'der

blun'der·buss'

blunt'ly

blur, blurred, blur'ring

blurb

blur'ry

blurt

blush'er

blus'ter

blus'ter·y *also* blus'ter·
  ous

bo'a

boar *(animal)*
  ♦*bore*

board *(piece of wood)*
  ♦*bored*

board'er *(lodger)*
  ♦*border*

board'ing house *also*
  board'ing·house'

board'walk'

boast'ful

boat'house'

boat'load'

boat'man

boat'swain *also* bo"-
  s'n, bo'sun

bob, bobbed, bob'bing

bob'bin

bob'ble, -bled, -bling

bob'by

bob'by·sox'er

bob'cat'

bob'o·link'

bob'sled', -sled'ded,
  -sled'ding

bob'tail'

bob·white'

bode, bod'ed, bod'ing

bod'ice

bod'i·ly

bod'kin

bod'y

bod'y·build'er

bod'y·guard'

bod'y·surf'

bog, bogged, bog'ging

bo'gey *(golf score),* pl.
  -geys

♦*bogie, bogy*

bog'gle, -gled, -gling

bog'gy

bo'gie *(railroad car)*,
    also bo'gy
    ♦*bogey*

bo'gus

bo'gy *(hobglobin)*, also
    bo'gey, bo'gie

Bo·he'mi·an *also* bo·
    he'mi·an

boil'er

boil'er·mak'er

bois'ter·ous

bo'la *also* bo'las

bold'face', -faced',
    -fac'ing

bold'-faced' *adj.*

bold'ly

bole *(tree trunk)*
    ♦*boll, bowl*

bo·le'ro *pl.* -ros

Bo·liv'i·an

boll *(seed pod)*
    ♦*bole, bowl*

bol'lix

bo·lo'gna *(meat)*, also
    ba·lo'ney, bo·lo'ney

Bol'she·vik'

Bol'she·vism

bol'ster

bolt'er

bo'lus *pl.* -lus·es

bomb

bom·bard'

bom'bar·dier'

bom·bard'ment

bom'bast'

bom·bas'tic

bom'ba·zine'

bomb'er

bomb'proof'

bomb'shell'

bomb'sight'

bo'na fide'

bo·nan'za

bon'bon'

bond'age

bond'hold'er

bond'ing

bond'ser'vant

bonds'man

bone, boned, bon'ing

bone'black'

bone'-dry'

bone'fish' *pl.* -fish' or
    -fish'es

bone'head'

bon'er

bon'fire'

bong

bon'go *pl.* -gos

bon'ho·mie'

bo·ni'to *pl.* -to *or* -tos

bon' mot' *pl.* bons'
    mots'

bon'net

bon'ny *also* bon'nie

bon·sai' *pl.* -sai'

bo'nus *pl.* -nus·es

bon vi·vant' *pl.* bons
    vi·vants'

bon voy·age'

bon'y

boo *pl.* boos

boo, booed, boo'ing

boo'-boo *pl.* -boos

boo'by

boo'dle, -dled, -dling

boog'ie-woog'ie

book'bind'er·y

book'bind'ing

book'case'

book'end' *also* book
    end

book'ie

book'ing

book'ish

book'keep'er

book'keep'ing

book'let

book'mak'er

book'mark'

book'mo·bile'

book'plate'

book'rack'

book'sell'er

book'shelf'

book'stall'

book'stand'

book'store'

book'worm'

boom

boo'mer·ang'

boon'docks'

boon'dog'gle, -gled,
    -gling

boor'ish

boost'er

boot'black'

boot'ee *(baby shoe),*
  also boot'ie
  ♦*booty*
booth *pl.* booths
boot'jack'
boot'leg', -legged',
  -leg'ging
boot'leg'ger
boot'lick'
boot'strap'
boo'ty *(plunder)*
  ♦*bootee*
booze, boozed, booz'-
  ing
booz'er
booz'y
bop, bopped, bop'ping
bo'rate'
bo'rax'
Bor·deaux' *pl.* -deaux
bor·del'lo *pl.* -los
bor'der *(margin)*
  ♦*boarder*
bor'der·land'
bor'der·line'
bore *(to drill, tire),*
  bored, bor'ing
  ♦*boar*
bore *(wave)*
  ♦*boar*
bo're·al
bore'dom
bor'er
bo'ric
bor'ing
born *(brought into life)*
  ♦*borne, bourn*

born'-a·gain' *adj.*
borne *(carried)*
  ♦*born, bourn*
bo'ron'
bor'ough *(town)*
  ♦*burro, burrow*
bor'row
borscht *also* borsht,
  borsch
bor'zoi'
bosh
bosk'y
bos'om
bo'son
boss'ism
boss'y
bo·tan'i·cal *also* bo·
  tan'ic
bot'a·nist
bot'a·ny
botch'er
bot'fly'
both
both'er
both'er·a'tion
both'er·some
bot'tle, -tled, -tling
bot'tle·neck'
bot'tle-nosed' dol-
  phin
bot'tom
bot'tom·less
bot'u·lism'
bou'doir'
bouf·fant'
bou'gain·vil'le·a
bough *(branch)*

♦*bow (section of a*
  ship, a bending)
bouil'la·baisse'
bouil'lon' *(broth)*
  ♦*bullion*
boul'der *(rock)*
  ♦*bolder*
boul'e·vard'
bounce, bounced,
  bounc'ing
bounc'er
bound
bound'a·ry
bound'en
bound'er
boun'te·ous
boun'ti·ful
boun'ty
bou·quet'
bour'bon
bour·geois' *pl.* -geois'
bour·geoi·sie'
bourn *(stream), also*
  bourne
  ♦*born, borne*
bourse
bout
bou·tique'
bou·ton·niere' *also*
  bou'ton·nière'
bo'vine'
bow *(section of a ship,*
  a bending)
  ♦*bough*
bow *(weapon)*
  ♦*beau*
bowd'ler·i·za'tion

bowd'ler·ize', -ized',
   -iz'ing
bow'el
bow'er
bow'fin'
bow'ie knife
bowl *(dish, ball, game)*
   ♦*bole, boll*
bow'leg'
bow'leg'ged
bow'ler
bow'line
bowl'ing
bow'sprit'
bow'string'
bow'-wow'
box'car'
box'er
box'ing
box'-of'fice *adj.*
box'wood'
boy *(male child)*
   ♦*buoy*
boy'cott'
boy'friend'
boy'hood'
boy'sen·ber'ry
bra
brace, braced, brac'ing
brace'let
brac'er
brach'i·o·pod'
brack'en
brack'et
brack'ish
bract
brad

brae *(hillside)*
   ♦*bray*
brag, bragged, brag'-
   ging
brag'ga·do'ci·o *pl.* -os
brag'gart
brag'ger
Brah'ma
Brah'man *also* Brah'-
   min
braid'ing
Braille *also* braille
brain'pan'
brain'storm'
brain'wash'
brain'y
braise *(to cook)*,
   braised, brais'ing
   ♦*braze*
brake *(fern, thicket)*
   ♦*break*
brake *(to reduce)*,
   braked, brak'ing
   ♦*break*
brake'age
bram'ble
bram'bly
bran
branch
bran'dish
brand'-new'
bran'dy, -died, -dy·ing
brant *pl.* brant *or*
   brants
brash'ly
bras·siere' *or* bras·
   sière'

brass'y
brat'ty
brat'wurst'
bra·va'do *pl.* -does *or*
   -dos
brave, brav'er, brav'est
brave, braved, brav'ing
brav'er·y
bra'vo *pl.* -voes *or* -vos
bra·vu'ra
brawl'er
brawn'y
bray *(harsh cry)*
   ♦*brae*
bray'er
braze *(to solder)*,
   brazed, braz'ing
   ♦*braise*
bra'zen
bra'zier
Bra·zil'ian
Bra·zil' nut
breach *(violation, gap)*
   ♦*breech*
bread *(food)*
   ♦*bred*
bread'-and-but'ter
   adj.
bread'bas'ket
bread'board'
bread'fruit'
bread'stuff'
breadth *(width)*
   ♦*breath*
bread'win'ner
break *(to crack)*,

broke, bro′ken,
break′ing
♦*brake*
break′a·ble
break′age
break′down′ *n.*
break′er
break′fast
break′front′
break′neck′ *adj.*
break′through′ *n.*
break′up′ *n.*
break′wa′ter
bream *pl.* bream *or*
  breams
breast′bone′
breast′plate′
breast′work′
breath *(air)*
  ♦*breadth*
breathe, breathed,
  breath′ing
breath′er
breath′less
breath′tak′ing
breath′y
breech *(buttocks)*
  ♦*breach*
breech′cloth′
breech′es
breech′load′er
breed, bred, breed′ing
breed′er
breeze, breezed,
  breez′ing
breeze′way′
breez′y

breth′ren
bre·vet′
bre′vi·ar·y
brev′i·ty
brew′er
brew′er·y
brew′ing
bri′ar *(shrub, pipe),*
  also bri′er
bribe, bribed, brib′ing
brib′er·y
bric′-a-brac′
brick′bat′
brick′lay′er
brick′work′
brick′yard′
bri′dal *(wedding)*
  ♦*bridle*
bride′groom′
brides′maid′
bridge, bridged,
  bridg′ing
bridge′a·ble
bridge′head′
bridge′work′
bri′dle *(to restrain),*
  -dled, -dling
  ♦*bridal*
Brie
brief′case′
brief′ing
bri′er *(plant), also*
  bri′ar
brig
bri·gade′
brig′a·dier′ general

  pl. brig′a·dier′ gener-
    als
brig′and
brig′and·age
brig′an·tine′
bright′en
bright′ness
bril′liance *also* bril′-
  lian·cy
bril′liant
bril′lian·tine′
brim′ful′
brim′stone′
brin′dle
brin′dled
brine
bring, brought, bring′-
  ing
brink
brin′y
bri′o
bri·oche′
bri·quette′ *also* bri·
  quet′
bris′ket
brisk′ly
bris′ling
bris′tle, -tled, -tling
bris′tly
bri·tan′nia metal
britch′es
Brit′i·cism *also* Brit′-
  ish·ism
Brit′ish
Brit′on *(person)*
  ♦*Britain*
brit′tle

broach *(to introduce)*
  ♦*brooch*
broad'ax' *also* broad'-
  axe'
broad'cast', -cast' *or*
  -cast'ed, -cast'ing
broad'cloth'
broad'en
broad'leaf'
broad'-leaved' *also*
  broad'-leafed'
broad'loom'
broad'-mind'ed
broad'side'
broad'sword'
broad'tail'
Broad'way'
bro·cade', -cad'ed,
  -cad'ing
broc'co·li
bro·chette'
bro·chure'
bro'gan
brogue
broil'er
bro'ken
bro'ken-down'
bro'ken·heart'ed
bro'ker
bro'ker·age
bro·me'li·ad'
bro'mic acid
bro'mide'
bro·mid'ic
bro'mine'
bron'chi·a *sing.* -chi·
  um

bron'chi·al
bron'chi·ole'
bron·chi'tis
bron'cho·pneu·mon'-
  ia
bron'cho·scope'
bron'chus *pl.* -chi'
bron'co *pl.* -cos
bron'co·bust'er
bron'to·saur' *also*
  bron'to·sau'rus
bronze, bronzed,
  bronz'ing
brooch *(pin)*
  ♦*broach*
brood'er
brood'y
brook
broom *(sweeper)*
  ♦*brougham*
broom'corn'
broom'stick'
broth
broth'el
broth'er
broth'er·hood'
broth'er-in-law' *pl.*
  broth'ers-in-law'
brougham *(carriage)*
  ♦*broom*
brou'ha·ha'
brow'beat', -beat',
  -beat'en, -beat'ing
brown'ie
brown'out' *n.*
brown'stone'

browse, browsed,
  brows'ing
bru'cel·lo'sis
bru'in
bruise *(to injure)*,
  bruised, bruis'ing
  ♦*brews*
bruis'er
bruit *(to spread news)*
  ♦*brute*
brunch
bru·net' *fem.* bru·
  nette'
brunt
brush'-off' *n.*
brush'wood'
brush'work'
brusque *also* brusk
Brus'sels sprouts
bru'tal
bru·tal'i·ty
bru'tal·ize', -ized', -iz'-
  ing
brute *(beast)*
  ♦*bruit*
brut'ish
bry'o·phyte'
bub'ble, -bled, -bling
bub'bly
bu'bo *pl.* -boes
bu·bon'ic
buc'ca·neer'
buck'a·roo' *pl.* -roos',
  also buck'er·oo' *pl.*
  -oos
buck'board'
buck'et

buck′eye′

buck′le, -led, -ling

buck′ler

buck′ram

buck′saw′

buck′shot′

buck′skin′

buck′tooth′ *pl.* -teeth′

buck′toothed′

buck′wheat′

bu·col′ic

bud, bud′ded, bud′-
ding

bud′der

Bud′dha

Bud′dhism

Bud′dhist

bud′dy

budge, budged, budg′-
ing

budg′er·i·gar′

budg′et

budg′et·ar′y

buff

buf′fa·lo′ *also* -loes′ *or*
-los′ *or* ′-lo

buff′er

buf·fet′ *(sideboard)*

buf′fet *(blow)*

buf′fle·head′

buf·foon′

buf·foon′er·y

bug, bugged, bug′ging

bug′a·boo′ *pl.* -boos′

bug′bear′

bug′-eyed′

bug′ger

bug′gy

bu′gle, -gled, -gling

bu′gler

build *(to erect),* built,
build′ing

♦*billed*

build′er

build′ing

build′-up′ *n., also*
build′up′

built′-in′

built′-up′

bulb

bul′bar

bul′bous

bul′bul′

Bul·gar′i·an

bulge, bulged, bulg′ing

bulg′y

bulk′head′

bulk′y

bull′dog′, -dogged′,
-dog′ging

bull′doze′, -dozed′,
-doz′ing

bull′doz′er

bul′let

bul′le·tin

bul′let·proof′

bull′fight′

bull′fight′er

bull′finch′

bull′frog′

bull′head′

bull′head′ed

bul′lion *(metal)*
♦*bouillon*

bull′ish

bull′necked′

bul′lock

bull′pen′

bull′ring′

bull′roar′er

bull′s eye *also* bull′s′-
eye′

bul′ly, -lied, -ly·ing

bul′rush′

bul′wark

bum, bummed, bum′-
ming

bum′ble, -bled, -bling

bum′ble·bee′

bump′er

bump′kin

bump′tious

bump′y

bun

bunch′y

bun′co *pl.* -cos, *also*
bun′ko *pl.* -kos

bun′dle, -dled, -dling

bun′ga·low′

bung′hole′

bun′gle, -gled, -gling

bun′ion

bunk

bun′ker

bunk′house′

bun′kum *also* bun′-
combe

bun′ny

Bun′sen burner

bunt'ing

bunt'line

buoy *(float)*
    ♦*boy*

buoy•an•cy

buoy'ant

bur *(seed), also* burr

bur'ble', -bled, -bling

bur'den

bur'den•some

bur'dock'

bu'reau *pl.* -reaus *or*
    reaux

bu•reauc'ra•cy

bu'reau•crat'

bu'reau•crat'ic

bu•rette' *also* bu•ret'

burg *(town)*
    ♦*burgh*

bur'geon

burg'er *(hamburger)*
    ♦*burgher*

bur'gess

burgh *(town)*
    ♦*burg*

burgh'er *(citizen)*
    ♦*burger*

bur'glar

bur'glar•ize', -ized',
    -iz'ing

bur'gla•ry

bur'gle, -gled, -gling

bur'go•mas'ter

bur'gun•dy *(red color)*

Bur'gun•dy *(wine)*

bur'i•al

bu'rin

burl

bur'lap'

bur•lesque', -lesqued',
    -lesqu'ing

bur'ly

Bur•mese' *adj.,*
    also Bur'man

Bur•mese' *pl.* -mese'

burn, burned *or* burnt,
    burn'ing

burn'er

bur'nish

bur•noose' *also* bur•
    nous'

burn'out' *n.*

burp

bur *(prickly seed) also*
    burr
    ♦*birr*

burr *(edge, trill,*
    washer), also bur
    ♦*birr, bur*

bur'ro *(donkey), pl.*
    -ros
    ♦*borough, burrow*

bur'row *(hole)*
    ♦*borough, burro*

bur•sa' *pl.* -sae *or* -sas

bur'sar

bur•si'tis

burst, burst, burst'ing

bur'y *(to inter),* -ied,
    -y'ing
    ♦*berry*

bus *(motor vehicle), pl.*
    bus'es *or* bus'ses

    ♦*buss*

bus *(to transport),*
    bused *or* bussed,
    bus'ing *or* bus'sing
    ♦*buss*

bus'by

bushed

bush'el

bush'ing

bush'-league' *adj.*

bush'mas'ter

bush'whack'

bush'y

busi'ness

busi'ness•like'

busi'ness•man'

busi'ness•wom'an

bus'kin

buss *(kiss)*
    ♦*bus*

bus'tard

bust'er

bus'tle, -tled, -tling

bust'y

bus'y, -ied, -y'ing

bus'y•bod'y

but *conj.*
    ♦*butt*

bu'ta•di'ene'

bu'tane'

butch'er

butch'er•y

but'ler

butt *(target, end)*
    ♦*but*

butt *(to hit, join)*
    ♦*but*

butte
but′ter
but′ter-and-eggs′
but′ter·cup′
but′ter·fat′
but′ter·fin′gered
but′ter·fin′gers
but′ter·fish′ *pl.* -fish′
  or -fish′es
but′ter·fly′
but′ter·milk′
but′ter·nut′
but′ter·scotch′
but′ter·y
but′tock
but′ton
but′ton·hole′, -holed′,
  -hol′ing
but′ton·hook′
but′ton·wood′
but′tress
bu′tyl
bu·tyr′ic
bux′om
buy (*to purchase*),
  bought, buy′ing
  ♦*by, bye*
buy′er
buz′zard
buzz′er
by *prep.*
  ♦*buy, bye*
by′-and-by′ *n.*
bye (*position*)
  ♦*buy, by*
bye′-bye′

by′-e·lec′tion *also*
  bye′-e·lec′tion
by′gone′
by′law′
by′-line′, -lined′, -lin′-
  ing, *also* by′line′
by·lin′er
by′-pass′ *also* by′pass′
by′-path′
by′-play′
by′-prod′uct
by′road′
bys′sus *pl.* -sus·es *or*
  -si
by′stand′er
byte (*computer unit*)
  ♦*bight, bite*
by′way′
by′word′
Byz′an·tine′

C

cab
ca·bal′, -balled′, -ball′-
  ing
cab·al·le′ro *pl.* -ros
ca·ban′a *also* ca·ba′ña
cab′a·ret′
cab′bage
cab′by
cab′in
cab′i·net
cab′i·net·mak′er
cab′i·net·work′

ca′ble, -bled, -bling
ca′ble·gram′
cab′o·chon′
ca·boo′dle
ca·boose′
ca·ca′o *pl.* -os
cach′a·lot′
cache (*to hide*), cached,
  cach′ing
  ♦*cash*
ca·chet′
cack′le, -led, -ling
cac′o·mis′tle
ca·coph′o·nous
ca·coph′o·ny
cac′tus *pl.* -ti′ *or* -tus·
  es
cad
ca·dav′er
ca·dav′er·ous
cad′die (*to carry golf
  clubs*), -died, -dy·ing,
  also cad′dy
cad′dis fly *also* cad′-
  dice fly
cad′dish
cad′dy (*box*)
  ♦*caddie*
ca′dence
ca·den′za
ca·det′
cadge, cadged, cadg′-
  ing
cad′mic
cad′mi·um
cad′re
ca·du′ce·us *pl.* -ce·i′

Cae·sar′e·an *also* cae·
 sar′e·an section
cae·su′ra *pl.* -ras *or*
 -rae
cae·su′ral *also* cae·su′-
 ric
ca·fé′
caf′e·te′ri·a
caf·feine′ *also* caf·fein′
caf′tan
cage, caged, cag′ing
cag′ey *also* cag′y
ca·hoots′
cai′man *pl.* -mans, *also*
 cay′man
cairn
cairn′gorm′
Cairn terrier
cais′son′
cai′tiff
ca·jole′, -joled′, -jol′ing
ca·jol′er·y
cake, caked, cak′ing
cake′walk′
cal′a·bash′
cal′a·boose′
ca·la′di·um
cal′a·mine′
ca·lam′i·tous
ca·lam′i·ty
cal·car′e·ous
cal·cif′er·ous
cal′ci·fi·ca′tion
cal′ci·fy′, -fied′, -fy′ing
cal′ci·mine′
cal′ci·na′tion

cal·cine′, -cined′, -cin′-
 ing
cal′cite′
cal·cit′ic
cal′ci·um
cal′cu·la·ble
cal′cu·late′, -lat′ed,
 -lat′ing
cal′cu·la′tion
cal′cu·la′tor
cal′cu·lus *pl.* -li′ *or*
 -lus·es
cal′dron *also* caul′dron
cal′en·dar *(time)*
cal′en·der *(press)*
cal′ends *pl.* -ends
calf *pl.* calves
calf′skin′
cal′i·ber
cal′i·brate′, -brat′ed,
 -brat′ing
cal′i·bra′tion
cal′i·bra′tor
cal′i·co *pl.* -coes *or*
 -cos
Cal′i·for′nian
cal′i·for′ni·um
cal′i·per *also* cal′li·per
ca′liph *also* ca′lif
ca′liph·ate′
cal′is·then′ics
cal′la
call′board′
call′er
cal·lig′ra·pher *also*
 cal·lig′ra·phist
cal′li·graph′ic

cal·lig′ra·phy ←
call′ing
cal′li·o·pe′
cal·los′i·ty
cal′lous *(unfeeling)*
 ♦*callus*
cal′low
cal′lus *(hard tissue)*
 ♦*callous*
calm′ly
cal′o·mel′
ca·lor′ic
cal′o·rie
cal′o·rif′ic
cal′o·rim′e·ter
cal′u·met′
ca·lum′ni·ate′, -at′ed,
 -at′ing
ca·lum′ni·a′tion
ca·lum′ni·a′tor
ca·lum′ni·ous
cal′um·ny
cal′va·ry
calve, calved, calv′ing
Cal′vin·ism
Cal′vin·ist
ca·lyp′so
ca·lyx′ *pl.* -lyx·es *or* -ly·
 ces′
cam
ca′ma·ra′de·rie
cam′as *also* cam′ass
cam′ber
cam′bi·um
Cam·bo′di·an
cam′bric
cam′el

ca·mel'lia
ca·mel'o·pard'
Cam'e·lot'
cam'el's-hair' *adj.*
Cam'em·bert'
cam·e·o' *pl.* -os'
cam'er·a
cam'er·al
cam'er·a·man'
cam'i·sole'
cam'ou·flage',
  -flaged', -flag'ing
cam'ou·flag'er
cam·paign'
cam·pa·ni'le *pl.* -les or
  -li
camp'fire'
camp'ground'
cam'phor
cam'phor·ate', -at'ed,
  -at'ing
cam·phor'ic
camp'site'
cam'pus *pl.* -pus·es
cam'shaft'
can *auxiliary, past*
  tense could
can *(to preserve),*
  canned, can'ning
Ca·na'di·an
ca·naille'
ca·nal'
ca·nal'i·za'tion
ca·nal'ize', -ized', -iz'-
  ing
can'a·pé' *(appetizer)*
  ♦canopy

ca·nard'
ca·nar'y
ca·nas'ta
can'can'
can'cel, -celed or
  -celled, -cel·ing or
  -cel·ling
can'cel·a·ble
can'cel·la'tion *also*
  can'ce·la'tion
can'cer *(tumor)*
Can'cer *(constellation)*
can'cer·ous
can·del'a
can·de·la'brum *pl.*
  -bra *or* -brums, *also*
  can·de·la'bra *pl.*
  -bras
can'did
can'di·da·cy *also* can'-
  di·da·ture'
can'di·date'
can'died
can'dle
can'dle·hold'er
can'dle·light'
can'dle·pin'
can'dle·pow'er
can'dle·stick'
can'dle·wick'
can'dor
can'dy, -died, -dy·ing
cane, caned, can'ing
cane'brake'
can'er
ca'nine'
can'is·ter

can'ker
can'ker·ous
can'ker·worm'
can'na
can'na·bis
can'nel
can'nel·lo'ni
can'ner·y
can'ni·bal
can'ni·bal·ism
can'ni·bal·is'tic
can'ni·bal·i·za'tion
can'ni·bal·ize', -ized',
  -iz'ing
can'ning
can'non *(gun), pl.* -non
  or -nons
  ♦canon
can'non·ade', -ad'ed,
  -ad'ing
can'non·ball'
can'non·eer'
can'not
can'ny
ca·noe', -noed', -noe'-
  ing
ca·noe'ist
can'on *(ecclesiastical*
  law, clergyman)
  ♦cannon
ca·non'i·cal *also* ca·
  non'ic
can·on·ic'i·ty
can'on·i·za'tion
can'on·ize', -ized', -iz'-
  ing

can'o•py *(to cover),*
  -pied, -py•ing
  ♦*canapé*

cant *(slope, whining
  speech)*

can't *contraction*

can'ta•bi•le'

can'ta•loupe' *also*
  can'ta•loup'

can•tan'ker•ous

can•ta'ta

can•teen'

can'ter *(gait)*
  ♦*cantor*

Can'ter•bur'y bells

can'thus *pl.* -thi'

can'ti•cle

can'ti•le'ver

can•ti'na

can'tle

can'to *pl.* -tos

can'ton

Can'ton•ese' *pl.* -ese'

can'tor *(singer)*
  ♦*canter*

Ca•nuck'

can'vas *(fabric)*
  ♦*canvass*

can'vas•back'

can'vass *(poll)*
  ♦*canvas*

can'yon

cap, capped, cap'ping

ca'pa•bil'i•ty

ca'pa•ble

ca•pa'cious

ca•pac'i•tance

ca•pac'i•tate', -tat'ed,
  -tat'ing

ca•pac'i•tive

ca•pac'i•tor

ca•pac'i•ty

ca•par'i•son

ca'per

cape'skin'

cap'il•lar'i•ty

cap'il•lar'y

cap'i•tal *(city, wealth,
  top of a column)*
  ♦*capitol*

cap'i•tal•ism

cap'i•tal•ist

cap'i•tal•is'tic

cap'i•tal•i•za'tion

cap'i•tal•ize', -ized',
  -iz'ing

cap'i•ta'tion

cap'i•tol *(building)*
  ♦*capital*

ca•pit'u•late', -lat'ed,
  -lat'ing

ca•pit'u•la'tion

ca•pit'u•la'tor

ca•pit'u•la•to'ry

ca'pon'

ca•pric'cio *pl.* -cios *or*
  -ci

ca•price'

ca•pri'cious

Cap'ri•corn'

cap'ri•ole', -oled', -ol'-
  ing

cap•size', -sized', -siz'-
  ing

cap'stan

cap'stone'

cap'su•lar

cap'su•late' *also* cap'-
  su•lat'ed

cap'su•la'tion

cap'sule

cap'tain

cap'tain•cy

cap'tion

cap'tious

cap'ti•vate', -vat'ed,
  -vat'ing

cap'ti•va'tion

cap'ti•va'tor

cap'tive

cap•tiv'i•ty

cap'tor

cap'ture, -tured, -tur•
  ing

cap'u•chin

cap'y•ba'ra

car

car'a•cal'

car'a•cole' *also* car'a•
  col'

ca•rafe'

car'a•mel

car'a•mel•ize', -ized',
  -iz'ing

car'a•pace'

car'at *(weight)*
  ♦*caret, carrot*

car'a•van'

car'a•van'sa•ry *also*
  car'a•van'se•rai'

car'a•vel'

car'a·way'
car'bide'
car'bine'
car'bo·hy'drate'
car'bo·lat'ed
car·bol'ic acid
car'bon
car'bo·na'ceous
car'bon·ate', -at'ed, -at'ing
car'bon·a'tion
car'bon·a'tor
car·bon'ic acid
car'bon·if'er·ous *(of carbon)*
Car'bon·if'er·ous *(geologic period)*
car'bon·i·za'tion
car'bon·ize', -ized', -iz'ing
car'bon·yl'
Car'bo·run'dum®
car·box'yl
car·box'yl'ic
car'boy'
car'bun'cle
car·bun'cu·lar
car'bu·re'tor
car'cass
car·cin'o·gen
car·cin'o·gen'ic
car·ci·no'ma *pl.* -mas *or* -ma·ta
car'da·mom *or* car'da·mum, *also* car'da·mon
card'board'

car'di·ac'
car'di·gan
car'di·nal
car'di·nal·ate
car'di·o·gram'
car'di·o·graph'
car'di·ol'o·gist
car'di·ol'o·gy
car'di·o·pul'mon·ar'y
car'di·o·vas'cu·lar
card'sharp' *also* card'-sharp'er
care, cared, car'ing
ca·reen' *(to tilt, swerve)*
ca·reer' *(life work)*
ca·reer' *(to rush head-long)*
care'free'
care'ful
care'less
ca·ress'
car'et *(proofreading mark)*
    ♦carat, carrot
care'tak'er
care'worn'
car'fare'
car'go *pl.* -goes *or* -gos
car'hop'
Car'ib·be'an
car'i·bou' *pl.* -bou' *or* -bous'
car'i·ca·ture', -tured', -tur'ing
car'i·ca·tur'ist
car'ies *(decay)*
    ♦carries

car'il·lon'
car'i·ous
car'load'
Car'mel·ite'
car'mine
car'nage
car'nal
car·nal'i·ty
car·na'tion
car·nel'ian
car'ni·val
car'ni·vore'
car·niv'o·rous
car·no'tite'
car'ob
car'ol *(to sing)*, -oled *or* -olled, -ol'ing *or* -ol·ling
    ♦carrel
Car'o·lin'i·an
car'om
car'o·tene'
ca·rot'e·noid'
ca·rot'id
ca·rous'al *(revelry)*
    ♦carousel
ca·rouse', -roused', -rous'ing
car'ou·sel' *(mer-ry-go-round)*, *or* car'-rou·sel'
    ♦carousal
ca·rous'er
carp *(fish)*, *pl.* carp *or* carps
carp *(to complain)*
car'pal *(of the carpus)*

car'pel *(flower part)*
car'pen·ter
car'pen·try
car'pet
car'pet·bag'
car'pet·bag'ger
car'-pool'
car'-pool'er
car'port'
car'pus *pl.* -pi'
car'rel *(library nook)*
♦*carol*
car'riage
car'ri·er
car'ri·on
car'rot *(vegetable)*
♦*carat, caret*
car'ry, -ried, -ry·ing
car'ry-all'
car'ry-o'ver
car'sick'
cart'age
carte blanche'
car·tel'
car'ti·lage
car'ti·lag'i·nous
car·tog'ra·pher
car'to·graph'ic *also*
  car'to·graph'i·cal
car·tog'ra·phy
car'ton
car·toon'
car·toon'ist
car'tridge
cart'wheel'
carve, carved, carv'ing
carv'er

car'y·at'id *pl.* -ids *or*
  -i·des'
car'y·op'sis *pl.* -ses' *or*
  -si·des'
ca·sa'ba
Cas·a·no'va
cas·cade', -cad'ed,
  -cad'ing
cas·car'a
case, cased, cas'ing
case'hard'en
ca'sein'
case'ment
case'work'
case'work'er
cash *(money)*
♦*cache*
cash'ew
cash·ier' *(financial offi-*
  cer)
ca·shier' *(to dismiss)*
cash'mere'
cas'ing
ca·si'no *pl.* -nos
cask
cas'ket
Cas·san'dra
cas·sa'va
cas'se·role'
cas·sette'
cas'sia
cas'sock
cas·so·war'y
cast *(to throw)*, cast,
  cast'ing
♦*caste*
cas'ta·nets'

cast'a·way'
caste *(social class)*
♦*cast*
cas'tel·lat'ed
cast'er *(wheel)*, *also*
  cas'tor
cas'ti·gate', -gat'ed,
  -gat'ing
cas'ti·ga'tion
cas'ti·ga'tor
cast'-i'ron *adj.*
cas'tle, -tled, -tling
cast'off' *n.*
cast'-off' *adj.*
cas'tor *(oil)*
♦*caster*
cas'trate', -trat'ed,
  -trat'ing
cas·tra'tion
cas'u·al
cas'u·al·ty
cas'u·ist
cas'u·is'tic
cas'u·ist'ry
ca'sus bel'li'
cat
cat·a·bol'ic
ca·tab'o·lism
cat'a·clysm
cat'a·clys'mic *also*
  cat'a·clys'mal
cat'a·combs'
cat'a·falque'
cat'a·lep'sy
cat'a·lep'tic
cat'a·logue', -logued',

-logu'ing, *also* cat'a·
  log', -loged', -log'ing
cat'a·logu'er *also* cat'-
  a·log'er
ca·tal'pa
ca·tal'y·sis *pl.* -ses'
cat'a·lyst
cat'a·lyt'ic
cat'a·lyze', -lyzed',
  -lyz'ing
cat'a·ma·ran'
cat'a·mount'
cat'a·pult'
cat'a·ract'
ca·tarrh'
ca·tarrh'al *also* ca·
  tarrh'ous
ca·tas'tro·phe
cat'a·stroph'ic
cat'a·to'ni·a
cat'a·ton'ic
cat'bird'
cat'boat'
cat'call'
catch, caught, catch'-
  ing
catch'all'
catch'er
catch'word'
catch'y
cat'e·chism
cat'e·chist
cat'e·chi·za'tion
cat'e·chize', -chized',
  -chiz'ing
cat'e·chu'men
cat'e·gor'i·cal

cat'e·go·ri·za'tion
cat'e·go·rize', -rized',
  -riz'ing
cat'e·go'ry
cat'e·nate', -nat·ed,
  -nat'ing
cat'e·na'tion
ca'ter
cat'er-cor'nered *also*
  cat'er-cor'ner, cat'ty-
  cor'nered
cat'er·pil'lar
cat'er·waul'
cat'fish' *pl.* -fish' *or*
  -fish'es
cat'gut'
ca·thar'sis *pl.* -ses'
ca·thar'tic
ca·the'dral
cath'e·ter
cath'ode'
cath'ode-ray' tube
cath'o·lic *(universal)*
Cath'o·lic *(of the*
  Catholic Church)
Ca·thol'i·cism
cath'o·lic'i·ty
cat'i'on
cat'i·on'ic
cat'kin'
cat'like'
cat'nip'
cat'-o'-nine'-tails'
cat's'-eye'
cat's'-paw' *also* cats'-
  paw'
cat'tail'

cat'tle
cat'ty
cat'walk'
Cau·ca'sian
Cau'ca·soid'
cau'cus *pl.* -cus·es *or*
  -cus·ses
cau'cus, -cused *or*
  -cussed, -cus·ing *or*
  -cus·sing
cau'dal
cau'date' *also* cau'-
  dat'ed
cau'li·flow'er
caulk *also* calk
caus'al
cau·sal'i·ty
cau·sa'tion
caus'a·tive
cause, caused, caus'ing
cause cé·lè'bre *pl.*
  causes célè'bres
cause'way'
caus'tic
cau'ter·i·za'tion
cau'ter·ize', -ized',
  -iz'ing
cau'tion
cau'tion·ar'y
cau'tious
cav'al·cade'
cav'a·lier'
cav'al·ry
cave, caved, cav'ing
ca've·at'
cave'-in' *n.*
cav'ern

cav'ern·ous
cav'i·ar' *also* cav'i·are'
cav'il, -iled *or* -illed,
  -il·ing *or* -il·ling
cav'i·ta'tion
cav'i·ty
ca·vort'
caw
cay *(islet)*
  ♦*key, quay*
cay·enne' pepper
Cay·use' *pl.* -use' *or*
  -us·es
cease, ceased, ceas'ing
cease'-fire'
ce'cal
ce·cro'pi·a moth
ce'cum *pl.* -ca, *also*
  cae'cum
ce'dar
cede *(to yield)*, ced'ed,
  ced'ing
  ♦*seed*
ce·dil'la
ceil'ing
cel'an·dine'
cel'e·brant
cel'e·brate', -brat'ed,
  -brat'ing
cel'e·bra'tion
cel'e·bra'tor
ce·leb'ri·ty
ce·ler'i·ty
cel'er·y
ce·les'ta *also* ce·leste'
ce·les'tial
ce'li·ac' *also* coe'li·ac'

cel'i·ba·cy
cel'i·bate
cell *(room, unit)*
  ♦*sell*
cel'lar *(storage room)*
  ♦*seller*
cel'list
cel'lo *pl.* -los
cel'lo·phane'
cel'lu·lar
cel'lu·loid'®
cel'lu·lose'
Cel'si·us
Celt'ic *also* Kelt'ic
ce·ment'
cem'e·ter'y
cen'o·bite'
cen'o·bit'ic *also* cen'o·
  bit'i·cal
cen'o·taph'
cen'o·taph'ic
Ce'no·zo'ic
cen'ser *(vessel)*
cen'sor *(examiner)*
cen·so'ri·al
cen·so'ri·ous
cen'sor·ship'
cen'sur·a·ble
cen'sure, -sured, -sur·
  ing
cen'sus *pl.* -sus·es
cent *(coin)*
  ♦*scent, sent*
cen'taur'
cen·tav'o *pl.* -vos
cen'te·nar'i·an
cen·ten'a·ry

cen·ten'ni·al
cen'ter
cen'ter·board'
cen'ter·fold'
cen'ter·piece'
cen'ti·grade'
cen'ti·gram'
cen'ti·li'ter
cen'time'
cen'ti·me'ter
cen'ti·pede'
cen'tral
cen'tral·ism
cen'tral·ist
cen'tral·is'tic
cen·tral'i·ty
cen'tral·i·za'tion
cen'tral·ize', -ized',
  -iz'ing
cen·trif'u·gal
cen·trif'u·ga'tion
cen'tri·fuge'
cen'tri·ole'
cen·trip'e·tal
cen'trist
cen'troid'
cen'tro·some'
cen·tu'ri·on
cen'tu·ry
ce·phal'ic
ceph'a·lo·pod'
ce·ram'ic
ce·ram'ist
ce're·al *(grain)*
  ♦*serial*
cer'e·bel'lum *pl.* -lums
  or -la

cer'e·bral
cer'e·bro·spi'nal
cer'e·brum *pl.* -brums
 or -bra
cere'cloth'
cere'ment
cer'e·mo'ni·al
cer'e·mo'ni·ous
cer'e·mo'ny
ce·rise'
ce'ri·um
cer'met'
cer'tain
cer'tain·ty
cer'ti·fi'a·ble
cer·tif'i·cate', -cat'ed,
 -cat'ing
cer'ti·fi·ca'tion
cer'ti·fy', -fied', -fy'ing
cer'ti·tude'
ce·ru'le·an
cer'vi·cal
cer'vine'
cer'vix *pl.* -vix·es *or*
 -vi·ces'
ce'si·um *also* cae'si·um
ces·sa'tion
ces'sion *(surrendering)*
 ♦*session*
cess'pool'
ce·ta'ce·an
Cha·blis'
cha'-cha'
chafe, chafed, chaf'ing
chaff
chaff'er *(one who
 teases)*

chaff'er *(to bargain)*
chaf'finch
chaf'ing dish
cha·grin'
chain'-re·act' *v.*
chain'-smoke',
 -smoked', -smok'ing
chair'man
chair'per'son
chair'wom'an
chaise' longue' *pl.*
 chaise' longues' *or*
 châises' longues'
chal'ce·don'ic
chal·ced'o·ny
chal'co·cite'
chal'co·py'rite'
cha·let'
chal'ice
chalk'board'
chalk'y
chal'lenge, -lenged,
 -leng·ing
chal'lenge·a·ble
chal'leng·er
chal'lis
cham'ber
cham'ber·lain
cham'ber·maid'
cham'bray'
cha·me'leon
cham'fer
cham'ois' *(animal), pl.*
 -ois
cham'ois *(leather), pl.*
 -ois, *also* cham'my

cham'o·mile' *or* cam'-
 o·mile'
champ
cham·pagne' *(wine)*
cham·paign' *(plain)*
cham'pi·on
cham'pi·on·ship'
chance, chanced,
 chanc'ing
chan'cel
chan'cel·ler·y
chan'cel·lor
chan'cer·y
chan'cre
chanc'y
chan'de·lier'
chan'dler
chan'dler·y
change, changed,
 chang'ing
change'a·ble
change'ling
change'o'ver
chan'nel
chan'son
chant'er
chan·teuse'
chan'tey *(song), pl.*
 -teys, *also* chant'y,
 shant'y
chan'ti·cleer'
Cha'nu·kah *also* Ha'-
 nuk·kah, Ha'nuk·kah
cha·os'
cha·ot'ic
chap, chapped, chap'-
 ping

chap′ar·ral′
chap′book′
cha·peau′ *pl.* -peaux′
  or -peaus′
chap′el
chap′er·on *also* chap′-
  er·one′
chap′lain
chap′let
chaps
chap′ter
char, charred, char′-
  ring
char′a·banc′
char′ac·ter
char′ac·ter·is′tic
char′ac·ter·i·za′tion
char′ac·ter·ize′, -ized′,
  -iz′ing
cha·rades′
char′coal′
chard *(beet)*
  ♦*shard*
charge, charged,
  charg′ing
charge′a·ble
char·gé′ d′af·faires′
  pl. char·gés′ d′af·
  faires′
charg′er
char′i·ly
char′i·ness
char′i·ot
char′i·o·teer′
cha·ris′ma
char′is·mat′ic
char′i·ta·ble

char′i·ty
char′la·tan
char′ley horse
char′lotte
charm′er
char′nel
chart
char′ter
char·treuse′
char′wom′an
char′y
chase, chased, chas′ing
chas′er
chasm
chas′mal
Chas′sid *pl.* -si′dim,
  also Has′sid, Ha′sid
chas′sis *pl.* -sis
chaste *(pure),* chast′er,
  chast′est
  ♦*chased*
chas′ten
chas·tise′, -tised′, -tis′-
  ing
chas′ti·ty
chas′u·ble
chat, chat′ted, chat′-
  ting
cha·teau′ *pl.* -teaux′,
  also châ·teau′
chat′e·laine′
chat′tel
chat′ter
chat′ter·box′
chat′ty
chauf′feur
chau′vin·ism

chau′vin·ist
chau′vin·is′tic
cheap *(inexpensive)*
  ♦*cheep*
cheap′en
cheap′skate′
cheat′er
check *(halt, restraint,*
  verification, bank or-
  der, pattern)
  ♦*Czech*
check′a·ble
check′book′
check′er
check′er·board′
check′ered
check′ers
check′mate′, -mat′ed,
  -mat′ing
check′-out′ *n.*
check′point′
check′room′
check′up′ *n.*
Ched′dar *also* ched′-
  dar
cheek′bone′
cheek′y
cheep *(chirp)*
  ♦*cheap*
cheer′ful
cheer′lead′er
cheer′y
cheese′burg′er
cheese′cake′
cheese′cloth′
chees′y
chee′tah

chef-d'oeu'vre *pl.*
  chefs-d'oeu'vre
chef's salad
chem'i·cal
Chemical Mace®
chem'i·lu·mi·nes'-
  cence
che·mise'
chem'ist
chem'is·try
che'mo·syn'the·sis
che'mo·syn·thet'ic
che'mo·tax·on'o·my
che'mo·ther'a·py
chem·ur'gic *also*
  chem·ur'gi·cal
chem'ur·gy
che·nille'
cher'ish
che·root'
cher'ry
cher'ry·stone'
cher'ub *pl.* -u·bim'
che·ru'bic
cher'vil
chesh'ire cheese
chess'board'
chess'man'
chest
ches'ter·field'
chest'nut'
chev'a·lier'
chev'i·ot
chev'ron
chew'ing gum
che·wink'
Chi·an'ti

chi·a'ro·scu'ro *pl.* -ros
chic *(stylish)*
  ♦*chick, sheik*
chi·can'er·y
Chi·ca'no *pl.* -nos
chick *(young bird)*
  ♦*chic*
chick'a·dee'
chick'en
chick'en-heart'ed
chick'en-liv'ered
chick'pea'
chick'weed'
chic'le
chic'o·ry
chide, chid'ed *or* chid,
  chid'ed *or* chid *or*
  chid'den, chid'ing
chief'ly
chief'tain
chif·fon'
chif·fo·nier'
chig'ger
chi·gnon'
Chi·hua'hua
chil'blain'
child *pl.* chil'dren
child'bear'ing
child'birth'
child'hood'
child'ish
child'like'
Chil'e·an
chil'e con car'ne *also*
  chil'i con car'ne
chil'i *(pepper), pl.* -ies,

  also chil'e, chil'li *pl.*
  -lies
chill'y *(cold)*
  ♦*chili*
chime, chimed, chim'-
  ing
chim'er
chi·me'ra
chi·mer'i·cal
chim'ney *pl.* -neys
chimp
chim'pan·zee'
chin, chinned, chin'-
  ning
chi'na
chi'na·ber'ry
Chi'na·town'
chi'na·ware'
chinch
chin·chil'la
chine
Chi·nese' *pl.* -nese'
chink
chi'no *pl.* -nos
chi·nook'
chin'qua·pin'
chintz'y
chip, chipped, chip'-
  ping
chip'munk'
Chip'pen·dale'
chip'per
chi·ro·man'cy
chi·rop'o·dist
chi·rop'o·dy
chi·ro·prac'tic
chi·ro·prac'tor

chirp′er
chirr *(trill)*
  ♦*churr*
chir′rup
chis′el, -eled *or* -elled,
  -el·ing *or* -el·ling
chi′-square′
chit′chat′, -chat′ted,
  -chat′ting
chi′tin *(hornlike sub-
  stance)*
chi′ton *(mollusk)*
chit′ter
chit′ter·lings *also*
  chit′lins, chit′lings
chi·val′ric
chiv·al·rous
chiv·al·ry
chive
chlo′ral
chlo′rate′
chlor′dane′ *also*
  chlor′dan′
chlo′ride′
chlo′rin·ate′, -at′ed,
  -at′ing
chlo′rine′
chlo′rite′
chlo′ro·form′
chlo′ro·phyll *also*
  chlo′ro·phyl
chlo′ro·plast′
chlo·ro′sis
chlor′tet·ra·cy′cline′
chock′-a-block′
chock′-full′
choc′o·late

choice, choic′er,
  choic′est
choir *(singers)*
  ♦*quire*
choir′boy′
choke, choked, chok′-
  ing
choke′cher′ry
choke′damp′
chok′er
chol′er *(anger)*
  ♦*collar*
chol′er·a
chol′er·ic
cho·les′ter·ol′
choose, chose, cho′sen,
  choos′ing
choos′er
choos′y *also* choos′ey
chop, chopped, chop′-
  ping
chop′house′
chop′per
chop′py
chop′sticks′
chop su′ey
cho′ral *(of a chorus)*
  ♦*coral*
cho·rale′ *(hymn), also*
  cho·ral′
  ♦*corral*
chord *(musical tones,
  line segment)*
  ♦*cord*
chor′date′
chore
cho·re′a

cho′re·o·graph′
cho′re·og′ra·pher
cho′re·o·graph′ic
cho′re·og′ra·phy
cho′ric
cho′rine′
cho′ri·on′
cho′ris·ter
cho′roid′ *also* cho·roi′-
  de·a
chor′tle, -tled, -tling
cho′rus *pl.* -rus·es
cho′rus, -rused *or*
  -russed, -rus·ing *or*
  -rus·sing
cho′sen
chow′der
chow′ mein′
chrism
chris′ten
Chris′ten·dom
Chris′tian
Chris′ti·an′i·ty
Christ′mas
chro′mate′
chro·mat′ic
chro·mat′i·cism
chro′ma·tin
chro′ma·tog′ra·phy
chrome
chro′mic
chro′mite′
chro′mi·um
chro′mo·lith′o·graph′
chro′mo·li·thog′ra·
  phy
chro′mo·so′mal

chro′mo·some′
chro′mo·sphere′
chron′ic
chron′i·cle, -cled,
 -cling
chron′i·cler
chron′o·log′i·cal also
 chron′o·log′ic
chro·nol′o·gist
chro·nol′o·gy
chro·nom′e·ter
chrys′a·lid
chrys′a·lis pl. chrys·a·
 lis·es or chry·sal′i·
 des′
chry·san′the·mum
chub′by
chuck
chuck′le, -led, -ling
chuck′le·head′
chug, chugged, chug′-
 ging
chuk′ka
chum, chummed,
 chum′ming
chum′my
chump
chunk′y
church′go′er
church′war′den
church′yard′
churl′ish
churn′ing
churr (trill)
 ♦chirr
chute (trough)
 ♦shoot, shute

chut′ney pl. -neys
chutz′pah
chyle
chyme
ci·ca′da
cic′a·trix′ pl. cic′a·tri′-
 ces
cic′e·ro′ne′ pl. -nes or
 -ni
ci′der
ci′gar′
cig′a·rette′ also cig′a·
 ret′
cig′a·ril′lo pl. -los
cil′i·a sing. -i·um
cil′i·ar′y
cil′i·ate also cil′i·at′ed
cinch
cin·cho′na
cinc′ture, -tured, -tur·
 ing
cin′der
Cin′der·el′la
cin′e·ma
cin′e·mat′ic
cin′e·ma·tog′ra·pher
cin′e·ma·tog′ra·phy
ci′né·ma′ vé′ri·té′
cin′na·bar′
cin′na·mon
cinque′foil′
ci′pher also cy′pher
cir′ca
cir·ca′di·an
cir′cle, -cled, -cling
cir′clet
cir′cuit

cir·cu′i·tous
cir′cuit·ry
cir′cu·lar
cir′cu·lar′i·ty
cir′cu·lar·ize′, -ized′,
 -iz′ing
cir′cu·late′, -lat′ed,
 -lat′ing
cir′cu·la′tion
cir′cu·la′tor
cir′cu·la·to′ry
cir′cum·cise′, -cised′,
 -cis′ing
cir′cum·ci′sion
cir·cum′fer·ence
cir′cum·flex′
cir′cum·lo·cu′tion
cir′cum·loc′u·to′ry
cir′cum·nav′i·gate′,
 -gat′ed, -gat′ing
cir′cum·nav′i·ga′tion
cir′cum·nav′i·ga′tor
cir′cum·po′lar
cir′cum·scribe′,
 -scribed′, -scrib′ing
cir′cum·scrip′tion
cir′cum·spect′
cir′cum·spec′tion
cir′cum·stance′
cir′cum·stan′tial
cir′cum·stan′ti·ate′,
 -at′ed, -at′ing
cir′cum·stan′ti·a′tion
cir′cum·vent′
cir′cum·ven′tion
cir′cus
cirque

cir·rho'sis
cir·rhot'ic
cir'ro·cu'mu·lus
cir'ro·stra'tus
cir'rus *pl.* -ri'
cis·lu'nar
cis'tern
cis·ter'nal
cit'a·del
ci·ta'tion
cite *(to quote),* cit'ed, cit'ing
  ♦*sight, site*
cit'i·fy', -fied', -fy'ing
cit'i·zen
cit'i·zen·ry
cit'i·zen·ship'
cit'rate'
cit'ric
cit'ron
cit'ro·nel'la
cit'rus *pl.* -rus·es *or* -rus
cit'y
cit'y-state'
civ'et
civ'ic
civ'ics
civ'il
ci·vil'ian
ci·vil'i·ty
civ'i·liz'a·ble
civ'i·li·za'tion
civ'i·lize', -lized', -liz'ing
civ'vies *also* civ'ies
clab'ber

clack *(noise)*
  ♦*claque*
cald, clad, clad'ding
claim'ant
clair·voy'ance
clair·voy'ant
clam, clammed, clam'ming
clam'bake'
clam'ber
clam'my
clam'or
clam'or·ous
clamp
clam'shell'
clan
clan·des'tine
clang
clan'gor
clank
clan'nish
clans'man
clap, clapped, clap'ping
clap'board
clap'per
clap'trap'
claque *(group)*
  ♦*clack*
clar'et
clar'i·fi·ca'tion
clar'i·fy'', -fied', -fy'ing
clar'i·net'
clar'i·net'ist *also* clar'i·net'tist
clar'i·on

clar'i·ty
clash
clasp
class'-con'scious *adj.*
clas'sic
clas'si·cal
clas'si·cism
clas'si·cist
clas'si·fi'a·ble
clas'si·fi·ca'tion
clas'si·fi·ca·to'ry
clas'si·fy', -fied', -fy'ing
class'mate'
class'room'
class'y
clat'ter
clause *(words)*
  ♦*claws*
claus'tro·pho'bi·a
claus'tro·pho'bic
clav'i·chord'
clav'i·cle
cla·vic'u·lar
cla·vier'
claw
clay'ey *or* clay'ish
clean'-cut'
cleanse, cleansed, cleans'ing
cleans'er
clean'-shav'en
clean'up' *n.*
clear'ance
clear'-cut'
clear'-eyed'
clear'ing

clear'ing-house' *also*
  clear'ing·house'
clear'-sight'ed
cleat
cleav'age
cleave *(to split),* cleft
  or cleaved *or* clove,
  cleft *or* cleaved *or*
  clo'ven, cleav'ing
cleave *(to adhere),*
  cleaved *or* clove,
  cleaved, cleav'ing
cleav'er
clef
cleft
clem'a·tis
clem'en·cy
clem'ent
clench
cler'gy
cler'gy·man
cler'ic
cler'i·cal
cler'i·cal·ism
clerk
clev'er
clew *(ball of yarn, cor-*
  ner of a sail)
  ♦*clue*
cli·ché'
click *(sound)*
  ♦*clique*
click'er
cli'ent
cli'en·tele'
cliff'hang'er
cli·mac'ter·ic

cli·mac'tic
cli'mate
cli·mat'ic *also* cli·mat'-
  i·cal
cli'ma·to·log'ic *also*
  cli'ma·to·log'i·cal
cli'ma·tol'o·gist
cli'ma·tol'o·gy
cli'max'
climb *(ascent)*
  ♦*clime*
climb'a·ble
clime *(climate)*
  ♦*climb*
clinch'er
cline
cling, clung, cling'ing
cling'stone'
clin'ic
clin'i·cal
cli·ni'cian
clink'er
clip, clipped, clip'ping
clip'board'
clip'per
clip'ping
clique *(exclusive group)*
  ♦*click*
cliqu'ey *also* cliqu'y,
  cliqu'ish
clit'o·ral
clit'o·ris
clo·a'ca *pl.* -cae'
cloak'-and-dag'ger
  adj.
cloak'room'
clob'ber

cloche
clock'wise'
clock'work'
clod'dish
clod'hop'per
clog, clogged, clog'ging
cloi'son·né'
clois'ter
clois'tral
clone, cloned, clon'ing
clop, clopped, clop'-
  ping
close, clos'er, clos'est
close *(to shut),* closed,
  clos'ing
  ♦*clothes*
closed'-cir'cuit *adj.*
close'-fist'ed
close'-grained'
close'-mouthed'
close'-out' *n.*
clos'et
close'-up' *n.*
clos·trid'i·um *pl.* -i·a
clo'sure *(a closing)*
  ♦*cloture*
clot, clot'ted, clot'ting
cloth *pl.* cloths
cloth'bound'
clothe, clothed *or* clad,
  cloth'ing
clothes *(apparel)*
  ♦*close*
clothes'horse'
clothes'line'
clothes'pin'
cloth'ier

cloth'ing
clo'ture *(parliamentary procedure)*, also clo'-sure
cloud'burst'
cloud'y
clout
clove
clo'ven-hoofed'
clo'ver
clo'ver·leaf'
clown
cloy'ing
club, clubbed, club'-bing
club'by
club'foot'
club'foot'ed
club'house'
cluck
clue *(to give guiding information)*, clued, clue'ing or clu'ing, *also* clew
clump
clum'sy
clus'ter
clutch
clut'ter
Clydes'dale'
coach'man
co'ad·ju'tor
co·ag'u·lant
co·ag'u·lase'
co·ag'u·late', -lat'ed, -lat'ing
co·ag'u·la'tion

co·ag'u·la'tor
coal *(fuel)*
　♦*kohl*
co'a·lesce', -lesced', -lesc'ing
co'a·les'cence
co'a·les'cent
co'a·li'tion
co'-an'chor
coarse *(rough)*, coars'-er, coars'est
　♦*course*
coars'en
coast'al
coast'er
coast'line'
coat *(garment)*
　♦*cote*
co·a'ti *pl.* -tis
coat'ing
coat of arms *pl.* coats of arms
coat of mail *pl.* coats of mail
coat'room'
coat'tail'
co-au'thor
coax
co·ax'i·al
cob
co'balt'
cob'ble, -bled, -bling
cob'bler
cob'ble·stone'
CO'BOL' *or* Co'bol'
co'bra
cob'web'

co'ca
co·caine' *also* co·cain'
coc'coid' *also* coc'cal
coc'cus *pl.* -ci'
coc'cyx *pl.* coc·cy'ges
coch'i·neal'
coch'le·a *pl.* -ae'
cock·ade'
cock'a·ma'mie *also* cock'a·ma'my
cock'-and-bull' story
cock'a·too' *pl.* -toos'
cock'a·trice
cock'chaf'er
cock'crow'
cock'er·el
cock'er spaniel
cock'eyed'
cock'fight'
cock'le
cock'le·bur'
cock'le·shell'
cock'ney *pl.* -neys
cock'pit'
cock'roach'
cocks'comb'
cock'sure'
cock'tail'
cock'y
co'co *(palm tree)*, *pl.* -cos
co'coa *(beverage)*
co'co·nut' *also* co'coa·nut'
co·coon'
cod *pl.* cod *or* cods
co'da

cod′dle, -dled, -dling
code, cod′ed, cod′ing
co′deine′
co′dex′ *pl.* -di·ces′
cod′fish′ *pl.* -fish′ *or* -fish′es
codg′er
cod′i·cil
cod′i·fi·ca′tion
cod′i·fy′, -fied′, -fy′ing
cod′ling
cod′-liv′er oil
co′ed′ *or* co′-ed′
co′ed·u·ca′tion *also* co-ed·u·ca′tion
co′ed·u·ca′tion·al
co′ef·fi′cient
coe′la·canth′
coe′len·ter·ate′
co·en′zyme′
co·e′qual
co′e·qual′i·ty
co·erce′, -erced′, -erc′ing
co·erc′i·ble
co·er′cion
co·er′cive
co·e′val
co′ex·ist′
co′ex·is′tence
co′ex·is′tent
co′ex·tend′
co′ex·ten′sive
cof′fee
coffee house *also* cof′fee·house′
cof′fee·pot′

cof′fer
cof′fer·dam′
cof′fin
cog
co·gen′cy
co′gent
cog′i·tate′, -tat′ed, -tat′ing
cog′i·ta′tion
cog′i·ta′tor
co′gnac′
cog′nate′
cog·ni′tion
cog′ni·tive
cog′ni·za·ble
cog′ni·zance
cog′ni·zant
cog·no′men *pl.* -no′mens *or* -nom′i·na
co′gno·scen′te *pl.* -ti
cog′wheel′
co·hab′it
co·hab′i·tant
co·hab′i·ta′tion
co·here′ (*to stick together*), -hered′, -her′ing
♦*adhere*
co·her′ence *also* co·her′en·cy
co·her′ent
co·he′sion
co·he′sive
co′hort′
coif·feur′ (*hairdresser*)
coif·fure′ (*to style hair*), -fured′, -fur′ing

coil
coin (*money*)
♦*quoin*
coin′age
co′in·cide′, -cid′ed, -cid′ing
co·in′ci·dence
co·in′ci·dent
co·in′ci·den′tal
co′i·tus *also* co·i′tion
coke (*fuel*)
Coke® (*beverage*)
co′la
col′an·der
cold′-blood′ed
co·le·op′ter·an *also* co′le·op′ter·on
cole′slaw′
co′le·us *pl.* -us·es
col′ic
col′ick·y
col′i·se′um
co·li′tis
col·lab′o·rate′, -rat′ed, -rat′ing
col·lab′o·ra′tion
col·lab′o·ra′tion·ism
col·lab′o·ra′tion·ist
col·lab′o·ra′tor
col·lage′
col′la·gen
col·lapse′, -lapsed′, -laps′ing
col·laps′i·ble *also* col·laps′a·ble
col′lar (*neckpiece*)
♦*choler*

col·lar·bone'
col'lard
col·late', -lat'ed, -lat'-
  ing
col·lat'er·al
col·la'tion
col·la'tor
col·league'
col·lect'
col·lect'i·ble *also* col·
  lect'a·ble
col·lec'tion
col·lec'tive
col·lec'tiv·ism
col·lec'tiv·ist
col·lec'tiv·i·za'tion
col·lec'tiv·ize', -ized',
  -iz'ing
col·lec'tor
col'leen'
col'lege
col·le'gi·al'i·ty
col·le'gian
col·le'giate
col·lide', -lid'ed, -lid'-
  ing
col'lie
col'lier
col'lier·y
col·lin'e·ar
col·li'sion
col'lo·cate', -cat'ed,
  -cat'ing
col'lo·ca'tion
col·lo'di·on *also* col·
  lo'di·um
col'loid'

col·loi'dal
col·lo'qui·al
col·lo'qui·al·ism
col·lo'qui·um *pl.* -qui·
  ums *or* -qui·a
col'lo·quy
col·lude', -lud'ed,
  -lud'ing
col·lu'sion
col·lu'sive
co·logne'
Co·lom'bi·an *(native
  of Colombia)*
  ♦*Columbian*
co'lon *(punctuation
  mark*
co'lon *(intestine)*, *pl.*
  -lons *or* -la
colo'nel *(officer)*
  ♦*kernel*
colo'nel·cy
co·lo'ni·al
co·lo'ni·al·ism
co·lo'ni·al·ist
col'o·nist
col'o·ni·za'tion
col'o·nize', -nized',
  -niz'ing
col'o·niz'er
col'on·nade'
col'on·nad'ed
col'o·ny
col'o·phon'
col'or
Col'o·ra'dan
col'or·a'tion
col'or·a·tu'ra

col'or·blind'
col'or·cast', -cast' *or*
  -cast'ed, -cast'ing
col'ored
col'or·fast'
col'or·ful
col'or·im'e·ter
col'or·ing
col'or·ist
col'or·less
co·los'sal
co·los'sus *pl.* -si' *or*
  -sus·es
colt'ish
Co·lum'bi·an *(of the
  U.S.)*
  ♦*Colombian*
co·lum'bic
co·lum'bine'
co·lum'bi·um
Co·lum'bus Day
col'umn
co·lum'nar
col'um·nist
co'ma *pl.* -mas
co'ma·tose'
comb
com·bat' *v.*
com'bat' *n.*
com·bat'ant
com·bat'ive
com·bi·na'tion
com·bine', -bined',
  -bin'ing
com'bine' *n.*
com·bin'er
comb'ings

com'bo *pl.* -bos
com·bus'ti·bil'i·ty
com·bus'ti·ble
com·bus'tion
com·bus'tive
come, came, come,
  com'ing
come'back' *n.*
co·me'di·an
co·me'dic
co·me'di·enne'
com'e·do' *pl.* com'e·
  dos' *or* com'e·do'nes
come'down' *n.*
com'e·dy
come'ly
come'-on' *n.*
com'er
co·mes'ti·ble
com'et
come'up'pance
com'fit
com'fort
com'fort·a·ble
com'fort·er
com'fy
com'ic
com'i·cal
com'ing-out' *n.*
com'i·ty *pl.* -ties
com'ma
com·mand'
com'man·dant'
com'man·deer'
com·mand'er
commander in chief

pl. commanders in
  chief
com·mand'ing
com·mand'ment
com·man'do *pl.* -dos
  or -does
com·me'di·a dell'ar'·
  te
com·mem'o·rate',
  -rat'ed, -rat'ing
com·mem'o·ra'tion
com·mem'o·ra·tive
com·mem'o·ra'tor
com·mem'o·ra·to'ry
com·mence',
  -menced', -menc'ing
com·mence'ment
com·mend'
com·mend'a·ble
com'men·da'tion
com·men'da·to'ry
com·men'sal
com·men'sal·ism
com·men'su·ra·ble
com·men'su·rate
com·ment'
com'men·tar'y
com'men·tate', -tat'·
  ed, -tat'ing
com'men·ta'tor
com'merce
com·mer'cial
com·mer'cial·ism
com·mer'cial·i·za'·
  tion
com·mer'cial·ize',
  -ized', -iz'ing

com·mer'cial·ly
com·min'gle, -gled,
  -gling
com·mis'er·ate', -at'·
  ed, -at'ing
com·mis'er·a'tion
com·mis'er·a'tive
com·mis'er·a'tor
com'mis·sar'
com'mis·sar'i·at
com'mis·sar'y
com·mis'sion
com·mis'sion·er
com·mit', -mit'ted,
  -mit'ting
com·mit'ment
com·mit'tal
com·mit'tee
com·mix'
com·mix'ture
com·mode'
com·mo'di·ous
com·mod'i·ty
com'mo·dore'
com'mon
com'mon·al·ty
com'mon·er
com'mon-law' *adj.*
com'mon·place'
com'mons
com'mon·weal'
com'mon·wealth'
com·mo'tion
com·mu'nal
com'mu'nal·ism
com'mu·nal'i·ty
com·mune' *n.*

com·mune′, -muned′,
  -mun′ing
com·mu′ni·ca·bil′i·ty
com·mu′ni·ca·ble
com·mu′ni·cant
com·mu′ni·cate′,
  -cat′ed, -cat′ing
com·mu′ni·ca′tion
com·mu′ni·ca′tive
com·mu′ni·ca′tor
com·mun′ion
com·mu′ni·qué′
com′mu·nism
Com′mu·nist *also*
  com′mu·nist
com′mu·nis′tic
com·mu′ni·ty
com′mu·ni·za′tion
com′mu·nize′, -nized′,
  -niz′ing
com′mu·ta′tion
com′mu·ta′tive
com′mu·ta′tor
com·mute′, -mut′ed,
  -mut′ing
com·mut′er
com·pact′ *adj. & v.*
com′pact′ *n.*
com·pac′tor
com·pa′dre
com·pan′ion
com·pan′ion·a·ble
com·pan′ion·ship′
com·pan′ion·way′
com′pa·ny
com′pa·ra·bil′i·ty
com′pa·ra·ble

com·par′a·tive
com·pare′, -pared′,
  -par′ing
com·par′i·son
com·part′ment
com·part·men′tal·
  ize′, -ized′, -iz′ing
com′pass
com·pas′sion
com·pas′sion·ate
com·pat′i·bil′i·ty
com·pat′i·ble
com·pa′tri·ot
com·peer′
com·pel′, -pelled′,
  -pel′ling
com·pen′di·ous
com·pen′di·um *pl.*
  -di·ums *or* -di·a
com·pen′sate′, -sat′ed,
  -sat′ing
com′pen·sa′tion
com′pen·sa′tor
com·pen′sa·to′ry
com·pete′, -pet′ed,
  -pet′ing
com′pe·tence *also*
  com′pe·ten·cy
com′pe·tent
com′pe·ti′tion
com·pet′i·tive
com·pet′i·tor
com′pi·la′tion
com·pile′, -piled′,
  -pil′ing
com·pla′cen·cy *also*
  com·pla′cence

com·pla′cent *(smug)*
  ♦*complaisant*
com·plain′
com·plain′ant
com·plaint′
com·plai′sance *(com-
  pliance)*
  ♦*complacence*
com·plai′sant *(oblig-
  ing)*
  ♦*complacent*
com′ple·ment *(full
  amount)*
  ♦*compliment*
com′ple·men′ta·ry
  (completing)
  ♦*complimentary*
com·plete′, -plet′ed,
  -plet′ing
com·ple′tion
com·plex′ *adj.*
com′plex′ *n.*
com·plex′ion
com·plex′i·ty
com·pli′ance *also*
  com·pli′an·cy
com·pli′ant
com′pli·cate′, -cat′ed,
  -cat′ing
com′pli·cat′ed
com′pli·ca′tion
com·plic′i·ty
com′pli·ment *(praise)*
  ♦*complement*
com′pli·men′ta·ry
  (flattering)
  ♦*complementary*

com‧plin *also* com‧-
  pline
com‧ply', -plied',
  -ply'ing
com‧po'nent
com‧port'
com‧port'ment
com‧pose', -posed',
  -pos'ing
com‧pos'er
com‧pos'ite
com‧po‧si'tion
com‧pos'i‧tor
com‧post'
com‧po'sure
com‧pote'
com‧pound *adj. & n.*
com‧pound' *v.*
com‧pre‧hend'
com‧pre‧hend'i‧ble
com‧pre‧hen'si‧bil'i‧
  ty
com‧pre‧hen'si‧ble
com‧pre‧hen'sion
com‧pre‧hen'sive
com‧press' *n.*
com‧press' *v.*
com‧press'i‧bil'i‧ty
com‧press'i‧ble
com‧pres'sion
com‧pres'sive
com‧pres'sor
com‧prise', -prised',
  -pris'ing
com‧pro‧mise',
  -mised', -mis'ing
com‧pro‧mis'er

com‧pul'sion
com‧pul'sive
com‧pul'so‧ry
com‧put'a‧bil'i‧ty
com‧put'a‧ble
com‧pu‧ta'tion
com‧pute', -put'ed,
  -put'ing
com‧put'er
com‧put'er‧i‧za'tion
com‧put'er‧ize',
  -ized', -iz'ing
com'rade
Com'sat'
con, conned, con'ning
con‧cat'e‧nate', -nat-
  ed, -nat'ing
con‧cat'e‧na'tion
con‧cave'
con‧cav'i‧ty
con‧ceal'
con‧ceal'ment
con‧cede', -ced'ed,
  -ced'ing
con‧ceit'
con‧ceit'ed
con‧ceiv'a‧bil'i‧ty
con‧ceiv'a‧ble
con‧ceive', -ceived',
  -ceiv'ing
con‧cel'e‧brant
con‧cel'e‧brate',
  -brat'ed, -brat'ing
con‧cen'trate', -trat'-
  ed, -trat'ing
con‧cen‧tra'tion

con‧cen‧tra'tor
con‧cen'tric
con‧cen‧tric'i‧ty
con'cept'
con‧cep'tion
con‧cep'tu‧al
con‧cep'tu‧al‧ism
con‧cep'tu‧a‧list
con‧cep'tu‧al‧i‧za'‧
  tion
con‧cep'tu‧al‧ize',
  -ized', -iz'ing
con‧cern'
con‧cern'ing
con'cert' *n. & adj.*
con‧cert' *v.*
con‧cert'ed
con‧cer‧ti'na
con‧cer‧ti'no *pl.* -nos
con‧cert'mas'ter
con‧cer'to *pl.* -tos *or*
  -ti
con‧ces'sion
con‧ces'sion‧aire'
con‧ces'sive
conch *(mollusk), pl.*
  conchs *or* conch'es
  ♦conk
con‧cierge'
con‧cil'i‧ate', -at'ed,
  -at'ing
con‧cil'i‧a'tion
con‧cil'i‧a'tor
con‧cil'i‧a‧to'ry
con‧cise'
con'clave'

con·clude', -clud'ed,
  -clud'ing
con·clu'sion
con·clu'sive
con·coct'
con·coc'tion
con·com'i·tance
con·com'i·tant
con·cord *(harmony)*
  ♦*Concorde*
con·cor'dance
con·cor'dant
con·cor'dat'
Con·corde' *(plane)*
  ♦*concord*
con'course'
con·cres'cence
con·crete' *adj.*
con'crete' *n.*
con·crete', -cret'ed,
  -cret'ing
con·cre'tion
con'cu·bine'
con·cu'pis·cence
con·cu'pis·cent
con·cur', -curred',
  -cur'ring
con·cur'rence
con·cur'rent
con·cus'sion
con·demn'
con·dem'na'tion
con·dem'na·to'ry
con·dens'a·ble *also*
  con·dens'i·ble
con·den·sa'tion

con·dense', -densed',
  -dens'ing
con·dens'er
con·de·scend'
con·de·scen'sion
con·dign'
con·di·ment
con·di'tion
con·di'tion·al
con·di'tioned
con·di'tion·er
con·di'tion·ing
con·dole', -doled',
  -dol'ing
con·do'lence
con·do·min'i·um
con·do·na'tion
con·done', -doned',
  -don'ing
con'dor
con·duce', -duced',
  -duc'ing
con·du'cive
con'duct' *n.*
con·duct' *v.*
con·duc'tance
con·duct'i·ble
con·duc'tion
con·duc'tive
con'duc·tiv'i·ty
con·duc'tor
con'duit
cone
con'fab', -fabbed',
  -fab'bing
con·fab'u·late', -lat'-
  ed, -lat'ing

con·fab'u·la'tion
con·fab'u·la'tor
con·fec'tion
con·fec'tion·er'y
con·fed'er·a·cy
con·fed'er·ate', -at'ed,
  -at'ing
con·fed'er·a'tion
con·fed'er·a'tive
con·fer', -ferred', -fer'-
  ring
con'fer·ee'
con'fer·ence
con·fess'
con·fes'sion
con·fes'sion·al
con·fes'sor
con·fet'ti
con'fi·dant' *(friend)*,
  fem. con'fi·dante'
  ♦*confident*
con·fide', -fid'ed, -fid'-
  ing
con'fi·dence
con'fi·dent *(self-as-
  sured)*
  ♦*confidant*
con'fi·den'tial
con'fi·den'ti·al'i·ty
con·fig'u·ra'tion
con·fig'u·ra'tive
con·fine', -fined', -fin'-
  ing
con·fine'ment
con·firm'
con'fir·ma'tion

con′fis·cate′, -cat′ed,
  -cat′ing
con·fis·ca′tion
con·fis′ca·tor
con′fla·gra′tion
con·flict′ *n.*
con·flict′ *v.*
con·flic′tive
con′flu·ence *also* con′-
  flux
con′flu·ent
con·form′
con·form′a·ble
con·for·ma′tion
con·form′ist
con·form′i·ty *also*
  con·for′mance
con·found′
con′fra·ter′ni·ty
con′frere
con·front′
con′fron·ta′tion
Con·fu′cian
Con·fu′cian·ism
con·fuse′, -fused′,
  -fus′ing
con·fus′ed·ly
con·fu′sion
con·fu·ta′tion
con·fute′, -fut′ed,
  -fut′ing
con′ga
con·geal′
con·ge′ner
con·gen′ial
con·ge′ni·al′i·ty
con·gen′i·tal

con′ger
con·ge′ries
con·gest′
con·ges′tion
con·ges′tive
con·glom′er·ate′, -at′-
  ed, -at′ing
con·glom′er·a′tion
Con·go·lese′ *pl.* -lese′
con·grat′u·late′, -lat′-
  ed, -lat′ing
con·grat′u·la′tion
con·grat′u·la′tor
con·grat′u·la·to′ry
con′gre·gate′, -gat′ed,
  -gat′ing
con′gre·ga′tion
con′gre·ga′tion·al
con′gre·ga′tion·al·
  ism
Con′gre·ga′tion·al·ist
con′gre·ga′tor
con′gress
con·gres′sion·al
con′gress·man
con′gress·wom′an
con′gru·ence *also*
  con′gru·en·cy
con′gru·ent
con·gru′i·ty
con′gru·ous
con′ic *also* con′i·cal
con′i·fer
co·nif′er·ous
con·jec′tur·al
con·jec′ture, -tured,
  -tur·ing

con·join′
con·joint′
con′ju·gal
con′ju·gate′, -gat′ed,
  -gat′ing
con′ju·ga′tion
con′ju·ga′tor
con·junct′
con·junc′tion
con·junc·ti′va *pl.* -vas
  or -vae
con·junc·ti′val
con·junc′tive
con·junc·ti·vi′tis
con·junc′ture
con′ju·ra′tion
con·jure, -jured, -jur·
  ing
con′jur·er *also* con′jur·
  or
conk *(to hit)*
  ♦*conch*
con′nate′
con·nect′
con·nec′tion
con·nec′tive
con·nec′tor
con′ning tower
con·nip′tion
con·niv′ance
con·nive′, -nived′,
  -niv′ing
con·nois·seur′
con′no·ta′tion
con′no·ta′tive
con·note′, -not′ed,
  -not′ing

con·nu'bi·al
con'quer
con'quer·a·ble
con'quer·or
con'quest
con·quis'ta·dor
con·san·guin'e·ous
con·san·guin'i·ty
con'science
con·sci·en'tious —
con'scious
con'scious·ness
con'scious·ness-rais'-
  ing
con'script' *n.*
con'script' *v.*
con·scrip'tion
con'se·crate', -crat'ed,
  -crat'ing
con'se·cra'tion
con'se·cra'tor
con·sec'u·tive
con·sen'sus
con·sent'
con'se·quence
con'se·quent
con'se·quen'tial
con·serv'a·ble
con'ser·va'tion
con'ser·va'tion·ist
con·ser'va·tism
con·ser'va·tive
con·ser'va·tor
con·ser'va·to'ry
con·serve', -served',
  -serv'ing
con·sid'er

con·sid'er·a·ble
con·sid'er·ate
con·sid'er·a'tion
con·sign'
con·sign·ee'
con·sign'ment
con·sig'nor *also* con·
  sign'er
con·sist'
con·sis'ten·cy *also*
  con·sis'tence
con·sis'tent
con'sis·to'ri·al
con·sis'to·ry
con·sol'a·ble
con'so·la'tion
con·sol'a·to'ry
con'sole' *n.*
con·sole', -soled',
  -sol'ing
con·sol'i·date', -dat'-
  ed, -dat'ing
con·sol'i·da'tion
con·sol'i·da'tor
con'som·mé'
con'so·nance
con'so·nant
con'so·nan'tal
con'sort' *n.*
con·sort' *v.*
con·sor'ti·um *pl.* -ti·a
con·spec'tus
con·spic'u·ous
con·spir'a·cy
con·spir'a·tor
con·spir'a·to'ri·al

con·spire', -spired',
  -spir'ing
con'sta·ble
con·stab'u·lar'y
con'stan·cy
con'stant
con·stel·la'tion
con·ster·na'tion
con'sti·pate', -pat'ed,
  -pat'ing
con'sti·pa'tion
con·stit'u·en·cy
con·stit'u·ent
con'sti·tute', -tut'ed,
  -tut'ing
con'sti·tu'tion
con'sti·tu'tion·al
con'sti·tu'tion·al'i·ty
con'sti·tu'tive
con·strain'
con·straint'
con·strict'
con·stric'tion
con·stric'tive
con·stric'tor
con·struct'
con·struc'tion
con·struc'tive
con·struc'tor *also* con·
  struct'er
con·strue', -strued',
  -stru'ing
con'sul
con'su·lar
con'su·late
con·sult'
con·sul'tant

con·sul·ta'tion
con·sul'ta·tive
con·sum'a·ble
con·sume', -sumed',
  -sum'ing
con·sum'er
con·sum'er·ism
con·sum'er·ist
con·sum'mate *adj.*
con·sum·mate', -mat'-
  ed, -mat'ing
con·sum·ma'tion
con·sump'tion
con·sump'tive
con·tact'
con·ta'gion
con·ta'gious
con·tain'
con·tain'er
con·tain·er·i·za'tion
con·tain·er·ize', -ized',
  -iz'ing
con·tain'ment
con·tam'i·nant
con·tam'i·nate', -nat'-
  ed, -nat'ing
con·tam'i·na'tion
con·tam'i·na'tor
con'tem·plate', -plat'-
  ed, -plat'ing
con'tem·pla'tion
con'tem'pla·tive
con'tem·pla'tor
con·tem'po·ra'ne·ous
con·tem'po·rar'y
con·tempt'
con·tempt'i·ble

con·temp'tu·ous
con·tend'
con·tent' *adj. & v.*
con·tent' *n.*
con·tent'ed
con·ten'tion
con·ten'tious
con·tent'ment
con·ter'mi·nous
con·test' *n.*
con·test' *v.*
con·test'a·ble
con·test'ant
con'text
con·tex'tu·al
con'ti·gu'i·ty
con·tig'u·ous
con'ti·nence
con'ti·nent
con'ti·nen'tal
con·tin'gen·cy
con·tin'gent
con·tin'u·al
con·tin'u·ance
con·tin'u·a'tion
con·tin'ue, -ued,
  -u·ing
con·tin'u·er
con'ti·nu'i·ty
con·tin'u·o' *pl.* -os
con·tin'u·ous
con·tin'u·um *pl.* -u·a
  or -u·ums
con·tort'
con·tor'tion
con·tor'tion·ist
con·tor'tion·is'tic

con'tour
con'tra·band'
con'tra·bass'
con'tra·bas·soon'
con'tra·cep'tion
con'tra·cep'tive
con'tract' *n.*
con·tract' *v.*
con·tract'i·ble
con·trac'tile
con·trac'tion
con·trac'tor
con·trac'tu·al
con'tra·dict'
con'tra·dict'er *also*
  con'tra·dic'tor
con'tra·dic'tion
con'tra·dic'to·ry
con'tra·dis·tinc'tion
con·trail'
con·tral'to *pl.* -tos
con·trap'tion
con'tra·pun'tal
con'tra·pun'tist
con'tra·ri'e·ty
con'trar·i·wise'
con'trar'y
con'trast' *n.*
con·trast' *v.*
con'tra·vene', -vened',
  -ven'ing
con'tra·ven'tion
con'tre·temps'
con·trib'ute, -ut·ed,
  -ut·ing
con'tri·bu'tion
con·trib'u·tive

con·trib′u·tor
con·trib′u·to′ry
con·trite′
con·tri′tion
con·tri′vance
con·trive′, -trived′,
  -triv′ing
con·triv′ed·ly
con·trol′, -trolled′,
  -trol′ling
con·trol′la·ble
con·trol′ler *also* comp·
  trol′ler
con′tro·ver′sial
con′tro·ver′sy
con′tro·vert′
con′tro·vert′i·ble
con·tu·ma′cious
con′tu·ma·cy
con·tu·me′li·ous
con′tu·me·ly
con·tuse′, -tused′,
  -tus′ing
con·tu′sion
co·nun′drum
con′ur·ba′tion
con′va·lesce′, -lesced′,
  -lesc′ing
con′va·les′cence
con′va·les′cent
con·vec′tion
con·vec′tor
con·vene′, -vened′,
  -ven′ing
con·ven′ience
con·ven′ient
con′vent

con·ven′tion
con·ven′tion·al
con·ven′tion·al′i·ty
con·ven′tion·eer′
con·verge′, -verged′,
  -verg′ing
con·ver′gence *also*
  con·ver′gen·cy
con·ver′gent
con·ver′sant
con′ver·sa′tion
con′ver·sa′tion·al
con′ver·sa′tion·al·ist
con·verse′ *adj.*
con′verse′ *n.*
con·verse′, -versed′,
  -vers′ing
con·ver′sion
con·vert′ *n.*
con·vert′ *v.*
con·vert′er *also* con·
  ver′tor
con·vert′i·bil′i·ty
con·vert′i·ble
con′vex
con·vex′i·ty
con·vey′
con·vey′ance
con·vey′er *also* con·
  vey′or
con·vict′ *n.*
con·vict′ *v.*
con·vic′tion
con·vince′, -vinced′,
  -vinc′ing
con·vinc′i·ble
con·viv′i·al

con·viv′i·al′i·ty
con′vo·ca′tion
con·voke′, -voked′,
  -vok′ing
con′vo·lute′, -lut′ed,
  -lut′ing
con′vo·lu′tion
con′voy′
con·vulse′, -vulsed′,
  -vuls′ing
con·vul′sion
con·vul′sive
co′ny *also* co′ney *pl.*
  -neys
coo (*murmuring sound*),
  pl. coos
  ♦*coup*
coo (*to make a mur-
  muring sound*),
  cooed, coo′ing
  ♦*coup*
cook′book′
cook′er
cook′er·y
cook′out′
cook′y *or* cook′ie
cool′ant
cool′er
cool′-head′ed
coo′lie (*laborer*), *also*
  coo′ly
  ♦*coulee*
cool′ly (*in a cool man-
  ner*)
  ♦*coulee*
coon′hound′
coon′skin′

coop *(cage)*
 ♦*coupe*
co-op′ *(cooperative)*
coo′per
coo′per·age
co·op′er·ate′, -at′ed,
 -at′ing
co·op′er·a′tion
co·op′er·a·tive
co·op′er·a′tor
co-opt′
co·or′di·nate′, -nat′ed,
 -nat′ing
co·or′di·na′tion
co·or′di·na′tor
coot
coo′tie
cop, copped, cop′ping
co′pal
co·part′ner
cope, coped, cop′ing
co′pe·pod′
Co·per′ni·can
cop′i·er
co′pi·lot
cop′ing
co′pi·ous
co·pla′nar
co·pol′y·mer
cop′-out′ *n.*
cop′per
cop′per·as
cop′per·head′
cop′per·plate′
cop′per·smith′
cop′pice
cop′ra

copse
cop′ter
cop′u·la
cop′u·lar
cop′u·late′, -lat′ed,
 -lat′ing
cop′u·la′tion
cop′u·la·tive
cop′y, -ied, -y·ing
cop′y·book′
cop′y·cat′
cop′y·ed′it
cop′y·ist
cop′y·read′er
cop′y·right′
cop′y·writ′er
coq au vin′
co′quet·ry
co·quette′
co·quet′tish
co·quille′
co·qui′na
cor′a·cle
cor′al *(marine skeleton)*
 ♦*choral*
cor′al-bells′
cor′bel
cord *(rope)*
 ♦*chord*
cord′age
cor′dial
cor·dial′i·ty
cor·dil·le′ra
cor·dil·le′ran
cord′ite′
cor′don
cor′do·van

cor′du·roy
cord′wood′
core *(to remove the
 center),* cored, cor′-
 ing
 ♦*corps*
cor′er
co′re·spon′dent *(adul-
 terer)*
 ♦*correspondent*
co′ri·an′der
co·ri′um *pl.* -ri·a
cork′er
cork′screw′
cork′y
corm
cor′mo·rant
corn′cob′
corn′crib′
cor·ne′a
cor′ne·al
cor′ne·ous
cor′ner
cor′ner·back′
cor′ner·stone′
cor′net′
cor·net′ist *also* cor·
 net′tist
corn′field′
corn′flow′er
corn′husk′
cor′nice
corn′meal′
corn′stalk′
corn′starch′
cor·nu·co′pi·a
cor·nu·co′pi·an

corn′y
co•rol′la
cor•ol•lar′y
co•ro′na *pl.* -nas *or*
　-nae
cor•o′nar′y
cor•o•na′tion
cor•o•ner
cor•o•net′
cor′po•ral
cor′po•rate
cor•po•ra′tion
cor•po′re•al
corps *(troops)*
　♦*core*
corpse *(body)*
cor′pu•lence
cor′pu•lent
cor′pus *pl.* po•ra
cor′pus•cle
cor•pus′cu•lar
corpus de•lic′ti
cor•ral′ *(to capture or
　pen up),* -ralled′,
　-ral′ling
　♦*chorale*
cor•rect′
cor•rec′tion
cor•rec′tion•al
cor•rec′tive
cor•re•late′, -lat′ed,
　-lat′ing
cor•re•la′tion
cor•rel′a•tive
cor•re•spond′
cor•re•spon′dence

cor•re•spon′dent
　(writer)
　♦*corespondent*
cor•ri•dor
cor•ri•gen′dum *pl.* -da
cor•rob′o•rate′, -rat′-
　ed, -rat′ing
cor•rob′o•ra′tion
cor•rob′o•ra′tive
cor•rob′o•ra′tor
cor•rode′, -rod′ed,
　-rod′ing
cor•rod′i•ble *or* cor•
　ro′si•ble
cor•ro′sion
cor•ro′sive
cor′ru•gate′, -gat′ed,
　-gat′ing
cor′ru•ga′tion
cor•rupt′
cor•rup′ter *or* cor•
　rup′tor
cor•rupt′i•ble
cor•rup′tion
cor•rup′tive
cor•sage′
cor′sair
cor′set
Cor′si•can
cor•tege′
cor′tex *pl.* -ti•ces′ *or*
　-tex•es
cor′ti•cal
cor′ti•sone′
co•run′dum
cor•us•cate′, -cat′ed,
　-cat′ing

cor•us•ca′tion
cor•vette′
cor′vine′
co•ry′za
co•se′cant
co•sign′ *(to sign
　jointly)*
co′sine′ *(mathematical
　function)*
cos•met′ic
cos•me•tol′o•gist
cos•me•tol′o•gy
cos′mic *also* cos′mi•cal
cos•mog′o•ny
cos•mog′ra•phy
cos•mo•log′i•cal
cos•mol′o•gist
cos•mol′o•gy
cos′mo•naut
cos•mo•pol′i•tan
cos′mos
co•spon′sor
Cos′sack
cos′set
cost
cos′ta *pl.* -tae
co′star′ *also* co′-star′
Cos′ta Ri′can
cost′-ef•fec′tive
cost′-ef•fi′cient
cost′ly
cost′-plus′
cost′-push′
cos′tume, -tumed,
　-tum•ing
cos′tum•er
cot

co·tan'gent
cote *(shelter)*
 ♦*coat*
co'te·rie
co·til'lion
cot'tage
cot'tag·er
cot'ter
cot'ton
cot'ton·mouth'
cot'ton·seed'
cot'ton·tail'
cot'ton·wood'
cot'y·le'don
cot'y·le'don·al *also*
 cot'y·le'do·nous
couch
cou'gar
cough
could'n't
cou'lee *(ravine)*
 ♦*coolie, coolly*
cou'lomb'
coun'cil *(assembly)*
 ♦*counsel*
coun'cil·or *(council
 member), also* coun'-
 cil·lor
 ♦*counselor*
coun'sel *(to advise),*
 -seled *or* -selled, -sel·
 ing *or* -sel·ling
 ♦*council*
coun'sel·or *(adviser),
 also* coun'sel·lor
 ♦*councilor*
count'a·ble

count'down'
coun'te·nance,
 -nanced, -nanc·ing
coun'ter *(contrary)*
count'er *(serving table,
 game piece, one that
 counts)*
coun'ter·act'
coun'ter·ac'tion
coun'ter·ac'tive
coun'ter·at·tack'
coun'ter·bal'ance *n.*
coun'ter·bal'ance,
 -anced, -anc·ing
coun'ter·claim' *n.*
coun'ter·claim' *v.*
coun'ter·clock'wise'
coun'ter·cul'ture
coun'ter·es'pi·o·nage'
coun'ter·feit'
coun'ter·foil'
coun'ter·in·tel'li·
 gence
coun'ter·ir'ri·tant
coun'ter·mand'
coun'ter·mea'sure
coun'ter·of·fen'sive
coun'ter·pane'
coun'ter·part'
coun'ter·point'
coun'ter·poise' *n.*
coun'ter·poise',
 -poised', -pois'ing
coun'ter·pro·duc'tive
coun'ter·rev'o·lu'tion
coun'ter·shaft'
coun'ter·sign'

coun'ter·sink', -sunk',
 -sink'ing
coun'ter·spy'
coun'ter·ten'or
coun'ter·weight'
count'ess
count'less
coun'try
coun'try·side'
coun'ty
coup *(masterstroke)*
 ♦*coo*
coup' de grâce' *pl.*
 coups' de grâce'
coup' d'é·tat' *pl.*
 coups' d'é·tat'
coupe *(dessert)*
 ♦*coop*
cou·pé' *(car), also*
 coupe
cou'ple, -pled, -pling
cou'plet
cou'pon'
cour'age
cou·ra'geous
cou'ri·er
course *(to flow),*
 coursed, cours'ing
 ♦*coarse*
cours'er
court
cour'te·ous
cour'te·san
cour'te·sy
court'house'
court'i·er
court'ly

court'-mar'tial *pl.*
  courts'-mar'tial
court'-mar'tial,
  -tialed *or* -tialled,
  -tial·ing *or* -tial·ling
court'room'
court'ship'
court'yard'
cous'in *(relative)*
  ♦*cozen*
cou·ture'
cou·tu'ri·er
co·va'lence *also* co·
  va'len·cy
co·va'lent
cove
cov'en
cov'e·nant
cov'er
cov'er·age
cov'er·alls'
cov'er·ing
cov'er·let
cov'ert
cov'er-up' *n. also* cov'-
  er·up'
cov'et
cov'et·ous
cov'ey *pl.* -eys
cow'ard
cow'ard·ice
cow'bell'
cow'bird'
cow'boy'
cow'catch'er
cow'er
cow'girl'

cow'hand'
cow'herd'
cow'hide'
cow'lick'
cowl'ing
co'work'er
cow'poke'
cow'pox'
cow'punch'er
cow'ry *also* cow'rie
cow'skin'
cow'slip'
cox'comb'
cox'swain'
coy'ly
coy·o'te
coz'en *(to deceive)*
  ♦*cousin*
co'zy *also* co'sy
crab, crabbed, crab'-
  bing
crab'bed *adj.*
crab'by
crab'grass'
crack'brain'
crack'down' *n.*
crack'er
crack'er-bar'rel *adj.*
crack'er·jack'
crack'ing
crack'le, -led, -ling
crack'pot'
crack'up' *n.*
cra'dle, -dled, -dling
cra'dle·song'
crafts'man
craft'y

crag'gy
cram, crammed, cram'-
  ming
cramp
cram'pon
cran'ber'ry
crane, craned, cran'ing
cra'ni·al
cra·ni·ot'o·my
cra'ni·um *pl.* -ni·ums
  or -ni·a
crank'case'
crank'shaft'
crank'y
cran'ny
crap'pie
craps
crap'shoot'er
crap'u·lence
crash'-land' *v.*
crass
crate, crat'ed, crat'ing
crat'er *(one that crates)*
cra'ter *(pit)*
cra·vat'
crave, craved, crav'ing
cra'ven
crav'er
craw'fish' *pl.* -fish' *or*
  -fish'es
crawl'y
cray'fish' *pl.* -fish' *or*
  -fish'es
cray'on
craze, crazed, craz'ing
cra'zy

creak *(squeaking sound)*
 ♦*creek*
creak'y
cream'er
cream'er·y
crease, creased, creas'ing
cre·ate', -at'ed, -at'ing
cre·a'tion
cre·a'tive
cre·a·tiv'i·ty
cre·a'tor
crea'ture
crèche
cre'dence
cre·den'tial
cre·den'za
cred'i·bil'i·ty
cred'i·ble
cred'it
cred'it·a·bil'i·ty
cred'it·a·ble
cred'i·tor
cre'do *pl.* -dos
cre·du'li·ty
cred'u·lous
creed
creek *(stream)*
 ♦*creak*
creel
creep, crept, creep'ing
creep'er
creep'y
cre'mate', -mat'ed, -mat'ing
cre·ma'tion

cre·ma'tor
cre·ma·to'ri·um *pl.* -ri·ums *or* -ri·a
cre'ma·to'ry
crème' de ca·ca'o'
crème' de la crème'
crème' de menthe'
cre·nate' *also* cre·nat'ed
Cre'ole'
cre'o·sol'
cre'o·sote'
crepe *also* crêpe
crêpe' de Chine'
crêpe' su·zette'
cre·pus'cu·lar
cres·cen'do *pl.* -dos *or* -di
cres'cent
cre'sol'
cress
cres'set
crest'fall'en
Cre·ta'ceous
cre'tin
cre'tin·ism
cre·tonne'
cre·vasse' *(deep crack)*
crev'ice *(narrow opening)*
crew'-cut' *adj.*
crew'el *(yarn)*
 ♦*cruel*
crib, cribbed, crib'bing
crib'bage
crick
crick'et

cri'er
crime
Cri·me'an
crim'i·nal
crim'i·nal'i·ty
crim'i·no·log'i·cal
crim'i·nol'o·gist
crim'i·nol'o·gy
crimp
crim'son
cringe, cringed, cring'ing
crin'kle, -kled, -kling
crin'o·line
crip'ple, -pled, -pling
cri'sis *pl.* -ses'
crisp'er
crisp'y
criss'cross'
cri·te'ri·on *pl.* -ri·a *or* -ri·ons
crit'ic
crit'i·cal
crit'i·cism
crit'i·cize', -cized', -ciz'ing
~ cri·tique'
crit'ter
croak
cro·chet', -cheted', -chet'ing
crock'er·y
croc'o·dile'
croc'o·dil'i·an
cro'cus *pl.* -cus·es *or* -ci'
croft'er

crois·sant′
Cro-Mag′non
crom′lech′
crone
cro′ny
crook′ed
crook′neck′
croon′er
crop, cropped, crop′-
　ping
crop′per
cro·quet′ (game)
cro·quette′ (food)
cro′sier also cro′zier
cross′bar′
cross′bones′
cross′bow′
cross′breed′, -bred′,
　-breed′ing
cross′check′
cross′-coun′try
cross′cur′rent
cross′cut′, -cut′,
　-cut′ting
cross′-ex·am′i·na′-
　tion
cross′-ex·am′ine,
　-ined, -in·ing
cross′-eye′
cross′-eyed′
cross′-fer′ti·li·za′tion
cross′-fer′ti·lize′,
　-lized′, -liz′ing
cross′fire′
cross′-grained′
cross′hatch′
cross′-leg′ged

cross′ing
cross′o·ver n.
cross′piece′
cross′-pol′li·nate′,
　-nat′ed, -nat′ing
cross′-pol′li·na′tion
cross′-pur′pose′
cross′-re·fer′, -ferred′,
　-fer′ring
cross′-ref′er·ence
cross′road′
cross′-stitch′
cross′town′
cross′walk′
cross′wise′ also cross′-
　ways′
cross′word′ puzzle
crotch′et
crotch′et·y
crouch
croup
crou′pi·er
crou′ton′
crow (bird)
crow, crowed, crow′ing
crow′bar′
crowd
crow′foot′ pl. -foots′
　or -feet′
crown′-of-thorns′
crow′s′-foot′ pl. -feet′
crow′s′-nest′
cru′cial
cru′ci·ble
cru′ci·fix′
cru′ci·fix′ion
cru′ci·form′

cru′ci·fy′, -fied′, -fy′-
　ing
crud′dy
crude, crud′er, crud′est
crude′ly
cru′di·ty
cru′el (merciless, pain-
　ful)
　♦crewel
cru′el·ty
cru′et
cruise (to sail), cruised,
　cruis′ing
　♦crews, cruse
cruis′er
crul′ler
crumb
crum′ble, -bled,
　-bling
crum′my
crum′pet
crum·ple, -pled, -pling
crunch′y
cru·sade′, -sad′ed,
　-sad′ing
cru·sad′er
cruse (jar)
　♦crews, cruise
crush′a·ble
crus·ta′cean
crus·ta′ceous
crust′y
crutch
crux pl. crux′es or cru′-
　ces
cry, cried, cry′ing
cry′ba·by

cry'o·bi·ol'o·gy
cry'o·gen
cry'o·gen'ic
cry'o·gen'ics
cry·on'ics
cry'o·sur'geon
cry'o·sur'ger·y
cry'o·sur'gi·cal
crypt
cryp'tic
cryp'to·gram'
cryp'to·graph'
cryp·tog'ra·pher
cryp'to·graph'ic
cryp·tog'ra·phy
crys'tal
crys'tal·line
crys'tal·li·za'tion
crys'tal·lize', -lized',
   -liz'ing
crys'tal·log'ra·pher
crys'tal·log'ra·phy
crys'tal·loid'
cten'o·phore'
Cu'ban
cub'by·hole'
cube, cubed, cub'ing
cu'bic
cu'bi·cal (cubic)
cu'bi·cle (small com-
   partment)
cub'ism
cub'ist
cu'bit
cuck'old
cuck'oo
cu'cum'ber

cud
cud'dle, -dled, -dling
cud'dle·some
cudg'el, -eled or -elled,
   -el·ing or -el·ling
cue (rod, hint)
   ♦queue
cue (to hit a ball, sig-
   nal), cued, cu'ing
   ♦queue
cuff
cui·rass'
cui·sine'
cul'-de-sac' pl. -sacs'
cu'li·nar'y
cull
cul'mi·nate', -nat'ed,
   -nat'ing
cul'mi·na'tion
cu·lottes'
cul'pa·bil'i·ty
cul'pa·ble
cul'prit
cul'tic
cult'ist
cul'ti·va·ble also cul'-
   ti·vat'a·ble
cul'ti·vate', -vat'ed,
   -vat'ing
cul'ti·va'tion
cul'ti·va'tor
cul'tur·al
cul'ture, -tured, -tur·
   ing
cul'vert
cum'ber
cum'ber·some

cum'brance
cum'brous
cum'in
cum lau'de
cum'mer·bund'
cu'mu·la'tive
cu'mu·lo·nim'bus pl.
   -bus·es or -bi'
cu'mu·lous adj.
cu'mu·lus pl. -li'
cu'ne·i·form'
cun'ning
cup, cupped, cup'ping
cup'board
cup'cake'
cu'pel, -peled or
   -pelled, -pel·ing or
   -pel·ling
cup'ful pl. -fuls'
Cu'pid
cu·pid'i·ty
cu'po·la
cu'pric
cu'prous
cur
cur'a·ble
cu·ra're or cu·ra'ri
cu'rate
cur'a·tive
cu·ra'tor
curb'ing
curb'stone'
curd
cur'dle, -dled, -dling
cure (to remedy, pre-
   serve), cured, cur'ing
cu·ré' (parish priest)

cure'-all'
cu'ret·tage'
cu·rette' *also* cu·ret'
cur'few
cu'ri·a *pl.* -ae'
cu'rie
cu'ri·o' *pl.* -os'
cu'ri·os'i·ty
cu'ri·ous
cu'ri·um
curl'er
cur'lew
curl'i·cue *also* curl'y·
　cue
curl'ing
curl'y
cur·mudg'eon
cur'rant *(berry)*
　♦*current*
cur'ren·cy
cur'rent *(prevalent)*
　♦*currant*
cur'rent *(electric
　charge)*
　♦*currant*
cur·ric'u·lar
cur·ric'u·lum *pl.* -la *or*
　-lums
cur'ry, -ried, -ry·ing
cur'ry·comb'
curse, cursed *or* curst,
　curs'ing
curs'ed *adj. also* curst
curs'er *(one that
　curses)*
　♦*cursor*
cur'sive

cur'sor' *(indicator)*
　♦*curser*
cur'so·ry
cur·tail'
cur·tail'ment
cur'tain
curt'ly
curt'sy, -sied, -sy·ing
cur·va'ceous
cur'va·ture
curve, curved, curv'ing
curv'ed·ly
cur'vet
cur·vi·lin'e·ar
cush'ion
cush'y
cusp
cus'pid
cus'pi·date'
cus'pi·dor'
cuss
cuss'ed *adj.*
cus'tard
cus·to'di·al
cus·to'di·an
cus'to·dy
cus'tom
cus'tom·ar'y
cus'tom-built'
cus'tom·er
cus'tom·house'
cus'tom·ize', -ized',
　-iz'ing
cus'tom-made'
cut, cut, cut'ting
cut'-and-dried'
cu·ta'ne·ous

cut'a·way'
cut'back'
cute, cut'er, cut'est
cute'ly
cu'ti·cle
cut'-in' *(film shot)*
cu'tin *(waxlike sub-
　stance)*
cut'lass
cut'ler·y
cut'let
cut'off' *n.*
cut'out' *n.*
cut'-rate'
cut'ter
cut'throat'
cut'ting
cut'tle·bone'
cut'tle·fish' *pl.* -fish'
　or -fish'es
cut'up' *n.*
cut'worm'
cy'an *(blue)*
　♦*scion*
cy·an'ic
cy'a·nide', -nid'ed,
　-nid'ing
cy·an'o·gen
cy'a·no'sis
cy'a·not'ic
cy'ber·net'ic
cy'ber·net'ics
cyc'la·mate'
cyc'la·men
cyc·la'mic' acid
cy'cle, -cled, -cling
cy'clic *also* cy'cli·cal

cy'clist *also* cy'cler
cy'cloid'
cy'clone'
cy'clon'ic
cy'clo•pe'di•a *also* cy'-
  clo•pae'di•a
Cy'clops' *pl.* Cy•clo'-
  pes
cy'clo•ram'a
cy'clo•tron'
cyg'net *(swan)*
  ♦*signet*
cyl'in•der
cy•lin'dri•cal *also* cy•
  lin'dric
cym'bal *(percussion in-
  strument)*
  ♦*symbol*
cyn'ic
cyn'i•cal
cyn'i•cism
cy'no•sure'
cy'press
Cyp'ri•an
cyp'ri•noid'
Cyp'ri•ot *also* Cyp'ri•
  ote
Cy•ril'lic
cyst
cys'tic
cys•ti'tis
cy'to•gen'e•sis
cy'to•log'i•cal
cy•tol'o•gist
cy•tol'o•gy
cy'to•plasm
cy'to•plas'mic

cy'to•plast'
cy'to•sine'
czar *also* tsar, tzar
czar'e•vitch
cza•rev'na
cza•ri'na
czar'ism
czar'ist
Czech *(inhabitant)*
  ♦*check*
Czech'o•slo'vak *also*
  Czech'o•slo•va'ki•an

D

dab, dabbed, dab'bing
dab'ber
dab'ble, -bled, -bling
da ca'po
dace *pl.* dace *or* dac'es
da'cha
dachs'hund'
Da'cron'®
dac'tyl
dac•tyl'ic
Da'da *or* da'da, *also*
  Da'da•ism
dad'dy
daddy long'legs' *pl.*
  daddy long'legs'
da'do *pl.* -does
daf'fo•dil
daf'fy
daft
dag'ger

da•guerre'o•type'
dahl'ia
dai'ly
dain'ty
dai'qui•ri *pl.* -ris
dair'y
dair'y•ing
dair'y•maid'
dair'y•man
da'is
dai'sy
Da•ko'tan
dale
dal'li•ance
dal'ly, -lied, -ly•ing
Dal•ma'tian
dam *(barrier, female
  parent)*
  ♦*damn*
dam *(to restrain)*,
  dammed, dam'ming
  ♦*damn*
dam'age, -aged, -ag•
  ing
dam'as•cene', -cened',
  -cen'ing
dam'ask
dame
damn *(to condemn)*
  ♦*dam*
dam'na•ble
dam•na'tion
damned *(condemned)*
  ♦*dammed*
damp'en
damp'er
dam'sel

dam'sel·fly'
dam'son
dance, danced, danc'-
  ing
danc'er
dan·de·li·on
dan'der
Dan'die Din'mont'
dan'di·fi·ca'tion
dan'di·fy', -fied', -fy'-
  ing
dan'dle, -dled, -dling
dan'druff
dan'dy
Dane *(native of Den-
  mark)*
  ♦*deign*
dan'ger
dan'ger·ous
dan'gle, -gled, -gling
Dan'ish
dank'ness
dan·seur'
dan·seuse'
daph'ni·a *pl.* -ni·a
dap'per
dap'ple, -pled, -pling
dare, dared, dar'ing
dare'dev'il
dar'er
dar'ing
Dar·jee'ling
dark'en
dark'ness
dark'room'
dar'ling
darn

dar'nel
darn'ing needle
dart
dart'er
dar'tle, -tled, -tling
Dar·win'i·an
Dar'win·ism
dash'board'
dash'er
da·shi'ki
dash'ing
das'tard
da'ta *sing.* -tum
dat'a·ble *or* date'a·ble
date, dat'ed, dat'ing
date'line'
da'tive
daub'er
daugh'ter
daugh'ter-in-law' *pl.*
  daugh'ters-in-law'
daunt'less
dau'phin
dav'en·port'
dav'it
daw
→daw'dle, -dled, -dling
dawn
day'book'
day'break'
day'-care' *adj.*
day'dream', -dreamed'
  or -dreamt', -dream'-
  ing
day'flow'er
Day'-Glo'®
day'light'

day'light'-sav'ing
  time
day'long'
day'star'
day'time'
day'-to-day'
daze *(to stun)*, dazed,
  daz'ing
  ♦*days*
daz'zle, -zled, -zling
de'-ac·ces'sion
dea'con
dea'con·ry
de·ac'ti·vate', -vat'ed,
  -vat'ing
de·ac'ti·va'tion
dead'beat'
dead'en
dead'-end' *adj.*
dead'head'
dead'line'
dead'lock'
dead'ly
dead'pan'
dead'wood'
deaf'en
deaf'-mute'
deal, dealt, deal'ing
deal'er
deal'er·ship'
dean'er·y
dear *(beloved)*
  ♦*deer*
dearth
death'bed'
death'blow'
death'less

death'ly
death's'-head'
death'trap'
death'watch'
de·ba'cle
de·bar', -barred', -bar·ring
de·bark'
de'bar·ka'tion
de·base', -based', -bas'ing
de·base'ment
de·bat'a·ble
de·bate', -bat'ed, -bat·ing
de·bauch'
de·bauch'er·y
de·ben'ture
de·bil'i·tate', -tat'ed, -tat'ing
de·bil'i·ta'tion
de·bil'i·ta'tive
de·bil'i·ty
deb'it
deb'o·nair' also deb'o·naire'
de·brief'
de·bris' also dé·bris'
debt'or
de·bug', -bugged', -bug'ging
de·bunk'
de·but' also dé·but'
deb'u·tante' also dé·bu·tante'
dec'ade'

dec'a·dence also dec'a·den·cy
dec'a·dent
dec'a·gon'
dec'a·gram' or dek'a·gram'
dec'a·he'dral
dec'a·he'dron pl. -drons or -dra
de'cal'
de·cal'ci·fi·ca'tion
de·cal'ci·fy', -fied', -fy'ing
de·cal·co·ma'ni·a
Dec'a·logue' or Dec'a·log'
dec'a·me'ter or dek'a·me'ter
de·camp'
de·cant'
de·can·ta'tion
de·cant'er
de·cap'i·tate', -tat'ed, -tat'ing
de·cap'i·ta'tion
de·cap'i·ta·tor
de·car'bon·ate', -at'ed, -at'ing
de·cath'lon
de·cay'
de·cease', -ceased', -ceas'ing
de·ce'dent
de·ceit'
de·ceit'ful
de·ceive', -ceived', -ceiv'ing

de·ceiv'er
de·cel'er·ate', -at'ed, -at'ing
de·cel'er·a'tion
De·cem'ber
de'cen·cy
de'cent (proper)
♦descent, dissent
de·cen'tral·i·za'tion
de·cen'tral·ize', -ized', -iz'ing
de·cep'tion
de·cep'tive
dec'i·bel
de·cide', -cid·ed, -cid·ing
de·cid'u·ous
dec'i·gram'
dec'i·li'ter
de·cil'lion
de·cil'lionth
dec'i·mal
dec'i·mate', -mat'ed, -mat'ing
dec'i·ma'tion
dec'i·ma'tor
dec'i·me'ter
de·ci'pher
de·ci'pher·a·ble
de·ci'sion
de·ci'sive
deck'house'
deck'le, -led, -ling
deck'le-edged'
de·claim'
dec'la·ma'tion
de·clam'a·to'ry

de·clar'a·ble
dec'la·ra'tion
de·clar'a·tive
de·clare', -clared',
 -clar'ing
de·clas'si·fi·ca'tion
de·clas'si·fy', -fied',
 -fy'ing
de·clen'sion
dec'li·na'tion
de·cline', -clined',
 -clin'ing
de·cliv'i·ty
de·coct'
de·coc'tion
de·code', -cod'ed,
 -cod'ing
de·cod'er
dé·colle·tage'
dé·colle·té'
de'com·mis'sion
de'com·pos'a·ble
de'com·pose', -posed',
 -pos'ing
de'com·po·si'tion
de'com·press'
de'com·pres'sion
de'con·tam'i·nate',
 -nat'ed, -nat'ing
de'con·tam'i·na'tion
de'con·trol', -trolled',
 -trol'ling
dé'cor' *also* de'cor'
dec'o·rate', -rat'ed,
 -rat'ing
dec'o·ra'tion
dec'o·ra·tive

dec'o·ra'tor
dec'o·rous
de·co'rum
de·coy'
de·crease' *n.*
de·crease', -creased',
 -creas'ing
de·cree'
dec're·ment
de·crep'it
de·crep'i·tude'
de·cre·scen'do *pl.*
 -dos
de·cre'tal
de·crim'i·nal·i·za'-
 tion
de·crim'i·nal·ize',
 -ized', -iz'ing
de·cry', -cried', -cry'-
 ing
de·cus'sate', -sat'ed,
 -sat'ing
ded'i·cate', -cat'ed,
 -cat'ing
ded'i·ca'tion
ded'i·ca'tor
de·duce', -duced',
 -duc'ing
de·duc'i·ble
de·duct'
de·duct'i·ble
de·duc'tion
de·duc'tive
deed
deem
deep'en
Deep'freeze'®

deep'-fry', -fried',
 -fry'ing
deep'-root'ed
deep'-sea' *adj.*
deep'-seat'ed
deer *(animal)* pl. deer
 or deers
 ♦*dear*
deer'hound'
deer'skin'
deer·stalk'er
de'-es·ca·late', -lat'ed,
 -lat'ing
de'-es·ca·la'tion
de·face', -faced', -fac'-
 ing
de·face'ment
de fac'to
de·fal'cate', -cat'ed,
 -cat'ing
de'fal·ca'tion
de'fal·ca'tor
def'a·ma'tion
de·fam'a·to'ry
de·fame', -famed',
 -fam'ing
de·fault'
de·feat'
de·feat'ism
de·feat'ist
def'e·cate', -cat'ed,
 -cat'ing
def'e·ca'tion
def'e·ca'tor
de'fect' *n.*
de·fect' *v.*
de·fec'tion

de·fec'tive
de·fec'tor
de·fend'
de·fen'dant
de·fense'
de·fen'si·ble
de·fen'sive
de·fer', -ferred', -fer'-
 ring
def'er·ence *(respect)*
 ♦*difference*
def'er·ent
def'er·en'tial
de·fer'ment *also* de·
 fer'ral
de·fer'ra·ble
de·fer'rer
de·fi'ance
de·fi'ant
de·fi'cien·cy
de·fi'cient
def'i·cit
de·file', -filed', -fil'ing
de·file'ment
de·fil'er
de·fin'a·ble
de·fine', -fined', -fin'-
 ing
de·fin'er
def'i·nite *(clear)*
 ♦*definitive*
def'i·ni'tion
de·fin'i·tive *(final)*
 ♦*definite*
de·flate', -flat'ed,
 -flat'ing
de·fla'tion

de·fla'tor
de·flect'
de·flect'a·ble
de·flec'tion
de·flec'tive
de·flec'tor
de·fo'li·ant
de·fo'li·ate', -at'ed,
 -at'ing
de·fo'li·a'tion
de·fo'li·a'tor
de·for'est
de·for·es'ta'tion
de·form'
de'for·ma'tion
de·form'i·ty
de·fraud'
de·fray'
de·fray'a·ble
de·fray'al
de·frock'
de·frost'
de·frost'er
deft'ly
de·funct'
de·func'tive
de·fuse', -fused', -fus'-
 ing
de·fy', -fied', -fy'ing
de·gauss'
de·gen'er·a·cy
de·gen'er·ate', -at'ed,
 -at'ing
de·gen'er·a'tion
de·gen'er·a·tive
de·glu'ti·nate', -nat'-
 ed, -nat'ing

de·glu'ti·na'tion
de'glu·ti'tion
deg'ra·da'tion
de·grade', -grad'ed,
 -grad'ing
de·grad'er
de·grease', -greased',
 -greas'ing
de·gree'
de·gree'-day'
de·hisce', -hisced',
 -hisc'ing
de·his'cence
de·his'cent
de·hu'man·i·za'tion
de·hu'man·ize', -ized',
 -iz'ing
de'hu·mid'i·fi·ca'tion
de'hu·mid'i·fi'er
de'hu·mid'i·fy', -fied',
 -fy'ing
de·hy'drate', -drat'ed,
 -drat'ing
de'hy·dra'tion
de·hy'dra'tor
de·hy'dro·ge·nate',
 -nat'ed, -nat'ing
de·hy'dro·ge·na'tion
de·ice', -iced', -ic'ing
de·ic'er
de'i·fi·ca'tion
de'i·fy', -fied', -fy'ing
deign *(to condescend)*
 ♦*Dane*
de'ism
de'ist
de·is'tic

de'i·ty
dé·jà vu'
de·ject'
de·jec'tion
de ju're
Del·a·war'e·an
de·lay'
de·lec'ta·bil'i·ty
de·lec'ta·ble
de'lec·ta'tion
del'e·gate', -gat·ed,
   -gat'ing
del'e·ga'tion
de·lete', -let·ed, -let'ing
del'e·te'ri·ous
de·le'tion
delft'ware'
del'i pl. -is
de·lib'er·ate', -at·ed,
   -at'ing
de·lib'er·a'tion
de·lib'er·a'tive
del'i·ca·cy
del'i·cate
del'i·ca·tes'sen
de·li'cious
de·light'
de·light'ful
de·lim'it
de·lim'i·ta'tion
de·lin'e·ate', -at·ed,
   -at'ing
de·lin'e·a'tion
de·lin'e·a'tive
de·lin'e·a'tor
de·lin'quen·cy
de·lin'quent

del'i·quesce',
   -quesced', -quesc'ing
del'i·ques'cence
del'i·ques'cent
de·lir'i·ous
de·lir'i·um pl. -i·ums
   or -i·a
de·liv'er
de·liv'er·a·ble
de·liv'er·ance
de·liv'er·y
de·louse', -loused',
   -lous'ing
del·phin'i·um
del'ta
del·ta'ic also del'tic
del'toid
de·lude', -lud·ed, -lud'-
   ing
del'uge, -uged, -ug'ing
de·lu'sion
de·lu'sive also de·lu'-
   so·ry
de luxe' also de·luxe'
delve, delved, delv'ing
delv'er
de·mag'net·i·za'tion
de·mag'net·ize',
   -ized', -iz'ing
dem'a·gog'ic also
   dem'a·gog'i·cal
dem'a·gogue'
dem'a·gogu'er·y
dem'a·go'gy
de·mand'
de·mand'-pull' adj.

de·mar'cate', -cat'ed,
   -cat'ing
de'mar·ca'tion
de'mar·ca'tor
dé·marche'
de·mean'
de·mean'or
de·ment'ed
de·men'tia
dementia prae'cox'
de·mer'it
de·mesne'
dem'i·god'
dem'i·john'
de·mil'i·ta·ri·za'tion
de·mil'i·ta·rize',
   -rized', -riz'ing
dem'i·mon·daine'
dem'i·monde'
de·mise', -mised',
   -mis'ing
dem'i·tasse'
de·mo'bil·i·za'tion
de·mo'bil·ize', -ized',
   -iz'ing
de·moc'ra·cy
dem'o·crat'
dem'o·crat'ic
de·moc'ra·ti·za'tion
de·moc'ra·tize',
   -tized', -tiz'ing
de·mod'u·late', -lat'-
   ed, -lat'ing
de·mod'u·la'tion
de·mod'u·la'tor
de·mog'ra·pher

dem'o•graph'ic *also*
  dem'o•graph'i•cal
dem'o•graph'ics
de•mog'ra•phy
dem'oi•selle'
de•mol'ish
dem'o•li'tion
de'mon
de•mo'ni•ac' *also* de'-
  mo•ni'a•cal
de•mon'ic
de'mon•ol'o•gist
de'mon•ol'o•gy
de•mon'stra•ble
dem'on•strate',
  -strat'ed, -strat'ing
dem'on•stra'tion
de•mon'stra•tive
de•mon'stra•tor
de•mor'al•i•za'tion
de•mor'al•ize', -ized',
  -iz'ing
de•mote', -mot'ed,
  -mot'ing
de•mo'tion
de•mount'
de•mul'cent
de•mur' *(to object)*,
  -murred', -mur'ring
de•mure' *(modest)*
de•mur'ra•ble
de•mur'rage
de•mur'rer
de•mys'ti•fi•ca'tion
de•mys'ti•fy', -fied',
  -fy'ing
den

de•na'tion•al•i•za'tion
de•na'tion•al•ize',
  -ized', -iz'ing
de•nat'u•ral•i•za'tion
de•nat'u•ral•ize',
  -ized', -iz'ing
de•na'tur•ant
de•na'ture, -tured,
  -tur•ing
den'drite'
den•drol'o•gy
den'gue
de•ni'al
de•ni'er *(one who de-*
  nies)
den•ier' *(yarn gauge)*
den'i•grate', -grat'ed,
  -grat'ing
den'i•gra'tion
den'i•gra'tor
den'im
de•ni'tri•fi•ca'tion
de•ni'tri•fy', -fied',
  -fy'ing
den'i•zen
de•nom'i•nate', -nat'-
  ed, -nat'ing
de•nom'i•na'tion
de•nom'i•na'tion•al•
  ism
de•nom'i•na'tive
de•nom'i•na'tor
de•no'ta'tion
de•no'ta•tive
de•note', -not'ed,
  -not'ing

dé'noue•ment' *also*
  de'noue•ment'
de•nounce',
  -nounced', -nounc'-
  ing
dense, dens'er, dens'-
  est
dense'ly
den'si•ty
dent
den'tal
den'tate'
den•tic'u•late *also*
  den•tic'u•lat'ed
den'ti•frice
den'ti•nal
den'tine' *also* den'tin
den'tist
den'tist•ry
den•ti'tion
den'ture
de•nude', -nud'ed,
  -nud'ing
de•num'er•a•ble
de•nun'ci•a'tion
de•ny', -nied', -ny'ing
de•o'dor•ant
de•o'dor•ize', -ized',
  -iz'ing
de•o'dor•iz'er
de•ox'i•di•za'tion
de•ox'i•dize', -dized',
  -diz'ing
de•ox'y•gen•ate', -at'-
  ed, -at'ing
de•ox'y•ri•bo•nu•cle'-
  ic acid

de·part′
de·part′ment
de′part·men′tal
de·par′ture
de·pend′
de·pend′a·bil′i·ty
de·pend′a·ble
de·pend′ence *also* de·pend′ance
de·pend′en·cy *also* de·pend′an·cy
de·pend′ent *also* de·pend′ant
de·per′son·al·i·za′tion
de·pict′
de·pic′tion
de·pil′a·to′ry
de·plane′ -planed′, -plan′ing
de·plet′a·ble
de·plete′, -plet′ed, -plet′ing
de·ple′tion
de·plor′a·ble
de·plore′, -plored′, -plor′ing
de·ploy′
de·ploy′ment
de·po′lar·i·za′tion
de·po′lar·ize′, -ized′, -iz′ing
de·po′nent
de·pop′u·late′, -lat′ed, -lat′ing
de·pop′u·la′tion
de·pop′u·la·tor

de·port′
de′port·ee′
de′por·ta′tion
de·port′ment
de·pos′a·ble
de·pos′al
de·pose′, -posed′, -pos′ing
de·pos′it
dep′o·si′tion
de·pos′i·tor
de·pos′i·to′ry
de′pot
dep′ra·va′tion *(corruption)*
♦*deprivation*
de·prave′, -praved′, -prav′ing
de·prav′i·ty
dep′re·cate′, -cat′ed, -cat′ing
dep′re·ca′tion
dep′re·ca′tor
dep′re·ca·to′ry *also* dep′re·ca′tive
de·pre′ci·ate′, -at′ed, -at′ing
de·pre′ci·a′tion
de·pre′ci·a′tor
de·pre′ci·a·to′ry
dep′re·date′, -dat′ed, -dat′ing
dep′re·da′tion
de·press′
de·pres′sant
de·pres′sion
de·pres′sive

de·pres′sor
dep′ri·va′tion *(loss)*, *also* de·priv′al
♦*depravation*
de·prive′, -prived′, -priv′ing
de·pro′gram′, -grammed′ *or* -gramed′, -gram′ming *or* -gram′ing
de·pro′gram′mer *or* de·pro′gram′er
depth
dep′u·ta′tion
de·pute′, -put′ed, -put′ing
dep′u·tize′, -tized′, -tiz′ing
dep′u·ty
de·rail′
de·rail′ment
de·range′, -ranged′, -rang′ing
de·range′ment
der′by
de·reg′u·late′, -lat′ed, -lat′ing
de·reg′u·la′tion
de·reg′u·la′tor
de·reg′u·la·to′ry
der′e·lict
der′e·lic′tion
de·ride′, -rid′ed, -rid′ing
de·ri′sion
de·ri′sive
de·riv′a·ble

der'i·va'tion
de·riv'a·tive
de·rive', -rived', -riv'ing
der'ma *(skin)*, also derm, der'mis
der'ma *(food)*
der'mal
der·ma·ti'tis
der'ma·tol'o·gist
der'ma·tol'o·gy
der'o·gate', -gat'ed, -gat'ing
der'o·ga'tion
de·rog'a·to·ry
der'rick
der·ri·ère' *also* der'ri·ere'
der'ring-do'
der'rin·ger
der'vish
de·sal'i·nate', -nat'ed, -nat'ing
de·sal'i·na'tion
de·sal'i·ni·za'tion
de·sal'in·ize', -ized', -iz'ing
de·salt'
des'cant
de·scend'
de·scen'dant *(off-spring)*
de·scen'dent *(descending)*, also de·scen'dant
de·scend'i·ble *also* de·scend'a·ble

de·scent' *(downward incline)*
◆decent, dissent
de·scrib'a·ble
de·scribe', -scribed', -scrib'ing
de·scrip'tion
de·scrip'tive
de·scry', -scried', -scry'ing
des'e·crate', -crat'ed, -crat'ing
des'e·cra'tion
de·seg're·gate', -gat'ed, -gat'ing
de·seg're·ga'tion
de·sen'si·ti·za'tion
de·sen'si·tize', -tized', -tiz'ing
des'ert *(barren region)*
de·sert' *(deserved reward)*
◆dessert
de·sert' *(to leave)*
◆dessert
de·ser'tion
de·serve', -served', -serv'ing
de·serv'ed·ly
des'ic·cant
des'ic·cate', -cat'ed, -cat'ing
des'ic·ca'tion
des'ic·ca'tive
de·sid'er·a'tum *pl.* -ta
de·sign'

des'ig·nate', -nat'ed, -nat'ing
des'ig·na'tion
des'ig·na·tive *also* des'ig·na·to'ry
des'ig·na'tor
de·sign'ed·ly
des'ig·nee'
de·sign'er
de·sir'a·bil'i·ty
de·sir'a·ble
de·sire', -sired', -sir'ing
de·sir'er
de·sir'ous
de·sist'
desk
des'o·late', -lat'ed, -lat'ing
des'o·la'tion
de·spair'
des'per·a'do *pl.* -does *or* -dos
des'per·ate *(hopeless)*
◆disparate
des'per·a'tion
des'pi·ca·ble
de·spise', -spised', -spis'ing
de·spis'er
de·spite'
de·spoil'
de·spo'li·a'tion
de·spond'
de·spon'den·cy *also* de·spon'dence
de·spon'dent
des'pot

des·pot'ic
des'pot·ism
des·sert' *(food)*
  ♦*desert (deserved re-
  ward; to leave)*
des·sert'spoon'
des'ti·na'tion
des'tine, -tined, -tin·
  ing
des'ti·ny
des'ti·tute'
des'ti·tu'tion
de·stroy'
de·stroy'er
de·struct'
de·struc'ti·bil'i·ty
de·struc'ti·ble
de·struc'tion
de·struc'tive
des'ue·tude'
des'ul·to·ry
de·tach'
de·tach'a·ble
de·tach'ment
de·tail'
de·tain'
de·tain'ment
de·tect'
de·tect'a·ble *also* de·
  tect'i·ble
de·tec'tion
de·tec'tive
de·tec'tor
dé·tente'
de·ten'tion
de·ter', -terred', -ter'-
  ring

de·ter'gent
de·te'ri·o·rate', -rat'-
  ed, -rat'ing
de·te'ri·o·ra'tion
de·ter'ment
de·ter'min·a·ble
de·ter'mi·nant
de·ter'mi·nate
de·ter'mi·na'tion
de·ter'mi·na'tive
de·ter'mine, -mined,
  -min·ing
de·ter'min·er
de·ter'min·ism
de·ter'rence
de·ter'rent
de·test'
de·test'a·ble
de'tes·ta'tion
de·throne', -throned',
  -thron'ing
det'o·nate', -nat'ed,
  -nat'ing
det'o·na'tion
det'o·na'tor
de'tour'
de·tox'i·fi·ca'tion
de·tox'i·fy', -fied',
  -fy'ing *also* de·tox'i·
  cate', -cat'ed, -cat'ing
de·tract'
de·trac'tion
de·trac'tor
de·train'
det'ri·ment
det'ri·men'tal
de·tri'tus

deuce
deuc'ed
de'us ex mach'i·na'
deu·te'ri·um
deu'ter·on
de·val'u·ate', -at'ed,
  -at'ing, *also* de·val'-
  ue, -ued, -u·ing
de·val'u·a'tion
dev'as·tate', -tat'ed,
  -tat'ing
dev'as·ta'tion
de·vel'op
de·vel'op·ment
de·vel'op·men'tal
de·vi'ance
de·vi'ant
de·vi'ate', -at'ed, -at'-
  ing
de·vi·a'tion
de·vi·a'tor
de·vice' *(contrivance)*
  ♦*devise*
dev'il, -iled *or* -illed,
  -il·ing *or* -il·ling
dev'il·fish' *pl.* -fish' *or*
  -fish'es
dev'il·ish
dev'il-may-care'
dev'il·ment
dev'il's-food' cake
dev'il·try *also* dev'il·ry
de'vi·ous
de·vis'a·ble
de·vise' *(to invent),*
  -vised', -vis'ing
  ♦*device*

de·vi'tal·ize', -ized',
-iz'ing
de·void'
dev'o·lu'tion
de·volve', -volved',
-volv'ing
de·vote', -vot'ed, -vot'-
ing
dev'o·tee'
de·vo'tion
de·vour'
de·vout'
dew (moisture)
♦do (what should be
done, party; to per-
form), due
dew'ber'ry
dew'drop'
dew'fall'
dew'lap'
dew'y
dew'y-eyed'
dex·ter'i·ty
dex'ter·ous also dex'-
trous
dex'tral
dex'trin also dex'trine
dex'trose'
di'a·be'tes
diabetes mel·li'tus
di'a·bet'ic
di'a·bol'ic also di'a·
bol'i·cal
di·ac'e·tyl·mor'phine'
di'a·chron'ic
di'a·crit'i·cal also di'a·
crit'ic

di'a·dem'
di'ag·nose', -nosed',
-nos'ing
di'ag·no'sis pl. -ses'
di'ag·nos'tic
di'ag·nos'ti·cian
di·ag'o·nal
di'a·gram', -grammed'
or -gramed', -gram'-
ming or -gram'ing
di'a·gram·mat'ic also
di'a·gram·mat'i·cal
di'al, -aled or -alled,
-al·ing or -al·ling
di'a·lect'
di'a·lec'tal
di'a·lec'tic
di'a·lec'ti·cal
di'a·lec'ti'cian
di'al·er
di'a·logue' also di'a·
log'
di·al'y·sis pl. -ses'
di'a·lyze', -lyzed',
-lyz'ing
di'a·mag·net'ic
di·am'e·ter
di'a·met'ri·cal also
di'a·met'ric
dia'mond
dia'mond·back'
di'a·pa'son
di'a·per
di·aph'a·nous
di'a·pho·re'sis
di'a·pho·ret'ic
di'a·phragm'

di'a·rist
di'ar·rhe'a also di'ar·
rhoe'a
di'a·ry
Di·as'po·ra also di·as'-
po·ra
di'a·stase'
di·a·sta'sic
di·as'to·le'
di'a·stol'ic
di'a·stroph'ic
di·as'tro·phism
di'a·ther'my
di'a·tom'
di'a·to·ma'ceous
di'a·tom'ic
di·at'o·mite'
di'a·ton'ic
di'a·tribe'
di·az'e·pam'
di·ba'sic
dib'ble, -bled, -bling
dice sing. die
dice, diced, dic'ing
dic'er
di·chlo'ride
di·chot'o·mize',
-mized', -miz'ing
di·chot'o·mous
di·chot'o·my
di·chro'mate'
di'chro·mat'ic
dick'ens
dick'er
dick'ey pl. -eys, also
dick'ie, dick'y
di·cli'nous

di'cot'y•le'don *also* di'cot
di'cot'y•le'don•ous
Dic'ta•phone'®
dic'tate', -tat'ed, -tat'- ing
dic•ta'tion
dic'ta•tor
dic'ta•to'ri•al
dic•ta'tor•ship'
dic'tion
dic'tion•ar'y
dic'tum *pl.* -ta *or* -tums
di•dac'tic *also* di•dac'- ti•cal
di•dac'ti•cism
did'dle, -dled, -dling
did'n't
di•dym'i•um
die *(to expire),* died, dy'ing
♦*dye*
die *(to stamp),* died, die'ing
♦*dye*
die'-hard' *also* die'hard'
di•e•lec'tric
di•er'e•sis *pl.* -ses', *also* di•aer'e•sis
die'sel engine
di'et
di'e•tar'y
di'e•tet'ic
di•eth'yl ether

di•e•ti'tian *also* di'e•ti'- cian
dif'fer
dif'fer•ence *(diversity)* ♦*deference*
dif'fer•ent
dif'fer•en'tial
dif'fer•en'ti•ate', -at'- ed, -at'ing
dif'fer•en'ti•a'tion
dif'fi•cult'
dif'fi•cul'ty
dif'fi•dence'
dif'fi•dent'
dif•fract'
dif•frac'tion
dif•frac'tive
dif•fuse', -fused', -fus'- ing
dif•fus'er
dif•fus'i•ble
dif•fu'sion
dif•fu'sive
dig, dug, dig'ging
di•gest' *n.*
di•gest' *v.*
di•gest'i•ble
di•ges'tion
di•ges'tive
dig'ger
dig'gings
dig'it
dig'i•tal
dig'i•tal'is
dig'i•tal•i•za'tion
dig'ni•fy', -fied', -fy'- ing

dig'ni•tar'y
dig'ni•ty
di'graph'
di•gress'
di•gres'sion
di•gres'sive
di•he'dral
dike, diked, dik'ing, *also* dyke, dyked, dyk'ing
di•lap'i•dat'ed
di•lap'i•da'tion
di•lat'a•ble
dil'a•ta'tion
di•late', -lat'ed, -lat'ing
di•la'tion
di•la'tive
di•la'tor *also* di•lat'er, dil'a•ta•tor
dil'a•to'ry
di•lem'ma
dil'et•tante' *pl.* -tantes' *or* -tan'ti
dil'et•tan'tism
dil'i•gence'
dil'i•gent'
dill
dil'ly
dil'ly-dal'ly, -lied, -ly• ing
di•lute', -lut'ed, -lut'- ing
di•lu'tion
di•lu'vi•al *also* di•lu'vi• an
dim, dim'mer, dim'- mest

dim, dimmed, dim'-
  ming
dime
di·men'sion
di·men'sion·al
dim'er·ous
di·min'ish
di·min'u·en'do *pl.*
  -dos
dim'i·nu'tion
di·min'u·tive
dim'i·ty
dim'mer
di·morph'
di·mor'phic *also* di·
  mor'phous
di·mor'phism
dim'-out' *n.*
dim'ple, -pled, -pling
dim'wit'
din, dinned, din'ning
di·nar'
dine *(to eat),* dined,
  din'ing
  ♦*dyne*
din'er
di·nette'
ding'bat'
ding'-dong'
din'ghy
din'go *pl.* -goes
din'gus
din'gy
din'ky
din'ner
din'ner·ware'
di'no·saur'

dint
di·oc'e·san
di'o·cese
di'ode'
di'o·ram'a
di'o·rite'
di·ox'ide'
dip, dipped, dip'ping
diph·the'ri·a
diph·the·rit'ic *also*
  diph·ther'ic, diph·
  the'ri·al
diph'thong'
dip'lo·coc'cus *pl.* -ci'
dip'loid'
di·plo'ma
di·plo'ma·cy
dip'lo·mat'
dip'lo·mat'ic
di·plo'ma·tist
di'pole'
dip'per
dip'py
dip'so·ma'ni·a
dip'so·ma'ni·ac
dip'stick'
dip'ter·ous
dip'tych
dire *(disastrous),* dir'er,
  dir'est
  ♦*dyer*
di·rect'
di·rec'tion
di·rec'tion·al
di·rec'tive
di·rect'ly
di·rec'tor

di·rec'tor·ate
di·rec'tor·ship'
di·rec'to·ry
dirge
dir'i·gi·ble
dirn'dl
dirt'-cheap'
dirt'y
dis·a·bil'i·ty
dis·a'ble, -bled, -bling
dis·a·buse', -bused',
  -bus'ing
di·sac'cha·ride'
dis·ad·van'tage,
  -taged, -tag·ing
dis·ad·van'taged
dis·ad·van·ta'geous
dis·af·fect'
dis·af·fec'tion
dis·af·fil'i·ate, -at'ed,
  -at'ing
dis·af·firm'
dis·af·fir'mance *also*
  dis·af·fir·ma'tion
dis·a·gree'
dis·a·gree'a·ble
dis·a·gree'ment
dis·al·low'
dis·al·low'a·ble
dis·ap·pear'
dis·ap·pear'ance
dis·ap·point'
dis·ap·point'ment
dis·ap'pro·ba'tion
dis·ap·prov'al
dis·ap·prove',
  -proved', -prov'ing

dis•arm′
dis•ar′ma•ment
dis•arm′ing
dis•ar•range′,
　-ranged′, -rang′ing
dis•ar•ray′
dis•as•sem′ble, -bled,
　-bling
dis•as•sem′bly
dis•as•so′ci•ate′, -at′-
　ed, -at′ing
dis•as•so′ci•a′tion
dis•as′ter
dis•as′trous
dis•a•vow′
dis•a•vow′al
dis•band′
dis•bar′, -barred′,
　bar′ring
dis•be•lief′
dis•be•lieve′, -lieved′,
　-liev′ing
dis•be•liev′er
dis•bud′, -bud′ded,
　-bud′ding
dis•bur′den
dis•burse′ (to pay out),
　-bursed′, -burs′ing
　◆disperse
dis•burse′ment also
　dis•bur′sal
disc (record), also disk
dis′card′ n.
dis•card′ v.
dis•cern′
dis•cern′i•ble
dis•cern′ment

dis′charge′ n.
dis′charge′ -charged′,
　-charg′ing
dis•ci′ple
dis•ci•pli•nar′i•an
dis•ci•pli•nar′y
dis•ci•pline, -plined,
　-plin•ing
dis•claim′
dis•close′, -closed′,
　-clos′ing
dis•clo′sure
dis′co′ pl. -cos′
dis•cog′ra•pher
dis•cog′ra•phy
dis•coid′
dis•col′or
dis•col′or•a′tion
dis′com•bob′u•late′,
　-lat′ed, -lat′ing
dis•com′fit (to frus-
　trate)
　◆discomfort
dis•com′fi•ture
dis•com′fort (to make
　uneasy)
　◆discomfit
dis′com•mode′,
　-mod′ed, -mod′ing
dis′com•pose′,
　-posed′, -pos′ing
dis′com•po′sure
dis′con•cert′
dis′con•nect′
dis′con•nec′tion
dis•con′so•late
dis′con•tent′

dis′con•tin′u•ance
dis′con•tin′u•a′tion
dis′con•tin′ue, -ued,
　-u•ing
dis′con•ti•nu′i•ty
dis′con•tin′u•ous
disc′o•phile′
dis′cord′ n.
dis•cord′ v.
dis•cor′dance also dis•
　cor′dan•cy
dis•cor′dant
dis′co•theque′ also
　dis′co•thèque′
dis•count′
dis•count′a•ble
dis•coun′te•nance,
　-nanced, -nanc•ing
dis•cour′age, -aged,
　-ag•ing
dis•cour′age•ment
dis•course′ n.
dis•course′, -coursed′,
　-cours′ing
dis•cour′te•ous
dis•cour′te•sy
dis•cov′er
dis•cov′er•a•ble
dis•cov′er•y
dis•cred′it
dis•cred′it•a•ble
dis•creet′ (judicious)
　◆discrete
dis•crep′an•cy
dis•crep′ant
dis•crete′ (separate)
　◆discreet

dis·cre'tion
dis·cre'tion·ar'y
dis·crim'i·nate', -nat'-
  ed, -nat'ing
dis·crim'i·na'tion
dis·crim'i·na'tive
dis·crim'i·na'tor
dis·crim'i·na·to'ry
dis·cur'sive
dis'cus *(disk)*, pl. -cus·
  es
dis·cuss' *(to speak
  about)*
dis·cuss'ant
dis·cuss'i·ble
dis·cus'sion
dis·dain'
dis·dain'ful
dis·ease', -eased',
  -eas'ing
dis'em·bark'
dis·em'bar·ka'tion
dis'em·bar'rass
dis'em·bod'i·ment
dis'em·bod'y, -ied,
  -y·ing
dis'em·bow'el
dis'en·chant'
dis'en·chant'ment
dis'en·cum'ber
dis'en·gage', -gaged',
  -gag'ing
dis'en·gage'ment
dis'en·tan'gle, -gled,
  -gling
dis'es·tab'lish
dis'es·teem'

dis·fa'vor
dis·fig'ure, -ured, -ur·
  ing
dis·fran'chise',
  -chised', -chis'ing,
dis·fran'chise'ment
dis·gorge', -gorged',
  -gorg'ing
dis·grace', -graced',
  -grac'ing
dis·grace'ful
dis·grun'tle, -tled,
  -tling
dis·guise', -guised',
  -guis'ing
dis·gust'
dish
dis'ha·bille' *also* des'-
  ha·bille'
dis'har·mo'ni·ous
dis·har'mo·ny
dish'cloth'
dis·heart'en
di·shev'el, -eled *or*
  -elled, -el'ing *or* -el·
  ling
di·shev'eled
dis·hon'est
dis·hon'es·ty
dis·hon'or
dis·hon'or·a·ble
dish'pan'
dish'rag'
dish'tow'el
dish'wash'er
dish'wa'ter
dis'il·lu'sion

dis'il·lu'sion·ment
dis'in·cli·na'tion
dis'in·cline', -clined',
  -clin'ing
dis'in·fect'
dis'in·fec'tant
dis'in·gen'u·ous
dis'in·her'it
dis·in'te·grate', -grat'-
  ed, -grat'ing
dis·in'te·gra'tion
dis·in'te·gra'tor
dis'in·ter', -terred',
  -ter'ring
dis·in'ter·est
dis·in'ter·est·ed
dis·join'
dis·joint'
dis·junc'tion
dis·junc'tive
disk *(plate)*, *also* disc
disk·ette'
dis·like', -liked', -lik'-
  ing
dis'lo·cate', -cat'ed,
  -cat'ing
dis'lo·ca'tion
dis·lodge', -lodged',
  -lodg'ing
dis·lodge'ment *also*
  dis·lodg'ment
dis·loy'al
dis·loy'al·ty
dis'mal
dis·man'tle, -tled,
  -tling
dis·may'

dis•mem′ber
dis•mem′ber•ment
dis•miss′
dis•miss′al
dis•miss′i•ble
dis•mount′
dis′o•be′di•ence
dis′o•be′di•ent
dis′o•bey′
dis′o•blige′, -bliged′,
   -blig′ing
dis•or′der
dis•or′der•ly
dis•or′gan•i•za′tion
dis•or′gan•ize′, -ized′,
   -iz′ing
dis•o′ri•ent′
dis•o′ri•en•ta′tion
dis•own′
dis•par′age, -aged,
   -ag•ing
dis′pa•rate (separate)
   ♦desperate
dis•par′i•ty
dis•pas′sion•ate
dis•patch′ also des•
   patch′
dis•patch′er
dis•pel′, -pelled′, -pel′-
   ling
dis•pen′sa•bil′i•ty
dis•pen′sa•ble
dis•pen′sa•ry
dis•pen•sa′tion
dis•pen′sa•to′ry
dis•pense′, -pensed′,
   -pens′ing

dis•pens′er
dis•per′sal
dis•perse′ (to scatter),
   -persed′, -pers′ing
   ♦disburse
dis•pers′i•ble
dis•per′sion
dis•pir′it
dis•place′, -placed′,
   -plac′ing
dis•place′a•ble
dis•place′ment
dis•play′
dis•please′, -pleased′,
   -pleas′ing
dis•pleas′ure
dis•port′
dis•pos′a•bil′i•ty
dis•pos′a•ble
dis•pos′al
dis•pose′, -posed′,
   -pos′ing
dis′po•si′tion
dis′pos•sess′
dis′pos•ses′sion
dis′pos•ses′sor
dis•proof′
dis′pro•por′tion
dis′pro•por′tion•al
dis′pro•por′tion•ate
dis•prove′, -proved′,
   -prov′ing
dis•put′a•bil′i•ty
dis•put′a•ble
dis•pu′tant
dis′pu•ta′tion
dis′pu•ta′tious

dis•pute′, -put′ed,
   -put′ing
dis•qual′i•fi•ca′tion
dis•qual′i•fy′, -fied′,
   -fy′ing
dis•qui′et
dis•qui′e•tude′
dis′qui•si′tion
dis′re•gard′
dis′re•pair′
dis•rep′u•ta•ble
dis′re•pute′
dis′re•spect′
dis′re•spect′ful
dis•robe′, -robed′,
   -rob′ing
dis•rupt′
dis•rupt′er also dis•
   rup′tor
dis•rup′tion
dis•rup′tive
dis•sat′is•fac′tion
dis•sat′is•fac′to•ry
dis•sat′is•fy′, -fied′,
   -fy′ing
dis•sect′
dis•sec′tion
dis•sec′tor
dis•sem′ble, -bled,
   -bling
dis•sem′i•nate′, -nat′-
   ed, -nat′ing
dis•sem′i•na′tion
dis•sem′i•na′tor
dis•sen′sion
dis•sent′ (to differ)
   ♦decent, descent

dis·sent′er
dis·ser·ta′tion
dis·serv′ice
dis·sev′er
dis′si·dence
dis′si·dent
dis·sim′i·lar
dis·sim′i·lar′i·ty
dis·si·mil′i·tude′
dis·sim′u·late′, -lat′ed,
  -lat′ing
dis·sim′u·la′tion
dis′si·pate′, -pat′ed,
  -pat′ing
dis′si·pat′er also dis′si·
  pa′tor
dis′si·pa′tion
dis·so′ci·ate′, -at′ed,
  -at′ing
dis·so′ci·a′tion
dis·sol′u·ble
dis′so·lute′
dis′so·lu′tion
dis·solv′a·ble
dis·solve′, -solved′,
  -solv′ing
dis′so·nance also dis′·
  so·nan·cy
dis′so·nant
dis·suade′, -suad′ed,
  -suad′ing
dis·sua′sion
dis·sua′sive
dis·taff′
dis′tal
dis′tance, -tanced,
  -tanc·ing

dis′tant
dis·taste′
dis·taste′ful
dis·tem′per
dis·tend′
dis·ten′si·ble
dis·ten′tion also dis·
  ten′sion
dis·till′
dis′til·late′
dis′til·la′tion
dis·till′er·y
dis·tinct′
dis·tinc′tion
dis·tinc′tive
dis·tin′guish
dis·tin′guish·a·ble
dis·tort′
dis·tor′tion
dis′tract′
dis·trac′tion
dis·traught′
dis·tress′
dis·trib′ute, -ut·ed,
  -ut·ing
dis′tri·bu′tion
dis·trib′u·tive
dis·trib′u·tor
dis′trict′
dis·trust′
dis·trust′ful
dis·turb′
dis·tur′bance
di·sul′fide′
dis·un′ion
dis′u·nite′, -nit′ed,
  -nit′ing

dis·u′ni·ty
dis·use′
ditch
dith′er
dit′to pl. -tos
dit′ty
di′u·ret′ic
di·ur′nal
di′va
di·va′lent
di·van′
dive, dived or dove,
  dived, div′ing
dive′-bomb′
div′er
di·verge′, -verged′,
  -verg′ing
di·ver′gence also di·
  ver′gen·cy
di·ver′gent
di′vers (various)
di·verse′ (unlike)
di·ver′si·fi·ca′tion
di·ver′si·fy′, -fied′,
  -fy′ing
di·ver′sion
di·ver′sion·ar′y
di·ver′si·ty
di·vert′
di·ver′tisse·ment
di·vest′
di·vid′a·ble
di·vide′, -vid′ed, -vid′·
  ing
div′i·dend′
di·vid′er
div′i·na′tion

di·vine′, -vined′, -vin′-
  ing
di·vin′er
di·vin′i·ty
di·vis′i·bil′i·ty
di·vis′i·ble
di·vi′sion
di·vi′sive
di·vi′sor
di·vorce′, -vorced′,
  -vorc′ing
di·vor·cée′
div′ot
di·vulge′, -vulged′,
  -vulg′ing
di·vul′gence
di·vulg′er
div′vy, -vied, -vy·ing
Dix′ie
Dix′ie·land′
diz′zy, -zied, -zy·ing
do *(what should be
  done, party),* pl. do′s
  or dos
  ♦*dew, due*
do *(musical tone),* pl.
  dos
  ♦*doe, dough*
do *(to perform),* did,
  done, do′ing
  ♦*dew, due*
dob′bin
Do′ber·man pin′-
  scher
do′cent
doc′ile
do·cil′i·ty

dock′age
dock′et
dock′hand′
dock′yard′
doc′tor
doc′tor·al
doc′tor·ate
doc′tri·naire′
doc′trin·al
doc′trine
doc′u·ment
doc′u·men′ta·ry
doc′u·men·ta′tion
dod′der
do·dec′a·gon′
do·de·cag′o·nal
do·dec′a·he′dral
do·dec′a·he′dron pl.
  -drons *or* -dra
dodge, dodged, dodg′-
  ing
dodg′er
do′do pl. -does *or* -dos
doe *(deer),* pl. doe *or*
  does
  ♦*do (musical tone),
  dough*
do′er
doe′skin′
does′n′t
doff
dog, dogged, dog′ging
dog′cart′
dog′catch′er
dog′-ear′
dog′fight′

dog′fish′ pl. -fish′ *or*
  -fish′es
dog′ged
dog′ger·el
dog′gy bag *or* dog′gie
  bag
dog′house′
do′gie *also* do′gy
dog′ma
dog·mat′ic
dog′ma·tism
dog′ma·tist
do′-good′er
dog′-tired′
dog′trot′
dog′watch′
dog′wood′
doi′ly
do′-it-your·self′
Dol′by System®
dol′drums
dole, doled, dol′ing
doll
dol′lar
dol′lop
dol′ly
dol′man *(robe)*
dol′men *(monument)*
dol′o·mite′
do′lor
do′lor·ous
dol′phin
dolt′ish
do·main′
dome, domed, dom′ing
do·mes′tic

do·mes′ti·cate′, -cat′-
  ed, -cat′ing
do·mes′ti·ca′tion
do′mes·tic′i·ty
dom′i·cile′, -ciled′,
  -cil′ing
dom′i·nance
dom′i·nant
dom′i·nate′, -nat′ed,
  -nat′ing
dom′i·na′tion
dom′i·na′tor
dom′i·neer′
Do·min′i·can
do·min′ion
dom′i·no′ pl. -noes′ or
  -nos′
don, donned, don′ning
do·nate′, -nat′ed,
  -nat′ing
do·na′tion
do′na·tor
done (finished)
  ♦dun
don′jon (tower)
  ♦dungeon
don′key pl. -keys
don′ny·brook′
do′nor
do′-noth′ing adj.
doo′dad′
doo′dle, -dled, -dling
doo′dle·bug′
doo′hick′ey pl. -eys
doom
dooms′day′
door′bell′

door′jamb′
door′keep′er
door′knob′
door′man′
door′mat′
door′nail′
door′step′
door′stop′
door′way′
dope, doped, dop′ing
dop′ey also dop′y
dor′man·cy
dor′mant
dor′mer
dor′mi·to′ry
dor′mouse′ pl. -mice′
dor′sal
do′ry
dos′age
dose, dosed, dos′ing
do·sim′e·ter
dos′si·er′
dot, dot′ted, dot′ting
do′tage
do′tard
dote, dot′ed, dot′ing
dot′tle
dot′ty
dou′ble, -bled, -bling
dou′ble-bar′reled
dou′ble-breast′ed
dou′ble-check′ v.
dou′ble-cross′
dou′ble-deal′er
dou′ble-deal′ing
dou′ble-deck′er
dou′ble-dig′it adj.

dou′ble-edged′
dou′ble-en·ten′dre
dou′ble-faced′
dou′ble-head′er
dou′ble-joint′ed
dou′ble·knit′ adj.
dou′ble-park′
dou′ble-quick′
dou′ble-reed′
dou′ble-space′,
  -spaced′, -spac′ing
dou′blet
dou′ble-time′,
  -timed′, -tim′ing
dou·bloon′
dou′bly
doubt′ful
doubt′less
douche, douched,
  douch′ing
dough (bread mixture,
  money)
  ♦do (musical tone),
  doe
dough′boy′
dough′nut′ also do′-
  nut′
dough·ty
dough′y
dour′ly
douse (to extinguish),
  doused, dous′ing
douse (to immerse),
  doused, dous′ing,
  also dowse, dowsed,
  dows′ing

dove'cote' *also* dove'-
cot'
dove'tail'
dow'a·ger
dow'dy
dow'el, -eled *or* -elled,
-el·ing *or* -el·ling
dow'er
down'beat'
down'cast'
down'er
down'fall'
down'grade', -grad'-
ed, -grad'ing
down'heart'ed
down'hill'
down'pour'
down'range'
down'right'
down'stage'
down'stairs'
down'stream'
down'swing'
down'time'
down'-to-earth'
down'town'
down'trod'den
down'turn'
down'ward *also*
down'wards
down'wind'
down'y
dow'ry
dowse *(to divine),*
dowsed, dows'ing,
also douse, doused,
dous'ing

dows'er
dox·ol'o·gy
doze, dozed, doz'ing
doz'en
doz'enth
drab, drab'ber, drab'-
best
drab'ly
dra·cae'na
dra·co'ni·an *also* dra·
con'ic
draft·ee'
draft'ing
drafts'man
draft'y
drag, dragged, drag'-
ging
drag'ger
drag'gle, -gled, -gling
drag'net'
drag'on
drag'on·fly'
dra·goon'
drain'age
drain'pipe'
drake
dram
dra'ma
dra·mat'ic
dra·mat'ics
dram'a·tis per·so'nae
dram'a·tist
dram'a·ti·za'tion
dram'a·tize', -tized',
-tiz'ing
dram'a·tur'gy

drape, draped, drap'-
ing
drap'er·y
dras'tic
draw, drew, drawn,
draw'ing
draw'back'
draw'bridge'
draw'er
draw'knife'
drawl
draw'string'
dray'age
dread'ful
dread'nought'
dream, dreamed *or*
dreamt, dream'ing
dream'land'
dream'y
drear'y
dredge, dredged,
dredg'ing
dregs
drench'er
Dres'den china
dres·sage'
dress'er
dress'ing
dress'mak'er
dress'y
drib'ble, -bled, -bling
drib'let
dri'er *(one that dries),*
also dry'er
drift'er
drift'wood'
drill'mas'ter

drink, drank, drunk,
drink'ing
drink'a·ble
drip, dripped, drip'ping
drip'-dry' adj.
drip'pings
drip'py
drive, drove, driv'en,
driv'ing
drive'-in'
driv'el, -eled or -elled,
-el·ing or -el·ling
driv'er
drive'way'
driz'zle, -zled, -zling
drogue
droll'er·y
drom'e·dar'y
drone, droned, dron'-
ing
drool
droop (to sag)
♦drupe
droop'y
drop, dropped, drop'-
ping
drop'-kick' v.
drop'-leaf' adj.
drop'let
drop'out' n.
drop'per
drop'pings
drop'sy
dross
drought also drouth
drove (herd)
drov'er

drown
drowse, drowsed,
drows'ing
drows'y
drub, drubbed, drub'-
bing
drudge, drudged,
drudg'ing
drudg'er·y
drug, drugged, drug'-
ging
drug'gist
drug'store'
dru'id also Dru'id
drum, drummed,
drum'ming
drum'beat'
drum'head'
drum'lin
drum'mer
drum'stick'
drunk'ard
drunk'en
dru·pa'ceous
drupe (fruit)
♦droop
dry, dri'er or dry'er,
dri'est or dry'est
dry, dried, dry'ing
dry'ad
dry'-clean' v.
dry'-dock' v.
dry'er (appliance)
♦drier
du'al (double)
♦duel
du'al·ism

du'al·ist (one who be-
lieves in dualism)
♦duelist
du'al·is'tic
du·al'i·ty
dub, dubbed, dub'bing
du·bi'e·ty
du'bi·ous
du'cal
duc'at
duch'ess
duch'y
duck'board'
duck'ling
duck'pin'
duck'weed'
duct (passage)
♦ducked
duc'tile
duc·til'i·ty
dud
dude
dudg'eon
duds
due (payable)
♦dew, do (what
should be done; to
perform)
du'el (to fight), -eled or
-elled, -el·ing or -el·
ling
♦dual
du'el·er also du'el·ist
du·et'
duf'fel
duf'fer
du'gong'

dug'out'
duke'dom
dul'cet
dul'ci·mer
dull'ard
dull'ness *also* dul'ness
dul'ly
du'ly
dumb'bell'
dumb'wait·er
dum'-dum *(person)*
dum'dum' bullet
dum'found' *or* dumb'-
　found'
dum'my
dump'ling
dump'y
dun *(dull brown)*
　♦*done*
dun *(to demand pay-
　ment)*, dunned, dun'-
　ning
　♦*done*
dunce
dun'der·head'
dune
dun'ga·ree'
dun'geon *(prison)*
　♦*donjon*
dung'hill'
dunk
du'o *pl.* -os
du'o·dec'i·mal
du'o·dec'i·mo' *pl.* -os'
du'o·de'nal
du'o·de'num *pl.* -na
dupe, duped, dup'ing

dup'er·y
du'ple
du'plex'
du'pli·cate *adj.*
du'pli·cate', -cat'ed,
　-cat'ing
du'pli·ca'tion
du'pli·ca'tor
du·plic'i·ty
du'ra·bil'i·ty
du'ra·ble
du'ra ma'ter
du'rance
du·ra'tion
du·ress'
dur'ing
du'rum
dusk'y
dust'bin'
dust'er
dust'pan'
dust'up'
dust'y
Dutch
du'te·ous
du'ti·a·ble
du'ti·ful
du'ty
du'ty-free' *adj. & adv.*
dwarf *pl.* dwarfs *or*
　dwarves
dwarf'ism
dwell, dwelt *or*
　dwelled, dwell'ing
dwin'dle, -dled, -dling
dy'ad
dy·ad'ic

dye *(to color)*, dyed,
　dye'ing
　♦*die*
dyed'-in-the-wool'
dy'er *(colorer)*
　♦*dire*
dye'stuff'
dy'ing *(declining)*
　♦*dyeing*
dy·nam'ic *also* dy·
　nam'i·cal
dy·nam'ics
dy'na·mism
dy'na·mist
dy'na·mis'tic
dy'na·mite', -mit'ed,
　-mit'ing
dy'na·mo' *pl.* -mos'
dy'na·mo'e·lec'tric
　also dy'na·mo'e·lec'-
　tri·cal
dy'na·mom'e·ter
dy'nast'
dy·nas'tic
dy'nas·ty
dyne *(unit of force)*
　♦*dine*
Dy·nel'®
dys'en·ter'ic
dys'en·ter'y
dys·func'tion
dys·gen'ic
dys·lec'tic
dys·lex'i·a
dys·lex'ic
dys·pep'sia
dys·pep'tic

dys·pha'sia
dys·pro'si·um
dys·troph'ic
dys·tro·phy *also* dys·
  tro'phi·a

E

each
ea'ger
ea'gle
ea'gle-eyed'
ea'glet
ear'ache'
ear'drum'
eared
ear'flap'
ear'lap'
earl'dom
ear'ly
ear'mark'
ear'muff'
earn *(to gain)*
  ♦*urn*
ear'nest
earn'ings
ear'phone'
ear'ring
ear'shot'
ear'split'ting
earth'bound'
earth'en
earth'en·ware'
earth'ling

earth'ly *(not spiritual,*
  possible)
  ♦*earthy*
earth'quake'
earth'shak'ing
earth'ward *also* earth'-
  wards
earth'work'
earth'worm'
earth'y *(of the soil,*
  uninhibited)
  ♦*earthly*
ear'wax'
ear'wig'
ease, eased, eas'ing
ea'sel
ease'ment
eas'i·ly
east'bound'
Eas'ter
east'er·ly
east'ern
east'ern·most'
East'er·tide'
east'ward *also* east'-
  wards
eas'y
eas'y·go'ing *also* eas'-
  y-go'ing
eat, ate, eat'en, eat'ing
eat'a·ble
eat'er·y
eau' de co·logne' *pl.*
  eaux' de co·logne'
eaves'drop',
  -dropped', -drop'-
  ping

eaves'drop'per
ebb
eb'on·ite'
eb'on·y
e·bul'lience
e·bul'lient
eb'ul·li'tion
ec·cen'tric
ec·cen'tric'i·ty
ec·cle'si·as'tic
ec·cle'si·as'ti·cal
ech'e·lon'
e·chid'na
e·chi'no·derm'
ech'o *pl.* -oes
ech'o, -oed, -o·ing
ech'o·lo·ca'tion
é·clair'
é·clat'
e·clec'tic
e·clec'ti·cism
e·clipse', e·clipsed',
  e·clips'ing
e·clip'tic
ec'logue'
ec'o·cide'
ec'o·log'i·cal
e·col'o·gist
e·col'o·gy
e·con'o·met'rics
e'co·nom'ic
e'co·nom'i·cal
e'co·nom'ics
e·con'o·mist
e·con'o·mize',
  -mized', -miz'ing
e·con'o·miz'er

e·con'o·my
ec'o·spe'cies
ec'o·sys'tem
ec'o·type'
ec'ru
ec'sta·sy
ec·stat'ic
ec'to·derm'
ec'to·plasm
Ec'ua·dor'i·an
ec'u·men'i·cal
ec'u·men'ism
ec'ze·ma
ec·zem'a·tous
E'dam cheese
ed'dy, died, -dy·ing
e'del·weiss'
e·de'ma *pl.* -mas *or*
  -ma·ta
E'den
e·den'tate'
edge, edged, edg'ing
edge'wise' *also* edge'-
  ways'
edg'y
ed'i·bil'i·ty
ed'i·ble
e'dict'
ed'i·fi·ca'tion
ed'i·fice
ed'i·fy', -fied', -fy'ing
ed'it
e·di'tion *(publication)*
  ♦*addition*
ed'i·tor
ed'i·to'ri·al

ed'i·to'ri·al·ize',
  -ized', -iz'ing
ed'i·to'ri·al·iz'er
ed'i·tor·ship'
ed'u·ca·ble
ed'u·cate', -cat'ed,
  -cat'ing
ed'u·ca'tion
ed'u·ca'tion·al
ed'u·ca'tor
e·duce', e·duced',
  e·duc'ing
e·duc'i·ble
eel *pl.* eel *or* eels
e'er *(ever)*
  ♦*air, are (metric
  unit), ere, heir*
ee'rie *(weird), or* ee'ry
  ♦*aerie*
ef·face', -faced', -fac'-
  ing
ef·fect' *(result)*
  ♦*affect*
ef·fec'tive
ef·fec'tu·al
ef·fec'tu·ate', -at'ed,
  -at'ing
ef·fem'i·na·cy
ef·fem'i·nate'
ef'fer·ent
ef'fer·vesce', -vesced',
  -vesc'ing
ef'fer·ves'cence
ef'fer·ves'cent
ef·fete'
ef'fi·ca'cious
ef'fi·ca·cy

ef·fi'cien·cy
ef·fi'cient
ef'fi·gy
ef'flo·resce', -resced',
  -resc'ing
ef'flo·res'cence
ef'flo·res'cent
ef'flu·ence
ef'flu·ent
ef·flu'vi·al
ef·flu'vi·um *pl.* -vi·a
  or -vi·ums
ef'flux'
ef'fort
ef·front'er·y
ef·ful'gence
ef·ful'gent
ef·fuse', -fused', -fus'-
  ing
ef·fu'sion
ef·fu'sive
eft
e·gad'
e·gal'i·tar'i·an
e·gal'i·tar'i·an·ism
egg'beat'er
egg'head'
egg'nog'
egg'plant'
egg'shell'
eg'lan·tine'
e'go *pl.* e'gos
e'go·cen'tric
e'go·ism
e'go·ist
e'go·is'tic *also* e'go·is'-
  ti·cal

e•go•tism

e•go•tist

e•go•tis'tic *also* e'go•tis'ti•cal

e'go•trip', -tripped', -trip'ping

e•gre'gious

e'gress

e'gret

E•gyp'tian

E•gyp•tol'o•gist

E•gyp•tol'o•gy

ei'der

ei'der•down'

eight *(number)*
♦*ate*

eight•een'

eight•eenth'

eighth

eight'i•eth

eight'y

ein•stein'i•um

ei'ther

e•jac'u•late', -lat'ed, -lat'ing

e•jac'u•la'tion

e•jac'u•la'tor

e•ject'

e•jec'tion

e•jec'tor

eke, eked, ek'ing

e•lab'o•rate', rat'ed, -rat'ing

e•lab'o•ra'tion

e'land

e•lapse', e•lapsed', e•laps'ing

e•las'tic

e•las'tic'i•ty

e•late', e•lat'ed, e•lat'ing

e•la'tion

el'bow

el'bow•room'

eld'er *(older person)*

el'der *(shrub)*

el'der•ber'ry

e•lect'

e•lec'tion

e•lec'tion•eer'

e•lec'tive

e•lec'tor

e•lec'tor•al

e•lec'tor•ate

e•lec'tric *or* e•lec'tri•cal

e•lec•tri'cian

e•lec•tric'i•ty

e•lec'tri•fi•ca'tion

e•lec'tri•fy', -fied', -fy'ing

e•lec'tro•car'di•o•gram'

e•lec'tro•car'di•o•graph'

e•lec'tro•chem'i•cal

e•lec'tro•chem'is•try

e•lec'tro•cute', -cut'ed, -cut'ing

e•lec'tro•cu'tion

e•lec'trode'

e•lec'tro•dy•nam'ics

e•lec'tro•dy•na•mom'e•ter

e•lec'tro•en•ceph'a•lo•gram'

e•lec'tro•en•ceph'a•lo•graph'

e•lec•trol'y•sis

e•lec'tro•lyte'

e•lec'tro•lyt'ic

e•lec'tro•lyze', -lyzed', -lyz'ing

e•lec'tro•mag•net'ic

e•lec'tro•mag'net•ism

e•lec•trom'e•ter

e•lec'tro•mo'tive

e•lec'tron'

e•lec'tro•neg'a•tive

e•lec•tron'ic

e•lec•tron'ics

e•lec'tro•plate', -plat'ed, -plat'ing

e•lec'tro•pos'i•tive

e•lec'tro•scope'

e•lec'tro•scop'ic

e•lec'tro•shock'

e•lec'tro•stat'ic

e•lec'tro•stat'ics

e•lec'tro•ther'a•py

e•lec'tro•type', -typed', -typ'ing

e•lec'tro•va'lence *also* e•lec'tro•va'len•cy

e•lec'tro•va'lent

el'ee•mos'y•nar'y

el'e•gance

el'e•gant

el'e•gi'ac

el'e•gize', -gized', -giz'ing

el′e·gy
el′e·ment
el′e·men′tal
el′e·men′ta·ry
el′e·phant
el′e·phan·ti·a·sis
el′e·phan′tine
el′e·vate′, -vat′ed,
　-vat′ing
el′e·va′tion
el′e·va′tor
e·lev′en
e·lev′enth
elf pl. elves
elf′in
e·lic′it (to draw out)
　♦illicit
e·lic′i·ta′tion
e·lic′i·tor
e·lide′, e·lid′ed, e·lid′-
　ing
el′i·gi·bil′i·ty
el′i·gi·ble
e·lim′i·nate′, -nat′ed,
　-nat′ing
e·lim′i·na′tion
e·lim′i·na′tor
e·li′sion
e·lite′ or é·lite′
e·lit′ism′ or é·lit′ism′
e·lit′ist or é·lit′ist
e·lix′ir
E·liz′a·be′than
elk pl. elks or elks
elk′hound′
ell
el·lipse′

el·lip′sis pl. -ses′
el·lip′soid′
el′lip·soid′al
el·lip′tic or el·lip′ti·cal
elm
el′o·cu′tion
el′o·cu′tion·ar′y
el′o·cu′tion·ist
e·lon′gate′, -gat′ed,
　-gat′ing
e·lon′ga′tion
e·lope′, e·loped′,
　e·lop′ing
e·lope′ment
el′o·quence
el′o·quent
else′where′
e·lu′ci·date′, -dat′ed,
　-dat′ing
e·lu′ci·da′tion
e·lu′ci·da′tor
e·lude′ (to avoid),
　e·lud′ed, e·lud′ing
　♦allude
e·lu′sive (evasive)
　♦allusive, illusive
el′ver
E·ly′sian
e·ma′ci·ate′, -at′ed,
　-at′ing
e·ma′ci·a′tion
em′a·nate′, -nat′ed,
　-nat′ing
em′a·na′tion
em′a·na′tive
e·man′ci·pate′, -pat′-
　ed, -pat′ing

e·man′ci·pa′tion
e·man′ci·pa′tor
e·mas′cu·late′, -lat′ed,
　-lat′ing
e·mas′cu·la′tion
e·mas′cu·la′tor
em·balm′
em·bank′
em·bank′ment
em·bar′go pl. -goes
em·bark′
em·bar·ka′tion also
　em·bark′ment
em·bar′rass
em·bar′rass·ment
em′bas·sy
em·bat′tle, -tled, -tling
em·bed′, -bed′ded,
　-bed′ding
em·bel′lish
em′ber
em·bez′zle, -zled,
　-zling
em·bez′zle·ment
em·bit′ter
em·blaze′, -blazed′,
　-blaz′ing
em·bla′zon
em′blem
em′ble·mat′ic or em′-
　blem·at′i·cal
em·bod′i·ment
em·bod′y, -ied, -y·ing
em·bold′en
em·bol′ic
em′bo·lism
em′bo·lus pl. -li′

em′bon·point′
em·bos′om
em·boss′
em′bou·chure′
em·bow′er
em·brace′, -braced′,
　-brac′ing
em·bra′sure
em·broi′der
em·broi′der·y
em·broil′
em′bry·o′ *pl.* -os′
em′bry·o·log′ic *also*
　em′bry·o·log′i·cal
em′bry·ol′o·gist
em′bry·ol′o·gy
em′bry·on′ic
em·cee′, -ceed′, -cee′-
　ing
e·mend′ *(to edit)*
　♦amend
e·men·da′tion
e′men·da′tor
e·men′da·to·ry
em′er·ald
e·merge′, e·merged′,
　e·merg′ing
e·mer′gence
e·mer′gen·cy
e·mer′gent
e·mer′i·tus
em′er·y
e·met′ic
em′i·grant *(one who*
　leaves one's native
　land)
　♦immigrant

em′i·grate′ *(to leave*
　one's native land),
　-grat′ed, -grat′ing
　♦immigrate
em′i·gra′tion *(depar-*
　ture from one's native
　land)
　♦immigration
é′mi·gré′
em′i·nence
em′i·nent *(prominent)*
　♦immanent, imminent
e·mir′ *or* e·meer′, *also*
　amir′, a·meer′
e·mir′ate
em′is·sar′y
e·mis′sion
e·mis′sive
e·mit′, e·mit′ted,
　e·mit′ting
e·mit′ter
e·mol′lient
e·mol′u·ment
e·mote′, e·mot′ed,
　e·mot′ing
e·mo′tion
e·mo′tion·al
e·mo′tion·al·ism
e·mo′tive
em′pa·thet′ic
em·path′ic
em′pa·thize′, -thized′,
　-thiz′ing
em′pa·thy
em′per·or
em′pha·sis *pl.* -ses′

em′pha·size′, -sized′,
　-siz′ing
em·phat′ic
em′phy·se′ma
em′pire′
em·pir′i·cal
em·pir′i·cism
em·pir′i·cist
em·place′ment
em·ploy′
em·ploy′a·ble
em·ploy′ee
em·ploy′er
em·ploy′ment
em·po′ri·um *pl.* -ri·
　ums *or* -ri·a
em·pow′er
em·press
emp′ty, -tied, -ty·ing
emp′ty-hand′ed
em′py·re′an
e′mu *pl.* e′mus
em′u·late′, -lat′ed,
　-lat′ing
em′u·la′tion
em′u·la′tor
em′u·lous
e·mul′si·fi·ca′tion
e·mul′si·fy′, -fied′,
　-fy′ing
e·mul′sion
en·a′ble, -bled, -bling
en·act′
en·act′ment
en·ac′tor
e·nam′el, -eled *or*

-elled, -el·ing or -el·
ling
e·nam'el·ware'
en·am'or
en·camp'
en·camp'ment
en·cap'su·late', -lat'-
ed, -lat'ing, also in·
cap'su·late'
en·cap'su·la'tion
en·case', -cased', -cas'-
ing, also in·case'
en·caus'tic
en'ce·phal'ic
en·ceph'a·lit'ic
en·ceph'a·li'tis
en·ceph'a·lo·gram'
en·ceph'a·lo·my'e·li'-
tis
en·ceph'a·lon' pl. -la
en·chain'
en·chant'
en·chant'ment
en·chant'ress
en'chi·la'da
en·ci'pher
en·cir'cle, -cled, -cling
en'clave'
en·close', -closed',
-clos'ing, also in·
close'
en·clo'sure
en·code', -cod'ed,
-cod'ing
en·cod'er
en·co'mi·um pl. -mi·
ums or -mi·a

en·com'pass
en·core', -cored', -cor'-
ing
en·coun'ter
en·cour'age, -aged,
-ag·ing
en·cour'age·ment
en·croach'
en·croach'ment
en·crust' also in·crust'
en·crust·a'tion
en·cum'ber
en·cum'brance
en·cyc'li·cal
en·cy'clo·pe'di·a or
en·cy'clo·pae·di·a
en·cy'clo·pe'dic or en·
cy'clo·pae'dic
end
en·dan'ger
en·dear'
en·dear'ment
en·deav'or
en·dem'ic
end'ing
en'dive'
end'less
en'do·blast' also en'to·
blast'
en'do·carp'
en'do·crine
en'do·cri·nol'o·gist
en'do·cri·nol'o·gy
en'do·derm'
en'do·der'mis
en'do·me'tri·um pl.
-tri·a

en'do·morph'
en'do·mor'phic
en'do·plasm
en·dorse', -dorsed',
-dors'ing, also in·
dorse'
en·dorse'ment
en·dors'er also en·
dor'sor
en'do·skel'e·ton
en'do·the'li·al
en'do·the'li·um pl.
-li·a
en'do·ther'mic also
en'do·ther'mal
en·dow'
en·dow'ment
end'plate'
en·due', -dued', -du'-
ing, also in·due'
en·dur'a·ble
en·dur'ance
en·dure', -dured',
-dur'ing
end'wise' also end'-
ways'
en'e·ma
en'e·my
en'er·get'ic
en'er·gize', -gized',
-giz'ing
en'er·giz'er
en'er·gy
en'er·vate', -vat·ed,
-vat'ing
en'er·va'tion
en'er·va'tor

en·fee′ble, -bled,
-bling
en·fee′ble·ment
en′fi·lade′
en·fold′
en·force′, -forced′,
-forc′ing
en·force′a·ble
en·force′ment
en·forc′er
en·fran′chise′,
-chised′, -chis′ing
en·fran′chise′ment
en·gage′, -gaged′,
-gag′ing
en·gage′ment
en garde′
en·gen′der
en′gine
en′gi·neer′
en′gi·neer′ing
Eng′lish
en·gorge′, -gorged′,
-gorg′ing
en·graft′
en·grave′, -graved′,
-grav′ing
en·grav′er
en·gross′
en·gulf′
en·hance′, -hanced′,
-hanc′ing
en·hance′ment
en·har·mon′ic
e·nig′ma
en·ig·mat′ic or en·ig·
mat′i·cal

en·join′
en·joy′
en·joy′a·ble
en·joy′ment
en·kin′dle, -dled,
-dling
en·lace′, -laced′, -lac′-
ing, *also* in·lace′
en·large′, -larged′,
-larg′ing
en·large′ment
en·larg′er
en·light′en
en·light′en·ment
en·list′
en·list′ment
en·li′ven
en masse′
en·mesh′
en′mi·ty
en·no′ble, -bled,
-bling
en·nui′
e·nor′mi·ty
e·nor′mous
e·nough′
en·plane′, -planed′,
-plan′ing
en·rage′, -raged′, -rag′-
ing
en·rap′ture, -tured,
-tur·ing
en·rich′
en·rich′ment
en·roll′, -rolled′, -roll′-
ing, *also* en·rol′,
-rolled′, -rol′ling

en·roll′ment *or* en·
rol′ment
en route′
en·sconce′, -sconced′,
-sconc′ing
en·sem′ble
en·shrine′, -shrined′,
-shrin′ing, *also* in·
shrine′
en·shroud′
en′sign
en′si·lage
en·sile′, -siled′, -sil′ing
en·slave′, -slaved′,
-slav′ing
en·snare′, -snared′,
-snar′ing, *also* in·
snare′
en·sue′, -sued′, -su′ing
en·sure′ *(to make cer-
tain)*, -sured′, -sur′-
ing
♦assure, insure
en·tab′la·ture′
en·tail′
en·tan′gle, -gled,
-gling
en·tan′gle·ment
en·tente′
en′ter
en·ter′ic
en·ter·i′tis
en′ter·prise′
en′ter·pris′ing
en′ter·tain′
en′ter·tain′er
en′ter·tain′ment

en·thrall' *or* in·thrall'
en·throne', -throned',
  -thron'ing, *also* in·
  throne'
en·thuse', -thused',
  -thus'ing
en·thu'si·asm
en·thu'si·ast'
en·thu'si·as'tic
en·tice', -ticed', -tic'ing
en·tice'ment
en·tire'
en·tire'ty
en·ti'tle, -tled, -tling
en·ti'tle·ment
en'ti·ty
en·tomb'
en'to·mo·log'ic *also*
  en'to·mo·log'i·cal
en'to·mol'o·gist
en'to·mol'o·gy
en'tou·rage'
en'tr'acte'
en'trails'
en·train'
en'trance *n.*
en·trance', -tranced',
  -tranc'ing
en'trant
en·trap', -trapped',
  -trap'ping
en·trap'ment
en·treat' *also* in·treat'
en·treat'y
en·trée' *or* en'tree
en·trench' *or* in·
  trench'

en'tre nous'
en'tre·pre·neur'
en'tro·py
en·trust' *or* in·trust'
en'try
en'try·way'
en·twine', -twined',
  -twin'ing, *also* in·
  twine'
e·nu'mer·ate', -at·ed,
  -at'ing
e·nu'mer·a'tion
e·nu'mer·a'tive
e·nu'mer·a'tor
e·nun'ci·ate', -at·ed,
  -at'ing
e·nun'ci·a'tion
e·nun'ci·a'tor
en·u·re'sis
en·vel'op *v.*
en've·lope' *n.*
en·ven'om
en'vi·a·ble
en'vi·ous
en·vi'ron·ment
en·vi'ron·men'tal·ist
en·vi'rons
en·vis'age, -aged, -ag·
  ing
en·vi'sion
en'voi *(closing stanza)*,
  also en'voy
en'voy *(diplomat)*
en'vy, -vied, -vy'ing
en·wrap', -wrapped',
  -wrap'ping, *also* in·
  wrap'

en'zy·mat'ic
en'zyme'
E'o·cene'
e'o·hip'pus
e'o·lith'
E'o·lith'ic
e'on'
e'o·sin'
ep'au·let' *also* ep'au·
  lette'
é·pée' *also* e·pee'
e·phed'rine
e·phem'er·al
ep'ic *(poem)*
  ♦epoch
ep'i·can'thic fold
ep'i·cen'ter
ep'i·cure'
ep'i·cu·re'an *also* Ep'i·
  cu·re'an
ep'i·dem'ic
ep'i·de·mi·ol'o·gist
ep'i·der'mal
ep'i·der'mis
ep'i·glot'tis *pl.* -glot'·
  tis·es *or* -glot'ti·des'
ep'i·gram'
ep'i·gram·mat'ic
ep'i·graph'
ep'i·graph'ic *also* ep'i·
  graph'i·cal
ep'i·lep'sy
ep'i·lep'tic
ep'i·logue' *also* ep'i·
  log'
E·piph'a·ny
ep'i·phyte'

ep'i·phyt'ic
e·pis'co·pa·cy
e·pis'co·pal
E·pis'co·pa'li·an
e·pis'co·pate'
ep'i·sode'
ep'i·sod'ic
e·pis'te·mo·log'i·cal
e·pis'te·mol'o·gy
e·pis'tle
e·pis'to·lar'y
ep'i·taph'
ep'i·the'li·um pl. -li·
  ums or -li·a
ep'i·thet'
ep·it'o·me
e·pit'o·mize', -mized',
  -miz'ing
ep'och (era)
  ♦epic
ep'och·al
ep'ode'
ep'o·nym'
e·pon'y·mous
ep·ox'y
ep'si·lon'
Ep'som salts
eq·ua·bil'i·ty
eq'ua·ble
e'qual, e'qualed or
  e'qualled, e'qualing
  or e'qual·ling
e·qual'i·ty
e'qual·ize', -ized', -iz'-
  ing
e'qua·nim'i·ty

e·quate', e·quat'ed,
  e·quat'ing
e·qua'tion
e·qua'tor
e'qua·to'ri·al
eq'uer·ry
e·ques'tri·an
e·ques'tri·enne'
e'qui·an'gu·lar
e'qui·dis'tant
e'qui·lat'er·al
e'qui·lib'ri·um
e'quine'
e'qui·noc'tial
e'qui·nox'
e·quip', e·quipped',
  e·quip'ping
eq'ui·page
e·quip'ment
e'qui·poise'
eq'ui·ta·ble
eq'ui·ta'tion
eq'ui·ty
e·quiv'a·lence also
  e·quiv'a·len·cy
e·quiv'a·lent
e·quiv'o·cal
e·quiv'o·cate', -cat'ed,
  -cat'ing
e·quiv'o·ca'tion
e'ra
e·rad'i·ca·ble
e·rad'i·cate', -cat'ed,
  -cat'ing
e·rad'i·ca'tion
e·rad'i·ca'tor
e·ras'a·ble

e·rase', e·rased', e·ras'-
  ing
e·ras'er
e·ra'sure
er'bi·um
ere (before)
  ♦air, are (metric
  unit), e'er, heir
e·rect'
e·rec'tion
e·rec'tor
er'e·mite'
erg
er'go
er'got
er'mine
e·rode', e·rod'ed,
  e·rod'ing
e·rog'e·nous also er'o·
  gen'ic
e·ro'sion
e·ro'sive
e·rot'ic
e·rot'i·cism
err
er'rand
er'rant
er·rat'ic
er·ra'tum pl. -ta
er·ro'ne·ous
er'ror
er'satz'
erst'while'
e·ruct'
e·ruc'ta'tion
er'u·dite'
er'u·di'tion

e·rupt'
e·rup'tion
e·rup'tive
er'y·sip'e·las
e·ryth'ro·blast'
e·ryth'ro·cyte'
e·ryth'ro·my'cin
es'ca·drille'
es·ca·late', -lat'ed,
   -lat'ing
es·ca·la'tion
es·ca·la'tor
es·cap'a·ble
es·ca·pade'
es·cape', -caped',
   -cap'ing
es·cap'ee'
es·cap'ism
es·cap'ist
es·car·got'
es·ca·role'
es·carp'ment
es·chat'o·log'i·cal
es·chew'
es·cort' n.
es·cort' v.
es·cri·toire'
es·crow'
es·cutch'eon
es'ker
Es'ki·mo' pl. -mo' or
   -mos'
e·soph'a·ge'al
e·soph'a·gus pl. -gi'
es·o·ter'ic
es·pa·drille'
es·pal'ier

es·par'to pl. -tos
es·pe'cial
Es·pe·ran'to
es·pi·o·nage'
es·pla·nade'
es·pou'sal
es·pouse', -poused',
   -pous'ing
es·pres'so pl. -sos
es·prit' de corps'
es·py', -pied', -py'ing
es·quire'
es·say' (to attempt)
   ♦assay
es'say n.
es'sence
es·sen'tial
es·tab'lish
es·tab'lish·ment
es·tate'
es·teem'
es'ter
es'ti·ma·ble
es'ti·mate', -mat'ed,
   -mat'ing
es'ti·ma'tion
es'ti·ma'tor
Es·to'ni·an
es·trange', -tranged',
   -trang'ing
es'tro·gen
es'tro·gen'ic
es'trous adj.
es'trus n.
es'tu·ar'y
é'ta·gère' also e'ta·
   gere'

et cet'er·a
etch'ing
e·ter'nal
e·ter'ni·ty
eth'ane'
eth'a·nol'
e'ther
e·the're·al
eth'ic
eth'i·cal
eth'ics
E'thi·o'pi·an
eth'nic
eth·nic'i·ty
eth'no·cen'tric
eth'no·graph'ic
eth·nog'ra·phy
eth'no·log'ic also eth'-
   no·log'i·cal
eth·nol'o·gist
eth·nol'o·gy
e'thos'
eth'yl
eth'yl·ene'
e'ti·o·log'ic also e'ti·o·
   log'i·cal
e'ti·ol'o·gist
e'ti·ol'o·gy
et'i·quette'
E·trus'can
e'tude'
et'y·mo·log'i·cal
et'y·mol'o·gist
et'y·mol'o·gy
eu·ca·lyp'tus pl. -tus·
   es or -ti'
Eu'cha·rist

eu'chre
Eu·clid'e·an
eu·gen'ics
eu'lo·gis'tic
eu'lo·gize', -gized',
 -giz'ing
eu'lo·gy
eu'nuch
eu'phe·mism
eu'phe·mis'tic
eu·pho'ni·ous
eu·pho'ni·um
eu'pho·ny
eu·pho'ri·a
eu·phor'ic
Eur·a'sian
eu·re'ka
eu'ro·cur'ren·cy
Eu'ro·dol'lar
Eu'ro·pe'an
eu·ro'pi·um
Eu·sta'chian tube
eu'tha·na'sia
eu·then'ics
e·vac'u·ate', -at'ed,
 -at'ing
e·vac'u·a'tion
e·vac'u·a'tor
e·vac'u·ee'
e·vade', e·vad'ed,
 e·vad'ing
e·val'u·ate', -at'ed,
 -at'ing
e·val'u·a'tion
ev'a·nes'cence
ev'a·nes'cent

e·van·gel'i·cal *also*
 e'van·gel'ic
e·van'gel·ism
e·van'gel·ist
e·van'gel·is'tic
e·van'gel·ize', -ized',
 -iz'ing
e·vap'o·rate', -rat'ed,
 -rat'ing
e·vap'o·ra'tion
e·vap'o·ra'tor
e·va'sion
e·va'sive
eve
e'ven
eve'ning *(night)*
e'ven·ing *(smoothing)*
e·vent'
e·vent'ful
e'ven·tide'
e·ven'tu·al
e·ven'tu·al'i·ty
e·ven'tu·ate', -at'ed,
 -at'ing
ev'er
ev'er·glade'
ev'er·green'
ev'er·last'ing
ev'er·more'
e·vert'
eve'ry
eve'ry·bod'y
eve'ry·day'
eve'ry·one' *pron.*
eve'ry·place'
eve'ry·thing'
eve'ry·where'

e·vict'
e·vic'tion
e·vic'tor
ev'i·dence, -denced,
 -denc·ing
ev'i·dent
ev'i·den'tial
e'vil
e'vil·do'er
e'vil-mind'ed
e·vince', e·vinced',
 e·vinc'ing
e·vin'ci·ble
e·vis'cer·ate', -at'ed,
 -at'ing
e·vis'cer·a'tion
ev'o·ca'tion
e·voc'a·tive
e·voke', e·voked',
 e·vok'ing
ev'o·lu'tion
ev'o·lu'tion·ar'y
ev'o·lu'tion·ism
ev'o·lu'tion·ist
e·volve', e·volved',
 e·volv'ing
ewe *(female sheep)*
 ♦*yew, you*
ew'er
ex·ac'er·bate', -bat'ed,
 -bat'ing
ex·ac'er·ba'tion
ex·act'
ex·ac'tion
ex·act'i·tude'
ex·ac'tor

ex·ag'ger·ate', -at'ed,
　-at'ing
ex·ag'ger·a'tion
ex·ag'ger·a'tor
ex·alt'
ex'al·ta'tion
ex·am'
ex·am'i·na'tion
ex·am'ine, -ined, -in·
　ing
ex·am'in·er
ex·am'ple
ex·as'per·ate', -at'ed,
　-at'ing
ex·as'per·a'tion
ex ca·the'dra
ex·ca'vate', -vat'ed,
　-vat'ing
ex'ca·va'tion
ex'ca·va'tor
ex·ceed' *(to surpass)*
　♦*accede*
ex·ceed'ing·ly
ex·cel', -celled', -cel'-
　ling
ex'cel·lence
Ex'cel·len·cy
ex'cel·lent
ex·cel'si·or
ex·cept' *(to exclude)*
　♦*accept*
ex·cept'ing
ex·cep'tion
ex·cep'tion·al
ex'cerpt'
ex·cess' *(superfluity)*
　♦*access*

ex·ces'sive
ex·change', -changed',
　-chang'ing
ex·change'a·ble
ex·cheq'uer
ex'cise' *(tax)*
ex·cise' *(to cut)*,
　-cised', -cis'ing
ex·ci'sion
ex·cit'a·bil'i·ty
ex·cit'a·ble
ex'ci·ta'tion
ex·cite', -cit'ed, -cit'ing
ex·cite'ment
ex·claim'
ex'cla·ma'tion
ex·clam'a·to'ry
ex'clave'
ex·clud'a·ble *also* ex·
　clud'i·ble
ex·clude', -clud'ed,
　-clud'ing
ex·clu'sion
ex·clu'sive
ex'com·mu'ni·cate',
　-cat'ed, -cat'ing
ex'com·mu'ni·ca'tion
ex'com·mu'ni·ca'tor
ex·co'ri·ate', -at'ed,
　-at'ing
ex·co'ri·a'tion
ex'cre·ment
ex·cres'cence
ex·cres'cent
ex·cre'ta
ex·cre'tal

ex·crete', -cret'ed,
　-cret'ing
ex·cre'tion
ex'cre·to'ry
ex·cru'ci·at'ing
ex'cul·pate', -pat'ed,
　-pat'ing
ex'cul·pa'tion
ex·cul'pa·to'ry
ex·cur'sion
ex·cus'a·ble
ex·cuse', -cused', -cus'-
　ing
ex'e·cra·ble
ex'e·crate', -crat'ed,
　-crat'ing
ex'e·cra'tion
ex'e·cra'tor
ex'e·cute', -cut'ed,
　-cut'ing
ex'e·cu'tion
ex'e·cu'tion·er
ex·ec'u·tive
ex·ec'u·tor
ex·ec'u·trix'
ex'e·ge'sis *pl.* -ses
ex·em'plar
ex·em'pla·ry
ex·em'pli·fi·ca'tion
ex·em'pli·fy', -fied',
　-fy'ing
ex·empt'
ex·empt'i·ble
ex·emp'tion
ex'er·cise' *(to exert)*,
　-cised', -cis'ing
　♦*exorcise*

ex'er·cis'er
ex·ert'
ex·er'tion
ex'e·unt
ex·fo'li·ate', -at'ed,
  -at'ing
ex·fo'li·a'tion
ex·ha·la'tion
ex·hale', -haled', -hal'-
  ing
ex·haust'
ex·haust'i·ble
ex·haus'tion
ex·haus'tive
ex·hib'it
ex'hi·bi'tion
ex'hi·bi'tion·ism
ex'hi·bi'tion·ist
ex'hi·bi'tion·is'tic
ex·hib'i·tor
ex·hil'a·rate', -rat'ed,
  -rat'ing
ex·hil'a·ra'tion
ex·hort'
ex·hor·ta'tion
ex·hor'ta·tive *also* ex·
  hor'ta·to'ry
ex'hu·ma'tion
ex·hume', -humed',
  -hum'ing
ex'i·gen·cy *also* ex'i·
  gence
ex'i·gent
ex'ile', -iled', -il'ing
ex·ist'
ex·is'tence
ex·is'tent

ex'is·ten'tial
ex'is·ten'tial·ism
ex'is·ten'tial·ist
ex'it
ex li'bris
ex·o·bi·ol'o·gy
ex'o·crine'
ex'o·dus
ex·og'e·nous
ex·on'er·ate', -at'ed,
  -at'ing
ex·on'er·a'tion
ex·or'bi·tant
ex·or·cise' *(to expel)*,
  -cised', -cis'ing
  ◆*exercise*
ex'or·cis'er
ex'or·cism
ex'or·cist'
ex·o·skel'e·ton
ex'o·sphere'
ex·o·ther'mic *also* ex'-
  o·ther'mal
ex·ot'ic
ex·pand'
ex·panse'
ex·pan'sion
ex·pan'sion·ism
ex·pan'sion·ist
ex·pan'sive
ex par'te
ex·pa'ti·ate', -at'ed,
  -at'ing
ex·pa'ti·a'tion
ex·pa'tri·ate', -at'ed,
  -at'ing
ex·pa'tri·a'tion

ex·pect'
ex·pec'tan·cy
ex·pec'tant
ex·pec·ta'tion
ex·pec'to·rant
ex·pec'to·rate', -rat'-
  ed, -rat'ing
ex·pec'to·ra'tion
ex·pe'di·en·cy *also* ex·
  pe'di·ence
ex·pe'di·ent
ex·pe'di·en'tial
ex'pe·dite', -dit'ed,
  -dit'ing
ex'pe·dit'er *also* ex'pe·
  di'tor
ex'pe·di'tion
ex'pe·di'tion·ar'y
ex'pe·di'tious
ex·pel', -pelled', -pel'-
  ling
ex·pend'
ex·pend'a·ble
ex·pen'di·ture
ex·pense'
ex·pen'sive
ex·pe'ri·ence, -enced,
  -enc·ing
ex·per'i·ment
ex·per'i·men'tal
ex·per'i·men·ta'tion
ex'pert'
ex'per·tise'
ex'pi·ate', -at'ed, -at'-
  ing
ex'pi·a'tion
ex'pi·a'tor

ex·pi·ra'tion
ex·pire', -pired', -pir'-
  ing
ex·plain'
ex·plain'a·ble
ex'pla·na'tion
ex·plan'a·to'ry
ex'ple·tive
ex'pli·ca·ble
ex'pli·cate', -cat'ed,
  -cat'ing
ex'pli·ca'tion
ex'pli·ca'tor
ex·plic'it
ex·plode', -plod'ed,
  -plod'ing
ex'ploit' n.
ex·ploit' v.
ex·ploit'a·ble
ex'ploi·ta'tion
ex·ploit'a·tive
ex'plo·ra'tion
ex·plor'a·to'ry
ex·plore', -plored',
  -plor'ing
ex·plor'er
ex·plo'sion
ex·plo'sive
ex·po'nent
ex'po·nen'tial
ex'port' n.
ex·port' v.
ex·pose', -posed',
  -pos'ing
ex·po·sé'
ex'po·si'tion
ex·pos'i·tor

ex·pos'i·to'ry
ex' post fac'to
ex·pos'tu·late', -lat'ed,
  -lat'ing
ex·pos'tu·la'tion
ex·po'sure
ex·pound'
ex·press'
ex·press'i·ble
ex·pres'sion
ex·pres'sion·ism
ex·pres'sion·ist
ex·pres'sion·is'tic
ex·pres'sive
ex·press'way'
ex·pro'pri·ate', -at'ed,
  -at'ing
ex·pro'pri·a'tion
ex·pro'pri·a'tor
ex·pul'sion
ex·punge', -punged',
  -pung'ing
ex'pur·gate', -gat'ed,
  -gat'ing
ex'pur·ga'tion
ex'pur·ga'tor
ex'qui·site
ex'tant (existing)
♦extent
ex·tem'po·ra'ne·ous
ex·tem'po·rar'y
ex·tem'po·re
ex·tem'po·rize',
  -rized', -riz'ing
ex·tend'
ex·tend'i·bil'i·ty
ex·tend'i·ble

ex·ten'si·ble
ex·ten'sion
ex·ten'sive
ex·ten'sor
ex·tent' (size)
♦extant
ex·ten'u·ate', -at'ed,
  -at'ing
ex·ten'u·a'tion
ex·te'ri·or
ex·ter'mi·nate', -nat'-
  ed, -nat'ing
ex·ter'mi·na'tion
ex·ter'mi·na'tor
ex·ter'nal
ex·ter'nal·i·za'tion
ex·ter'nal·ize', -ized',
  -izing
ex·tinct'
ex·tinc'tion
ex·tin'guish
ex·tin'guish·er
ex'tir·pate', -pat'ed,
  -pat'ing
ex'tir·pa'tion
ex'tir·pa'tor
ex·tol', -tolled', -tol'-
  ling
ex·tol'ler
ex·tort'
ex·tor'tion
ex·tor'tion·ist
ex'tra
ex'tract' n.
ex·tract' v.
ex·trac'tion
ex·trac'tive

ex·trac′tor
ex′tra·cur·ric′u·lar
ex′tra·dite′, -dit·ed, -dit′ing
ex′tra·di′tion
ex′tra·ga·lac′tic
ex′tra·mar′i·tal
ex·tra·ne·ous
ex·traor′di·nar′y
ex·trap′o·late′, -lat·ed, -lat′ing
ex·trap′o·la′tion
ex′tra·sen′so·ry
ex′tra·ter·res′tri·al
ex′tra·ter·ri·to′ri·al
ex·trav′a·gance
ex·trav′a·gant
ex·trav′a·gan′za
ex′tra·ve·hic′u·lar ac-tivity
ex·treme′
ex·trem′ism
ex·trem′ist
ex·trem′i·ty
ex·tri′ca·ble
ex′tri·cate′, -cat′ed, -cat′ing
ex′tri·ca′tion
ex·trin′sic
ex′tro·ver′sion
ex′tro·ver′sive
ex′tro·vert′
ex·trude′, -trud′ed, -trud′ing
ex·tru′sion
ex·tru′sive
ex·u′ber·ance

ex·u′ber·ant
ex′u·da′tion
ex·ude′, -ud·ed, -ud′-ing
ex·ult′
ex·ul′tant
ex′ul·ta′tion
eye *(to look)*, eyed, eye′ing *or* ey′ing
♦*aye, I*
eye′ball′
eye′bolt′
eye′brow′
eye′cup′
eye′drop′per
eye′ful′
eye′glass′
eye′lash′
eye′let *(hole)*
♦*islet*
eye′lid′
eye′piece′
eye′shot′
eye′sight′
eye′sore′
eye′spot′
eye′stalk′
eye′strain′
eye′tooth′
eye′wash′
eye′wit′ness

F

fa′ble
fa′bled

fab′ric
fab′ri·cate′, -cat·ed, -cat′ing
fab′ri·ca′tion
fab′ri·ca′tor
fab′u·list
fab′u·lous
fa·çade′ *also* fa·cade′
face, faced, fac′ing
face′lift′ing *also* face′-lift′
face′-off′ *n.*
fac′et
fa·ce′tious
fa′cial
fac′ile
fa·cil′i·tate′, -tat′ed, -tat′ing
fa·cil′i·ta′tion
fa·cil′i·ty
fac′ing
fac·sim′i·le
fact′-find′er
fact′-find′ing
fac′tion
fac′tion·al·ism
fac′tious
fac·ti′tious *(artificial)*
♦*fictitious*
fac′tor
fac′tor·a·ble
fac·to′ri·al
fac′tor·i·za′tion
fac′to·ry
fac·to′tum
fac′tu·al
fac′ul·ty

fad′dish

fad′dist

fade, fad′ed, fad′ing

fade′-in′ *n.*

fade′-out′ *n.*

fa·e′ri·e *also* fa′er·y

fag, fagged, fag′ging

fag′ot *also* fag′got

fag′ot·ing *also* fag′got·
ing

Fahr′en·heit′

fa·ience′ *also* fa·ïence′

fail *(to be unsuccessful)*
  ♦*faille*

faille *(fabric)*
  ♦*fail, file*

fail′-safe′

fail′ure

fain *(gladly)*
  ♦*feign*

faint *(indistinct)*
  ♦*feint*

faint′-heart′ed

fair *(lovely, pale, just)*
  ♦*fare*

fair *(market)*
  ♦*fare*

fair′ground′ *also* fair′-
  grounds′

fair′-haired′

fair′ly

fair′-mind′ed

fair′-spo′ken

fair′-trade′, -trad′ed,
  -trad′ing

fair′way′

fair′-weath′er *adj.*

fair′y

fair′y·land′

faith′ful

faith′less

fake, faked, fak′ing

fak′er *(imposter)*
  ♦*fakir*

fak′er·y

fa·kir′ *(beggar)*
  ♦*faker*

fal′con

fal′con·ry

fall, fell, fall′en, fall′ing

fal·la′cious

fal′la·cy

fal′li·bil′i·ty

fal′li·ble

fall′ing-out′ *pl.* fall′-
  ings-out′ *or or* fall′-
  ing-outs′

Fal·lo′pi·an tube

fall′out′ *n.*

fal′low

false, fals′er, fals′est

false′-heart′ed

false′hood′

fal′set′to *pl.* -tos

fal′si·fi·ca′tion

fal′si·fy′, -fied′, -fy′ing

fal′si·ty

fal′ter

fame, famed, fam′ing

fa·mil′ial

fa·mil′iar

fa·mil′i·ar′i·ty

fa·mil′iar·ize′, -ized′,
  -iz′ing

fam′i·ly

fam′ine

fam′ished

fa′mous

fan, fanned, fan′ning

fa·nat′ic

  ♦*fakir*

fa·nat′i·cal

fa·nat′i·cism

fan′cied

fan′ci·er

fan′ci·ful

fan′cy, -cied, -cy·ing

fan′cy-free′

fan′cy·work′

fan·dan′go *pl.* -gos

fan′fare′

fang

fan′light′

fan′tail′

fan·ta′sia

fan·ta·size′, -sized′,
  -siz′ing

fan·tas′tic

fan′ta·sy

far, far′ther *or* fur′-
  ther, far′thest *or*
  fur′thest

far′ad

far′a·day′

far′a·way′

farce

far·ceur′

far′ci·cal

fare *(charge)*
  ♦*fair*

fare *(to get along)*,
  fared, far′ing

♦*fair*
fare•well'
far'-fetched'
far'-flung'
fa•ri'na
far'i•na'ceous
farm'er
farm'house'
farm'land'
farm'stead'
farm'yard'
far'o
far'-off'
far'-out'
far•ra'go *pl.* -goes
far'-reach'ing
far'row
far'see'ing
far'-sight'ed
far'ther *(to a greater distance)*
♦*further*
far'thest *(to the most distant point)*
♦*furthest*
far'thing
far'thin•gale'
fas'ci•a *pl.* -ci•ae'
fas'ci•cle
fas•cic'u•late' *also* fas•cic'u•lat'ed
fas'ci•nate', -nat'ed, -nat'ing
fas'ci•na'tion
fas'ci•na'tor
fas'cism
fas'cist

fash'ion
fash'ion•a•ble
fast'back'
fas'ten
fas'ten•er
fast'-food' *adj.*
fas•tid'i•ous
fast'ness
fat, fat'ter, fat'test
fa'tal
fa'tal•ism
fa'tal•ist
fa'tal•is'tic
fa•tal'i•ty
fat'back'
fate *(destiny)*
♦*fete*
fat'ed
fate'ful
fa'ther
fa'ther•hood'
fa'ther-in-law' *pl.* fa'-thers-in-law'
fa'ther•land'
fa'ther•ly
fath'om *pl.* -om *or* -oms
fath'om•a•ble
fa•tigue', -tigued', -tigu'ing
fat'-sol'u•ble
fat'ten
fat'ty
fa•tu'i•ty
fat'u•ous
fau'cet
fault'find'er

fault'find'ing
fault'y
faun *(deity)*
♦*fawn*
fau'na *pl.* -nas *or* -nae'
fauv'ism
faux pas' *pl.* faux pas'
fa'vor
fa'vor•a•ble
fa'vor•ite
fa'vor•it•ism
fawn *(deer)*
♦*faun*
fawn *(to grovel)*
♦*faun*
faze *(to upset),* fazed, faz'ing
♦*phase*
fe'al•ty
fear'ful
fear'less
fear'some
fea'si•bil'i•ty
fea'si•ble
feast
feat *(exploit)*
♦*feet*
feath'er
feath'er•bed', -bed'-ded, -bed'ding
feath'er•brain'
feath'er•stitch'
feath'er•weight'
feath'er•y
fea'ture, -tured, -tur•ing
feb'rile

Feb′ru·ar′y
fe′cal
fe′ces *also* fae′ces
feck′less
fe′cund
fe·cun·date′, -dat′ed,
  -dat′ing
fe·cun′di·ty
fed′er·al
fed′er·al·ism
fed′er·al·ist
fed′er·al·i·za′tion
fed′er·al·ize′, -ized′,
  -iz′ing
fed′er·ate′, -at′ed, -at′-
  ing
fed′er·a′tion
fe·do′ra
fee
fee′ble
fee′ble-mind′ed
feed, fed, feed′ing
feed′back′
feed′bag′
feed′er
feel, felt, feel′ing
feel′er
feign *(to pretend)*
  ◆*fain*
feint *(strategem)*
  ◆*faint*
feist′y
feld′spar′ *also* fel′spar′
fe·lic′i·tate′, -tat′ed,
  -tat′ing
fe·lic′i·ta′tion
fe·lic′i·ta′tor

fe·lic′i·tous
fe·lic′i·ty
fe′line
fell
fel′low
fel′low·ship′
fel′ly *also* fel′loe
fel′on
fe·lo′ni·ous
fel′o·ny
felt′ing
fe′male
fem′i·nine
fem′i·nin′i·ty
fem′i·nism
fem′i·nist
femme fa·tale′ *pl.*
  femmes fa·tales′
fem′o·ral
fe′mur *pl.* fe′murs *or*
  fem′o·ra
fen
fence, fenced, fenc′ing
fenc′er
fend
fend′er
fen′es·tra′tion
fen′nel
fe′ral
fer′-de-lance′
fer′ment′ *n.*
fer·ment′ *v.*
fer·men·ta′tion
fer′mi·um
fern′er·y *pl.* -ies
fern′y
fe·ro′cious

fe·roc′i·ty
fer′ret *(animal)*
fer′ret *(tape)*, *also* fer′-
  ret·ing
fer′ric
Fer′ris wheel *also*
  fer′ris wheel
fer′rite′
fer′ro·al′loy′
fer′ro·mag·net′ic
fer′ro·mag′ne·tism
fer′ro·man′ga·nese′
fer′ro·type′
fer′rous
fer′rule *(metal ring)*
  ◆*ferule*
fer′ry, -ried, -ry·ing
fer′ry·boat′
fer′tile
fer·til′i·ty
fer′til·i·za′tion
fer′til·ize′, -ized′, -iz′-
  ing
fer′til·iz′er
fer′ule *(stick)*
  ◆*ferrule*
fer′ven·cy
fer′vent
fer′vid
fer′vor
fes′tal
fes′ter
fes′ti·val
fes′tive
fes·tiv′i·ty
fes·toon′
fe′tal *also* foe′tal

fetch'ing

fete *(festival), also* fête
♦*fate*

fete *(to honor),* fet'ed,
fet'ing, *also* fête, fêt'-
ed, fêt'ing
♦*fate*

fet'id

fet'ish

fet'ish·ism

fet'ish·ist

fet'lock'

fet'ter

fet'tle

fe'tus *pl.* -tus·es, *also*
foe'tus

feud

feu'dal

feu'dal·ism

feu'dal·ist

feu'dal·is'tic

feu'da·to'ry

fe'ver

fe'ver·ish

few

fey

fez *pl.* fez'zes

fi·an·cé' *fem.* fi·an·cée'

fi·as'co *pl.* -coes *or*
-cos

fi'at'

fib, fibbed, fib'bing

fib'ber

fi'ber

fi'ber·board'

Fi'ber·fil'®

Fi'ber·glas'®

fi'bril

fib·ril·la'tion

fi'brin

fi·brin'o·gen

fi'broid'

fi·bro'sis

fi'brous

fib'u·la *pl.* -lae *or* -las

fick'le

fic'tion

fic·ti'tious *(imaginary)*
♦*factitious*

fid'dle, -dled, -dling

fid'dler

fid'dle·sticks'

fi·del'i·ty

fidg'et

fidg'et·y

fi·du'ci·ar'y

fie

fief

field'er

field'stone'

fiend'ish

fierce, fierc'er, fierc'est

fier'y

fi·es'ta

fife

fif·teen'

fif·teenth'

fifth

fif'ti·eth

fif'ty

fif'ty-fif'ty

fig

fight, fought, fight'ing

fight'er

fig'ment

fig·ur·a'tion

fig'ur·a·tive

fig'ure, -ured, -ur·ing

fig'ure·head'

fig'u·rine'

Fi'ji·an

fil'a·ment

fil'bert

filch'er

file *(collection, tool)*
♦*faille*

file *(to catalogue,
smooth),* filed, fil'ing
♦*faille*

fi'let mi·gnon'

fil'i·al

fil'i·bus'ter

fil'i·gree',
-greed',-gree'ing

fil'ing

Fil'i·pi'no *pl.* -nos

fill'er

fil'let *(ribbon)*

fil'let' *(meat), also* fi·
let'

fil'let *(to bind),* -let·ed,
-let·ing

fil'let *(to bone),*
-leted', -let'ing, *also*
fi·let'

fill'-in' *n.*

fill'ing

fil'lip

fil'ly

film'go'er

film'strip'

film′y
fil′ter *(strainer)*
  ♦*philter*
fil′ter•a•bil′i•ty
fil′ter•a•ble *also* fil′tra•ble
filth′y
fil′trate′, -trat′ed, -trat′ing
fil•tra′tion
fin
fi•na′gle, -gled, -gling
fi′nal
fi•na′le
fi′nal•ist
fi•nal′i•ty
fi′nal•ize′, -ized′, -iz′ing
fi′nal•ly
fi•nance′, -nanced′, -nanc′ing
fi•nan′cial
fin′an•cier′
finch
find, found, find′ing
find′er
fine, fin′er, fin′est
fine, fined, fin′ing
fine′-drawn′
fine′-grained′
fin′er•y
fi•nesse′
fin′ger
fin′ger•board′
fin′ger•ing
fin′ger•ling
fin′ger•nail′

fin′ger-paint′
fin′ger•print′
finger tip *also* fin′ger•tip′
fin′i•al
fin′i•cal
fin′ick•y
fi′nis
fin′ish
fi′nite′
fin′nan had′die
finned
Finn′ish
fin′ny
fir *(tree)*
  ♦*fur*
fire, fired, fir′ing
fire′arm′
fire′ball′
fire′boat′
fire′box′
fire′brand′
fire′break′
fire′brick′
fire′bug′
fire′crack′er
fire′damp′
fire′dog′
fire′fight′er
fire′fly′
fire′guard′
fire′house′
fire′light′
fire′man
fire′place′
fire′plug′
fire′pow′er

fire′proof′
fire′side′
fire′trap′
fire′wa′ter
fire′weed′
fire′wood′
fire′works′
fir′ing
fir′kin
fir′ma•ment
firm′ly
first′-born′
first′-class′ *adj. & adv.*
first′hand′
first′-rate′
first′-string′
firth
fis′cal
fish *pl.* fish *or* fish′es
fish′bowl′
fish′er *(one that fishes)*
  ♦*fissure*
fish′er•man
fish′er•y
fish′eye′
fish′hook′
fish′meal′
fish′net′
fish′pond′
fish′tail′
fish′wife′
fish′y
fis′sile
fis′sion
fis′sion•a•ble
fis′sure *(crack)*
  ♦*fisher*

fist'ful' *pl.* -fuls'
fist'i·cuffs'
fis'tu·la *pl.* -las *or* -lae'
fis'tu·lous
fit, fit'ter, fit'test
fit, fit'ted *or* fit, fit'ting
fit'ful
five'-and-dime' *n.*
five'-and-ten' *n.*
five'fold'
fix'a·ble
fix'ate', -at'ed, -at'ing
fix·a'tion
fix'a·tive
fixed
fix'ed·ly
fix'ings
fix'ture
fizz
fiz'zle, -zled, -zling
fjord *or* fiord
flab'ber·gast'
flab'by
flac'cid
flack (*press agent*)
  ♦*flak*
flac'on
flag, flagged, flag'ging
flag'el·lant
flag'el·late', -lat'ed,
  -lat'ing
flag'el·la'tion
fla·gel'lum *pl.* -la
flag'eo·let'
flag'ging
flag'on
flag'pole'

fla'gran·cy *also* fla-
  grance
fla'grant
flag'ship'
flag'staff'
flag'stone'
flail
flair (*knack*)
  ♦*flare*
flak (*artillery, criticism*)
  ♦*flack*
flake, flaked, flak'ing
flak'y
flam·bé', -béed', -bé-
  ing
flam·boy'ance *also*
  flam·boy'an·cy
flam·boy'ant
flame, flamed, flam'-
  ing
fla·men'co
flame'out' *n.*
flam'ing
fla·min'go *pl.* -gos *or*
  -goes
flam'ma·bil'i·ty
flam'ma·ble
flange
flank'er·back'
flan'nel
flan'nel·ette'
flap, flapped, flap'ping
flap'jack'
flap'per
flare (*to flame*), flared,
  flar'ing
  ♦*flair*

flare'-up' *n.*
flash'back' *n.*
flash'cube'
flash'light'
flash'y
flask
flat, flat'ter, flat'test
flat, flat'ted, flat'ting
flat'boat'
flat'car'
flat'fish' *pl.* -fish' *or*
  -fish'es
flat'foot' (*fallen arch*),
  pl. -feet'
flat'foot' (*policeman*),
  pl. -foots'
flat'foot'ed
flat'i'ron
flat'ten
flat'ter
flat'ter·y
flat'top'
flat'u·lence
flat'u·lent
flat'ware'
flat'worm'
flaunt (*to show off*)
  ♦*flout*
flau'tist
fla'vor
flaw'less
flax'en
flax'seed'
flay'er
flea (*insect*)
  ♦*flee*
flea'-bit'ten

fleck

fledge, fledged, fledg'ing

fledg'ling *also* fledge'-ling

flee *(to run)*, fled, flee'-ing
♦*flea*

fleece, fleeced, fleec'-ing

fleec'y

fleet'ing

Flem'ing

Flem'ish

flesh'ly *(of the body, physical)*

flesh'y *(of flesh, plump)*

fleur'-de-lis' *pl.* fleurs'-de-lis', *or* fleur'-de-lys' *pl.* fleurs'-de-lys'

flex'i·bil'i·ty

flex'i·ble

flex'ion *also* flec'tion

flex'or *(muscle)*
♦*flexure*

flex'time'

flex'ure *(bend)*
♦*flexor*

flib'ber·ti·gib'bet

flick'er

fli'er *also* fly'er

flight'less

flight'y

flim'flam', -flammed', -flam'ming

flim'sy

flinch

fling, flung, fling'ing

flint'lock'

flint'y

flip, flipped, flip'ping

flip'-flop'

flip'pan·cy

flip'pant

flip'per

flirt

flir·ta'tion

flir·ta'tious

flit, flit'ted, flit'ting

float'er

float'ing

flock

floe *(ice mass)*
♦*flow*

flog, flogged, flog'ging

flog'ger

flood'gate'

flood'light', -light'ed *or* -lit', -light'ing

floor'board'

floor'ing

floor'-through'

floor'walk'er

flop, flopped, flop'ping

flop'house'

flop'py

flo'ra *pl.* -ras *or* -rae'

flo'ral

Flor'en·tine'

flo·res'cence

flo'ret

flo'ri·cul'ture

flor'id

flo'rist

floss'y

flo·ta'tion *also* floa·ta'tion

flo·til'la

flot'sam

flounce, flounced, flounc'ing

floun'der

flour *(powder)*
♦*flower*

flour'ish

flour'y *(covered with flour)*
♦*flowery*

flout *(to scoff)*
♦*flaunt*

flow *(stream)*
♦*floe*

flow'er *(blossom)*
♦*flour*

flow'er·pot'

flow'er·y *(like flowers, fancy)*
♦*floury*

flu *(influenza)*
♦*flew, flue*

fluc'tu·ate', -at'ed, -at'ing

fluc'tu·a'tion

flue *(pipe)*
♦*flew, flu*

flu'en·cy

flu'ent

fluff'y

flu'id

flu·id'ics

flu·id'i·ty
fluke
fluke *(blade, stroke of luck)*
fluke *(fish), pl.* fluke
fluk'y
flume
flum'mer·y
flum'mox
flunk
flun'ky *also* flun'key *pl.* -keys
flu·o·resce', -resced', -resc'ing
flu·o·res'cence
flu·o·res'cent
fluor'i·date', -dat'ed, -dat'ing
fluor'i·da'tion
flu'o·ride'
flu'o·rine'
fluor'ite'
flu·o·ro·car'bon
fluor'o·scope'
fluor'o·scop'ic
flu'o·ros'co·py
flur'ry, -ried, -ry·ing
flush
flus'ter
flute, flut'ed, flut'ing
flut'ist
flut'ter
flu'vi·al
flux
fly *(to move through air),* flew, flown, fly'ing

fly *(to hit a baseball),* flied, flied, fly'ing
fly'a·way'
fly'blown'
fly'by' *pl.* -bys'
fly'-by-night'
fly'catch'er
fly'ing
fly'leaf'
fly'pa·per
fly'speck'
fly'trap'
fly'weight'
fly'wheel'
f'-num'ber
foal
foam'y
fob, fobbed, fob'bing
fo'cal
fo'cus *pl.* -cus·es *or* -ci'
fo'cus, -cused *or* -cussed, -cus·ing *or* -cus·sing
fod'der
foe
fog, fogged, fog'ging
fog'gy
fog'horn'
fo'gy *also* fo'gey *pl.* -geys
foi'ble
foil
foist
fold'er
fol'de·rol'
fo'li·age
fo'li·ate', -at'ed, -at'ing

fo'li·a'tion
fo'lic acid
fo'li·o' *pl.* -os'
fo'li·um *pl.* -li·a
folk *pl.* folk *or* folks
folk'lore'
folk'lor'ist
folk'sy
folk'way'
fol'li·cle
fol'low
fol'low·er
fol'low-through' *n.*
fol'low-up' *n.*
fol'ly
fo·ment'
fo'men·ta'tion
fond
fon'dant
fon'dle, -dled, -dling
fond'ness
fon·due' *also* fon·du'
font
food'stuff'
fool'er·y
fool'har'dy
fool'ish
fool'proof'
fools'cap'
foot *pl.* feet
foot'age
foot'-and-mouth' disease
foot'ball'
foot'board'
foot'bridge'
foot'-can'dle

foot'fall'
foot'gear'
foot'hill'
foot'hold'
foot'ing
foot'less
foot'lights'
foot'ling
foot'lock'er
foot'loose'
foot'man
foot'note'
foot'path'
foot'-pound'
foot'print'
foot'rest'
foot'sore'
foot'step'
foot'stool'
foot'wear'
foot'work'
fop'per•y
fop'pish
for *prep. & conj.*
　♦*fore, four*
for'age, -aged, -ag•ing
for'ag•er
fo•ra'men *pl.* -ram'i•na
　or -ra'mens
for'as•much' as
for'ay'
for•bear' *(to refrain)*,
　-bore', -borne',
　-bear'ing
　♦*forebear*
for•bear'ance
for•bid', -bade' *or*
-bad', -bid'den *or*
-bid', -bid'ding
force, forced, forc'ing
force'a•ble
force'ful
force'meat'
for'ceps *pl.* -ceps
for'ci•ble
ford
fore *(at or toward the*
front)
　♦*for, four*
fore'-and-aft' *adj.*
fore•arm' *v.*
fore'arm' *n.*
fore'bear' *(ancestor)*,
　also forbear
fore•bode', -bod'ed,
　-bod'ing
fore'brain'
fore•cast', -cast' *or*
-cast'ed, -cast'ing
fore•cas•tle
fore•close', -closed',
　-clos'ing
fore•clo'sure
fore'court'
fore•doom'
fore'fa'ther
fore'fin'ger
fore'foot'
fore'front'
fore•go' *(to precede)*,
　-went', -gone', -go'-
ing
　♦*forgo*
fore'ground'
fore'hand'
fore'head'
for'eign
fore•knowl'edge
fore'leg'
fore'limb'
fore'lock'
fore'man
fore'mast'
fore'most'
fore'name'
fore'noon'
fo•ren'sic
fore•or•dain'
fore'part'
fore'quar'ter
fore'run'ner
fore'sail'
fore•see', -saw', -seen',
　-see'ing
fore•see'a•ble
fore•shad'ow
fore'shore'
fore•short'en
fore'sight'
fore'skin'
for'est
fore•stall'
for'est•ry
fore'taste' -tast'ed,
　-tast'ing
fore•tell', -told', -tell'-
ing
fore'thought'
fore•to'ken
for•ev'er
for•ev'er•more'

fore·warn'
fore'wing'
fore'word' (preface)
 ♦forward
for'feit
for'fei·ture'
for·gath'er also fore·
 gath'er
forge, forged, forg'ing
forg'er
forg'er·y
for·get', -got', -got'ten
 or -got', -get'ting
for·get'ful
for·get'-me-not'
for·get'ta·ble
for·get'ter
for·giv'a·ble
for·give', -gave', -giv'-
 en, -giv'ing
for·go' (to relinquish),
 -went', -gone', -go'-
 ing, also fore·go'
for·go'er
fork'-ful pl. fork'fuls
 or forks'ful
for·lorn'
form
for'mal
for·mal'de·hyde'
for'mal·ism
for'mal·ist
for'mal·is'tic
for·mal'i·ty
for'mal·ize', -ized',
 -iz'ing

for'mal·ly (in a formal
 manner)
 ♦formerly
for'mat
for·ma'tion
for'ma·tive
form'er (one that
 forms)
for'mer (earlier)
for'mer·ly (once)
 ♦formally
form'fit'ting
For·mi'ca®
for'mic acid
for'mi·da·bil'i·ty
for'mi·da·ble
for'mu·la pl. -las or
 -lae'
for'mu·la'ic
for'mu·late', -lat'ed,
 -lat'ing
for'mu·la'tion
for'mu·la'tor
for'ni·cate', -cat'ed,
 -cat'ing
for'ni·ca'tion
for·sake', -sook', -sak'-
 en, -sak'ing
for·sooth'
for·swear', -swore',
 -sworn', -swear'ing,
 also fore·swear'
for·syth'i·a
fort (fortified place)
forte (strong point)
for'te' (musical direc-
 tion)

forth (forward)
 ♦fourth
forth·com'ing
forth'right'
forth·with'
for'ti·eth
for'ti·fi·ca'tion
for'ti·fy', -fied', -fy'ing
for·tis'si·mo' pl. -mos'
for'ti·tude'
fort'night'
FOR'TRAN'
for'tress
for·tu'i·tous
for·tu'i·ty
for'tu·nate
for'tune
for'tune·tell'er
for'tune·tell'ing
for'ty
for'ty-five'
for'ty-nin'er
fo'rum pl. -rums or -ra
for'ward (toward the
 front), also for'wards
 ♦foreword
fos'sil
fos'sil·ize', -ized', -iz'-
 ing
fos'ter
foul (offensive)
 ♦fowl
fou·lard'
foul'-mouthed'
foul'-up' n.
foun·da'tion
found'er n.

foun'der *v.*
found'ling
foun'dry
fount
foun'tain
foun'tain·head'
four *(number)*
  ♦*for, fore*
four'-di·men'sion·al
four'-flush'er
four'fold'
four'hand'ed
Four'-H' Club
four'-in-hand'
four'-leaf' clover
four'-o'clock' *(plant)*
four'-post'er
four'score'
four'some
four'square'
four·teen'
four·teenth'
fourth *(number)*
  ♦*forth*
fo've·a *pl.* -ae'
fowl *(bird), pl.* fowl *or*
  fowls
  ♦*foul*
foxed
fox'glove'
fox'hole'
fox'hound'
fox'trot', -trot'ted,
  -trot'ting
fox'y
foy'er
fra'cas

frac'tion
frac'tion·al
frac'tion·ate', -at'ed,
  -at'ing
frac'tious
frac'ture, -tured, -tur·
  ing
frag'ile
fra·gil'i·ty
frag'ment
frag'men·tar'y
frag'men·ta'tion
fra'grance
fra'grant
frail'ty
frame, framed, fram·
  ing
fram'er
frame'-up' *n.*
frame'work'
franc *(money)*
  ♦*frank*
fran'chise', -chised',
  -chis'ing
fran'chi·see'
fran'chis·er
Fran·cis'can
fran'ci·um
fran'gi·ble
fran·gi·pan'i
frank *(straightforward)*
  ♦*franc*
Frank'en·stein'
frank'furt·er
frank'in·cense'
fran'tic
frap·pé'

fra·ter'nal
fra·ter'nal·ism
fra·ter'ni·ty
frat'er·ni·za'tion
frat'er·nize', -nized',
  -niz'ing
frat'ri·cid'al
frat'ri·cide'
Frau *pl.* Frau'en
fraud'u·lence
fraud'u·lent
fraught
Fräu'lein' *pl.* -lein'
fray
fraz'zle, -zled, -zling
freak'ish
freck'le, -led, -ling
free, fre'er, fre'est
free, freed, free'ing
free'bie *also* free'bee
free'board'
free'boot'er
free'born'
free'dom
free'-for-all'
free'form'
free'hand'
free'hand'ed
free'hold'
free'-lance' *adj.*
free'-lance', -lanced',
  -lanc'ing
free'-lanc'er *or* free'
  lance
free'load'
free'load'er
free'man

free'ma'son
free'ma'son·ry
free'sia
free'-soil'
free'stand'ing
free'stone'
free'think'er
free'think'ing
free'-throw' line
free'way'
free'wheel'ing
free'will' *adj.*
freeze *(to chill)*, froze,
　fro'zen, freez'ing
　♦*frieze*
freeze'-dry', -dried',
　-dry'ing
freez'er
freight'age
freight'er
French
French'-Ca·na'di·an
fre·net'ic *also* fre·net'i·
　cal
fren'zied
fren'zy
Fre'on'®
fre'quence
fre'quen·cy
fre'quent *adj.*
fre·quent' *v.*
fre·quen'ta·tive
fres'co *pl.* -coes *or* -cos
fresh'en
fresh'et
fresh'man
fresh'wa'ter

fret, fret'ted, fret'ting
fret'work'
Freu'di·an
fri'a·bil'i·ty
fri'a·ble
fri'ar *(monk)*
　♦*fryer*
fric'as·see'
fric'a·tive
fric'tion
Fri'day
friend'ly
friend'ship'
frieze *(ornament)*
　♦*freeze*
frig'ate
fright'en
fright'ful
frig'id
fri·gid'i·ty
fri·jol' *pl.* -jo'les, *also*
　fri·jo'le
frill'y
fringe, fringed, fring'-
　ing
Fris'bee®
frisk'y
frit'il·lar'y
frit'ter
fri·vol'i·ty
friv'o·lous
frizz
friz'zle, -zled, -zling
friz'zy
fro
frock
frog'gy

frog'man'
frol'ic, -icked, -ick·ing
frol'ick·er
frol'ic·some
from
frond
front'age
fron'tal
fron·tier'
fron·tiers'man
fron'tis·piece'
front'-page' -paged',
　-pag'ing
front'-run'ner
frost'bite', -bit', -bit'-
　ten, -bit'ing
frost'ed
frost'ing
frost'y
froth'y
frown
frow'zy *also* frow'sy
fro'zen
fruc'tose'
fru'gal
fru·gal'i·ty
fruit *pl.* fruit *or* fruits
fruit'cake'
fruit'ful
fru·i'tion
fruit'less
fruit'y
frump'ish
frump'y
frus'trate', -trat'ed,
　-trat'ing
frus·tra'tion

frus'tum *pl.* -tums *or*
  -ta
fry, fried, fry'ing
fry'er *(one that fries),*
  also fri'er
  ♦*friar*
f'-stop'
fuch'sia
fud'dle, -dled, -dling
fud'dy-dud'dy
fudge, fudged, fudg'-
  ing
fu'el, fu'eled *or* -elled,
  -el'ing *or* -el'ling
fu'gal
fu'gi·tive
fugue
füh'rer *also* fueh'rer
ful'crum *pl.* -crums *or*
  -cra
ful·fill' *also* ful·fil',
  -filled', -fill'ing
ful·fill'ment
full'back'
full'-blood'ed
full'-blown'
full'-bod'ied
full'er
full'-fash'ioned
full'-fledged'
full'-length'
full'ness *also* ful'ness
full'-scale'
full'-size' *adj., also*
  full'-sized'
full'-time' *adj. & adv.*
ful'ly

ful'mi·nate', -nat'ed,
  -nat'ing
ful'mi·na'tion
ful'mi·na'tor
ful'some
fum'ble, -bled, -bling
fume, fumed, fum'ing
fu'mi·gate', -gat'ed,
  -gat'ing
fu'mi·ga'tion
fu'mi·ga'tor
fun
func'tion
func'tion·al
func'tion·al·ism
func'tion·ar'y
fund
fun'da·men'tal
fun'da·men'tal·ism
fun'da·men'tal·ist
fu'ner·al
fu'ner·ar'y
fu·ne're·al
fun'gal
fun'gi·cide'
fun'gous *(of a fungus)*
fun'gus *(plant), pl.* -gi'
  or -gus·es
fu·nic'u·lar
funk'y
fun'nel
fun'ny
fur *(pelt)*
  ♦*fir*
fur·be·low'
fur'bish
Fu'ries

fu'ri·ous
furl
fur'long'
fur'lough
fur'nace
fur'nish
fur'nish·ings
fur'ni·ture
fu'ror'
furred
fur'ri·er
fur'ring
fur'row
fur'ry *(like fur)*
  ♦*fury*
fur'ther *(more)*
  ♦*farther*
fur'ther·ance
fur'ther·more'
fur'ther·most'
fur'thest *(to the great-
  est degree)*
  ♦*farthest*
fur'tive
fu'ry *(rage)*
  ♦*furry*
furze *(shrub)*
  ♦*firs, furs*
fuse *(lighting device,
  circuit breaker)*
  ♦*fuze*
fuse *(to melt, blend)*
  fused, fus'ing
  ♦*fuze*
fu·see' *also* fu·zee'
fu'se·lage'
fu'sel oil

fus'i·ble

fu'sil·lade'

fu'sion

fuss'-budg·et

fuss'y

fus'tian

fus'ty

fu'tile

fu·til'i·ty

fu'ture

fu'tur·ism

fu'tur·ist

fu'tur·is'tic

fu·tu'ri·ty

fu·tu·rol'o·gy

fuze *(detonator)*, also
   fuse

fuzz'y

G

gab, gabbed, gab'bing

gab'ar·dine'

gab'ber

gab'ble, -bled, -bling

gab'by

gab'fest'

ga'ble

gad, gad'ded, gad'ding

gad'a·bout'

gad'fly'

gadg'et

gadg'a·teer'

gadg'et·ry

gad'o·lin'i·um

Gael *(Celt)*
   ♦*gale*

Gael'ic

gaff *(hook)*

gaffe *(error)*

gag, gagged, gag'ging

ga'ga'

gage *(pledge)*
   ♦*gauge*

gag'gle

gag'man'

gai'e·ty

gai'ly

gain'ful

gain·say', -said', -say'-
   ing

gait *(motion)*
   ♦*gate*

gai'ter

ga'la

ga·lac'tic

gal'an·tine'

gal'ax·y

gale *(wind)*
   ♦*Gael*

ga·le'na

Gal'i·le'an *also* Gal'i·
   lae'an

gall

gal'lant

gal'lant·ry

gall'blad'der

gal'le·on

gal'ler·y

gal'ley *pl.* -leys

Gal'lic

gal'li·mau'fry

gal'li·na'ceous

gall'ing

gal'li·um

gal'li·vant'

gal'lon

gal'lop

gal'lows

gall'stone'

ga·lore'

ga·losh'

gal·van'ic

gal'va·nism

gal'va·ni·za'tion

gal'va·nize', -nized',
   -niz'ing

gal'va·nom'e·ter

gam'bit

gam'ble *(to bet)*, -bled,
   -bling

gam'bol *(to play)*,
   -boled *or* -bolled,
   -bol·ing *or* -bol·ling

game, gam'er, gam'est

game, gamed, gam'ing

game'cock'

game'keep'er

games'man·ship'

gam'ete'

ga·me'to·cyte'

gam'in

gam'ma

gam'mon

gam'ut

gam'y

gan'der

gang *(group)*
   ♦*gangue*

gang'bus'ter
gan'gling *also* gan'gly
gan'gli•on *pl.* -gli•a *or*
  -gli•ons
gang'plank'
gang'punch'
gan'grene'
gan'gre•nous
gang'ster
gangue *(rock), also*
  gang
gang'way'
gan'net
gant'let *(track), also*
  gaunt'let
gan'try
gap, gapped, gap'ping
gape, gaped, gap'ing
gar
ga•rage', -raged', -rag'-
  ing
garb
gar'bage
gar'ble, -bled, -bling
gar'çon'
gar'den
gar'den•er
gar•de'nia
gar'fish' *pl.* -fish' *or*
  -fish'es
gar•gan'tu•an
gar'gle, -gled, -gling
gar'goyle'
gar'ish
gar'land
gar'lic
gar'lick•y

gar'ment
gar'ner
gar'net
gar'nish
gar'nish•ee', -eed',
  -ee'ing
gar'nish•ment
gar'ni•ture
gar'ret
gar'ri•son
gar•rote', -rot'ed, -rot'-
  ing, *or* gar•rotte',
  -rot'ted, -rot'ting
gar•ru'li•ty
gar'ru•lous
gar'ter
gas *pl.* gas'es *or* gas'ses
gas, gassed, gas'sing
gas'e•ous
gash
gas'ket
gas'light
gas'o•hol'
gas'o•line'
gasp
gas'ser
gas'sy
gas'tric
gas•tri'tis
gas'tro•en'ter•i'tis
gas'tro•in•tes'ti•nal
gas'tro•nom'ic *also*
  gas'tro•nom'i•cal
gas•tron'o•my
gas'tro•pod'
gas•trop'o•dan *also*
  gas•trop'o•dous

gas'tru•la *pl.* -las *or*
  -lae'
gas'works'
gate *(opening)*
  ♦*gait*
gate'crash'er
gate'fold'
gate'keep'er
gate'post'
gate'way'
gath'er
gath'er•ing
Gat'or•ade'®
gauche *(awkward)*
  ♦*gouache*
gau'che•rie'
gaud'y
gauge *(scale)*
  ♦*gage*
gauge *(to measure),*
  gauged, gaug'ing
  ♦*gage*
gaunt
gaunt'let *(glove), also*
  gant'let
gauss *pl.* gauss *or*
  gauss'es
gauze
gauz'y
gav'el
ga'vi•al
ga•votte'
gawk'y
gay
gaze, gazed, gaz'ing
ga•ze'bo *pl.* -bos *or*
  -boes

ga·zelle'
ga·zette'
gaz'et·teer'
gear·box
gear'ing
gear'shift'
gear'wheel'
geck'o pl. -os or -oes
gee'zer
ge·fil'te fish
Gei'ger counter
gei'sha pl. -sha or
  -shas
gel (jelly)
  ♦jell
gel'a·tin
  also gel'a·tine
ge·lat'i·nous
geld'ing
gel'id
Gem'i·ni'
gem'o·log'i·cal
gem·ol'o·gist
gem·ol'o·gy or gem·
  mol'o·gy
gems'bok'
gem'stone'
gen'darme'
gen'der
gene
ge'ne·a·log'i·cal
ge'ne·al'o·gist
ge'ne·al'o·gy
gen'er·al
gen'er·al·ist
gen'er·al'i·ty
gen'er·al·i·za'tion

gen'er·al·ize', -ized',
  -iz'ing
gen'er·al·ly
gen'er·al-pur'pose
  adj.
gen'er·al·ship'
gen'er·ate', -at'ed,
  -at'ing
gen'er·a'tion
gen'er·a'tive
gen'er·a'tor
ge·ner'ic
gen'er·os'i·ty
gen'er·ous
gen'e·sis pl. -ses'
gen·et'
ge·net'ic also ge·net'i·
  cal
ge·net'i·cist
ge·net'ics
gen'ial
ge'ni·al'i·ty
ge'nie
gen'i·tal
gen'i·ta'li·a
gen'i·tals
gen'i·tive
gen'i·tor
gen'i·to·u'ri·nar'y
gen'ius (gifted person),
  pl. -ius·es
  ♦genus
gen'o·cid'al
gen'o·cide'
Gen'o·ese' pl. -ese'
gen'o·type'
gen'o·typ'ic

gen're
gent
gen·teel'
gen'tian
Gen'tile
gen·til'i·ty
gen'tle
gen'tle·folk' also gen'-
  tle·folks'
gen'tle·man
gen'tle·wom'an
gen'try
gen'u·flect'
gen'u·flec'tion
gen'u·ine
ge'nus (classification),
  pl. gen'er·a
  ♦genius
ge'o·cen'tric
ge'o·chem'is·try
ge'o·chro·nol'o·gy
ge'ode'
ge'o·des'ic
ge·od'e·sy
ge'o·det'ic also ge'o·
  det'i·cal
ge·og'ra·pher
ge'o·graph'ic also ge'-
  o·graph'i·cal
ge·og'ra·phy
ge'o·log'ic also ge'o·
  log'i·cal
ge·ol'o·gist
ge·ol'o·gy
ge'o·mag·net'ic
ge'o·mag'ne·tism
ge·om'e·ter

ge·o·met′ric *also* ge′o·
  met′ri·cal
ge·om′e·tri′cian *also*
  ge·om′e·ter
ge·om′e·try
ge′o·mor′phic
ge′o·mor′pho·log′ic
  also ge′o·mor′pho·
  log′i·cal
ge′o·mor·phol′o·gy
ge′o·phys′i·cal
ge′o·phys′i·cist
ge′o·phys′ics
ge′o·po·lit′i·cal
ge′o·pol′i·tics
Geor·gette′ crepe
Geor′gian
ge′o·tac′tic
ge′o·tax′is
ge′o·ther′mal *also* ge′-
  o·ther′mic
ge′o·tro′pic
ge·ot′ro·pism
ge·ra′ni·um
ger′bil
ger·i·at′ric
ger·i·at′rics
germ
Ger′man
ger·mane′
Ger·man′ic
ger·ma′ni·um
ger′mi·cid′al
ger′mi·cide′
ger′mi·nal
ger′mi·nant

ger′mi·nate′, -nat′ed,
  -nat′ing
ger′mi·na′tion
ge·ron′to·log′i·cal
  also ge·ron′to·log′ic
ger′on·tol′o·gy
ger′ry·man′der
ger′und
ge·run′dive
ges′so
ge·stalt′ *pl.* -stalts′ *or*
  -stalt′en, *or* Ge·stalt′
Ge·sta′po
ges′tate′, -tat′ed, -tat′-
  ing
ges·ta′tion
ges·tic′u·late′, -lat′ed,
  -lat′ing
ges·tic′u·la′tion
ges·tic′u·la′tor
ges′ture, -tured, -tur·
  ing
get, got, got *or* got′ten,
  get′ting
get′a·ble *also* get′ta·ble
get′a·way′ *n.*
get′ter
get′-to·geth′er *n.*
get′-up′ *n.*
get′-up′-and-go′ *n.*
gew′gaw′
gey′ser
Gha·na′ian *also* Gha′-
  ni·an
ghast′ly
gher′kin
ghet′to *pl.* -tos *or* -toes

ghost′ly
ghost′write′, -wrote′,
  -writ′ten, -writ′ing
ghost′writ′er
ghoul′ish
GI *pl.* GIs *or* GI′s
gi′ant
gib′ber
gib′ber·ish
gib′bet, -bet·ed *or*
  -bet·ted, -bet·ing *or*
  -bet·ting
gib′bon
gib′bous
gibe *(to taunt),* gibed,
  gib′ing, *also* jibe,
  jibed, jib′ing
gib′let
gid′dy
gift′ed
gig, gigged, gig′ging
gig′a·bit′
gi·gan′tic
gi·gan′tism
gig′gle, -gled, -gling
gig′ot
gigue
Gi′la monster
gild *(to cover with
  gold),* gild′ed *or* gilt,
  gild′ing
  ♦*guild*
gill
gil′ly·flow′er
gilt *(layer of gold)*
  ♦*guilt*

gilt'-edged' *also* gilt'-
-edge'
gim'bals
gim'crack'
gim'let
gim'mick
gim'mick•ry
gim'mick•y
gimp'y
gin, ginned, gin'ning
gin'ger
gin'ger•bread'
gin'ger•snap'
ging'ham
gin•gi'val
gin•gi•vi'tis
gink'go pl. -goes, *also*
ging'ko pl. -koes
gin'seng
gi•raffe'
gird, gird'ed *or* girt,
gird'ing
gird'er
gir'dle, -dled, -dling
girl'friend' *also* girl
friend
girl'ish
girth
gis'mo pl. -mos, *also*
giz'mo
gist *(essence)*
♦jest
give, gave, giv'en, giv'-
ing
give'-and-take' n.
give'a•way' n.
giv'en

giz'zard
gla•cé'
gla'cial
gla'cier *(ice)*
♦glazier
gla•ci•ol'o•gy
glad, glad'der, glad'-
dest
glad'den
glade
glad'-hand' n.
glad'i•a'tor
glad'i•a•to'ri•al
glad'i•o'lus pl. -li' *or*
-lus•es
glam'or•i•za'tion
glam'or•ize', -ized',
-iz'ing, *also* glam'-
our•ize'
glam'or•ous *also*
glam'our•ous
glam'our *also* glam'or
glance, glanced,
glanc'ing
gland
glan'ders
glan'du•lar
glare, glared, glar'ing
glass'ful' pl. -fuls'
glass•ine'
glass'ware'
glass'work'
glass'y
glau•co'ma
glau•co'ma•tous
glaze, glazed, glaz'ing

glaz'er *(one that
glazes)*
gla'zier *(glass worker)*
♦glacier
gleam
glean
glee'ful
glen
glib, glib'ber, glib'best
glide, glid'ed, glid'ing
glid'er
glim'mer
glimpse, glimpsed,
glimps'ing
glint
glis•sade', -sad'ed,
-sad'ing
glis•san'do pl. -di *or*
-dos
glis'ten
glis'ter
glitch
glit'ter
gloam'ing
gloat
glob
glob'al
glo'bate' *also* glo'bat'-
ed
globe'fish' pl. -fish' *or*
-fish•es
globe'trot'ter
glob'u•lar
glob'ule
glob'u•lin
glock'en•spiel'
gloom'y

glo'ri·fi·ca'tion
glo'ri·fy', -fied', -fy'ing
glo'ri·ous
glo'ry, -ried, -ry·ing
glos'sa·ry
gloss'y
glot'tal
glot'tis *pl.* -tis·es *or* -ti·
des'
glove, gloved, glov'ing
glov'er
glow'er
glow'ing
glow'worm'
glox·in'i·a
glu'cose'
glue, glued, glu'ing
glum, glum'mer,
glum'mest
glut, glut'ted, glut'ting
glu'ten
glu'te·nous *(of gluten)*
♦*glutinous*
glu'te·us *pl.* -te·i'
glu'ti·nous *(adhesive)*
♦*glutenous*
glut'ton
glut'ton·ous
glut'ton·y
glyc'er·in
glyc'er·ol'
gly'co·gen
gly'co·gen'ic
gly'col'
glyph
G'-man'
gnarl

gnash
gnat
gnaw *(to chew)*,
gnawed, gnawed *or*
gnawn, gnaw'ing
♦*naw*
gneiss *(rock)*
♦*nice*
gneiss'ic *also* gneiss'-
oid', gneiss'ose'
gnoc'chi
gnome
gno'mon
gnu *(antelope)*
♦*knew, new*
go, went, gone, go'ing
go *pl.* goes
go'a
goad
go'-a·head'
goal'ie
goal'keep'er
goat·ee'
goat'skin'
gob
gob'ble, -bled, -bling
gob'ble·dy·gook' *also*
gob'ble·de·gook'
go'-be·tween' *n.*
gob'let
gob'lin
go'-cart'
god'child'
god'daugh'ter
god'dess
god'fa'ther
god'for·sak'en

god'head'
god'hood'
god'less
god'like'
god'moth'er
god'par'ent
god'send'
god'son'
God'speed'
go'fer *(errand runner)*
also go'-fer
♦*gopher*
go'-get'ter
gog'gle, -gled, -gling
go'ing
goi'ter *also* goi'tre
gold'brick'
gold'en
gold'en·rod'
gold'-filled'
gold'finch'
gold'fish' *pl.* -fish' *or*
-fish'es
gold'smith'
golf'er
Go·li'ath
go'nad'
gon'do·la
gon'do·lier'
gon'er
gon'fa·lon'
gong
gon'o·coc'cus *pl.* -ci'
gon'or·rhe'a
gon'or·rhe'al *also*
gon'or·rhe'ic
goo'ber

good, bet′ter, best
good-by′ or good-bye′
good′-for-noth′ing
good′heart′ed
good′-hu′mored
good′-look′ing
good′ly
good′-na′tured
good′ness
goods
Good Sa·mar′i·tan
good′-sized′
good′-tem′pered
good will also good′-will′
good′y-good′y
goo′ey
goof′y
goo′gol′
goo′gol·plex′
gook
goon
goose pl. geese
goose′ber′ry
goose′neck′
goose′-step′, -stepped′, -step′ping
go′pher (animal)
♦gofer
gore, gored, gor′ing
gorge, gorged, gorg′ing
gor′geous
Gor′gon·zo′la
go·ril′la (animal)
♦guerilla
gorse
gor′y

gos′hawk′
gos′ling
gos′pel
gos′sa·mer
gos′sip
Goth′ic
gouache (painting)
♦gauche
Gou′da
gouge, gouged, goug-ing
gou′lash
gourd
gour′mand
gour·met′
gout′y
gov′ern
gov′ern·a·ble
gov′ern·ance
gov′ern·ess
gov′ern·ment
gov′er·nor
governor general pl. governors general
gown
grab, grabbed, grab′-bing
grab′ber
grace, graced, grac′ing
grace′ful
Grac′es
gra′cious
grack′le
grad
gra′date′, -dat′ed, -dat′ing
gra·da′tion

grade, grad′ed, grad-ing
gra′di·ent
grad′u·al
grad′u·al·ism
grad′u·al·ist
grad′u·ate′, -at′ed, -at′ing
grad′u·a′tion
graf·fi′to pl. -ti
graft
gra′ham
grail also Grail
grain′y
gram·at′om
gram′i·ci·din
gram′mar
gram·mar′i·an
gram·mat′i·cal
gram′-mo·lec′u·lar weight
gram′o·phone′
gram′pus pl. -pus·es
gran′a·ry
gran′dam′ also gran′-dame′
grand′aunt′
grand′child′
grand′dad′
grand′dad′dy also gran′dad′dy
grand′daugh′ter
gran·dee′
gran′deur
grand′fa′ther
gran·dil′o·quence
gran·dil′o·quent

gran'di·ose'
gran'di·os'i·ty
grand'ma'
grand'moth'er
grand'neph'ew
grand'niece'
grand'pa'
grand'par'ent
grand'sire'
grand'son'
grand'stand'
grand'un·cle
grange
gran'ite
gran'ny or gran'nie
gra·no'la
grant·ee'
gran'tor
gran'u·lar
gran'u·lar'i·ty
gran'u·late', -lat'ed,
   -lat'ing
gran'u·la'tion
gran'ule
grape'fruit'
grape'shot'
grape'vine'
graph'eme'
graph'ic also graph'i·
   cal
graph'ics
graph'ite'
gra·phit'ic
grap'nel
grap'ple, -pled, -pling
grasp'ing
grass'hop'per

grass'land'
grass'roots'
grass'y
grate *(framework)*,
   ♦great
grate *(to rub)*, grat'ed,
   grat'ing
   ♦great
grat'er *(one that grates)*
   ♦greater
grat'i·fi·ca'tion
grat'i·fy, -fied', -fy'ing
grat'is
grat'i·tude'
gra·tu'i·tous
gra·tu'i·ty
grave, grav'er, grav'est
grave, graved, grav'en,
   grav'ing
grave'dig'ger
grav'el, -eled or -elled,
   -el·ing or -el·ling
grave'stone'
grave'yard'
grav'id
gra·vim'e·ter
grav'i·met'ric also
   grav'i·met'ri·cal
grav'i·tate', -tat'ed,
   -tat'ing
grav'i·ta'tion
grav'i·ton'
grav'i·ty
gra·vure'
gra'vy
gray also grey
gray'beard'

gray'ling pl. -ling or
   -lings
graze, grazed, graz'ing
grease, greased, greas'-
   ing
greas'y
great *(large)*
   ♦grate
great'-aunt'
great'coat'
great'er *(larger)*
   ♦grater
great'-grand'child'
great'-grand'daugh'-
   ter
great'-grand'fa'ther
great'-grand'moth'er
great'-grand'par'ent
great'-grand'son'
great'heart'ed
great'-neph'ew
great'-niece'
great'-un'cle
grebe
Gre'cian
Grec'o-Ro'man
greed'y
Greek
green'back'
green'belt'
green'er·y
green'-eyed'
green'gage'
green'gro'cer
green'horn'
green'house'
green'room'

green'sward'
green'wood'
greet'ing
gre·gar'i·ous
grem'lin
gre·nade'
gren'a·dier'
gren'a·dine'
grey'hound'
grid'dle, -dled, -dling
grid'dle·cake'
grid'i'ron
grief
griev'ance
grieve, grieved, griev'-
ing
griev'ous
grif'fin *also* grif'fon,
gryph'on
grill *(utensil)*
grille *(grating), also*
grill
grill'room'
grim, grim'mer, grim'-
mest
grim'ace, -aced, -ac·
ing
grime
grim'y
grin, grinned, grin'ning
grind, ground, grind'-
ing
grind'er
grind'stone'
grin'go *pl.* -gos
grip *(to grasp),*
gripped, grip'ping

gripe *(to complain),*
griped, grip'ing
grippe *(influenza), also*
grip
gris'ly *(gruesome)*
♦*gristly, grizzly*
grist
gris'tle
gris·tly *(fatty)*
♦*grisly, grizzly*
grist'mill'
grit, grit'ted, grit'ting
grits
grit'ty
griz'zle, -zled, -zling
griz'zly *(bear)*
♦*grisly, gristly*
groan *(to complain)*
♦*grown*
groats
gro'cer
gro'cer·y
grog
grog'gy
grog'ram
groin
grom'met
groom
grooms'man
groove, grooved,
groov'ing
groov'y
grope, groped, grop'-
ing
gros'beak'
gros'grain'
gross'ly

gro·tesque'
grot'to *pl.* -toes *or* -tos
grouch'y
ground'less
ground'nut'
ground'work'
group'er *pl.* -per *or*
-pers
group'ie
group'ing
grouse *pl.* grouse
grouse, groused,
grous'ing
grout
grove
grov'el, -eled *or* -elled,
-el·ing *or* -el·ling
grow, grew, grown,
grow'ing
growl
grown'-up'
growth
grub, grubbed, grub'-
bing
grub'by
grub'stake'
grudge, grudged,
grud'ging
gru'el
gru'el·ing
grue'some *also* grew'-
some
gruff'ly
gruff'ness
grum'ble, -bled, -bling
grump'y
grun'ion

grunt
Gru·yère'
gua'ca·mo'le
gua·na'co *pl.* -cos
gua'nine'
gua'no *pl.* -nos
guar'an·tee' *(to se-
    cure)*, -teed', -tee'ing
    ◆*guaranty*
guar'an·tor
guar'an·ty *(pledge)*
    ◆*guarantee*
guard'ed
guard'house'
guard'i·an
guard'rail'
guard'room'
guards'man
Gua·te·ma'lan
gua'va
gu·ber·na·to'ri·al
gudg'eon
Guern'sey *pl.* -seys
guer·ril'la *(soldier)*, or
    gue·ril'la
    ◆*gorilla*
guess'work'
guest *(visitor)*
    ◆*guessed*
guff
guf·faw'
guid'ance
guide, guid'ed, guid'-
    ing
guide'book'
guide'line'
guide'post'

gui'don'
guild *(association)*
    ◆*gild*
guild'hall'
guile'less
guil'lo·tine', -tined',
    -tin'ing
guilt *(remorse)*
    ◆*gilt*
guilt'y
guimpe
guin'ea
guise *(appearance)*
    ◆*guys*
gui·tar'
gui·tar'ist
gulch
gulf'weed'
gull
gul'let
gul'li·bil'i·ty
gul'li·ble
gul'ly
gulp
gum, gummed, gum'-
    ming
gum ar·a·bic
gum'bo *pl.* -bos
gum'boil'
gum'drop'
gum'my
gump'tion
gum'shoe'
gum'wood'
gun, gunned, gun'ning
gun'boat'
gun'cot'ton

gun'fight'
gun'fire'
gun'lock'
gun'man
gun'met'al
gun'ner
gun'ner·y
gun'ny
gun'pow'der
gun'run'ner
gun'shot'
gun'-shy'
gun'sling'er
gun'smith'
gun'wale *also* gun'nel
gup'py
gur'gle, -gled, -gling
gu'ru
gush'er
gush'y
gus'set
gus'ta·to'ry
gus'to *pl.* -toes
gust'y
gut, gut'ted, gut'ting
guts'y
gut'ta-per'cha
gut'ter
gut'ter·snipe'
gut'tur·al
guy
guz'zle, -zled, -zling
gym·na'si·um *pl.* -si·
    ums *or* -si·a
gym'nast'
gym·nas'tics
gym'no·sperm'

gy·ne·co·log'i·cal *also*
  gy'ne·co·log'ic
gy'ne·col'o·gist
gy'ne·col'o·gy
gyp, gypped, gyp'ping,
  also gip, gipped,
  gip'ping
gyp'sum
Gyp'sy *also* Gip'sy
gy'rate', -rat'ed, -rat'-
  ing
gy·ra'tion
gy'ra'tor
gyr'fal'con
gy'ro *pl.* -ros
gy'ro·com'pass
gy'ro·scope'
gy'ro·scop'ic
gy'ro·sta'bi·liz'er

H

ha'be·as cor'pus
hab'er·dash'er
hab'er·dash'er·y
hab'it
hab'i·ta·bil'i·ty
hab'it·a·ble
hab'i·tat'
hab'i·ta'tion
hab'it-form'ing
ha·bit'u·al
ha·bit'u·ate', -at'ed,
  -at'ing
ha·bit'u·a'tion

hab'i·tude'
ha·bit'u·é'
ha'ci·en'da
hack'er
hack'ie
hack'le
hack'ney *pl.* -neys
hack'neyed
hack'saw'
had'dock -dock *or*
  -docks
Ha'des
haf'ni·um
haft
hag
hag'fish' *pl.* -fish *or*
  -fish'es
hag'gard
hag'gis
hag'gle, -gled, -gling
hag'i·og'ra·pher
hag'i·o·graph'ic *also*
  hag'i·o·graph'i·cal
hag'i·og'ra·phy
hai'ku *pl.* -ku
hail *(precipitation,*
  shout)
  ♦*hale*
hail'stone'
hail'storm'
hair *(threadlike growth)*
  ♦*hare*
hair'breadth'
hair'brush'
hair'cloth'
hair'cut'
hair'do' *pl.* -dos'

hair'dress'er
hair'dress'ing
hair'line'
hair'pin'
hair'-rais'ing
hairs'breadth' *or*
  hair's'-breadth', *also*
  hair'breadth'
hair'split'ting
hair'spring'
hair'-trig'ger *adj.*
hair'y *(covered with*
  hair)
  ♦*harry*
Hai'tian
hake *pl.* hake *or* hakes
ha·la'tion
hal'berd
hal'cy·on
hale *(healthy),* hal'er,
  hal'est
  ♦*(hail)*
hale *(to compel),* haled,
  hal'ing
  ♦*hail*
half *pl.* halves
half'-and-half'
half'back'
half'-baked'
half'-breed'
half'-caste'
half'-cocked'
half'heart'ed
half'-hour'
half'-life'
half'-line'
half'-mast'

half'-moon'
half'-slip'
half'-staff'
half'-tim'bered *also*
  half'-tim'ber
half'tone'
half'-track'
half'-truth'
half'way'
half'-wit'
half'-wit'ted
hal'i·but *pl.* -but *or*
  -buts
hal'ide'
hal'ite'
hal'i·to'sis
hall *(corridor)*
  ♦*haul*
hal'le·lu'jah
hall'mark'
hal·loo', -looed', -loo'-
  ing
hal'low
Hal'low·een' *also*
  Hal'low·e'en'
hal·lu'ci·nate', -nat'-
  ed, -nat'ing
hal·lu'ci·na'tion
hal·lu'ci·na·to'ry
hal·lu'cin·o·gen
hal·lu'cin·o·gen'ic
hall'way'
ha'lo *pl.* -los *or* -loes
hal'o·gen
hal'o·phyte'
hal'o·phyt'ic
hal'ter

halt'ing
halve *(to divide into
  two parts),* halved,
  halv'ing
  ♦*have*
hal'yard
ham, hammed, ham'-
  ming
ham'burg·er
ham'let
ham'mer
ham'mer·head'
ham'mock
ham'per
ham'ster
ham'string', -strung',
  -string'ing
hand'bag'
hand'ball'
hand'bill'
hand'book'
hand'breadth' *also*
  hand's'-breath' *or*
  hand's' breath'
hand'car'
hand'cart'
hand'clasp'
hand'cuff'
hand'ful' *pl.* -fuls'
hand'gun'
hand'i·cap' -capped',
  -cap'ping
hand'i·cap'per
hand'i·craft'
hand'i·work'
hand'ker·chief
han'dle, -dled, -dling

han'dle·bar'
hand'made' *(prepared
  by hand)*
hand'maid' *(atten-
  dant),* also hand'-
  maid'en
hand'-me-down'
hand'-off' *n.*
hand'out' *n.*
hand'-pick'
hand'rail'
hand'shake'
hand'some *(good-look-
  ing)*
  ♦*hansom*
hand'spring'
hand'stand'
hand'-to-hand' *adj.*
hand'-to-mouth' *adj.*
hand'work'
hand'writ'ing
hand'y
hand'y·man'
hang, hung *or* hanged,
  hang'ing
han'gar *(shed)*
  ♦*hanger*
hang'dog'
hang'er *(device for
  hanging something)*
  ♦*hangar*
hang'er-on' *pl.* hang'-
  ers-on'
hang'nail'
hang'out' *n.*
hang'o'ver
hang'-up' *n.*

hank

han'ker

han'ky-pan'ky

han'som *(carriage)*

 ♦*handsome*

hap·haz'ard

hap'less

hap'loid'

hap'pen

hap'pen·ing

hap'pen·stance'

hap'py

hap'py-go-luck'y

ha'ra-ki'ri

ha·rangue', -rangued',

 -rangu'ing

ha·rass'

ha·rass'ment

har'bin·ger

har'bor

har'bor·mas'ter

hard'back'

hard'ball'

hard'-bit'ten

hard'board'

hard'-boiled'

hard'-core' *adj.,* also

 hard'core'

hard'-edge' *adj.*

hard'en

hard'hat' *adj.*

hard'head'ed

hard'heart'ed

har·di·hood

hard'-line' *adj.,* also

 hard'line'

hard'-lin'er

hard'ly

hard'ness

hard'pan'

hard'-shell' also hard'-

 -shelled'

hard'ship'

hard'tack'

hard'top'

hard'ware'

hard'wood'

har'dy

hare *(animal)*

 ♦*hair*

hare'brained'

hare'lip'

hare'lipped'

har'em

har'i·cot'

hark

har'le·quin

har'lot

harm'ful

har·mon'ic

har·mon'i·ca

har·mon'ics

har·mo'ni·ous

har·mo'ni·um

har'mo·nize', -nized',

 -niz'ing

har'mo·ny

har'ness

harp'ist

har·poon'

harp'si·chord'

har'py

har'que·bus

har'ri·dan

har'ri·er *(hawk, hound)*

 ♦*hairier*

har'row

har'row·ing

har'ry *(to disturb),*

 -ried, -ry·ing

 ♦*hairy*

harsh'ly

hart *(deer), pl.* harts or

 hart

 ♦*heart*

har'te·beest'

har'um-scar'um

har'vest

has'-been'

ha'sen·pfef'fer

hash

hash'ish' also hash'-

 eesh'

hasp

has'sle, -sled, -sling

has'sock

haste

has'ten

hast'y

hat'box'

hatch'back'

hatch'er·y

hatch'et

hatch'way'

hate, hat'ed, hat'ing

hate'ful

ha'tred

hau'berk

haugh'ty

haul *(to drag)*

 ♦*hall*

haul'age
haunch
haunt'ed
haut'boy'
hau·teur'
have *auxiliary,* had,
   hav'ing, has
   ♦*halve*
ha'ven
have'-not' *n.*
hav'er·sack'
hav'oc
Ha·wai'ian
hawk'er
hawk'-eyed'
hawks'bill'
hawk'-weed'
haw'ser
haw'thorn'
hay *(grass)*
   ♦*hey*
hay'fork'
hay'loft'
hay'mow'
hay'rack'
hay'seed'
hay'stack'
hay'wire'
haz'ard
haz'ard·ous
haze, hazed, haz'ing
ha'zel
ha'zel·nut'
haz'y
H'-bomb'
he
head'ache'

head'band'
head'board'
head'cheese'
head'dress'
head'first'
head'gear'
head'-hunt'er
head'-hunt'ing
head'ing
head'land
head'light'
head'line', -lined',
   -lin'ing
head'lin'er
head'lock'
head'long'
head'mas'ter
head'mis'tress
head'-on'
head'phone'
head'piece'
head'quar'ters
head'rest'
head'room'
head'set'
head'stall'
head'stock'
head'stone'
head'strong'
head'wait'er
head'wa'ters
head'way'
head'work'
head'y
heal *(to cure)*
   ♦*heel, he'll*
health'y

heap'ing
hear *(to listen to),*
   heard, hear'ing
   ♦*here*
hear'ing
hark'en *also* hark'en
hear'say'
hearse
heart *(organ)*
   ♦*hart*
heart'ache'
heart'beat'
heart'break'
heart'bro'ken
heart'burn'
heart'en
heart'felt'
hearth'stone'
heart'land'
heart'less
heart'-rend'ing
hearts'ease' *also*
   heart's'-ease'
heart'sick'
heart'strings'
heart'-to-heart'
heart'wood'
heart'y
heat'er
heath
hea'then *pl.* -thens *or*
   -then
heath'er
heave, heaved *or* hove,
   heav'ing
heav'en

heav'en·ward *also*
　heav'en·wards
heav'y
heav'y-dut'y
heav'y-foot'ed
heav'y-hand'ed
heav'y-heart'ed
heav'y·set'
heav'y·weight'
He·bra'ic *also* He·
　bra'i·cal
He'brew
heck'le, -led, -ling
hec'tare'
hec'tic
hec'to·gram'
hec'to·graph'
hec'to·li'ter
hec'to·me'ter
hec'tor
hedge, hedged, hedg'-
　ing
hedge'hog'
hedge'hop', -hopped',
　-hop'ping
hedge'row'
he'don·ism
he'don·ist
he'don·is'tic
hee'bie-jee'bies
heed *(attention)*
　♦*he'd*
heed'less
hee'haw'
heel *(part of the foot, a
　tilting)*
　♦*heal, he'll*

heft'y
he·gem'o·ny
heif'er
height'en
hei'nous
heir *(inheritor)*
　♦*air, are (metric
　unit), e'er, ere*
heir apparent *pl.*
　heirs apparent
heir'ess
heir'loom'
heir presumptive *pl.*
　heirs presumptive
heist
hel'i·cal
hel'i·con'
hel'i·cop'ter
he'li·o·cen'tric
he'li·o·cen'tric'i·ty
he'li·o·graph'
he'li·og'raph·er
he'li·og'raph·y
he'li·o·trope'
he'li·ot'ro·pism
hel'i·pad'
hel'i·port'
he'li·um
he'lix *pl.* he'lix·es *or*
　hel'i·ces'
hell'-bent'
hell'cat'
hel'le·bore'
Hel·len'ic
Hel'le·nism
hell'gram·mite'
hell'hole'

hel'lion
hel·lo', -loed', -lo'ing
hel·lo' *pl.* -los
helm
hel'met
helms'man
hel'ot
help'ful
help'ing
help'less
help'mate'
help'meet'
hel'ter-skel'ter
helve
hem, hemmed, hem'-
　ming
he'-man'
hem'a·tite'
he'ma·to·log'i·cal
he'ma·tol'o·gist
he'ma·tol'o·gy
heme
hem'i·sphere'
hem'i·spher'ic *also*
　hem'i·spher'i·cal
hem'lock'
he'mo·glo'bin
he'mo·phil'i·a
he'mo·phil'i·ac'
hem'or·rhage,
　-rhaged, -rhag·ing
hem'or·rhag'ic
hem'or·rhoid'
he'mo·stat'
hemp
hem'stitch'
hen'bane'

hence'forth' *also*
  hence·for'ward
hench'man
hen'na
hen'peck'
hen'ry -ries *or* -rys
hep'a·rin
he·pat'i·ca
hep'a·ti'tis
Hep'ple·white'
hep'ta·gon'
hep·tag'o·nal
hep·tam'e·ter
her
her'ald
he·ral'dic
her'ald·ry
her·ba'ceous
herb'age
herb'al
herb'al·ist
her·bar'i·um *pl.*
  -i·ums *or* -i·a
her·bi·cid'al
her'bi·cide'
her·biv'o·rous
her·cu'le·an
Her'cu·les'
herd *(group)*
  ♦*heard*
herds'man
here *(at this place)*
  ♦*hear*
here'a·bout' *also*
  here'a·bouts'
here·af'ter

here·by'
he·red'i·tar'y
he·red'i·ty
Here'ford
here·in'
here'in·af'ter
here·of'
here·on'
her'e·sy
her'e·tic
he·ret'i·cal
here·to'
here·to·fore'
here·un'to
here'up·on'
here·with'
her'i·ta·ble
her'i·tage
her·maph'ro·dite'
her·maph'ro·dit'ic
her·met'ic *also* her·
  met'i·cal
her'mit
her'mit·age
her·ni·a *pl.* -ni·as *or*
  -ni·ae'
he'ro *pl.* -roes
he·ro'ic *also* he·ro'i·cal
her'o·in *(narcotic)*
her'o·ine *(female char-
  acter)*
her'o·ism
her'on
her'pes'
her·pet'ic
her·pe·tol'o·gist
her·pe·tol'o·gy

her'ring *pl.* -ring *or*
  -rings
her'ring·bone'
hers
her·self'
hertz *(unit)*
  ♦*hurts*
hes'i·tan·cy
hes'i·tant
hes'i·tate', -tat'ed,
  -tat'ing
hes'i·tat'er
hes'i·ta'tion
het'er·o·dox'
het'er·o·dox'y
het'er·o·dyne',
  -dyned', -dyn'ing
het'er·og'a·mous
het'er·o·ge·ne'i·ty
het'er·o·ge'ne·ous
  also het'er·og'e·nous
het'er·o·nym'
het'er·o·sex'u·al
het'er·o·sex'u·al'i·ty
heu·ris'tic
hew *(to cut)*, hewed,
  hewn *or* hewed,
  hew'ing
  ♦*hue*
hex
hex'a·chlo'ro·phene'
hex'a·gon'
hex·ag'o·nal
hex'a·gram'
hex'a·he'dral
hex'a·he'dron *pl.*
  -drons *or* -dra

hex·am'e·ter

hex·ane'

hex'a·pod'

hey interj.
  ◆hay

hey'day'

hi interj.
  ◆hie, high

hi·a'tus pl. -tus·es or
  -tus

hi·ba'chi -chis

hi'ber·nate', -nat·ed,
  -nat'ing

hi'ber·na'tion

hi'ber·na'tor

hi·bis'cus

hic'cup, -cupped, -cup·
  ping, also hic'cough

hick

hick'o·ry

hi·dal'go pl. -gos

hide, hid, hid'den or
  hid, hid'ing

hide'-and-seek'

hide'a·way'

hide'bound'

hid'e·ous

hide'-out' n.

hie (to hasten), hied,
  hie'ing or hy'ing
  ◆hi, high

hi'er·ar'chi·cal also
  hi'er·ar'chic

hi'er·ar'chy

hi'er·o·glyph'ic adj.,
  also hi'er·o·glyph'i·
  cal

hi'er·o·glyph'ic n.,
  also hi'er·o·glyph'

hi'-fi'

high (tall)
  ◆hi, hie

high'ball'

high'born'

high'boy'

high'bred'

high'brow'

high'chair'

high'-class'

high'er-up'

high'fa·lu'tin or hi'fa·
  lu'tin

high'-fi·del'i·ty adj.

high'-flown'

high'-grade' adj.

high'hand'ed

high'-hat', -hat'ted,
  -hat'ting

high'land

high'land·er

high'light', -light'ed,
  -light'ing

high'-mind'ed

high'ness

high'-oc'tane'

high'-pitched'

high'-pres'sure,
  -sured, -sur·ing

high'-rise'

high'road'

high'-school' adj.

high'-sound'ing

high'-spir'it·ed

high'-strung'

high'tail'

high'-ten'sion

high'-test'

high'-toned'

high'-wa'ter mark

high'way'

high'way'man

hi'jack'

hike, hiked, hik'ing

hik'er

hi·lar'i·ous

hi·lar'i·ty

hill'bil'ly

hill'ock

hill'side'

hill'top'

hilt

him pron.
  ◆hymn

him·self'

hin'der

Hin'di

hind'most' also hin'-
  der·most'

hind'quar'ter

hin'drance

hind'sight'

Hin'du

Hin'du·ism

hinge, hinged, hing'ing

hint

hin'ter·land'

hip, hip'per, hip'pest

hip'bone'

hip'-hug'gers

hip'pie also hip'py

hip'po pl. -pos

Hip'po•crat'ic oath
hip'po•drome'
hip'po•pot'a•mus pl.
  -mus•es or -mi'
hire, hired, hir'ing
hire'ling
hir'sute'
his
His•pan'ic
hiss
his'ta•mine'
his'ta•min'ic
his'to•log'i•cal
his•tol'o•gist
his•tol'o•gy
his•tol'y•sis
his'to•lyt'ic
his•to'ri•an
his•tor'ic (famous)
his•tor'i•cal (concerned
  with history)
his•to'ri•og'ra•pher
his•to'ri•og'ra•phy
his'to•ry
his'tri•on'ic also his'-
  tri•on'i•cal
his'tri•on'ics
hit, hit, hit'ting
hit'-and-run'
hitch'hike', -hiked',
  -hik'ing
hitch'hik'er
hith'er
hith'er•to'
hit'-or-miss' adj.
hit'ter
hive, hived, hiv'ing

hives
ho interj.
  ♦hoe
hoa'gie
hoar
hoard (cache)
  ♦horde
hoar'frost'
hoarse (grating),
  hoars'er, hoars'est
  ♦horse
hoar'y
hoax
hob'ble, -bled, -bling
hob'by
hob'by•horse'
hob'by•ist
hob'gob'lin
hob'nail'
hob'nob', -nobbed',
  -nob'bing
ho'bo pl. -boes or -bos
hock
hock'ey
ho'cus-po'cus
hod
hodge'podge'
hoe (to weed), hoed,
  hoe'ing
  ♦ho
hoe'cake'
hoe'-down'
hog, hogged, hog'ging
hog'back'
hogs'head'
hog'-tie', -tied', -ty'ing

  or -tie'ing, also hog'-
  tie'
hog'wash'
hoist'er
hoi'ty-toi'ty
ho'kum
hold, held, hold'ing
hold'er
hold'out' n.
hold'o'ver n.
hold'up' n.
hole (cavity)
  ♦whole
hole (to puncture),
  holed, hol'ing
  ♦whole
hol'i•day'
ho'li•er-than-thou'
  adj
ho'li•ness
ho'lism
ho•lis'tic
hol'lan•daise' sauce
Hol'land•er
hol'ler
hol'low
hol'ly
hol'ly•hock'
Hol'ly•wood'
hol'mi•um
hol'o•caust'
Hol'o•cene'
hol'o•gram'
hol'o•graph'
hol'o•graph'ic also
  hol'o•graph'i•cal
ho•log'ra•phy

Hol'stein
hol'ster
ho'ly *(sacred)*
   ♦*wholly*
ho'ly•stone'
hom'age
hom'bre
Hom'burg *also* hom'-
   burg'
home, homed, hom'ing
home'bod'y
home'bred'
home'-brew'
home'com'ing
home'land'
home'ly
home'made'
home'mak'er
ho'me•o•path' *also*
   ho'me•op'a•thist
ho'me•o•path'ic
ho'me•op'a•thy
ho'me•o•sta'sis
ho'me•o•stat'ic
hom'er
Ho•mer'ic
home'room'
home'sick'
home'spun'
home'stead'
home'stretch'
home'ward *also*
   home'wards
home'work'
home'y, hom'i•er,
   hom'i•est, *also* hom•y
hom'i•cid'al

hom'i•cide'
hom'i•let'ic *also* hom'-
   i•let'i•cal
hom'i•ly
hom'ing pigeon
hom'i•nid
hom'i•noid'
hom'i•ny
ho'mo•ge•ne'i•ty
ho'mo•ge'ne•ous
ho•mog'en•i•za'tion
ho•mog'en•ize', -ized,
   -iz'ing
ho•mog'en•iz'er
hom'o•graph'
ho•mol'o•gous
hom'o•logue' *also*
   hom'o•log'
ho•mol'o•gy
hom'o•nym'
hom'o•nym'ic
ho•mon'y•mous
hom'o•phone'
hom'o•phon'ic
ho•moph'o•ny
ho•mop'ter•ous
Ho'mo sa'pi•ens'
ho'mo•sex'u•al
ho'mo•sex'u•al'i•ty
ho•mun'cu•lus
hon'cho *pl.* -chos
hon'cho, -choed, -cho•
   ing
Hon•du'ran
hone, honed, hon'ing
hon'est
hon'es•ty

hon'ey *pl.* -eys
hon'ey•bee'
hon'ey•comb'
hon'ey•dew'
hon'eyed
hon'ey•moon'
hon'ey•suck'le
honk'er
hon'ky-tonk'
hon'or
hon'or•a•ble
hon'o•rar'i•um *pl.*
   -i•ums *or* -i•a
hon'or•ar'y
hon'or•if'ic
hood'ed
hood'lum
hood'wink'
hoo'ey
hoof *pl.* hooves *or*
   hoofs
hoo'kah
hook'-and-lad'der
   truck
hook'up' *n.*
hook'worm'
hook'y
hoo'li•gan
hoop *(circle)*
   ♦*whoop*
hoop'la'
hoo'poe
hoose'gow'
Hoo'sier
hoot
hoot'en•an'ny
hop, hopped, hop'ping

hope, hoped, hop'ing
hope'ful
hop'per
hop'sack'ing
hop'scotch'
horde *(throng)*
　♦*hoard*
hore'hound'
ho·ri'zon
hor'i·zon'tal
hor·mon'al *also* hor·
　mon'ic
hor'mone'
horn'bill'
horn'blende'
horn'book'
horned
hor'net
horn'pipe'
hor'o·loge'
hor'o·log'ic *also* hor'o·
　log'i·cal
ho·rol'o·gy
hor'o·scope'
ho·ros'co·py
hor·ren'dous
hor'ri·ble
hor'rid
hor·rif'ic
hor'ri·fy', -fied', -fy'-
　ing
hor'ror
hors d'oeuvre' *pl.*
　hors d'oeuvres' *or*
　hors d'oeuvre'
horse *(animal)*
　♦*hoarse*

horse *(to play roughly),*
　horsed, hors'ing
　♦*hoarse*
horse'back'
horse'car'
horse'flesh'
horse'fly'
horse'hair'
horse'hide'
horse'laugh'
horse'man
horse'man·ship'
horse'play'
horse'pow'er
horse'rad'ish
horse'shoe'
horse'tail'
horse'whip',
　-whipped', -whip'-
　ping
horse'wom'an
hors'y *also* hors'ey
hor'ta·tive
hor'ta·to'ry
hor'ti·cul'tur·al
hor'ti·cul'ture
hor'ti·cul'tur·ist
ho·san'na
hose *pl.* hose *or* hos'es
hose, hosed, hos'ing
ho'sier·y
hos'pice
hos'pi·ta·ble
hos'pi·tal
hos'pi·tal'i·ty
hos'pi·tal·i·za'tion

hos'pi·tal·ize', -ized',
　-iz'ing
host
hos'tage
hos'tel *(lodging)*
　♦*hostile*
host'ess
hos'tile *(antagonistic)*
　♦*hostel*
hos·til'i·ty
hos'tler
hot, hot'ter, hot'test
hot'bed'
hot'-blood'ed
hotch'potch'
hot'-dog', -dogged',
　-dog'ging
ho·tel'
hot'foot' *pl.* -foots'
hot'head'ed
hot'house'
hot'shot'
hound
hound's'-tooth'
　check
hour *(time)*
　♦*our*
hour'glass'
hour'ly
house, housed, hous'-
　ing
house'boat'
house'break'ing
house'bro'ken
house'coat'
house'fly'
house'hold'

house'hus'band
house'keep'er
house'maid'
house'moth'er
house'top'
house'warm'ing
house'wife'
house'work'
hous'ing
hov'el
hov'er
Hov'er·craft'®
how'dah
how'dy
how·ev'er
how'it·zer
howl'er
howl'ing
how'so·ev'er
hoy'den
hub'bub'
hub'cap'
hu'bris
huck'le·ber'ry
huck'ster
hud'dle, -dled, -dling
hue *(color, outcry)*
 ♦*hew*
huff'y
hug, hugged, hug'ging
huge, hug'er, hug'est
hug'ger
hug'ger·mug'ger *or*
 hug'ger-mug'ger
Hu'gue·not'
hu'la
hulk'ing

hull
hul'la·ba·loo'
hum, hummed, hum'-
 ming
hu'man
hu·mane'
hu'man·ism
hu'man·ist
hu'man·is'tic
hu·man'i·tar'i·an
hu·man'i·tar'i·an·ism
hu·man'i·ty
hu'man·i·za'tion
hu'man·ize', -ized',
 -iz'ing
hu'man·kind'
hu'man·ly
hu'man·oid'
hum'ble, -bled, -bling
hum'bug', -bugged',
 -bug'ging
hum'bug'ger
hum'ding'er
hum'drum'
hu'mer·al
hu'mer·us *(bone)*, *pl.*
 -mer·i'
 ♦*humorous*
hu'mid
hu·mid'i·fi·ca'tion
hu·mid'i·fi'er
hu·mid'i·fy', -fied',
 -fy'ing
hu·mid'i·ty
hu'mi·dor
hu·mil'i·ate', -at'ed,
 -at'ing

hu·mil'i·a'tion
hu·mil'i·ty
hum'ming·bird'
hum'mock
hu'mor
hu'mor·esque'
hu'mor·ist
hu'mor·ous *(funny)*
 ♦*humerus*
hump'back'
humph
hu'mus
hunch'back'
hunch'backed'
hun'dred *pl.* -dred *or*
 -dreds
hun'dredth
hun'dred·weight' *pl.*
 -weight' *or* -weights'
Hun·gar'i·an
hun'ger
hun'gry
hunk
hun'ker
hun'ky-do'ry
hunt'er
hunt'ing
hunts'man
hur'dle *(to jump over),*
 -dled, -dling
 ♦*hurtle*
hur'dy-gur'dy
hurl'er
hur'ly-bur'ly
hur·rah' *also* hoo·ray',
 hur·ray'
hur'ri·cane'

hur'ry, -ried, -ry·ing

hurt, hurt, hurt'ing

hur'tle *(to throw)*,
  -tled, -tling
  ♦*hurdle*

hus'band

hus'band·ry

hush'-hush'

hush'pup'py

husk'er

husk'y *(hoarse, burly)*

hus'ky *(dog)*

hus·sar'

hus'sy

hus'tle, -tled, -tling

hut

hutch

hy'a·cinth

hy'a·line

hy'a·lite'

hy'brid

hy'brid·ism

hy'brid·i·za'tion

hy'brid·ize', -ized',
  -iz'ing

hy·dran'ge·a

hy'drant

hy'drate', -drat·ed,
  -drat'ing

hy·dra'tion

hy'dra'tor

hy·drau'lic

hy·drau'lics

hy'dra·zine'

hy'dride'

hy'dro·car'bon

hy'dro·ce·phal'ic

hy'dro·ceph'a·lus

hy'dro·chlo'ric acid

hy'dro·cor'ti·sone'

hy'dro·dy·nam'ic

hy'dro·dy·nam'ics

hy'dro·e·lec'tric

hy'dro·e·lec'tric'i·ty

hy'dro·flu·or'ic acid

hy'dro·foil'

hy'dro·gen

hy'dro·gen·ate', -at'-
  ed, -at'ing

hy'dro·gen·a'tion

hy·drog'e·nous

hy·drog'ra·pher

hy·drog'ra·phy

hy'dro·log'ic

hy·drol'o·gist

hy·drol'o·gy

hy·drol'y·sis

hy'dro·lyt'ic

hy'dro·lyze', -lyzed',
  -lyz'ing

hy·drom'e·ter

hy'dro·pho'bi·a

hy'dro·plane'

hy'dro·pon'ics

hy'dro·sphere'

hy'dro·stat'ic *also* hy'-
  dro·stat'i·cal

hy'dro·stat'ics

hy'dro·ther'a·py

hy·drot'ro·pism

hy'drous

hy·drox'ide'

hy·drox'yl

hy·e'na *also* hy·ae'na

hy'giene'

hy·gi·en'ic

hy·gien'ist

hy·grom'e·ter

hy·gro·met'ric

hy·grom'e·try

hy'gro·scope'

hy'gro·scop'ic

hy'men

hy'me·ne'al

hymn *(song)*
  ♦*him*

hym'nal

hym'no·dy

hy'oid'

hype, hyped, hyp'ing

hy'per·ac'id

hy'per·ac·id'i·ty

hy'per·ac'tive

hy·per'bo·la *(curve)*

hy·per'bo·le *(exagger-
  ation)*

hy'per·bol'ic

hy·per'bo·re'an

hy'per·crit'i·cal *(over-
  critical)*
  ♦*hypocritical*

hy'per·gly·ce'mi·a

hy'per·o'pi·a

hy'per·sen'si·tive

hy'per·son'ic

hy'per·ten'sion

hy'per·thy'roid

hy'per·thy'roid·ism

hy'per·ven'ti·la'tion

hy'phen

hy′phen•ate′, -at′ed,
-at′ing
hy′phen•a′tion
hyp•no′sis *pl.* -ses′
hyp•no′ther•a•py
hyp•not′ic
hyp′no•tism
hyp′no•tist
hyp′no•tize′, -tized′,
-tiz′ing
hy′po *pl.* -pos
hy′po•chon′dri•a
hy′po•chon′dri•ac′
hyp•poc′ri•sy
hyp′o•crite′
hyp′o•crit′i•cal *(insin-
cere)*
♦*hypercritical*
hy′po•der′mic
hy′po•der′mis *also*
hy′po•derm′
hy′po•gly•ce′mi•a
hy′pot′e•nuse′
hy′po•thal′a•mus
hy•poth′e•sis *pl.* -ses′
hy•poth′e•size′,
-sized′, -siz′ing
hy′po•thet′i•cal *also*
hy′po•thet′ic
hy′po•thy′roid•ism
hy′rax′ *pl.* -rax′es *or*
-ra•ces
hys′sop
—hys•ter•ec′to•my
hys•ter•e′sis *pl.* -ses′
hys•ter′i•a
hys•ter′ic

hys•ter′i•cal
hys•ter′ics

I

i′amb′
i•am′bic
i′bex′
i′bis
ice, iced, ic′ing
ice′berg′
ice′boat′
ice′bound′
ice′box′
ice′break•er′
ice′-cream′ cone
Ice′land•er
Ice′land′ic
ice′-skate′, -skat′ed,
-skat′ing
ich•neu′mon
ich′thy•o•log′ic *also*
ich′thy•o•log′i•cal
ich′thy•ol′o•gist
ich′thy•ol′o•gy
ich′thy•o•saur′ *also*
ich′thy•o•sau′rus *pl.*
-sau′ri′
i′ci•cle
ic′ing
i′con *also* i′kon
i•con′o•clasm
i•con′o•clast′
i•con′o•clas′tic
ic′y

id
i•de′a
i•de′al
i•de′al•ism
i•de′al•ist
i•de′al•is′tic
i•de′al•i•za′tion
i•de′al•ize′, -ized′, -iz′-
ing
i•de′ate′, -at′ed, -at′ing
i′de•a′tion
i•dée fixe′ *pl.* i•dées
fixes′
i•den′ti•cal
i•den′ti•fi′a•ble
i•den′ti•fi•ca′tion
i•den′ti•fy′, -fied′, -fy′-
ing
i•den′ti•ty
id′e•o•gram′ *also* id′e•
o•graph′
i′de•o•log′i•cal
i′de•ol′o•gy
ides
id′ est′
id′i•o•cy
id′i•om
id′i•o•mat′ic
id′i•o•syn′cra•sy
id′i•o•syn•crat′ic
id′i•ot
id′i•ot′ic
i′dle *(to move lazily)*,
i′dled, i′dling
♦*idol, idyll*
i′dol *(image)*
♦*idle, idyll*

i·dol'a·ter
i·dol'a·trous
i·dol'a·try
i'dol·ize', -ized', -iz'ing
i'dyll *(poem), also* i'dyl
♦*idle, idol*
i·dyl'lic
if
ig'loo *pl.* -loos
ig'ne·ous
ig·nite', -nit'ed, -nit'-
ing
ig·ni'tion
ig·no'ble
ig'no·min'i·ous
ig'no·min'y
ig'no·ra'mus
ig'no·rance
ig'no·rant
ig·nore', -nored', -nor'-
ing
i·gua'na
il'e·ac'
il'e·al
il'e·i'tis
il'e·um *(intestine), pl.*
-e·a
♦*ilium*
Il'i·ad
il'i·um *(bone), pl.* -i·a
♦*ileum*
ilk
ill, worse, worst
ill'-ad·vised'
ill'-bred'
il·le'gal
il'le·gal'i·ty

il·leg'i·bil'i·ty
il·leg'i·ble
il·le·git'i·ma·cy
il·le·git'i·mate
ill'-fat'ed
ill'-fa'vored
ill'-got'ten
ill'-hu'mored
il·lib'er·al
il·lic'it *(unlawful)*
♦*elicit*
il·lim'it·a·ble
Il·li·nois'an
il·liq'uid
il·lit'er·a·cy
il·lit'er·ate
ill'-man'nered
ill'-na'tured
ill'ness
il·log'i·cal
ill'-o'mened
ill'-starred'
ill'-tem'pered
ill'-timed'
ill'-treat'
il·lu'mi·nate', -nat'ed,
-nat'ing
il·lu'mi·na'tion
il·lu'mi·na'tor
il·lu'mine, -mined,
-min·ing
ill'-use' *n., also* ill'-us'-
age
ill'-use', -used', -us'ing
il·lu'sion *(misconcep-
tion)*
♦*allusion*

il·lu'sion·ist
il·lu'sive *(deceptive)*
♦*allusive, elusive*
il·lu'so·ry
il·lus'trate', -trat'ed,
-trat'ing
il·lus'tra'tion
il·lus'tra·tive
il·lus'tra·tor
il·lus'tri·ous
il'ly
im'age, -aged, -ag·ing
im'age·ry
i·mag'i·na·ble
i·mag'i·nar'y
i·mag'i·na'tion
i·mag'i·na·tive
i·mag'ine, -ined, -in·
ing
i·ma'go *pl.* -goes *or*
-gi·nes
im·bal'ance
im'be·cile
im'be·cil'i·ty
im·bibe', -bibed',
-bib'ing
im·bro'glio *pl.* -glios
im·brue', -brued',
-bru'ing
im·bue', -bued', -bu'-
ing
im'i·tate', -tat'ed,
-tat'ing
im'i·ta'tion
im'i·ta'tive
im'i·ta'tor
im·mac'u·late

im'ma·nent *(within)*
 ♦*eminent, imminent*
im'ma·te'ri·al
im'ma·ture'
im'ma·tur'i·ty
im·meas'ur·a·ble
im·me'di·a·cy
im·me'di·ate
im·me·mo'ri·al
im·mense'
im·men'si·ty
im·merse', -mersed',
 -mers'ing
im·mer'sion
im'mi·grant
im'mi·grate', -grat'ed,
 -grat'ing
im'mi·gra'tion
im'mi·nence
im'mi·nent *(impend-
 ing)*
 ♦*eminent, immanent*
im·mo'bile
im·mo·bil'i·ty
im·mo·bi·li·za'tion
im·mo·bi·lize', -lized',
 -liz'ing
im·mod'er·ate
im·mod'er·a'tion
im·mod'est
im·mod'es·ty
im·mo·late', -lat'ed,
 -lat'ing
im'mo·la'tion
im'mo·la'tor
im·mor'al
im·mor·al'i·ty

im·mor'tal
im·mor·tal'i·ty
im·mor'tal·ize', -ized',
 -iz'ing
im·mov'a·bil'i·ty
im·mov'a·ble
im·mune'
im·mu'ni·ty
im'mu·ni·za'tion
im'mu·nize', -nized',
 -niz'ing
im'mu·nol'o·gist
im'mu·nol'o·gy
im·mure', -mured',
 -mur'ing
im·mu·ta·bil'i·ty
im·mu'ta·ble
imp
im·pact' *n.*
im·pact' *v.*
im·pact'ed
im·pac'tion
im·pair'
im·pair'ment
im·pa'la
im·pale', -paled', -pal'-
 ing
im·pal'pa·ble
im·pan'el, -eled *or*
 -elled, -el·ing *or* -el·
 ling
im·part'
im·par'tial
im·par·ti·al'i·ty
im·pass'a·ble *(impos-
 sible to cross)*
 ♦*impassible*

im·passe
im·pas'si·ble *(unfeel-
 ing)*
 ♦*impassable*
im·pas'sioned
im·pas'sive
im·pas·siv'i·ty
im·pa'tience
im·pa'tient
im·peach'
im·peach'ment
im·peach'a·ble
im·pec'ca·bil'i·ty
im·pec'ca·ble
im·pe·cu'ni·ous
im·pe'dance
im·pede', -ped'ed,
 -ped'ing
im·ped'i·ment
im·ped'i·men'ta
im·pel', -pelled', -pel'-
 ling
im·pend'ing
im·pen'e·tra·bil'i·ty
im·pen'e·tra·ble
im·pen'i·tence
im·pen'i·tent
im·per'a·tive
im'per·cep'ti·bil'i·ty
im'per·cep'ti·ble
im'per·cep'tive
im·per'fect
im'per·fec'tion
im'per·fec'tive
im·per'fo·rate
im·pe'ri·al
im·pe'ri·al·ism

im·pe'ri·al·ist
im·pe'ri·al·is'tic
im·per·il, -iled *or*
 -illed, -il·ing *or* -il·
 ling
im·pe'ri·ous
im·per'ish·a·bil'i·ty
im·per'ish·a·ble
im·per'ma·nence
im·per'ma·nent
im·per'me·a·ble
im·per'son·al
im·per'son·al'i·ty
im·per'son·ate', -at'-
 ed, -at'ing
im·per'son·a'tion
im·per'son·a'tor
im·per'ti·nence
im·per'ti·nent
im·per·turb'a·bil'i·ty
im·per·turb'a·ble
im·per'vi·ous
im·pe·ti'go
im·pet·u·os'i·ty
im·pet'u·ous
im·pe'tus *pl.* -tus·es
im·pi'e·ty
im·pinge', -pinged',
 -ping'ing
im·pi'ous
imp'ish
im·pla·ca·bil'i·ty
im·pla'ca·ble
im'plant' *n.*
im·plant' *v.*
im'plan·ta'tion
im·plau'si·bil'i·ty

im·plau'si·ble
im'ple·ment
im'ple·men·ta'tion
im'pli·cate', -cat'ed,
 -cat'ing
im'pli·ca'tion
im·plic'it
im·plied'
im·plode', -plod'ed,
 -plod'ing
im·plore', -plored',
 -plor'ing
im·plo'sion
im·plo'sive
im·ply', -plied', -ply'-
 ing
im'po·lite'
im·pol'i·tic
im·pon'der·a·ble
im'port' *n.*
im·port' *v.*
im·por'tance
im·por'tant
im'por·ta'tion
im·port'er
im·por'tu·nate
im'por·tune', -tuned',
 -tun'ing
im'por·tu'ni·ty
im·pose', -posed',
 -pos'ing
im'po·si'tion
im·pos'si·bil'i·ty
im·pos'si·ble
im'post'
im·pos'tor
im·pos'ture

im'po·tence
im'po·tent
im·pound'
im·pov'er·ish
im·prac'ti·ca·bil'i·ty
im·prac'ti·ca·ble
im·prac'ti·cal
im'pre·cate', -cat'ed,
 -cat'ing
im'pre·ca'tion
im'pre·ca'tor
im'pre·ca·to'ry
im'pre·cise'
im'pre·ci'sion
im·preg'na·ble
im·preg'nate', -nat'ed,
 -nat'ing
im'preg·na'tion
im·preg'na'tor
im'pre·sa'ri·o' *pl.* -os'
im'press' *n.*
im·press' *v.*
im·pres'sion
im·pres'sion·a·bil'i·ty
im·pres'sion·a·ble
im·pres'sion·ism
im·pres'sion·ist
im·pres'sion·ist'ic
im·pres'sive
im'pri·ma'tur'
im'print' *n.*
im·print' *v.*
im·pris'on
im·pris'on·ment
im·prob'a·bil'i·ty
im·prob'a·ble
im·promp'tu

im·prop'er
im·pro·pri'e·ty
im·prove', -proved',
   -prov'ing
im·prove'ment
im·prov'i·dence
im·prov'i·dent
im·prov'i·sa'tion
im'pro·vise', -vised',
   -vis'ing
im·pru'dence
im·pru'dent
im·pu'dence
im·pu'dent
im·pugn'
im·pulse'
im·pul'sion
im·pul'sive
im·pu'ni·ty
im·pure'
im·pu'ri·ty
im·put'a·ble
im·pu·ta'tion
im·pute', -put'ed,
   -put'ing
in *(within)*
   ♦*inn*
in'a·bil'i·ty
in' ab·sen'tia
in·ac·ces'si·ble
in·ac'cu·ra·cy
in·ac'cu·rate
in·ac'tion
in·ac'tive
in·ac·tiv'i·ty
in·ad'e·qua·cy
in·ad'e·quate

in'ad·mis'si·bil'i·ty
in'ad·mis'si·ble
in'ad·ver'tence
in'ad·ver'tent
in'ad·vis'a·bil'i·ty
in'ad·vis'a·ble
in·al'ien·a·ble
in·ane'
in·an'i·mate
in·an'i·ty
in·ap'pli·ca·bil'i·ty
in·ap'pli·ca·ble
in·ap·pre'cia·ble
in·ap·pro'pri·ate
in·arch'
in·ar·tic'u·late
in'as·much' as
in'at·ten'tion
in'at·ten'tive
in·au'di·ble
in·au'gu·ral
in·au'gu·rate', -rat'ed,
   -rat'ing
in·au'gu·ra'tion
in·au'gu·ra'tor
in'aus·pi'cious
in'-be·tween' *adj. & n.*
in'board'
in'born'
in'bound'
in'breed', -bred',
   -breed'ing
In'ca *pl.* -ca *or* -cas
in·cal'cu·la·bil'i·ty
in·cal'cu·la·ble
In'can
in·can·des'cence

in'can·des'cent
in'can·ta'tion
in·ca·pa·bil'i·ty
in·ca'pa·ble
in·ca·pac'i·tate', -tat'-
   ed, -tat'ing
in·ca·pac'i·ta'tion
in·ca·pac'i·ty
in·car'cer·ate', -at'ed,
   -at'ing
in·car·cer·a'tion
in·car'cer·a'tor
in·car·nate', -nat'ed,
   -nat'ing
in·car·na'tion
in·cau'tious
in·cen'di·ar'y
in·cense' *n.*
in·cense', -censed',
   -cens'ing
in·cen'tive
in·cep'tion
in·cep'tive
in·cer'ti·tude'
in·ces'sant
in·cest'
in·ces'tu·ous
in·cho'ate
inch'worm'
in'ci·dence
in'ci·dent
in'ci·den'tal
in·cin'er·ate', -at'ed,
   -at'ing
in·cin'er·a'tion
in·cin'er·a'tor

in·cip'i·en·cy *also* in·
  cip'i·ence
in·cip'i·ent
in·cise', -cised', -cis'ing
in·ci'sion
in·ci'sive
in·ci'sor
in·cite' *(to provoke)*,
  -cit'ed, -cit'ing
  ♦*insight*
in·cite'ment
in·clem'en·cy
in·clem'ent
in'cli·na'tion
in·cline', -clined',
  -clin'ing
in'cli·nom'e·ter
in·clude', -clud'ed,
  -clud'ing
in·clu'sion
in·clu'sive
in'cog·ni'to
in'co·her'ence *also*
  in'co·her'en·cy
in'co·her'ent
in·com·bus'ti·ble
in'come'
in'com'ing
in·com·men'su·ra·ble
in·com·men'su·rate
in'com·mode', -mod'-
  ed, -mod'ing
in'com·mo'di·ous
in'com·mu'ni·ca·ble
in'com·mu'ni·ca'do
in'com·mu'ni·ca'tive
in·com'pa·ra·ble

in'com·pat'i·bil'i·ty
in'com·pat'i·ble
in·com'pe·tence *also*
  in·com'pe·ten·cy
in·com'pe·tent
in'com·plete'
in'com'pre·hen'si·
  bil'i·ty
in'com'pre·hen'si·ble
in'com'pre·hen'sion
in'com·press'i·bil'i·ty
in'com·press'i·ble
in'con·ceiv'a·bil'i·ty
in'con·ceiv'a·ble
in'con·clu'sive
in·con'gru·ent
in'con·gru'i·ty
in·con'gru·ous
in·con'se·quent
in·con'se·quen'tial
in'con·sid'er·a·ble
in'con·sid'er·ate
in'con·sis'ten·cy
in'con·sis'tent
in'con·sol'a·bil'i·ty
in'con·sol'a·ble
in·con'so·nant
in'con·spic'u·ous
in·con'stan·cy
in·con'stant
in'con·test'a·bil'i·ty
in'con·test'a·ble
in·con'ti·nence
in·con'ti·nent
in'con·tro·vert'i·bil'i·
  ty
in'con·tro·vert'i·ble

in'con·ven'ience,
  -ienced, -ienc·ing
in'con·ven'ient
in'con·vert'i·bil'i·ty
in'con·vert'i·ble
in·cor'po·rate', -rat'-
  ed, -rat'ing
in·cor'po·ra'tion
in·cor'po·ra'tor
in'cor·po're·al
in'cor·rect'
in·cor'ri·gi·bil'i·ty
in·cor'ri·gi·ble
in'cor·rupt'i·bil'i·ty
in'cor·rupt'i·ble
in·creas'a·ble
in'crease' *n.*
in·crease', -creased',
  -creas'ing
in·cred'i·bil'i·ty
in·cred'i·ble *(unbeliev-*
  able)
  ♦*incredulous*
in·cre·du'li·ty
in·cred'u·lous *(skepti-*
  cal)
  ♦*incredible*
in'cre·ment
in·crim'i·nate', -nat'-
  ed, -nat'ing
in·crim'i·na'tion
in·crim'i·na'tor
in·crim'i·na·to'ry
in'cu·bate', -bat'ed,
  -bat'ing
in'cu·ba'tion
in'cu·ba'tor

in'cu·bus *pl.* -bus·es *or*
  -bi'
in·cul'cate', -cat'ed,
  -cat'ing
in·cul·ca'tion
in·cul·ca'tor
in·cul'pa·ble
in·cul'pate', -pat'ed,
  -pat'ing
in·cum'ben·cy
in·cum'bent
in·cu·nab'u·lum *pl.*
  -la
in·cur', -curred', -cur'-
  ring
in·cur'a·ble
in·cu'ri·ous
in·cur'sion
in·cus *pl.* in·cu'des
in·debt'ed
in·de·cen·cy
in·de'cent
in·de·ci'pher·a·bil'i·
  ty
in'de·ci'pher·a·ble
in·de·ci'sion
in·de·ci'sive
in·dec'o·rous
in·deed'
in'de·fat'i·ga·bil'i·ty
in'de·fat'i·ga·ble
in'de·fen'si·bil'i·ty
in'de·fen'si·ble
in·de·fin'a·ble
in·def'i·nite
in'de·his'cence
in'de·his'cent

in·del'i·bil'i·ty
in·del'i·ble
in·del'i·ca·cy
in·del'i·cate
in·dem'ni·fi·ca'tion
in·dem'ni·fy', -fied',
  -fy'ing
in·dem'ni·ty
in·dent'
in'den·ta'tion
in·den'tion
in·den'ture, -tured,
  -tur·ing
in'de·pend'ence
in'de·pend'ent
in'-depth'
in'de·scrib'a·bil'i·ty
in'de·scrib'a·ble
in'de·struc'ti·bil'i·ty
in'de·struc'ti·ble
in'de·ter'min·a·ble
in'de·ter'mi·na·cy
in'de·ter'mi·nate
in'de·ter'mi·na'tion
in·dex' *pl.* -dex·es *or*
  -di·ces'
In'di·a ink
In'di·an
In'di·an'i·an
in'di·cate', -cat'ed,
  -cat'ing
in'di·ca'tion
in·dic'a·tive
in'di·ca'tor
in·dict' *(to accuse)*
  ♦indite

in·dict'er *also* in·dict'-
  or
in·dif'fer·ence
in·dif'fer·ent
in'di·gence
in·dig'e·nous
in'di·gent
in'di·gest'i·bil'i·ty
in'di·gest'i·ble
in'di·ges'tion
in·dig'nant
in'dig·na'tion
in·dig'ni·ty
in'di·go' *pl.* -gos' *or*
  -goes'
in'di·rect'
in'di·rec'tion
in'dis·creet' *(imprudent)*
in'dis·crete' *(unified)*
in'dis·cre'tion
in'dis·crim'i·nate
in'dis·pen'sa·bil'i·ty
in'dis·pen'sa·ble
in'dis·pose', -posed',
  -pos'ing
in'dis·po·si'tion
in'dis·put'a·ble
in'dis·sol'u·bil'i·ty
in'dis·sol'u·ble
in'dis·tinct'
in'dis·tin'guish·a·bil'-
  i·ty
in'dis·tin'guish·a·ble
in·dite' *(to compose)*,
  -dit'ed, -dit'ing
  ♦indict

in'di•um
in'di•vid'u•al
in'di•vid'u•al•ism
in'di•vid'u•al•ist
in'di•vid'u•al•is'tic
in'di•vid'u•al'i•ty
in'di•vid'u•al•ize',
    -ized', -iz'ing
in'di•vis'i•bil'i•ty
in'di•vis'i•ble
In'do•chi•nese' *pl.*
    •nese'
in•doc'tri•nate', -nat'-
    ed, -nat'ing
in•doc'tri•na'tion
In'do-Eu•ro•pe'an
in'do•lence
in'do•lent
in•dom'i•ta•ble
In'do•ne'sian
in'door'
in•doors'
in'drawn'
in•du'bi•ta•ble
in•duce', -duced',
    -duc'ing
in•duce'ment
in•duct'
in•duc'tance
in'duc•tee'
in•duc'tion
in•duc'tive
in•duc'tor
in•dulge', -dulged',
    -dulg'ing
in•dul'gence
in•dul'gent

in•dus'tri•al
in•dus'tri•al•ism
in•dus'tri•al•ist
in•dus'tri•al•i•za'tion
in•dus'tri•al•ize',
    -ized', -iz'ing
in•dus'tri•ous
in'dus•try
in•e'bri•ate', -at'ed,
    -at'ing
in•e'bri•a'tion
in•ed'i•ble
in•ef'fa•bil'i•ty
in•ef'fa•ble
in'ef•face'a•bil'i•ty
in'ef•face'a•ble
in'ef•fec'tive
in'ef•fec'tu•al
in'ef•fi'cien•cy
in'ef•fi'cient
in'e•las'tic
in•el'e•gance
in•el'e•gant
in•el'i•gi•bil'i•ty
in•el'i•gi•ble
in'e•luc'ta•bil'i•ty
in'e•luc'ta•ble
in•ept'
in•ept'i•tude'
in'e•qual'i•ty
in•eq'ui•ta•ble
in•eq'ui•ty *(injustice)*
    ♦*iniquity*
in•ert'
in•er'tia
in•er'tial
in'es•cap'a•ble

in•es'ti•ma•ble
in•ev'i•ta•bil'i•ty
in•ev'i•ta•ble
in'ex•act'
in'ex•cus'a•ble
in'ex•haust'i•bil'i•ty
in'ex•haust'i•ble
in•ex'o•ra•ble
in'ex•pen'sive
in'ex•pe'ri•ence
in'ex•pe'ri•enced
in•ex'pert'
in'ex•pli•ca•bil'i•ty
in•ex'pli•ca•ble
in'ex•press'i•bil'i•ty
in'ex•press'i•ble
in'ex•tin'guish•a•ble
in•ex'tri•ca•bil'i•ty
in•ex'tri•ca•ble
in•fal'li•bil'i•ty
in•fal'li•ble
in'fa•mous
in'fa•my
in'fan•cy
in'fant
in•fan'ti•cide'
in'fan•tile'
in'fan•til•ism
in'fan•try
in'fan•try•man
in•fat'u•ate', -at'ed,
    -at'ing
in•fat'u•a'tion
in•fect'
in•fec'tion
in•fec'tious
in•fec'tive

in·fe·lic′i·tous
in′fe·lic′i·ty
in·fer′, -ferred′, -fer-
  ring
in·fer′a·ble
in′fer·ence
in′fer·en′tial
in·fe′ri·or
in·fe′ri·or′i·ty
in·fer′nal
in·fer′no *pl.* -nos
in·fest′
in·fer′tile
in′fer·til′i·ty
in·fest′
in′fes·ta′tion
in′fi·del
in′fi·del′i·ty
in′field′
in′fight′ing
in′fil·trate′, -trat′ed,
  -trat′ing
in′fil·tra′tion
in′fi·nite
in·fin′i·tes′i·mal
in·fin′i·tive
in·fin′i·ty
in·firm′
in·fir′ma·ry
in·fir′mi·ty
in′fix′ *n.*
in·fix′ *v.*
in·flame′, -flamed′,
  -flam′ing
in·flam′ma·ble
in′flam·ma′tion
in·flam′ma·to′ry

in·flate′, -flat′ed, -flat′-
  ing
in·fla′tion
in·fla′tion·ar′y
in·flect′
in·flec′tion
in·flec′tor
in·flex′i·bil′i·ty
in·flex′i·ble
in·flict′
in·flic′tion
in′flo·res′cence
in′flo·res′cent
in′flu·ence, -enced,
  -enc·ing
in′flu·en′tial
in′flu·en′za
in′flux′
in·form′
in·for′mal
in′for·mal′i·ty
in·for′mant
in′for·ma′tion
in·for′ma·tive
in·formed′
in·frac′tion
in·fra′red′
in′fra·son′ic
in′fra·struc′ture
in·fre′quence *also* in·
  fre′quen·cy
in·fre′quent
in·fringe′, -fringed′,
  -fring′ing
in·fringe′ment
in·fu′ri·ate′, -at′ed,
  -at′ing

in·fuse′, -fused′, -fus′-
  ing
in·fus′i·ble
in·fu′sion
in·gen′ious *(clever)*
  ♦*ingenuous*
in′gé·nue′
in′ge·nu′i·ty
in·gen′u·ous *(innocent)*
  ♦*ingenious*
in·gest′
in·ges′tion
in·glo′ri·ous
in′got
in·grain′
in·grate′
in·gra′ti·ate′, -at′ed,
  -at′ing
in·gra′ti·a′tion
in·grat′i·tude′
in·gre′di·ent
in′gress′
in′-group′
in′grown′
in′gui·nal
in·hab′it
in·hab′it·a·bil′i·ty
in·hab′it·a·ble
in·hab′i·tan·cy
in·hab′i·tant
in·ha′lant
in′ha·la′tion
in′ha·la′tor
in·hale′, -haled′, -hal′-
  ing
in′har·mo′ni·ous

in·here′, -hered′, -her-
  ing
in·her′ence
in·her′ent
in·her′it
in·her′it·a·ble
in·her′i·tance
in·her′i·tor
in·hib′it
in′hi·bi′tion
in·hib′i·tor
in·hib′i·to′ry
in·hos′pi·ta·ble
in′-house′ *adj.*
in·hu′man
in·hu·mane′
in′hu·man′i·ty
in·im′i·cal
in·im′i·ta·bil′i·ty
in·im′i·ta·ble
in·iq′ui·tous
in·iq′ui·ty *(sin)*
  ♦*inequity*
in·i′tial, -tialed *or*
  -tialled, -tial·ing *or*
  -tial·ling
in·i′ti·ate′, -at′ed, -at′-
  ing
in·i′ti·a′tion
in·i′ti·a·tive
in·i′ti·a·tor
in·ject′
in·jec′tion
in·jec′tor
in′ju·di′cious
in·junc′tion
in′jure, -jured, -jur·ing

in·ju′ri·ous
in′ju·ry
in·jus′tice
ink′blot′
ink′horn′
ink′ling
ink′stand′
ink′well′
ink′y
in′laid′
in′land
in′-law′
in′lay′ *n.*
in·lay′, -laid′, -lay′ing
in′let′
in′mate′
in me′di·as′ res′
in′ me·mo′ri·am
in′most′
inn *(hotel)*
  ♦*in*
in′nards′
in·nate′
in′ner
in′ner-cit′y *adj.*
in′ner·most′
in′ning
inn′keep′er
in′no·cence
in′no·cent
in·noc′u·ous
in′no·vate′, -vat′ed,
  -vat′ing
in′no·va′tion
in′no·va′tive
in′no·va′tor
in·nu·en′do *pl.* -does

in·nu′mer·a·ble
in·oc′u·late′, -lat′ed,
  -lat′ing
in·oc′u·la′tion
in·of·fen′sive
in·op′er·a·ble
in·op′er·a·tive
in·op′por·tune′
in·or′di·nate
in·or·gan′ic
in·pa′tient
in′put′
in′quest′
in·qui′e·tude′
in·quire′, -quired′,
  -quir′ing
in·quir′y
in·qui·si′tion
in·quis′i·tive
in·quis′i·tor
in·quis′i·to′ri·al
in′road′
in′rush′
in·sane′
in·san′i·ty
in·sa′tia·bil′i·ty
in·sa′tia·ble
in·sa′ti·ate
in·scribe′, -scribed′,
  -scrib′ing
in·scrip′tion
in·scru·ta·bil′i·ty
in·scru′ta·ble
in′sect′
in·sec′ti·cide′
in·sec′ti·vore′
in′sec·tiv′o·rous

in·se·cure'
in·se·cu'ri·ty
in·sem'i·nate', -nat'ed,
 -nat'ing
in·sem'i·na'tion
in·sem'i·na'tor
in·sen'sate'
in·sen'si·bil'i·ty
in·sen'si·ble
in·sen'si·tive
in·sen'si·tiv'i·ty
in·sen'tience
in·sen'tient
in·sep'a·ra·bil'i·ty
in·sep'a·ra·ble
in·sert' v.
in·sert' n.
in·ser'tion
in·set', -set', -set'ting
in·set' n.
in·shore'
in·side'
in·sid'er
in·sid'i·ous
in'sight' (understand-
 ing)
 ♦incite
in·sig'ni·a pl. -ni·a or
 -ni·as, also in·sig'ne
in'sig·nif'i·cance
in'sig·nif'i·cant
in'sin·cere'
in'sin·cer'i·ty
in·sin'u·ate', -at'ed,
 -at'ing
in·sin'u·a'tion
in·sin'u·a'tor

in·sip'id
in·sist'
in·sis'tence also in·
 sis'ten·cy
in·sis'tent
in·so·bri'e·ty
in·so·far'
in·sole'
in'so·lence
in'so·lent
in·sol'u·bil'i·ty
in·sol'u·ble
in·sol'ven·cy
in·sol'vent
in·som'ni·a
in·som'ni·ac'
in'so·much'
in·sou'ci·ance
in·sou'ci·ant
in·spect'
in·spec'tion
in·spec'tor
in'spi·ra'tion
in'spi·ra'tion·al
in·spire', -spired',
 -spir'ing
in·spir'it
in'sta·bil'i·ty
in·stall' also in·stal',
 -stalled', -stall'ing
in·stal·la'tion
in·stall'ment
In'sta·mat'ic®
in'stance, -stanced,
 -stanc'ing
in'stant
in'stan·ta'ne·ous

in·stead'
in'step'
in'sti·gate', -gat'ed,
 -gat'ing
in'sti·ga'tion
in'sti·ga'tor
in·still'
in'stil·la'tion
in'stinct'
in·stinc'tive
in'sti·tute', -tut'ed,
 -tut'ing
in'sti·tu'tion
in'sti·tu'tion·al·i·za'-
 tion
in'sti·tu'tion·al
in'sti·tu'tion·al·ize',
 -ized', -iz'ing
in'sti·tu'tor
in·struct'
in·struc'tion
in·struc'tive
in·struc'tor
in'stru·ment
in'stru·men'tal
in'stru·men'tal·ist
in'stru·men·tal'i·ty
in'stru·men·ta'tion
in'sub·or'di·nate
in'sub·or·di·na'tion
in'sub·stan'tial
in'sub·stan'ti·al'i·ty
in·suf'fer·a·ble
in'suf·fi'cien·cy
in'suf·fi'cient
in'su·lar
in'su·lar'i·ty

in'su•late', -lat'ed,
  -lat'ing
in'su•la'tion
in'su•la'tor
in'su•lin
in•sult' n.
in•sult' v.
in•su'per•a•bil'i•ty
in•su'per•a•ble
in•sup•port'a•ble
in•sur'a•ble
in•sur'ance
in•sure' (to protect with
  insurance, guarantee),
  -sured', -sur'ing
  ♦assure, ensure
in•sur'gence
in•sur'gen•cy
in•sur'gent
in•sur•mount'a•ble
in•sur•rec'tion
in•sur•rec'tion•ist
in•tact'
in•ta'glio pl. -glios
in•take'
in•tan•gi•bil'i•ty
in•tan'gi•ble
in'te•ger
in'te•gral
in'te•grate', -grat'ed,
  -grat'ing
in'te•gra'tion
in'te•gra'tive
in'te•gra'tor
in•teg'ri•ty
in•teg'u•ment
in'tel•lect'

in'tel•lec'tu•al
in'tel•lec'tu•al•i•za'-
  tion
in'tel•lec'tu•al•ize',
  -ized', -iz'ing
in•tel'li•gence
in•tel'li•gent
in•tel'li•gent'si•a
in•tel'li•gi•bil'i•ty
in•tel'li•gi•ble
in•tem'per•ance
in•tem'per•ate
in•tend'
in•tense'
in•ten'si•fi•ca'tion
in•ten'si•fi'er
in•ten'si•fy', -fied',
  -fy'ing
in•ten'si•ty
in•ten'sive
in•tent'
in•ten'tion
in•ten'tion•al
in•ter', -terred', -ter'-
  ring
in'ter•act'
in'ter•ac'tion
in'ter•ac'tive
in'ter a'li•a
in'ter•breed', -bred',
  -breed'ing
in•ter'ca•lar'y
in•ter'ca•late', -lat'ed,
  -lat'ing
in•ter'ca•la'tion
in'ter•cede', -ced'ed,
  -ced'ing

in'ter•cel'lu•lar
in'ter•cept'
in'ter•cep'tion
in'ter•cep'tive
in'ter•cep'tor also in'-
  ter•cept'er
in'ter•ces'sion
in'ter•ces'sor
in'ter•ces'so•ry
in'ter•change' n.
in'ter•change',
  -changed', -chang'ing
in'ter•change'a•ble
in'ter•col•le'giate
in'ter•com'
in'ter•com•mu'ni•
  cate', -cat'ed, -cat'-
  ing
in'ter•con•nect'
in'ter•con'ti•nen'tal
in'ter•cos'tal
in'ter•course'
in'ter•de•nom'i•na'-
  tion•al
in'ter•de•pend'ence
in'ter•de•pend'ent
in'ter•dict'
in'ter•dic'tion
in'ter•dic'tor
in'ter•est
in'ter•face', -faced',
  -fac'ing
in'ter•fere', -fered',
  -fer'ing
in'ter•fer'ence
in'ter•fer'on'
in'ter•ga•lac'tic

in·ter·im
in·te'ri·or
in'ter·ject'
in'ter·jec'tion
in'ter·jec'tor
in'ter·lace', -laced',
   -lac'ing
in'ter·lard'
in'ter·leaf'
in'ter·leave', -leaved',
   -leav'ing
in'ter·line', -lined',
   -lin'ing
in'ter·lin'e·ar
in'ter·lock'
in'ter·loc'u·tor
in'ter·loc'u·to'ry
in'ter·lope', -loped',
   -lop'ing
in'ter·lude'
in'ter·lu'nar
in'ter·mar'riage
in'ter·mar'ry, -ried,
   -ry·ing
in'ter·me'di·ar'y
in'ter·me'di·ate
in·ter'ment
in'ter·mez'zo pl. -zos
   or -zi
in·ter'mi·na·ble
in'ter·min'gle, -gled,
   -gling
in'ter·mis'sion
in'ter·mit', -mit'ted,
   -mit'ting
in'ter·mit'tence
in'ter·mit'tent

in'ter·mix'
in'ter·mix'ture
in'tern' also in'terne'
in·ter'nal
in·ter'nal-com·bus'-
   tion engine
in·ter'nal·i·za'tion
in·ter'nal·ize', -ized',
   -iz'ing
in'ter·na'tion·al
in'ter·na'tion·al·ism
in'ter·na'tion·al·ist
in'ter·na'tion·al·i·za'-
   tion
in'ter·na'tion·al·ize',
   -ized', -iz'ing
in'ter·nec'ine'
in'tern·ee'
in·ter'nist
in·tern'ment
in'ter·per'son·al
in'ter·plan'e·tar'y
in'ter·play'
in·ter'po·late', -lat'ed,
   -lat'ing
in·ter'po·la'tion
in·ter'po·la'tor
in'ter·pose', -posed',
   -pos'ing
in'ter·po·si'tion
in·ter'pret
in·ter'pret·a·bil'i·ty
in·ter'pret·a·ble
in·ter'pre·ta'tion
in·ter'pre·ta'tive also
   in·ter'pre·tive
in·ter'pret·er

in'ter·ra'cial
in'ter·reg'nal
in'ter·reg'num pl.
   -nums or -na
in'ter·re·late', -lat'ed,
   -lat'ing
in'ter·re·la'tion
in'ter·re·la'tion·ship
in·ter'ro·gate', -gat'ed,
   -gat'ing
in·ter'ro·ga'tion
in'ter·rog'a·tive
in·ter'ro·ga'tor
in·ter'rog'a·to'ry
in'ter·rupt'
in'ter·rupt'er also in'-
   ter·rup'tor
in'ter·rup'tion
in'ter·scho·las'tic
in'ter·sect'
in'ter·sec'tion
in'ter·sperse',
   -spersed', -spers'ing
in'ter·sper'sion
in'ter·state' (between
   states)
♦intrastate
in'ter·stel'lar
in·ter'stice pl. -sti·ces'
in'ter·sti'tial
in'ter·twine', -twined',
   -twin'ing
in·ter·ur'ban
in'ter·val
in'ter·vene', -vened',
   -ven'ing
in'ter·ven'tion

in·ter·ven·tion·ism
in·ter·ven·tion·ist
in·ter·view'
in·ter·weave', -wove',
 -wov'en, weav'ing
in·tes·ta·cy
in·tes·tate'
in·tes·ti·nal
in·tes·tine
in·ti·ma·cy
in·ti·mate *adj. & n.*
in·ti·mate', -mat'ed,
 -mat'ing
in·ti·ma'tion
in·tim'i·date', -dat'ed,
 -dat'ing
in·tim'i·da'tion
in·tim'i·da'tor
in'to
in·tol'er·a·bil'i·ty
in·tol'er·a·ble
in·tol'er·ance
in·tol'er·ant
in·to·na'tion
in·tone', -toned', -ton'-
 ing
in to'to
in·tox'i·cant
in·tox'i·cate', -cat'ed,
 -cat'ing
in·tox'i·ca'tion
in·tox'i·ca'tor
in'tra·cel'lu·lar
in·trac'ta·bil'i·ty
in·trac'ta·ble
in'tra·mu'ral
in·tran'si·gence

in·tran'si·gent
in·tran'si·tive
in'tra·state' *(within a
 state)*
 ♦*interstate*
in'tra·u'ter·ine
in'tra·ve'nous
in·trep'id
in'tre·pid'i·ty
in'tri·ca·cy
in'tri·cate
in·trigue' *n.*
in·trigue', -trigued',
 -trigu'ing
in·trin'sic
in'tro·duce', -duced',
 -duc'ing
in'tro·duc'tion
in'tro·duc'to·ry
in'tro·it *also* In'tro·it
in'tro·spec'tion
in'tro·spec'tive
in'tro·ver'sion
in'tro·vert'
in·trude', -trud'ed,
 -trud'ing
in·tru'sion
in·tru'sive
in·tu'it
in'tu·i'tion
in·tu'i·tive
in'u·lin
in·un·date', -dat'ed,
 -dat'ing
in·un·da'tion
in·un·da'tor

in·ure', -ured', -ur'ing,
 also en·ure'
in·vade', -vad'ed,
 -vad'ing
in'va·lid *(ill)*
in·val'id *(null)*
in·val'i·date', -dat'ed,
 -dat'ing
in·val'i·da'tion
in·val'i·da'tor
in·val'u·a·ble
in·var'i·a·bil'i·ty
in·var'i·a·ble
in·var'i·ance
in·var'i·ant
in·va'sion
in·vec'tive
in·veigh'
in·vei'gle, -gled, -gling
in·vent'
in·ven'tion
in·ven'tive
in·ven'tor
in'ven·to'ry, -ried, -ry·
 ing
in·verse'
in·ver'sion
in·vert'
in·ver'te·brate
in·vest'
in·ves'ti·gate', -gat'ed,
 -gat'ing
in·ves'ti·ga'tion
in·ves'ti·ga'tive *also*
 in·ves'ti·ga·to'ry
in·ves'ti·ga'tor
in·ves'ti·ture'

in·vest'ment
in·ves'tor
in·vet'er·a·cy
in·vet'er·ate
in·vid'i·ous
in·vig'o·rate', -rat'ed,
  -rat'ing
in·vig'o·ra'tion
in·vin·ci·bil'i·ty
in·vin'ci·ble
in·vi'o·la·bil'i·ty
in·vi'o·la·ble
in·vi'o·late
in·vis·i·bil'i·ty
in·vis'i·ble
in'vi·ta'tion
in·vite', -vit'ed, -vit'ing
in'vo·ca'tion
in'voice', -voiced',
  -voic'ing
in·voke', -voked',
  -vok'ing
in·vol'un·tar'y
in'vo·lu'tion
in·volve', -volved',
  -volv'ing
in·volve'ment
in·vul'ner·a·bil'i·ty
in·vul'ner·a·ble
in'ward also in'wards
in'ward·ly
i'o·dide'
i'o·dine'
i'o·dize', -dized', -diz'-
  ing
i'on
i·on'ic

i'on·i·za'tion
i'on·ize', -ized', -iz'ing
i·on'o·sphere'
i·o'ta
IOU pl. IOU's or
  IOUs
I'o·wan
ip'e·cac'
ip'so fac'to
I·ra'ni·an
I·raq'i pl. I·raq'i or
  I·raq'is
i·ras·ci·bil'i·ty
i·ras'ci·ble
i·rate'
ire
ir'i·des'cence
ir'i·des'cent
i·rid'i·um
i'ris pl. i'ris·es or i'ri·
  des'
I'rish
irk'some
i'ron
i'ron·bound'
i'ron·clad'
i·ron'ic also i·ron'i·cal
i'ron·ing
i'ron·stone'
i'ron·ware'
i'ron·wood'
i'ron·work'
i'ron·works'
i'ro·ny
ir·ra'di·ate', -at'ed,
  -at'ing
ir·ra'di·a'tion

ir·ra'di·a'tor
ir·ra'tion·al
ir·ra'tion·al'i·ty
ir're·claim'a·ble
ir'rec·on·cil'a·ble
ir're·cov'er·a·ble
ir're·deem'a·ble
ir're·duc'i·ble
ir·ref'u·ta·bil'i·ty
ir·ref'u·ta·ble
ir·reg'u·lar
ir·reg'u·lar'i·ty
ir·rel'e·vance
ir·rel'e·vant
ir're·lig'ious
ir're·me'di·a·ble
ir're·mov'a·ble
ir·rep'a·ra·ble
ir're·place'a·ble
ir're·pres'si·bil'i·ty
ir're·pres'si·ble
ir're·proach'a·ble
ir're·sist'i·bil'i·ty
ir're·sist'i·ble
ir·res'o·lute'
ir're·spec'tive
ir're·spon'si·bil'i·ty
ir're·spon'si·ble
ir're·triev'a·ble
ir·rev'er·ence
ir·rev'er·ent
ir're·vers'i·bil'i·ty
ir're·vers'i·ble
ir·rev'o·ca·bil'i·ty
ir·rev'o·ca·ble
ir'ri·gate', -gat'ed,
  -gat'ing

ir'ri•ga'tion
ir'ri•ga'tor
ir•ri•ta•bil'i•ty
ir'ri•ta•ble
ir'ri•tant
ir'ri•tate', -tat'ed, -tat'-
  ing
ir'ri•ta'tion
ir'ri•ta'tor
ir•rupt'
ir•rup'tion
ir•rup'tive
is
is'chi•um *pl.* -chi•a
i'sin•glass'
Is'lam
Is•lam'ic
is'land
isle *(island)*
  ♦*aisle, I'll*
is'let *(small island)*
  ♦*eyelet*
is'n't
i'so•bar'
i'so•bar'ic
i'so•gam'ete'
i'so•gon'ic *also* i•sog'o•
  nal
i'so•late', -lat'ed, -lat'-
  ing
i•so•la'tion
i'so•la'tion•ism
i'so•la'tion•ist
i'so•la'tor
i'so•mer
i'so•mer'ic
i•som'er•ism

i'so•met'ric *also* i'so•
  met'ri•cal
i'so•mor'phic
i'so•mor'phism
i'so•mor'phous
i'so•oc'tane
i'so•prene'
i'so•pro'pyl alcohol
i•sos'ce•les'
i'so•therm'
i'so•ther'mal
i'so•tope'
i'so•top'ic
i'so•trop'ic
i•sot'ro•py *also* i•sot'-
  ro•pism
Is•rae'li *pl.* -rael'i *or*
  -rael'is
Is'ra•el•ite'
is'su•ance
is'sue, -sued, -su•ing
isth'mi•an
isth'mus *pl.* -mus•es *or*
  -mi'
it
I•tal'ian
i•tal'ic
i•tal'i•ci•za'tion
i•tal'i•cize', -cized',
  -ciz'ing
itch'y
i'tem
i'tem•i•za'tion
i'tem•ize', -ized', -iz'-
  ing
it'er•ate', -at'ed, -at'-
  ing

it'er•a'tion
it'er•a'tive
i•tin'er•ant
i•tin'er•ar'y
its *pron.*
it's *contraction*
it•self'
i'vied
i'vo•ry
i'vy

J

jab, jabbed, jab'bing
jab'ber
jab•ot'
jac'a•ran'da
jack'al
jack'a•napes'
jack'ass'
jack'boot'
jack'daw'
jack'et
jack'ham'mer
jack'-in-the-box' *pl.*
  jack'-in-the-box'es *or*
  jacks'-in-the-box'
jack'-in-the-pul'pit
jack'knife', -knifed',
  -knif'ing
jack'-of-all'-trades'
  pl. jacks'-of-all'-
  trades'
jack'-o'-lan'tern
jack'pot'

jack'screw'
jack'straw'
jac'quard' also Jac'-
    quard'
jad'ed
jade'ite'
jag, jag·ged, jag'ging
jag'uar'
jai' a·lai'
jail'bird'
jail'break'
jail'er also jail'or
ja·lop'y
ja'lou·sie (shutter)
    ♦jealousy
jam (preserves)
    ♦jamb
jam (to wedge),
    jammed, jam'ming
    ♦jamb
Ja·mai'can
jamb (door post)
    ♦jam
jam'bo·ree'
jam'-pack' v.
jam'-up' n.
jan'gle, -gled, -gling
jan'i·tor
Jan'u·ar'y
ja·pan', -panned',
    -pan'ning
Ja(•)'a·nese' pl. -nese'
jape, japed, jap'ing
jap'er·y
ja·pon'i·ca
jar, jarred, jar'ring
jar'di·nière'

jar'ful' pl. -fuls'
jar'gon
jas'mine also jes'sa·
    mine
jas'per
jaun'dice
jaun'diced
jaunt
jaun'ty
Jav'a·nese' pl. -nese'
jave'lin
jaw'bone', -boned',
    -bon'ing
jaw'break'er
Jay'cee'
jay'hawk'er
jay'vee'
jay'walk'
jazz'y
jeal'ous
jeal'ous·y (suspicion)
    ♦jalousie
jeans
jeep
jeer
Je·ho'vah
je·june'
je·ju'num pl. -na
jell (to congeal)
    ♦gel
jel'lied
Jell'-O®
jel'ly, -lied, -ly·ing
jel'ly·bean'
jel'ly·fish' pl. -fish' or
    -fish'es
jen'net

jen'ny
jeop'ard·ize', -ized',
    -iz'ing
jeop'ard·y
jer'e·mi'ad
jerk
jer'kin
jerk'wa'ter
jerk'y
jer'ry·build', -built',
    -build'ing
jer'sey pl. -seys
Je·ru'sa·lem arti-
    choke
jest (joke)
    ♦gist
Jes'u·it
jet, jet'ted, jet'ting
jet'lin'er
jet'port'
jet'-pro·pelled'
jet'sam
jet'ti·son
jet'ty
jew'el, -eled or -elled,
    -el·ing or -el·ling
jew'el·ry
jew'el·weed'
Jew'ish
Jew'ry
jew's'-harp' also
    jews'-harp'
jez'e·bel'
jib, jibbed, jib'bing
jibe (to shift a sail,
    agree), jibed, jib'ing
    ♦gibe

jif'fy
jig, jigged, jig'ging
jig'ger
jig'gle, -gled, -gling
jig'saw'
jilt
jim'my, -mied, -my·ing
jim'son·weed'
jin'gle, -gled, -gling
jin'go pl. -goes
jin'go·ish
jin'go·ism
jin'go·ist
jin'go·is'tic
jin'ni pl. jinn
jin·rik'sha or jin·rick'-
    sha
jinx
jit'ney pl. -neys
jit'ter
jit'ter·bug', -bugged',
    -bug'ging
jit'ter·y
jive
job, jobbed, job'bing
job'ber
job'ber·y
job'hold'er
jock'ey
jock'ey pl. -eys
jock'strap'
jo·cose'
jo·cos'i·ty
joc'u·lar
joc'u·lar'i·ty
joc'und
jo·cun'di·ty

jodh'purs
jog, jogged, jog'ging
jog'ger
jog'gle, -gled, -gling
john'ny·cake'
John'ny-come'-late'-
    ly
joie de vi'vre
join'er
joint'ed
joint'er
join'ture
joist
joke, joked, jok'ing
jok'er
joke'ster
jol'li·fi·ca'tion
jol'li·ty
jol'ly
jolt
jon'quil
Jor·da'ni·an
josh
jos'tle, -tled, -tling
jot, jot'ted, jot'ting
joule
jounce, jounced,
    jounc'ing
jour'nal
jour'nal·ese'
jour'nal·ism
jour'nal·ist
jour'nal·is'tic
jour'ney pl. -neys
jour'ney·man
joust
jo'vi·al

jo'vi·al'i·ty
jowl
joy'ful
joy'ous
ju'bi·lance
ju'bi·lant
ju'bi·la'tion
ju'bi·lee'
Ju·da'ic also Ju·da'i·
    cal
Ju'da·ism
Ju'das
judge, judged, judg'ing
judge advocate pl.
    judge advocates
judge'ship'
judg'ment also judge'-
    ment
ju'di·ca·ble
ju'di·ca·to'ry
ju'di·ca·ture'
ju·di'cial (of the law)
    ♦judicious
ju·di'ci·ar'y
ju·di'cious (wise)
    ♦judicial
ju'do
jug
jug'ger·naut'
jug'gle, -gled, -gling
jug'gler
jug'u·lar
juice, juiced, juic'ing
juic'er
juic'y
ju·jit'su also ju·jut'su,
    jiu·jit'su, jiu·jut'su

ju'jube'
juke box
ju'lep
Jul'ian calendar
ju'li•enne'
Ju•ly'
jum'ble, -bled, -bling
jum'bo pl. -bos
jump'er
jump'-start'
jump'y
jun'co pl. -cos
junc'tion
junc'ture
June
jun'gle
jun'ior
ju'ni•per
junk
jun'ket
junk'ie also junk'y
jun'ta
Ju'pi•ter
ju•rid'i•cal
ju•ris•dic'tion
ju'ris•pru'dence
ju'rist
ju'ror
ju'ry
just
jus'tice
jus'ti•fi'a•ble
jus'ti•fi•ca'tion
jus'ti•fy,' -fied', -fy'ing
just'ly
jut, jut'ted, jut'ting
jute

ju've•nile'
ju've•nil'i•ty
jux'ta•pose', -posed',
   -pos'ing
jux'ta•po•si'tion

K

ka•bob'
ka•bu'ki
Kai'ser
kale
ka•lei'do•scope'
ka•lei'do•scop'ic
ka•mi•ka'ze
kan'ga•roo' pl. -roos'
Kan'san
ka•o'•lin also ka•o•line
ka'pok'
kap'pa
ka•put'
kar'a•kul
kar'at (measure), also
   car'at
   ♦caret, carrot
ka•ra'te
kar'ma
ka'sha
ka'ty•did'
kay'ak'
ka•zoo' pl. -zoos'
ke•bab' also ke•bob'
ked'ger•ee'
keel'boat'
keel'haul'

keen'ly
keep, kept, keep'ing
keep'er
keep'sake'
keg
kelp
kel'vin
ken, kenned or kent,
   ken'ning
ken'nel
ke'no
Ken•tuck'i•an
kep'i pl. -is
ker'a•tin
ke•rat'i•nous
ker'chief
ker'nel (grain)
   ♦colonel
ker'o•sene' also ker'o•
   sine'
kes'trel
ketch
ketch'up also catch'up,
   cat'sup
ket'tle
ket'tle•drum'
key (implement, island)
   ♦cay, quay
key'board'
key'hole'
key'note', -not'ed,
   -not'ing
key'stone'
key'stroke'
khak'i pl. -is
khan
kib•butz' pl. -but•zim'

kib'itz
ki'bosh'
kick'back' n.
kick'off' n.
kid, kid'ded, kid'ding
kid'dy also kid'die
kid'nap', -naped or
  -napped', -nap'ing or
  -nap'ping
kid'nap'er or kid'nap'-
  per
kid'ney pl. -neys
kid'skin'
kill (to slay)
  ♦kiln
kill'deer' pl. -deer' or
  -deers'
kil'li·fish' pl. -fish' or
  -fish'es
kill'joy'
kiln (oven)
  ♦kill
ki'lo pl. -los
ki'lo·bit'
ki'lo·cy·cle
kil'o·gram'
kil'o·gram'-me'ter
ki'lo·hertz'
kil'o·me'ter
kil'o·met'ric
kil'o·ton'
kil'o·watt'
kil'o·watt'-hour'
kilt
kil'ter
ki·mo'no pl. -nos
kin

kin'der·gar'ten
kind'heart'ed
kin'dle, -dled, -dling
kin'dling
kind'ly
kind'ness
kin'dred
kin'e·mat'ics
kin'e·scope'
kin·es·the'sia
ki·net'ic
ki·net'ics
king'bird'
king'bolt'
king'dom
king'fish'er
kin'folk' also kins'-
  folk', kin'folks'
king'pin'
king'-size' also
  king'-sized'
kink'a·jou'
kink'y
kin'ship'
kins'man
kins'wom'an
ki·osk'
kip'per
kirsch
kis'met
kiss'er
kit
kitch'en
kitch'en·ette'
kitch'en·ware'
kite, kit'ed, kit'ing
kith

kitsch
kit'ten
kit'ty
kit'ty-cor'nered
ki'wi
Klans'man
Kleen'ex'®
klep'to·ma'ni·a
klep'to·ma'ni·ac'
klieg light
klutz
knack
knack'wurst' also
  knock'wurst'
knap'sack'
knave (roque)
  ♦nave
knav'er·y
knav'ish
knead (to mix)
  ♦need
knee'cap'
knee'-deep'
knee'-high'
knee'hole'
kneel, knelt or
  kneeled, kneel'ing
knee'pad'
knell
knick'er·bock'ers
knick'ers
knick'knack'
knife pl. knives
knife, knifed, knif'ing
knife'-edge'
knight (soldier)
  ♦night

knight′hood′

knish

knit *(to intertwine yarn),* knit or knit′-ted, knit′ting

♦*nit*

knob′by

knock′a·bout′

knock′down′ *adj. & n.*

knock′-knee′

knock-kneed″

knock′off′ *n.*

knock′out′ *n.*

knoll

knot *(to tie),* knot′ted, knot′ting

♦*not*

knot′hole′

knot′ty

know *(to perceive),* knew, known, know′ing

♦*no*

know′-how′

know′-it-all′

knowl′edge

knowl′edge·a·ble

know′-noth′ing

knuck′le, -led, -ling

knuck′le·bone′

knurl

KO *pl.* KO′s

KO, KO′d, KO′ing

ko·a′la

Ko′di·ak bear

kohl *(comestic)*

♦*coal*

kohl·ra′bi *pl.* -bies

kook′a·bur′ra

kook′y

Ko·ran′

Ko·re′an

ko′sher

kow′tow′

kraal

krill

Kru′ger·rand′

kryp′ton′

ku′dos′

Ku′ Klux′ Klan′

küm′mel

kum′quat′

kung′ fu′

kwash′i·or′kor

ky′mo·graph′

Kyr′i·e′

L

la′bel, -beled *or* -belled, -bel·ing *or* -bel·ling

la′bi·al

la′bi·um *pl.* -bi·a

la′bor

lab′o·ra·to′ry

la·bo′ri·ous

la′bor·ite′

la′bor·sav′ing

Lab′ra·dor retriever

la·bur′num

lab′y·rinth′

lab′y·rin′thine′

lac *(resin)*

♦*lack*

lace, laced, lac′ing

lac′er·ate′, -at′ed, -at′-ing

lac′er·a′tion

lac′er·a′tive

lace′wing′

lach′ry·mal

lach′ry·mose′

lack *(deficiency)*

♦*lac*

lack′a·dai′si·cal

lack′ey *pl.* -eys

lack′lus′ter

la·con′ic

lac′quer

la·crosse′

lac′ta·ry

lac′tase′

lac′tate′, -tat′ed, -tat′-ing

lac·ta′tion

lac′te·al

lac′tic

lac·tif′er·ous

lac′to·ba·cil′lus *pl.* -li′

lac′tose′

la·cu′na *pl.* -nae *or* -nas

lac′y

lad

lad′der

lade *(to load),* lad′ed,

lad′en *or* lad′ed,
  lad′ing
  ♦*laid*
la′dle, -dled, -dling
la′dy
la′dy•bird′
la′dy•bug′
la′dy•fin′ger
la′dy•love′
lady in waiting *pl.* la-
  dies in waiting
la′dy-kill′er
la′dy•like′
la′dy•ship′
la′dy′s-slip′per
La′e•trile′
lag, lagged, lag′ging
la′ger
lag′gard
la•gniappe′
la•goon′
la′ic *also* la′i•cal
lair
laird
lais′sez faire′
la′i•ty
lake
lam *(to thrash, escape),*
  lammed, lam′ming
  ♦*lamb*
la′ma *(monk)*
  ♦*llama*
La•maze′
lamb *(young sheep)*
  ♦*lam*
lam•baste′, -bast′ed,
  -bast′ing

lamb′da
lam′ben•cy
lam′bent
lamb′skin′
lame *(disabled),* lam′er,
  lam′est
lame *(to cripple),*
  lamed, lam′ing
la•mé′ *(metallic fabric)*
la•mel′la *pl.* -lae′ *or*
  -las
la•mel′late′
lam•el•la′tion
la•ment′
lam′en•ta•ble
lam′en•ta′tion
lam′i•na *pl.* -nae′ *or*
  -nas
lam′i•nar *also* lam′i•
  nal
lam′i•nate′, -nat′ed,
  -nat′ing
lam′i•na′tion
lam′i•na′tor
lamp′black′
lamp′light′
lam•poon′
lam•poon′er *also* lam•
  poon′ist
lam•poon′er•y
lamp′post′
lam′prey′ *pl.* -preys
la•na′i′ *pl.* -is′
Lan•cas′tri•an
lance, lanced, lanc′ing
lance′let
lan′cet

lan′dau
land′fall′
land′-grant′ *adj.*
land′hold′er
land′ing
land′la′dy
land′locked′
land′lord′
land′lub′ber
land′mark′
land′own′er
land′-poor′ *adj.*
land′scape′, -scaped′,
  -scap′ing
land′scap′ist
land′slide′
land′ward *also* land′-
  wards
lane *(road)*
  ♦*lain*
lan′guage
lan′guid
lan′guish
lan′guor
lank′y
lan′o•lin
lan′tern
lan′tha•nide′
lan′tha•num
lan′yard
Lao *pl.* Lao *or* Laos,
  also La•o′tian
lap *(to fold),* lapped,
  lap′ping
  ♦*Lapp*
la•pel′
lap′i•dar′i•an

lap'i·dar'y

lap'in

lap'is laz'u·li

Lapp *(native of Lap-
land)*

♦*lap*

lap'per

lap'pet

lapse, lapsed, laps'ing

lap'wing'

lar'board

lar'ce·nous

lar'ce·ny

larch

lard

lar'der

large, larg'er, larg'est

large'ly

large'mouth' bass

large-scale'

lar·gess' *also* lar·gesse'

larg'ish

lar'go *pl.* -gos

lar'i·at

lark'spur'

lar'rup

lar'va *pl.* -vae

lar'val

la·ryn'ge·al *also* la·
ryn'gal

lar'yn·gi'tis

la·ryn'go·scope'

lar'ynx *pl.* la·ryn'ges
or lar'ynx·es

la·sa'gna *also* la·sa'gne

las·civ'i·ous

la'ser

lash'ing

lass

las'sie

las'si·tude'

las'so *pl.* -sos *or* -soes

Las'tex®

last'ing

latch'key'

latch'string'

late, lat'er, lat'est

late'com'er

la·teen'

late'ly

la'ten·cy

la'tent

lat'er·al

la'tex' *pl.* -ti·ces' *or*
-tex·es

lath *(narrow strip), pl.*
laths

lathe *(shaping machine)*

lathe *(to shape)*, lathed,
lath'ing

lath'er

lath'er·y *adj.*

Lat'in

Lat'in-A·mer'i·can

lat'i·tude'

lat'i·tu'din·al

lat'i·tu'di·nar'i·an

lat'i·tu'di·nar'i·an·
ism

la·trine'

lat'ter

lat'ter-day'

Lat'ter-day' Saints

lat'tice

lat'tice·work'

Lat'vi·an

laud'a·bil'i·ty

laud'a·ble

lau'da·num

laud'a·to'ry

laugh'a·ble

laugh'ing·stock'

laugh'ter

launch'er

laun'der

laun'dress

Laun'dro·mat'®

laun'dry

lau're·ate

lau'rel

la'va

lav'a·liere'

lav'a·to'ry

lave, laved, lav'ing

lav'en·der

lav'ish

law'-a·bid'ing

law'break'er

law'ful

law'giv'er

law'less

law'mak'er

lawn

law·ren'ci·um

law'suit'

law'yer

lax'a·tive

lax'i·ty

lay *(to place)*, laid, lay'-
ing

♦*lei*

lay *(secular)*
　♦*lei*
lay *(ballad)*
　♦*lei*
lay'a•way' *n.*
lay'er
lay•ette'
lay'man
lay'off' *n.*
lay'out' *n.*
lay'o'ver *n.*
lay'-up' *n.*
laze, lazed, laz'ing
la'zy
la'zy•bones'
lea *(meadow)*
　♦*lee*
leach *(to percolate away)*
　♦*leech*
lead *(element)*
　♦*led*
lead *(to guide),* led, lead'ing
　♦*lied (song)*
lead'en
lead'er *(guide)*
　♦*lieder*
lead'er•ship'
lead'-in' *n.*
lead'ing
lead'off' *adj. & n.*
lead'-time'
leaf *(plant part),* pl. leaves
　♦*lief*
leaf'hop'per

leaf'let
leaf'stalk'
leaf'y
league, leagued, leagu'ing
leak *(escape)*
　♦*leek*
leak'age
leak'y
lean *(thin)*
　♦*lien*
lean *(to incline),* leaned or leant, lean'ing
　♦*lien*
lean'-to' *pl.* -tos'
leap, leaped or leapt, leap'ing
leap'frog', -frogged', -frog'ging
learn, learned or learnt, learn'ing
learn'ed *adj.*
lease, leased, leas'ing
lease'hold'
leash
least'wise'
leath'er
leath'er•neck'
leath'er•y
leave, left, leav'ing
leaved *adj.*
leav'en
leave'-tak'ing
leav'ings
Leb'a•nese' *pl.* -nese'
lech'er
lech'er•ous

lech'er•y
lec'i•thin
lec'tern
lec'tor
lec'ture, -tured, -tur•ing
ledge
ledg'er
lee *(shelter)*
　♦*lea*
leech *(blood-sucker, parasite)*
　♦*leach*
leek *(plant)*
　♦*leak*
leer'y
lees
lee'ward
lee'way'
left'-hand' *adj.*
left'-hand'ed
left'-hand'er
left'ist
left'o'ver *adj.*
left'o'vers
left'-wing' *adj.*
left'y
leg, legged, leg'ging
leg'a•cy
le'gal
le'gal•ism
le'gal•ist
le'gal•is'tic
le•gal'i•ty
le'gal•i•za'tion
le'gal•ize', -ized', -iz'-ing

leg'ate
leg'a·tee'
le·ga'tion
le·ga'to *pl.* -tos
leg'end
leg'en·dar'y
leg'er·de·main'
leg'ged
leg'ging
leg'gy
leg'horn'
leg'i·bil'i·ty
leg'i·ble
le'gion
le'gion·ar'y
le'gion·naire'
leg'is·late', -lat'ed,
   -lat'ing
leg'is·la'tion
leg'is·la'tive
leg'is·la'tor
leg'is·la'ture
le·git'
le·git'i·ma·cy
le·git'i·mate
le·git'i·mize', -mized',
   -miz'ing
leg'-of-mut'ton
leg'ume'
le·gu'mi·nous
leg'work'
lei *(garland)*
   ◆*lay*
lei'sure
lei'sured
leit'mo·tif' *also* leit'-
   mo·tiv'

lem'ma *pl.* -mas *or*
   ma·ta
lem'ming
lem'on
lem'on·ade'
le'mur
lend, lent, lend'ing
length'en
length'wise'
length'y
le'ni·en·cy *also* le'ni·
   ence
le'ni·ent
Len'in·ist
len'i·tive
lens
Lent'en
len'til
len'to
Le'o
le'o·nine'
leop'ard
le'o·tard'
lep'er
lep'i·dop'ter·ist
lep're·chaun'
lep'ro·sy
lep'rous
lep'ton'
les'bi·an
le'sion
less
les·see'
less'en *(to decrease)*
   ◆*lesson*
less'er *(smaller)*
   ◆*lessor*

les'son *(instruction)*
   ◆*lessen*
les'sor *(landlord)*
   ◆*lesser*
lest
let, let, let'ting
let'down' *n.*
le'thal
le·thal'i·ty
le·thar'gic
leth'ar·gy
let'ter
let'ter·box'
let'ter·head'
let'ter·ing
let'ter-per'fect
let'ter·press'
let'tuce
let'up' *n.*
leu'co·plast'
leu·ke'mi·a
leu'ko·cyte' *also* leu'-
   co·cyte'
le·va'tor *pl.* lev'a·to'res
lev·ee *(embankment)*
   ◆*levy*
lev'el, -eled *or* -elled,
   -el·ing *or* -el·ling
lev'el·er *also* lev'el·ler
lev'el·head'ed
lev'er
lev'er·age
le·vi'a·than
Le'vi's'®
lev'i·tate', -tat'ed,
   -tat'ing
lev'i·ta'tion

lev'i•ta'tor
lev'i•ty
lev'y *(to tax)*, -ied,
    -y•ing
    ♦*levee*
lewd'ly
lex'i•cal
lex'i•cog'ra•pher
lex'i•co•graph'ic *also*
    lex'i•co•graph'i•cal
lex'i•cog'ra•phy
lex'i•con'
li'a•bil'i•ty
li'a•ble *(responsible)*
    ♦*libel*
li'ai•son'
li•an'a *also* li•ane'
li'ar *(one who lies)*
    ♦*lyre*
li•ba'tion
li'bel *(to defame)*,
    -beled *or* -belled,
    -bel•ing *or* -bel•ling
    ♦*liable*
li'bel•ous
lib'er•al
lib'er•al•ism
lib'er•al'i•ty
lib'er•al•i•za'tion
lib'er•al•ize', -ized',
    -iz'ing
lib'er•a'tion
lib'er•a'tion•ist
lib'er•a'tor
lib'er•tar'i•an

lib'er•tine'
lib'er•ty
li•bid'i•nal
li•bid'i•nous
li•bi'do *pl.* -dos
Li'bra
li•brar'i•an
li'brar•y
li•bret'tist
li•bret'to *pl.* -tos *or* -ti
Lib'y•an
li'cens•a•ble
li'cense, -censed,
    -cens•ing
li'cen•see'
li•cen'ti•ate
li•cen'tious
li'chen *(plant)*
    ♦*liken*
lic'it
lick'e•ty-split'
lick'ing
lic'o•rice
lid
lie *(to recline)*, lay, lain,
    ly'ing
    ♦*lye*
lie *(to deceive)*, lied, ly'-
    ing
    ♦*lye*
lied *(song)*, *pl.* lie'der
    ♦*lead (to guide)*
lief *(readily)*
    ♦*leaf*
liege
lien *(claim)*
    ♦*lean*

lieu
lieu•ten'an•cy
lieu•ten'ant
life *pl.* lives
life'blood'
life'boat'
life'guard'
life'less
life'like'
life line *also* life'line'
life'long'
life'sav'er
Life Saver®
life'-size' *also* life'-
    sized'
life'style' *also* life'-
    style', life' style'
life'time'
life'work'
lift'off' *n.*
lig'a•ment
lig'a•ture
light, light'ed *or* lit,
    light'ing
light'en
light'er
light'face'
light'faced'
light'-fin'gered
light'-foot'ed
light'head'ed
light'heart'ed
light'house'
light'ing
light'ness
light'ning
light'ship'

light'some
light'weight'
light'-year'
lig'ne·ous
lig'nin
lig'nite'
lig'ro·in
lik'a·ble *also* like'a·ble
like, liked, lik'ing
like'li·hood'
like'ly
like'-mind'ed
lik'en *(to compare)*
 ♦*lichen*
like'ness
like'wise
lik'ing
li'lac
Lil'li·pu'tian
lilt
lil'y
lily of the valley *pl.*
 lil'ies of the valley
lil'y-white'
li'ma bean
limb *(appendage)*
 ♦*limn*
lim'ber
lim'bo *pl.* -bos
Lim'burg'er cheese
lime'ade'
lime'light'
lim'er·ick
lime'stone'
lim'it
lim'it·a·ble
lim'i·ta'tion

lim'it·ed
limn *(to draw)*
 ♦*limb*
lim'ner
li'mo·nite'
lim'ou·sine'
lim'pet
lim'pid
lim·pid'i·ty
limp'ly
lim'y
lin'age *(number of
 lines)*
 ♦*lineage*
linch'pin'
lin'den
line, lined, lin'ing
lin'e·age *(ancestry)*
 ♦*linage*
lin'e·al
lin'e·a·ment
lin'e·ar
line'back'er
line'man
lin'en
lin'er
lines'man
line'-up' *n., also*
 line'up'
ling *pl.* ling *or* lings
lin'ger
lin'ge·rie'
lin'go *pl.* -goes
lin'gua fran'ca
lin'gual
lin·gui'ne *also* lin·gui'-
 ni

lin'guist
lin·guis'tic
lin·guis'tics
lin'i·ment
lin'ing
link'age
links *(golf course)*
 ♦*lynx*
lin'net
li·no'le·um
Li'no·type'®, -typed',
 -typ'ing
lin'seed'
lint
lin'tel
li'on
li'on·ess
li'on·heart'ed
li'on·i·za'tion
li'on·ize', -ized', -iz'ing
lip
lip'ase'
lip'id *also* lip'ide'
lip'oid' *also* li·poi'dal
lip'-read', -read',
 -read'ing
lip'stick'
lip'synch'
liq'ue·fac'tion
liq'ue·fy', -fied', -fy'-
 ing
li·queur'
liq'uid
liq'ui·date', -dat'ed,
 -dat'ing
liq'ui·da'tion
li·quid'i·ty

liq'uor
li'ra *pl.* -re *or* -ras
lisle
lisp
lis'some
lis'ten
list'ing
list'less
lit'a•ny
li'tchi *also* li'chee, ly'-
　chee
li'ter
lit'er•a•cy
lit'er•al *(verbatim)*
　♦*littoral*
lit'er•al•ism
lit'er•ar'y
lit'er•ate
lit'er•a'ti
lit'er•a•ture'
lithe, lith'er, lith'est
lithe'some
lith'i•um
lith'o•graph'
li•thog'ra•pher
lith'o•graph'ic *also*
　lith'o•graph'i•cal
li•thog'ra•phy
li•thol'o•gy
lith'o•sphere'
Lith•u•a'ni•an
lit'i•gant
lit'i•gate', -gat'ed,
　-gat'ing
lit'i•ga'tion
lit'i•ga'tor
li•ti'gious

lit'mus
lit'ter
lit'ter•bug'
lit'tle, lit'tler *or* less,
　lit'tlest *or* least
lit'tle•neck'
lit'to•ral *(coastal re-
　gion)*
　♦*literal*
li•tur'gi•cal
lit'ur•gy
liv'a•ble *also* live'a•ble
live, lived, liv'ing
live'-in' *adj.*
live'li•hood'
live'long'
live'ly
li'ven
liv'er
liv'er•ied
liv'er•wort'
liv'er•wurst'
liv'er•y
live'stock'
liv'id
liv'ing
liz'ard
lla'ma *(animal)*
　♦*lama*
lla'no *pl.* -nos
lo *interj.*
　♦*low*
load *(weight)*
　♦*lode*
load'ed
loaf *pl.* loaves

loaf, loafed, loaf'ing,
　loafs
loaf'er
loam'y
loan *(money, borrow-
　ing)*
　♦*lone*
loan'-word' *also*
　loan'word'
loath *(reluctant)*
loathe *(to detest),*
　loathed, loath'ing
loath'some
lob, lobbed, lob'bing
lo'bar
lob'by, -bied, -by•ing
lob'by•ist
lobe
lobed
lo•be'li•a
lob'lol'ly
lo•bot'o•my
lob'ster
lo'cal
lo•cale'
lo•cal'i•ty
lo'cal•i•za'tion
lo'cal•ize', -ized',
　-iz'ing
lo'cate', -cat'ed, -cat'-
　ing
lo•ca'tion
loc'a•tive
lo'ca'tor
loch *(lake)*
lock *(mechanism,
　strand of hair)*

lock′er
lock′et
lock′jaw′
lock′out′ *n.*
lock′smith′
lock′up′ *n.*
lo′co *pl.* -cos
lo′co•mo′tion
lo′co•mo′tive
lo′co•weed′
lo′cus *pl.* -ci′
lo′cust
lo•cu′tion
lode *(ore deposit)*
  ♦*load*
lode′star′
lode′stone′
lodge, lodged, lodg′ing
lodg′ment *also* lodge′-ment
lo′ess
loft
loft′y
log, logged, log′ging
lo′gan•ber′ry
log′a•rithm′
log′a•rith′mic *also* log′a•rith′mi•cal
log′book′
loge
log′ger
log′ger•head′
log•gi•a
log′ging
log′ic
log′i•cal
lo•gi′cian

lo•gis′tic *also* lo•gis′ti•cal
lo•gis′tics
log′jam′
lo′go *pl.* -gos
lo′go•type′
log′roll′ing
lo′gy
loin′cloth′
loi′ter
loll
lol′la•pa•loo′za
lol′li•pop′ *also* lol′ly•pop′
lone *(solitary)*
  ♦*loan*
lone′ly
lon′er
lone′some
long′boat′
long′bow′
long′-dis′tance *adj.*
lon•gev′i•ty
long′hair′
long′haired′
long′hand′
long′horn′
long′ing
lon′gi•tude′
lon•gi•tu′di•nal
long′leaf′ pine
long′-lived′
long′-play′ing
long′-range′
long′shore′man
long′-sight′ed
long′-stand′ing

long′-suf′fer•ing
long′-term′
long′-time′
long′-wind′ed
look′ing glass
look′out′ *n.*
look′-up′
loom
loon′y
loop *(circular or oval figure)*
  ♦*loupe*
loop′hole′
loose, loos′er, loos′est
loose′-joint′ed
loose′-leaf′
loos′en
loot *(spoils)*
  ♦*lute*
lop, lopped, lop′ping
lope, loped, lop′ing
lop′-eared′
lop′sid′ed
lo•qua′cious
lo•quac′i•ty
lo′ran′
lord′ly
lord′ship′
lore
lor•gnette′
lor′ry
lose, lost, los′ing
loss
lost
lot
lo′tion
lot′ter•y

lot'to

lo'tus *pl.* -tus•es

loud'ly

loud'mouth'

loud'mouthed'

loud'speak'er

lounge, lounged, loung'ing

loupe *(magnifying glass)*
  ♦*loop*

louse *pl.* lice

louse, loused, lous'ing

lous'y

lout'ish

lou'ver *also* lou'vre

lov'a•ble *also* love'a•ble

love, loved, lov'ing

love'bird'

love'less

love'lorn'

love'ly

lov'er

love'sick'

lov'ing

low *(having little height)*
  ♦*lo*

low *(to moo)*
  ♦*lo*

low'born'

low'boy'

low'brow'

low'-down' *adj.*

low'down' *n.*

low'er *(below)*

low'er *(to scowl), also* lour

low'er-case', -cased', -cas'ing

low'er-class' *adj.*

low'er•most'

low'-key'

low'-keyed'

low'land

low'ly

low'-mind'ed'

low'-pres'sure *adj.*

low'-rise'

low'-test' *adj.*

lox *(smoked salmon)*
  ♦*locks*

loy'al

loy'al•ist

loy'al•ty

loz'enge

lu•au'

lub'ber

lu'bri•cant

lu'bri•cate', -cat'ed, -cat'ing

lu'bri•ca'tion

lu'bri•ca'tor

lu•bri'cious

lu'cent

lu'cid

lu•cid'i•ty

Lu'ci•fer

Lu'cite'®

luck'y

lu'cra•tive

lu'cre

lu•di•crous

lug, lugged, lug'ging

lug'gage

lu•gu'bri•ous

luke'warm'

lull

lull'a•by'

lum•ba'go

lum'bar *(of the back)*

lum'ber *(wood)*

lum'ber *(to move heav•ily)*

lum'ber•jack'

lum'ber•yard'

lu'men *pl.* -mens *or* -mi•na

lu'mi•nance

lu'mi•nar'y

lu'mi•nes'cence

lu'mi•nes'cent

lu'mi•nos'i•ty

lu'mi•nous

lum'mox

lump'y

lu'na•cy

lu'nar

lu'na•tic

lunch'eon

lunch'eon•ette'

lunch'room'

lu•nette'

lunge, lunged, lung'ing

lung'fish' *pl.* -fish' *or* -fish'es

lu'pine *also* lu'pin

lu'pus

lurch

lure, lured, lur'ing

lu'rid
lurk
lus'cious
lush
lust
lus'ter
lus'trous
lust'y
lute *(musical instrument)*
   ♦*loot*
lu·te'ti·um *also* lu·te'·ci·um
Lu'ther·an
lux·u'ri·ance
lux·u'ri·ant
lux·u'ri·ate', -at'ed, -at'ing
lux·u'ri·ous
lux'u·ry
ly·ce'um
lye *(chemical)*
   ♦*lie*
lymph
lym·phat'ic
lym'pho·cyte'
lym'phoid'
lynch
lynx *(cat)*
   ♦*links*
lyre *(harp)*
   ♦*liar*
lyre'bird'
lyr'ic
lyr'i·cism
lyr'i·cist

ly·ser'gic ac'id di'·eth·yl·am'ide'
ly'sin
ly'sine'

M

ma·ca'bre
mac·ad'am
mac·a·da'mi·a nut
mac·ad'am·ize', -ized', -iz'ing
mac·a·ro'ni *pl.* -ni
mac·a·roon'
ma·caw'
mace
mac'er·ate', -at'ed, -at'ing
mac'er·a'tion
mac'er·a'tor *also* mac'er·at'er
ma·chet'e
Mach'i·a·vel'li·an
mach'i·na'tion
ma·chine', -chined', -chin'ing
ma·chine'-gun', -gunned', -gun'ning
ma·chine'-read'a·ble
ma·chin'er·y
ma·chin'ist
ma·chis'mo
Mach number
ma'cho *pl.* -chos
mack'er·el *pl.* -el *or* -els

mack'i·naw'
mack'in·tosh' *(raincoat),* also mac'in·tosh'
   ♦*McIntosh*
mac'ra·mé'
mac'ro' *pl.* -ros'
mac'ro·bi·ot'ics
mac'ro·cosm
mac'ro·cos'mic
ma·crog'ra·phy
mac'ro·mol'e·cule
ma'cron'
mac'ro·scop'ic *also* mac'ro·scop'i·cal
mac'u·la *pl.* -lae'
mac'u·lar
mac'u·late', -lat'ed, -lat'ing
mac'u·la'tion
mad, mad'der, mad'dest
Mad'am *pl.* Mes·dames'
Mad'ame *pl.* Mes·dames'
mad'cap'
mad'den
mad'der
Ma·dei'ra
Mad'e·moi·selle' *pl.* Mes'de·moi·selles'
made'-to-or'der
made'-up' *adj.*
mad'house'
mad'man'

mad′ness
Ma·don′na
ma′dras
mad′ri·gal
ma′dri·lène′ *also* ma′-
　dri·lene′
mael′strom
mae′nad′
maes′tro *pl.* -tros
Ma′fi·a
Ma′fi·o′so′ *pl.* -si′
mag′a·zine′
ma·gen′ta
mag′got
Ma′gi′
mag′ic
mag′i·cal
ma·gi′cian
mag′is·te′ri·al
mag′is·tra·cy
mag′is·trate′
mag′ma *pl.* mag′ma·ta
　or mag′mas
mag′na cum lau′de
mag′na·nim′i·ty
mag·nan′i·mous
mag′nate′ *(influential
　person)*
　♦*magnet*
mag·ne′sia
mag·ne′si·um
mag′net *(something
　that attracts)*
　♦*magnate*
mag·net′ic
mag′net·ism
mag′net·ite′

mag′net·i·za′tion
mag′net·ize′, -ized′,
　-iz′ing
mag·ne′to *pl.* -tos
mag·ne·tom′e·ter
mag·ne′to·sphere′
mag·ne′tron′
mag′ni·fi·ca′tion
mag·nif′i·cence
mag·nif′i·cent *(splen-
　did)*
　♦*munificent*
mag′ni·fi′er
mag′ni·fy′, -fied′, -fy′-
　ing
mag·nil′o·quence
mag·nil′o·quent
mag′ni·tude′
mag·no′lia
mag′num
mag′num o′pus
mag′pie
Mag′yar′
ma·ha·ra′jah *or* ma′-
　ha·ra′ja
ma·ha·ra′ni *or* ma·ha·
　ra′nee
ma·hat′ma
mah′jong′ *also* mah′-
　jongg′
ma·hog′a·ny
maid *(girl, servant)*
　♦*made*
maid′en
maid′en·hair′
maid′en·hood′

maid of honor *pl.*
　maids of honor
maid′ser′vant
mail *(postal material,
　armor)*
　♦*male*
mail′bag′
mail′box′
mail′man′
mail′-or′der house
maim
main *(principal)*
　♦*mane*
main′land′
main′line′, -lined′,
　-lin′ing
main′mast
main′sail
main′sheet′
main′spring′
main′stay′
main′stream′
main·tain′
main′te·nance
main′top′
main top′mast
maî′tre d′hô·tel′ *pl.*
　maî′tres d′hô·tel′
maize *(grain)*
　♦*maze*
ma·jes′tic
maj′es·ty
ma·jol′i·ca
ma′jor
ma′jor-do′mo *pl.*
　-mos
ma′jor·ette′

ma·jor'i·ty
ma'jor-league' *adj.*
ma'jor-med'i·cal *adj.*
ma·jus'cule
make, made, mak'ing
make'-be·lieve' *n. &*
   adj.
make'-read'y *n.*
make'shift'
make'-up' *n., also*
   make'up'
make'-work'
mal'a·chite'
mal'ad·just'ed
mal'ad·just'ment
mal'a·droit'
mal'a·dy
Mal'a·gas'y *pl.* -gas'y
   or -gas'ies
mal·aise'
mal'a·mute' *or* mal'e·
   mute'
mal'a·prop·ism
mal'a·pro·pos'
ma·lar'i·a
ma·lar'i·al *also* ma·
   lar'i·an, ma·lar'i·ous
ma·lar'key *also* ma·
   lar'ky
Ma'lay
Ma·lay'an
mal'con·tent'
male *(masculine)*
   ♦*mail*
mal'e·dic'tion
mal'e·fac'tion
mal'e·fac'tor

ma·lef'ic
ma·lev'o·lence
ma·lev'o·lent
mal·fea'sance
mal·fea'sant
mal'for·ma'tion
mal·formed'
mal·func'tion
mal'ice
ma·li'cious
ma·lign'
ma·lig'nan·cy
ma·lig'nant
ma·lig'ni·ty
ma·lin'ger
mall *(promenade)*
   ♦*maul*
mal'lard
mal'le·a·bil'i·ty
mal'le·a·ble
mal'let
mal'le·us *pl.* -le·i'
mal'low
malm'sey *pl.* -seys
mal·nour'ished
mal'nu·tri'tion
mal'oc·clu'sion
mal·o'dor·ous
mal·prac'tice
mal'prac·ti'tion·er
malt
mal'tase'
malt'ed milk
Mal·tese' *pl.* -tese'
mal'tose'
mal·treat'
ma'ma *also* mam'ma

mam'ba *(snake)*
mam'bo *(dance), pl.*
   -bos
mam'mal
mam·ma'li·an
mam'ma·ry
mam'mo·gram'
mam·mog'ra·phy
mam'moth
mam'my
man *pl.* men
man, manned, man'-
   ning, mans
man'a·cle, -cled, -cling
man'age, -aged, -ag·
   ing
man'age·a·bil'i·ty
man'age·a·ble
man'age·ment
man'ag·er
man'a·ge'ri·al
man'-at-arms' *pl.*
   men'-at-arms'
Man·chu'ri·an
man·da'mus
man'da·rin
man·date', -dat'ed,
   -dat'ing
man'da·to'ry
man'di·ble
man'do·lin'
man'drake'
man'drel *(spindle), or*
   man'dril
man'drill *(baboon)*
mane *(hair)*
   ♦*main*

man'-eat'er
man'-eat'ing
ma·neu'ver
ma·neu'ver·a·bil'i·ty
ma·neu'ver·a·ble
man'ful
man'ga·nese'
mange
man'ger
man'gle, -gled, -gling
man'go *pl.* -goes *or*
  -gos
man'grove'
man'gy
man'han'dle, -dled,
  -dling
Man·hat'tan
man'hole'
man'hood'
man'-hour' *pl.* man'-
  hours'
man'hunt'
ma·ni·a
ma·ni·ac'
ma·ni'a·cal
man'ic
man'ic-de·pres'sive
man'i·cot'ti
man'i·cure', -cured',
  -cur'ing
man'i·cur'ist
man'i·fest'
man'i·fes·ta'tion
man'i·fes'to *pl.* -toes
  or -tos
man'i·fold

man'i·kin *(dwarf)*, *or*
  man'ni·kin
  ♦*mannequin*
Ma·nil'a paper
man'i·oc' *also* man'i·
  o'ca
man'i·ple
ma·nip'u·late', -lat'ed,
  -lat'ing
ma·nip'u·la'tion
ma·nip'u·la'tive
ma·nip'u·la'tor
man'kind'
man'ly
man'made'
man'na
man'ne·quin *(model)*
  ♦*manikin*
man'ner *(behavior)*
  ♦*manor*
man'nered
man'ner·ism
man'ner·ly
man'nish
man'-of-war' *pl.*
  men'-of-war'
ma·nom'e·ter
man'or *(estate)*
  ♦*manner*
ma·no'ri·al
man'pow'er
man·qué'
man'sard
manse
man'ser'vant *pl.*
  men'ser'vants
man'sion

man'-sized' *also* man'-
  -size'
man'slaugh'ter
man'ta
man'tel *(shelf)*, *also*
  man'tle
man'tel·piece' *also*
  man'tle·piece'
man·til'la
man'tis
man·tis'sa
man'tle *(to cloak)*,
  -tled, -tling
  ♦*mantel*
man'tra
man'u·al
man'u·fac'to·ry
man'u·fac'ture,
  -tured, -tur·ing
man'u·fac'tur·er
man'u·mis'sion
man'u·mit', -mit'ted,
  -mit'ting
ma·nure'
man'u·script'
Manx
Manx cat *or* manx cat
man'y, more, most
Mao'ist
Mao'ri *pl.* -ri *or* -ris
map, mapped, map'-
  ping
ma'ple
mar, marred, mar'ring
mar'a·bou'
ma·ra'ca
mar'a·schi'no

mar'a·thon'
ma·raud'
mar'ble, -bled, -bling
mar'ble·ize', -ized', -iz'ing
march *(journey, border)*
March *(month)*
mar'chion·ess
Mar'di gras'
mare *(female horse)*
ma're *(region of the moon)*, pl. -ri·a
mar'ga·rine
mar'ga·ri'ta
mar'gin
mar'gin·al
mar'gi·na'li·a
mar'gue·rite'
mar'i·gold'
mar'i·jua'na or mar'i·hua'na
ma·rim'ba
ma·ri'na
mar'i·nade'
mar'i·nate', -nat'ed, -nat'ing
ma·rine'
mar'i·ner
mar'i·o·nette'
mar'i·po'sa
mar'i·tal
mar'i·time'
mar'jo·ram
marked
mark'ed·ly
mark'er
mar'ket

mar'ket·a·ble
mar'ket·place'
mark'ing
marks'man
marks'man·ship'
mark'up' *n.*
marl
mar'lin *(fish)*
mar'line *(rope)*
mar'line·spike'
mar'ma·lade'
mar'mo're·al
mar'mo·set'
mar'mot
ma·roon'
mar·quee' *(tent, entrance)*
  ♦*marquis, marquise*
mar'que·try *also* mar'que·terie
mar'quis *(nobleman),* pl. -quis *or* -quis·es
  ♦*marquee, marquise*
mar·quise' *(noblewoman, ring)*
  ♦*marquee, marquis*
mar'qui·sette'
mar'riage
mar'riage·a·ble
mar'ried
mar'row
mar'row·bone'
mar'ry, -ried, -ry·ing
Mars
marsh
mar'shal *(to organize),*

-shaled *or* -shalled, -shal·ing *or* -shal·ling
  ♦*martial*
marsh'land'
marsh'mal'low
marsh'y
mar·su'pi·al
mart
mar'ten *(animal)*
  ♦*martin*
mar'tial *(warlike)*
  ♦*marshall*
Mar'tian
mar'tin *(bird)*
  ♦*marten*
mar'ti·net'
mar'tin·gale'
mar·ti'ni pl. -nis
mar'tyr
mar'tyr·dom
mar'vel, -veled *or* -velled, -vel·ing *or* -vel·ling
mar'vel·ous *also* mar'vel·lous
Marx'i·an
Marx'ism
Marx'ist
mar'zi·pan'
mas·car'a
mas'cot
mas'cu·line
mas'cu·lin'i·ty
ma'ser
mash'ie
mask *(covering)*
  ♦*masque*

mas'o·chism
mas'o·chist
mas'o·chis'tic
ma'son
Ma·son'ic
Ma'son·ite'®
Mason jar
ma'son·ry
masque *(drama), also*
 mask
mas'quer·ade', -ad'ed,
 -ad'ing
mass *(matter)*
Mass *(Eucharist cere-*
 mony), also mass
mas'sa·cre, -cred,
 -cring
mas'sage', saged',
 -sag'ing
mas·seur'
mas·seuse'
mas·sif' *(mountain)*
mas'sive *(large)*
mass'-pro·duce',
 -duced', -duc'ing
mast
mas·tec'to·my
mas'ter
mas'ter-at-arms' *pl.*
 mas'ters-at-arms'
mas'ter·ful
mas'ter·ly
mas'ter·mind'
mas'ter·piece'
mas'ter·stroke'
mas'ter·work'
mas'ter·y

mast'head'
mas'tic
mas'ti·cate', -cat'ed,
 -cat'ing
mas'ti·ca'tion
mas'ti·ca'tor
mas'tiff
mas'to·don
mas'toid'
mas'toid·i'tis
mas'tur·bate', -bat'ed,
 -bat'ing
mas'tur·ba'tion
mat *(to cover, tangle, or*
 border), mat'ted,
 mat'ting
 ♦*matte*
mat'a·dor'
match'book'
match'box'
match'less
match'lock'
match'mak'er
match'mak'ing
mate, mat'ed, mat'ing
ma'ter
ma·te'ri·al *(substance)*
 ♦*materiel*
ma·te'ri·al·ism
ma·te'ri·al·ist
ma·te'ri·al·is'tic
ma·te'ri·al·i·za'tion
ma·te'ri·al·ize', -ized',
 -iz'ing
ma·te'ri·el' *(equip-*
 ment), or ma·té'ri·el'
 ♦*material*

ma·ter'nal
ma·ter'ni·ty
math'e·mat'i·cal *also*
 math'e·mat'ic
math'e·ma·ti'cian
math'e·mat'ics
mat'i·nee' *or* mat'i·
 née'
mat'ins
ma'tri·arch'
ma'tri·ar'chal
ma'tri·ar'chy
mat'ri·ci'dal
mat'ri·cide'
ma·tric'u·late', -lat'ed,
 -lat'ing
ma·tric'u·la'tion
mat'ri·mo'ni·al
mat'ri·mo'ny
ma'trix *pl.* -tri·ces' *or*
 -trix·es
ma'tron
matron of honor *pl.*
 matrons of honor
mat'ter
mat'ter-of-fact' *adj.*
mat'ting
mat'tock
mat'tress
mat'u·rate', -rat'ed,
 -rat'ing
mat'u·ra'tion
mat'u·ra'tive
ma·ture', tured', -tur'-
 ing
ma·tur'i·ty

mat'zo *pl.* -zoth *or*
-zos *or* -zot'
maud'lin
maul *(hammer), also*
mall
maun'der
Mau·ri·ta'ni·an
Mau·ri'ti·an
mau·so·le'um *pl.* -le'-
ums *or* -le'a
mauve
mav'er·ick
maw
mawk'ish
max'i *pl.* -is
max'il·la *pl.* -lae *or*
-las
max'il·lar
max'il·lar'y
max'im
max'i·mal
max'i·mi·za'tion
max'i·mize', -mized',
-miz'ing
max'i·mum *pl.* -mums
or -ma
may *auxiliary, past*
tense might
May *(month)*
Ma'ya *pl.* -ya *or* -yas
Ma'yan
may'be
may'day' *(signal)*
May Day *(May 1)*
may'flow'er
may'fly'
may'hem'

may·on·naise'
may'or
may'or·al
may'or·al·ty
May'pole' *also* may'-
pole'
maze *(labyrinth)*
◆*maize*
ma·zur'ka
Mc·Car'thy·ism
Mc'In·tosh'(apple)
◆*mackintosh*
me *pron.*
◆*mi*
mead *(beverage,*
meadow)
◆*meed*
mead'ow
mead'ow·lark'
mea'ger *also* mea'gre
meal'time'
meal'y-mouthed'
mean *(low)*
◆*mien*
mean *(midpoint)*
◆*mien*
mean *(to signify),*
meant, mean'ing
◆*mien*
me·an'der
mean'ing·ful
mean'ing·less
mean'time'
mean'while'
mea'sles
mea'sly
meas'ur·a·ble

meas'ure, -ured, -ur·
ing
meas'ure·ment
meat *(food)*
◆*meet, mete*
meat'ball'
meat'y
mec'ca
me·chan'ic
me·chan'i·cal
me·chan'ics
mech'a·nism
mech'a·nis'tic
mech'a·ni·za'tion
mech'a·nize', -nized',
-niz'ing
med'al *(award)*
◆*meddle*
me·dal'lion
med'dle *(to interfere),*
-dled, -dling
◆*medal*
med'dle·some
me'di·al
me'di·an
me'di·ate', -at'ed, -at'·
ing
me'di·a'tion
me'di·a'tor
med'ic
Med'i·caid' *also* med'-
i·caid'
med'i·cal
me·dic'a·ment
Med'i·care' *also* med'-
i·care'

med′i•cate′, -cat′ed,
  -cat′ing
med′i•ca′tion
me•dic′i•nal
med′i•cine
med′i•co′ *pl.* -cos′
me′di•e′val *also* me′di•
  ae′val
mè′di•e′val•ist *also*
  me′di•ae′val•ist
me′di•o′cre
me′di•oc′ri•ty
med′i•tate′, -tat′ed,
  -tat′ing
med′i•ta′tion
med′i•ta′tive
med′i•ta′tor
me′di•um *pl.* -di•a *or*
  -di•ums
med′ley *pl.* -leys
me•dul′la *pl.* -las *or*
  -lae
medulla ob′lon•ga′ta
  pl. medulla ob′lon•
  ga′tas *or* medullae
  ob′lon•ga′tae
me•dul′lar *also* med′-
  ul•lar′y
meed *(reward)*
  ♦*mead*
meek′ly
meer′schaum
meet *(fitting)*
  ♦*meat, mete*
meet *(to come upon)*,
  met, meet′ing
  ♦*meat, mete*

meg′a•bit′
meg′a•buck′
meg′a•byte′
meg′a•cy′cle
meg′a•death′
meg′a•hertz′
meg′a•lith′
meg′a•lith′ic
meg′a•lo•ma′ni•a
meg′a•lo•ma′ni•ac′
meg′a•lop′o•lis
meg′a•phone′
meg′a•spore′
meg′a•ton′
me′grim
mei•o′sis *pl.* -ses′
mei•ot′ic
Meis′sen
mel′a•mine′
mel′an•cho′li•a
mel′an•chol′ic
mel′an•chol′y
Mel′a•ne′sian
mé•lange′ *also* me•
  lange′
mel′a•nin
mel′a•no′ma *pl.* -mas
  or -ma•ta
Mel′ba toast
meld
me′lee′ *also* mê•lée′
mel′io•rate′, -rat′ed,
  -rat′ing
mel′io•ra′tion
mel•lif′lu•ous
mel′low
me•lo′de•on

me•lod′ic
me•lo′di•ous
mel′o•dra′ma
mel′o•dra•mat′ic
mcl′o•dy
mel′on
melt′down′
melt′ing point
mem′ber
mem′ber•ship′
mem′brane′
mem′bra•nous
me•men′to *pl.* -tos *or*
  -toes
mem′o *pl.* -os
mem′oir′
mem′o•ra•bil′i•a
mem′o•ra•ble
mem′o•ran′dum *pl.*
  -dums *or* -da
me•mo′ri•al
me•mo′ri•al•i•za′tion
me•mo′ri•al•ize′,
  -ized′, -iz′ing
mem′o•ri•za′tion
mem′o•rize′, -rized′,
  -riz′ing
mem′o•ry
men•ace′, -aced, -ac′ing
mé•nage′
me•nag′er•ie
mend
men•da′cious
men•dac′i•ty
men′de•le′vi•um
men′di•cant
mend′ing

men·ha′den *pl.* -den
   or -dens
me′ni·al
men′in·gi′tis
me′ninx *pl.* me·nin′ges
me·nis′cal *also* me·
   nis′cate, me·nis′-
   coid′, men′is·coi′dal
me·nis′cus *pl.* -ci′ *or*
   -cus·es
men′o·paus′al
men′o·pause′
men′sal
men′ses
men′stru·al
men′stru·ate′, -at·ed,
   -at′ing
men′stru·a′tion
men′su·ra·bil′i·ty
men′su·ra·ble
men′su·ra′tion
men′su·ra′tive
men′tal
men·tal′i·ty
men′thol′
men′tho·lat′ed
men′tion
men′tor
men′u
me·ow′
Meph′i·stoph′e·les′
me·phit′ic *also* me·
   phit′i·cal
me·phi′tis
mer′can·tile′
mer′can·til·ism
mer′can·til′ist

mer′ce·nar′y
mer′cer
mer′cer·ize′, -ized′,
   -iz′ing
mer′chan·dise′,
   -dised′, -dis′ing
mer′chan·dis′er
mer′chant
mer′ci·ful
mer′ci·less
mer·cu′ri·al
mer·cu′ri·al·ism
mer·cu′ric
mer·cu′ro·chrome′®
mer·cu′rous
mer′cu·ry *(element)*
Mer′cu·ry *(god,
   planet)*
mer′cy
mere *superl.* mer′est
mer′e·tri′cious
mer·gan′ser
merge, merged, merg′-
   ing
merg′er
me·rid′i·an
me·ringue′
me·ri′no *pl.* -nos
mer′it
mer′i·toc′ra·cy
mer′it·o·crat′
mer′i·to′ri·ous
mer′maid′
mer′man′
mer′ri·ment
mer′ry
mer′ry-go-round′

mer′ry·mak′er
mer′ry·mak′ing
Mer·thi′o·late′®
me′sa
mes·cal′
mes′ca·line′
mes′en·ter′ic
mes′en·ter′y *also*
   mes′en·ter′i·um
   pl. -i·a
mesh′work′
mes′mer·ism
mes′mer·ize′, -ized′,
   -iz′ing
mes′o·derm′
Mes′o·lith′ic
mes′on′
Mes·o·po·ta′mi·an
mes′o·sphere′
mes′o·spher′ic
Mes′o·zo′ic
mes·quite′
mess
mes′sage
mes′sen·ger
Mes·si′ah
mes′si·an′ic
mess′y
met′a·bol′ic
me·tab′o·lism
me·tab′o·lize′, -lized′,
   -liz′ing
met′a·car′pal
met′a·car′pus
met′al *(element)*
   ♦*mettle*
me·tal′lic

met'al·loid'

met'al·lur'gic *also*
  met'al·lur'gi·cal

met'al·lur'gist

met'al·lur'gy

met'al·work'

met'a·mor'phic *also*
  met'a·mor'phous

met'a·mor'phism

met'a·mor'phose',
  -phosed', -phos'ing

met'a·mor'pho·sis *pl.*
  -ses'

met'a·phase'

met'a·phor'

met'a·phor'ic *also*
  met'a·phor'i·cal

met'a·phys'i·cal

met'a·phy·si'cian

met'a·phys'ics

me·tas'ta·sis *pl.* -ses'

me·tas'ta·size', -sized',
  -siz'ing

met'a·tar'sal

met'a·tar'sus *pl.* -si'

met'a·zo'an

mete *(to distribute)*,
  met'ed, met'ing
  ♦*meat, meet*

me·tem'psy·cho'sis
  pl. -ses'

me'te·or

me'te·or'ic

me'te·or·ite'

me'te·or·oid'

me'te·or·o·log'i·cal

me'te·or·ol'o·gist

me'te·or·ol'o·gy

me'ter

meth'a·done' hydro-
  chloride

meth'ane'

meth'a·nol'

me·thinks'

meth'od

me·thod'i·cal *also* me·
  thod'ic

Meth'od·ist

meth'od·o·log'i·cal

meth'od·ol'o·gy

meth'yl

meth'yl·at'ed

me·tic'u·lous

mé·tier'

met'o·nym'

me·ton'y·my

met'ric

met'ri·cal

met'ri·ca'tion

met'ri·fi·ca'tion

met'ri·fy', -fied', -fy'-
  ing

met'ro *pl.* -ros

me·trol'o·gy

met'ro·nome'

met'ro·nom'ic

me·trop'o·lis *pl.* -lis·es

met'ro·pol'i·tan

met'tle *(spirit)*
  ♦*metal*

mewl *(to cry)*
  ♦*mule*

mews *(street)*
  ♦*muse, Muse*

Mex'i·can

me·zu'zah, *also* me·
  zu'za

mez'za·nine'

mez'zo *pl.* -zos

mez'zo-so·pran'o *pl.*
  -os

mez'zo·tint'

mho *(electrical unit)*,
  pl. mhos
  ♦*mow*

mi *(musical tone)*
  ♦*me*

mi·as'ma *pl.* -mas *or*
  -ma·ta

mi·as'mal *also* mi'as·
  mat'ic, mi·as'mic

mi'ca

mi'crobe'

mi'cro'bi·cide'

mi'cro·bi·o·log'i·cal
  also mi'cro·bi·o·log'ic

mi'cro·bi·ol'o·gist

mi'cro·bi·ol'o·gy

mi'cro·chip'

mi'cro·cir'cuit

mi'cro·com·put'er

mi'cro·cosm

mi'cro·cos'mic *also*
  mi'cro·cos'mi·cal

mi'cro·fiche'

mi'cro·film'

mi'cro·groove'®

mi·crom'e·ter

mi·crom'e·try

mi'cron' *pl.* -crons *or*

-cra, *also* mi'kron' *pl.*
-krons' *or* -kra
Mi'cro·ne'sian
mi'cro·nu'cle·us *pl.*
  -cle·i' *or* -cle·us·es
mi'cro·or'gan·ism
mi'cro·phone'
mi'cro·pho'to·graph'
mi'cro·pho·tog'ra·
  phy
mi'cro·proc'es·sor
mi'cro·scope'
mi'cro·scop'ic *also*
  mi'cro·scop'i·cal
mi·cros'co·pist
mi·cros'co·py
mi'cro·sur'ger·y
mi'cro·wave'
mid'air'
mid'course'
mid'day'
mid'dle
mid'dle-aged' *adj.*
mid'dle·brow'
mid'dle-class' *adj.*
mid'dle·man'
mid'dle·weight'
mid'dling
mid'dy *(blouse)*
  ♦*midi*
midge
midg'et
mid'i *(skirt), pl.* -is
  ♦*middy*
mid'land
mid'most'
mid'night'

mid'point'
mid'rib'
mid'riff'
mid'sec'tion
mid'ship'man
midst
mid'stream'
mid'sum'mer
mid'term'
mid'town'
mid'way'
mid'week'
mid'wife'
mid'wife'ry
mid'win'ter
mid'year'
mien *(bearing)*
  ♦*mean*
miff
might *(power)*
  ♦*mite*
might'y
mi'gnon·ette'
mi'graine'
mi'grant
mi'grate', -grat'ed,
  -grat'ing
mi·gra'tion
mi'gra·to'ry
mi·ka'do *pl.* -dos
mike, miked, mik'ing
mil *(unit of length)*
  ♦*mill*
mi·la'dy
milch
mil'dew
mild'ly

mile'age
mile'post'
mil'er
mile'stone'
mi·lieu'
mil'i·tan·cy
mil'i·tant
mil'i·ta·rism
mil'i·ta·rist
mil'i·ta·ris'tic
mil'i·ta·rize', -rized',
  -riz'ing
mil'i·tar'y
mil'i·tate', -tat'ed,
  -tat'ing
mi·li'tia
milk'maid'
milk'man'
milk'sop'
milk'weed'
milk'y
Milk'y Way
mill *(grinder, money)*
  ♦*mil*
mill'dam'
mil'le·nar'i·an
mil'le·nar'y *(thousand)*
  ♦*millinery*
mil·len'ni·al
mil·len'ni·um *pl.* -ni·
  ums *or* -ni·a
mil'let
mil'liard
mil'li·gram'
mil'li·li'ter
mil'li·me'ter
mil'li·ner

mil'li·ner'y *(hats)*
♦millenary
mill'ing
mil'lion *pl.* -lion *or*
-lions
mil'lion·aire'
mil'lionth
mil'li·pede' *or* mil'le·
pede'
mill'race'
mill'stone'
mill'stream'
mi·lord'
milque'toast'
milt
mime, mimed, mim'-
ing
mim'e·o·graph'
mi·me'sis
mi·met'ic
mim'ic, -icked, -ick·ing
mim'ick·er
mim'ic·ry
mi·mo'sa
min'a·ret'
min'a·to'ry
mince, minced, minc'-
ing
mince'meat'
mind *(intelligence, to
heed)*
♦mined
mind'-blow'ing
mind'ful
mind'less
mine, mined, min'ing
mine *pron.*

mine'field'
min'er *(one that mines)*
♦minor
min'er·al
min'er·a·log'i·cal
min'er·al'o·gist
min'er·al'o·gy
min'e·stro'ne
min'gle, -gled, -gling
min'i *pl.* -is
min'i·a·ture
min'i·a·tur'i·za'tion
min'i·a·tur·ize', -ized',
-iz'ing
min'i·bus'
min'i·cab'
min'i·com·put'er
min'im
min'i·mal'
min'i·mal·ism
min'i·mal·ist
min'i·mi·za'tion
min'i·mize', -mized',
-miz'ing
min'i·mum *pl.* -mums
or -ma
min'ing
min'ion
min'i·se'ries
min'i·skirt'
min'is·ter
min'is·te'ri·al
min'is·trant
min'is·tra'tion
min'is·try
mink *pl.* mink *or*
minks

Min'ne·so'tan
min'now *pl.* -now *or*
-nows
mi'nor *(smaller)*
♦miner
mi·nor'i·ty
mi'nor-league' *adj.*
Min'o·taur'
min'strel
min'strel·sy
mint'age
min'u·end'
min'u·et'
mi'nus
mi·nus'cu·lar
mi·nus'cule'
mi·nute' *(small)*
min'ute *(unit of time)*
mi·nute'ly *(on a small
scale)*
min'ute·ly *(once a
minute)*
min'ute·man'
mi·nu'ti·a *pl.* -ti·ae'
minx
Mi'o·cene'
mir'a·cle
mi·rac'u·lous
mi·rage'
mire, mired, mir'ing
mir'ror
mirth'ful
mis'ad·ven'ture
mis'al·li'ance
mis·an'thrope' *also*
mis·an'thro·pist

mis′an·throp′ic *also*
  mis′an·throp′i·cal
mis′an′thro·py
mis′ap·pli·ca′tion
mis′ap·ply′, -plied′,
  -ply′ing
mis′ap·pre·hend′
mis′ap·pre·hen′sion
mis′ap·pro′pri·ate′,
  -at′ed, -at′ing
mis′ap·pro′pri·a′tion
mis·be·got′ten
mis·be·have′, -haved′,
  -hav′ing
mis·be·hav′ior
mis·cal′cu·late′, -lat′-
  ed, -lat′ing
mis′cal·cu·la′tion
mis·call′
mis·car′riage
mis·car′ry, -ried, -ry·
  ing
mis·cast′, -cast′, -cast′-
  ing
mis′ce·ge·na′tion
mis′cel·la′ne·ous
mis′cel·la′ny
mis·chance′
mis′chief
mis′chie·vous
mis′ci·bil′i·ty
mis′ci·ble
mis·con·ceive′,
  -ceived′, -ceiv′ing
mis′con·cep′tion
mis·con′duct
mis·con·struc′tion

mis·con·strue′,
  -strued′, -stru′ing
mis·count′ *n.*
mis·count′ *v.*
mis·cre′ant
mis·deal′ *n.*
mis·deal′, -dealt′,
  -deal′ing
mis·deed′
mis′de·mean′or
mis′di·rect′
mis·do′ing
mi′ser
mis′er·a·ble
mis′er·y
mis·fea′sance
mis·fea′sor
mis·fire′, -fired′, -fir′-
  ing
mis·fit′
mis·for′tune
mis·giv′ing
mis·gov′ern
mis·guid′ance
mis·guide′, -guid′ed,
  -guid′ing
mis·han′dle, -dled,
  -dling
mis·hap′
mis·hear′, -heard′,
  -hear′ing
mish′mash′
mis·in·form′
mis′in·for·ma′tion
mis·in·ter′pret
mis′in·ter′pre·ta′tion

mis·judge′, -judged′,
  -judg′ing
mis·judg′ment
mis·lay′, -laid′, -lay′-
  ing
mis·lead′, -led′, -lead′-
  ing
mis·man′age, -aged,
  -ag·ing
mis·man′age·ment
mis·match′
mis·name′, -named′,
  -nam′ing
mis·no′mer
mi·sog′a·my
mi·sog′y·nist
mi·sog′y·nous
mi·sog′y·ny
mis·place′, -placed′,
  -plac′ing
mis·play′
mis′print′ *n.*
mis·print′ *v.*
mis·pri′sion
mis·pro·nounce′,
  -nounced′, -nounc′-
  ing
mis·pro·nun′ci·a′tion
mis′quo·ta′tion
mis·quote′, -quot′ed,
  -quot′ing
mis·read′, -read′,
  -read′ing
mis′rep·re·sent′
mis′rep·re·sen·ta′tion
mis·rule′, -ruled′, -rul′-
  ing

miss
mis'sal *(prayer book)*
 ♦*missile*
mis·shape', -shaped',
 -shap'ing
mis·shap'en
mis'sile *(weapon)*
 ♦*missal*
mis'sile·ry *also* mis'sil·
 ry
miss'ing
mis'sion
mis'sion·ar'y
Mis'sis·sip'pi·an
mis'sive
Mis·sou'ri·an
mis·spell', -spelled' *or*
 -spelt', -spell'ing
mis·spend', -spent',
 -spend'ing
mis·state', -stat'ed,
 -stat'ing
mis·step'
mist
mis·tak'a·ble
mis·take', -took',
 -tak'en, -tak'ing
Mis'ter
mis'tle·toe'
mis'tral
mis·treat'
mis·treat'ment
mis'tress
mis·tri'al
mis·trust'
mist'y

mis·un·der·stand',
 -stood', -stand'ing
mis·use', -used', -us'-
 ing
mite *(organism, small
 amount)*
 ♦*might*
mi'ter
mit'i·gate', -gat'ed,
 -gat'ing
mit'i·ga'tion
mit'i·ga'tor
mi·to·chon'dri·on *pl.*
 -dri·a
mi·to'sis
mi·tot'ic
mitt
mit'ten
mixed
mix'er
mix'ture
mix'-up' *n.*
miz'zen *or* miz'en
miz'zen·mast *or* miz'-
 en·mast
mne·mon'ic
moan *(sound)*
 ♦*mown*
moat *(ditch)*
 ♦*mote*
mob, mobbed, mob'-
 bing
mo'bile
mo·bil'i·ty
mo'bi·li·za'tion
mo'bi·lize', -lized',
 -liz'ing

Mö'bi·us strip
mob'ster
moc'ca·sin
mo'cha
mock'er·y
mock'-he·ro'ic
mock'ing·bird'
mock'up' *n., also*
 mock'-up'
mod
mo'dal
mo·dal'i·ty
mode
mod'el
mod'er·ate', -at'ed,
 -at'ing
mod'er·a'tion
mod'e·ra'to *pl.* -tos
mod'er·a'tor
mod'ern
mod'ern·ism
mod'ern·ist
mod'ern·ist'ic
mod'ern·i·za'tion
mod'ern·ize', -ized',
 -iz'ing
mod'est
mod'es·ty
mod'i·cum
mod'i·fi·ca'tion
mod'i·fi'er
mod'i·fy', -fied', -fy'-
 ing
mod'ish
mod'u·lar'i·ty

mod'u·late', -lat'ed,
-lat'ing
mod'u·la'tion
mod'u·la'tive *also*
mod'u·la·to'ry
mod'u·la'tor
mod'ule
mo'gul *(magnate)*
Mo'gul *(Indian Moslem)*
mo'hair'
Mo·ham'med·an
moi'e·ty
moil
moi·ré' *also* moire
moist
mois'ten
mois'ture
mo'lar
mo·las'ses
mold'a·ble
mold'ing
mold'y
mo·lec'u·lar
mol'e·cule'
mole'hill'
mole'skin'
mo·lest'
mo'les·ta'tion
moll
mol'li·fi'a·ble
mol'li·fi·ca'tion
mol'li·fy', -fied', -fy'-
ing
mol'lusk *also* mol'lusc
mol'ly

mol'ly·cod'dle, -dled,
-dling
molt
mol'ten
mo·lyb'de·num
mom
mo'ment
mo'men·tar'i·ly
mo'men·tar'y
mo·men'tous
mo·men'tum *pl.* -ta *or*
-tums
Mon'a·can
mo'nad'
mo·nad'ic *also* mo·
nad'i·cal
mon'arch
mon·ar'chic *also* mon·
ar'chi·cal
mon'ar·chism
mon'ar·chist
mon'ar·chis'tic
mon'ar·chy
mon·as·te'ri·al
mon'as·ter'y
mo·nas'tic
mo·nas'ti·cism
mon'a·tom'ic
mon·au'ral
mon'a·zite'
Mon'day
mon'e·tar'y
mon'ey *pl.* -eys *or* -ies
mon'ey·bag'
mon'ey·chang'er
mon'eyed *also* mon'-
ied

mon'ey·lend'er
mon'ey·mak'er
mon'ey·mak'ing
mon'ger
Mon'gol
Mon·go'li·an
mon'gol·ism
mon'gol·oid' *(charac-
terized by mongolism)*
Mon'gol·oid' *(of an
ethnic division)*
mon'goose' *pl.* -goos'-
es
mon'grel
mon'i·ker *or* mon'ick·
er
mo'nism
mo'nist
mo·nis'tic
mo·ni'tion
mon'i·tor
mon'i·to'ry
mon'key *pl.* -keys
mon'key·shine'
monk'ish
monks'hood'
mon'o·chro·mat'ic
also mon'o·chro'ic
mon'o·chrome'
mon'o·chro'mic
mon'o·cle
mon'o·cot'y·le'don
also mon'o·cot'
mon'o·cot'y·le'don·
ous
mo·noc'u·lar
mo·nod'ic

mon'o·dist
mon'o·dy
mo·nog'a·mist
mo·nog'a·mous
mo·nog'a·my
mon'o·gram',
  -grammed' or
  -gramed', -gram'-
  ming or -gram'ing
mon'o·graph'
mo·nog'ra·pher
mon'o·graph'ic
mon'o·lith'
mon'o·lith'ic
mo·nol'o·gist
mon'o·logue'
mon'o·ma'ni·a
mon'o·ma'ni·ac'
mon'o·ma'ni·a·cal
mon'o·mer
mo·no'mi·al
mon'o·nu'cle·o'sis
mon'o·phon'ic
mon'o·plane'
mo·nop'o·list
mo·nop'o·lis'tic
mo·nop'o·li·za'tion
mo·nop'o·lize',
  -lized', -liz'ing
mo·nop'o·ly
mon'o·rail'
mon'o·so'di·um glu'-
  ta·mate'
mon'o·syl·lab'ic
mon'o·syl'la·ble
mon'o·the·ism
mon'o·the·ist

mon'o·the·is'tic
mon'o·tone'
mo·not'o·nous
mo·not'o·ny
Mon'o·type'®
mon·ox'ide'
Mon·sieur' pl. Mes'-
  sieurs
Mon·si'gnor also
  mon·si'gnor
mon·soon'
mon'ster
mon'strance
mon·stros'i·ty
mon'strous
mon·tage'
Mon·tan'an
mon'tane'
month'ly
mon'u·ment
mon'u·men'tal
moo, mooed, moo'ing
moo pl. moos
mooch'er
mood'y
moon'beam'
moon'calf'
moon'light', -light'ed,
  -light'ing
moon'scape'
moon'shine', -shined',
  -shin'ing
moon'stone'
moon'struck' also
  moon'strick'en
moon'y
moor (open land)

moor (to secure)
Moor (North African)
moor'age
Moor'ish
moose (animal), pl.
  moose
  ♦mousse
moot
mop, mopped, mop'-
  ping
mope, moped, mop'ing
mop'pet
mo·raine'
mor'al
mo·rale'
mor'al·ist
mor'al·is'tic
mo·ral'i·ty
mor'al·i·za'tion
mor'al·ize', -ized', -iz'-
  ing
mo·rass'
mor'a·to'ri·um pl. -ri·
  ums or -ri·a
mo'ray
mor'bid
mor·bid'i·ty
mor·da'cious
mor·dac'i·ty
mor'dan·cy
mor'dant (caustic)
mor'dent (melodic or-
  nament)
more superl. most
mo·rel'
more·o'ver
mo'res

mor′ga·nat′ic

morgue

mor′i·bund′

Mor′mon

morn *(morning)*
 ♦*mourn*

morn′ing *(dawn)*
 ♦*mourning*

morn′ing-glo′ry

Mo·roc′can

mo·roc′co *(leather), pl.*
 -cos

mo′ron′

mo·ron′ic

mo·rose′

mor′pheme′

Mor′phe·us

mor′phine′

mor·pho·log′i·cal *also*
 mor′pho·log′ic

mor·phol′o·gist

mor·phol′o·gy

mor′row

Morse code

mor′sel

mor′tal

mor·tal′i·ty

mor′tar

mor′tar·board′

mort′gage, -gaged,
 -gag·ing

mort′ga·gee′

mort′ga·gor′

mor·ti′cian

mor′ti·fi·ca′tion

mor′ti·fy′, -fied′, -fy′-
 ing

mor′tise, -tised, -tis·
 ing, *also* mor′tice,
 -ticed, -tic·ing

mor′tu·ar′y

mo·sa′ic

mo′sey, -seyed, -sey·
 ing, -seys

Mos′lem

mosque

mos·qui′to *pl.* -toes *or*
 -tos

moss′back′

moss′y

most′ly

mote *(speck)*
 ♦*moat*

mo·tel′

mo·tet′

moth *pl.* moths

moth′ball′ *n.*

moth′-ball′ *v.*

moth′-eat′en

moth′er

moth′er·hood′

moth′er-in-law′ *pl.*
 moth′ers-in-law′

moth′er·land′

moth′er·ly

moth′er-of-pearl′

mo·tif′ *(design), also*
 mo′tive

mo′tile

mo·til′i·ty

mo′tion

mo′tion·less

mo′ti·vate′, -vat·ed,
 -vat′ing

mo′ti·va′tion

mo′tive *(reason, im-*
 pulse)
 ♦*motif*

mot′ley

mo′tor

mo′tor·bike′

mo′tor·boat′

mo′tor·cade′

mo′tor·car′

mo′tor·cy′cle, -cled,
 -cling

mo′tor·cy′clist

mo′tor·ist

mo′tor·i·za′tion

mo′tor·ize′, -ized′, -iz′-
 ing

mot′tle, -tled, -tling

mot′to *pl.* -toes *or* -tos

mound

mount′a·ble

moun′tain

moun′tain·eer′

moun′tain·ous

moun′tain·side′

moun′te·bank′

mount′ing

mourn *(to grieve)*
 ♦*morn*

mourn′ing *(grief)*
 ♦*morning*

mouse *pl.* mice

mouse, moused,
 mous′ing

mouse′trap′

mousse *(dessert)*
 ♦*moose*

mousse·line′
mous′y
mouth *pl.* mouths
mouth′ful′ *pl.* -fuls′
mouth′piece′
mouth′wash′
mou′ton′ *(sheepskin)*
  ♦*mutton*
mov′a·ble *also* move′a·
  ble
move, moved, mov′ing
move′ment
mov′er
mov′ie
mov′ie·mak′er
mow *(to cut down)*,
  mowed, mowed *or*
  mown, mow′ing
  ♦*mho*
moz′za·rel′la
much, more, most
mu′ci·lage
mu′ci·lag′i·nous
muck′rake′, -raked′,
  -rak′ing
mu′cous *adj., also*
  mu′cose′
mu′cus *n.*
mud′dle, -dled, -dling
mud′dle-head′ed
mud′dy, -died, -dy·ing
mud′guard′
mud′sling′er
mud′sling′ing
muff
muf′fin
muf′fle, -fled, -fling

muf′fler
muf′ti
mug, mugged, mug′-
  ging
mug′ger
mug′gy
muk′luk′
mu·lat′to *pl.* -tos *or*
  -toes
mul′ber′ry
mulch *(covering)*
mulct *(penalty)*
mule *(animal, slipper)*
  ♦*mewl*
mule′skin′ner
mu′le·teer′
mul′ish
mull
mul′lein
mul′let *pl.* -let *or* -lets
mul′li·gan
mul′li·ga·taw′ny
mul′lion
mul′ti·col′ored
mul′ti·di·men′sion·al
mul′ti·eth′nic
mul′ti·far′i·ous
mul′ti·form′
mul′ti·lat′er·al
Mul′ti·lith′®
mul′ti·me′di·a
mul·ti·mil·lion·aire′
mul′ti·na′tion·al
mul′ti·ple
mul′ti·ple-choice′ *adj.*
multiple scle·ro′sis
mul′ti·plex′

mul′ti·pli·cand′
mul′ti·pli·ca′tion
mul′ti·pli·ca′tive
mul′ti·plic′i·ty
mul′ti·pli′er
mul′ti·ply′, -plied′,
  -ply′ing
mul′ti·pur′pose
mul′ti·stage′
mul′ti·tude′
mul′ti·tu′di·nous
mul′ti·va′lent
mum′ble, -bled, -bling
mum′ble·ty-peg′
mum′bo jum′bo
mum′mer
mum′mer·y
mum′mi·fi·ca′tion
mum′mi·fy′, -fied′,
  -fy′ing
mum′my
mumps
munch
mun·dane′
mu·nic′i·pal
mu·nic′i·pal′i·ty
mu·nif′i·cence
mu·nif′i·cent *(gener-
  ous)*
  ♦*magnificent*
mu·ni′tions
mu′ral
mu′ral·ist
mur′der
mur′der·er
mur′der·ous

mu'rex' *pl.* -ri·ces' or
-rex'es
murk'y
mur'mur
mur'rain
mus'ca·tel'
mus'cle *(to force)*,
-cled, -cling
♦*mussel, muzzle*
mus'cle-bound'
mus'co·vite'
mus'cu·lar
muscular dys'tro·
phy
mus·cu·lar'i·ty
mus'cu·la·ture'
muse *(to ponder)*,
mused, mus'ing
♦*mews*
Muse *(goddess)*
♦*mews*
mu·se'um
mush'room'
mush'y
mu'sic
mu'si·cal *(of music)*
mu'si·cale' *(concert)*
mu·si'cian
mu·si'cian·ship'
mu'si·col'o·gist
mu'si·col'o·gy
musk
mus'kel·lunge' *pl.*
-lunge' or -lung'es
mus'ket
mus'ket·eer'
mus'ket·ry

musk'mel'on
musk'rat'
Mus'lim
mus'lin
muss
mus'sel *(shellfish)*
♦*muscle, muzzle*
must
mus'tache' also mous'·
tache'
mus·ta'chio *pl.* -chios
mus'tang'
mus'tard *(plant)*
♦*mustered*
mus'ter
must'y
mu·ta·bil'i·ty
mu'ta·ble
mu'tant
mu'tate', -tat'ed, -tat'·
ing
mu·ta'tion
mu'ta·tive
mute, mut'er, mut'est
mute, mut'ed, mut'ing
mu'ti·late', -lat'ed,
-lat'ing
mu'ti·la'tion
mu'ti·la'tor
mu'ti·neer'
mu'ti·nous
mu'ti·ny, -nied, -ny·
ing
mutt
mut'ter
mut'ton *(sheep)*
♦*mouton*

mu'tu·al
mu'tu·al'i·ty
muu'muu'
muz'zle *(to restrain)*,
-zled, -zling
♦*muscle, mussel*
my
my'as·the'ni·a
my·ce'li·um *pl.* -li·a
my'co·log'i·cal also
my'co·log'ic
my·col'o·gist
my·col'o·gy
my·co'sis *pl.* -ses'
my'e·lin also my'e·line
my'na or my'nah
my'o·car'di·al
my'o·car'di·um
my·o'pi·a
my·op'ic
myr'i·ad
myr'mi·don'
myrrh
myr'tle
my·self'
mys·te'ri·ous
mys'ter·y
mys'tic
mys'ti·cal
mys'ti·cism
mys'ti·fi·ca'tion
mys'ti·fy', -fied', -fy'·
ing
mys·tique'
myth'i·cal
myth'o·log'i·cal also
myth'o·log'ic

my·thol'o·gist
my·thol'o·gy

N

nab, nabbed, nab'bing
na'bob'
na·celle'
na'cre
na'cre·ous
na'dir
nag, nagged, nag'ging
nag'ger
nai'ad *pl.* -a·des' *or*
  -ads
nail
na·ive' *or* na·ïve', *also*
  na·if' *or* na·ïf'
na·ive·té' *or* na·ïve·té'
na'ked
nam'a·ble *also* name'-
  a·ble
nam'by-pam'by
name, named, nam'ing
name'less
name·ly
name'sake'
nan·keen'
nan'ny
nap, napped, nap'ping
na'palm'
nape
na'per·y
naph'tha
naph'tha·lene'

nap'kin
na·po'le·on *(pastry)*
Na·po'le·on'ic
nar'cis·sism
nar'cis·sist
nar'cis·sis'tic
nar·cis'sus *pl.* -sus·es
  or -si'
nar·co'sis
nar·cot'ic
nard
nar·rate', -rat'ed, -rat'-
  ing
nar·ra'tion
nar·ra·tive
nar·ra'tor *also* nar'-
  rat'er
nar'row
nar'row-gauge' *also*
  nar'row-gauged'
nar'row-mind'ed
nar'whal
nar'y
na'sal
na·sal'i·ty
nas'cence
nas'cent
na·stur'tium
nas'ty
na'tal
na'tion
na'tion·al
na'tion·al·ism
na'tion·al·ist
na'tion·al·is'tic
na'tion·al·i·ty
na'tion·al·i·za'tion

na'tion·al·ize', -ized',
  -iz'ing
na'tion·wide'
na'tive
na'tive-born' *adj.*
na·tiv'i·ty
nat'ty
nat'u·ral
nat'u·ral·ism
nat'u·ral·ist
nat'u·ral·is'tic
nat'u·ral·i·za'tion
nat'u·ral·ize', -ized',
  -iz'ing
nat'u·ral·ly
na'ture
naught *also* nought
naugh'ty
nau'se·a
nau'se·ate', -at'ed,
  -at'ing
nau'seous *(causing
  sickness)*
nau'ti·cal
nau'ti·lus *pl.* -lus·es *or*
  -li'
na'val *(nautical)*
  ♦navel
nave *(part of a church)*
  ♦knave
na'vel *(bellybutton)*
  ♦naval
nav'i·ga·bil'i·ty
nav'i·ga·ble
nav'i·gate', -gat'ed,
  -gat'ing
nav'i·ga'tion

nav'i·ga'tor
na'vy
nay *(no)*
♦*née, neigh*
Na'zi *pl.* -zis
Na'zism *also* Na'zi·ism
Ne·an'der·thal'
Ne·a·pol'i·tan
neap tide
near'by'
near'ly
near'sight'ed
neat'ly
neat's'-foot' oil
neb'bish
Ne·bras'kan
neb·u'la *pl.* -lae' *or*
  -las
neb'u·lar
neb'u·los'i·ty
neb'u·lous
nec'es·sar'i·ly
nec'es·sar'y
ne·ces'si·tate', -tat'ed,
  -tat'ing
ne·ces'si·ta'tion
ne·ces'si·tous
ne·ces'si·ty
neck'er·chief
neck'lace
neck'line'
neck'piece'
neck'tie'
neck'wear'
ne·crol'o·gy
nec'ro·man'cer
nec'ro·man'cy

ne·crop'o·lis *pl.* -lis·es
  or -leis'
nec'tar
nec'tar·ine'
née *(born), also* nee
  ♦*nay, neigh*
need *(requirement)*
  ♦*knead, kneed*
nee'dle, -dled, -dling
nee'dle·fish' *pl.* -fish'
  or -fish'es
nee'dle·point'
need'less
nee'dle·work'
need'n't
need'y
ne'er'-do-well'
ne·far'i·ous
ne·gate', -gat'ed, -gat'-
  ing
ne·ga'tion
neg'a·tive, -tived, -tiv·
  ing
neg'a·tiv·ism
neg'a·tiv·ist
neg'a·tiv·is'tic
ne·glect'
ne·glect'ful
neg'li·gee' *also* neg'li·
  gée'
neg'li·gence
neg'li·gent
neg'li·gi·bil'i·ty
neg'li·gi·ble
ne·go'tia·bil'i·ty
ne·go'tia·ble

ne·go'ti·ate', -at'ed,
  -at'ing
ne·go'ti·a'tion
ne·go'ti·a'tor
Ne'gro *pl.* -groes
Ne'groid'
neigh *(horse's cry)*
  ♦*nay, née*
neigh'bor
neigh'bor·hood'
neigh'bor·ly
nei'ther *(not either)*
  ♦*nether*
nek'ton
nek·ton'ic
nel'son
nem'a·to·cyst'
nem'a·tode'
Nem'bu·tal'®
nem'e·sis *pl.* -ses'
ne'o·clas'sic *also* ne'o·
  clas'si·cal
ne'o·clas'si·cism
ne'o·clas'si·cist
ne'o·co·lo'ni·al·ist
ne'o·dym'i·um
ne'o·im·pres'sion·ism
ne'o·im·pres'sion·ist
Ne'o·lith'ic
ne·ol'o·gism
ne'o·my'cin
ne'on'
ne'o·na'tal
ne'o·nate'
ne'o·phyte'
ne'o·plasm
ne'o·prene'

Nep'al·ese' *pl.* -ese'
ne·pen'the
neph'ew
neph'rite'
ne·phri'tis
nep'o·tism
nep'o·tis'tic *also* nep'-
 o·tis'ti·cal
Nep'tune'
nep·tu'ni·um
ner·va'tion
nerve'less
nerve'-rack'ing *also*
 nerve'-wrack'ing
nerv'ous
nerv'y
nes'tle, -tled, -tling
nest'ling *(young bird)*
net, net'ted, net'ting
neth'er *(below)*
 ♦neither
neth'er·most'
net'su·ke'
net'ting
net'tle, -tled, -tling
net'tle·some
net'work'
Neuf'châ·tel'
neu'ral
neu·ral'gia
neu·ral'gic
neu·ras·the'ni·a
neu·ri'tis
neu·ro·bi·ol'o·gy
neu'ro·chem'is·try
neu'ro·log'i·cal
neu·rol'o·gist

neu·rol'o·gy
neu'ron'
neu'ro·pa·thol'o·gy
neu·rop'ter·an
neu·ro'sis *pl.* -ses'
neu·rot'ic
neu'ter
neu'tral
neu'tral·ism
neu'tral·ist
neu·tral'i·ty
neu'tral·i·za'tion
neu'tral·ize', -ized',
 -iz'ing
neu·tri'no *pl.* -nos
neu'tron'
Ne·vad'an
nev'er
nev'er·more'
nev'er·the·less'
ne'void'
ne'vus *pl.* -vi'
new *(recent)*
 ♦gnu, knew
new'born'
new'com'er
new'el
New Eng'land·er
new'fan'gled
New'found·land·er
New Hamp'shir·ite'
New Jer'sey·ite'
new'ly-wed' *also*
 new'ly·wed'
New Mex'i·can
news'boy'
news'cast'

news'let'ter
news'man'
news'pa'per
news'print'
news'reel'
news'stand'
news'wor'thy
news'y
newt
new'ton
New York'er
next
nex'us *pl.* -us *or* -us·es
ni'a·cin
nib
nib'ble, -bled, -bling
Nic'a·ra'guan
nice *(pleasing)*, nic'er,
 nic'est
 ♦gneiss
ni'ce·ty
niche *(recess)*
nick *(notch)*
nick'el
nick'el·o'de·on
nick'name', -named',
 -nam'ing
nic'o·tine'
nic'o·tin'ic
niece
nif'ty
Ni·ger'i·an
nig'gard·ly
nig'gling
nigh
night *(darkness)*
 ♦knight

night'cap'
night'clothes'
night'club'
night'dress'
night'fall'
night'gown'
night'hawk'
night'in·gale'
night'mare'
night'rid'er
night'shade'
night'shirt'
night'spot'
night'stick'
night'time'
ni'hil·ism
ni'hil·ist
ni'hil·is'tic
nil
nim'ble
nim'bo·stra'tus
nim'bus *pl.* -bi' *or*
 -bus·es
nin'com·poop'
nine'pin'
nine·teen'
nine·teenth'
nine'ti·eth
nine'ty
nin'ny
ninth
ni·o'bi·um
nip, nipped, nip'ping
nip'per
nip'ple
nip'py
nir·va'na

Ni·sei' *pl.* -sei' *or* -seis'
nit *(insect egg)*
 ♦knit
ni'ter
nit'-pick'
ni'trate', -trat'ed,
 -trat'ing
ni·tra'tion
ni'tric
ni'tride'
ni·tri·fi·ca'tion
ni'tri·fy', -fied', -fy'ing
ni'trite'
ni'tro·bac·te'ri·a
ni'tro·ben'zene'
ni'tro·cel'lu·lose'
ni'tro·gen
ni·trog'e·nous
ni'tro·glyc'er·in *also*
 ni'tro·glyc'er·ine
ni'trous
nit'ty-grit'ty
nit'wit'
nix
no *pl.* noes
no·bel'i·um
No·bel' Prize
no·bil'i·ty
no'ble
no'ble·man
no·blesse' o·blige'
no'ble·wom'an
no'bod'y
noc·tur'nal
noc'turne'
nod, nod'ded, nod'ding
nod'al

nod'der
node
nod'u·lar
nod'ule
No·ël' *also* No·el'
no'-fault' *adj.*
nog'gin
no'-hit'ter
noise, noised, nois'ing
noise'less
noise'mak'er
noi'some
nois'y
no'mad'
no·mad'ic
nom' de plume'
no'men·cla'ture
nom'i·nal
nom'i·nate', -nat'ed,
 -nat'ing
nom'i·na'tion
nom'i·na'tive
nom'i·na'tor
nom'i·nee'
non'age
non'a·ge·nar'i·an
non'a·gon'
non'a·ligned'
nonce
non'cha·lance'
non'cha·lant'
non'com'
non'com·bat'ant
non'com·mis'sioned
 officer
non'com·mit'tal
non'com·pli'ance

non'con·duc'tor
non'con·form'ist
non'con·form'i·ty
non'de·nom'i·na'-
    tion·al
non'de·script'
none *(not one)*
    ♦*nun*
non·en'ti·ty
none'such'
none'the·less'
non'-Eu·clid'e·an
non'ex·ist'ence
non'ex·ist'ent
non·fea'sance
non·fer'rous
non·fic'tion
non·flam'ma·ble *(not
    easily burned)*
    ♦*flammable, inflam-
    mable*
no·nil'lion
no·nil'lionth
non'in·ter·ven'tion
non'in·ter·ven'tion·
    ist
non·ju'ror
non·met'al
non'me·tal'lic
non·ob·jec'tive
no-non'sense' *adj.*
non'pa·reil'
non·par'ti·san
non·plus', -plused' *or*
    -plussed', -plus'ing
    or -plus'sing
non'pro·duc'tive

non·prof'it
non'pro·lif'er·a'tion
non'rep·re·sen·ta'-
    tion·al
non·res'i·dent
non're·sis'tant
non're·stric'tive
non·sched'uled
non'sec·tar'i·an
non·sense'
non·sen'si·cal
non se'qui·tur
non'sked'
non'skid'
non·smok'er
non·smok'ing
non·stan'dard
non·stop'
non'sup·port'
non·un'ion
non·ver'bal
non·vi'o·lence
non·vi'o·lent
noo'dle
nook
noon'day'
no one *also* no'-one'
noon'tide'
noon'time'
noose
no'-par' *adj.*
nor
Nor'dic
norm
nor'mal
nor'mal·cy
nor·mal'i·ty

nor'mal·i·za'tion
nor'mal·ize', -ized',
    -iz'ing
nor'ma·tive
Norse *pl.* Norse
Norse'man
North A·mer'i·can
north'bound'
North Car·o·lin'i·an
North Da·ko'tan
north·east'
north·east'er
north·east'er·ly
north·east'ern
north·east'ward *also*
    north·east'wards
north'er·ly
north'ern
north'ern·er
north'ern·most'
north'land'
north'-north·east'
north'-north·west'
north'ward *also*
    north'wards
north·west'
north·west'er·ly
north·west'ern
north·west'ward *also*
    north·west'wards
Nor·we'gian
nose, nosed, nos'ing
nose'bleed'
nose'-dive', -dived' *or*
    -dove', -div'ing
nose'gay'
nose'piece'

nosh
no'-show' *n.*
nos•tal'gi•a
nos•tal'gic
nos'tril
nos'trum
nos'y *also* nos'ey
not *(in no way)*
♦*knot*
no'ta be'ne
no•ta•bil'i•ty
no'ta•ble
no'ta•ri•za'tion
no'ta•rize', -rized',
-riz'ing
no'ta•ry
notary public *pl.* no-
taries public
no•ta'tion
notch
note, not'ed, not'ing
note'book'
note'wor'thy
noth'ing
noth'ing•ness
no'tice, -ticed, -tic•ing
no'tice•a•ble
no'ti•fi•ca'tion
no'ti•fy', -fied', -fy'ing
no'tion
no'to•chord'
no•to•ri'e•ty
no•to'ri•ous
no'-trump'
not'with•stand'ing
nou'gat
noun

nour'ish
nour'ish•ment
nou'veau riche' *pl.*
nou'veaux riches'
no'va *pl.* -vae *or* -vas
No'va Sco'tian
nov'el
nov'el•ette'
nov'el•ist
nov'el•is'tic
no•vel'la *pl.* -las *or* -le
nov'el•ty
No•vem'ber
no•ve'na *pl.* -nas *or*
-nae
nov'ice
no•vi'ti•ate
now'a•days'
no'way' *also* no'ways'
no'where'
no'wise'
nox'ious
noz'zle
nu'ance'
nub'bin
nub'ble
nu'bile
nu'cle•ar
nu'cle•ase'
nu'cle•ate', -at'ed, -at'-
ing
nu'cle•a'tion
nu•cle'ic acid
nu•cle'o•lar
nu•cle'o•lus *pl.* -li'
nu'cle•on'
nu'cle•on'ic

nu'cle•on'ics
nu'cle•o•pro'tein
nu'cle•o•side'
nu'cle•o•tide'
nu'cle•us *pl.* -cle•i'
nude
nudge, nudged, nudg'-
ing
nud'ism
nud'ist
nu'di•ty
nug'get
nui'sance
nuke
null
nul'li•fi•ca'tion
nul'li•fi'er
nul'li•fy', -fied', -fy'ing
nul'li•ty
numb *(insensible)*,
numb'er, numb'est
num'ber *(integer, sym-
bol, quantity)*
num'ber•less
numb'ness
nu'mer•a•ble
nu'mer•al
nu'mer•ate', -at'ed,
-at'ing
nu'mer•a'tion
nu'mer•a'tor
nu•mer'i•cal *also* nu•
mer'ic
nu'mer•o•log'i•cal
nu'mer•ol'o•gist
nu'mer•ol'o•gy
nu'mer•ous

nu'mis·mat'ic
nu'mis·mat'ics
nu·mis'ma·tist
num'skull' *also*
  numb'skull'
nun *(religious sister)*
  ♦none
nun'ci·o' *pl.* -os'
nun'ner·y
nup'tial
nurse, nursed, nurs'ing
nurse'maid' *also*
  nurs'er·y·maid'
nurs'er·y
nurs'er·y·man
nurs'ling
nur'ture, -tured, -tur·
  ing
nut'crack'er
nut'hatch'
nut'meat'
nut'meg'
nu·tri·a
nu'tri·ent
nu'tri·ment
nu·tri·men'tal
nu·tri'tion
nu·tri'tion·al
nu·tri'tion·ist
nu·tri'tious
nu'tri·tive
nut'shell'
nut'ty
nuz'zle, -zled, -zling
ny'lon'
nymph
nym·phet'

nym'pho·ma'ni·a
nym'pho·ma'ni·ac'

O

oaf *pl.* oafs
oak'en
oa'kum
oar *(pole)*
  ♦o'er, or, ore
oar'lock'
oars'man
o·a'sis *pl.* -ses'
oat'en
oath *pl.* oaths
oat'meal'
ob'du·ra·cy
ob'du·rate
o·be'di·ence
o·be'di·ent
o·bei'sance
o·bei'sant
ob'e·lisk
o·bese'
o·be·si·ty
o·bey'
ob·fus'cate', -cat'ed,
  -cat'ing
ob'fus·ca'tion
o'bi *pl.* o'bis
o'bit
o'bi·ter dic'tum *pl.*
  o'bi·ter dic'ta
o·bit'u·ar'y
ob'ject *n.*

ob·ject' *v.*
ob·jec'tion
ob·jec'tion·a·ble
ob·jec'tive
ob·jec·tiv'i·ty
ob·jec'tor
o'blast
ob'late'
ob·la'tion
ob'li·gate', -gat'ed,
  -gat'ing
ob'li·ga'tion
ob'li·ga'tor
o·blig'a·to'ry
o·blige', o·bliged',
  o·blig'ing
o·blique'
o·bliq'ui·ty
o·blit'er·ate', -at'ed,
  -at'ing
o·blit'er·a'tion
o·blit'er·a'tor
o·bliv'i·on
o·bliv'i·ous
ob'long'
ob'lo·quy
ob·nox'ious
o'boe
o'bo·ist
ob·scene'
ob·scen'i·ty
ob·scur'ant
ob·scur'ant·ism
ob·scure', -scur'er,
  -scur'est
ob·scure', -scured',
  -scur'ing

ob·scu'ri·ty
ob·se'qui·ous
ob'se·quy
ob·serv'a·ble
ob·ser'vance
ob·ser'vant
ob·ser·va'tion
ob·ser'va·to'ry
ob·serve', -served',
 -serv'ing
ob·sess'
ob·ses'sion
ob·ses'sive
ob·sid'i·an
ob'so·les'cence
ob'so·les'cent
ob'so·lete'
ob'sta·cle
ob·stet'ric *also* ob·
 stet'ri·cal
ob·ste·tri'cian
ob·stet'rics
ob'sti·na·cy
ob'sti·nate
ob·strep'er·ous
ob·struct'
ob·struct'er *also* ob·
 struc'tor
ob·struc'tion
ob·struc'tion·ism
ob·struc'tion·ist
ob·struc'tive
ob·tain'
ob·tain'a·ble
ob·trude', -trud'ed,
 -trud'ing
ob·tru'sion

ob·tru'sive
ob·tuse'
ob·verse' *adj.*
ob'verse' *n.*
ob·vert'
ob'vi·ate', -at·ed, -at'-
 ing
ob'vi·a'tion
ob'vi·a'tor
ob'vi·ous
oc'a·ri'na
oc·ca'sion
oc·ca'sion·al
oc'ci·dent *also* Oc'ci·
 dent
oc'ci·den'tal *or* Oc'ci·
 den'tal
oc·cip'i·tal
oc·clude', -clud'ed,
 -clud'ing
oc·clu'sion
oc·clu'sive
oc·cult'
oc'cul·ta'tion
oc·cult'ism
oc·cult'ist
oc'cu·pan·cy
oc'cu·pant
oc'cu·pa'tion
oc'cu·pa'tion·al
oc'cu·pi'er
oc'cu·py', -pied', -py'-
 ing
oc·cur', -curred', -cur'-
 ring
oc·cur'rence
oc·cur'rent

o'cean
o'ce·an'ic
o'cean·og'ra·pher
o'cean·o·graph'ic *also*
 o'cean·o·graph'i·cal
o'cean·og'ra·phy
oc'e·lot'
o'cher *or* o'chre
o'clock'
o'co·ti'llo *pl.* -llos
oc'ta·gon'
oc·tag'o·nal
oc'ta·he'dral
oc'ta·he'dron *pl.*
 -drons *or* -dra
oc'tane'
oc'tant
oc'tave
oc·ta'vo *pl.* -vos
oc'tet'
oc·til'lion
Oc·to'ber
oc'to·ge·nar'i·an
oc'to·pus *pl.* -pus·es *or*
 -pi'
oc'u·lar
oc'u·list
o'da·lisque' *also* o'da·
 lisk'
odd'ball'
odd'i·ty
odd'ment
odds
ode *(poem)*
 ♦owed
o'di·ous
o'di·um

o•dom′e•ter
o′dor
o′dor•if′er•ous
o′dor•ous
od′ys•sey *(journey), pl.*
-seys
Od′ys•sey *(epic)*
oed′i•pal *also* Oed′i•
pal
Oed′i•pus complex
o′er *(over)*
♦*oar, or, ore*
of
of′fal *(refuse)*
♦*awful*
off′beat′
off′-Broad′way′
off′-col′or
of•fend′
of•fense′ *(violation)*
of′fense′ *(attacking)*
of•fen′sive
of•fer
of′fer•er *also* of′fer•or
of′fer•to•ry
off′hand′
of′fice
of′fice•hold′er
of′fi•cer
of•fi′cial *(authorized)*
♦*officious*
of•fi′cial•dom
of•fi′ci•ant
of•fi′ci•ate′, -at′ed,
-at′ing
of•fi′ci•a′tor

of•fi′cious *(meddle-*
some)
♦*official*
off′ing
off′-line′
off′set′, -set′, -set′ting
off′shoot′
off′shore′
off′side′
off′spring′
off′-stage′
off′-the-rec′ord *adj.*
off′-the-wall′ *adj.*
off′-track′
off′-white′
oft
of′ten
of′ten•times′ *also* oft′-
times′
o′gee′
o′gle, o′gled, o′gling
o′gre
oh *(exclamation)*
♦*owe*
O•hi′o•an
ohm
ohm′me′ter
oil′cloth′
oil′skin′
oil′stone′
oil′y
oint′ment
O.K. *or* OK *or* o•kay′
pl. O.K.'s *or* OK's *or*
o•kays′
O.K. *or* OK *or* o•kay′,
O.K.'d *or* OK'd *or* o•

kayed′, O.K.'ing *or*
OK'ing *or* o•kay′ing
o•ka′pi *pl.* -pi *or* -pis
O′kla•ho′man
o′kra
old′en
old′-fash′ioned *adj.*
old′-line′
old′ster
old′-time′
old′-tim′er
old′-world′ *also* Old′-
-World′
o′le•ag′i•nous
o′le•an′der
o′le•fin
o•le′ic
o′le•o•mar′ga•rine
o′le•o•res′in
ol•fac′to•ry
ol′i•garch′
ol′i•gar′chic *also* ol′i•
gar′chi•cal
ol′i•gar′chy
Ol′i•go•cene′
ol′i•gop′o•ly
o′li•o′ *pl.* -os
ol′ive
ol′i•vine′
O•lym′pi•ad′
O•lym′pi•an
O•lym′pic
om′buds•man
o•me′ga
om′e•let *also* om′e•
lette
o′men

om'i·nous
o·mis'sion
o·mit', o·mit'ted,
o·mit'ting
om·ni·bus' *pl.* -bus'es
om·nip'o·tence *also*
om·nip'o·ten·cy
om·nip'o·tent
om·ni·pres'ence
om·ni·pres'ent
om·nis'cience *also*
om·nis'cien·cy
om·nis'cient
om'ni·vore'
om·niv'o·rous
on·board' *adj.*
once'-o'ver
on'com'ing
one *(single)*
♦won
one'-on-one'
on'er·ous
one·self'
one'-sid'ed
one'time'
one'-to-one'
one'-track'
one-up'man·ship'
one'-way'
on'go'ing
on'ion
on'ion·skin'
on'-line' *adj.*
on'look'er
on'ly
on·o·mat'o·poe'ia
on·o·mat'o·poe'ic

also on'o·mat'o·po·
et'ic
on'rush'
on'set'
on'shore'
on'slaught'
on'to'
on·to·log'i·cal
on·tol'o·gy
o'nus
on'ward *also* on'wards
on'yx
oo'dles
oo'long'
oomph
ooze, oozed, ooz'ing
ooz'y
o·pac'i·ty
o'pal
o'pal·es'cence
o'pal·es'cent
o·paque'
op art
op-ed' page
o'pen
o'pen-air'
o'pen-and-shut' *adj.*
o'pen-end'
o'pen-end'ed
o'pen·er
o'pen-eyed'
o'pen·hand'ed
o'pen-heart' *adj.*
o'pen·heart'ed
o'pen-hearth'
o'pen·ing
o'pen-mind'ed

o'pen·work'
op'er·a
op'er·a·bil'i·ty
op'er·a·ble
op'er·and
op'er·ate', -at'ed, -at'-
ing
op'er·at'ic
op'er·a'tion
op'er·a'tion·al
op'er·a·tive
op'er·a'tor
op'e·ret'ta
o·phid'i·an
oph·thal'mic
oph·thal'mo·log'ic
also oph·thal'mo·
log'i·cal
oph'thal·mol'o·gist
oph'thal·mol'o·gy
o'pi·ate', -at'ed, -at'ing
o·pine', o·pined',
o·pin'ing
o·pin'ion
o·pin'ion·at'ed
o'pi·um
o·pos'sum *pl.* -sum *or*
-sums, *also* pos'sum
op·po'nent
op'por·tune'
op'por·tun'ism
op'por·tun'ist
op'por·tun·is'tic
op'por·tu'ni·ty
op·pos'a·ble
op·pose', -posed',
-pos'ing

op′po•site
op′po•si′tion
op•press′
op•pres′sion
op•pres′sive
op•pres′sor
op•pro′bri•ous
op•pro′bri•um
opt
op′tic
op′ti•cal
op•ti′cian
op′tics
op′ti•mal
op′ti•mism
op′ti•mist
op′ti•mis′tic
op′ti•mum *pl.* -ma *or*
-mums
op′tion
op′tion•al
op•tom′e•trist
op•tom′e•try
op′u•lence *also* op′u•
len•cy
op′u•lent
o′pus *pl.* op′er•a *or*
o′pus•es
or *conj.*
 ♦*oar, o′er, ore*
or′a•cle *(seer)*
 ♦*auricle*
o•rac′u•lar
o′ral *(spoken)*
 ♦*aural*
or′ange
or′ange•ade′

o•rang′u•tan′ *also*
o•rang′ou•tan′
o•rate′, o•rat′ed, o•rat′-
ing
o•ra′tion
or′a•tor
or′a•tor′i•cal
or′a•to′ri•o′ *pl.* -os′
or′a•to′ry
orb
or•bic′u•lar
or′bit
or′bit•al
or′chard
or′ches•tra
or•ches′tral
or′ches•trate′, -trat′ed,
-trat′ing
or′ches•tra′tion
or′chid
or•dain′
or•deal′
or′der
or′der•ly
or′di•nal
or′di•nance *(com-*
mand)
 ♦*ordnance*
or′di•nar′i•ly
or′di•nar′y
or′di•nate
or′di•na′tion
ord′nance *(military*
supplies)
 ♦*ordinance*
Or′do•vi′cian
or′dure

ore *(mineral)*
 ♦*oar, o′er, or*
o•reg′a•no
Or′e•go′ni•an
or′gan
or′gan•dy *also* or′gan•
die
or′gan•elle′
or•gan′ic
or•gan′i•cism
or′gan•ism
or′gan•is′mal
 also or′gan•is′mic
or′gan•ist
or′gan•i•za′tion
or′gan•ize′, -ized′, -iz′-
ing
or•gan′za
or′gasm
or′gi•as′tic
or′gy
o′ri•el
o′ri•ent *(to align)*
O′ri•ent *(Asia)*
o′ri•en′tal *also* O′ri•
en′tal
o′ri•en•ta′tion
or′i•fice
o′ri•ga′mi
or′i•gin
o•rig′i•nal
o•rig′i•nal′i•ty
o•rig′i•nate′, -nat′ed,
-nat′ing
o•rig′i•na′tion
o•rig′i•na′tor
o′ri•ole′

Or'lon'®
or'mo·lu'
or'na·ment
or'na·men'tal
or'na·men·ta'tion
or·nate'
or'ner·y
or'ni·tho·log'ic *also*
  or'ni·tho·log'i·cal
or'ni·thol'o·gist
or'ni·thol'o·gy
o'ro·tund'
or'phan
or'phan·age
or'pi·ment
or'ris·root'
or'thi·con'
or'tho·clase'
or'tho·don'tia
or'tho·don'tic
or'tho·don'tist
or'tho·dox'
or'tho·dox'y
or·thog'o·nal
or'tho·graph'ic
or·thog'ra·phy
or'tho·pe'dic
or'tho·pe'dics
or'tho·pe'dist
o'ryx *pl.* o'ryx·es *or* o'-
  ryx
Os'car
os'cil·late' *(to swing
  back and forth),* -lat'-
  ed, -lat'ing
  ♦*osculate*
os'cil·la'tion

os'cil·la'tor
os'cil·la·to'ry
os·cil'lo·scope'
os·cil'lo·scop'ic
os'cine
os'cu·late' *(to kiss),*
  -lat'ed, -lat'ing
  ♦*oscillate*
os'cu·la'tion
o'sier
os'mi·um
os·mo'sis
os·mot'ic
os'prey *pl.* -preys
os'se·ous
os·si·fi·ca'tion
os'si·fy', -fied', -fy'ing
os·ten'si·ble
os·ten·ta'tion
os·ten·ta'tious
os'te·o·path'
os'te·o·path'ic
os'te·op'a·thy
os'tra·cism
os'tra·cize', -cized',
  -ciz'ing
os'trich
Os'tro·goth'
oth'er
oth'er·wise'
oth'er·world'ly
o'ti·ose'
o'to·lar'yn·gol'o·gy
o·tol'o·gy
ot'ter *pl.* -ter *or* -ters
ot'to·man *pl.* -mans
ou'bli·ette'

ouch
ought *auxiliary*
  ♦*aught*
ounce
our *pron.*
  ♦*hour*
ours *pron.*
  ♦*hours*
our·self'
our·selves'
oust'er
out'-and-out' *adj.*
out'back'
out·bid', -bid', -bid'-
  den *or* -bid', -bid'-
  ding
out'board'
out'bound'
out'break'
out'build'ing
out'burst'
out'cast'
out'class'
out'come'
out·crop', -cropped',
  -crop'ping
out'cry'
out·dat'ed
out·dis'tance, -tanced,
  -tanc·ing
out·do', -did', -done',
  -do'ing
out'door'
out'doors'
out'er
out'er·most'

out·face′, -faced′,
  -fac′ing
out′field′
out′fit′, -fit′ted, -fit′-
  ting
out′fit′ter
out·flank′
out′flow′
out·fox′
out′go′ *pl.* -goes′
out·go′, -went′, -gone′,
  -go′ing
out·grow′, -grew′,
  -grown′, -grow′ing
out′growth′
out·guess′
out′house′
out′ing
out·land′ish
out·last′
out′law′
out′lay′
out′let′
out·line′, -lined′, -lin′-
  ing
out·live′, -lived′, -liv′-
  ing
out′look′
out′ly′ing
out·ma·neu′ver
out·mod′ed
out·num′ber
out′-of-date′ *adj.*
out′pa′tient
out′play′
out′post′
out′pour′ing

out′put′
out·rage′, -raged′,
  -rag′ing
out·ra′geous
out·rank′
out′reach′
out′rid′er
out′rig′ger
out′right′
out·run′, -ran′, -run′,
  -run′ning
out·sell′, -sold′, -sell′-
  ing
out′set′
out·shine′, -shone′,
  -shin′ing
out′side′
out′sid′er
out′size′ *also* out′sized′
out′skirts′
out·smart′
out·spo′ken
out′spread′ *adj.*
out′spread′ *n.*
out·spread′, -spread′,
  -spread′ing
out′stand′ing
out·sta′tion
out′stay′
out·stretch′
out·strip′, -stripped′,
  -strip′ping
out′ward *also* out′-
  wards
out·wear′, -wore′,
  -worn′, -wear′ing
out·weigh′

out·wit′, -wit′ted,
  -wit′ting
out′work′ *n.*
out·work′ *v.*
ou′zel
o′val
o·var′i·an *also* o·var′i·
  al
o′va·ry
o′vate′
o·va′tion
ov′en
ov′en·bird′
o′ver
o′ver·a·bun′dance
o′ver·a·bun′dant
o′ver·a·chieve′,
  -chieved′, -chiev′ing
o′ver·act′
o′ver·age′ *adj.*
o′ver·age′ *n.*
o′ver·all′ *also* o′ver-all′
o′ver·alls′
o′ver·arm′
o′ver·awe′, -awed′,
  -aw′ing
o′ver·bal′ance,
  -anced, -anc·ing
o′ver·bear′ing
o′ver·bid′ *n.*
o′ver·bid′, -bid′, -bid′-
  den *or* -bid′, -bid′-
  ding
o′ver·bite′
o′ver·blown′
o′ver·board′
o′ver·book′

o'ver·bur'den

o'ver·call' n.

o'ver·call' v.

o'ver·cap'i·tal·ize', -ized', -iz'ing

o'ver·cast' adj. & n.

o'ver·cast', -cast'ed, -cast'ing

o'ver·charge' n.

o'ver·charge', -charged', -charg'ing

o'ver·coat'

o'ver·come', -came', -come', -com'ing

o'ver·com'pen·sate', -sat'ed, -sat'ing

o'ver·com'pen·sa'tion

o'ver·con'fi·dence

o'ver·de·vel'op

o'ver·do' (to do to excess), -did', -done', -do'ing
♦overdue

o'ver·dose' n.

o'ver·dose', -dosed', -dos'ing

o'ver·draft'

o'ver·draw', -drew', -drawn', -draw'ing

o'ver·dress'

o'ver·drive' n.

o'ver·drive', -drove', -driv'en, -driv'ing

o'ver·due' (unpaid, past due)
♦overdo

o'ver·eat', -ate', -eat'-ing

o'ver·ed'u·cate', -cat'-ed, -cat'ing

o'ver·em'pha·sis

o'ver·es'ti·mate', -mat'ed, -mat'ing

o'ver·es'ti·ma'tion

o'ver·ex·ert'

o'ver·ex·er'tion

o'ver·ex·pose', -posed', -pos'ing

o'ver·ex·po'sure

o'ver·ex·tend'

o'ver·ex·ten'sion

o'ver·flow' n.

o'ver·flow' v.

o'ver·grow', -grew', -grown', -grow'ing

o'ver·growth'

o'ver·hand'

o'ver·hang' n.

o'ver·hang', -hung', -hang'ing

o'ver·haul' n.

o'ver·haul' v.

o'ver·head' adj. & n.

o'ver·head' adv.

o'ver·hear', -heard', -hear'ing

o'ver·heat'

o'ver·in·dulge', -dulged', -dulg'ing

o'ver·in·dul'gence

o'ver·in·dul'gent

o'ver·joyed'

o'ver·kill'

o'ver·land'

o'ver·lap' n.

o'ver·lap', -lapped', -lap'ping

o'ver·lay' n.

o'ver·lay', -laid', -lay'-ing

o'ver·leap', -leaped' or -leapt', -leap'ing

o'ver·lie', -lay', -lain', -lay'ing

o'ver·load' n.

o'ver·load' v.

o'ver·long'

o'ver·look' n.

o'ver·look' v.

o'ver·lord'

o'ver·ly

o'ver·mas'ter

o'ver·match' n.

o'ver·match' v.

o'ver·much'

o'ver·night' adj.

o'ver·night' adv.

o'ver·pass' n.

o'ver·pass', -passed' or -past', -pass'ing

o'ver·pay', -paid', -pay'ing

o'ver·pay'ment

o'ver·play'

o'ver·pop'u·la'tion

o'ver·pow'er

o'ver·price', -priced', -pric'ing

o'ver·print' n.

o'ver·print' v.

o'ver•pro•duce',
-duced', -duc'ing
o'ver•pro•duc'tion
o'ver•pro•tec'tive
o'ver•qual'i•fied
o'ver•rate', -rat'ed,
-rat'ing
o'ver•reach'
o'ver•re•act'
o'ver•re•ac'tion
o'ver•ride', -rode',
-rid'den, -ri(•)ing
o'ver•rule', -ruled',
-rul'ing
o'ver•run' n.
o'ver•run', -ran', -run',
-run'ning
o'ver•seas' (abroad)
♦oversees
o'ver•see', -saw',
-seen', -see'ing
o'ver•se'er
o'ver•sell', -sold',
-sell'ing
o'ver•shad•ow
o'ver•shoe'
o'ver•shoot', -shot',
-shoot'ing
o'ver•shot' adj.
o'ver•sight'
o'ver•sim'pli•fi•ca'-
tion
o'ver•sim'pli•fy',
-fied', -fy'ing
o'ver•size' adj., also
o'ver•sized'
o'ver•size' n.

o'ver•skirt'
o'ver•sleep', -slept',
-sleep'ing
o'ver•state', -stat'ed,
-stat'ing
o'ver•stay'
o'ver•step', -stepped',
-step'ping
o'ver•stock'
o'ver•stuff'
o'ver•sub•scribe',
-scribed', -scrib'ing
o'ver•sub•scrip'tion
o•vert'
o'ver•take', -took',
-tak'en, -tak'ing
o'ver•tax'
o'ver-the-count'er
adj.
o'ver•throw' n.
o'ver•throw', -threw',
-thrown', -throw'ing
o'ver•time'
o'ver•tone'
o'ver•top', -topped',
-top'ping
o'ver•trick'
o'ver•trump'
o'ver•ture'
o'ver•turn' n.
o'ver•turn' v.
o'ver•use', -used', -us'-
ing
o'ver•view'
o'ver•ween'ing
o'ver•weigh'
o'ver•weight'

o'ver•whelm'
o'ver•work' n.
o'ver•work' v.
o'ver•wrought'
o'vi•duct'
o'vine'
o'vi•par'i•ty
o•vip'a•rous
o'vi•pos'i•tor
o•void' also o•voi'dal
o'vo•vi•vip'a•rous
o'vu•lar
o'vu•late', -lat'ed,
-lat'ing
o'vu•la'tion
o'vule
o'vum pl. o'va
owe (to be indebted),
ōwed, ow'ing
♦oh
owl'et
owl'ish
own'er
own'er•ship'
ox pl. ox'en
ox•al'ic acid
ox'al•is
ox'blood' red
ox'bow'
ox'eye'
ox'ford
ox'i•dant
ox'i•da'tion
ox'i•da'tive
ox'ide'
ox'i•di•za'tion

ox'i·dize', -dized',
-diz'ing
ox'lip'
Ox·o'ni·an
ox'tail'
ox'y·a·cet'y·lene
ox'y·gen
ox'y·gen·ate', -at'ed,
-at'ing
ox'y·gen·a'tion
ox'y·gen'ic *also* ox·
yg'e·nous
ox'y·mo'ron' *pl.* -ra
o'yez'
oys'ter
o'zone'
o·zo'no·sphere'

P

pab'u·lum
pace, paced, pac'ing
pace'mak'er
pace'set'ter
pace'set'ting
pach'y·derm'
pach'y·san'dra
pa·cif'ic
pac'i·fi·ca'tion
pac'i·fi'er
pac'i·fism
pac'i·fist
pac'i·fy', -fied', -fy'ing
pack'age, -aged, -ag·
ing

pack'er
pack'et
pack'ing
pack'sack'
pack'sad'dle
pact *(treaty)*
♦*packed*
pad, pad'ded, pad'ding
pad'dle, -dled, -dling
pad'dle·fish' *pl.* -fish'
or -fish'es
pad'dock
pad'dy
pad'lock'
pa'dre
pae'an *(song)*
♦*peon*
pa·el'la
pa'gan
pa'gan·ism
page, paged, pag'ing
pag'eant
pag'eant·ry
page'boy'
pag'i·nate', -nat'ed,
-nat'ing
pag'i·na'tion
pa·go'da
pail *(bucket)*
♦*pale*
pain *(suffering)*
♦*pane*
pain'ful
pain'kill'er
pain'kill'ing
pain'less
pains'tak'ing

paint'brush'
paint'er
paint'ing
pair *(set of two)*
♦*pare, pear*
pais'ley
pa·ja'mas
Pak·i·stan'i *pl.* -stan'is
or -stan'i
pal, palled, pal'ling
pal'ace
pal'a·din
pal'an·quin'
pal'at·a·bil'i·ty
pal'at·a·ble
pal'a·tal
pal'ate *(roof of the
mouth)*
♦*palette, pallet*
pa·la'tial
pa·lat'i·nate'
pal'a·tine'
pa·lav'er
pale *(wan)*, pal'er, pal'-
est
♦*pail*
pale *(picket)*
♦*pail*
pale *(to blanch, fence
in)*, paled, pal'ing
♦*pail*
pale'face'
Pa'le·o·cene'
pa'le·og'ra·pher
pa'le·o·graph'ic *also*
pa'le·o·graph'i·cal
pa'le·og'ra·phy

Pa′le·o·lith′ic
pa′le·on·tol′o·gist
pa′le·on·tol′o·gy
Pa′le·o·zo′ic
Pal′es·tin′i·an
pal′ette *(board for
　paint)*
　♦*palate, pallet*
pal′frey *pl.* -freys
pal′i·mo′ny
pal′imp·sest′
pal′in·drome′
pal′ing
pal′i·node′
pal′i·sade′
pall *(coffin cover)*
　♦*pawl*
pall *(to grow dull)*
　♦*pawl*
pal·la′di·um
pall′bear′er
pal′let *(tool, bed)*
　♦*palate, palette*
pal′li·ate′, -at′ed, -at′-
　ing
pal′li·a′tion
pal′li·a′tive
pal′lid
pal′lor
palm
pal′mate′ *also* pal′-
　mat·ed
pal·met′to *pl.* -tos *or*
　-toes
palm′ist *also* palm′is·
　ter
palm′is·try

palm′y
pal′o·mi′no *pl.* -nos
palp
pal′pa·bil′i·ty
pal′pa·ble
pal′pate′ *(to examine
　by touch)*, -pat′ed,
　-pat′ing
pal′pi·tate′ *(to throb)*,
　-tat′ed, -tat′ing
pal′pi·ta′tion
pal′sied
pal′sy
pal′ter
pal′try *(petty)*
　♦*poultry*
pam′pa *pl.* -pas
pam′per
pam′phlet
pam′phlet·eer′
pan *(to wash, cook,
　move a camera)*,
　panned, pan′ning
Pan *(god)*
pan′a·ce′a
pa·nache′
Pan·a·ma′ni·an
Pan′-A·mer′i·can
pan′a·tel′a
pan′-broil′
pan′cake′ *(griddle
　cake)*
Pan′-Cake′ Make′-
　Up′®
pan′chro·mat′ic
pan′cre·as
pan′cre·at′ic

pan′da
pan·dem′ic
pan′de·mo′ni·um
pan′der
Pan·do′ra's box
pan′dow′dy
pane *(sheet of glass)*
　♦*pain*
pan′e·gyr′ic
pan′e·gyr′i·cal
pan′e·gyr′ist
pan′el, -eled *or* -elled,
　-el·ing *or* -el·ling
pan′el·ist
pan′-fry′, -fried′, -fry′-
　ing
pang
pan·go′lin
pan′han′dle, -dled,
　-dling
pan′ic, -icked, -ick·ing
pan′ick·y
pan′i·cle
pan′ic-strick′en
pan′nier
pan′o·ply
pan′o·ram′a
pan′o·ram′ic
pan′pipe′
pan′sy
pant
pan′ta·lets′ *also* pan′-
　ta·lettes′
pan′ta·loons′
pan′the·ism
pan′the·ist

pan'the·is'tic *also*
  pan'the·is'ti·cal
pan'the·on'
pan'ther
pant'ies
pan'to·mime',
  -mimed', -mim'ing
pan'try
pants
pant'suit' *also* pants
  suit
pant'y·hose' *pl.* -hose'
pant'y·waist'
pan'zer
pap
pa'pa
pa'pa·cy
pa'pal
pa'pa·raz'zo *pl.* -zi
pa'paw' *also* paw'paw'
pa·pa'ya
pa'per
pa'per·back'
pa'per·board'
pa'per·bound'
pa'per·hang'er
pa'per·knife'
pa'per·weight'
pa'per·work'
pa'pier-mâ·ché'
pa·pil'la *pl.* -lae
pap'il·lar'y
pa'pist
pa·poose'
pa·pri'ka
Pap'u·an New
  Guin'e·an

pa·py'rus *pl.* -rus·es *or*
  -ri'
par
par'a·ble
pa·rab'o·la
par'a·bol'ic *also* par'a·
  bol'i·cal
par'a·chute', -chut'ed,
  -chut'ing
par'a·chut'ist
pa·rade', -rad'ed,
  -rad'ing
par'a·digm'
par'a·dise'
par'a·dox'
par'a·dox'i·cal
par'af·fin
par'a·gon'
par'a·graph'
Par'a·guay'an
par'a·keet'
par·al'de·hyde'
par'a·le'gal
par·al·lax'
par·al·lel', -leled' *or*
  -lelled', -lel·ing *or*
  -lel'ling
par·al·lel'e·pi'ped
par·al·lel·ism'
par·al·lel'o·gram'
pa·ral'y·sis *pl.* -ses'
par'a·lyt'ic
par'a·lyze', -lyzed',
  -lyz'ing
par'a·me'ci·um *pl.* -ci·
  a *or* -ci·ums
par'a·med'ic

par'a·med'i·cal
pa·ram'e·ter *(constant,*
  limit)
  ♦perimeter
par'a·mil'i·tar'y
par'a·mount'
par'a·mour'
par'a·noi'a
par'a·noi'ac'
par'a·noid'
par'a·pet
par'a·pher·na'lia
par'a·phrase',
  -phrased', -phras'ing
par'a·ple'gi·a
par'a·ple'gic
par'a·pro·fes'sion·al
par'a·psy·chol'o·gy
par'a·site'
par'a·sit'ic *also* par'a·
  sit'i·cal
par'a·sit·ism'
par'a·sit·ize', -ized',
  -iz'ing
par'a·sol'
par'a·sym'pa·thet'ic
  nervous system
par'a·thi'on
par'a·thy'roid' gland
par'a·troop'er
par'a·troops'
par'a·ty'phoid' fever
par'boil'
par'cel *(to divide)*,
  -celed *or* -celled,
  -cel·ing *or* -cel·ling
  ♦partial

parch
Par·chee′si®
parch′ment
par′don
par′don·a·ble
pare *(to peel)*, pared,
  par′ing
  ♦*pair, pear*
par′e·gor′ic
pa·ren′chy·ma
par′ent
par′ent·age
pa·ren′tal
pa·ren′the·sis *pl.* -ses′
par′en·thet′i·cal *also*
  par′en·tinet′ic
par′ent·hood′
par′ent·ing
pa·re′sis
pa·ret′ic
par′ ex′cel·lence′
par·fait′
pa·ri′ah
pa·ri′e·tal
par′i·mu′tu·el
par′ish *(adminstrative*
  unit)
  ♦*perish*
pa·rish′ion·er
Pa·ri′sian
par′i·ty
par′ka
Par′kin·son's disease
park′way′
par′lance
par′lay′ *(bet)*

par′ley *(discussion), pl.*
  -leys
par′lia·ment
par′lia·men·tar′i·an
par′lia·men·ta·ry
par′lor
par′lous
Par′me·san′
pa·ro′chi·al
pa·ro′chi·al·ism
par′o·dy, -died, -dy·
  ing
pa·role′, -roled′, -rol′-
  ing
pa·rol′ee′
pa·rot′id gland
par′ox·ysm
par′ox·ys′mal
par·quet′, -queted′,
  -quet′ing
par·quet′ry
par′ri·cid′al
par′ri·cide′
par′rot
par′ry, -ried, -ry·ing
parse, parsed, pars′ing
par′sec′
par′si·mo′ni·ous
par′si·mo′ny
pars′ley
pars′nip′
par′son
par′son·age
Par′sons table
par·take′, -took′, -tak-
  en, -tak′ing
part′ed

par·terre′
par′tial *(incomplete)*
  ♦*parcel*
par′ti·al′i·ty
par·tic′i·pance
par·tic′i·pant
par·tic′i·pate′, -pat′ed,
  -pat′ing
par·tic′i·pa′tion
par·tic′i·pa′tor
par′ti·cip′i·al
par′ti·ci·ple
par′ti·cle
par·ti-col′ored
par·tic′u·lar
par·tic′u·lar′i·ty
par·tic′u·lar·i·za′tion
par·tic′u·lar·ize′,
  -ized′, -lz′ing
par·tic′u·lar·ly
part′ing
par′ti·san
par′tite′
par·ti′tion
part′ly
part′ner
part′ner·ship′
par′tridge
part′-time′ *adj.*
par·tu′ri·en·cy
par·tu′ri·ent
par·tu·ri′tion
par′ty
par·ve·nu′
pas′chal
pas′ de deux′ *pl.* pas′
  de deux′

pa'sha
pasque'flow'er
pass'a·ble *(capable of being passed)*
 ♦*passible*
pas'sage
pas'sage·way'
pas'sant
pass'book'
pas·sé'
pas'sen·ger
pas'ser-by' *pl.* pas'-sers-by', *also* pas'ser·by'
pas'ser·ine'
pas'si·ble *(sensitive)*
 ♦*passable*
pas'sim
pass'ing
pas'sion
pas'sion·ate
pas'sion·flow'er
pas'sive
pas·siv'i·ty
pass'key'
Pass'o'ver
pass'port'
pass'word'
past *(ago)*
 ♦*passed*
pas'ta
paste, past'ed, past'ing
paste'board'
pas·tel'
pas·tel'ist
pas'tern
paste'-up' *n.*

pas'teur·i·za'tion
pas'teur·ize', -ized', -iz'ing
pas·tiche'
pas·tille'
pas'time'
pas'tor
pas'tor·al
pas'tor·ate
pas·tra'mi
pas'try
pas'tur·age
pas'ture, -tured, -tur·ing
past'y *(pale)*
pas'ty *(pie)*
pat, pat'ted, pat'ting
patch'ou·li *pl.* -lis, *also* patch'ou·ly, pach'ou·li *pl.* -lis
patch'work'
pate *(head)*
pâ·té' *(meat paste)*
 ♦*patty*
pâ·té' de foie gras'
pa·tel'la *pl.* -lae
pa·tel'lar *also* pa·tel'-late
pat'en
pat'ent
pat'ent·ee'
pa'ter·fa·mil'i·as
pa·ter'nal
pa·ter'nal·ism
pa·ter'nal·is'tic
pa·ter'ni·ty
pa'ter·nos'ter

path *pl.* paths
pa·thet'ic
path'find'er
path'o·gen
path'o·gen'ic
path'o·log'i·cal
pa·thol'o·gist
pa·thol'o·gy
pa'thos'
path'way'
pa'tience
pa'tient
pat'i·na
pat'i·o' *pl.* -os'
pa'tis·se·rie'
pat'ois *pl.* -ois'
pa'tri·arch
pa'tri·ar'chal
pa'tri·ar'chy
pa·tri'cian
pat'ri·cid'al
pat'ri·cide'
pat'ri·mo'ni·al
pat'ri·mo'ny
pa'tri·ot
pa'tri·ot'ic
pa'tri·ot·ism
pa·trol', -trolled', -trol'ling
pa·trol'man
pa'tron
pa'tron·age
pa'tron·ize', -ized', -iz'ing
pat'ro·nym'ic
pa·troon'
pat'sy

pat'ter
pat'tern
pat'ty *(small cake or pie)*
  ♦*pâté*
pau'ci·ty
paunch'y
pau'per·ism
pau'per·i·za'tion
pau'per·ize', -ized', -iz'ing
pause *(to stop briefly)*, paused, paus'ing
  ♦*paws*
pa·vane' *also* pa·van'
pave, paved, pav'ing
pave'ment
pa·vil'ion
paw
pawl *(hinged device)*
  ♦*pall*
pawn'bro'ker
pawn'shop'
pay, paid, pay'ing
pay'a·ble
pay'check'
pay'day'
pay·ee'
pay'load'
pay'mas'ter
pay'ment
pay·off' *n.*
pay·o'la
pay'roll'
pea
peace *(calm)*
  ♦*piece*

peace'a·ble
peace'ful
peace'mak'er
peace'time'
pcach'y
pea'cock'
pea'fowl' *pl.* -fowl *or* -fowls'
pea'hen'
peak *(point)*
  ♦*peek, pique*
peaked *(pointed)*
peak'ed *(pale)*
peal *(ringing)*
  ♦*peel*
pea'nut'
pear *(fruit)*
  ♦*pair, pare*
pcarl *(gem)*
  ♦*purl*
pearl'y
peas'ant
peas'ant·ry
pea'shoot'er
peat
pea'vey *pl.* -veys, *also* pea'vy
peb'ble, -bled, -bling
peb'bly
pe·can'
pec'ca·dil'lo *pl.* -loes *or* -los
pec'ca·ry
peck
peck'ing order
pec'tic *also* pec'tin·ous
pec'tin

pec'to·ral
pec·u·late', -lat'ed, -lat'ing
pec·u·la'tion
pec·u·la'tor
pe·cu'liar
pe·cu'li·ar'i·ty
pe·cu'ni·ar'y
ped·a·gog'ic *also* ped'·a·gog'i·cal
ped'a·gogue'
ped'a·go'gy
ped'al *(to operate a foot lever)*, -aled *or* alled, -al·ing *or* -al·ling
  ♦*peddle*
ped'ant
pe·dan'tic
ped'ant·ry
ped'dle *(to sell)*, -dled, -dling
  ♦*pedal*
ped'es·tal
pe·des'tri·an
pe'di·at'ric
pe'di·a·tri'cian
pe'di·at'rics
ped'i·cure', -cured', -cur'ing
ped'i·cur'ist
ped'i·gree'
ped'i·greed'
ped'i·ment
pe·dom'e·ter
peek *(brief look)*
  ♦*peak, pique*

peek'a·boo'
peel *(skin, rind)*
◆*peal*
peen
peep'hole'
peep'ing Tom
peep'show' *also* peep
show
peer *(nobleman)*
◆*pier*
peer *(to look)*
◆*pier*
peer'age
peer'less
peeve, peeved, peev'-
ing
pee'vish
pee'wee *(small thing)*
◆*pewee*
peg, pegged, peg'ging
peg'board'
peg'ma·tite'
pei·gnoir'
pe·jo'ra·tive
Pe'king·ese' *pl.* -ese',
also Pe'kin·ese'
pe'koe *(tea)*
◆*picot*
pel'age
pe·lag'ic
pelf
pel'i·can
pe·lisse'
pel·lag'ra
pel·lag'rous
pel'let

pell'-mell' *also* pell'-
mell'
pel·lu'cid
pelt
pel'vic
pel'vis *pl.* -vis·es *or*
-ves'
pem'mi·can
pen *(to confine),*
penned *or* pent,
pen'ning
pen *(to write),* penned,
pen'ning
pe'nal
pe'nal·ize', -ized', -iz'-
ing
pen'al·ty
pen'ance
pen'chant
pen'cil, -ciled *or*
-cilled, -cil·ing *or*
-cil·ling
pen'dant *n., also* pen'-
dent
pen'dent *adj., also*
pen'dant
pend'ing
pen'du·lar
pen'du·lous
pen'du·lum
pen'e·tra·bil'i·ty
pen'e·tra·ble
pen'e·trate', -trat'ed,
-trat'ing
pen'e·tra'tion
pen'e·tra'tive
pen'guin

pen'i·cil'lin
pen·in'su·la
pen·in'su·lar
pe'nis *pl.* -nis·es *or*
-nes'
pen'i·tence
pen'i·tent
pen'i·ten'tial
pen'i·ten'tia·ry
pen'knife'
pen'man
pen'man·ship'
pen name *also*
pen'name'
pen'nant
pen'ni·less
pen'non
Penn'syl·va'nian
pen'ny *(British coin),*
pl. pen'nies *or* pence
pen'ny *(U.S. coin), pl.*
-nies
pen'ny-pinch'ing
pen'ny·roy'al
pen'ny·weight'
pen'ny-wise'
pen'ny·worth'
pe·nol'o·gist
pe·nol'o·gy
pen'sion
pen'sive
pen'ta·cle
pen'tad'
pen'ta·gon'
pen·tag'o·nal
pen·tam'e·ter
pen'tane'

Pen'ta·teuch'
pen·tath'lon
pen'ta·ton'ic scale
Pen'te·cost'
Pcn'te·cos'tal
pent'house'
pen'to·bar'bi·tal so-
dium
pent'-up' adj.
pe·nu'che also pe·nu'-
chi
pe'nult'
pe·nul'ti·mate
pe·num'bra pl. -brae
or -bras
pe·nu'ri·ous
pen'u·ry
pe'on (laborer)
♦paean
pe'on·age
pe'o·ny
peo'ple pl. -ple or
-ples
peo'ple, -pled, -pling
pep, pepped, pep'ping
pep'lum
pep'per
pep'per-and-salt' adj.
pep'per·corn'
pep'per·mint'
pep'per·o'ni
pep'per·y
pep'py
pep'sin
pep'tic
pep'tide' also pep'tid
pep'tone'

per'ad·ven'ture
per·am'bu·late', -lat'-
ed, -lat'ing
per·am'bu·la'tion
per·am'bu·la'tor
per·am'bu·la·to'ry
per an'num
per·cale'
per cap'i·ta
per·ceiv'a·ble
per·ceive', -ceived',
-ceiv'ing
per cent also per·cent'
per·cent'age
per·cen'tile'
per·cep'ti·bil'i·ty
per·cep'ti·ble
per·cep'tion
per·cep'tive
per·cep'tu·al
perch (fish), pl. perch
or perch'es
perch (roost)
per'chance
per·cip'i·ence
per·cip'i·en·cy
per·cip'i·ent
per·co·late', -lat'ed,
-lat'ing
per·co·la'tion
per·co·la'tor
per·cus'sion
per·cus'sion·ist
per·cus'sive
per di'em
per·di'tion

per'e·gri·nate', -nat'-
ed, -nat'ing
per'e·gri·na'tion
per'e·grine
per·emp'to·ry
per·en'ni·al
per'fect adj. & n.
per·fect' v.
per·fect'i·ble
per·fec'tion
per·fec'tion·ism
per·fec'tion·ist
per'fect·ly
per·fec'to pl. -tos
per·fer'vid
per·fid'i·ous
per'fi·dy
per'fo·rate', -rat'ed,
-rat'ing
per'fo·ra'tion
per'fo·ra'tor
per·force'
per·form'
per·form'ance
per·fume' n.
per·fume', -fumed',
-fum'ing
per·fum'er·y
per·func'to·ry
per·go'la
per·haps'
per'i·car'di·al
per'i·car'di·um pl.
-di·a
per'i·gee'
per'i·he'li·on pl. -li·a
per'il

per'il·ous
pe·rim'e·ter *(boundary)*
♦*parameter*
pe'ri·od
pe'ri·od'ic
pe'ri·od'i·cal
pe'ri·o·dic'i·ty
pe'ri·o·don'tal
per'i·pa·tet'ic
pe·riph'er·al
pe·riph'er·y
per'i·scope'
per'ish *(to die)*
♦*parish*
per'ish·a·ble
per'i·stal'sis *pl.* -ses'
per'i·stal'tic
per'i·to·ne'al
per'i·to·ne'um *pl.*
-ne'a, *also* per'i·to·
nae'um *pl.* -nae'a
per'i·to·ni'tis
per'i·wig'
per'i·win'kle
per'jure, -jured, -jur·
ing
per'ju·ry
perk'y
per'ma·frost'
per'ma·nence
per'ma·nen·cy
per'ma·nent
per·man'ga·nate'
per'me·a·bil'i·ty
per'me·a·ble

per'me·ate', -at'ed,
-at'ing
per'me·a'tion
per·mis'si·ble
per·mis'sion
per·mis'sive
per·mit' *n.*
per·mit', -mit'ted,
-mit'ting
per·mit'ter
per'mu·ta'tion
per·mute', -mut'ed,
-mut'ing
per·ni'cious
per'o·ra'tion
per·ox'ide, -id'ed,
-id'ing
per'pen·dic'u·lar
per'pe·trate', -trat'ed,
-trat'ing
per'pe·tra'tion
per'pe·tra'tor
per·pet'u·al
per·pet'u·ate', -at'ed,
-at'ing
per·pet'u·a'tion
per·pet'u·a'tor
per'pe·tu'i·ty
per·plex'
per·plex'i·ty
per'qui·site *(benefit)*
♦*prerequisite*
per se'
per'se·cute' *(to ha·
rass)*, -cut'ed, -cut'·
ing
♦*prosecute*

per'se·cu'tor
per'se·ver'ance
per'se·vere', -vered',
-ver'ing
Per'sian
per·sim'mon
per·sist'
per·sist'ence *also* per·
sist'en·cy
per·sist'ent
per·snick'e·ty
per'son
per·so'na *pl.* -nae *or*
-nas
per'son·a·ble
per'son·age
per'son·al *(private)*
♦*personnel*
per'son·al'i·ty *(char·
acter)*
♦*personalty*
per'son·al·ize', -ized',
-iz'ing
per'son·al·ty *(prop·
erty)*
♦*personality*
per·so'na non gra'ta
pl. per·so'nae non
gra'tae
per·son'i·fi·ca'tion
per·son'i·fy', -fied',
-fy'ing
per'son·nel' *(employ·
ees)*
♦*personal*
per·spec'tive *(view)*
♦*prospective*

per·spi·ca'cious
per·spi·cac'i·ty
per·spi·cu'i·ty
per·spic'u·ous
per·spi·ra'tion
per·spire', -spired',
   -spir'ing
per·suad'a·ble
per·suade', -suad'ed,
   -suad'ing
per·sua'si·ble
per·sua'sion
per·sua'sive
pert
per·tain'
per'ti·na'cious
per'ti·nac'i·ty
per'ti·nence also per'-
   ti·nen·cy
per'ti·nent
per·turb'
per'tur·ba'tion
pe·ruke'
pe·rus'a·ble
pe·rus'al
pe·ruse', -rused', -rus'-
   ing
pe·rus'er
Pe·ru'vi·an
per·vade', -vad'ed,
   -vad'ing
per·va'sion
per·va'sive
per·verse'
per·ver'sion
per·ver'si·ty
per·vert' n.

per·vert' v.
per·vert'ed
per'vi·ous
pe·se'ta
pes'ky
pe'so pl. -sos
pes'si·mism
pes'si·mist
pes'si·mis'tic
pest
pes'ter
pes'ti·cide'
pes·tif'er·ous
pes'ti·lence
pes'ti·lent also pes'ti·
   len'tial
pes'tle
pet, pet'ted, pet'ting
pet'al
pet'aled also pet'alled
pe·tard'
pet'cock'
pe'ter
pet'i·ole'
pet'it (lesser)
   ♦petty
pe·tite' (small)
pet'it four' pl. pet'its
   fours' or pet'it fours'
pe·ti'tion
pet'it point'
pet'rel (sea bird)
   ♦petrol
pet'ri·fac'tion
pet'ri·fy', -fied', -fy'ing
pet'ro·chem'i·cal
pet'ro·dol'lar

pe·trog'ra·phy
pet'rol (gasoline)
   ♦petrel
pet'ro·la'tum
pe·tro'le·um
pet'ro·log'ic also pet'-
   ro·log'i·cal
pe·trol'o·gy
pet'ti·coat'
pet'ti·fog'ger
pet'tish
pet'ty (small)
   ♦petit
pet'u·lance
pet'u·lant
pe·tu'ni·a
pew
pe'wee (bird), also
   pee'wee
pe'wit'
pew'ter
pe·yo'te
pha'e·ton
pha'lanx' pl. pha'-
   lanx'es or pha·lan'-
   ges
phal'a·rope'
phal'lic
phal'lus pl. -li' or -lus·
   es
phan'tasm
phan·tas'ma·go'ri·a
   also phan·tas'ma·go'-
   ry
phan·tas'mal also
   phan·tas'mic
phan'tom

Phar'aoh *also* phar'-
  aoh
phar'i·sa'ic *also* phar'-
  i·sa'i·cal
phar'i·see
phar·ma·ceu'ti·cal
  also phar'ma·ceu'tic
phar'ma·ceu'tics
phar'ma·cist
phar'ma·col'o·gy
phar'ma·co·poe'ia
phar'ma·cy
pha·ryn'ge·al
phar'ynx *pl.* pha·ryn'-
  ges *or* phar'ynx·es
phase *(to progress in*
  stages), phased,
  phas'ing
  ♦*faze*
pheas'ant *pl.* -ants *or*
  -ant
phe'no·bar'bi·tal
phe'nol'
phe'nol·phthal'ein'
phe·nom'e·nal
phe·nom'e·non' *pl.*
  -na *or* -nons'
phe'no·type'
phe'no·typ'ic
phen'yl
Phi' Be'ta Kap'pa
Phil'a·del'phi·an
phi·lan'der
phil'an·throp'ic
phi·lan'thro·pist
phi·lan'thro·py
phil'a·tel'ic

phi·lat'e·list
phi·lat'e·ly
phil'har·mon'ic
Phil'ip·pine'
Phil'is·tine'
phil'o·den'dron *pl.*
  -drons *or* -dra
phi·lol'o·ger
phi·lol'o·gy
phi·los'o·pher
phil'o·soph'i·cal *also*
  phil'o·soph'ic
phi·los'o·phize',
  -phized', -phiz'ing
phi·los'o·phy
phil'ter *(potion),* also
  phil'tre
  ♦*filter*
phle·bi'tis
phle·bot'o·my
phlegm
phleg·mat'ic
phlo·em'
phlox *pl.* phlox *or*
  phlox'es
pho'bi·a
pho'bic
phoe'be
Phoe·ni'cian
phoe'nix
phone, phoned, phon'-
  ing
pho'neme'
pho·ne'mic
pho·net'ic
pho'ne·ti'cian
pho·net'ics

phon'ic
pho'no·graph'
pho'no·graph'ic
pho·nog'ra·phy
pho·nol'o·gy
pho'non'
pho'ny *also* pho'ney
  pl. -neys
phos'gene'
phos'phate'
phos'phat'ic
phos'phor
phos'pho·resce',
  -resced', -resc'ing
phos'pho·res'cence
phos'pho·res'cent
phos·pho'ric
phos'pho·rous *(of*
  phosphorus)
phos'pho·rus *(ele-*
  ment)
pho'to *pl.* -tos
pho'to·cell'
pho'to·cop'i·er
pho'to·cop'y, -ied,
  -y'ing
pho'to·e·lec'tric *also*
  pho'to·e·lec'tri·cal
pho'to·e·lec'tron
pho'to·en·grave',
  -graved', -grav'ing
pho'to·flash'
pho'to·flood'
pho'to·gen'ic
pho'to·graph'
pho·tog'ra·pher
pho'to·graph'ic

pho·tog'ra·phy
pho'to·gra·vure'
pho'to·jour'na·lism
pho'to·me·chan'i·cal
pho·tom'e·ter
pho·tom'e·try
pho'to·mi'cro·graph'
pho'to·mon·tage'
pho'ton'
pho'ton'ic
pho'to·re·cep'tive
pho'to·re·cep'tor
pho'to·sen'si·tive
pho'to·sen'si·tiv'i·ty
pho'to·sen'si·tize',
　-tized', -tiz'ing
pho'to·sphere'
Pho'to·stat'®
pho'to·syn'the·sis
pho'to·syn'the·size',
　-sized', -siz'ing
pho'to·syn·thet'ic
pho·tot'ro·pism
phras'al
phrase, phrased,
　phras'ing
phra'se·ol'o·gy
phre·nol'o·gist
phre·nol'o·gy
phy·lac'ter·y
phy'lum *pl.* -la
phys'ic (*to act as a ca-*
　thartic), -icked, -ick·
　ing
　♦*physique, psychic*
phys'i·cal
phy·si'cian

phys'i·cist
phys'ics
phys'i·og·nom'ic *also*
　phys'i·og·nom'i·cal
phys'i·og'no·my
phys'i·o·log'i·cal
phys'i·ol'o·gist
phys'i·ol'o·gy
phys'i·o·ther'a·peu'-
　tic
phys'i·o·ther'a·py
phy·sique' (*body*)
　♦*physic, psychic*
pi (*Greek letter*), *pl.* pis
　♦*pie*
pi (*jumbled type*), *pl.*
　pis, *also* pie
pi'a ma'ter
pi'a·nis'si·mo' *pl.*
　-mos'
pi·an'ist
pi·an'o *pl.* -os
pi·an'o·for'te
pi·az'za *pl.* -zas *or* -ze
pi'ca (*type size*)
　♦*pika*
pic'a·dor' *pl.* pic'a·
　dors' *or* pic'a·do'res
pic'a·resque'
pic'a·yune'
pic·ca·lil'li *pl.* -lis
pic'co·lo' *pl.* -los'
pick'ax' *also* pick'axe'
pick'er·el *pl.* -el *or* -els
pick'et
pick'le, -led, -ling
pick'lock'

pick'-me-up'
pick'pock'et
pick'up' *n.*
pic'nic, -nicked, -nick·
　ing
pic'nick·er
pi'cot (*loop*)
　♦*pekoe*
pic'ric acid
Pict (*Britannic tribes-*
　man)
　♦*picked*
pic'to·graph'
pic'to·graph'ic
pic·tog'ra·phy
pic·to'ri·al
pic'ture, -tured, -tur·
　ing
pic·tur·esque'
pid'dle, -dled, -dling
pidg'in (*language*)
　♦*pigeon*
pie (*pastry*)
　♦*pi*
pie'bald'
piece (*to join parts of*),
　pieced, piec'ing
　♦*peace*
pièce de ré·sis·tance'
piece'meal'
piece'work'
pied
pied-à-terre' *pl.*
　pieds-à-terre'
pied'mont'
pier (*wharf*)
　♦*peer*

pi′e·tism
pierce, pierced, pierc′-
  ing
pi′e·ty
pi·e′zo·e·lec′tric
pi·e′zo·e·lec·tric′i·ty
pif′fle, -fled, -fling
pig
pi′geon (bird)
  ♦pidgin
pi′geon·hole′, -holed′,
  -hol′ing
pi′geon-toed′
pig′gish
pig′gy·back′
pig′head·ed
pig′let
pig′ment
pig′men·ta′tion
pig′nut′
pig′pen′
pig′skin′
pig′sty′
pig′tail′
pi′ka (animal)
  ♦pica
pike (fish), pl. pike or
  pikes
pik′er
pike′staff′ pl. -staves′
pi·laf′ or pi·laff′
pi′las′ter
pil′chard
pile, piled, pil′ing
pil′fer
pil′fer·age
pil′grim

pil′grim·age, -aged,
  -ag·ing
pil′lage, -laged, -lag·
  ing
pil′lar
pill′box′
pill′lion
pil′lo·ry, -ried, -ry·ing
pil′low
pil′low·case′
pi′lot
pi′lot·house′
pi′ma cotton
pi·mien′to pl. -tos,
  also pi·men′to
pim′per·nel′
pim′ple
pim′pled also pim′ply
pin, pinned, pin′ning
pi′ña co·la′da
pin′a·fore′
pi·ña′ta
pin′ball′
pince-nez′ pl. -nez′
pin′cers also pinch′ers
pinch′beck′
pinch′-hit′, -hit′, -hit′-
  ting
pin′cush′ion
pine, pined, pin′ing
pin′e·al
pine′ap′ple
pin′feath′er
ping
Ping′-Pong′®
pin′head′
pin′hole′

pin′ion (wing, gear-
  wheel)
  ♦piñon
pink′eye′
pink′ie also pink′y
pin′nace
pin′na·cle
pin′nate′
pi′noch′le or pi′noc·le
pi·ñon (tree), also pin′-
  yon′
  ♦pinion
pin′point′
pin′prick′
pin′set′ter
pin′stripe′
pin′to pl. -tos or -toes
pint′size′ also
  pint′sized′
pin′up′ n. & adj.
pin′wale′
pin′wheel′
pin′worm′
pin′y also pine′y
Pin′yin′ or pin′yin′
pi′o·neer′
pi′ous
pip, pipped, pip′ping
pipe, piped, pip′ing
pipe′line′
pi·pette′ (glass tube)
  ♦pipit
pip′it (bird)
  ♦pipette
pip′kin
pip′pin
pip′-squeak′

pi′quan·cy
pi′quant
pique (to provoke),
  piqued, piqu′ing
  ♦peak, peek
pi·qué′ (fabric)
pi·quet′ (card game),
  also pic·quet′
pi′ra·cy
pi·ra′nha also pi·ra′ña
pi′rate, -rat·ed, -rat·ing
pi·rat′i·cal
pir′ou·ette′, -et·ted,
  -et′ting
pis·ca·to′ri·al also
  pis·ca·to′ry
Pi′sces
pi′scine′
pis′mire′
pis·ta′chi·o′ pl. -os′
pis′til (flower part)
pis′tol (gun)
pis′tol-whip′,
  -whipped′, -whip′-
  ping
pis′ton
pit, pit′ted, pit′ting
pit′a·pat′, -pat·ted,
  -pat′ting
pitch′-black′
pitch′blende′
pitch′-dark′
pitch′er
pitch′fork′
pitch′out′
pit′e·ous
pit′fall′

pith′e·can′thro·pus
pith′y
pit′i·a·ble
pit′i·ful
pit′i·less
pi′ton′
pit′tance
pit′ter-pat′ter
pi·tu′i·tar′y
pit′y, -ied, -y·ing
piv′ot
piv′ot·al
pix′y or pix′ie
piz′za
piz·zazz′
piz·ze·ri′a
piz·zi·ca′to pl. -tos
plac′ard′
pla′cate, -cat·ed, -cat′-
  ing
pla·ca′tion
pla·ca·to′ry
place (to set), placed,
  plac′ing
  ♦plaice
pla·ce′bo pl. -bos or
  -boes
place′-kick′ v.
place′ment
pla·cen′ta pl. -tas or
  -tae
pla·cen′tal
plac′er
plac′id
pla·cid′i·ty
plack′et
pla′gia·rism

pla′gia·rist
pla′gia·rize′, -rized′,
  -riz′ing
pla·gi·o·clase′
plague, plagued,
  plagu′ing
plaice (fish), pl. plaice
  or plaic′es
  ♦place
plaid
plain (clear)
  ♦plane
plain (level region)
  ♦plane
plain′chant′
plain′clothes′ man
  also plain′clothes′-
  man
plains′man
plain′song′
plaint
plain′tiff (complainant)
plain′tive (mournful)
plait (braid)
  ♦plat, plate
plan, planned, plan′-
  ning
pla′nar (flat)
  ♦planer
pla·nar′i·an
pla·nar′i·ty
plane (surface, air-
  plane, tool, tree)
  ♦plain
plane (to smooth, soar),
  planed, plan′ing
  ♦plain

plan'et
plan'e·tar'i·um *pl.*
-i·ums *or* -i·a
plan'e·tar'y
plan'e·toid'
plank'ing
plank'ton
plank'ton'ic
plan'ner
plan'tain
plan'tar *(of the sole of the foot)*
◆*planter*
plan·ta'tion
plant'er *(container, tool, one that plants)*
◆*plantar*
plaque
plash
plas'ma *also* plasm
plas·mat'ic *also* plas'mic
plas·mo'di·um *pl.*
-di·a
plas'ter
plas'ter·board'
plaster of Par'is
plas'tic
plas·tic'i·ty
plas'tid
plas'tron
plat *(to braid),* plat'ted,
plat'ting
◆*plait, plate*
plate *(to coat),* plat'ed,
plat'ing
◆*plait, plat*

pla·teau' *pl.* -teaus' *or*
-teaux'
plate'ful' *pl.* -fuls'
plate'let
plat'en
plat'form'
plat'ing
plat'i·num
plat'i·tude'
plat'i·tu'di·nous
Pla·ton'ic
Pla'to·nism
pla·toon'
plat'ter
plat'y *pl.* -ys *or* -ies
plat'y·pus *pl.* -pus·es
plau'dit
plau·si·bil'i·ty
plau'si·ble
pla'ya
play'a·ble
play'-act'
play'back' *n.*
play'bill'
play'boy'
play'-by-play'
play'er
play'fel'low'
play'ful
play'go'er
play'ground'
play'house'
play'let'
play'mate'
play'-off' *n.*
play'pen'
play'room'

play'thing'
play'wright'
pla'za
plea
plea'-bar'gain *v.*
plead, plead'ed *or*
pled, plead'ing
pleas'ant
pleas'ant·ry
please, pleased, pleas'ing
pleas'ur·a·ble
pleas'ure, -ured, -ur·ing
pleat
plebe
ple·be'ian
pleb'i·scite'
plec'trum *pl.* -trums *or*
-tra
pledge, pledged,
pledg'ing
pledg·ee'
Pleis'to·cene'
ple'na·ry
plen'i·po·ten'ti·ar'y
plen'i·tude'
plen'te·ous
plen'ti·ful
plen'ty
ple'si·o·sau'rus *pl.*
-sau'ri, *also* ple'si·o·saur'
pleth'o·ra
ple·tho'ric
pleu'ra *pl.* -rae'
pleu'ral

pleu'ri·sy
Plex'i·glas'®
plex'us *pl.* -us *or* -us·es
pli'a·bil'i·ty
pli'a·ble
pli'an·cy
pli'ant
pli'cate' *also* pli'cat'ed
pli'ers
plight
plinth
Pli'o·cene'
plis·sé'
plod, plod'ded, plod'-
  ding
plod'der
plop, plopped, plop'-
  ping
plot, plot'ted, plot'ting
plot'ter
plov'er
plow *also* plough
plow'man
plow'share'
ploy
pluck'y
plug, plugged, plug'-
  ging
plug'-ug'ly
plum *(fruit)*
  ♦plumb
plum'age
plumb *(weight)*
  ♦plum
plumb'er
plumb'ing

plume, plumed, plum'-
  ing
plum'met
plump'ness
plum'y
plun'der
plunge, plunged,
  plung'ing
plunk
plu·per'fect
plu'ral
plu'ral·ism
plu'ral·ist
plu'ral'i·ty
plus
plush
Plu'to
plu·toc'ra·cy
plu'to·crat'
plu'to·crat'ic
plu·to'ni·um
plu'vi·al *also* plu'vi·an
plu'vi·al
ply, plied, ply'ing
ply'wood'
pneu·mat'ic
pneu·mo'nia
pneu·mon'ic
poach'er
pock'et
pock'et·book'
pock'et·ful' *pl.* pock'-
  el·fuls' *or* pock'ets·
  ful'
pock'et·knife'
pock'mark'
pod

po·di'a·trist
po·di'a·try
po'di·um *pl.* -di·a *or*
  -di·ums
po'em
po'e·sy
po'et
po'et·as'ter
po·et'ic *also* po·et'i·cal
poet lau're·ate *pl.* po-
  ets lau're·ate *or* poet
  lau're·ates
po'et·ry
po'go stick
po·grom'
poi
poign'ance *also*
  poign'an·cy
poign'ant
poin·set'ti·a
point'blank'
point'er
poin'til·lism
poin'til·list
point'less
poise, poised, pois'ing
poi'son
poi'son·ous
poke, poked, pok'ing
poke'ber'ry
pok'er
pok'er·faced'
poke'weed'
po'key *(jail),* *pl.* -keys
pok'y *(slow),* *also*
  poke'y
po'lar

Po·lar'is
po·lar'i·ty
po'lar·i·za'tion
po'lar·ize', -ized', -iz'-
  ing
Po'lar·oid'®
pole *(axis point, rod)*
  ♦*poll*
pole *(to propel with a*
  pole), poled, pol'ing
  ♦*poll*
Pole *(inhabitant of Po-*
  land)
  ♦*poll*
pole·ax' *or* pole'axe'
pole'cat'
po·lem'ic *n.*
po·lem'ic *also* po·lem'-
  i·cal
po·lem'i·cist *also* po·
  lem'ist
pole'star'
pole'-vault' *v.*
pole'-vault'er
po·lice' *pl.* -lice'
po·lice', -liced', -lic'ing
po·lice'man
po·lice'wom'an
pol'i·clin'ic *(outpatient*
  department)
  ♦*polyclinic*
pol'i·cy
pol'i·cy·hold'er
po'li·o'
po'li·o·my'e·li'tis
pol'ish *(shine)*
Po'lish *(of Poland)*

pol'it·bu'ro
po·lite', -lit'er, -lit'est
pol'i·tic *(shrewd)*
  ♦*politick*
po·lit'i·cal
pol'i·ti'cian
pol'i·tick' *(to talk poli-*
  tics)
  ♦*politic*
po·lit'i·co' *pl.* -cos'
pol'i·tics
pol'i·ty
pol'ka
poll *(election)*
  ♦*pole, Pole*
pol'len
pol'li·nate', -nat'ed,
  -nat'ing
pol'li·na'tion
pol'li·na'tor
pol'li·wog' *also* pol'ly·
  wog'
poll'ster
pol·lut'ant
pol·lute', -lut'ed, -lut'-
  ing
pol·lu'tion
Pol'ly·an'na
po'lo
pol'o·naise'
po·lo'ni·um
pol'ter·geist'
pol·troon'
pol'y·an'drous
pol'y·an'dry
pol'y·chro·mat'ic
pol'y·chrome'

pol'y·clin'ic *(hospital)*
  ♦*policlinic*
pol'y·es'ter
pol'y·eth'yl·ene'
po·lyg'a·mist
po·lyg'a·mous
po·lyg'a·my
pol'y·glot'
pol'y·gon'
po·lyg'o·nal
pol'y·graph'
pol'y·he'dral
pol'y·he'dron *pl.*
  -drons *or* -dra
pol'y·mer
pol'y·mer'ic
po·lym'er·i·za'tion
pol'y·mer·ize', -ized',
  -iz'ing
pol'y·mor'phism
Pol'y·ne'sian
pol'y·no'mi·al
pol'yp
pol'y·phon'ic
po·lyph'o·ny
pol'y·sac'cha·ride'
  also pol'y·sac'cha·rid,
  pol'y·sac'cha·rose'
pol'y·sty'rene
pol'y·syl·lab'ic
pol'y·syl'la·ble
pol'y·tech'nic
pol'y·the'ism
pol'y·the'ist
pol'y·the·is'tic
pol'y·un·sat'u·rat'ed
pol'y·u're·thane'

pol'y·va'lence
pol'y·va'lent
pol'y·vi'nyl
po·made'
po'man·der
pome'gran'ate
pom'mel
pomp
pom'pa·dour'
pom·pa·no' pl. -no' or
  -nos'
pom'pon' also pom'-
  pom'
pom·pos'i·ty
pom'pous
pon'cho pl. -chos
pond
pon'der
pon·der·o'sa pine
pon'der·ous
pone
pon·gee'
pon'iard
pons pl. pon'tes
pon'tiff
pon·tif'i·cal
pon·tif'i·cate', -cat·ed,
  -cat'ing
pon·tif'i·ca'tor
pon·toon'
po'ny
po'ny·tail'
pooch
poo'dle
pooh'-pooh' v.
pool'room'
poop

poor'house'
poor'ly
pop, popped, pop'ping
pop art
pop'corn'
pope
pop'er·y
pop'eyed'
pop'gun'
pop'in·jay'
pop'ish
pop'lar (tree)
  ♦popular
pop'lin
pop'o·ver
pop'per
pop'py
pop'py·cock'
pop'u·lace (masses)
  ♦populous
pop'u·lar (well-liked)
  ♦poplar
pop'u·lar'i·ty
pop'u·lar·i·za'tion
pop'u·lar·ize', -ized',
  -iz'ing
pop'u·late', -lat'ed,
  -lat'ing
pop'u·la'tion
pop'u·lism
pop'u·list
pop'u·lous (thickly set-
  tled)
  ♦populace
por'ce·lain
porch
por'cine'

por'cu·pine'
pore (opening)
  ♦pour
pore (to study), pored,
  por'ing
  ♦pour
por'gy pl. -gy or -gies
pork'er
pork'pie'
por·nog'ra·pher
por·no·graph'ic
por·nog'ra·phy
po·ros'i·ty
po'rous
por'phy·ry
por'poise
por'ridge
por'rin·ger
port
port'a·bil'i·ty
port'a·ble
port'age, -aged, -ag·
  ing
por'tal
por'tal-to-por'tal adj.
port·cul'lis
porte'-co·chère' or
  porte'-co·chere'
por·tend'
por·tent'
por·ten'tous
por'ter
por'ter·house'
port·fo'li·o pl. -os
port'hole'
por'ti·co' pl. -coes' or
  -cos'

por·tière′ *or* por·tiere′
por′tion
port′ly
port·man′teau *pl.*
-teaus *or* -teaux
por′trait
por′trait·ist
por′trai·ture′
por·tray′
por·tray′al
Por·tu·guese′ *pl.*
-guese′
pose, posed, pos′ing
pos′er *(one who poses,
baffling question)*
po·seur′ *(affected per-
son)*
posh
pos·it
po·si′tion
pos′i·tive
pos′i·tiv·ism
pos′i·tiv·ist
pos′i·tron′
pos′se
pos·sess′
pos·ses′sion
pos·ses′sive
pos·ses′sor
pos·si·bil′i·ty
pos′si·ble
post′age
post′al
post′box′
post-card *also*
post′card′

post·date′, -dat′ed,
-dat′ing
post·doc′tor·al
post′er
pos·te′ri·or
pos·ter′i·ty
pos′tern
post·grad′u·ate
post′haste′
post′hu·mous
post′hyp·not′ic sug-
gestion
pos·til′ion *also* pos·
til′lion
post′im·pres′sion·ism
post′im·pres′sion·ist
post′man
post′mark′
post′mas′ter
postmaster general
pl. postmasters gen-
eral
post′me·rid′i·an *(in
the afternoon)*
post′ me·rid′i·em *(af-
ter twelve noon)*
post·mor′tem
post·na′sal
post·na′tal
post·op′er·a·tive
post·or′bi·tal
post′paid′
post·par′tum
post·pone′, -poned′,
-pon′ing
post·pone′ment
post′script′

pos′tu·lant
pos′tu·late′, -lat′ed,
-lat′ing
pos′tu·la′tion
pos′tu·la′tor
pos′tur·al
pos′ture, -tured, -tur·
ing
post′war′
po′sy
pot, pot′ted, pot′ting
po′ta·ble
pot′ash
po·tas′si·um
po·ta′tion
po·ta′to *pl.* -toes
pot-au-feu′
pot·bel′lied
pot·bel′ly
pot·boil′er
po′ten·cy
po′tent
po′ten·tate′
po·ten′tial
po·ten′ti·al′i·ty
po·ten′ti·om′e·ter
poth′er
pot′herb′
pot′hole′
pot′hook′
po′tion
pot′latch′
pot′luck′
pot′pie′
pot·pour·ri′ *pl.* -ris′
pot′sherd′ *also* pot′-
shard′

pot'tage
pot'ted
pot'ter
pot'ter·y
pouch
pouf
poul'tice
poul'try *(fowl)*
  ◆*paltry*
pounce, pounced,
  pounc'ing
pound *(weight)*, *pl.*
  pound *or* pounds
pound *(to hammer)*
pound'age
pound'-fool'ish *adj.*
pour *(to flow)*
  ◆*poor*
pour·boire'
pousse'-ca·fé'
pout *(sulky expression)*
pout *(fish)*, *pl.* pout *or*
  pouts
pov'er·ty
pow'der
pow'der·y
pow'er
pow'er·boat'
pow'er·ful
pow'er·house'
pow'er·less
pow'wow'
pox *(disease)*
  ◆*pocks*
prac'ti·ca·bil'i·ty
prac'ti·ca·ble *(possi-
  ble)*

prac'ti·cal *(useful, sen-
  sible)*
prac'ti·cal'i·ty
prac'ti·cal·ly
prac'tice, -ticed, -tic·
  ing
prac·ti'tio·ner
prae'tor
prae·to'ri·an
prag·mat'ic
prag'ma·tism
prag'ma·tist
prai'rie
praise, praised, prais'-
  ing
praise'wor'thy
pra·line'
pram
prance, pranced,
  pranc'ing
prank'ster
pra'se·o·dym'i·um
prate, prat'ed, prat'ing
prat'fall'
prat'tle, -tled, -tling
prawn
pray *(to implore)*
  ◆*prey*
pray'er *(one who
  prays)*
prayer *(petition)*
preach'er
pre'ad·o·les'cence
pre'ad·o·les'cent
pre'am'ble
pre·am'pli·fi'er

pre'ar·range, -ranged',
  -rang'ing
Pre·cam'bri·an
pre·car'i·ous
pre·cau'tion
pre·cau'tion·ar'y
pre·cede' *(to come or
  go before)*, -ced'ed,
  -ced'ing
  ◆*proceed*
prec'e·dence
prec'e·dent *(prior ex-
  ample)*
  ◆*president*
pre'cept'
pre·cep'tor
pre·ces'sion *(prece-
  dence, axial move-
  ment)*
  ◆*processional*
pre'cinct'
pre'cious
prec'i·pice
pre·cip'i·tance
pre·cip'i·tant
pre·cip'i·tate *(hasty)*
  ◆*precipitous*
pre·cip'i·tate' *(to hurl
  downward)*, -tat'ed,
  -tat'ing
pre·cip'i·ta'tion
pre·cip'i·ta'tor
pre·cip'i·tous *(steep)*
  ◆*precipitate*
pré·cis' *(summary)*, *pl.*
  -cis'
pre·cise' *(definite)*

pre·ci'sion

pre·clude', -clud'ed,
 -clud'ing

pre·clu'sion

pre·clu'sive

pre·co'cious

pre·coc'i·ty

pre·cog·ni'tion

pre·cog'ni·tive

pre'-Co·lum'bi·an

pre'con·ceive',
 -ceived', -ceiv'ing

pre'con·cep'tion

pre'con·di'tion

pre·cook'

pre·cur'sor

pre·cur'so·ry

pre·da'cious or pre·
 da'ceous

pre·date', -dat'ed,
 -dat'ing

pred'a·tor

pred'a·to'ry

pre'de·cease',
 -ceased', -ceas'ing

pred'e·ces'sor

pre·des'ti·na'tion

pre·des'tine, -tined,
 -tin·ing

pre'de·ter'mi·na'tion

pre'de·ter'mine,
 -mined, -min·ing

pred'i·ca·ble

pre·dic'a·ment

pred'i·cate', -cat'ed,
 -cat'ing

pred'i·ca'tion

pred'i·ca'tive

pre·dict'

pre·dict'a·bil'i·ty

pre·dict'a·ble

pre·dic'tion

pre·dic'tor

pred'i·lec'tion

pre'dis·pos'al

pre'dis·pose', -posed',
 -pos'ing

pre'dis·po·si'tion

pre·dom'i·nance

pre·dom'i·nant

pre·dom'i·nate', -nat'-
 ed, -nat'ing

pre·dom'i·na'tion

pre·dom'i·na'tor

pre-em'i·nence or pre·
 em'i·nence

pre-em'i·nent or pre·
 em'i·nent

pre-empt' or pre·empt'

pre-emp'tion or pre·
 emp'tion

pre-emp'tive or pre·
 emp'tive

pre-emp'tor or pre·
 emp'tor

pre-emp'to·ry or pre·
 emp'to·ry

preen

pre'-ex·ist' or pre'ex·
 ist'

pre·fab'

pre·fab'ri·cate', -cat'-
 ed, -cat'ing

pre·fab'ri·ca'tion

pre·fab'ri·ca'tor

pref'ace, -aced, -ac·ing

pref'a·to'ry

pre'fect' also prae'fect'

pre'fec'ture

pre·fer', -ferred', -fer'-
 ring

pref'er·a·ble

pref'er·ence

pref'er·en'tial

pre·fer'ment

pre·fig'ure, -ured, -ur·
 ing

pre'fix' n.

pre·fix' v.

pre'flight'

pre·fron'tal lobot-
 omy

preg'nan·cy

preg'nant

pre·heat'

pre·hen'sile

pre'his·tor'ic also
 pre'his·tor'i·cal

pre·his'to·ry

pre·judge', -judged',
 -judg'ing

prej'u·dice, -diced,
 -dic'ing

prej'u·di'cial

prel'a·cy

prel'ate

pre·lim'i·nar'y

pre·lit'er·ate

prel'ude', -ud'ed,
 -ud'ing

pre·mar'i·tal

pre·ma·ture'
pre·med'
pre·med'i·cal
pre·med'i·tate', -tat'-
    ed, -tat'ing
pre·med'i·ta'tion
pre·med'i·ta'tive
pre·med'i·ta'tor
pre'mier (first in im-
    portance)
pre·mier' (prime minis-
    ter)
pre·mière' (first
    presentation)
prem'ise, -ised, -is·ing
pre'mi·um
pre'mix'
pre'mo'lar
pre'mo·ni'tion
pre·na'tal
pre·oc'cu·pa'tion
pre·oc'cu·py', -pied',
    -py'ing
pre'or·dain'
prep, prepped, prep'-
    ping
pre'pack'age, -aged,
    -ag·ing
prep'a·ra'tion
pre·par'a·to'ry
pre·pare', -pared',
    -par'ing
pre·par'ed·ness
pre·pay', -paid', -pay'-
    ing
pre·pay'ment
pre·pon'der·ance

pre·pon'der·ant
pre·pon'der·ate', -at'-
    ed, -at'ing
prep'o·si'tion
prep'o·si'tion·al
pre'pos·sess'
pre'pos·ses'sion
pre·pos'ter·ous
prep'pie or prep'py
pre·pro'gram',
    -grammed' or
    -gramed', -gram'-
    ming or -gram'ing
pre'puce'
pre-Raph'a·el·ite'
pre·req'ui·site (prior
    requirement)
    ♦perquisite
pre·rog'a·tive
pres'age n.
pre·sage', -saged',
    -sag'ing
pres'by·ter
Pres'by·te'ri·an
pres'by·ter'y
pre'school'
pre'sci·ence
pre'sci·ent
pre·scribe' (to order,
    enjoin), -scribed',
    -scrib'ing
    ♦proscribe
pre'script'
pre·scrip'tion
pre·scrip'tive
pres'ence
pres'ent n. & adj.

pre·sent' v.
pre·sent'a·ble
pres'en·ta'tion
pres'ent-day' adj.
pre·sen'ti·ment (pre-
    monition)
    ♦presentment
pres'ent·ly
pre·sent'ment (presen-
    tation)
    ♦presentiment
pres'er·va'tion
pre·serv'a·tive
pres'er·va'tor
pre·serve', -served',
    -serv'ing
pre'shrunk'
pre·side', -sid'ed, -sid'-
    ing
pres'i·den·cy
pres'i·dent (chief ex-
    ecutive)
    ♦precedent
pres'i·dent-e·lect'
pres'i·den'tial
pre·sid'i·um pl. -i·a or
    -i·ums
pre'soak'
pre'sort'
press'ing
press'man
press'room'
press'run'
pres'sure, -sured, -sur·
    ing
pres'sur·i·za'tion

pres'sur·ize', -ized',
  -iz'ing
press'work'
pres'ti·dig'i·ta'tion
pres'ti·dig'i·ta'tor
pres·tige'
pres·tig'ious
pres'to *pl.* -tos
pre·sum'a·ble
pre·sume', -sumed',
  -sum'ing
pre·sum'ed·ly
pre·sump'tion
pre·sump'tive
pre·sump'tu·ous
pre'sup·pose', -posed',
  -pos'ing
pre'sup·po·si'tion
pre'teen'
pre·tend'
pre·tend'er
pre·tense'
pre·ten'sion
pre·ten'tious
pret'er·it *or* pret'er·ite
pre'ter·nat'u·ral
pre·test' *n.*
pre·test' *v.*
pre'text'
pre·tri'al
pret'ti·fy', -fied', -fy'-
  ing
pret'ty, -tied, -ty·ing
pret'zel
pre·vail'
prev'a·lence
prev'a·lent

pre·var'i·cate', -cat'-
  ed, -cat'ing
pre·var'i·ca'tion
pre·var'i·ca'tor
pre·vent'
pre·vent'a·ble *also*
  pre·vent'i·ble
pre·ven'tion
pre·ven'tive *also* pre·
  ven'ta·tive
pre'view' *also* pre'vue',
  -vued', -vu'ing
pre'vi·ous
pre'vo·cal'ic
pre'vo·ca'tion·al
pre'war'
prey *(victim)*
  ♦*pray*
price, priced, pric'ing
prick'le, -led, -ling
prick'ly
pride, prid'ed, prid'ing
prie·dieu' *pl.* -dieus' *or*
  -dieux'
pri'er *(one that pries)*,
  also pry'er
  ♦*prior*
priest
priest'hood'
prig'gish
prim, prim'mer, prim'-
  mest
pri'ma·cy
pri'ma don'na *pl.*
  pri'ma don'nas
pri'mal
pri·mar'i·ly

pri'mar'y
pri'mate'
prime, primed, prim'-
  ing
prim'er
pri·me'val
prim'i·tive
pri'mo·gen'i·tor
pri'mo·gen'i·ture'
pri·mor'di·al
primp
prim'rose'
prince'ly
prin'cess
prin'ci·pal *(foremost)*
  ♦*principle*
prin'ci·pal'i·ty
prin'ci·ple *(rule, law)*
  ♦*principal*
prin'ci·pled
print'a·ble
print'er
print'ing
print'-out' *n.*
pri'or *(before)*
  ♦*prier*
pri'or *(monk)*
  ♦*prier*
pri·or'i·ty
pri'or·y
prism
pris·mat'ic
pris'on
pris'on·er
pris'sy
pris'tine'
pri'va·cy

pri′vate
pri′va·teer′
pri′va′tion
priv′et
priv′i·lege, -leged,
  -leg·ing
priv′y
prix′ fixe′ *pl.* prix′
  fixes′
prize, prized, priz′ing
prize′fight′
prize′fight′er
prize′fight′ing
pro *pl.* pros
prob′a·bil′i·ty
prob′a·ble
pro′bate′, -bat·ed,
  -bat·ing
pro·ba′tion
pro·ba′tion·ar′y
pro·ba′tion·er
pro′ba·tive
probe, probed, prob′-
  ing
pro′bi·ty
prob′lem
prob′lem·at′i·cal *also*
  prob′lem·at′ic
pro·bos′cis *pl.* -cis·es
  or -cides′
pro·ce′dur·al
pro·ce′dure
pro·ceed′ *(to go for-*
  ward)
  ♦*precede*
pro·ceed′ings
pro·ceeds′

proc′ess′
pro·ces′sion *(parade)*
  ♦*precession*
pro·ces′sion·al
pro·claim′
proc′la·ma′tion
pro·cliv′i·ty
pro·con′sul
pro·con′su·lar
pro·con′su·late
pro·cras′ti·nate′,
  -nat·ed, -nat·ing
pro·cras′ti·na′tion
pro·cras′ti·na′tor
pro·cre·ate′, -at·ed,
  -at′ing
pro′cre·a′tion
pro′cre·a′tive
pro′cre·a′tor
pro·crus′te·an
proc′to·log′ic *also*
  proc′to·log′i·cal
proc·tol′o·gist
proc·tol′o·gy
proc′tor
proc′u·ra′tor
pro·cure′, -cured′,
  -cur′ing
pro·cure′ment
prod, prod′ded, prod′-
  ding
prod′der
prod′i·gal
prod′i·gal′i·ty
pro·di′gious
prod′i·gy
pro′duce *n.*

pro·duce′, -duced′,
  -duc′ing
pro·duc′er
pro·duc′i·ble
prod′uct
pro·duc′tion
pro·duc′tive
pro′duc·tiv′i·ty
pro′em′
prof′a·na′tion
pro·fane′, -faned′,
  -fan′ing
pro·fan′i·ty
pro·fess′
pro·fes′sion
pro·fes′sion·al
pro·fes′sion·al·ism
pro·fes′sor
pro′fes·so′ri·al
prof′fer
pro·fi′cien·cy
pro·fi′cient
pro′file′, -filed′, -fil′ing
prof′it *(gain)*
  ♦*prophet*
prof′it·a·bil′i·ty
prof′it·a·ble
prof′i·teer′
prof′li·ga·cy
prof′li·gate
pro for′ma
pro·found′
pro·fun′di·ty
pro·fuse′
pro·fu′sion
pro·gen′i·tor
prog′e·ny

pro·ges'ter·one'
prog·no'sis *pl.* -ses'
prog·nos'tic
prog·nos'ti·cate',
   -cat'ed, -cat'ing
prog·nos'ti·ca'tion
prog·nos'ti·ca'tor
pro'gram', -grammed'
   or -gramed', -gram'-
   ming *or* -gram'ing
pro'gram·mat'ic
pro'gram'mer *or* pro'-
   gram'er
prog'ress' *n.*
pro·gress' *v.*
pro·gres'sion
pro·gres'sive
pro·hib'it
pro·hi·bi'tion
pro·hib'i·tive *also* pro·
   hib'i·to'ry
proj'ect' *n.*
pro·ject' *v.*
pro·jec'tile
pro·jec'tion
pro·jec'tion·ist
pro·jec'tor
pro'le·tar'i·an
pro'le·tar'i·at
pro·lif'er·ate', -at'ed,
   -at'ing
pro·lif'er·a'tion
pro·lif'ic
pro·lix'
pro·lix'i·ty
pro'logue'
pro·long'

pro'lon·ga'tion
prom
prom'e·nade', -nad'-
   ed, -nad'ing
pro·me'thi·um
prom'i·nence
prom'i·nent
prom'is·cu'i·ty
pro·mis'cu·ous
prom'ise, -ised, -is·ing
prom'is·so'ry
prom'on·to'ry
pro·mote', -mot'ed,
   -mot'ing
pro·mo'tion
pro·mo'tion·al
prompt'book'
prompt'er
prom'ul·gate', -gat'ed,
   -gat'ing
prom'ul·ga'tion
prom'ul·ga'tor
prone'ness
prong'horn' *pl.* -horn'
   or -horns'
pro·nom'i·nal
pro'noun'
pro·nounce',
   -nounced', -nounc'-
   ing
pro·nounce'a·ble
pro·nounce'ment
pron'to
pro·nun'ci·a'tion
proof'read', -read',
   -read'ing

prop, propped, prop'-
   ping
prop'a·gan'da
prop'a·gan'dist
prop'a·gan'dize',
   -dized', -diz'ing
prop'a·gate', -gat'ed,
   -gat'ing
prop'a·ga'tor
pro'pane'
pro·pel', -pelled', -pel'-
   ling
pro·pel'lant *also* pro·
   pel'lent
pro·pel'ler *also* pro·
   pel'lor
pro·pen'si·ty
prop'er
prop'er·tied
prop'er·ty
pro'phase'
proph'e·cy *(prediction)*
proph'e·sy' *(to pre-
   dict)*, -sied', -sy'ing
proph'et *(seer)*
   ♦*profit*
pro·phet'ic
pro'phy·lac'tic
pro·pin'qui·ty
pro·pi'ti·ate', -at'ed,
   -at'ing
pro·pi'ti·a'tion
pro·pi'ti·a'tor
pro·pi'ti·a·to'ry
pro·pi'tious
pro·po'nent
pro·por'tion

pro•por'tion•al
pro•por'tion•al'i•ty
pro•por'tion•ate
pro•pos'al
pro•pose', -posed', -pos'ing
prop'o•si'tion
pro•pound'
pro•pri'e•tar'y
pro•pri'e•tor
pro•pri'e•tor•ship'
pro•pri'e•ty
pro•pul'sion
pro•pul'sive
pro'pyl•ene'
pro ra'ta
pro•rate', -rat'ed, -rat'-ing
pro•ra'tion
pro•ro•ga'tion
pro•rogue', -rogued', -rogu'ing
pro•sa'ic
pro•sce'ni•um *pl.* -ni•ums *or* -ni•a
pro•scribe' *(to forbid)*, -scribed', -scrib'ing
♦*prescribe*
pro•scrip'tion
pro•scrip'tive
prose
pros'e•cute' *(to try by law)*, -cut'ed, -cut'ing
♦*persecute*
pros'e•cu'tion
pros'e•cu'tor
pros'e•lyte'

pros'e•ly•tize', -tized', -tiz'ing
pro•sod'ic
pros'o•dy
pros'pect'
pro•spec'tive
pros'pec'tor
pro•spec'tus
pros'per
pros•per'i•ty
pros'per•ous
pros'tate' *(gland)*
♦*prostrate*
pros•the'sis *pl.* -ses'
pros•thet'ic
pros•thet'ics
pros'ti•tute', -tut'ed, -tut'ing
pros'ti•tu'tion
pros'ti•tu'tor
pros'trate' *(to throw down flat)*, -trat'ed, -trat'ing
♦*prostate*
pros•tra'tion
pros'tra'tor
pro'tac•tin'i•um
pro•tag'o•nist
pro'te•an
pro•tect'
pro•tec'tion
pro•tec'tion•ism
pro•tec'tive
pro•tec'tor *also* pro•tect'er
pro•tec'tor•ate
pro'té•gé' *masc.*

pro'té•gée' *fem.*
pro'tein'
pro tem'po•re
pro•te•ol'y•sis
pro'test' *n.*
pro•test' *v.*
Prot'es•tant
Prot'es•tant•ism
prot'es•ta'tion
pro'to•col'
pro'ton'
pro'to•plasm
pro'to•plas'mic *also* pro'to•plas'mal, pro'-to•plas•mat'ic
pro'to•typ'al *also* pro'to•typ'i•cal
pro'to•type'
pro'to•zo'an *adj., also* pro'to•zo'ic
pro'to•zo'an *pl.* -zo'-ans *or* -zo'a
pro•tract'
pro•trac'tile *also* pro•tract'i•ble
pro•trac'tion
pro•trac'tive
pro•trac'tor
pro•trude', -trud'ed, -trud'ing
pro•tru'sion
pro•tru'sive
pro•tu'ber•ance
pro•tu'ber•ant
proud'ly
prov'a•bil'i•ty
prov'a•ble

prove, proved, proved
  or prov'en, prov'ing
prov'e·nance
Pro·ven·çal'
prov'en·der
pro·ve'nience
prov'erb'
pro·ver'bi·al
pro·vide', -vid'ed,
  -vid'ing
prov'i·dence
prov'i·dent
prov'i·den'tial
prov'ince
pro·vin'cial
pro·vin'cial·ism
pro·vin·ci·al'i·ty
pro·vi'sion
pro·vi'sion·al
pro·vi'so pl. -sos or
  -soes
pro·vi'so·ry
prov'o·ca'tion
pro·voc'a·tive
pro·voke', -voked',
  -vok'ing
pro·vost'
prow
prow'ess
prowl'er
prox'i·mal
prox'·i·mate
prox·im'i·ty
prox'y
prude
pru'dence
pru'dent

pru·den'tial
prud'er·y
prud'ish
prune, pruned, prun'-
  ing
pru'ri·ence
pru'ri·ent
Prus'sian
prus'sic acid
pry, pried, pry'ing
psalm'ist
psalm'o·dy
Psal'ter also psal'ter
psal'ter·y
pseu'do
pseu'do·nym'
pseu·don'y·mous
pseu'do·po'di·um pl.
  -di·a, also pseu'do·
  pod'
pshaw
psit'ta·co'sis
pso·ri'a·sis
psy'che
psy'che·del'ic
psy·chi·at'ric
psy·chi'a·trist
psy·chi'a·try
psy'chic (of the mind),
  also psy'chi·cal
  ♦physic, physique
psy'chi·cal·ly
psy'cho pl. -chos
psy·cho·a·nal'y·sis
psy'cho·an'a·lyst
psy'cho·an'a·lyt'ic

  also psy'cho·an'a·
  lyt'i·cal
psy'cho·an'a·lyze',
  -lyzed', -lyz'ing
psy'cho·bi·ol'o·gy
psy'cho·dra'ma
psy'cho·his'to·ry
psy'cho·log'i·cal
psy·chol'o·gist
psy·chol'o·gy
psy'cho·met'rics
psy'cho·path'
psy'cho·path'ic
psy·cho'sis pl. -ses'
psy'cho·so·mat'ic
psy'cho·ther'a·peu'-
  tic
psy'cho·ther'a·pist
psy'cho·ther'a·py
psy·chot'ic
ptar'mi·gan pl. -gan
  or -gans
pte·rid'o·phyte'
pter'o·dac'tyl
pter'o·saur'
pto'maine' also pto'-
  main'
pty'a·lin
pub
pu'ber·ty
pu·bes'cence
pu·bes'cent
pu'bic
pu'bis pl. -bes'
pub'lic
pub'lic-ad·dress' sys-
  tem

pub'li·can
pub'li·ca'tion
pub'li·cist
pub·lic'i·ty
pub'li·cize', -cized',
  -ciz'ing
pub'lic·ly
pub'lic-spir'i·ted
pub'lish
pub'lish·a·ble
pub'lish·er
puce
puck (hockey disk)
Puck (sprite)
puck'er
pud'ding
pud'dle, -dled, -dling
pudg'y
pueb'lo pl. -los
pu'er·ile
pu'er·il'i·ty
pu·er'per·al
Puer'to Ri'can
puff'ball'
puff'er
puf'fin
puff'y
pug
pu'gi·lism
pu'gi·list
pu'gi·lis'tic
pug·na'cious
pug·nac'i·ty
puis'sance
puis'sant
pul'chri·tude'
pul'chri·tu·di·nous

pule, puled, pul'ing
Pul'it·zer Prize
pull'back' n.
pul'let
pul'ley pl. -leys
Pull'man
pull'out' n.
pull'o'ver n.
pull'-up' n.
pul'mo·nar'y
pul'pit
pulp'wood'
pulp'y
pul'sar'
pul'sate', -sat'ed, -sat'-
  ing
pul·sa'tion
pulse, pulsed, puls'ing
pul'ver·i·za'tion
pul'ver·ize', -ized',
  -iz'ing
pu'ma
pum'ice, -iced, -ic·ing
pum'mel, -meled or
  -melled, -mel·ing or
  -mel·ling
pump'er
pum'per·nick'el
pump'kin
pump'kin·seed'
pun, punned, pun'ning
punch'-drunk'
pun'cheon
punch'y
punc·til'i·o' pl. -os'
punc·til'i·ous
punc'tu·al

punc'tu·al'i·ty
punc'tu·ate', -at'ed,
  -at'ing
punc'tu·a'tion
punc'tu·a'tor
punc'ture, -tured, -tur·
  ing
pun'dit
pun'gen·cy
pun'gent
pun'ish
pun'ish·a·ble
pun'ish·ment
pu'ni·tive
punk
pun'ster
punt'er
pu'ny
pup
pu'pa pl. -pae or -pas
pu'pal (of a pupa)
  ♦pupil
pu'pate', -pat'ed,
  -pat'ing
pu·pa'tion
pu'pil (student)
  ♦pupal
pup'pet
pup'pet·eer'
pup'pet·ry
pup'py
pur'blind'
pur'chas·a·ble
pur'chase, -chased,
  -chas·ing
pure, pur'er, pur'est
pure'bred'

pu·rée'
pure'ly
pur·ga'tion
pur·ga·tive
pur·ga·to'ri·al
pur·ga·to'ry
purge, purged, purg-
  ing
pu·ri·fi·ca'tion
pu·rif·i·ca·to'ry
pu'ri·fi'er
pu'ri·fy', -fied', -fy'ing
Pu'rim
pur'ism
pur'ist
Pu'ri·tan *also* pu'ri·tan
pu'ri·tan'i·cal
Pu'ri·tan·ism *also* pu'-
  ri·tan·ism
pu'ri·ty
purl *(to ripple, knit)*
  ♦*pearl*
pur'lieu
pur·loin'
pur'ple
pur'plish
pur'port' *n.*
pur·port' *v.*
pur'pose, -posed, -pos-
  ing
pur'pose·ful
purr
purse, pursed, purs'ing
purs'er
pur·su'a·ble
pur·su'ance
pur·su'ant

pur·sue', -sued', -su'-
  ing
pur·suit'
pur·sui·vant
pu'ru·lence
pu'ru·lent
pur·vey'
pur·vey'ance
pur·vey'or
pur'view'
pus
push'-but'ton *adj.*
push'cart'
push'er
push'o'ver *n.*
push'pin'
push'up' *n.*
push'y
pu·sil·la·nim'i·ty
pu·sil·lan'i·mous
puss'y *(cat)*
pus'sy *(full of pus)*
puss'y·foot'
pus'tule'
put *(to place)*, put,
  put'ting
  ♦*putt*
pu'ta·tive
put'-down' *n.*
put'off' *n.*
put'-on' *n. & adj.*
put'out' *n.*
pu'tre·fac'tion
pu'tre·fac'tive
pu'tre·fy', -fied', -fy'-
  ing
pu'trid

pu·trid'i·ty
putsch
putt *(to hit a golf ball)*,
  putt'ed, putt'ing
  ♦*put*
putt·tee'
putt'er *(golf club)*
putt'er *(to occupy one-
  self aimlessly)*
put'ty, -tied, -ty·ing
put'-up' *adj.*
puz'zle, -zled, -zling
puz'zle·ment
Pyg·ma'lion
pyg'my *also* pig'my
py'lon'
py'or·rhe'a *also* py'or·
  rhoe'a
pyr'a·mid
py·ram'i·dal
pyre
py·re'thrum
py·ret'ic
Py'rex'®
pyr'i·dine'
pyr'i·dox'ine' *also*
  pyr'i·dox'in
py'rite'
py·ri'tes *pl.* -tes
py'ro·ma'ni·a
py'ro·ma'ni·ac'
py'ro·tech'nic *also*
  py'ro·tech'ni·cal
py'ro·tech'nics
Py·thag'o·re'an
py'thon'
pyx *also* pix

Q

quack'er•y
quad'ran'gle
quad'rant
quad'ra•phon'ic
quad'rate'
quad•rat'ic
quad•ren'ni•al
quad'ri•ceps'
quad'ri•lat'er•al
qua•drille'
quad•ril'lion
quad•ril'lionth
quad'ri•par'tite'
quad'ri•phon'ic *also*
   quad'ro•phon'ic
quad'ri•ple'gi•a
quad'ri•ple'gic
quad•roon'
quad•ru•ped'
quad•ru'ple, -pled,
   -pling
quad•ru'plet
quad•ru'pli•cate',
   -cat'ed, -cat'ing
quad•ru'pli•ca'tion
quaff
quag'gy
quag'mire'
qua'hog'
quail *pl.* quail *or*
   quails
quaint'ly
quake, quaked, quak'-
   ing

Quak'er
quak'y
qual'i•fi•ca'tion
qual'i•fi'er
qual'i•fy', -fied', -fy'-
   ing
qual'i•ta'tive
qual'i•ty
qualm
quan'da•ry
quan'ti•fi•ca'tion
quan'ti•fy', -fied', -fy'-
   ing
quan'ti•ta'tive
quan'ti•ty
quan'tum *pl.* -ta
quar'an•tine', -tined',
   -tin'ing
quark
quar'rel, -reled *or*
   -relled, -rel•ing *or*
   -rel•ling
quar'rel•er *or* quar'rel•
   ler
quar'rel•some
quar'ry, -ried, -ry•ing
quart
quar'ter
quar'ter•back'
quar'ter-deck'
quar'ter-fi'nal
quar'ter-hour' *also*
   quarter hour
quar'ter•ly
quar'ter•mas'ter
quar'tern

quar'ter•staff' *pl.*
   -staves'
quar•tet' *also* quar•
   tette'
quar'to *pl.* -tos
quartz *(mineral)*
   ♦*quarts*
quartz'ite'
qua'sar'
quash
qua'si'
qua'si'-stel'lar object
qua'ter•nar'y *(in
   fours)*
Qua'ter•nar'y *(geo-
   logic period)*
quat'rain'
quat're•foil'
qua'ver
quay *(wharf)*
   ♦*cay, key*
quea'sy
queen'ly
queer'ly
quell
quench'a•ble
que•nelle'
quer'u•lous
que'ry, -ried, -ry•ing
quest
ques'tion
ques'tion•a•ble
ques'tion•naire'
queue *(line)*
   ♦*cue*
quib'ble, -bled, -bling
quiche

quick′en
quick′-freeze′, -froze′,
   -fro′zen, -freez′ing
quick′ie
quick′lime′
quick′sand′
quick′sil′ver
quick′step′
quick′-tem′pered
quick′-wit′ted
quid *(money), pl.* quid
   or quids
quid′ pro quo′
qui·es′cence
qui·es′cent
qui′et
qui′e·tude′
qui·e′tus
quill
quilt′ing
quince
qui·nine′
quin·quen′ni·al
quin′sy
quint
quin′tal
quin·tes′sence
quin·tes·sen′tial
quin·tet′ *also* quin·
   tette′
quin·til′lion
quin·til′lionth
quin·tu′ple, -pled,
   -pling
quin·tu′plet

quip, quipped, quip′-
   ping
quip′ster
quire *(sheets of paper)*
   ♦*choir*
quirk′y
quis′ling
quit, quit *or* quit′ted,
   quit′ting
quit′claim′
quite
quit′rent′
quit′tance
quit′ter
quiv′er
qui vive′
quix·ot′ic *also* quix·
   ot′i·cal
quiz, quizzed, quiz′zing
quiz *pl.* quiz′zes
quiz′zi·cal
quiz′zi·cal′i·ty
quoin *(corner)*
   ♦*coin*
quoit
quon′dam
quo′rum
quo′ta
quot′a·ble
quo·ta′tion
quote, quot′ed, quot′-
   ing
quoth
quo·tid′i·an
quo′tient

R

rab′bet *(groove)*
   ♦*rabbit*
rab′bi *pl.* -bis
rab′bin·ate
rab·bin′i·cal *also* rab·
   bin′ic
rab′bit *(animal), pl.*
   -bit *or* -bits
   ♦*rabbet*
rab′ble
rab′ble-rous′er
Rab′e·lai′si·an
rab′id
ra·bid′i·ty
ra′bies
rac·coon′ *pl.* -coons′
   or -coon′
race, raced, rac′ing
race′course′
race′horse′
ra·ceme′
rac′er
race′track′
race′way′
ra′cial
ra′cism
rac′ist
rack *(framework)*
   ♦*wrack*
rack′et *(bat), also* rac′-
   quet
rack′et *(noise)*
rack′et·eer′
rac′on·teur′

rac'quet·ball'
rac'y
ra'dar'
ra'dar·scope'
ra'di·al
ra'di·an
ra'di·ance *also* ra'di·
 an·cy
ra'di·ant
ra'di·ate', -at'ed, -at'-
 ing
ra'di·a'tion
ra'di·a'tive
ra'di·a'tor
rad'i·cal
rad'i·cal·ism
rad'i·cal·i·za'tion
rad'i·cal·ize', -ized',
 -iz-'ing
rad'i·cand'
ra'di·o' *pl.* -os
ra'di·o', -oed', -o'ing
ra'di·o·ac'tive
ra'di·o·ac·tiv'i·ty
ra'di·o·car'bon
ra'di·o·chem'i·cal
ra'di·o·chem'is·try
ra'di·o·gram'
ra'di·o·graph'
ra'di·og'ra·pher
ra'di·o·graph'ic
ra'di·og'ra·phy
ra'di·o·i'so·tope'
ra'di·o·lar'i·an
ra'di·o·log'i·cal
ra'di·ol'o·gist
ra'di·ol'o·gy

ra'di·om'e·ter
ra'di·o·met'ric
ra'di·om'e·try
ra'di·o·phone'
ra'di·o·pho'to·graph'
 also ra'di·o·pho'to
ra'di·o·pho·tog'ra·
 phy
ra'di·o·scop'ic *also*
 ra'di·o·scop'i·cal
ra'di·os'co·py
ra'di·o·sen'si·tive
ra'di·o·tel'e·graph'
ra'di·o·tel'e·graph'ic
ra'di·o·te·leg'ra·phy
ra'di·o·tel'e·phone'
ra'di·o·tel'e·phon'ic
ra'di·o·te·leph'o·ny
ra'di·o·ther'a·py
rad'ish
ra'di·um
ra'di·us *pl.* -di·i' *or*
 -di·us·es
ra'dix *pl.* rad'i·ces' *or*
 ra'dix·es
rad'on'
raf'fi·a
raff'ish
raf'fle, -fled, -fling
raft
raf'ter
rag, ragged, rag'ging
ra'ga
rag'a·muf'fin
rage, raged, rag'ing
rag'ged
rag'lan

ra·gout'
rag'tag'
rag'time'
rag'weed'
rah
raid'er
rail'ing
rail'ler·y
rail'road'
rail'way'
rai'ment
rain *(precipitation)*
 ♦reign, rein
rain'bow'
rain'coat'
rain'drop'
rain'fall'
rain'mak'er
rain'mak'ing
rain'spout'
rain'storm'
rain'wat'er
rain'wear'
rain'y
raise *(to lift),* raised,
 rais'ing
 ♦rays, raze
rais'er *(one that raises)*
 ♦razor
rai'sin
rai'son d'ê'tre
ra'jah *or* ra'ja
rake, raked, rak'ing
rake'-off' *n.*
rak'ish
ral'ly, -lied, -ly·ing

ram, rammed, ram'-
  ming
ram'ble, -bled, -bling
ram·bunc'tious
ram'e·kin *also* ram'e·
  quin
ram'ie
ram'i·fi·ca'tion
ram'i·fy', -fied', -fy'ing
ram'jet'
ra'mose'
ramp
ram'page', -paged',
  -pag'ing
ram'pan·cy
ram'pant
ram'part'
ram'rod'
ram'shack'le
ranch'er
ran·che'ro *pl.* -ros
ran'cho *pl.* -chos
ran'cid
ran·cid'i·ty
ran'cor
ran'cor·ous
ran'dom
ran'dom·i·za'tion
ran'dom·ize', -ized',
  -iz'ing
range, ranged, rang'ing
rang'er
rang'y
ra'ni *pl.* -nis, *also* ra'-
  nee
rank'ing
ran'kle, -kled, -kling

ran'sack'
ran'som
rant
rap *(to knock),* rapped,
  rap'ping
  ♦*wrap*
ra·pa'cious
ra·pac'i·ty
rape, raped, rap'ing
rap'id
rap'id-fire'
ra·pid'i·ty
ra'pi·er
rap'ine
rap'ist
rap·pel', -pelled', -pel'-
  ling
rap·port'
rap'proche·ment'
rap·scal'lion
rapt *(enchanted)*
  ♦*rapped, wrapped*
rap·to'ri·al
rap'ture
rap'tur·ous
ra'ra a'vis *pl.* ra'ra
  a'vis·es *or* ra'rae
  a'ves
rare, rar'er, rar'est
rare'bit
rare'-earth' element
rar'e·fac'tion
rar'e·fy', -fied', -fy'ing
rar'ing
rar'i·ty
ras'cal
ras·cal'i·ty

rash'er
rasp'ber'ry
rasp'y
rat, rat'ted, rat'ting
rat'a·bil'i·ty
rat'a·ble
ratch'et
rate, rat'ed, rat'ing
rath'er
rat'i·fi·ca'tion
rat'i·fy', -fied', -fy'ing
ra'tio *pl.* -tios
ra'ti·oc'i·nate', -nat'-
  ed, -nat'ing
ra'ti·oc'i·na'tion
ra'ti·oc'i·na'tor
ra'tion
ra'tion·al *adj.*
ra'tion·ale' *n.*
ra'tion·al·ism
ra'tion·al·ist
ra'tion·al·is'tic
ra'tion·al'i·ty
ra'tion·al·i·za'tion
ra'tion·al·ize', -ized',
  -iz'ing
rat'ite'
rat'line *also* rat'lin
rat·tan'
rat'ter
rat'tle, -tled, -tling
rat'tle-brained'
rat'tler
rat'tle·snake'
rat'tle·trap'
rat'ty
rau'cous

rav′age, -aged, -ag·ing

rave, raved, rav′ing

rav′el, -eled or -elled,
  -el·ing or -el·ling

ra′ven

rav′en·ing

rav′en·ous

ra·vine′

rav′i·o·li

rav′ish

rav′ish·ing

raw′boned′

raw′hide′

ray (beam, fish)
  ♦re

ray′on′

raze (to demolish),
  razed, raz′ing
  ♦raise, rays

ra′zor (cutting instru-
  ment)
  ♦raiser

ra′zor·back′

raz′zle-daz′zle

razz′ma·tazz′

re (musical tone)
  ♦ray

re (concerning)
  ♦ray

reach

re·act′

re·ac′tance

re·ac′tant

re·ac′tion

re·ac′tion·ar·y

re·ac′ti·vate′, -vat·ed,
  -vat·ing

re·ac′tive

re·ac′tor

read (to peruse), read,
  read′ing
  ♦reed

read′a·bil′i·ty

read′a·ble

read′er

read′er·ship′

read′i·ly

read′ing

re·ad·just′

re·ad·just′ment

read′-out′ n.

read′y, -ied, -y·ing

read′y-made′

re·af·firm′

re·af·fir·ma′tion

re·a′gent

re·al (actual)
  ♦reel

re′al-es·tate′ adj.

re′al·ism

re′al·ist

re′al·is′tic

re·al′i·ty (actuality)
  ♦realty

re′al·iz′a·ble

re′al·i·za′tion

re′al·ize′, -ized′, -iz′ing

re′al·ly

realm

re′al-time′ adj.

Re′al·tor

re′al·ty (property)
  ♦reality

ream′er

reap′er

re′ap·por′tion

re′ap·por′tion·ment

re′ap·prais′al

re·arm′

re·ar′ma·ment

rear′most′

re′ar·range′, -ranged′,
  -rang′ing

rear′view′ mirror

rear′ward also rear′-
  wards

rea′son

rea′son·a·bil′i·ty

rea′son·a·ble

re′as·sur′ance

re′as·sure′, -sured′,
  -sur′ing

re·bate′, -bat·ed, -bat·
  ing

reb′el n.

re·bel′, -belled′, -bel′-
  ling

re·bel′lion

re·bel′lious

re·bind′, -bound′,
  -bind′ing

re·birth′

re·born′

re′bound′ n.

re·bound′ v.

re·broad′cast′, -cast′
  or -cast′ed, -cast′ing

re·buff′

re·build′, -built′,
  -build′ing

re·buke', -buked', -buk'ing

re'bus *pl.* -bus·es

re·but', -but'ted, -but'ting

re·but'tal

re·cal'ci·trance *also* re·cal'ci·tran·cy

re·cal'ci·trant

re·call'

re·call'a·ble

re·cant'

re'can·ta'tion

re'cap' *(tire, summary)*

re·cap' *(to rebond a tire)*, -capped', -cap'ping

re'cap' *(to summarize)*, -capped', -cap'ping

re'ca·pit'u·late', -lat'ed, -lat'ing

re'ca·pit'u·la'tion

re'ca·pit'u·la'tive *also* re·ca·pit'u·la;to'ry

re·cap'ture, -tured, -tur·ing

re'cast' *n.*

re·cast', -cast', -cast'ing

re·cede' *(to ebb)*, -ced'ed, -ced'ing

re-cede' *(to cede back)*, -ced'ed, -ced'ing

re·ceipt'

re·ceiv'a·ble

re·ceive', -ceived', -ceiv'ing

re·ceiv'er·ship'

re'cent

re·cep'ta·cle

re·cep'tion

re·cep'tion·ist

re·cep'tive

re'cep·tiv'i·ty

re·cep'tor

re'cess'

re·ces'sion *(withdrawal)*

re-ces'sion *(restoration)*

re·ces'sion·al

re·ces'sive

re'charge' *n.*

re·charge', -charged', charging

re·cher·ché'

re·cid'i·vism

re·cid'i·vist

re·cid'i·vis'tic

rec'i·pe

re·cip'i·ent

re·cip'ro·cal

re·cip'ro·cate', -cat'ed, -cat'ing

re·cip'ro·ca'tion

re·cip'ro·ca'tive

re·cip'ro·ca'tor

rec'i·proc'i·ty

re·cit'al

rec'i·ta'tion

rec'i·ta'tive *adj.*

rec'i·ta'tive' *n.*

re·cite', -cit'ed, -cit'ing

reck'less

reck'on

re·claim' *(to make usable)*

re-claim' *(to claim again)*

re·claim'a·ble

re·claim'ant

rec'la·ma'tion

re·cline', -clined', -clin'ing

re'cluse'

re·clu'sive

rec'og·ni'tion

rec'og·niz'a·ble

re·cog'ni·zance

re·cog'ni·zant

rec'og·nize', -nized', -niz'ing

re·coil'

rec'ol·lect' *(to remember)*

re'-col·lect' *(to collect again)*

rec'ol·lec'tion *(memory)*

re'-col·lec'tion *(new collection)*

rec'ol·lec'tive

re·com'bi·nant

re'com·bi·na'tion

rec'om·mend'

rec'om·mend'a·ble

rec'om·men·da'tion

rec'om·pense', -pensed', -pens'ing

re'com·pose', -posed', -pos'ing

rec′on·cil′a·ble

rec′on·cile′, -ciled′,
  -cil′ing

rec′on·cil′i·a′tion

rec′on·cil′i·a·to′ry

rec′on·dite′

re′con·di′tion

re′con·nais·sance

re′con·noi′ter

re′con·sid′er

re′con·sid′er·a′tion

re·con′sti·tute′, -tut′-
  ed, -tut′ing

re′con·struct′

re′con·struc′tion

rec′ord *n.*

re·cord′ *v.*

re·cord′er

re·cord′ing

re·count′ *(to narrate)*

re-count′ *(to count
  again)*

re·coup′

re·cov′er *(to regain)*

re-cov′er *(to cover
  anew)*

re·cov′er·a·ble

re·cov′er·y

rec′re·ant

rec′re·ate′ *(to refresh)*,
  -at′ed, -at′ing

re′-cre·ate′ *(to create
  anew)*, -at′ed, -at′ing

rec′re·a′tion *(refresh-
  ment)*

re′-cre·a′tion *(new cre-
  ation)*

rec′re·a′tion·al

re·crim′i·nate′, -nat′-
  ed, -nat′ing

re·crim′i·na′tion

re·crim′i·na′tor

re·crim′i·na·to′ry

re′cru·desce′, -desced′,
  -desc′ing

re′cru·des′cence

re′cru·des′cent

re·cruit′

re·cruit′ment

rec′tal

rec·tan′gle

rec·tan′gu·lar

rec·tan′gu·lar′i·ty

rec′ti·fi′a·ble

rec′ti·fi·ca′tion

rec′ti·fi′er

rec′ti·fy′, -fied′, -fy′ing

rec′ti·lin′e·ar

rec′ti·tude′

rec′to *pl.* -tos

rec′tor

rec′tor·ate

rec·to′ri·al

rec′to·ry

rec′tum *pl.* -tums *or*
  -ta

re·cum′bence

re·cum′bent

re·cu′per·ate′, -at′ed,
  -at′ing

re·cu′per·a′tion

re·cu′per·a′tive *also*
  re·cu′per·a·to′ry

re·cur′, -curred′, -cur-
  ring

re·cur′rence

re·cur′rent

re·cy′cle, -cled, -cling

red *(blood-colored)*,
  red′der, red′dest
  ♦read *(past tense)*

re·dact′

re·dac′tion

re·dac′tor

red′bird′

red′-blood′ed

red′breast′

red′cap′

red′coat′

red′den

red′dish

re·dec′o·rate′, -rat′ed,
  -rat′ing

re·dec′o·ra′tion

re·deem′

re·deem′a·ble

re′de·liv′er

re·demp′tion

re′de·vel′op

re′de·vel′op·ment

red′-hand′ed

red′head′

red′-hot′

red′in·gote′

re′di·rect′

re′dis·trib′ute, -ut·ed,
  -ut·ing

re′dis′trict

red′-let′ter *adj.*

red′neck′

re·do′, -did′, -done′,
-do′ing

red′o·lence *also* red′o·
len·cy

red′o·lent

re·dou′ble, -bled,
-bling

re·doubt′

re·doubt′a·ble

re·dound′

re·dress′

re·dress′er *also* re·
dres′sor

red′start′

re·duce′, -duced′,
-duc′ing

re·duc′i·bil′i·ty

re·duc′i·ble

re·duc′ti·o′ ad ab·
sur′dum

re·duc′tion

re·duc′tive

re·dun′dan·cy

re·dun′dant

re·du′pli·cate′, -cat′-
ed, -cat′ing

re·du′pli·ca′tion

re·du′pli·ca′tive

red′wing′

red′wood′

re-ech′o, -oed, -o·ing

reed *(grass, musical in-
strument)*
    ♦*read*

re-ed′u·cate′, -cat′ed,
-cat′ing

re-ed′u·ca′tion

reef

reek *(to smell)*
    ♦*wreak*

reel *(spool, whirling,
dance)*
    ♦*real*

re′-e·lect′ *or* re′e·lect′

re′-e·lec′tion *or* re′e·
lec′tion

re′-en·act′

re′-en·act′ment

re-en′ter *or* re·en′ter

re-en′trance *or*
re·en′trance

re-en′try *or* re·en′try

re′es·tab′lish

reeve *(bailiff, bird)*

reeve *(to fasten a rope)*,
reeved *or* rove,
reev′ing

re′-ex·am′i·na′tion *or*
re′ex·am′i·na′tion

re′-ex·am′ine, -ined,
-in·ing, *or* re′ex·am′-
ine

re·fec′tion

re·fec′to·ry

re·fer′, -ferred′, -fer′-
ring

ref′er·a·ble

ref′e·ree′

ref′er·ence

ref′er·en′dum *pl.*
-dums *or* -da

re·fer′ent

ref′er·en′tial

re·fer′ral

re·fer′rer

re′fill′ *n.*

re·fill′ *v.*

re·fi′nance, -nanced,
-nanc·ing

re·fine′, -fined′, -fin′-
ing

re·fine′ment

re·fin′er·y

re·fin′ish

re·fit′, -fit′ted, -fit′ting

re·flect′

re·flec′tance

re·flec′tion

re·flec′tive

re·flec′tor

re′flex′ *adj. & n.*

re·flex′ *v.*

re·flex′ive

re·for′est

re′for·es·ta′tion

re·form′ *(to improve)*

re-form′ *(to form
again)*

ref′or·ma′tion

re·for′ma·tive

re·for′ma·to·ry

re·form′er

re·fract′

re·frac′tion

re·frac′tive

re′frac·tiv′i·ty

re·frac′tor

re·frac′to·ry

re·frain′

re·fresh′

re·fresh′er

re·fresh'ment
re·frig'er·ant
re·frig'er·ate', -at'ed,
　-at'ing
re·frig'er·a'tion
re·frig'er·a'tor
re·fu'el
ref'uge
ref'u·gee'
re·ful'gence *also* re·
　ful'gen·cy
re·ful'gent
re·fund' *n.*
re·fund' *v.*
re·fund'a·ble
re·fut'a·bly
re·fur'bish
re·fus'al
ref·use (*trash*)
re·fuse' (*to decline*),
　-fused', -fus'ing
re·fut'a·bil'i·ty
re·fut'a·ble
ref'u·ta'tion *also* re·
　fu'tal
re·fute', -fut'ed, -fut'-
　ing
re·gain'
re'gal (*royal*)
re·gale' (*to delight*),
　-galed', -gal'ing
re·ga'lia
re·gard'
re·gard'ing
re·gard'less
re·gat'ta
re·gen·cy

re·gen'er·ate', -at'ed,
　-at'ing
re·gen'er·a'tion
re·gen'er·a'tive
re·gen'er·a'tor
re'gent
reg'i·cid'al
reg'i·cide'
re·gime'
reg'i·men
reg'i·ment
reg'i·men'tal
reg'i·men·ta'tion
re'gion
re'gion·al
reg'is·ter (*record*)
　♦*registrar*
reg'is·tered
reg'is·trant
reg'is·trar' (*officer*)
　♦*register*
reg'is·tra'tion
reg'is·try
reg'nant
re·gress' *n.*
re·gress' *v.*
re·gres'sion
re·gres'sive
re·gret', -gret'ted,
　-gret'ting
re·gret'ful·ly
re·gret'ta·ble
re·group'
reg'u·lar
reg'u·lar'i·ty
reg'u·lar·ize', -ized',
　-iz'ing

reg'u·late', -lat'ed,
　-lat'ing
reg'u·la'tion
reg'u·la'tive
reg'u·la'tor
reg'u·la·to'ry
re·gur'gi·tate', -tat'ed,
　-tat'ing
re·gur'gi·ta'tion
re·ha·bil'i·tate', -tat'-
　ed, -tat'ing
re·ha·bil'i·ta'tion
re·ha·bil'i·ta'tive
re'hash' *n.*
re·hash' *v.*
re·hear', -heard',
　-hear'ing
re·hears'al
re·hearse', -hearsed',
　-hears'ing
re·house', -housed',
　-hous'ing
Reich
reign (*sovereignty*)
　♦*rain, rein*
reign (*to rule*)
　♦*rain, rein*
re'im·burse', -bursed',
　-burs'ing
re'im·burse'ment
rein (*strap*)
　♦*rain, reign*
rein (*to hold back*)
　♦*rain, reign*
re'in·car'nate', -nat'-
　ed, -nat'ing
re'in·car·na'tion

rein'deer' *pl.* -deer *or* -deers'
re'in·forc'a·ble
re'in·force', -forced', -forc'ing
re'in·force'ment
re'in·state', -stat'ed, -stat'ing
re'in·state'ment
re'in·sure', -sured', -sur'ing
re'in·vest'
re·is'sue, -sued, -su·ing
re·it'er·ate', -at'ed, -at'ing
re·it'er·a'tion
re·it'er·a'tive
re'ject' *n.*
re·ject' *v.*
re·ject'er *also* re·jec'tor
re·jec'tion
re·joice', -joiced', -joic'ing
re·join' *(to respond)*
re-join' *(to reunite)*
re·join'der
re·ju've·nate', -nat'ed, -nat'ing
re·ju've·na'tion
re·ju've·na'tor
re'lapse' *n.*
re·lapse', -lapsed', -laps'ing
re·late', -lat'ed, -lat'ing
re·lat'er *also* re·la'tor
re·la'tion
re·la'tion·ship'

rel'a·tive
rel'a·tiv'i·ty
re·lax'
re·lax'ant
re·lax·a'tion
re·lay' *(to pass along)*, -laid' *or* -layed', -lay'ing
re-lay' *(to lay again)*, -laid', -lay'ing
re·leas'a·ble
re·lease' *(to set free)*, -leased', -leas'ing
re'-lease' *(to lease again)*, -leased', -leas'ing
rel'e·gate, -gat'ed, -gat'ing
rel'e·ga'tion
re·lent'
re·lent'less
rel'e·vance *also* rel'e·van·cy
rel'e·vant
re·li'a·bil'i·ty
re·li'a·ble
re·li'ance
re·li'ant
rel'ic
re·lief'
re·liev'a·ble
re·lieve', -lieved', -liev'ing
re·lig'ion
re·lig'i·os'i·ty
re·lig'ious
re·line', -lined', -lin'ing

re·lin'quish
rel'i·quar'y
rel'ish
re·live', -lived', -liv'ing
re·lo'cate', -cat'ed, -cat'ing
re·lo·ca'tion
re·luc'tance *also* re·luc'tan·cy
re·luc'tant
re·ly', -lied', -ly'ing
re·main'
re·main'der
re·mains'
re·make', -made', -mak'ing
re·mand'
re·mark'
re·mark'a·ble
re·mar'ry, -ried, -ry·ing
re·me'di·al
rem'e·dy, -died, -dy·ing
re·mem'ber
re·mem'ber·a·ble
re·mem'brance
re·mind'
re·mind'er
rem'i·nisce', -nisced', -nisc'ing
rem'i·nis'cence
rem'i·nis'cent
re·miss'
re·mis·si·bil'i·ty
re·mis'si·ble
re·mis'sion

re·mit′, -mit′ted, -mit′-
　ting
re·mit′tal
re·mit′tance
re·mit′tent
re·mit′ter
rem′nant
re·mod′el
re·mon′strance
re·mon′strant
re·mon′strate′, -strat′-
　ed, -strat′ing
re′mon·stra′tion
re·mon′stra·tive
re·mon′stra′tor
rem′o·ra
re·morse′
re·mote′, -mot′er,
　-mot′est
re·mount′
re·mov′a·ble
re·mov′al
re·move′, -moved′,
　-mov′ing
re·mu′ner·a·bil′i·ty
re·mu′ner·a·ble
re·mu′ner·ate′, -at′ed,
　-at′ing
re·mu′ner·a′tion
re·mu′ner·a′tive
re·mu′ner·a′tor
ren·ais·sance′ (rebirth)
　♦renascence
re′nal
re·nas′cence (renais-
　sance)
re·nas′cent

rend, rent or rend′ed,
　rend′ing
ren′der
ren′dez·vous′ pl.
　-vous′
ren·di′tion
ren′e·gade′
re·nege′, -neged′,
　-neg′ing
re·new′
re·new′a·ble
re·new′al
ren′net
ren′nin
re·nounce′, -nounced′,
　-nounc′ing
ren′o·vate′,
　-vat′ed, -vat′ing
ren′o·va′tion
ren′o·va′tor
re·nown′
re·nowned′
rent′al
re·num′ber
re·nun′ci·a′tion
re·nun′ci·a′tive
re·nun′ci·a·to′ry
re·o′pen
re·or′der
re·or′gan·i·za′tion
re·or′gan·ize′, -ized′,
　-iz′ing
rep (ribbed fabric), also
　repp
rep (representative)
re·pack′age, -aged,
　-ag·ing

re·pair′
re·pair′a·ble
re·pair′man′
rep′a·ra·bil′i·ty
rep′a·ra·ble
rep′a·ra′tion
re·par′a·tive also re·
　par′a·to′ry
rep′ar·tee′
re·past′
re·pa′tri·ate′, -at′ed,
　-at′ing
re·pa′tri·a′tion
re·pay′, -paid′, -pay′-
　ing
re·pay′a·ble
re·pay′ment
re·peal′
re·peat′
re·pel′, -pelled′, -pel′-
　ling
re·pel′lence also re·
　pel′len·cy
re·pel′lent
re·pent′
re·pen′tance
re·pen′tant
re·per·cus′sion
re·per·cus′sive
rep′er·toire′ (group of
　works), also rep′er·
　to′ry
rep′er·to′ry (theatrical
　company)
rep′e·ti′tion
rep′e·ti′tious
re·pet′i·tive

re·phrase′, -phrased′,
  -phras′ing
re·pine′, -pined′, -pin′-
  ing
re·place′, -placed′,
  -plac′ing
re·place′a·ble
re·place′ment
re′plant′ n.
re·plant′ v.
re′play′ n.
re·play′ v.
re·plen′ish
re·plen′ish·ment
re·plete′
re·ple′tion
rep′li·ca
rep′li·cate′, -cat′ed,
  -cat′ing
rep′li·ca′tion
re·ply′, -plied′, -ply′ing
re·port′
re·port′a·ble
re′port·age′
re·port′ed·ly
re·port′er
re·pos′al
re·pose′, -posed′,
  -pos′ing
re·pos′i·to′ry
re·pos·sess′
re·pos·ses′sion
rep′re·hend′
rep′re·hen′si·bil′i·ty
rep′re·hen′si·ble
rep′re·hen′sion
rep′re·sent′

rep′re·sen·ta′tion
rep′re·sen·ta′tion·al
rep′re·sen·ta′tive
re·press′
re·press′i·ble
re·pres′sion
re·pres′sive
re·pres′sor
re·priev′a·ble
re·prieve′, -prieved′,
  -priev′ing
rep′ri·mand′
re′print′ n.
re·print′ v.
re·pri′sal
re·prise′
re·proach′
re·proach′ful
rep′ro·bate′
rep′ro·ba′tion
re′pro·duce′, -duced′,
  -duc′ing
re′pro·duc′er
re′pro·duc′i·ble
re′pro·duc′tion
re′pro·duc′tive
re·proof′
re·prove′, -proved′,
  -prov′ing
rep′tile
rep·til′i·an
re·pub′lic
re·pub′li·can
re·pub′li·can·ism
re′pub·li·ca′tion
re·pub′lish

re·pu′di·ate′, -at′ed,
  -at′ing
re·pu′di·a′tion
re·pu′di·a′tor
re·pug′nance
re·pug′nant
re·pulse′, -pulsed′,
  -puls′ing
re·pul′sion
re·pul′sive
rep′u·ta·bil′i·ty
rep′u·ta·ble
rep′u·ta′tion
re·pute′, -put′ed, -put′-
  ing
re·quest′
re′qui·em
re·quire′, -quired′,
  -quir′ing
re·quire′ment
req′ui·site
req′ui·si′tion
re·quit′al
re·quite′, -quit′ed,
  -quit′ing
re·route′, -rout′ed,
  -rout′ing
re′run′ n.
re·run′, -ran′,
  -run′ning
re′sale′
re·scind′
re·scind′a·ble
re·scis′sion
res′cue, -cued, -cu·ing
re·search′
re·sec′tion

re·sem'blance
re·sem'ble, -bled,
　-bling
re·sent'
re·sent'ful
re·sent'ment
res'er·va'tion
re·serve', -served',
　-serv'ing
re·serv'ist
res'er·voir'
re·set', -set', -set'ting
re·shuf'fle, -fled, -fling
re·side', -sid'ed, -sid'-
　ing
res'i·dence
res'i·den·cy
res'i·dent
res'i·den'tial
re·sid'u·al
re·sid'u·ar'y
res'i·due'
re·sign' *(to give up)*
re·sign' *(to sign anew)*
res'ig·na'tion
re·sil'ience *also* re·sil'-
　ien·cy
re·sil'ient
res'in
res'in·ous
re·sist'
re·sis'tance
re·sis'tant
re·sist'er *(one that re-
　sists)*
re·sis'tor *(electrical de-
　vice)*

re·sol'u·ble
res'o·lute'
res'o·lu'tion
re·solv'a·bil'i·ty
re·solv'a·ble
re·solve', -solved',
　-solv'ing
res'o·nance
res'o·nant
res'o·nate', -nat'ed,
　-nat'ing
res'o·na'tion
res'o·na'tor
re·sort'
re·sound'
re'source'
re·source'ful
re·spect'
re·spect'a·bil'i·ty
re·spect'a·ble
re·spect'ful
re·spect'ful·ly *(defer-
　entially)*
　♦*respectively*
re·spec'tive
re·spec'tive·ly *(in or-
　der)*
　♦*respectfully*
re·spell', -spelled' *or*
　-spelt,' -spell'ing
res'pi·ra'tion
res'pi·ra'tor
res'pi·ra·to'ry
re·spire', -spired',
　-spir'ing
res'pite

re·splen'dence *or* re·
　splen'den·cy
re·splen'dent
re·spond'
re·spon'dent
re·sponse'
re·spon'si·bil'i·ty
re·spon'si·ble
re·spon'sive
rest *(quiet, remainder)*
　♦*wrest*
re·state', -stat'ed,
　-stat'ing
re·state'ment
res'tau·rant
res'tau·ra·teur'
rest'ful
res'ti·tu'tion
res'tive
rest'less
re·stock'
res'to·ra'tion
re·stor'a·tive
re·store', -stored',
　-stor'ing
re·strain'
re·straint'
re·strict'
re·stric'tion
re·stric'tive
re·sult'
re·sul'tant
re·sume' *(to begin
　again)*, -sumed',
　-sum'ing
rés'u·mé' *(summary)*
re·sump'tion

re·sur'gence
re·sur'gent
res'ur·rect'
res'ur·rec'tion
re·sur'vey' *n.*
re'sur·vey' *v.*
re·sus'ci·tate', -tat·ed,
-tat'ing
re·sus'ci·ta'tion
re·sus'ci·ta'tive
re·sus'ci·ta'tor
re'tail'
re·tain'
re'take' *n.*
re·take', -took', -tak'-
en, -tak'ing
re·tal'i·ate', -at'ed,
-at'ing
re·tal'i·a'tion
re·tal'i·a·to'ry
re·tard'
re·tar'date'
re'tar·da'tion
retch *(to vomit)*
  ♦*wretch*
re·tell', -told', -tell'ing
re·ten'tion
re·ten'tive
re·think', -thought',
-think'ing
ret'i·cence
ret'i·cent
re·tic'u·lar
re·tic'u·late
re·tic'u·la'tion
ret'i·cule'

ret'i·na *pl.* -nas *or*
  -nae'
ret'i·nal
ret'i·nue'
re·tire', -tired', -tir'ing
re·tire'ment
re·tool'
re·tort'
re·touch'
re·trace', -traced',
-trac'ing
re·trace'a·ble
re·tract'
re·tract'a·ble *also* re·
  tract'i·ble
re·trac'tile
re·trac'tion
re·trac'tor
re·tread' *n.*
re·tread' *(to fit a new
  tire tread)*, -tread'ed,
-tread'ing
re-tread' *(to tread
  again)*, -trod', -trod'-
den, -tread'ing
re·treat'
re·trench'
re·tri'al
ret'ri·bu'tion
re·trib'u·tive *also* re·
  trib'u·to'ry
re·triev'a·ble
re·triev'al
re·trieve', -trieved',
-triev'ing
ret'ro·ac'tive
ret'ro·grade'

ret'ro·gress'
ret'ro·gres'sion
ret'ro·gres'sive
ret'ro·rock'et
ret'ro·spect'
ret'ro·spec'tion
ret'ro·spec'tive
re·turn'
re·turn'a·ble
re·turn·ee'
re·un'ion
re'u·nite', -nit'ed,
-nit'ing
re'up·hol'ster
rev, revved, rev'ving
re·val'u·a'tion
re·vamp'
re·veal'
rev·eil'le
rev'el, -eled *or* -elled,
-el'ing *or* -el·ling
rev'e·la'tion
rev'el·er
rev'el·ry
re·venge', -venged',
-veng'ing
rev'e·nue'
re·ver'ber·ate', -at'ed,
-at'ing
re·ver'ber·a'tion
re·vere', -vered', -ver'-
ing
rev'er·ence
rev'er·end
rev'er·ent
rev'er·en'tial
rev'er·ie

re·ver′sal
re·verse′, -versed′,
　-vers′ing
re·vers′i·bil′i·ty
re·vers′i·ble
re·ver′sion
re·vert′
re·vert′i·ble
re·view′ *(examination)*
　♦*revue*
re·vile′, -viled′, -vil′ing
re·vis′a·ble
re·vise′, -vised′, -vis′-
　ing
re·vis′er *also* re·vi′sor
re·vi′sion
re·vi′sion·ism
re·vi′sion·ist
re·vis′it
re·vi′tal·i·za′tion
re·vi′tal·ize′, -ized′,
　-iz′ing
re·viv′al
re·viv′al·ist
re·vive′, -vived′, -viv′-
　ing
re·viv′i·fy′, -fied′, -fy′-
　ing
rev′o·ca·bil′i·ty
rev′o·ca·ble
rev′o·ca′tion
re·voke′, -voked′,
　-vok′ing
re·volt′
rev′o·lu′tion
rev′o·lu′tion·ar′y
rev′o·lu′tion·ist

rev′o·lu′tion·ize′,
　-ized′, -iz′ing
re·volv′a·ble
re·volve′, -volved′,
　-volv′ing
re·volv′er
re·vue′ *(musical show)*
　♦*review*
re·vul′sion
re·ward′
re′wind′ *n.*
re·wind′, -wound′,
　-wind′ing
re·wire′, -wired′, -wir′-
　ing
re·word′
re·work′
re′write′ *n.*
re·write′, -wrote′,
　-writ′ten, -writ′ing
re·zone′, -zoned′,
　-zon′ing
rhap·sod′ic *also* rhap·
　sod′i·cal
rhap′so·dist
rhap′so·dize′, -dized′,
　-diz′ing
rhap′so·dy
rhe′a
rhe′ni·um
rhe′o·stat′
rhe′sus monkey
rhet′o·ric
rhe·tor′i·cal
rhet′o·ri′cian
rheum *(mucus)*
　♦*room*

rheu·mat′ic
rheu′ma·tism
rheu′ma·toid′
rheum′y *(full of*
　rheum)
　♦*roomy*
rhine′stone′
rhi′no *pl.* -nos
rhi·noc′er·os *pl.* -os *or*
　-os·es
rhi′zoid′
rhi·zoi′dal
rhi′zome′
rho *(Greek letter)*
　♦*roe, row (series, boat*
　trip)
Rhode Is′land·er
Rho·de′sian
rho′di·um
rho·do·den′dron
rhom′bic
rhom′boid′
rhom·boi′dal
rhom′bus *pl.* -bus·es
　or -bi′
rhu′barb′
rhyme *(to compose*
　verse), rhymed,
　rhym′ing, *also* rime,
　rimed, rim′ing
rhyme′ster *also* rime′-
　ster
rhythm
rhyth′mi·cal *also*
　rhyth′mic
ri·al′to
ri·a′ta *also* re·a′ta

rib, ribbed, rib'bing

rib'ald

rib'ald·ry

rib'bon

ri'bo·fla'vin

ri'bo·nu'cle·ic acid

ri'bose'

ri·bo·so'mal

ri'bo·some

rice, riced, ric'ing

ric'er

rich'es

rich'ly

Rich'ter scale

rick'ets

rick'et·y

rick'rack'

ric'o·chet', -cheted' or
-chet'ted, -chet'ing or
-chetting

ri·cot'ta

rid, rid or rid'ded, rid'-
ding

rid'dance

rid'dle, -dled, -dling

ride, rode, rid'den,
rid'ing

rid'er

ridge, ridged, ridg'ing

rid'i·cule', -culed',
-cul'ing

ri·dic'u·lous

rid'ing

rife, rif'er, rif'est

rif'fle (to shuffle), -fled,
-fling
♦*rifle*

riff'raff'

ri'fle (to plunder, cut
grooves), -fled, -fling
♦*riffle*

rift

rig, rigged, rig'ging

rig'a·to'ni

rig'ger (one who rigs)
♦*rigor*

right (correct, not left)
♦*rite, write*

right'-an'gled

right'eous

right'ful

right'-hand' adj.

right'-hand'ed

right'ist

right'ly

right'-on' adj.

right'-wing' adj.

rig'id

ri·gid'i·ty

rig'ma·role also rig'a·
ma·role

rig'or (severity)
♦*rigger*

rigor mor'tis

rig'or·ous

rile, riled, ril'ing

rim, rimmed, rim'ming

rime (to cover with
frost), rimed, rim'ing
♦*rhyme*

rim'y

rind

ring (circle)
♦*wring*

ring (encircle), ringed,
ring'ing
♦*wring*

ring (to sound), rang,
rung, ring'ing
♦*wring*

ring'er

ring'lead'er

ring'let

ring'mas'ter

ring'-necked' pheas-
ant

ring'side'

ring'tail'

ring'-tailed'

ring'worm'

rink

rinse, rinsed, rins'ing

ri'ot

ri'ot·ous

rip, ripped, rip'ping

ri·par'i·an

rip'cord'

ripe, rip'er, rip'est

rip'en

rip'-off' n.

ri·poste', -post'ed,
-post'ing

rip'per

rip'ple, -pled, -pling

rip'ply

rip'-roar'ing also
rip'-roar'i·ous

rise, rose, ris'en, ris'ing

ris'er

ris'i·bil'i·ty

ris'i·ble

risk′y *(dangerous)*
  ♦*risqué*
ri·sot′to
ris·qué′ *(suggestive)*
  ♦*risky*
ris′sole
ri′tar·dan′do
rite *(ceremony)*
  ♦*right, write*
rit′u·al
rit′u·al·is′tic
ritz′y
ri′val, -valed, -val·ing
ri′val·ry
rive, rived, rived *or*
  riv′en, riv′ing
riv′er
riv′er·bed′
riv′er·boat′
riv′er·side′
riv′et
riv′u·let
roach *(fish) pl.* roach
  or roach′es
road *(way)*
  ♦*rode, rowed*
road′bed′
road′block
road′house′
road′run′ner
road′side′
road′stead′
road′ster
road′way′
road′work′
roam
roan

roar′ing
roast′er
rob, robbed, rob′bing
rob′ber
rob′ber·y
robe, robed, rob′ing
rob′in
ro′bot
ro·bust′
roc *(legendary bird)*
rock *(stone, swaying
  motion)*
rock′-bound′
rock′er
rock′et
rock′et·eer′
rock′et·ry
rock′fish′ *pl.* -fish′ *or*
  -fish′es
rock′ 'n' roll′ *also*
  rock′-and-roll′
rock′-ribbed′
rock′y
ro·co′co
rod
ro′dent
ro′de·o′ *pl.* -os′
roe *(fish eggs, deer)*
  ♦*rho, row (series,
  boat trip)*
roe′buck′
roent′gen
rog′er *interj.*
rogue
Rogue′fort cheese
rogu′er·y
rogu′ish

roil *(to muddy)*
  ♦*royal*
rois′ter
rois′ter·ous
role *(part), also* rôle
roll *(list, bread)*
roll *(to revolve)*
roll′a·way′
roll′back′ *n.*
roll′er
rol′ler·drome′
roll′er-skate′, -skat′ed,
  -skat′ing
rol′lick
rol′lick·ing
roll′-on′ *adj.*
roll′o·ver
ro′ly-po′ly
ro·maine
ro′man *(type)*
Ro′man *(of Rome)*
ro·mance′ *(story)*
Ro·mance′ *(languages)*
Ro′man·esque′
Roman numeral
ro·man′tic
ro·man′ti·cism
ro·man′ti·cist
ro·man′ti·cize′,
  -cized′, -ciz′ing
Rom′a·ny *pl.* -ny *or*
  -nies
Ro′me·o′ *pl.* -os′
romp′ers
ron′do *pl.* -dos
rood *(cross)*
  ♦*rude, rued*

roof'ing
rook'er•y
rook'ie
room (space)
 ♦rheum
room'er (lodger)
 ♦rumor
room•ette'
room'ful' pl. -fuls
room'mate'
room'y (spacious)
 ♦rheumy
roost'er
root (plant part, origin)
 ♦route
root (to dig, cheer)
 ♦route
root'stock'
rope, roped, rop'ing
rop'y
Roque'fort
Ror'schach test
ro'sa•ry
rose (flower)
ro•sé' (wine)
ro'se•ate
rose'bud'
rose'bush'
rose'-col'ored
rose'mar'y
ro•sette'
rose'wood'
Rosh' Ha•sha'nah
 also Rosh' Ha•sha'-
 na, Rosh' Ha•sho'na,
 Rosh' Ha•sho'nah
Ro'si•cru'cian

ros'in
ros'ter
ros'trum pl. -trums or
 -tra
ros'y
rot, rot'ted, rot'ting
Ro•tar'i•an
ro'ta•ry
ro'tate', -tat'ed, -tat'-
 ing
ro•ta'tion
ro'ta•tive
ro'ta•tor
ro'ta•to'ry
rote (repetition)
 ♦wrote
ro'ti•fer
ro•tis'se•rie
ro'to•gra•vure'
ro'tor
rot'ten
ro•tund'
ro•tun'da
ro•tun'di•ty
rou•é'
rouge, rouged, roug-
 ing
rough (uneven)
 ♦ruff
rough'age
rough'-and-read'y
 adj.
rough'-and-tum'ble
 adj.
rough'en
rough'hew' -hewed' or
 -hewn', -hew'ing

rough'house',
 -housed', -hous'ing
rough'neck'
rough'rid'er
rough'shod'
rou•lade'
rou•lette'
round'a•bout'
round'ed
roun'del
roun'de•lay'
round'house'
round'ly'
round'-shoul'dered
round'-the-clock'
round'-trip' adj.
round'up' n.
round'worm'
rouse, roused, rous'ing
roust'a•bout'
rout (retreat)
rout (to defeat, search)
route (way)
 ♦root
rou•tine'
roux (thickener)
 ♦rue
rove, roved, rov'ing
row (series, boat trip)
 ♦rho, roe
row (quarrel)
row'an
row'boat'
row'dy
row'el
roy'al (regal)
 ♦roil

roy'al·ist
roy'al·ty
rub, rubbed, rub'bing
rub'ber
rub'ber·ize', -ized',
  -iz'ing
rub'ber·neck'
rub'ber-stamp' *v.*
rub'ber·y
rub'bing
rub'bish
rub'ble
rub'down' *n.*
rube
ru·bel'la
ru'bi·cund
ru·bid'i·um
ru'bric
ru'by
ruche
ruck'sack'
ruck'us
rud'der
rud'dy
rude *(impolite)*, rud'er,
  rud'est
  ♦*rood, rued*
ru'di·ment
ru'di·men'ta·ry
rue *(to feel regret for)*,
  rued, ru'ing
  ♦*roux*
rue'ful
ruff *(collar)*
  ♦*rough*
ruf'fi·an
ruf'fle, -fled, -fling

rug
Rug'by
rug'ged
ru'in *(destruction)*
  ♦*rune*
ru'in·a'tion
ru'in·ous
rule, ruled, rul'ing
rul'er
rum
Ru·ma'ni·an *also* Ro·
  ma'ni·an, Rou·ma'ni·
  an
rum'ba *also* rhum'ba
rum'ble, -bled, -bling
ru'mi·nant
ru'mi·nate', -nat'ed,
  -nat'ing
ru'mi·na'tion
ru'mi·na'tive
ru'mi·na'tor
rum'mage, -maged,
  -mag·ing
rum'my
ru'mor *(gossip)*
  ♦*roomer*
ru'mor·mon'ger
rump
rum'ple, -pled, -pling
rum'pus
rum'run'ner
run, ran, run, run'ning
run'a·bout'
run'-a·round'
run'a·way'
run'back' *n.*
run'-down' *n. & adj.*

rune *(Germanic alpha-
  betic character)*
  ♦*ruin*
rung *(step)*
  ♦*wrung*
run'ic
run'-in' *n.*
run'let
run'nel
run'ner
run'ner-up'
run'ning
run'ny
run'-off' *n.*
run'-of-the-mill' *adj.*
run'-on' *n. & adj.*
runt
run'-through' *n.*
run'way'
rup'ture, -tured, -tur·
  ing
ru'ral
ruse
rush'er
rush'-hour' *adj.*
rus'set
Rus'sian
rust
rus'tic
rus'ti·cate', -cat'ed,
  -cat'ing
rus'ti·ca'tion
rus'ti·ca'tor
rus·tic'i·ty
rus'tle, -tled, -tling
rus'tler
rust'proof'

rust'y
rut, rut'ted, rut'ting
ru·ta·ba'ga
ru·the'ni·um
ruth'less
rut'ty
ry'a
rye *(grain, whiskey)*
 ◆*wry*

S

Sab'bath
sab·bat'i·cal
sa'ber
sa'ber-toothed' tiger
sa'ble
sa'bot'
sab'o·tage', -taged',
 -tag'ing
sab'o·teur'
sac *(pouch)*
 ◆*sack*
sac'cha·rin *n.*
sac'cha·rine *adj.*
sac'er·do'tal
sa'chem
sa·chet' *(perfume)*
 ◆*sashay*
sack *(bag, loot, wine)*
 ◆*sac*
sack *(to fire, loot)*
 ◆*sac*
sack'cloth'
sack'ing

sac'ra·ment
sac'ra·men'tal
sa'cred
sac'ri·fice', -ficed',
 -fic'ing
sac'ri·fi'cial
sac'ri·lege'
sac'ri·le'gious
sac'ris·tan
sac'ris·ty
sac'ro·il'i·ac'
sac'ro·sanct'
sa'crum *pl.* -cra
sad, sad'der, sad'dest
sad'den
sad'dle, -dled, -dling
sad'dle·bag'
sad'dle·bow'
sad'dle·cloth'
sad'dler
sad'i'ron
sa'dism
sa'dist
sa·dis'tic
sa·fa'ri *pl.* -ris
safe, saf'er, saf'est
safe'-con'duct *n.*
safe'crack'er
safe'-de·pos'it box.
safe'guard'
safe'keep'ing
safe'ty
saf'flow'er
saf'fron
sag, sagged, sag'ging
sa'ga
sa·ga'cious

sa·gac'i·ty
sag'a·more'
sage, sag'er, sag'est
sage'brush'
Sag·it·ta'ri·us
sa'go *pl.* -gos
sa·gua'ro *pl.* -ros, *also*
 sa·hua'ro
sa'hib
said
sail *(canvas)*
 ◆*sale*
sail'boat'
sail'cloth'
sail'fish' *pl.* -fish' *or*
 -fish'es
sail'ing
sail'or
saint'ed
saint'hood'
saint'ly
sake *(purpose)*
sa'ke *(liquor), also* sa'ki
sa·laam'
sal'a·bil'i·ty
sal'a·ble *also* sale'a·ble
sa·la'cious
sa·lac'i·ty
sal'ad
sal'a·man'der
sa·la'mi *pl.* -mis
sal am·mo'ni·ac'
sal'a·ried
sal'a·ry
sale *(exchange, bar-
 gain)*
 ◆*sail*

sales'clerk'
sales'man
sales'man·ship'
sales'per'son
sales'wom'an
sal'i·cyl'ic acid
sa'li·ence *also* sa'li·
   en·cy
sa'li·ent
sa'line'
sa·lin'i·ty
sa·li'va
sal'i·var'y
sal'i·vate', -vat'ed,
   -vat'ing
sal'i·va'tion
sal'low
sal'ly, -lied, -ly·ing
sal'ma·gun'di
salm'on *pl.* -on *or*
   -ons
sal'mo·nel'la *pl.* -nel'-
   lae, -nel'las, *or* -nel'-
   la
sa·lon' *(room, assem-*
   blage)
sa·loon' *(tavern)*
sa·loon'keep'er
salt'box'
salt'cel'lar
sal·tine'
salt'pe'ter
salt'shak'er
salt'-wa'ter *adj.*
salt'works'
salt'y
sa·lu'bri·ous

sa·lu'ki *pl.* -kis
sal'u·tar'y
sal'u·ta'tion
sa·lu'ta·to'ri·an
sa·lu'ta·to'ry
sa·lute', -lut'ed, -lut'-
   ing
sal'va·ble
sal'vage, -vaged, -vag·
   ing
sal'vage·a·ble
sal·vag'er
sal·va'tion
salve, salved, salv'ing
sal'ver
sal'vi·a
sal'vo *pl.* -vos *or* -voes
sam'a·ra
Sa·mar'i·tan
sa·mar'i·um
sam'ba
same
same'ness
sam'i·sen'
Sa·mo'an
sam'o·var'
Sam'o·yed' *also* Sam'-
   o·yede'
sam'pan'
sam'ple, -pled, -pling
sam'pler
sam'u·rai' *pl.* -rai' *or*
   -rais'
san'a·to'ri·um *(chro-*
   nic-treatment or recu-
   perative hospital), pl.
   -ri·ums *or* -ri·a

♦*sanitarium*
sanc'ti·fi·ca'tion
sanc'ti·fy', -fied', -fy'-
   ing
sanc'ti·mo'ni·ous
sanc'ti·mo'ny
sanc'tion
sanc'ti·ty
sanc'tu·ar'y
sanc'tum *pl.* -tums *or*
   -ta
san'dal
san'dal·wood'
san'da·rac'
sand'bag', -bagged',
   -bag'ging
sand'bar'
sand'blast'
sand'box'
sand'er
sand'hog'
sand'lot'
sand'man'
sand'pa'per
sand'pi'per
sand'stone'
sand'storm'
sand'wich
sand'y
sane *(rational)*, san'er,
   san'est
♦*seine*
San'for·ized'®
sang-froid'
san·gri'a
san·gui·nar'y
san'guine

san·i·tar'i·um *(health resort)*, *pl.* -i·ums or -i·a
♦*sanatorium*
san'i·tar'y
san'i·ta'tion
san'i·tize', -tized', -tiz'ing
san'i·ty
san·sei' *pl.* -sei' or -seis'
San'skrit'
sans ser'if
San'ta Claus'
sap, sapped, sap'ping
sa'pi·ence
sa'pi·ent
sap'ling
sap'o·dil'la
sap'phire
sap'py
sap'ro·phyte'
sap'ro·phyt'ic
sap'suck·er
sap'wood'
sa·ran' *also* Sa·ran'®
sar'casm'
sar·cas'tic
sar·co'ma *pl.* -ma·ta or -mas
sar·coph'a·gus *pl.* -gi' or -gus·es
sard
sar·dine'
Sar·din'i·an
sar·don'ic
sar·gas'so

sa'ri *pl.* -ris
sa·rong'
sar'sa·pa·ril'la
sar·to'ri·al
sash
sa·shay' *(to strut)*
♦*sachet*
sass
sas'sa·fras'
sas'sy
Sa'tan
sa·tan'ic *or* sa·tan'i·cal
satch'el
sate, sat'ed, sat'ing
sa·teen'
sat'el·lite'
sa·ti·a·bil'i·ty
sa·ti·a·ble
sa'ti·ate', -at'ed, -at'ing
sa'ti·a'tion
sa·ti'e·ty
sat'in
sat'in·wood'
sat'in·y
sat'ire
sa·tir'i·cal *or* sa·tir'ic
sat'i·rist
sat'i·rize', -rized', -riz'ing
sat'is·fac'tion
sat'is·fac'to·ry
sat'is·fi'er
sat'is·fy', -fied', -fy'ing
sa'trap'
sa'tra·py
sat'u·ra·ble

sat'u·rate', -rat'ed, -rat'ing
sat'u·ra'tion
sat'u·ra'tor
Sat'ur·day
Sat'urn
sat'ur·na'li·a
sat'ur·nine'
sat'yr
sa·ty·ri'a·sis
sauce, sauced, sauc'ing
sauce'pan'
sau'cer
sau'cy
Sau'di A·ra'bi·an
sau'er·bra'ten
sauer'kraut'
sau'na
saun'ter
sau'ri·an
sau'sage
sau·té', -téed', -té'ing
sau·terne' *or* Sau· terne'
sav'a·ble *also* save'a· ble
sav'age, -aged, -ag·ing
sav'age·ry
sa·van'na *also* sa·van'- nah
sa·vant'
save, saved, sav'ing
sav'ior *also* sav'iour
sa'voir-faire'
sa'vor
sa'vor·y
sav'vy, -vied, -vy·ing

saw, sawed, sawed *or*
  sawn, saw'ing
saw'bones' *pl.* -bones'
  or -bones'es
saw'buck'
saw'dust'
sawed'-off' *adj.*
saw'fish' *pl.* -fish' *or*
  -fish'es
saw'horse'
saw'mill'
saw'-toothed'
saw'yer
sax'horn'
sax'i·frage
sax'o·phone'
sax'o·phon'ist
say, said, say'ing
say'-so' *pl.* -sos'
scab, scabbed, scab'-
  bing
scab'bard
scab'by
sca'bies
scab'rous
scads
scaf'fold
scaf'fold·ing
sca'lar
scal'a·wag' *also* scal'-
  ly·wag'
scald
scale, scaled, scal'ing
sca'lene'
scal'lion
scal'lop *also* es·cal'lop
scal'pel

scalp'er
scal'y
scamp
scam'per
scam'pi
scan, scanned, scan'-
  ning
scan'dal
scan'dal·ize', -ized',
  -iz'ing
scan'dal·ous
Scan'di·na'vi·an
scan'di·um
scan'ner
scan'sion
scant'ling
scant'y
scape'goat'
scape'grace'
scap'u·la *pl.* -las *or*
  -lae'
scap'u·lar
scar, scarred, scar'ring
scar'ab
scarce, scarc'er, scarc'-
  est
scar'ci·ty
scare, scared, scar'ing
scare'crow'
scarf *pl.* scarfs *or*
  scarves
scar'let
scarp
scar'y
scat, scat'ted, scat'ting
scathe, scathed, scath'-
  ing

scat'o·log'i·cal
sca·tol'o·gy
scat'ter
scat'ter·brain'
scat'ter·brained'
scat'ter·shot'
scav'enge, -enged,
  -eng·ing
sce·nar'i·o' *pl.* -os'
sce·nar'ist
scene *(view)*
  ♦*seen*
scen'er·y
sce'nic
scent *(odor)*
  ♦*cent, sent*
scep'ter
sched'ule, -uled, -ul·
  ing
sche'ma *pl.* -ma·ta
sche·mat'ic
scheme, schemed,
  schem'ing
scher·zan'do *pl.* -dos
scher'zo *pl.* -zos *or* -zi
Schick test
schism
schis·mat'ic
schist
schis'tose' *also* schis'-
  tous
schiz'oid'
schiz'o·phre'ni·a
schiz'o·phren'ic
schle·miel'
schlep, schlepped,
  schlep'ping

schli•ma′zel

schlock

schmaltz

schmo *pl.* schmoes,
 also schmoe

schnapps

schnau′zer

schnit′zel

schnook

schol′ar

schol′ar•ship′

scho•las′tic

scho•las′ti•cism

school′book′

school′boy′

school′child′

school′girl′

school′house′

school′ing

school′marm′

school′mas′ter

school′mate′

school′mis′tress

school′room′

school′teach′er

schoo′ner

schot′tische

schuss

schwa

sci•at′ic

sci•at′i•ca

sci′ence

sci′en•tif′ic

sci′en•tism

sci′en•tist

sci′en•tol′o•gy

scim′i•tar

scin•til′la

scin′til•late′, -lat′ed,
 -lat′ing

scin′til•la′tion

sci′on *also* ci′on

scis′sile

scis′sion

scis′sors

scle′ra

scle•ro′sis *pl.* -ses′

scle•rot′ic

scoff

scoff′law′

scold′ing

sconce

scone

scoop

scoot′er

scope

sco•pol′a•mine′

scor•bu′tic

scorch

score, scored, scor′ing

score′card′

sco′ri•a *pl.* -ri•ae′

scorn′ful

Scor′pi•o′

scor′pi•on

Scot

scotch *(to stifle)*

Scotch *(people, whis-*
 key)

sco′ter

scot′-free′

Scots′man

Scot′tie

Scot′tish

scoun′drel

scourge, scourged,
 scourg′ing

scout′ing

scout′mas′ter

scow

scowl

scrab′ble *(to grope)*,
 -bled, -bling

Scrab′ble® *(game)*

scrag′gly

scrag′gy

scram, scrammed,
 scram′ming

scram′ble, -bled,
 -bling

scrap, scrapped,
 scrap′ping

scrap′book′

scrape, scraped,
 scrap′ing

scrap′per

scrap′ple

scrap′py

scratch′y

scrawl

scraw′ny

scream′er

screech′ing

screed

screen′ing

screen′play′

screen′-test′ *v.*

screen′writ′er

screw′ball′

screw′driv′er

screw′y

scrib′al
scrib′ble, -bled, -bling
scribe, scribed, scrib′-
ing
scrim
scrim′mage, -maged,
-mag·ing
scrimp
scrim′shaw′
scrip *(paper money)*
script *(writing, text)*
scrip′tur·al
Scrip′ture
script′writ′er
scriv′en·er
scrod
scrof′u·la
scrof′u·lous
scroll′work′
Scrooge
scro′tal
scro′tum *pl.* -ta *or*
-tums
scrounge, scrounged,
scroung′ing
scrub, scrubbed,
scrub′bing
scrub′ber
scrub′by
scrub′wom′an
scruff
scruff′fy
scrump′tious
scrunch
scru′ple, -pled, -pling
scru′pu·los′i·ty
scru′pu·lous

scru′ti·nize′, -nized′,
-niz′ing
scru′ti·ny
scu′ba
scud, scud′ded, scud′-
ding
scuff
scuf′fle, -fled, -fling
scull *(oar)*
   ♦*skull*
scul′ler·y
scul′lion
sculpt
sculp′tor
sculp′tress
sculp′tur·al
sculp′ture, -tured,
-tur·ing
scum
scup *pl.* scup *or* scups
scup′per
scup′per·nong′
scurf′y
scur·ril′i·ty
scur′ri·lous
scur′ry, -ried, -ry·ing
scur′vy
scut′tle, -tled, -tling
scut′tle·butt′
scythe, scythed, scyth′-
ing
sea *(water)*
   ♦*see, si*
Sea′bee′
sea′board′
sea′borne′
sea′coast′

sea′far′er
sea′far′ing
sea′food′
sea′go′ing
seal′er
seal′ing wax
seal′skin′
Sea′ly·ham′ terrier
seam *(junction)*
   ♦*seem*
sea′man *(sailor)*
   ♦*semen*
sea′man·ship′
seam′stress
seam′y
sé′ance′
sea′plane′
sea′port′
sear *(to dry up)*
   ♦*seer, sere*
search′light′
sea′scape′
sea′shell′
sea′shore′
sea′sick′
sea′side′
sea′son
sea′son·a·ble
sea′son·al
sea′son·ing
seat′ing
sea′ward *also* sea′-
wards
sea′way′
sea′weed′
sea′wor′thy
se·ba′ceous

se'cant

se·cede', -ced'ed,
   -ced'ing

se·ces'sion

se·ces'sion·ist

se·clude', -clud'ed,
   -clud'ing

se·clu'sion

se·clu'sive

sec'ond

sec'ond·ar'y

sec'ond-class' *adj. &
   adv.*

sec'ond-de·gree'
   burn

sec'ond-guess' *v.*

sec'ond·hand' *adj. &
   adv.*

second hand *(time-
   piece part)*

sec'ond-rate' *adj.*

se'cre·cy

se'cret *(concealed)*
   ♦*secrete*

se'cret *(something kept
   hidden)*
   ♦*secrete*

sec're·tar'i·al

sec're·tar'i·at

sec're·tar'y

sec're·tar'y-gen'er·al
   pl. sec're·tar'ies-gen'-
   er·al

se·crete' *(to exclude a
   substance, hide),*
   -cret'ed, -cret'ing
   ♦*secret*

se·cre'tion

se·cre'tive

se·cre'tor

se·cre'to·ry

sect

sec·tar'i·an

sec·tar'i·an·ism

sec'tile

sec'tion

sec'tion·al

sec'tion·al·ism

sec'tion·al·ist

sec'tor

sec·to'ri·al

sec'u·lar

sec'u·lar·ism

sec'u·lar·ist

sec'u·lar·i·ty

sec'u·lar·i·za'tion

sec'u·lar·ize', -ized',
   -iz'ing

se·cur'a·ble

se·cure', -cur'er, -cur-
   est

se·cure', -cured', -cur-
   ing

se·cu'ri·ty

se·dan'

se·date', -dat'ed, -dat'-
   ing

se·da'tion

sed'a·tive

sed'en·tar'y

Se'der *pl.* Se'ders *or*
   Se·dar'im

sedge

sed'i·ment

sed'i·men'ta·ry

sed'i·men·ta'tion

se·di'tion

se·di'tious

se·duce', -duced',
   -duc'ing

se·duce'a·ble *also* se·
   duc'i·ble

se·duc'tion

se·duc'tive

se·duc'tress

se·du'li·ty

sed'u·lous

se'dum

see *(bishopric)*
   ♦*sea, si*

see *(to perceive),* saw,
   seen, see'ing
   ♦*sea, si*

seed *(plant part),* pl.
   seeds *or* seed
   ♦*cede*

seed'case'

seed'ling

seed'y

seek, sought, seek'ing

seem *(to appear)*
   ♦*seam*

seem'ly

seep'age

seer *(prophet)*
   ♦*sear, sere*

seer'suck'er

see'saw'

seethe, seethed, seeth'-
   ing

see'-through' *adj.*

seg'ment
seg·men'tal
seg·men·ta'tion
seg·ment'ed
se'go pl. -gos
seg·re·gate', -gat'ed,
  -gat'ing
seg·re·ga'tion
seg·re·ga'tion·ist
seg·re·ga'tor
seign'ior
sei·gnio'ri·al
seine (to fish with a
  net), seined, sein'ing
  ♦sane
seis'mic
seis'mo·gram'
seis'mo·graph'
seis·mog'ra·pher
seis'mo·graph'ic
seis·mog'ra·phy
seis'mo·log'ic also
  seis'mo·log'i·cal
seis·mol'o·gist
seis·mol'o·gy
seis·mom'e·ter
seiz'a·ble
seize, seized, seiz'ing
sei'zure
sel'dom
se·lect'
se·lec'tion
se·lec'tive
se·lec·tiv'i·ty
se·lect'man
se·lec'tor
se·le'ni·um

self pl. selves
self'-ab·sorbed'
self'-ad·dressed'
self'-as·sur'ance
self'-as·sured'
self'-cen'tered
self'-con·fessed'
self'-con·fi·dence
self'-con·fi·dent
self'-con·scious
self'-con·tained'
self'-con·trol'
self'-con·trolled'
self'-de·feat'ing
self'-de·fense'
self'-de·ni'al
self'-de·ny'ing
self'-de·struct'
self'-de·struc'tive
self'-de·ter'mi·na'-
  tion
self'-dis·ci·pline
self'-ed'u·cat'ed
self'-ef·fac'ing
self'-em·ployed'
self'-es·teem'
self'-ev'i·dent
self'-ex·plan'a·to'ry
self'-ex·pres'sion
self'-gov'ern·ing
self'-gov'ern·ment
self'-im·por'tance
self'-im·por'tant
self'-im·prove'ment
self'-in·dul'gence
self'-in·dul'gent
self'-in'ter·est

self'ish
self'-knowl'edge
self'less
self'-made'
self'-pit'y
self'-por'trait
self'-pos·sessed'
self'-pos·ses'sion
self'-pres'er·va'tion
self'-re·li'ance
self'-re·li'ant
self'-re·spect'
self'-re·straint'
self'-right'eous
self'-rule'
self'-sac'ri·fice'
self'same'
self'-sat'is·fac'tion
self'-sat'is·fied'
self'-seek'ing
self'-serv'ice adj.
self'-start'er
self'-styled'
self'-suf·fi'cien·cy
self'-suf·fi'cient
self'-sup·port'
self'-sup·port'ing
self'-sus·tain'ing
self'-taught'
self'-will'
self'-willed'
self'-wind'ing
sell (to exchange for
  money), sold, sell'ing
  ♦cell
sell'er (vender)
  ♦cellar

sell'out' *n.*

selt'zer

sel'vage *also* sel'vedge

se·man'tic

se·man'ti·cist

se·man'tics

sem'a·phore',
  -phored', -phor'ing

sem'blance

se'men *(sperm)*
  ♦*seaman*

se·mes'ter

sem'i·an'nu·al *(twice
  a year)*
  ♦*biannual, biennial,
  biyearly, semiyearly*

sem'i·au'to·mat'ic

sem'i·cir'cle

sem'i·cir'cu·lar

sem'i·clas'si·cal

sem'i·co'lon

sem'i·con·duc'tor

sem'i·de·tached'

sem'i·fi'nal

sem'i·fi'nal·ist

sem'i·for'mal

sem'i·month'ly *(twice
  a month)*
  ♦*bimonthly*

sem'i·nal

sem'i·nar'

sem'i·nar'i·an

sem'i·nar'y

sem'i·of·fi'cial

sem'i·pre'cious

sem'i·pri'vate

sem'i·pro·fes'sion·al

sem'i·skilled'

sem'i·sol'id

Sem'ite'

Se·mit'ic

sem'i·tone'

sem'i·ton'ic

sem'i·trans·par'ent

sem'i·trop'i·cal

sem'i·vow'el

sem'i·week'ly *(twice a
  week)*
  ♦*biweekly*

sem'i·year'ly *(twice a
  year)*
  ♦*biannual, biennial,
  biyearly, semiannual*

sem'o·li'na

sen *pl.* sen

sen'ate *also* Sen'ate

sen'a·tor

sen'a·to'ri·al

send, sent, send'ing

send·off' *n.*

se'nile'

se·nil'i·ty

sen'ior

sen·ior'i·ty

sen'na

se·ñor' *pl.* -ño'res

se·ño'ra

se·ño'ri·ta

sen·sate' *also* sen'sat'-
  ed

sen·sa'tion

sen·sa'tion·al

sen·sa'tion·al·ism

sen·sa'tion·al·ist

sense *(to perceive),*
  sensed, sens'ing
  ♦*cents*

sense'less

sen'si·bil'i·ty

sen'si·ble

sen'si·tive

sen'si·tiv'i·ty

sen'si·ti·za'tion

sen'si·tize', -tized',
  -tiz'ing

sen'sor

sen'so·ry

sen'su·al

sen'su·al·ist

sen'su·al·is'tic

sen'su·al'i·ty

sen'su·ous

sen'tence, -tenced,
  -tenc·ing

sen·ten'tial

sen·ten'tious

sen'tience

sen'tient

sen'ti·ment

sen'ti·men'tal

sen'ti·men'tal·ism

sen'ti·men'tal·ist

sen'ti·men'tal'i·ty

sen'ti·men'tal·ize',
  -ized', -iz'ing

sen'ti·nel

sen'try

se'pal

sep'a·ra·ble

sep'a·rate', -rat'ed,
  -rat'ing

sep'a·ra'tion
sep'a·ra·tism
sep'a·ra·tist
sep'a·ra'tor
se'pi·a
sep'sis
sep'tal
Sep·tem'ber
sep·ten'ni·al
sep·tet' *also* sep·tette'
sep'tic
sep·ti·ce'mi·a
sep·til'lion
sep·til'lionth
sep'tu·a·ge·nar'i·an
Sep'tu·a·ges'i·ma
Sep'tu·a·gint'
sep'tum *pl.* -ta
se·pul'cher
se·pul'chral
se'quel
se'quence
se'quen'tial
se·ques'ter
se·ques'trate', -trat'ed,
   -trat'ing
se'ques·tra'tion
se'ques·tra'tor
se'quin
se·quoi'a
se·ra'glio *pl.* -glios
se·ra'pe *also* sa·ra'pe
ser'aph *pl.* -a·phim *or*
   -aphs
se·raph'ic
Serb
Serb'bi·an

Ser'bo-Cro·a'tian
sere *(withered)*
   ♦*sear, seer*
ser'e·nade', -nad'ed,
   -nad'ing
ser'en·dip'i·tous
ser'en·dip'i·ty
se·rene'
se·ren'i·ty
serf *(laborer)*
   ♦*surf*
serf'dom
serge *(cloth)*
   ♦*surge*
ser'gean·cy
ser'geant
se'ri·al *(of or in a se-
   ries)*
   ♦*cereal*
se'ri·al·i·za'tion
se'ri·al·ize', -ized', -iz'-
   ing
se'ri·a'tim
ser'i·cul'ture
se'ries *pl.* -ries
ser'if
ser'i·graph'
se·rig'ra·phy
se·ri·o·com'ic
se'ri·ous
ser'mon
ser'mon·ize', -ized',
   -iz'ing
ser'o·log'ic *also* ser'o·
   log'i·cal
se·rol'o·gist
se·rol'o·gy

ser'pent
ser'pen·tine'
ser'rate' *also* ser'rat'ed
ser·ra'tion
šer'ried
se'rum *pl.* -rums *or* -ra
ser'vant
serve, served, serv'ing
serv'ice, -iced, -ic·ing
serv'ice·a·bil'i·ty
serv'ice·a·ble
serv'ice·man'
ser'vile
ser·vil'i·ty
ser'vi·tor
ser'vi·tude'
ser'vo·mech'a·nism
ses'a·me
ses'qui·cen·ten'ni·al
ses'sile
ses'sion *(meeting)*
   ♦*cession*
ses·tet'
set, set, set'ing
se'ta *pl.* -tae'
set'back' *n.*
set'off' *n.*
set·tee'
set'ter
set'ting
set'tle, -tled, -tling
set'tle·ment
set'-to' *pl.* -tos'
set'up' *n.*
sev'en
sev'en·fold'
sev'en·teen'

sev'en·teenth'
sev'enth
sev'en·ti·eth
sev'en·ty
sev'en-up'
sev'er
sev'er·al
sev'er·ance
se·vere', -ver'er, -ver'-
est
se·ver'i·ty
Sè'vres
sew (to stitch), sewed,
sewn or sewed, sew'-
ing
♦so, sow (to scatter)
sew'age
sew'er
sew'er·age
sex'a·ge·nar'i·an
sex'ism
sex'ist
sex'tant
sex·tet'
sex·til'lion
sex·til'lionth
sex'ton
sex·tu'ple, -pled,
-pling
sex·tu'plet
sex'u·al
sex'u·al'i·ty
shab'by
shack
shack'le, -led, -ling
shad pl. shad or shads

shade, shad'ed, shad'-
ing
shad'ow
shad'ow·box'
shad'y
shaft'ing
shag'bark'
shag'gy
shah
shak'a·ble also shake'-
a·ble
shake, shook, shak'en,
shak'ing
shake'down' n. & adj.
shak'er (one that
shakes)
Shak'er (member of a
religious sect)
Shake·spear'e·an or
Shake·spear'i·an
shake·up' n.
shak'o pl. -os or -oes,
also shack'o
shak'y
shale
shall past tense should
shal·lot'
shal'low
sha·lom'
sham, shammed,
sham'ming
sha'man
sha'man·ism
sham'ble, -bled, -bling
shame, shamed,
sham'ing
shame'faced'

shame'ful
shame'less
sham·poo' pl. -poos'
sham'rock'
sha'mus
shang·hai' (to kidnap),
-haied', -hai'ing
shank
shan·tung'
shan'ty (shack)
♦chantey
shan'ty·town'
shape, shaped, shap'-
ing
shape'less
shape'ly
shape'up' n.
shard also sherd
share, shared, shar'ing
share'crop'per
share'hold'er
shark'skin'
sharp'en
sharp'er
sharp'-eyed'
sharp'ie
sharp'shoot'er
sharp'-tongued'
Shas'ta daisy
shat'ter
shat'ter·proof' glass
shave, shaved, shaved
or shav'en, shav'ing
shav'er
Sha'vi·an
shawl
shay

she
sheaf *pl.* sheaves
shear *(to clip),* sheared,
    sheared *or* shorn,
    shear'ing
    ♦*sheer*
shears
sheath *pl.* sheaths
sheathe, sheathed,
    sheath'ing
sheave, sheaved,
    sheav'ing
she·bang'
shed, shed, shed'ding
shed'der
sheen
sheep *pl.* sheep
sheep'fold'
sheep'herd'er
sheep'ish
sheep'skin'
sheer *(thin)*
    ♦*shear*
sheer *(to swerve)*
    ♦*shear*
sheet'ing
sheik *(Arab leader),*
    also sheikh
    ♦*chic*
sheik'dom
shek'el
shelf *pl.* shelves
shel·lac', -lacked',
    -lack'ing
shell'bark'
shell'fire'

shell'fish' *pl.* -fish' *or*
    -fish'es
shell'proof'
shell'-shocked'
shel'ter
shel'tie *also* shel'ty
shelve, shelved, shelv'-
    ing
she·nan'i·gans
shep'herd
Sher'a·ton
sher'bet
sher'iff
sher'ry
Shet'land
shib'bo·leth
shield
shift'less
shift'y
shill
shil·le'lagh *also* shil·
    la'lah
shil'ling
shil'ly-shal'ly, -lied,
    -ly·ing
shim
shim'mer
shim'my, -mied, -my·
    ing
shin, shinned, shin'-
    ning
shin'bone'
shin'dig'
shine, shone *or* shined,
    shin'ing
shin'er
shin'gle, -gled, -gling

shin'ny, -nied, -ny·ing
shin'plas'ter
Shin'to *also* Shin'to·
    ism
shin'y
ship, shipped, ship'-
    ping
ship'board'
ship'build'er
ship'build'ing
ship'load'
ship'mas'ter
ship'mate'
ship'ment
ship'per
ship'ping
ship'shape'
ship'wreck'
ship'yard'
shire
shirk
shirr
shirt'ing
shirt'tail'
shirt'waist'
shish' ke·bab' *also*
    shish' ke·bob', shish'
    ka·bob'
shiv'er
shiv'er·y
shoal
shoat *also* shote
shock
shock'ing
shod'dy
shoe *(to cover the foot),*

shod, shod or shod'-
den, shoe'ing
♦*shoo*
shoe'horn'
shoe'lace'
shoe'mak'er
shoe'mak'ing
shoe'string'
shoe'tree'
sho'far' pl. sho'fars' or
sho·froth'
sho'gun'
shoo interj.
♦*shoe*
shoo (to scare aware),
shooed, shoo'ing
♦*shoe*
shoo'fly' pie
shoo'-in' n.
shook-up' adj.
shoot (to fire a
weapon), shot,
shoot'ing
♦*chute*
shoot'-out' n., also
shoot'out'
shop, shopped, shop'-
ping
shop'keep'er
shop'lift'er
shop'lift'ing
shop'per
shop'talk'
shop'worn'
sho'ran'
shore, shored, shor'ing
shore'line'

short'age
short'bread'
short'cake'
short'change',
-changed', -chang'ing
short'-cir'cuit v.
short'com'ing
short'en
short'en·ing
short'fall'
short'hand'
short'-hand'ed
short'horn'
short'-lived'
short'ly
short'-or'der adj.
short'sight'ed
short'stop'
short'-tem'pered
short'-wave' adj.
short'-wind'ed
shot pl. shots or shot
shot'gun'
shot'-put'
shot'-put'ter
shoul'der
shout'er
shove, shoved, shov'-
ing
shov'el, -eled or -elled,
-el·ing or -el·ling
show, showed, shown
or showed, show'ing
show'boat'
show'case'
show'down'
show'er

show'girl'
show'man
show'man·ship'
show'off' n.
show'piece'
show'y
shrap'nel pl. -nel
shred, shred'ded or
shred, shred'ding
shred'der
shrew
shrewd'ly
shrew'ish
shriek'er
shrift
shrike
shrill'ness
shril'ly
shrimp pl. shrimp or
shrimps
shrine
shrink, shrank or
shrunk, shrunk or
shrunk'en, shrink'ing
shrink'a·ble
shrink'age
shrink'-pack'age,
-aged, -ag·ing
shrink'-wrap',
-wrapped', -wrap'-
ping
shrive, shrove or
shrived, shriv'en or
shrived, shriv'ing
shriv'el, -eled or -elled,
-el or ing·-el·ling
shroud

Shrove'tide'
shrub'ber•y
shrub'by
shrug, shrugged,
     shrug'ging
shuck
shucks
shud'der
shuf'fle, -fled, -fling
shuf'fle•board'
shun, shunned, shun'-
     ning
shun'ner
shun'pike'
shunt
shunt'-wound'
shush
shut, shut, shut'ting
shut'down' n.
shut'eye'
shut-in' adj.
shut'-in' n.
shut'off' n.
shut'out' n.
shut'ter
shut'ter•bug'
shut'tle, -tled, -tling
shut'tle•cock'
shy, shi'er or shy'er,
     shi'est or shy'est
shy, shied, shy'ing
shy'lock' also Shy'-
     lock'
shy'ly
shy'ster
si (musical tone)
     ♦sea, see

Si'a•mese'
     pl. -mese'
Si•be'ri•an
sib'i•lance also sib'i•
     lan•cy
sib'i•lant
sib'ling
sib'yl
sic (thus)
     ♦sick
sic (to urge on), sicced,
     sic'cing, also sick
Si•cil'ian
sick (ill)
     ♦sick
sick'bay'
sick'bed'
sick'en
sick'en•ing
sick'le
sick'ly
sick'ness
sick'-out' n.
sick'room'
side, sid'ed, sid'ing
side'arm' adj.
side'board'
side'burns'
side'car'
side'kick'
side'light'
side'line', -lined', -lin'-
     ing
side'long'
side'man'
si•de're•al
side'sad'dle

side'split'ting
side'step', -stepped',
     -step'ping
side'swipe', -swiped',
     -swip'ing
side'track'
side'walk'
side'ward also side'-
     wards
side'ways' also side'-
     way', side'wise'
side'-wheel'er
side'wind'er
sid'ing
si'dle, -dled, -dling
siege
si•en'na
si•er'ra
si•es'ta
sieve, sieved, siev'ing
sift'er
sift'ings
sigh
sight (vision)
     ♦cite
sight'ed
sight'less
sight'-read', -read',
     -read'ing
sight'see'ing
sight'se'er
sig'ma
sign (indication)
     ♦sine
sig'nal, -naled or
     -nalled, -nal•ing or
     -nal•ling

sig′nal•er *also* sig′nal•
ler

sig′nal•ize′, -ized′, -iz′-
ing

sig′nal•ly

sig′na•to′ry

sig′na•ture

sign′board′

sig′net *(seal)*
  ♦*cygnet*

sig•nif′i•cance

sig•nif′i•cant

sig•ni•fi•ca′tion

sig′ni•fy′, -fied′, -fy′ing

si•gnor′ *pl.* -gno′ri *or*
-gnors′

si•gno′ra *pl.* -re *or* -ras

si•gno′re *pl.* -ri

si′gno•ri′na *pl.* -ne *or*
-nas

sign′post′

si′lage

si′lence, -lenced, -lenc•
ing

si′lent

sil′hou•ette′, -et′ted,
-et′ting

sil′i•ca

sil′i•cate′

si•li′ceous

sil′i•con *(element)*

sil′i•cone′ *(polymer)*

sil′i•co′sis

silk′en

silk′-screen′ *v.*

silk′-stock′ing *adj.*

silk′worm′

silk′y

sill

sil′ly

si′lo *pl.* -los

silt

Si•lu′ri•an

sil′ver

sil′ver•fish′ *pl.* -fish′ *or*
-fish′es

sil′ver•smith′

sil′ver-tongued′

sil′ver•ware′

sil′ver•y

sim′i•an

sim′i•lar

sim′i•lar′i•ty

sim′i•le

si•mil′i•tude′

sim′mer

si′mon-pure′

sim′o•ny

sim•pa′ti•co′

sim′per

sim′ple

sim′ple-mind′ed

sim′ple•ton

sim•plic′i•ty

sim•pli•fi•ca′tion

sim′pli•fi′er

sim′pli•fy′, -fied′, -fy′-
ing

sim′ply

sim′u•late′, -lat′ed,
-lat′ing

sim′u•la′tion

sim′u•la′tive

sim′u•la′tor

si′mul•cast′, -cast′ed,
-cast′ing

si′mul•ta•ne′i•ty

si′mul•ta′ne•ous

sin, sinned, sin′ning

since

sin•cere′, -cer′er, -cer′-
est

sin•cer′i•ty

sine *(mathematical
function)*
  ♦*sign*

si′ne•cure′

si′ne•cur•ist

si′ne di′e

si′ne qua non′

sin′ew

sin′ew•y

sin′ful

sing, sang *or* sung,
sung, sing′ing,

singe, singed, singe′ing

sing′er

Sin′gha•lese′ *pl.* -lese′,
also Sin′ha•lese′

sin′gle, -gled, -gling

sin′gle-breast′ed

sin′gle-en′try *adj.*

sin′gle-hand′ed

sin′gle-mind′ed

sin′gle-space′,
-spaced′, -spac′ing

sin′gle•ton

sin′gly

sing′song′

sin′gu•lar

sin′gu•lar′i•ty

sin'is·ter
sin'is·tral
sink, sank *or* sunk,
   sunk *or* sunk'en,
   sink'ing
sink'a·ble
sink'hole'
sin'ner
Si·nol'o·gist
Si·nol'o·gy
sin'u·os'i·ty
sin'u·ous
si'nus
si'nus·i'tis
sip, sipped, sip'ping
si'phon *also* sy'phon
si'phon·al *also* si·
   phon'ic
sir
sire, sired, sir'ing
si'ren
sir'loin'
si·roc'co *pl.* -cos, *also*
   sci·roc'co
si'sal
sis'si·fied'
sis'sy
sis'ter
sis'ter·hood'
sis'ter-in-law' *pl.* sis'-
   ters-in-law'
sit, sat, sit'ting
si·tar'
sit'com' *also* sit'-com'
sit'-down' *n. & adj.*
site *(location)*
   ♦*cite, sight*

sit'-in' *n.*
sit'ter
sit'ting
sit'u·ate', -at'ed, -at'-
   ing
sit'u·a'tion
sit'-up' *n.*
sitz bath
six'-gun'
six'-pack'
six'pence
six'pen·ny
six'-shoot'er
six'teen'
six'teenth'
sixth
six'ti·eth'
six'ty
six'ty-fourth' note
siz'a·ble *also* size'a·ble
size, sized, siz'ing
siz'zle, -zled, -zling
skate, skat'ed, skat'ing
skate'board'
skeet
skein
skel'e·tal
skel'e·ton
skep'tic *also* scep'tic
skep'ti·cal
skep'ti·cism
sketch'book'
sketch'y
skew'bald'
skew'er
ski *pl.* skis
ski, skied, ski'ing

skid, skid'ded, skid'-
   ding
skiff
skilled
skil'let
skill'ful
skim, skimmed, skim'-
   ming
skim'mer
skimp'y
skin, skinned, skin'-
   ning
skin'-deep'
skin'-dive', -dived',
   -div'ing
skin'flint'
skink
skin'ner
skin'ny
skin'tight'
skip, skipped, skip'-
   ping
skip'per
skirl
skir'mish
skirt
skit
skit'ter
skit'tish
skit'tles
skiv'vy
skulk
skull *(head bones)*
   ♦*scull*
skull'cap'
skull·dug'ger·y *also*
   skul·dug'ger·y

skunk
sky, skied, sky'ing
sky'dive', -dived, -div'ing
Skye terrier
sky'-high'
sky'jack'
Sky'lab'
sky'lark'
sky'light'
sky'line'
sky'rock'et
sky'scrap'er
Sky'train'®
sky'ward *also* sky'-wards
sky'way'
sky'writ'er
sky'writ'ing
slab
slack'en
slag
slake, slaked, slak'ing
sla'lom
slam, slammed, slam'-ming
slan'der
slan'der·ous
slang'y
slant
slant'wise'
slap, slapped, slap'ping
slap'hap'py
slap'stick'
slash
slat
slate, slat'ed, slat'ing

slath'er
slat'ted
slat'tern
slaugh'ter
slaugh'ter·house'
Slav
slave, slaved, slav'ing
slav'er·y
Slav'ic
slav'ish
slaw
slay *(to kill),* slew, slain, slay'ing
    ♦*sleigh*
slea'zy
sled, sled'ded, sled'-ding
sledge, sledged, sledg'-ing
sledge'ham'mer
sleek
sleep, slept, sleep'ing
sleep'walk'er
sleep'walk'ing
sleep'y
sleep'y·head'
sleet
sleeve, sleeved, sleev'-ing
sleigh *(vehicle)*
    ♦*slay*
sleight *(dexterity, trick)*
    ♦*slight*
slen'der
slen'der·ize', -ized', -izing
sleuth'hound'

slew *(large number),* *also* slue
    ♦*slough (swamp)*
slice, sliced, slic'ing
slice'a·ble
slick'er
slide, slid, slid'ing
slight *(thin, scant)*
    ♦*sleight*
slight *(to ignore, shirk)*
    ♦*sleight*
slight'ly
slim, slim'mer, slim'-mest
slim, slimmed, slim'-ming
slime
slim'y
sling, slung, sling'ing
sling'shot'
slink, slunk, slink'ing
slink'y
slip, slipped, slip'ping
slip'case'
slip'cov'er
slip'knot'
slip'-on' *n.*
slip'o'ver
slip'page
slip'per
slip'per·y
slip'shod'
slip'stitch'
slip'stream'
slip'-up' *n.*
slit, slit, slit'ting
slith'er

sliv′er
sliv′o·vitz
slob′ber
sloe (fruit)
    ♦slow
sloe′-eyed′
slog, slogged, slog′ging
slo′gan
sloop
slop, slopped, slop′-
    ping
slope, sloped, slop′ing
slop′py
slosh
slot, slot′ted, slot′ting
sloth′ful
slouch
slough (swamp), also
    slew
    ♦slue
slough (dead tissue)
Slo′vak′
slov′en
Slo′vene′
slov′en·ly
slow (not quick)
    ♦sloe
slow′down′ n.
slow′-mo′tion adj.
slow′poke′
slow′wit′ted
sludge
sludg′y
slue (to twist), slued,
    slu′ing, also slew
    ♦slough (swamp)
slug, slugged, slug′ging

slug′fest′
slug′gard
slug′ger
slug′gish
sluice, sluiced, sluic′-
    ing
slum, slummed, slum′-
    ming
slum′ber
slum′ber·ous
slum′lord′
slump
slur, slurred, slur′ring
slurp
slur′ry
slush′y
slut′tish
sly, sli′er or sly′er, sli′-
    est or sly′est
smack′-dab′
smack′ing
small′-mind′ed
small′pox′
small′time′
smart al′eck
smart′-al′eck·y
smart′en
smash′ing
smash′up′ n.
smat′ter
smear′y
smell, smelled or
    smelt, smell′ing
smell′y
smelt (fish), pl. smelts
    or smelt
smelt (to melt)

smelt′er also smelt′er·y
smid′gen also smid′-
    geon, smid′gin
smi′lax′
smile, smiled, smil′ing
smirch
smirk
smite, smote, smit′ten
    or smote, smit′ing
smith
smith′er·eens′
smith′y
smock′ing
smog
smog′gy
smoke, smoked,
    smok′ing
smoke′house′
smoke′less
smoke′stack′
smok′y
smol′der also smoul′-
    der
smooch
smooth′bore′
smooth′en
smor′gas·bord′
smoth′er
smudge, smudged,
    smudg′ing
smudg′y
smug, smug′ger,
    smug′gest
smug′gle, -gled, -gling
smug′gler
smut′ty
snack

snaf'fle, -fled, -fling

sna·fu' *pl.* -fus

snag, snagged, snag'-
  ging

snag'gle·tooth'

snail

snake, snaked, snak'-
  ing

snake'bite'

snake'root'

snake'skin'

snak'y

snap, snapped, snap'-
  ping

snap'drag'on

snap'per

snap'pish

snap'py

snap'shot'

snare, snared, snar'ing

snarl

snatch'er

snaz'zy

sneak'ers

sneak'y

sneer

sneeze sneezed, sneez'-
  ing

snick'er

snide, snid'er, snid'est

sniff

snif'fle, -fled, -fling

snif'ter

snig'ger

snip, snipped, snip'-
  ping

snipe *pl.* snipe *or*
  snipes

snipe, sniped, snip'ing

snip'er

snip'pet

snip'pet·y

snip'py

snit

snitch

sniv'el, -eled *or* -elled,
  -el·ing *or* -el·ling

snob'ber·y

snob'bish

snob'bism

snood

snook'er

snoop'y

snoot'y

snooze, snoozed,
  snooz'ing

snore, snored, snor'ing

snor'kel

snort

snout

snow'ball'

snow'bird'

snow'blind' *also*
  snow'blind'ed

snow'bound'

snow'cap'

snow'capped'

snow'drift'

snow'drop'

snow'fall'

snow'flake'

snow'man'

snow'mo·bile'

snow'plow'

snow'shoe'

snow'storm'

snow'suit'

snow'-white' *adj.*

snow'y

snub, snubbed, snub'-
  bing

snub'-nosed'

snuff'box'

snuf'fle, -fled, -fling

snug, snug'ger, snug'-
  gest

snug'ger·y

snug'gle, -gled, -gling

so *(thus)*
  ♦*sew, sow (to scatter)*

soak'age

so'-and-so' *pl.* -sos'

soap'box'

soap'stone'

soap'suds'

soap'wort'

soap'y

soar *(to fly)*
  ♦*sore*

so·a've

sob, sobbed, sob'bing

so'ber

so·bri'e·ty

so'bri·quet'

so'-called' *adj.*

soc'cer

so'cia·bil'i·ty

so'cia·ble

so'cial

so'cial·ism

so'cial·ist
so'cial·is'tic
so'cial·ite'
so'cial·i·za'tion
so'cial·ize', -ized', -iz'-
 ing
so·ci'e·tal
so·ci'e·ty
so'ci·o·bi·ol'o·gy
so'ci·o·ec'o·nom'ic
so'ci·o·log'ic also so'-
 ci·o·log'i·cal
so'ci·ol'o·gist
so'ci·ol'o·gy
sock pl. socks or sox
sock'et
sock'eye' salmon
So·crat'ic
sod, sod'ded, sod'ding
so'da
so·dal'i·ty
sod'den
so'di·um
so'di·um-va'por
 lamp
Sod'om or sod'om
sod'om·y
so·ev'er
so'fa
soft'ball'
soft'-boiled'
sof'ten
sof'ten·er
soft'heart'ed
soft'ly
soft'-ped'al, -aled or

-alled, -al·ing or -al·
 ling
soft'-shell' also soft'-
 shelled'
soft'-shoe'
soft'-soap'
soft'-spo'ken
soft'ware'
soft'wood'
soft'y
sog'gy
soi·gne' also soi·gnée'
soil'age
soi·ree' also soi·rée'
so'journ
sol (musical tone)
 ♦Sol, sole, soul
Sol (the sun)
 ♦sol, sole, soul
sol'ace, -aced, -ac·ing
so'lar
so·lar'i·um pl. -i·a or
 -i·ums
sol'der
sol'dier
sole (single)
 ♦sol, Sol, soul
sole (shoe bottom)
 ♦sol, Sol, soul
sole (fish), pl. sole or
 soles
 ♦sol, Sol, soul
sole (to put a sole on),
 soled, sol'ing
 ♦sol, Sol, soul
sol'e·cism
sol'emn

so·lem'ni·ty
sol'em·ni·za'tion
sol'em·nize', -nized',
 -niz'ing
so'le·noid'
so·lic'it
so·lic'i·ta'tion
so·lic'i·tor
so·lic'i·tous
so·lic'i·tude'
sol'id
sol'i·dar'i·ty
so·lid'i·fi·ca'tion
so·lid'i·fy', -fied', -fy'-
 ing
so·lid'i·ty
sol'id-state' adj.
so·lil'o·quist
so·lil'o·quize',
 -quized', -quiz'ing
so·lil'o·quy
sol'ip·sism
sol'ip·sist
sol'ip·sis'tic
sol'i·taire'
sol'i·tar'y
sol'i·tude'
so'lo pl. -los
so'lo·ist
Sol'o·mon
sol'stice
sol'u·bil'i·ty
sol'u·ble
sol'ute'
so·lu'tion
solv'a·bil'i·ty
solv'a·ble

solve, solved, solv′ing
sol′ven•cy
sol′vent
So•ma′li *pl.* -li *or* -lis
so•mat′ic
som′ber
som•bre′ro *pl.* -ros
some *(a few)*
 ♦*sum*
some′bod′y
some′day′
some′how′
some′one′
some′place′
som′er•sault′
some′thing
some′time
some′times′
some′way′ *also* some′-
 ways′
some′what′
some′where′
som′me•lier′
som•nam′bu•late′,
 -lat′ed, -lat′ing
som•nam′bu•lism
som•nam′bu•list
som•nam′bu•lis′tic
 also som•nam′bu•lar
som•nif′er•ous
som′no•lence
som′no•lent
son *(offspring)*
 ♦*sun*
so′nar′
so•na′ta
song′bird′

song′fest′
song′ster
song′writ′er
son′ic
son′-in-law′ *pl.* sons′-
 in-law′
son′net
son′net•eer′
son′ny *(boy)*
 ♦*sunny*
so•nor′i•ty
so•no′rous
soon
soot
sooth *(truth)*
soothe *(to calm)*,
 soothed, sooth′ing
sooth′say′er
soot′y
sop, sopped, sop′ping
soph′ism
soph′ist
so•phis′tic *or* so•phis′-
 ti•cal
so•phis′ti•cate′, -cat′-
 ed, -cat′ing
so•phis′ti•ca′tion
so•phis′ti•ca′tor
soph′is•try
soph′o•more′
soph′o•mor′ic
so•po•rif′ic
sop′ping
sop′py
so•pran′o *pl.* -os
sor′cer•er
sor′cer•y

sor′did
sore *(painful)*, sor′er,
 sor′est
 ♦*soar*
sore′head′
sore′ly
sor′ghum
so•ror′i•ty
sor′rel
sor′row
sor′row•ful
sor′ry
sort′er
sor′tie
so′-so′
sot
sot′tish
sot′to vo′ce
sou
sou•brette′
souf•flé′
sough
soul *(entity)*
 ♦*sol, Sol, sole*
soul′ful
soul′-search′ing
sound′ing
sound′proof′
sound′track′
soup
soup′spoon′
soup′y
source
sour′dough′
sour′puss′
sou′sa•phone′
souse, soused, sous′ing

South Af·ri·can
South A·mer·i·can
south·bound'
South Car·o·lin'i·an
South Da·ko'tan
south·east'
south·east'er
south·east'er·ly
south·east'ern
south·east'ward *also*
  south·east'wards
south'er·ly
south'ern
south'ern·er
south'ern·most'
south'paw'
south'-south·east'
south'-south·west'
south'ward *also*
  south'wards
south·west'
south·west'er
south·west'er·ly
south·west'ern
south·west'ward *also*
  south·west'wards
sou've·nir'
sov'er·eign
sov'er·eign·ty
so'vi·et'
sow *(to scatter)*, sowed,
  sown *or* sowed, sow'-
  ing
  ♦*sew, so*
sow *(pig)*
soy'bean'
spa

space, spaced, spac'ing
space'craft' *pl.* -craft'
space'man'
space'port'
space'ship'
space'-time'
spac'ing
spa'cious
Spack'le®, -led, -ling
spade, spad'ed, spad'-
  ing
spade'work'
spa'dix *pl.* -di·ces'
spa·ghet'ti ←
span, spanned, span'-
  ning
span'gle, -gled, -gling
Span'iard
span'iel
Span'ish
Span'ish-A·mer'i·can
spank'er
spank'ing
span'ner
spar, sparred, spar'ring
spare, spar'er, spar'est
spare, spared, spar'ing
spare'ribs'
spark
spar'kle, -kled, -kling
spar'kler
spar'row
sparse, spars'er, spars'-
  est
Spar'tan
spasm
spas·mod'ic

spas'tic
spat *(gaiter, quarrel)*
spat *(larval oyster)*, *pl.*
  spat *or* spats
spat *(to quarrel,*
  spawn), spat'ted,
  spat'ting
spate
spathe
spa'tial
spat'ter
spat'u·la
spat'u·lar
spav'in
spav'ined
spawn
spay
speak, spoke, spok'en,
  speak'ing
speak'eas'y
speak'er
speak'er·phone'
spear'head'
spear'mint'
spe'cial
spe'cial·ist
spe·ci·al'i·ty *(charac-*
  teristic)
  ♦*specialty*
spe'cial·i·za'tion
spe'cial·ize', -ized',
  -iz'ing
spe'cial·ty *(distinctive*
  quality)
  ♦*speciality*
spe'cie *(coin)*
spe'cies *(kind)*, *pl.* -cies

spe•cif'ic
spec'i•fi•ca'tion
spec'i•fy', -fied', -fy'-
  ing
spec'i•men
spe'cious
speck'le, led, -ling
specs
spec'ta•cle
spec•tac'u•lar
spec'ta•tor
spec'ter
spec'tral
spec'tro•gram'
spec'tro•graph'
spec'tro•graph'ic
spec'trog'ra•phy
spec•trom'e•ter
spec'tro•met'ric
spec•trom'e•try
spec'tro•scope'
spec'tro•scop'ic *also*
  spec'tro•scop'i•cal
spec•tros'co•py
spec'trum *pl.* -tra *or*
  -trums
spec'u•late', -lat'ed,
  -lat'ing
spec'u•la'tion
spec'u•la•tive
spec'u•la'tor
speech'less
speech'mak'er
speech'mak'ing
speed, sped *or* speed'-
  ed, speed'ing
speed'boat'

speed'er
speed•om'e•ter
speed'-read', -read',
  -read'ing
speed'ster
speed'up' *n.*
speed'way'
speed'well'
speed'y
spell, spelled *or* spelt,
  spell'ing
spell'bind', -bound',
  -bind'ing
spell'er
spe•lun'ker
spe•lunk'ing
spend, spent, spend'-
  ing
spend'thrift'
Spen•se'ri•an sonnet
sperm
sper'ma•ce'ti
sper•mat'ic
sper•mat'o•gen'e•sis
sper'ma•to•ge•net'ic
sper'ma•to•phyte'
sper•mat'o•phyt'ic
sper•mat'o•zoid
sper•ma'to•zo'on *pl.*
  -zo'a
spew
sphag'num
sphe'noid
sphe•noi'dal
sphere
sphe•ric'i•ty
sphe'roid'

sphinc'ter
sphinx *pl.* sphinx'es *or*
  sphin'ges'
sphyg'mo•ma•nom'e•
  ter *also* sphyg•mom'-
  e•ter
spice, spiced, spic'ing
spick'-and-span' *adj.*
spic'u•lar *also* spic'u•
  late
spic'ule *also* spic'u•la
  pl. -lae'
spic'y
spi'der
spi'der•y
spiel
spiff'y
spig'ot
spike, spiked, spik'ing
spike'nard'
spik'y
spill, spilled *or* spilt,
  spill'ing
spill'age
spill'way'
spin, spun, spin'ning
spin'ach
spi'nal
spin'dle, -dled, -dling
spin'dly
spine'less
spin'et
spin'na•ker
spin'ner
spin'ner•et'
spin'ning
spin'-off' *n.*

spin'ster
spin'y
spir'a·cle
spi'ral, -raled *or*
    -ralled, -ral·ing *or*
    -ral·ling
spire
spi·ril'lum *pl.* -la
spir'it
spir'it·ed
spir'it·less
spir'i·tu·al
spir'i·tu·al·ism
spir'i·tu·al·ist
spir'i·tu·al·is'tic
spir'i·tu·al'i·ty
spir'i·tu·ous
spi'ro·chet'al
spi'ro·chete'
spi'ro·gy'ra
spit *(to eject from the*
    mouth), spat *or* spit,
    spit'ting
spit *(to place on a rod),*
    spit'ted, spit'ting
spite, spit'ed, spit'ing
spite'ful
spit'fire'
spit'tle
spit·toon'
splash'down'
splash'y
splat'ter
splay'foot'
splay'foot'ed
spleen
splen'did

splen·dif'er·ous
splen'dor
splice, spliced, splic'-
    ing
splint
splin'ter
splin'ter·y
split, split, split'ting
split'-lev'el
split'ting
splotch'y
splurge, splurged,
    splurg'ing
splut'ter
Spode
spoil, spoiled *or* spoilt,
    spoil'ing
spoil'age
spoil'sport'
spoke, spoked, spok'-
    ing
spo'ken
spoke'shave'
spokes'man
spokes'per'son
spokes'wom'an
spo'li·a'tion
spo'li·a'tor
spon·da'ic
spon'dee'
sponge, sponged,
    spong'ing
spon'gy
spon'sor
spon'sor·ship'
spon·ta·ne'i·ty
spon·ta'ne·ous

spoof
spook'y
spool
spoon
spoon'bill'
spoon'er·ism
spoon'-fed'
spoon'ful' *pl.* -fuls'
spoor *(animal track)*
    ♦*spore*
spo·rad'ic
spo·ran'gi·al
spo·ran'gi·um *pl.* -gi·a
spore *(reproductive or-*
    gan)
    ♦*spoor*
spor'ran
sport'ing
spor'tive
sports'man
sports'man·ship'
sports'wear'
sports'wom'an
sports'writ'er
sport'y
spot, spot'ted, spot'-
    ting
spot'-check' *v.*
spot'less
spot'light', -light'ed *or*
    -lit', -light'ing
spot'ter
spot'ty
spou'sal
spouse
spout
sprain

sprat
sprawl
spray'er
spread, spread, spread'ing
spread'-ea'gle, -gled, -gling
spree
sprig, sprigged, sprig'ging
spright'ly
spring, sprang or sprung, sprung, spring'ing
spring'board'
spring'bok' pl. -bok' or -boks'
spring'tide'
spring'time'
spring'y
sprin'kle, -kled, -kling
sprin'kler
sprint'er
sprit
sprite
sprock'et
sprout
spruce (neat), spruc'er, spruc'est
spruce (tree)
spruce (to neaten), spruced, spruc'ing
spry, spri'er or spry'er, spri'est or spry'est
spud
spume, spumed, spum'ing

spu•mo'ne also spu•mo'ni
spunk'y
spur, spurred, spur'ring
spurge
spu'ri•ous
spurn
spurt
sput'nik
sput'ter
spu'tum pl. -ta
spy, spied, spy'ing
spy'glass'
squab pl. squabs or squab
squab'ble, -bled, -bling
squad'ron
squal'id
squall
squal'or
squan'der
square, squar'er, squar'est
square, squared, squar'ing
square'-dance', -danced', -danc'ing
square'-rigged'
square'-rig'ger
squash'y
squat, squat'ter, squat'test
squat, squat'ted or squat, squat'ting
squat'ter

squaw
squawk
squeak'y
squeal'er
squea'mish
squee'gee'
squeeze, squeezed, squeez'ing
squelch'er
squib
squid pl. squids or squid
squig'gle, -gled, -gling
squint'er
squint'-eyed'
squire, squired, squir'ing
squire'ar•chy or squir'ar•chy
squirm'y
squir'rel
squirt
squish'y
stab, stabbed, stab'bing
sta'bile
sta•bil'i•ty
sta'bi•li•za'tion
sta'bi•lize', -lized', -liz'ing
sta'ble, -bled, -bling
stac•ca'to pl. -tos or -ti
stack
sta'di•um pl. -di•a or -di•ums
staff pl. staffs or staves
stag

stage, staged, stag'ing
stage'coach'
stage'craft'
stage'hand'
stage'-man·age,
  -aged, -ag·ing
stage'-struck'
stag·fla'tion
stag'ger
stag'ing
stag'nan·cy
stag'nant
stag'nate', -nat'ed,
  -nat'ing
stag·na'tion
stag'y
staid (sedate)
  ♦stayed
stained'-glass' adj.
stain'less
stair (steps)
  ♦stare
stair'case'
stair'way'
stair'well'
stake (to mark limits,
  gamble), staked,
  stak'ing
  ♦steak
sta·lac'tite' (downward
  deposit)
sta·lag'mite' (upward
  deposit)
stale, stal'er, stal'est
stale, staled, stal'ing
stale'mate', -mat'ed,
  -mat'ing

Sta'lin·ist
stalk'er
stalk'ing-horse'
stall
stal'lion
stal'wart
sta'men
stam'i·na
stam'mer
stamp
stam·pede', -ped'ed,
  -ped'ing
stance
stanch (to check)
  ♦staunch
stan'chion
stand, stood, stand'ing
stan'dard
stan'dard-bear'er
stan'dard·i·za'tion
stan'dard·ize', -ized',
  -iz'ing
stand'by' pl. -bys'
stand·ee'
stand'-in' n.
stand'ing
stand'-off' n.
stand·off'ish
stand'out' n.
stand'pipe'
stand'point'
stand'still'
stand'up' adj., also
  stand'-up'
stan'nic
stan'nous
stan'za

sta'pes' pl. sta'pes' or
  sta'pe·des'
staph'y·lo·coc'cal
staph'y·lo·coc'cus pl.
  -ci'
sta'ple, -pled, -pling
sta'pler
star, starred, star'ring
star'board
starch'y
star'dom
stare (to gaze fixedly),
  stared, star'ing
  ♦stair
star'fish' pl. -fish' or
  -fish'es
star'gaze', -gazed',
  -gaz'ing
star'gaz'er
stark'ly
star'let
star'light'
star'ling
star'lit'
star'-of-Beth'le·hem'
star'ry
star'ry-eyed'
start'er
star'tle, -tled, -tling
star·va'tion
starve, starved, starv'-
  ing
starve'ling
stash
sta'sis pl. -ses'
state, stat'ed, stat'ing
state'hood'

state'ly
state'ment
state'room'
state'side'
states'man
states'man·ship'
state'wide'
stat'ic
stat'ics
sta'tion
sta'tion·ar'y *(unmoving)*
   ♦*stationery*
sta'tion·er
sta'tion·er'y *(paper)*
   ♦*stationary*
sta'tion·mas'ter
sta·tis'tic
sta·tis'ti·cal
stat·is·ti'cian
sta·tis'tics
sta'tor
stat'u·ar'y
stat'ue
stat'u·esque'
stat'u·ette'
stat'ure
stat'us
status quo'
stat·ute
stat'u·to'ry
staunch *(firm)*
   ♦*stanch*
stave, staved *or* stove, stav'ing
stay
stead'fast'

stead'y, -ied, -y·ing
steak *(meat)*
   ♦*stake*
steak tar'tare'
steal *(to rob),* stole, stol'en, steal'ing
   ♦*steel*
stealth'y
steam'boat'
steam'er
steam'rol'ler
steam'ship'
steam'y
ste'a·tite'
steed
steel *(metal)*
   ♦*steal*
steel'work'
steel'work'er
steel'y
steel'yard'
steen'bok' *also* stein'-bok'
steep'en
stee'ple
stee'ple·chase'
stee'ple·jack'
steer'age
steers'man
steg'o·saur' *also* steg'-o·sau'rus
stein
ste'le *pl.* -les *or* -lae
stel'lar
stem, stemmed, stem'-ming
stem'less

stem'ware'
stem'-wind'er
stem'-wind'ing *adj.*
stench
sten'cil, -ciled *or* -cilled, -cil·ing *or* cil·ling
sten'o *pl.* -os
ste·nog'ra·pher
sten'o·graph'ic *also* sten'o·graph'i·cal
ste·nog'ra·phy
sten'o·type' *(shorthand symbol)*
Sten'o·type'® *(phonetic keyboard machine)*
sten·to'ri·an
step *(to walk),* stepped, step'ping
   ♦*steppe*
step'broth'er
step'child'
step'daugh'ter
step'-down' *adj. & n.*
step'fa'ther
step'-in' *adj. & n.*
step'lad'der
step'moth'er
step'par'ent
steppe *(plain)*
   ♦*step*
step'ping·stone'
step'sis'ter
step'son'
step'-up' *adj. & n.*
step'wise'

ste′re·o′ *pl.* -os′
ster′e·o·phon′ic
ster′e·op′ti·con′
ster′e·o·scope′
ster′e·o·scop′ic
ster′e·os′co·py
ster′e·o·tape′, -taped′,
　-tap′ing
ster′e·o·type′, -typed′,
　-typ′ing
ster′e·o·typ′ic *also*
　ster′e·o·typ′i·cal
ster′e·o·ty′py
ster′ile
ste·ril′i·ty
ster′il·i·za′tion
ster′il·ize′, -ized′, -iz′-
　ing
ster′ling
stern
ster′num *pl.* -na *or*
　-nums
stern′wheel′er
ster′oid′
ster′ol′
stet, stet′ted, stet′ting
steth′o·scope′
steth′o·scop′ic *also*
　steth′o·scop′i·cal
ste·thos′co·py
Stet′son®
ste·ve·dore′
stew
stew′ard
stew′ard·ess
stib′nite′
stick, stuck, stick′ing

stick′er
stick′le, -led, -ling
stick′le·back′
stick′ler
stick′pin′
stick-to′-it·ive·ness
stick′up′ *n.*
stick′y
stiff′en
stiff′en·er
stiff′-necked′
sti′fle, -fled, -fling
stig′ma *pl.* stig·ma·ta
　or stig′mas
stig·mat′ic
stig′ma·tism
stig′ma·ti·za′tion
stig′ma·tize′, -tized′,
　tiz′ing
stile *(steps, win-
　dow-frame part)*
　♦*style*
sti·let′to *pl.* -tos *or*
　-toes
still′birth′
still′born′
still′-life′ *adj.*
still′ness
stilt′ed
Stil′ton cheese
stim′u·lant
stim′u·late′, -lat′ed,
　-lat′ing
stim′u·lat′er *also*
　stim′u·la′tor
stim′u·la′tion
stim′u·la′tive

stim′u·lus *pl.* -li′
sting, stung, sting′ing
sting′ray′
stin′gy
stink, stank *or* stunk,
　stunk, stink′ing
stink′pot′
stink′weed′
stint
sti′pend′
stip′ple, -pled, -pling
stip′u·late′, -lat′ed,
　-lat′ing
stip′u·la′tion
stip′u·la′tor
stir, stirred, stir′ring
stir′rer
stir′rup
stir′rup-cup′
stitch′ing
sto′a *pl.* -ae′ *or* -as
stoat
stock·ade′
stock′bro′ker
stock′hold′er
stock′i·net′ *also*
　stock′i·nette′
stock′ing
stock′man
stock′pile′, -piled′,
　-pil′ing
stock′room′
stock′y
stock′yard′
stodg′y
sto′gy *or* sto′gie
sto′ic

sto'i·cal
sto'i·cism
stoke, stoked, stok'ing
stole
stol'id
sto·lid'i·ty
sto'ma *pl.* -ma·ta *or*
 -mas
stom'ach
stom'ach·ache'
stom'ach·er
stomp
stone, stoned, ston'ing
stone'cut'ter
stone'-deaf' *adj.*
stone'ma'son
stone'wall'
stone'ware'
stone'work'
ston'y
stooge
stool
stoop *(bending, stair-*
 case)
 ♦*stoup*
stop, stopped, stop'-
 ping
stop'cock'
stop'gap'
stop'light'
stop'o'ver
stop'page
stop'per
stop'watch'
stor'age
store, stored, stor'ing
store'-bought' *adj.*

store'front'
store'house'
store'keep'er
store'room'
sto'ried
stork
storm'y
sto'ry
sto'ry·book'
sto'ry·tell'er
stoup *(basin)*
 ♦*stoop*
stout'heart'ed
stove'pipe'
stow'age
stow'a·way' *n.*
stra·bis'mus
strad'dle, -dled, -dling
Strad'i·var'i·us
strafe, strafed, straf-
 ing
strag'gle, -gled, -gling
strag'gly
straight *(direct)*
 ♦*strait*
straight'-arm' *v.*
straight'-a·way'
straight'edge'
straight'en *(to make*
 straight)
 ♦*straiten*
straight·for'ward *also*
 straight·for'wards
straight'way'
strain'er
strait *(water)*
 ♦*straight*

strait'en *(to restrict)*
 ♦*straighten*
strait'jack'et
strait'-laced'
strand'ed
strange, strang'er,
 strang'est
stran'gle, -gled, -gling
stran'gler
stran'gu·late', -lat'ed,
 -lat'ing
stran'gu·la'tion
strap, strapped, strap'-
 ping
strap'hang'er
strat'a·gem
stra·te'gic
strat'e·gist
strat'e·gy
strat'i·fi·ca'tion
strat'i·fy', -fied', -fy'-
 ing
stra'to·cu'mu·lus *pl.*
 -li'
strat'o·sphere'
strat'o·spher'ic
stra'tum *pl.* -ta *or*
 -tums
stra'tus *pl.* -ti
straw'ber'ry
straw'-hat' *adj.*
stray
streak'y
stream'er
stream'line', -lined',
 -lin'ing
street'car'

street'scape'
street'walk'er
strength'en
stren'u·ous
strep'to·coc'cal
strep'to·coc'cus *pl.*
-ci'
strep'to·my'cin
stress
stretch'a·ble
stretch'er
stretch'er-bear'er
streu'sel
strew, strewed, strewn
or strewed, strew'ing
stri'a *pl.* -ae'
stri·ate' *also* stri'at'ed
stri·a'tion
strick'en
strict'ly
stric'ture
stride, strode, strid'-
den, strid'ing
stri'dence *also* stri'-
den·cy
stri'dent
strife
strike, struck, struck
or strick'en, strik'ing
strike'bound'
strike'break'er
strike'out' *n.*
strik'er
strik'ing
string, strung, string'-
ing
strin'gen·cy

strin'gent
string'er
string'y
strip, stripped, strip'-
ping
stripe, striped, strip'-
ing
strip'ling
strip'y
strive, strove, striv'en
or strived, striv'ing
strobe
strob'o·scope'
strob'o·scop'ic
stro'gan·off'
stroke, stroked, strok'-
ing
stroll'er
strong'-arm' *adj & v*
strong'box'
strong'hold'
strong'-mind'ed
stron'ti·um
strop, stropped, strop'-
ping
stro'phe
struc'tur·al
struc'ture, -tured, -tur·
ing
stru'del
strug'gle, -gled, -gling
strum, strummed,
strum'ming
strum'mer
strum'pet
strut, strut'ted, strut'-
ting

strych'nine'
stub, stubbed, stub'-
bing
stub'ble
stub'born
stub'by
stuc'co *pl.* -coes *or*
-cos
stuck'-up' *adj.*
stud, stud'ded, stud'-
ding
stud'book'
stu'dent
stu'di·o *pl.* -os
stu'di·ous
stud'y, -ied, -y·ing
stuff'ing
stuff'y
stul'ti·fi·ca'tion
stul'ti·fy', -fied', -fy'-
ing
stum'ble, -bled, -bling
stum'ble·bum'
stump
stun, stunned, stun'-
ning
stunt
stu'pe·fac'tion
stu'pe·fy', -fied', -fy'-
ing
stu·pen'dous
stu'pid
stu·pid'i·ty
stu'por
stu'por·ous
stur'dy
stur'geon

stut'ter

sty *(enclosure), pl.* sties

sty *(inflammation), pl.*
sties *or* styes

style *(to design),* styled,
styl'ing
♦*stile*

styl'ish

styl'ist

sty·lis'tic

styl·ize', -ized', -iz'ing

sty'lus *pl.* -lus·es *or* -li'

sty'mie, -mied, -mie·
ing, *also* sty'my,
-mied, -my·ing

styp'tic *also* styp'ti·cal

sty'rene

Sty'ro·foam'®

suave, suav'er, suav'est

suav'i·ty

sub, subbed, sub'bing

sub·al'tern

sub·a'tom'ic

sub'base'ment

sub'class'

sub'com·mit'tee

sub·con'scious

sub·con'ti·nent

sub'con'tract'

sub·con·trac'tor

sub·cu·ta'ne·ous

sub'deb'u·tante'

sub'di·vide', -vid'ed,
-vid'ing

sub'di·vi'sion

sub·dom'i·nant

sub·due', -dued', -du'-
ing

sub'e·qua·to'ri·al

sub'fam'i·ly

sub'ge'nus *pl.* -gen'er·
a

sub'group'

sub'head'

sub·hu'man

sub·ja'cent

sub'ject *adj. & n.*

sub·ject' *v.*

sub·jec'tion

sub·jec'tive

sub·jec'tiv·ism

sub·jec·tiv'i·ty

sub·join'

sub·ju·gate', -gat'ed,
-gat'ing

sub·ju·ga'tion

sub·ju·ga'tor

sub·junc'tive

sub'king'dom

sub·lease' *n.*

sub·lease', -leased',
-leas'ing

sub·let' *n.*

sub·let', -let', -let'ting

sub'li·mate', -mat'ed,
-mat'ing

sub'li·ma'tion

sub·lime'

sub·lim'i·nal

sub·lim'i·ty

sub·ma·chine' gun

sub'ma·rine'

sub·merge', -merged',
-merg'ing

sub·mer'gence

sub·mer'gi·bil'i·ty

sub·mer'gi·ble

sub·merse', -mersed',
-mers'ing

sub·mers'i·ble

sub·mer'sion

sub'mi'cro·scop'ic

sub·mis'sion

sub·mis'sive

sub·mit', -mit'ted,
-mit'ting

sub·mit'tal

sub·nor'mal

sub·or'der

sub·or'di·nate', -nat'-
ed, -nat'ing

sub·or'di·na'tion

sub·orn'

sub'or·na'tion

sub'phy·lum'

sub'plot'

sub·poe'na

sub ro'sa

sub·rou·tine'

sub·scribe', -scribed',
-scrib'ing

sub'script'

sub·scrip'tion

sub·sec'tion

sub'se·quence'

sub'se·quent

sub·ser'vi·ence'

sub·ser'vi·ent

sub'set'

sub·side', -sid'ed,
  -sid'ing
sub·si'dence
sub·sid'i·ar'y
sub·si·dize', -dized',
  -diz'ing
sub·si·dy
sub·sist'
sub·sis'tence
sub·soil'
sub·son'ic
sub·spe'cies
sub'stance
sub·stan'dard
sub·stan'tial
sub·stan'ti·al'i·ty
sub·stan'ti·ate', -at'-
  ed, -at'ing
sub·stan'ti·a'tion
sub·stan'tive
sub·sta'tion
sub·sti·tut'a·bil'i·ty
sub·sti·tut'a·ble
sub·sti·tute', -tut'ed,
  -tut'ing
sub·sti·tu'tion
sub·sti·tu'tive
sub'stra'tive
sub·stra'tum *pl.* -ta *or*
  -tums
sub·struc'ture
sub·sum'a·ble
sub·sume', -sumed',
  -sum'ing
sub·sys'tem
sub·ten'ant
sub·tend'

sub'ter·fuge'
sub'ter·ra'ne·an
sub·ti'tle
sub'tle
sub'tle·ty
sub'tly
sub·ton'ic
sub·to'tal
sub·tract'
sub·trac'tion
sub·trac'tive
sub'tra·hend'
sub·trop'i·cal
sub·trop'ics
sub·urb'
sub·ur'ban
sub·ur'ban·ite'
sub·ur'bi·a
sub·ver'sion
sub·ver'sive
sub·vert'
sub'way'
suc·ceed'
suc·cess'
suc·cess'ful
suc·ces'sion
suc·ces'sive
suc·ces'sor
suc·cinct'
suc'cor *(relief)*
  ♦*sucker*
suc'co·tash'
Suc'coth *also* Suk'koth
suc'cu·lence *also* suc'-
  cu·len·cy
suc'cu·lent
suc·cumb'

such'like'
suck'er *(dupe, lollipop)*
  ♦*succor*
suck'le, -led, -ling
su'crose'
suc'tion
Su'da·nese' *pl.* -nese'
sud'den
suds'y
sue, sued, su'ing
suede *also* suède
su'et
suf'fer
suf'fer·a·ble
suf'fer·ance
suf·fice', -ficed', -fic'-
  ing
suf·fi'cien·cy
suf·fi'cient
suf'fix'
suf'fo·cate', -cat'ed,
  -cat'ing
suf'fo·ca'tion
suf'frage
suf'fra·gette'
suf'fra·gist'
suf·fuse', -fused', -fus'-
  ing
suf·fu'sion
sug'ar
sug'ar-coat' *v.*
sug'ar·plum'
sug'ar·y
sug·gest'
sug·gest'i·bil'i·ty
sug·gest'i·ble
sug·ges'tion

sug·ges'tive
su'i·cid'al
su'i·cide'
suit (garments, cards, legal action)
   ♦suite (set of furniture)
suit'a·bil'i·ty
suit'a·ble
suit'case'
suite (retinue, set)
   ♦sweet
suite (set of furniture)
   ♦suit
suit'ing
suit'or
su'ki·ya'ki
sul'fa drug
sul'fa·nil'a·mide'
sul'fate'
sul'fide'
sul'fite'
sul'fon'a·mide'
sul'fur also sul'phur
sul'fu'ric
sul'fur·ous
sulk'y
sul'len
sul'ly, -lied, -ly·ing
sul'tan
sul'tan·a
sul'tan·ate'
sul'try
sum (to add, review), summed, sum'ming
   ♦some
su'mac' also su'mach'

sum'ma cum lau'de
sum·ma'ri·ly
sum·ma·ri·za'tion
sum·ma·rize', -rized', -riz'ing
sum·ma·ry (condensation)
   ♦summery
sum·ma'tion
sum'mer
sum'mer·house'
sum'mer·time'
sum'mer·y (of summer)
   ♦summary
sum'mit
sum'mon
sum'mons pl. -mons·es
sump
sump'tu·ar'y (regulating expenses)
sump'tu·ous (lavish)
sun (star)
   ♦son
sun (to bask in the sun), sunned, sun'ning
sun'bathe', -bathed', -bath'ing
sun'bath'er
sun'beam'
sun'bon'net
sun'burn', -burned' or -burnt', -burn'ing
sun'burst'
sun'dae (ice cream)

Sun'day' (Sabbath)
sun'der
sun'di·al
sun'down'
sun'dries
sun'dry
sun'fish' pl. -fish' or -fish'es
sun'flow'er
sun'glass'es
sunk'en
sun'light'
sun'lit'
sun'ny (full of sunlight, cheerful)
   ♦sonny
sun'rise'
sun'set'
sun'shade'
sun'shine'
sun'spot'
sun'stroke'
sun'struck'
sun'tan'
sun'tanned'
sun'up'
sup, supped, sup'ping
su'per
su'per·a·bun'dance
su'per·a·bun'dant
su'per·an·nu·at'ed
su·perb'
su'per·charge', -charged', -charg'ing
su'per·cil'i·ar'y
su'per·cil'i·ous

su'per·con'duc·tiv'i·ty

su'per·con·duc'tor

su'per·e'go

su'per·er'o·ga'tion

su'per·e·rog'a·to'ry

su'per·fi'cial

su'per·fi'ci·al'i·ty

su'per·fine'

su'per·flu·id'i·ty

su'per·flu'i·ty

su·per·flu·ous

su'per·heat'

su'per·high' fre-quency

su'per·high'way'

su'per·hu'man

su'per·im·pose', -posed', -pos'ing

su'per·im'po·si'tion

su'per·in·tend'

su'per·in·ten'dence

su'per·in·ten'dent

su·pe'ri·or

su·pe'ri·or'i·ty

su·per'la·tive

su'per·man'

su'per·mar'ket

su·per'nal

su'per·nat'u·ral

su'per·no'va pl. -vae' or -vas

su'per·nu'mer·ar'y

su'per·pow'er

su'per·sat'u·rate', -rat'ed, -rat'ing

su'per·scribe', -scribed', -scrib'ing

su'per·script'

su'per·scrip'tion

su'per·sede', -sed'ed, -sed'ing

su'per·son'ic

su'per·star'

su'per·sti'tion

su'per·sti'tious

su'per·struc'ture

su'per·ton'ic

su'per·vise', -vised', -vis'ing

su'per·vi'sion

su'per·vi'sor

su'per·vi'so·ry

su·pine'

sup'per

sup·plant'

sup'ple

sup'ple·ment

sup'ple·men'ta·ry also sup'ple·men'tal

sup'pli·ant

sup'pli·cant

sup'pli·cate', -cat'ed, -cat'ing

sup'pli·ca'tion

sup·pli'er

sup·ply', -plied', -ply'-ing

sup·port'

sup·port'a·ble

sup·por'tive

sup·pos'a·ble

sup·pose', -posed', -pos'ing

sup·pos'ed·ly

sup'po·si'tion

sup·pos'i·to'ry

sup·press'

sup·press'er also sup·pres'sor

sup·press'i·ble

sup·pres'sion

sup·pres'sive

sup'pu·rate', -rat'ed, -rat'ing

sup'pu·ra'tion

su'pra·re'nal

su·prem'a·cist

su·prem'a·cy

su·preme'

sur·cease'

sur·charge', -charged', -charg'ing

sur·cin'gle

sur'coat'

surd

sure, sur'er, sur'est

sure'-fire'

sure'-foot'ed

sure'ly

sure'ty

surf *(waves)*

 ♦serf

sur'face, -faced', -fac·ing

sur·fac'tant

surf'board'

sur'feit

surf'er

surf′ing

surge *(to billow)*,
　surged, surg′ing

sur′geon

Surgeon General *pl.*
　Surgeons General

sur′ger·y

sur′gi·cal

sur′ly

sur·mise′, -mised′,
　-mis′ing

sur·mount′

sur·mount′a·ble

sur·name′, -named′,
　-nam′ing

sur·pass′

sur′plice *(robe)*

sur′plus *(excess)*

sur′print′

sur·prise′, -prised′,
　-pris′ing

sur·re′al

sur·re′al·ism

sur·re′al·ist

sur·re′al·is′tic

sur·ren′der

sur·rep·ti′tious

sur′rey *pl.* -reys

sur′ro·gate

sur·round′

sur·round′ings

sur′tax′

sur·veil′lance

sur·vey′ *n.*

sur·vey′ *v.*

sur·vey′ing

sur·vey′or

sur·viv′al

sur·vive′, -vived′, -viv-
　ing

sur·vi′vor

sus·cep′ti·bil′i·ty

sus·cep′ti·ble

sus·cep′tive

sus·pect′ *n. & adj.*

sus·pect′ *v.*

sus·pend′

sus·pend′er

sus·pense′

sus·pen′sion

sus·pi′cion

sus·pi′cious

sus·tain′

sus·tain′a·ble

sus′te·nance

su′tra

sut·tee′

su′ture, -tured, -tur·ing

su′ze·rain

su′ze·rain·ty

svelte, svelt′er, svelt′est

swab, swabbed, swab′-
　bing, *also* swob,
　swobbed, swob′bing

swad′dle, -dled, -dling

swag

swage, swaged, swag′-
　ing

swag′ger

swain

swal′low

swal′low·tail′

swal′low-tailed′

swa′mi *pl.* -mis

swamp′land′

swamp′y

swan

swank *also* swank′y

swan′s′-down′ *also*
　swans′down′

swap, swapped, swap′-
　ping, *also* swop,
　swopped, swop′ping

sward *(turf)*
　♦*sword*

swarm

swarth′y

swash′buck′ler

swash′buck′ling

swas′ti·ka

swat, swat′ted, swat′-
　ting

swatch

swath *(stroke width)*,
　also swathe

swathe *(to wrap)*,
　swathed, swath′ing

swat′ter

sway′back′

swear, swore, sworn,
　swear′ing

swear′word′

sweat, sweat′ed *or*
　sweat, sweat′ing

sweat′band′

sweat′er

sweat′shop′

sweat′y

Swede

Swed′ish

sweep, swept, sweep'-
ing
sweep'stakes' *pl.*
-stakes', *also* sweep'-
stake'
sweet *(sugary)*
♦*suite (retinue, set)*
sweet'bread'
sweet'bri'er *also*
sweet'bri'ar
sweet'en
sweet'heart'
sweet'meat'
swell, swelled, swelled
or swol'len, swel'ling
swel'ter
swept'back'
swerve, swerved,
swerv'ing
swift'ly
swig, swigged, swig'-
ging
swill
swim, swam, swum,
swim'ming
swim'mer
swim'mer'et'
swim'suit'
swin'dle, -dled, -dling
swine *pl.* swine
swine'herd'
swing, swung, swing'-
ing
swin'ish
swipe, swiped, swip'-
ing
swirl

swish
Swiss
Swiss cheese
switch'blade'
switch'board'
switch'man
switch'yard'
swiv'el, -eled *or* -elled,
-el'ing *or* -el'ling
swiz'zle stick
swoon
swoop
sword *(weapon)*
♦*sward*
sword'fish' *pl.* -fish *or*
-fish'es
sword'play'
swords'man
sword'tail'
syb'a•rite *also* Syb'a•
rite
syb'a•rit'ic *also* syb'a•
rit'i•cal
syc'a•more'
syc'o•phan•cy
syc'o•phant
syc'o•phan'tic *also*
syc'o•phan'ti•cal
syl•lab'ic
syl•lab'i•cate', -cat'ed,
-cat'ing, *also* syl•lab'-
i•fy', -fied', -fy'ing
syl•lab'i•ca'tion
syl'la•ble
syl'la•bub' *also* sil'la•
bub'

syl'la•bus *pl.* -bus•es
or -bi'
syl'lo•gism
syl'lo•gis'tic
sylph
syl'van
sym'bi•o'sis
sym'bi•ot'ic
sym'bol *(sign)*
♦*cymbal*
sym•bol'ic *also* sym•
bol'i•cal
sym'bol•ism
sym'bol•ist
sym'bol•i•za'tion
sym'bol•ize', -ized',
-iz'ing
sym•bol'o•gy
sym•met'ric *also* sym•
met'ri•cal
sym'me•try
sym'pa•thet'ic
sym'pa•thize',
-thized', -thiz'ing
sym'pa•thy
sym•phon'ic
sym'pho•ny
sym•po'si•um *pl.* -si•
ums *or* -si•a
symp'tom
symp'to•mat'ic
syn'a•gogue' *also* syn'-
a•gog'
syn'apse'
syn•ap'sis *pl.* -ses'
syn•chro•cy'clo•tron'
syn'chro•ni•za'tion

syn'chro·nize',
 -nized', -niz'ing
syn'chro·nous
syn'chro·tron'
syn·cli'nal
syn'cline'
syn'co·pate', -pat'ed,
 -pat'ing
syn'co·pa'tion
syn'co·pa'tor
syn'co·pe
syn'cre·tism
syn'cre·tis'tic
syn'dic
syn'di·cate', -cat·ed,
 -cat·ing
syn'di·ca'tion
syn'drome'
syn'er·get'ic also syn·
 er'gic
syn'er·gism also syn'-
 er·gy
syn'er·gis'tic
syn'od
syn'o·nym'
syn·on'y·mous
syn·on'y·my
syn·op'sis pl. -ses'
sy·nop'tic also sy·
 nop'ti·cal
syn·tac'tic also syn·
 tac'ti·cal
syn'tax'
syn'the·sis pl. -ses'
syn'the·size', -sized',
 -siz'ing

syn·thet'ic also syn·
 thet'i·cal
syph'i·lis
syph'i·lit'ic
Syr'i·an
sy·ringe'
syr'inx pl. sy·rin'ges'
 or syr'inx·es
syr'up also sir'up
syr'up·y
sys'tem
sys'tem·at'ic also sys'-
 tem·at'i·cal
sys'tem·a·ti·za'tion
sys'tem·a·tize', -tized',
 -tiz'ing
sys'tem'ic
sys'to·le
sys'tol'ic

T

tab, tabbed, tab'bing
tab'ard
Ta·bas'co®
tab'by
tab'er·na'cle
ta'ble, -bled, -bling
tab·leau' pl. -leaux' or
 -leaus'
ta'ble·cloth'
ta'ble d'hôte' pl. ta'-
 bles d'hôte'
ta'ble·hop', -hopped',
 -hop'ing

ta'ble·land'
ta'ble·spoon' pl. -fuls'
tab'let
ta'ble·ware'
tab'loid'
ta·boo' pl. -boos', also
 ta·bu' pl. -bus'
ta·boo', -booed',
 -boo'ing, also ta·bu',
 -bued, -bu'ing
ta'bor
tab'u·lar
tab'u·la ra'sa
tab'u·late', -lat·ed,
 -lat'ing
tab'u·la'tion
tab'u·la'tor
ta'cet (musical direc-
 tion)
 ♦tacit
ta·chom'e·ter
tach'o·met'ric
tac'it (unspoken, im-
 plied)
 ♦tacet
tac'i·turn
tac'i·tur'ni·ty
tack
tack'le, -led, -ling
tack'y
ta'co pl. -cos
tac'o·nite'
tact (diplomacy)
 ♦tacked
tact'ful
tac'tic
tac'ti·cal

tac'ti'cian
tac'tics
tac'tile
tact'less
tad'pole'
taf'fe·ta
taf'fy
tag, tagged, tag'ging
Ta·hi'tian
tai'ga
tail *(hind part)*
  ♦*tale*
tail *(to follow)*
  ♦*tale*
tail'back'
tail'board'
tail'gate', -gat'ed,
  -gat'ing
tail'light'
tai'lor
tai'lor-made'
tail'piece'
tail'pipe'
tail'race'
tail'spin'
taint
take, took, tak'en, tak'-
  ing
take'down' *adj. & n.*
take'-home' pay
take'off' *n.*
take'o'ver *n. & adj.,*
  also take'-o'ver
talc
tal'cum
tale *(report)*
  ♦*tail*

tale'bear'er
tal'ent
tale'tell'er
tale'tell'ing
tal'is·man
tal'is·man'ic
talk'a·tive
talk'ie *(film)*
  ♦*talky*
talk'ing-to' *pl.* -tos
talk'y *(talkative)*
  ♦*talkie*
tall
tal'low
tal'ly, -lied, -ly·ing
tal'ly·ho' *pl.* -hos'
Tal'mud'
Tal·mu'dic *also* Tal·
  mu'di·cal
tal'on
ta'lus *(anklebone), pl.*
  -li'
ta'lus *(debris), pl.* -lus·
  es
tam
ta·ma'le
tam'a·rack'
tam'a·rind'
tam'a·risk'
tam'bour'
tam'bou·rine'
tame, tam'er, tam'est
tame, tamed, tam'ing
Tam'ma·ny
tam'-o'-shan'ter
tamp

tamp'er *(neutron re-*
  flector)
tam'per *(to interfere)*
tam'pon'
tan, tan'ner, tan'nest
tan, tanned, tan'ning
tan'a·ger
tan'bark'
tan'dem
tang
tan'ge·lo' *pl.* -los'
tan'gent
tan·gen'tial
tan'ger·ine'
tan'gi·bil'i·ty
tan'gi·ble
tan'gle, -gled, -gling
tan'go *pl.* -gos
tan'go, -goed, -go·ing
tang'y
tank'ard
tank'er
tan'ner
tan'ner·y
tan'nic
tan'nin
tan'ning
tan'sy
tan'ta·lite'
tan'ta·li·za'tion
tan'ta·lize', -lized',
  -liz'ing
tan'ta·lum
tan'ta·lus
tan'ta·mount'
tan'trum
Tao'ism

Tao′ist
tap, tapped, tap′ping
ta′pa
tap′-dance′, -danced′, -danc′ing
tape, taped, tap′ing
ta′per (candle)
♦tapir
ta′per (to diminish)
♦tapir
tape′-re·cord′ v.
tap′es·try
tape′worm′
tap′i·o′ca
ta′pir (animal)
♦taper
tap′room′
tap′root′
taps
tap′ster
tar, tarred, tar′ring
tar′an·tel′la
ta·ran′tu·la
tar′dy
tare (plant, weight)
♦tear (to split)
tar′get
tar′iff
tar′la·tan
tar′mac′
tar′nish
ta′ro (plant), pl. -ros
tar′ot (card)
tarp
tar′pa′per
tar·pau′lin

tar′pon pl. -pon or -pons
tar′ra·gon′
tar′ry, -ried, -ry·ing
tar′sal
tar′si·er
tar′sus pl. -si′
tart
tar′tan
tar′tar (acid compound, deposit, bad-tempered person)
Tar′tar (Mongol), also Ta′tar
tar·tar′ic
tar′tar·ous
tar′tar sauce also tar′-tare sauce
tart′ness
task′mas′ter
Tas·ma′ni·an
tas′sel, -seled or -selled, -sel·ing or -sel·ling
taste, tast′ed, tast′ing
taste′ful (showing good taste)
♦tasty
taste′less
tast′y (savory)
♦tasteful
tat, tat′ted, tat′ting
tat′ter
tat′ter·de·mal′ion
tat′tle, -tled, -tling
tat′tler
tat′tle·tale′

tat·too′ pl. -toos′
tat·too′, -tooed′, -too′-ing
taunt
taupe (brownish gray)
♦tope
Tau′rus
taut (tight)
♦taught
tau′to·log′i·cal also tau′to·log′ic
tau·tol′o·gy
tav′ern
taw
taw′dry
taw′ny
tax (levy)
♦tacks
tax·a·bil′i·ty
tax′a·ble
tax·a′tion
tax′-de·duct′i·ble
tax′-ex·empt′
tax′i pl. -is or -ies
tax′i, -ied, -i·ing or -y·ing
tax′i·cab′
tax′i·der′mist
tax′i·der′my
tax′i·me′ter
tax′ing
tax·o·nom′ic also tax′-o·nom′i·cal
tax·on′o·mist
tax·on′o·my
tax′pay′er
T′-bone′

tea *(beverage)*
  ♦*tee, ti*
tea'cart'
teach, taught, teach'-
  ing
teach'a·ble
teach'er
teach'-in' *n.*
teach'ing
tea'cup'
tea'cup'ful' *pl.* -fuls'
tea'house'
teak
tea'ket'tle
teal *pl.* teal *or* teals
team *(group)*
  ♦*teem*
team'mate'
team'ster
team'work'
tea'pot'
tear *(to split),* tore,
  torn, tear'ing
  ♦*tare*
tear *(to cry),* teared,
  tear'ing
  ♦*tier*
tear'drop'
tear'ful
tear'-jerk'er
tea'room'
tease, teased, teas'ing
tea'sel
tea'spoon'
tea'spoon·ful' *pl.*
  -fuls'
teat

tech·ne'ti·um
tech'nic
tech'ni·cal
tech'ni·cal'i·ty
tech·ni'cian
Tech'ni·col'or®
tech·nique'
tech·noc'ra·cy
tech'no·crat'
tech'no·crat'ic
tech'no·log'i·cal *also*
  tech'no·log'ic
tech·nol'o·gist
tech·nol'o·gy
tec·ton'ic
ted'dy bear *also* Ted'-
  dy bear
te'di·ous
te'di·um
tee *(golf peg)*
  ♦*tea, ti*
teem *(to abound)*
  ♦*team*
teen'-age' *also*
  teen'-aged'
teen'-ag'er
teens
tee'ny *also* teen'sy
teen'y·bop'per
tee'ter
tee'ter-tot'ter
teethe, teethed, teeth'-
  ing
tee'to'tal·er' *or* tee'to'-
  tal·ler
Tef'lon'®
teg'u·ment

tek'tite'
tel'e·cast', -cast' *or*
  -cast'ed, -cast'ing
tel'e·com·mu'ni·ca'-
  tion
tel'e·gram'
tel'e·graph'
te·leg'ra·pher *also* te·
  leg'ra·phist
tel'e·graph'ic *also* tel'-
  e·graph'i·cal
te·leg'ra·phy
tel'e·ki·ne'sis
tel'e·ki·net'ic
te·lem'e·ter
tel'e·met'ric *also* tel'e·
  met'ri·cal
te·lem'e·try
tel'e·o·log'i·cal
tel'e·ol'o·gy
tel'e·path'ic
te·lep'a·thist
te·lep'a·thy
tel'e·phone', -phoned',
  -phon'ing
tel'e·phon'ic
te·leph'o·ny
tel'e·pho'to *pl.* -tos
tel'e·pho'to·graph'
tel'e·pho'to·graph'ic
tel'e·pho·tog'ra·phy
tel'e·play'
tel'e·print'er
Tel'e·Promp'Ter®
tel'e·scope', -scoped',
  -scop'ing
tel'e·scop'ic

tel'e·thon'
Tel'e·type'®, -typed',
-typ'ing
tel'e·type'writ'er
tel'e·vise', -vised',
-vis'ing
tel'e·vi'sion
tel'ex'
tell, told, tell'ing
tell'tale'
tel'lu·ride'
tel·lu'ri·um
te'lo·phase'
Tel'star'
te·mer'i·ty
tem'per
tem'per·a
tem'per·a·ment
tem'per·a·men'tal
tem'per·ance
tem'per·ate
tem'per·a·ture
tem'pered
tem'pest
tem·pes'tu·ous
Tem'plar
tem'plate also tem'plet
tem'ple
tem'po pl. -pos or -pi
tem'po·ral
tem'po·ral'i·ty
tem'po·rar'y
tem'po·ri·za'tion
tem'po·rize', -rized',
-riz'ing
temp·ta'tion
tempt'ing

tempt'ress
tem'pu·ra
ten
ten'a·bil'i·ty
ten'a·ble
te·na'cious
te·nac'i·ty
ten'an·cy
ten'ant
tend
ten'den·cy
ten·den'tious
ten'der (soft)
ten'der (to offer)
tend'er (one who tends,
 boat)
ten'der·foot' pl.
 -foots' or -feet'
ten'der·heart'ed
ten'der·ize', -ized',
 -iz'ing
ten'der·iz'er
ten'der·loin'
ten'don
ten'dril
ten'e·ment
ten'et
ten'fold'
Ten'nes·se'an
ten'nis
ten'on
ten'or
ten'pin'
tense, tens'er, tens'est
tense, tensed, tens'ing
ten'sile
ten·sil'i·ty

ten'sion
Ten'sor® lamp
tent
ten'ta·cle
ten·tac'u·lar
ten'ta·tive
ten'ter
ten'ter·hook'
tenth
ten'u·ous
ten'ure
ten'ured
te'pee also tee'pee
tep'id
te·pid'i·ty
te·qui'la
ter'bi·um
ter'cen·ten'ar·y also
 ter'cen·ten'ni·al
ter'i·ya'ki
term
ter'ma·gant
ter'mi·na·ble
ter'mi·nal
ter'mi·nate', -nat'ed,
 -nat'ing
ter'mi·na'tion
ter'mi·na'tive
ter'mi·na'tor
ter'mi·no·log'i·cal
ter'mi·nol'o·gist
ter'mi·nol'o·gy
ter'mi·nus pl. -nus·es
 or -ni'
ter'mite'
tern (bird)
 ♦turn

ter'na·ry
Terp·sich'o·re
terp'si·cho·re'an
ter'race, -raced, -rac·
  ing
ter'ra cot'ta
ter'ra-cot'ta *adj.*
ter'ra fir'ma
ter·rain'
ter'ra·pin
ter·rar'i·um *pl.* -i·ums
  or -i·a
ter·raz'zo
ter·res'tri·al
ter'ri·ble
ter'ri·er
ter·ri'fic
ter'ri·fy', -fied', -fy'ing
ter'ri·to'ri·al
ter·ri·to·ri·al'i·ty
ter'ri·to'ry
ter'ror
ter'ror·ism
ter'ror·ist
ter'ror·i·za'tion
ter'ror·ize', -ized', -iz'-
  ing
ter'ry
terse, ters'er, ters'est
ter'tian
ter'ti·ar'y *(third)*
Ter'ti·ar'y *(geologic
  period)*
ter'za ri'ma *pl.* ter'ze
  ri'me
tes'sel·late', -lat'ed,
  -lat'ing

tes'sel·la'tion
test
tes'ta *pl.* -tae
tes'ta·cy
tes'ta·ment
tes'tate'
tes'ta'tor
tes·ta'trix
tes'ter *(canopy)*
test'er *(one that tests)*
tes'ti·cle
tes'ti·fy', -fied', -fy'ing
tes'ti·mo'ni·al
tes'ti·mo'ny
tes'ti·ness
tes'tis *pl.* -tes'
tes·tos'ter·one'
tes'ty
tet'a·nal
te·tan'ic
tet'a·nus
tête'-à-tête'
teth'er
teth'er·ball'
tet'ra
tet'ra·chlo'ride'
tet'ra·cy'cline'
tet'rad'
tet'ra·eth'yl lead *also*
  tet'ra·eth'yl·lead'
tet'ra·he'dral
tet'ra·he'dron *pl.*
  -drons *or* -dra
te·tram'e·ter
tet'rarch'
tet'rar'chy *also* tet'-
  rar'chate'

tet'ra·va'lent
Teu'ton
Teu·ton'ic
Tex'an
text'book'
tex'tile'
tex'tu·al
tex'tur·al
tex'ture
tex'tured
Thai *pl.* Thai
tha·lam'ic
thal'a·mus *pl.* -mi'
tha·las'sic
Tha·li'a
tha·lid'o·mide'
thal'li·um
thal'lo·phyte'
than
thane
thank'ful
thank'less
thanks'giv'ing
that *pl.* those
thatch
thaw
the *article*
  ♦*thee*
the'a·ter *also* the'a·tre
the'a·ter·go'er
the'a·ter-in-the-
  round' *pl.* the'a·ters-
  in-the-round'
the·at'ri·cal *also* the·
  at'ric
the·at'ri·cal'i·ty
the·at'rics

the'ca *pl.* -cae'
thee *pron.*
 ♦*the*
theft
their *pron.*
 ♦*there, they're*
theirs
the'ism
the'ist
the·is'tic *also* the·is'ti·
cal
them
the·mat'ic
theme
them·selves'
then
thence·forth'
thence·for'ward *also*
 thence·for'wards
the·oc'ra·cy
the'o·crat'
the'o·crat'ic *also* the'-
 o·crat'i·cal
the·o·lo'gi·an
the'o·log'i·cal *also*
 the'o·log'ic
the·ol'o·gy
the'o·rem
the'o·ret'i·cal *also*
 the'o·ret'ic
the'o·re·ti'cian
the'o·rist
the'o·ri·za'tion
the'o·rize', -rized',
 -riz'ing
the'o·ry
the'o·soph'i·cal

the·os'o·phist
the·os'o·phy
ther'a·peu'tic *also*
 ther'a·peu'ti·cal
ther'a·peu'tics
ther'a·pist
ther'a·py
there *(at that place)*
 ♦*their, they're*
there'a·bout' *also*
 there'a·bouts'
there·af'ter
there·at'
there·by'
there·for' *(for that)*
there·fore' *(hence)*
there·from'
there·in'
there·in·af'ter
there·of'
there·on'
there·to'
there·to·fore'
there·un·der'
there·un·to'
there·up·on'
there·with'
there·with·al'
ther'mal *also* ther'mic
therm'i'on
ther'mo·cou'ple
ther'mo·dy·nam'ic
ther'mo·dy·nam'ics
ther'mo·e·lec'tric *also*
 ther'mo·e·lec'tri·cal
ther'mo·e·lec'tric'i·ty
ther'mo·graph'

ther'mom'e·ter
ther'mo·met'ric
ther'mom'e·try
ther'mo·nu'cle·ar
ther'mo·plas'tic
Ther'mos® bottle
ther'mo·set'ting
ther'mo·sphere'
ther'mo·stat'
the·sau'rus *pl.* -rus·es
the'sis *pl.* -ses'
Thes'pi·an *also* thes'-
 pi·an
they
thi'a·mine *also* thi'a·
 min
thick'en
thick'et
thick'head'ed
thick'ness
thick'set'
thick'-skinned'
thick'-wit'ted
thief *pl.* thieves
thieve, thieved, thiev'-
 ing
thiev'er·y
thiev'ish
thigh'bone'
thim'ble
thim'ble·ful' *pl.* -fuls'
thim'ble·rig'
thin, thin'ner, thin'nest
thine
thing'a·ma·bob'
thing'a·ma·jig'

think, thought, think'-
  ing
think'a•ble
thin'ner
thin'-skinned'
thi•o•pen'tal sodium
third'-class' adj. &
  adv.
third'-de•gree' burn
thirst'•y
thir'teen'
thir'teenth'
thir'ti•eth
thir'ty
thir'ty-sec'ond note
this pl. these
this'tle
this'tle•down'
thith'er
thith'er•to'
thith'er•ward
thole'pin'
thong
Thor
tho•rac'ic
tho'rax' pl. -rax'es or
  -ra•ces'
tho'ri•um
thorn'y
thor'ough
thor'ough•bred'
thor'ough•fare'
thor'ough•go'ing
thou
though
thought'ful
thought'less

thou'sand
thou'sandth
thrall'dom also thral'-
  dom
thrash'ing
thread'bare'
thread'y
threat'en
three'-base' hit
three'-D' or 3-D
three'-deck'er
three'-di•men'sion•al
three'fold'
three'-piece'
three'-ply'
three'-ring' circus
three'score'
three'some
thren'o•dy
thresh'old'
thrice
thrift'y
thrill'er
thrive, throve or
  thrived, thrived or
  thriv'en, thriv'ing
throat'y
throb, throbbed,
  throb'bing
throe (pang)
  ♦throw
throm'bin
throm•bo'sis pl. -ses'
throm'bus pl. -bi'
throne (ceremonial
  chair)
  ♦thrown

throng
throt'tle, -tled, -tling
through (by way of)
  ♦threw
through•out'
throw (to hurl), threw,
  thrown, throw'ing
  ♦throe
throw'a•way' n. & adj.
throw'back' n.
thrum, thrummed,
  thrum'ming
thrush
thrust, thrust, thrust'-
  ing
thru'way' also
  through'way'
thud, thud'ded, thud'-
  ding
thug
thu'li•um
thumb'hole'
thumb'-in'dex v.
thumb'nail'
thumb'nut'
thumb'screw'
thumb'tack'
thump'ing
thun'der
thun'der•bird'
thun'der•bolt'
thun'der•clap'
thun'der•cloud'
thun'der•head'
thun'der•ous
thun'der•show'er
thun'der•stone'

thun'der•storm'
thun'der•struck'
thu'ri•ble
Thurs'day
thus
thwack
thwart
thy
thyme *(herb)*
♦*time*
thy'mic
thy'mus
thy'roid'
thy•rox'in *also* thy•rox'ine'
thy•self'
ti *(musical tone)*
♦*tea, tee*
ti•ar'a
Ti•bet'an
tib'i•a *pl.* -i•ae' *or* -i•as
tib'i•al
tic *(spasm)*
tick *(sound, mark, insect, casing)*
tick'er
tick'et
tick'ing
tick'le, -led, -ling
tick'ler
tick'lish
tick'tack'toe' *also* tick'-tack'-toe'
tid'al
tid'bit'
tid'dly•winks'

tide *(to rise and fall),* tid'ed, tid'ing
♦*tied*
tide'land'
tide'mark'
tide'wa'ter
tide'way'
tid'ings
ti'dy, -died, -dy•ing
tie, tied, ty'ing
tie'back'
tie'-dye', -dyed', -dye'-ing
tie'-in' *n.*
tier *(row)*
♦*tear (to cry)*
tierce
tie'-up' *n.*
tiff
Tif'fa•ny glass
ti'ger
ti'ger-eye'
tight'en
tight'fist'ed
tight'lipped'
tight'rope'
tights
tight'wad'
ti'gress
til'de
tile, tiled, til'ing
till'a•ble
till'age
till'er
tilt
tilth
tim'bale

tim'ber *(trees)*
♦*timbre*
tim'ber•land'
tim'ber•line'
tim'bre *(quality of sound)*
♦*timber*
time *(to clock),* timed, tim'ing
♦*thyme*
time'card'
time'-hon'ored
time'keep'er
time'-lapse' *adj.*
time'less
time'ly
time'-out' *n., also* time out
time'piece'
tim'er
time'sav'ing
time'serv'er
time'-shar'ing
time'ta'ble
time'worn'
tim'id
ti•mid'i•ty
tim'ing
tim'or•ous
tim'o•thy
tim'pa•ni *also* tym'pa•ni
tim'pa•nist
tin, tinned, tin'ning
tinc'ture
tin'der
tin'der•box'

tine
tin'foil'
tinge, tinged, tinge'ing
  or ting'ing
tin'gle, -gled, -gling
tin'gly
tin'horn'
tink'er
tin'kle, -kled, -kling
tin'ny
tin'-plate', -plat'ed,
  -pla'ting
tin'sel
tin'smith'
tint
tin'tin·nab'u·la'tion
tin'type'
tin'work'
ti'ny
tip, tipped, tip'ping
tip'-off' *n.*
tip'per
tip'pet
tip'ple, -pled, -pling
tip'ster
tip'sy
tip'toe', -toed', -toe'ing
tip'top'
ti'rade'
tire, tired, tir'ing
tire'less
tire'some
'tis
ti·sane'
tis'sue
tit
ti'tan *(giant)*

Ti'tan *(god)*
ti·tan'ic
ti·ta'ni·um
tithe, tithed, tith'ing
ti'tian
tit'il·late', -lat'ed, -lat'-
  ing
tit'il·la'tion
tit'il·la'tive
tit'lark
ti'tle, -tled, -tling
tit'mouse'
ti·tra'tion
tit'ter
tit'tle
tit'tle-tat'tle, -tled,
  -tling
tit'u·lar
tiz'zy
to *(toward)*
  ♦*too, two*
toad *(amphibian ani-
  mal)*
  ♦*toed, towed*
toad'fish', *pl.* -fish' or
  -fish'es
toad'stool'
toad'y, -ied, -y·ing
toast'er
toast'mas'ter
to·bac'co *pl.* -cos *or*
  -coes
to·bac'co·nist
to·bog'gan
to·bog'gan·ist
to'by *also* To'by
toc·ca'ta

toc'sin *(alarm)*
  ♦*toxin*
to·day' *also* to-day'
tod'dle, -dled, -dling
tod'dler
tod'dy
to-do' *pl.* -dos'
toe *(foot digit)*
  ♦*tow*
toed *(having toes)*
  ♦*ôad, towed*
toe'hold'
toe'nail'
tof'fee
tog, togged, tog'ging
to'ga
to·geth'er
to·geth'er·ness
tog'gle
togs
toil *(labor)*
toile *(fabric)*
toi'let
toi'let·ry
toi·lette'
To·kay'
to'ken
to'ken·ism
Tol·ec'
tol'er·a·bil'i·ty
tol'er·a·ble
tol'er·ance
tol'er·ant
tol'er·ate', -at'ed, -at'-
  ing
tol'er·a'tion
tol'er·a'tive

tol′er·a′tor
toll′booth′
toll′gate′
tol′u·ene′
tom′a·hawk′
tom·al′ley pl. -leys
to·ma′to pl. –toes
tomb
tom′boy′
tomb′stone′
tom′cat′
tom′cod′ pl. -cod′ or -cods′
tóme
tom′fool′
tom·fool′er·y
tom′my·rot′
to·mor′row
tom′tit′
tom′-tom′
ton (weight)
♦tun
to′nal
to·nal′i·ty
tone, toned, ton′ing
tongs
tongue, tongued, tongu′ing
tongue′-in-cheek′
tongue′-lash′ing
tongue′-tied′
ton′ic
to·night′ also to-night′
ton′nage
ton·neau′
ton′sil
ton′sil·lec′to·my

ton′sil·li′tis
ton·so′ri·al
ton′sure, -sured, -sur·ing
ton′tine′
too (also)
♦to, two
tool (implement)
♦tulle
tool′box′
tool′ing
toot
tooth pl. teeth
tooth′ache′
tooth′brush′
toothed
tooth′less
tooth′paste′
tooth′pick′
tooth′pow′der
tooth′some
tooth′y
top, topped, top′ping
to′paz′
top′coat′
top′-drawer′ adj.
tope (to drink), toped, top′ing
♦taupe
top′flight′ adj.
top·gal′lant
top′-heav′y
to′pi·ar′y
top′ic
top′i·cal
top′i·cal′i·ty
top′knot′

top′less
top′mast
top′most′
top′notch′
to·pog′ra·pher
top′o·graph′ic also top′o·graph′i·cal
to·pog′ra·phy
top′o·log′ic also top′o·log′i·cal
to·pol′o·gist
to·pol′o·gy
top′per
top′ping
top′ple, -pled, -pling
top′sail
top′-se′cret adj.
top′side′
top′soil′
top′stitch′
top′sy-tur′vy
toque
to′rah
torch′bear′er
tor′e·a·dor′
to·re′ro pl. -ros
tor′ment′ n.
tor·ment′ v.
tor·men′tor also tor·ment′er
tor·na′do pl. -does or -dos
tor·pe′do pl. -does
tor·pe′do, -doed, -do·ing
tor′pid
tor′por

torque
tor'rent
tor·ren'tial
tor'rid
tor'sion
tor'so *pl.* -sos *or* -si'
tort *(civil wrong)*
torte *(cake)*
tor·til'la
tor'toise
tor'toise·shell'
tor'tu·ous *(winding)*
　♦*torturous*
tor'ture, -tured, -tur·
　ing
tor'tur·ous *(painful)*
　♦*tortuous*
To'ry
toss'up' *n.*
tot, tot'ted, tot'ting
to'tal, -taled *or* -talled,
　-tal·ing *or* -tal·ling
to·tal'i·tar'i·an
to·tal'i·tar'i·an·ism
to·tal'i·ty
to'tal·iz'er
tote, tot'ed, tot'ing
to'tem
to'tem'ic
tot'ter
tou'can'
touch'-and-go' *adj.*
touch'back' *n.*
touch'down' *n.*
tou·ché'
touched
touch'-me-not'

touch'stone'
Touch'-Tone'®
touch'-type', -typed',
　-typ'ing
touch'up' *n.*
touch'y
tough *(strong)*
　♦*tuff*
tough'en
tough'-mind'ed
tou·pee'
tour' de force'
tour'ism
tour'ist
tour'ma·line
tour'na·ment
tour'ne·dos' *pl.* -dos'
tour'ney *pl.* -neys
tour'ni·quet
tou'sle, -sled, -sling
tout'er
tow *(dragging, flax)*
　♦*toe*
tow *(to pull)*
　♦*toe*
tow'age
to·ward' *also* to·wards
tow'el, -eled *or* -elled,
　-el·ing *or* -el·ling
tow'er
tow'head'
tow'head'ed
tow'hee'
tow'line'
town'ie'
towns'folk
town'ship'

towns'man
towns'peo'ple
towns'wom'an
tow'path'
tow'rope'
tox·e'mi·a
tox·e'mic
tox'ic
tox'i·cant
tox·ic'i·ty
tox'i·co·log'i·cal
tox'i·col'o·gist
tox'i·col'o·gy
tox'in *(poison)*
　♦*tocsin*
toy
trace, traced, trac'ing
trace'a·ble
trac'er·y
tra·che·a *pl.* -ae' *or* -as
tra'che·al
tra'che·ot'o·my
tra·cho'ma
trac'ing
track *(path)*
　♦*tract*
track'age
tract *(region, pamphlet)*
　♦*track*
trac'ta·bil'i·ty
trac'ta·ble
trac'tion
trac'tor
trade, trad'ed, trad'ing
trade'-in' *n.*
trade'mark'

trade'off' *n., also*
  trade'-off'
trades'man
tra·di'tion
tra·di'tion·al
tra·di'tion·al·ism
tra·di'tion·al·ist
tra·di'tion·al·is'tic
tra·duce', -duced',
  -duc'ing
traf'fic, -ficked, -fick·
  ing
traf'fick·er
tra·ge'di·an
tra·ge'di·enne'
trag'e·dy
trag'ic *also* trag'i·cal
trag'i·com'e·dy
trag'i·com'ic *also*
  trag'i·com'i·cal
trail'blaz'er
trail'blaz'ing
trail'er
train·ee'
train'er
train'load'
train'man
traipse, traipsed,
  traips'ing
trait
trai'tor
trai'tor·ous
tra·jec'to·ry
tram'mel, -meled *or*
  -melled, -mel·ing *or*
  -mel·ling
tramp

tram'ple, -pled, -pling
tram'po·line'
tram'way'
trance
tran'quil
tran·quil·i·za'tion
tran'quil·ize', -ized',
  -iz'ing, *also* tran'quil·
  lize', -lized', -liz'ing
tran'quil·iz'er
tran·quil'li·ty *or* tran·
  quil'i·ty
tran'quil·ly
trans·act'
trans·ac'tion
trans·ac'tor
trans·al'pine'
trans'at·lan'tic
tran·scend'
tran·scen'dent
tran'scen·den'tal
tran'scen·den'tal·ism
tran'scen·den'tal·ist
trans'con·ti·nen'tal
tran·scribe', -scribed',
  -scrib'ing
tran'script'
tran·scrip'tion
tran'sept'
trans'fer *n.*
trans·fer', -ferred',
  -fer'ring
trans·fer'a·bil'i·ty
trans·fer'a·ble
trans·fer'al *also* trans·
  fer'ral
trans·fer'ence

trans'fer·or'
trans·fig·u·ra'tion
trans·fig'ure, -ured,
  -ur·ing
trans·fi'nite'
trans·fix'
trans·form' *n.*
trans·form' *v.*
trans·for·ma'tion
trans·for·ma'tion·al
trans·for'ma·tive
trans·form'er
trans·fuse', -fused',
  -fus'ing
trans·fu'sion
trans·gress'
trans·gres'sion
trans·gres'sor
tran'sience *also* tran'·
  sien·cy
tran'sient
tran·sis'tor
tran·sis'tor·ize',
  -ized', -iz'ing
tran'sit
tran·si'tion
tran·si'tion·al
tran'si·tive
tran'si·to·ry
trans·lat'a·ble
trans·late', -lat'ed,
  -lat'ing
trans·la'tion
trans·la'tor
trans·lit'er·ate', -at'·
  ed, -at'ing
trans·lit'er·a'tion

trans·lu'cence *also*
　trans·lu'cen·cy
trans·lu'cent
trans·mi'grate', -grat'-
　ed, -grat'ing
trans'mi·gra'tion
trans·mis'si·bil'i·ty
trans·mis'si·ble
trans·mis'sion
trans·mit', -mit'ted,
　-mit'ting
trans·mit'ta·ble
trans·mit'tal
trans·mit'ter
trans·mut'a·bil'i·ty
trans·mut'a·ble
trans'mu·ta'tion
trans·mute', -mut'ed,
　-mut'ing
trans'o·ce·an'ic
tran'som
tran·son'ic
trans'pa·cif'ic
trans·par'en·cy *also*
　trans·par'ence
trans·par'ent
tran'spi·ra'tion
tran·spire', -spired',
　-spir'ing
trans'plant' *n.*
trans·plant' *v.*
trans'plan·ta'tion
trans·po'lar
trans'port' *n.*
trans·port' *v.*
trans·port'a·bil'i·ty
trans·port'a·ble

trans'por·ta'tion
trans·pos'a·ble
trans·pose', -posed',
　-pos'ing
trans'po·si'tion
trans·sex'u·al
trans·ship', -shipped',
　-ship'ping, *also* tran·
　ship'
trans·ship'ment
tran'sub·stan'ti·ate',
　-at'ed, -at'ing
tran'sub·stan'ti·a'-
　tion
trans'u·ran'ic
trans·ver'sal
trans·verse'
trans·ves'tite'
trap, trapped, trap'-
　ping
tra·peze'
tra·pe'zi·um *pl.* -zi·
　ums *or* -zi·a
trap'e·zoid'
trap'e·zoi'dal
trap'per
trap'pings
Trap'pist
trap'shoot'ing
trash'y
trau'ma *pl.* -mas *or*
　-ma·ta
trau·mat'ic
trau'ma·tize', -tized',
　-tiz'ing
tra·vail' *(toil, anguish)*
trav'el *(to journey),*

-eled *or* -elled, -el·ing
　or -el·ling
trav'el·er *also* trav'el·
　ler
trav'e·logue' *also*
　trav'e·log'
tra·vers'al
trav'erse *adj.*
tra·verse', -versed',
　-vers'ing
trav'er·tine'
trav'es·ty, -tied, -ty·
　ing
tra·vois' *pl.* -vois' *or*
　-vois'es
trawl'er
tray *(flat receptacle)*
　♦*trey*
treach'er·ous
treach'er·y
trea'cle
tread, trod, trod'den *or*
　trod, tread'ing
tread'le, -led, -ling
tread'mill'
trea'son
trea'son·a·ble
trea'son·ous
treas'ure, -ured, -ur·
　ing
treas'ur·er
treas'ure-trove'
treas'ur·y
trea'tise
treat'ment
trea'ty
treb'le, -led, -ling

treb'ly
tree, treed, tree'ing
tre'foil'
tree'top'
trek, trekked, trek'king
trel'lis
trem'ble, -bled, -bling
tre·men'dous
trem'o·lo' pl. -los'
trem'or
trem'u·lous
trench'an·cy
trench'ant
trench'er·man
trend'y
tre·pan', panned', -pan'ning
trep'a·na'tion
tre·pang'
treph'i·na'tion
tre·phine', -phined', -phin'ing
trep'i·da'tion
tres'pass
tres'pass·er
tress
tres'tle
trey (three)
♦tray
tri'ad'
tri·ad'ic
tri·age'
tri'al
tri'an'·gle
tri·an'gu·lar
tri·an'gu·late', -lat'ed, -lat'ing

tri·an'gu·la'tion
Tri·as'sic
trib'al
tribe
tribes'man
trib'u·la'tion
tri·bu'nal
trib·une'
trib'u·tar'y
trib'ute
trice
tri'ceps'
tri·cer'a·tops'
tri·chi'na pl. -nae or -nas
trich'i·no'sis
tri·chi'nous
trick'er·y
trick'le, -led, -ling
trick'ster
trick'y
tri·clin'ic
tri·col'or
tri·col'ored
tri'corn also tri'corne'
tri'cot
tri·cus'pid also tri·cus'pi·dal
tri'cy'cle
tri'dent
tried
tri·en'ni·al
tri'fle, -fled, -fling
tri·fo'cal
tri·fo'li·ate also tri·fo'·li·at'ed

tri·fur'cate also tri'fur·cat'ed
trig, trigged, trig'ging
trig'ger
trig'ger-hap'py
trig'o·no·met'ric also trig'o·no·met'ri·cal
trig'o·nom'e·try
trill
tril'lion
tril'lionth
tril'li·um
tri'lo·bite'
tril'o·gy
trim, trim'mer, trim'mest
trim, trimmed, trim'ming
tri·mes'ter
trim'mer
tri·mor'phic also tri·mor'phous
tri'nal
trine
Trin'i·tar'i·an
tri·ni'tro·tol'u·ene'
trin'i·ty
trin'ket
tri·no'mi·al
tri'o pl. -os
tri'ode'
tri·ox'ide'
trip, tripped, trip'ping
tri·par'tite'
tripe
tri'ple, -pled, -pling
trip'let

tri'plex'
trip'li•cate', -cat'ed,
   -cat'ing
trip'li•ca'tion
tri'ply
tri'pod'
trip'tych
tri'reme'
tri•sect'
tri'sec'tion
tri'sec'tor
trite, trit'er, trit'est
trit'i•um
tri'ton
tri'umph
tri•um'phal
tri•um'phant
tri•um'vir pl. -virs or
   vi•ri'
tri•um'vi•ral
tri•um'vi•rate
tri'une'
tri•va'lent
triv'et
triv'i•a
triv'i•al
triv'i•al'i•ty
tri•week'ly
tro'che (lozenge)
tro'chee (metrical foot)
trog'lo•dyte'
troi'ka
Tro'jan
troll
trol'ley pl. -leys, also
   trol'ly
trol'lop

trom•bone'
trom•bon'ist
tromp
troop (soldiers)
   ♦troupe
troop'er (soldier)
   ♦trouper
troop'ship'
trope
tro'phy
trop'ic
trop'i•cal
tro'pism
tro'po•sphere'
trot, trot'ted, trot'ting
troth
trot'ter
trou'ba•dour'
trou'ble, -led, -ling
trou'ble•mak'er
trou'ble-shoot'er
trou'ble•some
trough
trounce, trounced,
   trounc'ing
troupe (actors)
   ♦troop
troup'er (actor)
   ♦trooper
trou'sers
trous'seau pl. -seaux
   or -seaus
trout pl. trout or trouts
trow'el, -eled or -elled,
   -el•ing or -el•ling
troy
tru'an•cy

tru'ant
truce
truck'age
truck'er
truck'le, -led, -ling
truck'load'
truck'man
truc'u•lence
truc'u•lent
trudge, trudged,
   trudg'ing
true, tru'er, tru'est
true, trued, tru'ing or
   true'ing
true'blue' n.
true'-blue' adj.
true'love'
truf'fle
tru'ism
tru'ly
trump'er•y
trum'pet
trum'pet•er
trun'cate', -cat'ed,
   -cat'ing
trun'ca'tion
trun'cheon
trun'dle, -dled, -dling
trunk
truss'ing
trust'bust'er
trus•tee' (guardian)
   ♦trusty
trus•tee'ship'
trust'wor'thy
trust'y (dependable)
   ♦trustee

truth *pl.* truths
truth'ful
try, tried, try'ing
try'out' *n.*
try•pan'o•some'
tryst
tset'se fly
T'-shirt' *also* tee shirt
T'-square'
tsu•na'mi
tu'a•ta'ra
tub, tubbed, tub'bing
tu'ba
tub'by
tube
tube'less tire
tu'ber
tu'ber•cle
tu•ber'cu•lar
tu•ber'cu•lin
tu•ber'cu•loid'
tu•ber'cu•lo'sis
tu•ber'cu•lous
tube'rose'
tu'ber•os'i•ty *pl.* -ties
tu'ber•ous
tub'ing
tu'bu•lar
tu'bule
tuck'er
Tu'dor
Tues'day
tu'fa
tuff *(rock)*
  ♦*tough*
tuf'fet
tuft

tug, tugged, tug'ging
tug'boat'
tug'ger
tu•i'tion
tu•la•re'mi•a
tu'lip
tulle *(net)*
  ♦*tool*
tum'ble, -bled, -bling
tum'ble-down' *adj.*
tum'bler
tum'ble•weed'
tum'brel *also* tum'bril
tu'me•fac'tion
tu'me•fy', -fied', -fy'-
  ing
tu'mer•ic
tu•mes'cence
tu•mes'cent
tu'mid
tu•mid'i•ty
tum'my
tu'mor
tu'mult
tu•mul'tu•ous
tu'mu•lus *pl.* -li'
tun *(cask)*
  ♦*ton*
tu'na *pl.* -na *or* -nas
tun'a•ble *also* tune'a•
  ble
tun'dra
tune, tuned, tun'ing
tune'ful
tune'less
tun'er
tune'-up' *n.*

tung'sten
tu'nic
Tu•ni'sian
tun'nel, -neled *or*
  -nelled, -nel•ing *or*
  -nel•ling
tu'pe•lo' *pl.* -los'
tur'ban *(headdress)*
  ♦*turbine*
tur'bid
tur'bine *(engine)*
  ♦*turban*
tur'bo•charg'er
tur'bo•e•lec'tric
tur'bo•jet'
tur'bo•prop'
tur'bot *pl.* -bot *or*
  -bots
tur'bu•lence
tur'bu•lent
tu•reen'
turf
tur'gid
tur•gid'i•ty
Turk
tur'key *pl.* -keys
Tur'kic
Turk'ish
tur'moil
turn *(to rotate)*
  ♦*tern*
turn'a•bout'
turn'a•round' *n.*
turn'buck'le
turn'coat'
tur'nip
turn'key *pl.* -keys

turn'off' *n.*
turn'out' *n.*
turn'o'ver *n.*
turn'pike'
turn'stile'
turn'ta'ble
tur'pen•tine'
tur'pi•tude'
tur'quoise'
tur'ret
tur'ret•ed
tur'tle
tur'tle•dove'
tur'tle•neck'
tusk
tus'sah
tus'sle, -sled, -sling
tus'sock
tu'te•lage
tu'te•lar'y
tu'tor
tu•to'ri•al
tut'ti *pl.* -tis
tut'ti-frut'ti
tu'tu
tux•e'do *pl.* -dos
TV Dinner®
twad'dle, -dled, -dling
twain
twang
tweak
tweed'y
tweet'er
tweez'ers
twelfth
Twelfth'-night'
twelve'month

twelve'-tone'
twen'ti•eth
twen'ty
twen'ty-one'
twice
twid'dle, -dled, -dling
twig'gy
twi'light'
twill
twilled
twin
twine, twined, twin'ing
twinge, twinged,
  twing'ing
twi'night'
twin'kle, -kled, -kling
twin'-screw' *adj.*
twirl'ing
twist'a•ble
twist'er
twit, twit'ted, twit'ting
twitch
twit'ter
twixt
two *(number)*
  ◆*to, too*
two'-bag'ger
two'-bit' *adj.*
two'-by-four'
two'-di•men'sion•al
two'-edged'
two'-faced'
two'-fist'ed
two'fold'
two'-hand'ed
two'-ply'
two'some

two'-step'
two'-time', -timed',
  -tim'ing
two'-tim'er
two'-way'
ty•coon'
tyke *also* tike
tym•pan'ic *also* tym'-
  pa•nal
tym'pa•nist
tym'pa•num *pl.* -na *or*
  -nums, *also* tim'pa•
  num
type, typed, typ'ing
type'cast', -cast',
  -cast'ing
type'face'
type'script'
type'set'ter
type'set'ting
type'write', -wrote',
  -writ'ten, -writ'ing
type'writ'er
ty'phoid'
ty'phoon
ty'phous *adj.*
ty'phus *n.*
typ'i•cal *also* typ'ic
typ'i•cal'i•ty
typ'i•fi•ca'tion
typ'i•fy', -fied', -fy'ing
typ'ist
ty'po *pl.* -os
ty•pog'ra•pher
ty'po•graph'i•cal *also*
  ty'po•graph'ic
ty•pog'ra•phy

ty·pol'o·gy *pl.* -gies
ty·ran'ni·cal *also* ty·
  ran'nic
tyr'an·nize', -nized',
  -niz'ing
ty·ran'no·saur' *also*
  ty·ran'no·saur'us
tyr'an·nous
tyr'an·ny
ty'rant
ty'ro *pl.* -ros, *also* ti'ro
ty'ro·sine'

U

u·biq'ui·tous
u·biq'ui·ty
U'-boat'
ud'der
ug'ly
u·kase'
uke
U·krain'i·an
u·ku·le'le
ul'cer
ul'cer·ate', -at'ed, -at'-
  ing
ul'cer·a'tion
ul'cer·a'tive
ul'cer·ous
ul'na *pl.* -nae' *or* -nas
ul'nar
ul'ster
ul'te'ri·or
ul'ti·ma

ul'ti·mate
ul'ti·ma'tum *pl.* -tums
  or -ta
ul'ti·mo'
ul'tra
ul'tra·con·ser'va·tive
ul'tra·high'
ul'tra·ma·rine'
ul'tra·mi'cro·scope'
ul'tra·mod'ern
ul'tra·son'ic
ul'tra·son'ics
Ul'tra·suede'®
ul'tra·vi'o·let
ul'u·late', -lat'ed, -lat'-
  ing
ul'u·la'tion
U·lys'ses
um'bel
um'ber
um·bil'i·cal
um·bil'i·cus *pl.* -ci'
um'bra *pl.* -brae
um'brage
um·brel'la
u'mi·ak
um'laut'
um'pire', -pired', -pir'-
  ing
ump·teen'
ump·teenth'
un'a·bashed'
un'a·bash'ed·ly
un·a'ble
un·a·bridged'
un'ac·cent'ed
un'ac·cept'a·ble

un'ac·com'pa·nied
un'ac·count'a·ble
un'ac·cus'tomed
un'a·dorned'
un'a·dul'ter·at·ed
un'ad·vised'
un'ad·vis'ed·ly
un'af·fect'ed
un'a·fraid'
un·al'ien·a·ble
un'a·ligned'
un'al·loyed'
un·al'ter·a·ble
un·am·big'u·ous
un'-A·mer'i·can
u'na·nim'i·ty
u·nan'i·mous
un·an'swer·a·ble
un'an·tic'i·pat'ed
un'ap·proach'a·ble
un·armed'
un·asked'
un'as·sail'a·ble
un'as·sist'ed
un'as·sum'ing
un'at·tached'
un'at·test'ed
un'a·vail'ing
un'a·void'a·ble
un'a·ware'
un'a·wares'
un·bal'anced
un·bar', -barred',
  -bar'ring
un·bear'a·ble
un·beat'a·ble
un·beat'en

un'be·com'ing
un'be·knownst'
un'be·lief'
un'be·liev'a·ble
un'be·liev'er
un·bend', -bent',
 -bend'ing
un·bi'ased
un·bid'den
un·bind', -bound',
 -bind'ing
un·blessed' *also* un·
 blest'
un·blink'ing
un·blush'ing
un·bolt'
un·born'
un·bos'om
un·bound'ed
un·bowed'
un·bri'dled
un·bro'ken
un·buck'le, -led, -ling
un·bur'den
un·but'ton
un·called'-for'
un·can'ny
un·cap', -capped',
 -cap'ping
un·ceas'ing
un·cer'e·mo'ni·ous
un·cer'tain
un·cer'tain·ty
un·chain'
un·change'a·ble
un·char'i·ta·ble
un·chart'ed

un·chaste'
un·chris'tian
un'cial *also* Un'cial
un·ci'form'
un·cir'cum·cised'
un·civ'il
un·civ'i·lized'
un·clad'
un·clasp'
un·clas'si·fied'
un'cle
un·clean'
un·clear'
un·clench'
un·cloak'
un·close', -closed',
 -clos'ing
un·clothe', -clothed'
 or clad', cloth'ing
un·coil'
un·com'fort·a·ble
un'com·mit'ted
un·com'mon
un'com·mu'ni·ca'tive
un'com·plain'ing
un'com·pli·men'ta·ry
un'com'pro·mis'ing
un'con·cern'
un'con·cerned'
un'con·di'tion·al
un'con·di'tioned
un'con·nect'ed
un·con'quer·a·ble
un'con·scion·a·ble
un·con'scious
un'con·sid'ered
un'con·sti·tu'tion·al

un'con·sti·tu'tion·al'-
 i·ty
un'con·trol'la·ble
un'con·ven'tion·al
un'con·ven'tion·al'i·
 ty
un·cork'
un·count'ed
un·cou'ple, -pled,
 -pling
un·couth'
un·cov'er
un·crit'i·cal
un·cross'
unc'tion
unc·tu·os'i·ty
unc'tu·ous
un·cut'
un·daunt'ed
un'de·cid'ed
un'de·feat'ed
un'de·mon'stra·tive
un'de·ni'a·ble
un'der
un'der·a·chieve',
 -chieved', -chiev'ing
un'der·act'
un'der·age'
un'der·arm'
un'der·bel'ly
un'der·bid', -bid',
 -bid'ding
un'der·brush'
un'der·car'riage
un'der·charge' *n.*
un'der·charge',
 -charged', -charg'ing

un'der·class'man
un'der·clothes' *also*
  un'der·cloth'ing
un'der·coat'
un'der·cov'er
un'der·cur'rent
un'der·cut', -cut',
  -cut'ting
un'der·de·vel'oped
un'der·dog'
un'der·done'
un'der·drawers'
un'der·dressed'
un'der·es'ti·mate',
  -mat'ed, -mat'ing
un'der·es'ti·ma'tion
un'der·ex·pose',
  -posed', -pos'ing
un'der·ex·po'sure
un'der·feed', -fed',
  -feed'ing
un'der·foot'
un'der·gar'ment
un'der·gird', -gird'ed
  or girt, -gird'ing
un'der·go', -went',
  -gone', -go'ing
un'der·grad'u·ate
un'der·ground'
un'der·growth'
un'der·hand'
un'der·hand'ed
un'der·lay' *n.*
un'der·lay', -laid',
  -lay'ing
un'der·lie', -lay',
  -lain', -ly'ing

un'der·line', -lined',
  -lin'ing
un'der·ling'
un'der·mine', -mined',
  -min'ing
un'der·most'
un'der·neath'
un'der·nour'ish
un'der·nour'ished
un'der·pants'
un'der·pass'
un'der·pay', -paid',
  -pay'ing
un'der·pin'ning
un'der·play'
un'der·priv'i·leged
un'der·pro·duc'tion
un'der·rate', -rat'ed,
  -rat'ing
un'der·score',
  -scored', -scor'ing
un'der·sea' *adj.*
un'der·sea' *also* un'-
  der·seas'
un'der·sec're·tar'y
un'der·sell', -sold',
  -sell'ing
un'der·shirt'
un'der·shoot', -shot',
  -shoot'ing
un'der·shot' *adj.*
un'der·side'
un'der·signed'
un'der·sized' *also* un'-
  der·size'
un'der·skirt'
un'der·slung'

un'der·staffed'
un'der·stand', -stood',
  -stand'ing
un'der·stand'a·ble
un'der·state', -stat'ed,
  -stat'ing
un'der·state'ment
un'der·stud'y, -ied,
  -y·ing
un'der·take', -took',
  -tak'en, -tak'ing
un'der·tak'er
un'der·tak'ing *n.*
un'der-the-count'er
  adj.
un'der·tone'
un'der·tow'
un'der·val'ue, -ued,
  -u·ing
un'der·wa'ter *adj.*
un'der·wat'er *adv.*
un'der·wear'
un'der·weight'
un'der·world'
un'der·write', -wrote',
  -writ'ten, -writ'ing
un'der·writ'er
un'de·served'
un'de·serv'ed·ly
un'de·sir'a·ble
un'de·ter'mined
un'dies
un·dig'ni·fied'
un'dis·crim'i·nat'ing
un'dis·tin'guished
un'dis·turbed'

un·do' *(to reverse)*,
  -did', -done', -do'ing
  ♦*undue*
un·doubt'ed
un·dress'
un·due' *(excessive)*
  ♦*undo*
un'du·lant
un'du·late', -lat'ed,
  -lat'ing
un'du·la'tion
un·du'ly
un·dy'ing
un·earned'
un·earth'
un·earth'ly
un·eas'y
un·ed'u·cat'ed
un·e·mo'tion·al
un·em·ploy'a·ble
un·em·ployed'
un·em·ploy'ment
un·e'qual
un·e'qualed *also* un·
  e'qualled
un·e·quiv'o·cal
un·err'ing
un·es·sen'tial
un·e'ven
un·e·vent'ful
un·ex·am'pled
un·ex·cep'tion·a·ble
un·ex·cep'tion·al
un·ex·pect'ed
un·fail'ing
un·fair'
un·faith'ful

un'fa·mil'iar
un'fa·mil'i·ar'i·ty
un·fash'ion·a·ble
un·fas'ten
un·fath'om·a·ble
un·fa'vor·a·ble
un·feel'ing
un·feigned'
un·fet'tered
un·fin'ished
un·fit'
un·flap'pa·ble
un·fledged'
un·flinch'ing
un·fold'
un·fore·seen'
un·for·get'ta·ble
un·formed'
un·for'tu·nate
un·found'ed
un·fre·quent'ed
un·friend'ly
un·frock'
un·fruit'ful
un·furl'
un·gain'ly
un·glued'
un·god'ly
un·gov'ern·a·ble
un·gra'cious
un·gram·mat'i·cal
un·grate'ful
un·guard'ed
un'guent
un'gu·late
un·hal'lowed
un·hand'

un·hap'py
un·har'ness
un·health'y
un·heard'
un·heard'-of'
un·hes'i·tat'ing
un·hinge', -hinged',
  -hing'ing
un·hitch'
un·ho'ly
un·hook'
un·horse', -horsed',
  -hors'ing
u'ni·cam'er·al
u'ni·cel'lu·lar
u'ni·corn'
u'ni·cy'cle
un·i'den·ti·fied'
u'ni·di·rec'tion·al
u'ni·fi·ca'tion
u'ni·form'
u'ni·form'i·ty
u'ni·fy', -fied', -fy'ing
u'ni·lat'er·al
un·i·mag'in·a·ble
un·i·mag'i·na·tive
un·im·peach'a·ble
un·im·por'tance
un·im·por'tant
un·im·proved'
un·in·hab'it·ed
un·in·hib'i·ted
un·in·spired'
un·in·tel'li·gent
un·in·tel'li·gi·ble
un·in·ten'tion·al
un·in·ter·est·ed

un'in·vit'ed
un'ion
un'ion·ism
un'ion·ist
un'ion·i·za'tion
un'ion·ize', -ized', -iz'-
  ing
u·nique'
u'ni·sex'
u'ni·son
u'nit
U'ni·tar'i·an
u'ni·tar'y
u·nite', -nit'ed, -nit'ing
u'ni·ty
U'ni·vac'®
u'ni·va'lent
u'ni·valve'
u'ni·ver'sal
u'ni·ver·sal'i·ty
u'ni·verse'
u'ni·ver'si·ty
un·just'
un·kempt'
un·kind'
un·know'a·ble
un·know'ing
un·known'
un·lace', -laced', -lac'-
  ing
un·lad'y·like'
un·latch'
un·law'ful
un·lead'ed
un·learn', learned',
  -learn'ing
un·learn'ed *adj.*

un·leash'
un·leav'ened
un·less'
un·let'tered
un·li'censed
un·like'
un·like'ly
un·lim'ber
un·lim'it·ed
un·list'ed
un·load'
un·lock'
un·looked'-for'
un·loose', -loosed',
  -loos'ing
un·loos'en
un·love'ly
un·luck'y
un·made'
un·man'ly
un·manned'
un·man'nered
un·man'ner·ly
un·marked'
un·mar'ried
un·mask'
un·men'tion·a·ble
un·mer'ci·ful
un·mind'ful
un'mis·tak'a·ble
un·mit'i·gat'ed
un·mor'al
un·nat'u·ral
un·nec'es·sar'y
un·nerve', -nerved',
  -nerv'ing
un·num'bered

un'ob·tru'sive
un·oc'cu·pied'
un'of·fi'cial
un·or'gan·ized'
un·or'tho·dox'
un·pack'
un·paid'
un·pal'a·ta·ble
un·par'al·leled'
un·pin', -pinned',
  -pin'ning
un·pleas'ant
un·plug', -plugged',
  -plug'ging
un·pop'u·lar
un'pop·u·lar'i·ty
un·prec'e·dent'ed
un'pre·dict'a·ble
un·prej'u·diced
un'pre·med'i·tat'ed
un'pre·pared'
un'pre·pos·sess'ing
un'pre·ten'tious
un·prin'ci·pled
un·print'a·ble
un'pro·duc'tive
un'pro·fes'sion·al
un·prof'it·a·ble
un'pro·voked'
un·qual'i·fied'
un·ques'tion·a·ble
un·ques'tioned
un·quote', -quot'ed,
  -quot'ing
un·rav'el, -eled *or*
  -elled, -el'ing *or* -el'
  ling

un·read'
un·read'a·ble
un·read'y
un·re'al
un're·al·is'tic
un're·a'son·a·ble
un're·con·struct'ed
un·reel'
un're·gen'er·ate
un're·hearsed'
un're·lent'ing
un're·li'a·bil'i·ty
un·re'li·a·ble
un're·mark'a·ble
un're·mit'ting
un're·served'
un're·serv'ed·ly
un're·spon'sive
un·rest'
un're·strained'
un·ripe'
un·ri'valed
un·roll'
un·ruf'fled
un·ru'ly
un·sad'dle, -dled,
  -dling
un·safe'
un·salt'ed
un·san'i·tar'y
un·sat'is·fac'to·ry
un·sat'u·rat'ed
un·sa'vor·y
un·scathed'
un·schooled'
un'sci·en·tif'ic

un·scram'ble, -bled,
  -bling
un·screw'
un·scru'pu·lous
un·seal'
un·sea'son·a·ble
un·sea'soned
un·seat'
un·seem'ly
un·seen'
un·sel'fish
un·set'tle, -tled, -tling
un·shack'le, -led, -ling
un·shak'a·ble
un·shak'en
un·sheathe',
  -sheathed', -sheath'-
  ing
un·shod'
un·sight'ly
un·skilled'
un·skill'ful
un·snap', -snapped',
  -snap'ping
un·snarl'
un·so'cia·bil'i·ty
un·so'cia·ble
un'so·phis'ti·cat'ed
un·sound'
un·spar'ing
un·speak'a·ble
un·sta'ble
un·stead'y
un·stop', -stopped,
  -stopping
un·stressed'

un·string', -strung',
  -string'ing
un·struc'tured
un·stud'ied
un'sub·stan'tial
un'suc·cess'ful
un'suit'a·bil'i·ty
un·suit'a·ble
un·sul'lied
un·sung'
un'sur·passed'
un'sus·pect'ed
un'sus·pect'ing
un'sym·pa·thet'ic
un·tan'gle, -gled,
  -gling
un·ten'a·ble
un·think'a·ble
un·think'ing
un·ti'dy
un·tie', -tied', -ty'ing
un·til'
un·time'ly
un·tir'ing
un'to
un·told'
un·touch'a·ble
un'to·ward'
un·tried'
un·true'
un·truth'
un·truth'ful
un·tu'tored
un·twine', -twined',
  -twin'ing
un·twist'
un·used'

un·u'su·al
un·ut'ter·a·ble
un·var'nished
un·veil'
un·voiced'
un·war'i·ly
un·war'rant·ed
un·war'y
un·wel'come
un·well'
un·whole'some
un·wield'y
un·will'ing
un·wind', -wound',
 -wind'ing
un·wise', -wis'er, -wis'-
 est
un·wit'ting
un·wont'ed
un·world'ly
un·worn'
un·wor'thy
un·wrap', -wrapped',
 -wrap'ing
un·writ'ten
un·yield'ing
un·yoke', -yoked',
 -yok'ing
un·zip', -zipped', -zip'-
 ping
up'-and-com'ing
U·pan'i·shad'
up'beat'
up·braid'
up'bring'ing
up'com'ing
up'coun'try adj. & n.

up·coun'try adv.
up·date' n.
up·date', -dat'ed,
 -dat'ing
up'draft'
up·end'
up·grade', -grad'ed,
 -grad'ing
up·heav'al
up'hill'
up·hold', -held',
 -hold'ing
up·hol'ster
up·hol'ster·y
up'keep'
up'land
up'lift' adj. & n.
up·lift' v.
up·on'
up'per
up'per-case', -cased',
 -cas'ing
up'per-class'
up'per·class'man
up'per·cut'
up'per·most'
up'pi·ty
up·raise', -raised',
 -rais'ing
up'right'
up'ris'ing
up·riv'er
up·roar'
up·roar'i·ous
up·root'
up·set' n.
up·set', -set', -set'ting

up'shot'
up'side'-down'
up·stage' adj. & adv.
up·stage', -staged',
 -stag'ing
up·stairs' adj. & n.
up·stairs' adv.
up·stand'ing
up'start'
up'state'
up'stream'
up'surge' n.
up·surge' -surged',
 -surg'ing
up'sweep'
up'swept'
up'swing'
up'take'
up'tight' also up tight
up'-to-date'
up'town'
up'turn'
up'ward also up'wards
up'wind'
u·rae'us
u·ra'ni·um
U'ra·nus
ur'ban (of a city)
ur·bane' (suave)
ur'ban·ite'
ur·ban'i·ty
ur·ban·i·za'tion
ur'ban·ize', -ized', -iz'-
 ing
ur'chin
u·re'a
u·re'mi·a

u·re′ter
u·re′thra *pl.* -thras *or*
  -thrae
u·re′thral
urge, urged, urg′ing
ur′gen·cy
ur′gent
u′ric
u′ri·nal
u′ri·nal′y·sis
u′ri·nar′y
u′ri·nate′, -nat′ed,
  -nat′ing
u′rine
urn *(vase)*
  ♦*earn*
Ur′sa Major
Ursa Minor
ur′sine′
us
us′a·ble *also* use′a·ble
us′age
use *(to employ)*, used,
  us′ing
  ♦*yews*
use′ful
use′less
us′er
ush′er
u′su·al
u′su·fruct′
u′su·rer
u·su′ri·ous
u·surp′
u′sur·pa′tion
u′su·ry
u·ten′sil

u′ter·ine
u′ter·us
u·til′i·tar′i·an
u·til′i·tar′i·an·ism
u·til′i·ty
u·til·i·za′tion
u·til·ize′, -ized′, -iz′ing
ut′most′
u·to′pi·a
u·to′pi·an
ut′ter
ut′ter·ance
ut′ter·most′
U′-turn′
u′vu·la
u′vu·lar
ux·o′ri·al
ux·o′ri·ous

V

va′can·cy
va′cant
va′cate′, -cat′ed, -cat′-
  ing
va·ca′tion
vac′ci·nate′, -nat′ed,
  -nat′ing
vac′ci·na′tion
vac′ci·na′tor
vac·cine′
vac′il·late′, -lat′ed,
  -lat′ing
vac′il·la′tion
vac′il·la′tor

va·cu′i·ty
vac′u·ole′
vac′u·ous
vac′u·um *pl.* -u·ums *or*
  -u·a
vac′u·um-packed′
va′de me′cum *pl.* va′-
  de me′cums
vag′a·bond′
va′gar·y
va·gi′na *pl.* -nas *or*
  -nae
vag′i·nal
va′gran·cy
va′grant
vague, vagu′er, vagu′-
  est
vain *(unsuccessful, con-
  ceited)*
  ♦*vane, vein*
vain·glo′ri·ous
vain′glo′ry
val′ance *(drapery)*
  ♦*valence*
vale *(valley)*
  ♦*veil*
val′e·dic′tion
val′e·dic·to′ri·an
val′e·dic·to′ry
va′lence *(capacity to
  combine)*, *also* va′len·
  cy
  ♦*valance*
val′en·tine′
va·le′ri·an
val′et
val′e·tu′di·nar′i·an

val'e·tu·di·nar'i·an·
  ism
Val·hal'la
val'iant
val'id
val'i·date', -dat'ed,
  -dat'ing
val'i·da'tion
va·lid'i·ty
va·lise'
Val·kyr'ie
val'ley *pl.* -leys
val'or
val'or·ous
val'u·a·ble
val'u·a'tion
val'u·a'tor
val'ue, -ued, -u·ing
val'ue-add'ed tax
valve
val'vu·lar
va·moose', -moosed',
  -moos'ing
vamp
vam'pire'
vam'pir·ism
van
va·na'di·um
van'dal *(defacer)*
Van'dal *(tribesman)*
van'dal·ism
van'dal·ize', -ized',
  -iz'ing
Van·dyke'
vane *(wind indicator)*
  ♦*vain, vein*
van'guard'

va·nil'la
va·nil'lin
van'ish
van'i·ty
van'quish
van'tage
vap'id
va·pid'i·ty
va'por
va'por·iz'a·ble
va'por·i·za'tion
va'por·ize', -ized', -iz'-
  ing
va'por·ous
va·que'ro *pl.* -ros
var'i·a·bil'i·ty
var'i·a·ble
var'i·ance
var'i·ant
var'i·a'tion
var'i·col'ored
var'i·cose'
var'i·cos'i·ty
var'ied
var'i·e·gate', -gat'ed,
  -gat'ing
var'i·e·ga'tion
va·ri'e·ty
var'i·ous
var'let
var'mint
var'nish
var'si·ty
var'y *(to change)*, -ied,
  -y·ing
  ♦*very*
vas'cu·lar

vase
va·sec'to·my
Vas'e·line'®
vas'so·con·stric'tion
vas·so·con·stric'tor
vas'so·dil'a·ta'tion
  also va'so·di·la'tion
va'so·di·la'tor
vas'o·mo'tor
vas'sal
vas'sal·age
vast
vat
Vat'i·can
vaude'ville
vaude'vil'lian
vault'ing
vaunt'ed
veal
vec'tor
vec·to'ri·al
Ve'da
Ve·dan'ta
veep
veer
Ve'ga
veg'e·ta·ble
veg'e·tal
veg'e·tar'i·an
veg'e·tar'i·an·ism
veg'e·tate', -tat'ed,
  -tat'ing
veg'e·ta'tion
veg'e·ta'tive *also* veg'-
  e·tive
ve'he·mence *also* ve'-
  he·men·cy

ve'he·ment
ve'hi·cle
ve·hic'u·lar
veil *(covering)*
  ♦*vale*
vein *(vessel, strip, crack)*
  ♦*vain, vane*
ve'lar
veldt *also* veld
vel·le'i·ty
vel'lum *(parchment)*
  ♦*velum*
ve·loc'i·pede'
ve·loc'i·ty
ve·lour' *pl.* -lours', *or* ve·lours'
ve'lum *(membrane), pl.* -la
  ♦*vellum*
vel'vet
vel'vet·een'
vel'vet·y
ve'na ca'va *pl.* ve'nae' ca'vae'
ve'nal *(open to bribery)*
  ♦*venial*
ve·nal'i·ty
ve·na'tion
vend·ee'
vend'er *also* ven'dor
ven·det'ta
vend'i·ble *also* vend'a·ble
vend'ing machine
ve·neer'
ven'er·a·bil'i·ty

ven'er·a·ble
ven'er·ate', -at'ed, -at'ing
ven'er·a'tion
ven'er·a'tor
ve·ne're·al
Ve·ne'tian blind *also* ve·ne'tian blind
venge'ance
venge'ful
ve'ni·al *(minor)*
  ♦*venal*
ve·ni·al'i·ty
ve·ni're
ven'i·son
ven'om
ven'om·ous
ve'nous
vent
ven'ti·late', -lat'ed, -lat'ing
ven'ti·la'tion
ven'ti·la'tor
ven'tral
ven'tri·cle
ven'tri·cose *also* ven'-tri·cous
ven'tri·cos'i·ty
ven·tric'u·lar
ven·tril'o·quism *also* ven·tril'o·quy
ven·tril'o·quist
ven·tril'o·quis'tic
ven·tril'o·quize', -quized', -quiz'ing
ven'ture, -tured, -tur·ing

ven'ture·some
ven'tur·ous
ven'ue
Ve'nus
Ve·nu'sian
Ve'nus's-fly'trap'
ve·ra'cious *(truthful)*
  ♦*voracious*
ve·rac'i·ty
ve·ran'dah *or* ve·ran'-da
verb
ver'bal
ver'bal·ism
ver'bal·ist
ver'bal·i·za'tion
ver'bal·ize', -ized', -iz'ing
ver·ba'tim
ver·be'na
ver'bi·age
ver·bose'
ver·bos'i·ty
ver'dan·cy
ver'dant
ver'dict
ver'di·gris
ver'dure
verge, verged, verg'ing
verg'er
ver'i·fi'a·ble
ver'i·fi·ca'tion
ver'i·fi'er
ver'i·fy', -fied', -fy'ing
ver'i·ly
ver'i·si·mil'i·tude'
ver'i·ta·ble

ver·i·ty
ver'meil
ver·mi·cel'li
ver·mi·cide'
ver·mic'u·lar
ver·mic'u·lite'
ver·mi·form'
ver·mi·fuge'
ver·mil'ion *also* ver·
   mil'lion
ver'min *pl.* -min
ver'min·ous
Ver·mont'er
ver·mouth'
ver·nac'u·lar
ver'nal
ver'ni·er
ve·ron'i·ca
ver'sa·tile
ver'sa·til'i·ty
verse
versed
ver'si·cle
ver'si·fi·ca'tion
ver'si·fi'er
ver'si·fy', -fied', -fy'ing
ver'sion
ver'so *pl.* -sos
ver'sus
ver'te·bra *pl.* -brae *or*
   -bras
ver'te·bral
ver'te·brate'
ver'tex' *pl.* -tex'es *or*
   -ti·ces'
ver'ti·cal
ver'ti·cal'i·ty

ver·tig'i·nous
ver'ti·go' *pl.* -goes' *or*
   -gos'
verve
ver'y *(extremely)*
   ♦*vary*
ves'i·cant
ves'i·cate' -cat'ed,
   -cat'ing
ves'i·cle
ve·sic'u·lar
ves'per *(bell)*
Ves'per *(star)*
ves'pers *also* Ves'pers
ves'sel
ves'tal
vest'ed
ves·tib'u·lar
ves'ti·bule'
ves'tige
ves·tig'i·al
vest'ment
vest'-pock'et *adj.*
ves'try
ves'try·man
ves'ture
vetch
vet'er·an
Vet'er·ans Day
vet'er·i·nar'i·an
vet'er·i·nar'y
ve'to *pl.* -toes
ve'to, -toed, -to'ing
vex·a'tion
vex·a'tious
vexed
vi'a

vi·a·bil'i·ty
vi'a·ble
vi'a·duct'
vi'al *(container), also*
   phi'al
   ♦*vile, viol*
vi'and
vi·at'i·cum *pl.* -ca *or*
   -cums
vibes
vi'bran·cy
vi'brant
vi'bra·phone'
vi'bra·phon'ist
vi'brate', -brat'ed,
   -brat'ing
vi·bra'tion
vi'bra'to *pl.* -tos
vi'bra'tor
vi'bra·to'ry
vi·bur'num
vic'ar
vic'ar·age
vi·car'i·ous
vice *(evil, deputy)*
   ♦*vise*
vice-pres'i·den·cy
vice-pres'i·den'tial
vice·re'gal
vice'roy'
vice'roy·al·ty
vi'ce ver'sa
vi'chys·soise'
Vi'chy water
vic'i·nage
vi·cin'i·ty
vi'cious

vi'cious·ness
vi·cis'si·tude'
vic'tim
vic'tim·i·za'tion
vic'tim·ize', -ized',
  -iz'ing
vic'tim·iz'er
vic'tor
vic·to'ri·a
Vic·to'ri·an
vic·to'ri·ous
vic'to·ry
vict'ual
vi·cu'ña *also* vi·cu'na
vi'de
vi·del'i·cet
vid'e·o'
vie, vied, vy'ing
Vi'en·nese' *pl.* -nese'
Vi·et'cong' *pl.* -cong',
  also Vi·et' Cong'
Vi·et'minh' *pl.* -minh',
  also Vi·et' Minh'
Vi·et'nam·ese' *pl.*
  -ese'
view
view'er
view'point'
vi·ges'i·mal
vig'il
vig'i·lance
vig'i·lant
vig'i·lan'te
vi·gnette', -gnet'ted,
  gnet'ting
vig'or
vig'or·ous

Vi'king
vile *(hateful)*, vil'er,
  vil'est
  ♦*vial, viol*
vil'i·fi·ca'tion
vil'i·fy', -fied', -fy'ing
vil'la
vil'lage
vil'lag·er
vil'lain *(scoundrel)*
  ♦*villein*
vil'lain·ous
vil'lain·y
vil'la·nelle'
vil'lein *(serf)*
  ♦*villain*
vil'lein·age
vim
vin'ai·grette'
vin'ci·ble
vin'cu·lum *pl.* -lums
  or -la
vin'di·cate', -cat'ed,
  -cat'ing
vin'di·ca'tion
vin'di·ca'tor
vin·dic'tive
vin'e·gar
vin'e·gar·y
vine'yard
vin'i·cul'ture
vin' or·di·naire' *pl.*
  vins' or·di·naires'
vi'nous
vin'tage
vint'ner
vi'nyl

vi'ol *(instrument)*
  ♦*vial, vile*
vi·o'la
vi'o·la·bil'i·ty
vi'o·la·ble
vi'o·late', -lat'ed, -lat'-
  ing
vi'o·la'tion
vi'o·la'tive
vi'o·la'tor
vi'o·lence
vi'o·lent
vi'o·let
vi'o·lin'
vi'o·lin'ist
vi'o·list
vi'o·lon·cel'list
vi'o·lon·cel'lo *pl.* -los
VIP
vi'per
vi'per·ous
vi·ra'go -goes *or* -gos
vi'ral
vir'e·o' *pl.* -os'
vir'gin
vir'gin·al
Vir·gin'ian
vir·gin'i·ty
Vir'go
vir'gule
vir'ile
vi·ril'i·ty
vi·rol'o·gist
vi·rol'o·gy
vir'tu *(fine arts)*, *also*
  ver'tu
  ♦*virtue*

vir′tu·al

vir′tu·al·ly

vir′tue *(goodness)*
 ♦*virtu*

vir′tu·o′sic

vir′tu·os′i·ty

vir′tu·o′so *pl.* -sos *or*
 -si

vir′tu·ous

vi′ru·cide′

vir′u·lence

vir′u·lent

vi′rus *pl.* -rus·es

vi′sa

vis′age

vis′-à-vis′ *pl.* vis′-à-vis′

vis′cer·a

vis′cer·al

vis′cid

vis·cid′i·ty

vis′cose′

vis·cos′i·ty

vis′count′

vis′cous *(thick)*
 ♦*viscus*

vise *(clamp), also* vice

Vish′nu

vis′i·bil′i·ty

vis′i·ble

Vis′i·goth′

vi′sion

vi′sion·ar′y

vis′it

vis′i·tant

vis′i·ta′tion

vis′i·tor

vi′sor *also* vi′zor

vis′ta

vis′u·al

vis′u·al·i·za′tion

vis′u·al·ize′, -ized′,
 -iz′ing

vi′tal

vi·tal′i·ty

vi′tal·i·za′tion

vi′tal·ize′, -ized′, -iz′-
 ing

vi′ta·min

vi′ti·ate′, -at′ed, -at′ing

vi′ti·a′tion

vi′ti·a′tor

vit′i·cul′ture

vit′i·cul′tur·ist

vit′re·ous

vit′ri·fi′a·bil′i·ty

vit′ri·fi′a·ble

vit′ri·fi·ca′tion

vit′ri·fy′, -fied′, -fy′ing

vit′ri·ol′

vit′ri·ol′ic

vi·tu′per·ate′, -at′ed,
 -at′ing

vi·tu′per·a′tion

vi·tu′per·a·tive

vi·tu′per·a′tor

vi·va′cious

vi·vac′i·ty

vi′va vo′ce

vive

viv′id

viv′i·fi·ca′tion

viv′i·fy′, -fied′, -fy′ing

viv′i·par′i·ty

vi·vip′a·rous

viv′i·sect′

viv′i·sec′tion

viv′i·sec′tor

vix′en

viz′ard

vi·zier′ *also* vi·zir′

vo·cab′u·lar′y

vo′cal

vo·cal′ic

vo′cal·ist

vo′cal·i·za′tion

vo′cal·ize′, -ized′, -iz′-
 ing

vo·ca′tion

vo·ca′tion·al

voc′a·tive

vo·cif′er·ate′, -at′ed,
 -at′ing

vo·cif′er·a′tion

vo·cif′er·a′tor

vo·cif′er·ous

vod′ka

vogue

voice, voiced, voic′ing

voice′less

voice′-o′ver

voice′print′

void

void′a·ble

voi·là′

voile

vo′lant

vol′a·tile

vol′a·til′i·ty

vol′a·til·i·za′tion

vol′a·til·ize′, -ized′,
 -iz′ing

vol'a·tiz'a·ble
vol·can'ic
vol·ca'no pl. -noes or
　-nos
vole
vo·li'tion
vol'ley pl. -leys
vol'ley·ball'
volt'age
vol·ta'ic
vol·tam'e·ter
volt·am'me'ter
volt'-am·pere'
volt'me'ter
vol'u·bil'i·ty
vol'u·ble
vol'ume
vol'u·met'ric
vo·lu'mi·nous
vol'un·tar'y
vol'un·teer'
vo·lup'tu·ar'y
vo·lup'tu·ous
vo·lute'
vol'vox'
vom'it
voo'doo pl. -doos
voo'doo·ism
vo·ra'cious (greedy)
　♦veracious
vo·ra'ci·ty
vor'tex pl. -tex·es or
　-ti·ces'
vor'ti·cel'la
vot'a·ble also vote'a·
　ble
vo'ta·ry

vote, vot'ed, vot'ing
vo'tive
vouch'er
vouch'safe', -safed',
　-saf'ing
vow
vow'el
vox pop'u·li'
voy'age, -aged,
　-ag·ing
voy'ag·er (traveler)
vo·ya·geur' (boatman,
　guide), pl. -geurs
vo·yeur'
vo·yeur'ism
vo·yeur·is'tic
Vul'can
vul·ca·nite'
vul·can·i·za'tion
vul'can·ize', -ized',
　-iz'ing
vul'gar
vul'gar'i·an
vul'gar·ism
vul'gar'i·ty
vul'gar·i·za'tion
vul'gar·ize', -ized',
　-iz'ing
vul'gate' (speech)
Vul'gate' (Bible)
vul'ner·a·bil'i·ty
vul'ner·a·ble
vul'pine
vul'ture
vul'va pl. -vae
vy'ing

W

wack'y also whack'y
wad, wad'ded, wad'-
　ding
wad'dle, -dled, -dling
wade (to walk in wa-
　ter), wad'ed, wad'ing
　♦weighed
wa'di pl. -dis, also wa'-
　dy
wa'fer
waf'fle, -fled, -fling
waft
wag, wagged, wag'ging
wage, waged, wag'ing
wa'ger
wag'gish
wag'gle, -gled, -gling
Wag·ne'ri·an
wag'on
wag'on·ette'
waif
wail (cry)
　♦wale, whale
wain (wagon)
　♦wane
wain'scot, -scot·ed or
　-scot·ted, -scot·ing or
　-scot·ting
waist (middle)
　♦waste
waist'band'
waist'coat
waist'line'
wait (delay)
　♦weight

wait′er

wait′ress

waive *(to give up)*, waived, waiv′ing
♦*wave*

waiv′er *(relinquishment)*
♦*waver*

wake, woke *or* waked, waked *or* wok′en, wak′ing

wake′ful

wak′en

Wal′dorf′ salad

wale *(to mark with ridges)*, waled, wal′ing
♦*wail, whale*

walk′a•way′

walk′ie-talk′ie

walk′-in′ *adj. & n.*

walk′-on′ *n.*

walk′out′ *n.*

walk′-through′ *n.*

walk′up′ *n., also* walk′-up′

wal′la•by

wall′board′

wal′let

wall′eye′

wall′eyed′

wall′flow′er

Wal•loon′

wal′lop

wal′lop•ing

wal′low

wall′pa′per

wall′-to-wall′ *adj.*

wal′nut′

wal′rus *pl.* -rus *or* -rus•es

waltz

wam′pum

wan, wan′ner, wan′nest

wand

wan′der

wan′der•lust′

wane *(to decrease)*, waned, wan′ing
♦*wain*

wan′gle, -gled, -gling

want *(lack)*
♦*wont*

want′ing

wan′ton

wap′i•ti *pl.* -ti *or* -tis

war, warred, war′ring

war′ble, -bled, -bling

war′den

ward′er

ward′robe′

ward′room′

ward′ship′

ware *(articles)*
♦*wear, where*

ware′house′

war′fare′

war′head′

war′-horse′ *also* war horse

war′like′

war′lock′

war′lord′

warm′-blood′ed

warm′-heart′ed

war′mon′ger

warmth

warm′-up′ *n.*

warn′ing

warp

war′path′

war′plane′

war′rant

war′ran•tor

war′ran•ty

war′ren

war′ri•or

war′ship′

wart

war′time′

war′y

wash′a•ble

wash′-and-wear′

wash′board′

wash′bowl′

wash′cloth′

wash′day′

washed′-out′ *adj.*

washed′-up′ *adj.*

wash′er

wash′er•wom′an

wash′ing

Wash′ing•to′ni•an

wash′out′ *n.*

wash′room′

wash′stand′

wash′tub′

wasp′ish

wasp′waist′ed

was'sail

Was'ser·mann test

wast'age

waste *(to squander)*,
   wast'ed, wast'ing
   ♦*waist*

waste'bas'ket

waste'ful

waste'land'

wast'rel

watch'dog'

watch'ful

watch'mak'er

watch'man

watch'tow'er

watch'word'

wa'ter

wa'ter·borne'

wa'ter-col'or *adj.*

wa'ter-cool'

wa'ter·course'

wa'ter·cress'

wa'ter·fall'

wa'ter·fowl', *pl.* -fowl'
   or -fowls'

wa'ter·front'

Wa'ter·gate'

wa'ter·less

wa'ter-log', -logged',
   -log'ging

Wa'ter·loo'

wa'ter·mark'

wa'ter·mel'on

wa'ter·pow'er

wa'ter·proof'

wa'ter·re·pel'lent

wa'ter·re·sis'tant

wa'ter·shed'

wa'ter·side'

wa'ter-ski', -skied',
   -ski'ing

wa'ter·ski' *pl.* -skis' or
   -ski'

wa'ter-ski'er

wa'ter·spout'

wa'ter·tight'

wa'ter·way'

wa'ter·works'

wa'ter·y

watt

watt'age

watt'-hour'

wat'tle

wave *(water)*
   ♦*waive*

wave *(to flutter)*,
   waved, wav'ing
   ♦*waive*

wave'band'

wave'length'

wav'er *(one that waves)*
   ♦*waiver*

wa'ver *(to sway)*
   ♦*waiver*

wax

wax'en

wax'wing'

wax'work'

wax'y

wa'y

way *(course)*
   ♦*weigh, whey*

way'bill'

way'far'er

way'far'ing

way·lay', -laid', -lay'-
   ing

way'-out' *adj.*

way'side'

way'ward

we *pron.*
   ♦*wee*

weak *(feeble)*
   ♦*week*

weak'en

weak'fish' *pl.* -fish' or
   -fish'es

weak'ling

weak'ly *(sickly)*
   ♦*weekly*

weak'-mind'ed

weak'ness

weal *(prosperity, welt)*
   ♦*we'll, wheal, wheel*

wealth'y

wean

weap'on

weap'on·ry

wear *(to have on, dam-
   age, rub away)*, wore,
   worn, wear'ing
   ♦*ware, where*

wear'a·ble

wea'ri·some

wea'ry, -ried, -ry·ing

wea'sel

weath'er *(climate)*
   ♦*wether, whether*

weath'er-beat'en

weath'er·board'

weath'er·bound'

weath'er·cast'
weath'er·cock'
weath'ered
weath'er·ing
weath'er·man'
weath'er·proof'
weath'er-strip',
  -stripped', -strip'ping
weave *(to interlace)*,
  wove, wov'en, weav'-
  ing
  ♦*we've*
weav'er·bird'
web, webbed, web'bing
web'-foot'ed
wed, wed'ded, wed *or*
  wed'ded, wed'ding
wedge, wedged, wedg'-
  ing
wedg'ie
wed'lock'
Wednes'day
wee *(tiny)*, we'er, we'-
  est
  ♦*we*
weed *(plant)*
  ♦*we'd*
weed'y
week *(seven days)*
  ♦*weak*
week'day'
week'end'
week'end'er
week'ly *(once a week)*
  ♦*weakly*
wee'nie
weep, wept, weep'ing

weep'y
wee'vil
weft
weigh *(to determine
  weight)*
  ♦*way, whey*
weigh'-in' *n.*
weight *(measure of
  heaviness)*
  ♦*wait*
weight'less
weight'lift'ing
weight'y
weir *(dam)*
  ♦*we're*
weird'ness
weird'o *pl.* -oes
wel'come, -comed,
  -com·ing
weld
wel'fare'
wel'kin
well *(satisfactorily)*,
  bet'ter, best
well *(shaft)*
we'll *contraction*
  ♦*weal, wheal, wheel*
well'-bal'anced
well'-be'ing
well'-born'
well'-bred'
well'-dis·posed'
well'-done'
well'-fed'
well'-fixed'
well'-found'ed
well'-groomed'

well'-ground'ed
well'-known'
well'-man'nered
well'-mean'ing
well'-meant'
well'-nigh'
well'-off'
well'-read'
well'spring'
well-thought'-of'
well'-timed'
well'-to-do'
well'-turned'
well'-wish'er
well'-worn'
Wels'bach' burner
welsh *(to swindle)*, *also*
  welch
Welsh *(of Wales)*
Welsh'man
Welsh rab'bit *also*
  Welsh rare'bit
wel'ter
wel'ter·weight'
welt'ing
wen *(cyst)*
  ♦*when*
wench
wend
we're *contraction*
  ♦*weir*
were'wolf'
wes'kit
west'bound'
west'er·ly
west'ern
west'ern·er

west'ern•ize', -ized',
  -iz'ing
west'ern•most'
West In'di•an
west'-north'west'
west'-south'west'
West Vir•gin'ian
west'ward *also* west'-
  wards
wet *(damp)*, wet'ter,
  wet'test
  ♦*whet*
wet *(to dampen)*, wet'-
  ted, wet'ting
  ♦*whet*
wet'back'
weth'er *(sheep)*
  ♦*weather, whether*
wet'land'
we've *contraction*
  ♦*weave*
whack
whale *(mammal)*
  ♦*wail, wale*
whale'boat'
whale'bone'
whal'er
whal'ing
wham, whammed,
  wham'ming
wham'my
wharf *pl.* wharves *or*
  wharfs
wharf'age
what•ev'er
what'not'
what'so•ev'er

wheal *(swelling)*
  ♦*weal, we'll, wheel*
wheat'en
whee'dle, -dled, -dling
wheel *(disk)*
  ♦*weal, we'll, wheal*
wheel'bar'row
wheel'chair'
wheeled
wheel'er-deal'er
wheel'wright'
wheeze, wheezed,
  wheez'ing
wheez'y
whelk
whelm
whelp
when *(at what time)*
  ♦*wen*
whence'so•ev'er
when•ev'er
when'so•ev'er
where *(at what place)*
  ♦*ware, wear*
where'a•bouts'
where•as'
where•at'
where'by'
where'fore'
where'from'
where'in'
where•of'
where•on'
where'so•ev'er
where•to'
where'up•on'
wher•ev'er

where'with'
where'with•al'
wher'ry
whet *(to sharpen)*,
  whet'ted, whet'ting
  ♦*wet*
wheth'er *(if)*
  ♦*weather, wether*
whet'stone'
whey *(part of milk)*
  ♦*way, weigh*
whey'ey
which *pron.*
  ♦*witch*
which•ev'er
whiff
whif'fle•tree
Whig
while *(period of time)*
  ♦*wile*
while *(to spend idly)*,
  whiled, whil'ing
  ♦*wile*
whi'lom
whilst
whim
whim'per
whim'si•cal
whim'si•cal'i•ty
whim'sy *also* whim'sey
  pl. -seys
whine *(to complain)*,
  whined, whin'ing
  ♦*wine*
whin'ny, -nied, -ny•ing
whin'y

whip, whipped *or*
whipt, whip'ping
whip'cord'
whip'lash'
whip'per·snap'per
whip'pet
whip'poor·will' *also*
whip'-poor-will'
whip'saw'
whir, whirred, whir'-
ring
whirl'i·gig'
whirl'pool'
whirl'wind'
whirl'y·bird'
whisk'broom'
whisk'er
whis'key *pl.* -keys
whis'per
whist
whis'tle, -tled, -tling
whis'tle-stop',
-stopped', -stop'ping
whit *(particle)*
♦*wit*
white, whit'er, whit'est
white, whit'ed, whit'-
ing
white'cap'
white'-col'lar *adj.*
white'-faced'
white'fish' *pl.* -fish' *or*
-fish'es
white'-hot'
whit'en
white'ness
white'out' *n.*

white'-tailed' deer
white'wall'
white'wash'
whith'er *(where)*
♦*wither*
whit'ish
whit'low
Whit'sun·day
whit'tle, -tled, -tling
whiz, whizzed, whiz'-
zing, *also* whizz
who·dun'it
who·ev'er
whole *(complete)*
♦*hole*
whole'heart'ed
whole'sale', -saled',
-sal'ing
whole'sal'er
whole'some
whole'-wheat'
whol'ly *(totally)*
♦*holy*
whom·ev'er
whom·so·ev'er
whoop *(cough)*
♦*hoop*
whoop'ee
whoop'ing cough
whooping crane
whoops
whoosh
whop, whopped,
whop'ping
whop'per
whorl
who's *contraction*

whose *pron.*
who'so
who'so·ev'er
why *pl.* whys
wick
wick'ed
wick'er
wick'er·work'
wick'et
wick'i·up'
wide, wid'er, wid'est
wide'-an'gle lens
wide'-a·wake'
wide'-eyed'
wid'en
wide'-o'pen
wide'spread'
wid'geon *pl.* -geon *or*
-geons
wid'ow
wid'ow·er
wid'ow·hood'
width
wield'a·ble
wie'ner
Wie'ner schnit'zel
wie'ner·wurst'
wife *pl.* wives
wig, wigged, wig'ging
wig'gle, -gled, -gling
wig'wag', -wagged',
-wag'ging
wig'wam'
wild'cat'
wild'cat'ter
wil'de·beest'
wil'der·ness

wild'-eyed'
wild'fire'
wild'flow'er
wild'fowl' *pl.* -fowl' *or* -fowls'
wild'-goose' chase
wild'life'
wile *(to entice),* wiled, wil'ing
  ♦*while*
will *(volition)*
will *auxiliary, past tense* would
willed
will'ful *also* wil'ful
will'ing
will'-o'-the-wisp'
wil'low
wil'low•y
wil'ly-nil'ly
wilt
wi'ly
wim'ple
win, won, win'ning
wince, winced, winc'-ing
winch
wind *(air)*
wind *(to wrap around),* wound, wind'ing
wind'bag'
wind'-blown'
wind'break'
Wind'break'er®
wind'-chill' factor
wind'ed
wind'fall'

wind'flow'er
wind'jam'mer
wind'lass
wind'mill'
win'dow
win'dow-dress'er
win'dow-dress'ing
win'dow•pane'
win'dow-shop', -shopped', -shop'-ping
win'dow•sill'
wind'pipe'
wind'row'
wind'shield'
wind'sock'
Wind'sor tie
wind'storm'
wind'swept'
wind'-up' *n. & adj.*
wind'ward
wind'y
wine *(fermented juice)*
  ♦*whine*
wine'glass'
win'er•y
Wine'sap'
wine'skin'
wing'ding'
winged
wing'span'
wing'spread'
wink
win'kle
win'ner
win'ning
win'now

win'some
win'ter
win'ter•green'
win'ter•ize', -ized', -iz'ing
win'ter•time'
win'try *also* win'ter•y
wipe, wiped, wip'ing
wipe'out' *n.*
wire, wired, wir'ing
wire'-haired'
wire'less
wire'pull'er
wire'pull'ing
wire'tap', -tapped', -tap'ping
wir'ing
wir'y
wis'dom
wise, wis'er, wis'est
wise'a'cre
wise'crack'
wish'bone'
wish'ful
wish'y-wash'y
wisp'y
wis•ter'i•a *also* wis•tar'i•a
wist'ful
wit *(intelligence, humor)*
  ♦*whit*
witch *(hag)*
  ♦*which*
witch'craft'
with•al'

with·draw', -drew',
-drawn', -draw'ing
with·draw'al
withe
with'er *(to dry up)*
 ♦*whither*
with'ers
with·hold', -held',
-hold'ing
with·in'
with'-it' *adj.*
with·out'
with·stand', -stood',
-stand'ing
wit'less
wit'ness
wit'ti·cism
wit'ty
wiz'ard
wiz'ard·ry
wiz'ened
woad
wob'ble, -bled, -bling
wob'bly
woe'be·gone'
woe'ful
wok
wolf *pl.* wolves
wolf'hound'
wolf'ram
wol'ver·ine'
wom'an *pl.* wom'en
wom'an·hood'
wom'an·ish
wom'an·ize' -ized',
 -iz'ing
wom'an·kind'

womb
wom'bat'
wom'en·folk'
won'der
won'der·ful
won'der·land'
won'der·ment
won'der·work'er
won'drous
wont *(custom)*
 ♦*want*
wont'ed *(usual)*
 ♦*wanted*
won ton
woo
wood *(lumber)*
 ♦*would*
wood'bine'
wood'carv'ing
wood'chuck'
wood'cock' *pl.* -cock'
 or -cocks'
wood'craft'
wood'cut'
wood'cut'ter
wood'ed
wood'en
wood'land
wood'peck'er
wood'pile'
wood'shed'
woods'man
wood'wind'
wood'work'
wood'y
woof'er
wool'en *also* wool'len

wool'gath'er·ing
wool'ly *also* wool'y
wooz'y
Worces'ter·shire
word'age
word'book'
word'ing
word'less
word proc'ess·ing
word proc'es·sor
word'y
work'a·ble
work'a·day'
work'a·hol'ic
work'bench'
work'book'
work'box'
work'day'
work'er
work'horse'
work'house'
work'ing-class' *adj.*
work'ing·man'
work'load'
work'man
work'man·like' *also*
 work'man·ly
work'man·ship'
work'out' *n.*
work'room'
work'shop'
work'ta·ble
work'week'
world'ly
world'ly-wise'
world'-shak'ing
world'wide'

worm′-eat′en
worm′hole′
worm′wood′
worn′-out′ *adj.*
wor′ri•some
wor′ry, -ried, -ry•ing
wor′ry•wart′
worse
wors′en
wor′ship, -shiped *or*
　-shipped, -ship•ing *or*
　-ship•ping
wor′ship•er *or* wor′-
　ship•per
wor′ship•ful
worst *(most inferior)*
　♦*wurst*
wor′sted
worth′less
worth′while′
wor′thy
would *auxiliary*
　♦*wood*
would′-be′
wound
wow
wrack *(to ruin)*
　♦*rack*
wraith *(ghost)*
　♦*wrath*
wran′gle, -gled, -gling
wran′gler
wrap *(to enclose),*
　wrapped *or* wrapt,
　wrap′ping
　♦*rap*
wrap′a•round′

wrap′per
wrap′-up′ *n.*
wrath *(anger)*
　♦*wraith*
wreak *(to punish)*
　♦*reek*
wreath *pl.* wreaths
wreathe, wreathed,
　wreath′ing, wreathes
wreck *(to destroy)*
　♦*reck*
wreck′age
wren
wrench
wrest *(to obtain by
　force)*
　♦*rest*
wres′tle, -tled, -tling
wretch *(miserable per-
　son)*
　♦*retch*
wretch′ed
wrig′gle, -gled, -gling
wring *(to squeeze),*
　wrung, wring′ing
　♦*ring*
wring′er
wrin′kle, -kled, -kling
wrist′band′
writ *(order)*
write *(to compose),*
　wrote, writ′ten, writ′-
　ing
　♦*right, rite*
write′-in′ *n.*
write′-off′ *n.*
writ′er

write′-up′ *n.*
writhe, writhed,
　writh′ing
writ′ing
wrong′do′er
wrong′do′ing
wrong′-head′ed
wrought
wry *(crooked),* wri′er *or*
　wry′er, wri′est *or*
　wry′est
　♦*rye*
wurst *(sausage)*
　♦*worst*

X

x′-ax′is *pl.* -es
X′-chro′mo•some′
xe′non′
xen′o•phobe′
xen′o•pho′bi•a
xen′o•pho′bic
xe•rog′ra•pher
xer′o•graph′ic
xe•rog′ra•phy
Xer′ox®
X′mas
x′-ra′di•a′tion
X′-rat′ed
x′-ray′ *also* X′-ray′
xy′lem
xy′lo•phone′
xy′lo•phon′ist

Y

yacht'ing
yachts'man
ya'hoo pl. -hoos
Yah'weh also Yah'veh
yak (animal)
yak (to talk), yakked,
  yak'king
yam
yam'mer
yank (to pull)
Yank (Yankee)
Yan'kee
yap, yapped, yap'ping
yard'age
yard'arm'
yard'mas'ter
yard'stick'
yar'mul·ke also yar-
  mel·ke
yarn
yar'row
yaw
yawl
yawn'ing
yawp also yaup
yaws
y'-ax'is pl. -es
Y'-chro'mo·some'
ye
yea
yeah
year'book'
year'ling

year'long'
year'ly
yearn'ing
year'-round' adj.
yeast'y
yell'ing
yel'low
yel'low·ham'mer
yel'low·legs' pl. -legs'
yellow pages or Yel-
  low Pages
yel'low·tail'
yelp
yen
yen'ta
yeo'man
yeo'man·ry
yes pl. yes'es
yes, yessed, yes'sing
ye·shi'va or ye·shi'vah
yes'ter·day'
yes'ter·year'
yet
yet'i pl. -is
yew (tree)
  ♦ewe, you
Yid'dish
yield'ing
yip, yipped, yip'ping
yip'pee
yo'del, -deled or
  -delled, -del·ing or
  -del·ling
yo'ga
yo'gi pl. -gis
yo'gurt also yo'ghurt

yoke (to join), yoked,
  yok'ing
  ♦yolk
yo'kel
yolk (yellow of an egg)
  ♦yoke
Yom Kip'pur
yon'der
yoo'-hoo'
yore
York'shire' pudding
you pron.
  ♦ewe, yew
you'll contraction
  ♦Yule
young'ster
your possessive
you're contraction
yours
your·self' pl. -selves'
youth pl. youths
youth'ful
yowl
yo'-yo' pl. -yos'
yt·ter'bic
yt·ter'bi·um
yt'tric
yt'tri·um
yuc·ca
Yu'go·slav' or Yu'go·
  sla'vi·an
Yule (Christmas)
  ♦you'll
Yule'tide'
Yu'man
yum'my
yurt

Z

za′ba•glio′ne
za′ny
zap, zapped, zap′ping
zeal′ot
zeal′ous
ze′bra
ze′bu
zed
ze′nith
zeph′yr
zep′pe•lin *also* Zep′pe•
lin
ze′ro *pl.* -ros *or* -roes
ze′ro, -roed, -ro•ing
zest′ful
Zeus
zig′gu•rat′
zig′zag′, -zagged′,
-zag′ging
zilch
zil′lion
Zim•bab′we•an *also*
Zim•bab′wi•an
zinc

zin′fan•del′ *also* Zin′-
fan•del′
zing′er
zin′ni•a
Zi′on *also* Si′on
Zi′on•ism
Zi′on•ist
zip, zipped, zip′ping
Zip Code *also* zip
code, ZIP Code
zip′per
zip′py
zir′con′
zir•co′ni•um
zith′er *also* zith′ern
zo′di•ac
zo•di′a•cal
zom′bie *also* zom′bi *pl.*
-bis
zo′nal *also* zo′na•ry
zone, zoned, zon′ing
zonked
zoo *pl.* zoos
zo′o•ge•o•graph′ic
also zo′o•ge•o•graph′-
i•cal

zo′o•ge•og′ra•phy
zo′o•graph′ic *also* zo′-
o•graph′ic•al
zo•og′ra•phy
zo′oid′
zo•oid′al
zo′o•log′i•cal *also* zo′-
o•log′ic
zo•ol′o•gist
zo•ol′o•gy
zoom
zo′o•phyte′
zo′o•spore′
Zou•ave′
zuc•chi′ni *pl.* -ni
zwie′back′
zy′go•mat′ic
zy′go•spore′
zy′gote′
zy•got′ic
zy′mase′
zy′mo•gen
zy′mo•gen′ic *also* zy•
mog′e•nous
zy•mol′o•gy
zy′mur•gy
zyz′zy•va

GUIDE TO PLURALS

1. The plural of most nouns is formed by adding **-s** to the singular: *arm, arms; chief, chiefs; doll, dolls; epoch, epochs; jaw, jaws; log, logs; skate, skates; George, Georges;* the *Walkers;* the *Romanos.*

2. a. Common nouns ending in **ch** (*soft*), **sh, s, ss, x,** or **zz** usually form their plurals by adding **-es:** *church, churches; slash, slashes; gas, gasses; class, classes; fox, foxes; buzz, buzzes.*
   b. Proper nouns of this type always add **-es:** *Charles, Charleses;* the *Keaches;* the *Joneses;* the *Coxes.*

3. a. Common nouns ending in **y** preceded by a vowel usually form their plurals by adding **-s:** *bay, bays; guy, guys; key, keys; toy, toys.*
   b. Common nouns ending in **y** preceded by a consonant or by **qu** change the **y** to **i** and add **-es:** *baby, babies; city, cities; faculty, faculties; soliloquy, soliloquies.*
   c. Proper nouns ending in **y** form their plurals regularly, and do not change the **y** to **i** as common nouns do: both *Germanys;* the two *Kathys;* the *Connallys;* the two *Kansas Citys. Exceptions:* the *Alleghenies,* the *Ptolemies,* the *Rockies;* the *Two Sicilies.*

4. Most nouns ending in **f, ff,** or **fe** form their plurals regularly by adding **-s** to the singular. However, some nouns ending in **f** or **fe** change the **f** or **fe** to **v** and add **-es:** *calf, calves; half, halves; loaf, loaves; self, selves; thief, thieves; wife, wives; wolf, wolves.*
   Note: *Scarf, staff,* and *wharf* have two forms: *scarfs* or *scarves; staffs* or *staves; wharves* or *wharfs.* Sometimes different forms have different meanings, as in the case of *staffs* (members of an organization) and *staves* (long poles), or in the case of *beeves* (animals) and *beefs* (complaints).

5. a. Nouns ending in **o** preceded by a vowel form their plurals by adding **-s** to the singular: *cameo, cameos; duo, duos; studio, studios; zoo, zoos*.

b. Most nouns ending in **o** preceded by a consonant usually add **-es**: *echo, echoes; hero, heroes; tomato, tomatoes*.

Note: There are many exceptions to this rule since the consonant or cluster of consonants preceding the **o** does not determine whether the plural will add **-s** or **-es**: *alto, altos; ego, egos; piano, pianos; poncho, ponchos; silo, silos*.

c. Some nouns ending in **o** preceded by a consonant have two plural forms. In the following examples the preferred form is given first: *buffaloes* or *buffalos; cargoes* or *cargos; halos* or *haloes; zeros* or *zeroes*.

6. Most nouns ending in **i** form their plurals by adding **-s**: *alibi, alibis; rabbi, rabbis; ski, skis*.

Note: A few nouns add either **-s** or **-es**: *alkalis* or *alkalies; taxis* or *taxies*.

7. a. A few nouns undergo a change in the stem exhibiting a different medial vowel: *foot, feet; goose; geese; louse, lice; man, men; mouse, mice; tooth, teeth; woman, women*.

Note: Compounds in which one of these nouns is the final element form their plurals in the same way: *clubfoot, clubfeet; mailman, mailmen; dormouse, dormice; bucktooth, buckteeth; Englishwoman, Englishwomen;* but, *mongoose, mongooses*. Many words ending in **-man** are not compounds: *German, talisman, ottoman*, etc. These words form their plurals by adding **-s**: *Germans, talismans, ottomans*.

b. Only three nouns have plurals ending in **-en**: *ox, oxen; child, children; brother, brothers* (of the same parents), or *brethren* (a fellow member of a society, order, etc.).

8. Many nouns derived from a foreign language retain their foreign plurals, for example:

From Latin: *alumnus, alumni; bacillus, bacilli; genus, genera; series, series; species, species.*

From Greek: *analysis, analyses; basis, bases; crisis, crises; criterion, criteria or criterions; phenomenon, phenomena or phenomenons.*

From French: *adieu, adieux or adieus; beau, beaux or beaus; madame, mesdames.*

Miscellaneous: *paparazzo, papparazzi* (Italian); *cherub, cherubim* (Hebrew).

Many words of this class also have a regular **-s** or **-es** English plural that is often preferred; however, a foreign plural often signals a difference in meaning, for example: *antenna, antennas* (radio antennas) or *antennae* (the antennae of an insect).

9. a. Compounds written as a single word form their plurals like any other word of the same ending: *clothesbrush, clothesbrushes; dishcloth, dishcloths; housewife, housewives; mailman, mailmen; manhunt, manhunts.*

b. Sometimes both parts of the compound are made plural: *manservant, menservants.* This occurrence, however, is somewhat rare.

c. Compounds ending in **-ful** normally form their plurals by adding **-s** at the end: *cupful, cupfuls; handful, handfuls; tablespoonful, tablespoonfuls.*

d. Compounds words, written with or without a hyphen, that consist of a noun followed by an adjective or other qualifying expression form their plurals by making the same change in the noun as when the noun stands alone: *aide-de-camp, aides-de-camp; attorney-general, attorneys-general; court-martial, courts-martial; daughter-in-law, daughters-in-law; hanger-on, hangers-on; heir apparent, heirs apparent.*

10. Some nouns, mainly names of birds, fishes, and mammals, have the same form in the plural as in the singular: *deer, grouse, moose, swine, trout.* But some of these words, as well as a few others that ordinarily have no plural, as *coffee, flour,* *wheat,* have a plural differing from the singular (by adding **-s, -es, -ies, -ves,** etc.) to denote different varieties or species or kinds. In such cases the unchanged plural denotes that the idea is collective or is the form commonly used in the language of sportsmen: *deer, deer* or *deers; fish, fish* or *fishes; trout, trout* or *trouts.*

11. **a.** Many names of tribes, peoples, etc., have the same form in the plural as in the singular: *Iroquois; Sioux.*
    b. Similarly certain names of peoples, city inhabitants, etc., ending in **-ese** have the same form in the plural as in the singular: *Cantonese, Milanese, Portuguese, Siamese.*

12. Nouns ending in **-ics** are construed as singular when the word denotes a subject or a scientific study or treatise. They are construed as plural when the word denotes matters of practice, activities, or qualities.
    Mathematics is his chief interest but *The mathematics of the tax proposal were all wrong.*
    "Strategy wins wars, tactics wins battles" but *The union's tactics were discrediting the industry.*
    Acoustics is a difficult subject for the layman but *The acoustics of this room are excellent.*

13. Some nouns are rarely or never construed as singular: *cattle, clothes, scissors, pants, trousers.*

14. **a.** Plurals of letters, symbols, and numbers, and abbreviations are normally formed by adding an apostrophe and **s ('s):** *A's; ABC's; 2's; -'s; GI's; +'s*
    b. The plural of a word regarded as a word is indicated by an apostrophe and an **s ('s):** no *if's, and's,* or *but's.*
    Note: All entries in *The Word Book* will show plurals wherever needed.

A SOUND MAP FOR POOR SPELLERS

How can you look up a word to check its spelling when you have to know how to spell it in order to look it up? Most spelling difficulties are caused by speech sounds that can be spelled in more than one way since, as we noted in the section "Guide to Spelling," the standard alphabet has twenty-six characters to represent the forty or more sounds of the English language. The following chart, although far from comprehensive will translate sounds into their most common spellings. If you look up a word and cannot find it check the sound map and try another combination of letters that represent the same sound.

Sound	Spelling	In These Sample Words	Sound	Spelling	In These Sample Words
a (as in pat)	ai	plaid		ti	question
	al	half		tu	denture
	au	laugh	d (as in deed)	dd	muddle
				ed	mailed
a (as in mane)	ai	plain	e (as in pet)	a	any
	ao	gaol		ae	aesthetic
	au	gauge		ai	said
	ay	pay		ay	says
	e	suede, bouquet		ea	thread
	ea	break		ei	heifer
	ei	vein			

Sound	Spelling	Examples	Sound	Spelling	Examples
	eig	**feign**		eo	leopard
	eigh	**eight, neighbor**		ie	friendly
	ey	**fey**		oe	**Oedipus**
a (as in care)	ae	**aerial**		u	burial
	ai	**air**	e (as in be)	ae	Caesar
	ay	prayer, **Ayrshire**		ay	quay
	e	there		ea	**each, beach**
	ea	pear		ee	beet
	ei	**Eire**		ei	conceit
a (as in father)	ah	**ah**		eo	**people**
	al	balm		ey	key
	e	sergeant		i	piano
	ea	heart		ie	siege
b (as in bib)	bb	blubber		oe	phoenix
	bh	**bhang**	f (as in fife)	ff	stiff
	pb	**cupboard**, raspberry		gh	enough
ch (as in church)	c	cello		lf	half
	Cz	**Czech**		ph	**photo, graph**
	tch	latch	g (as in gag)	gg	bragged
				gh	**ghost**
				gu	**guest**
				gue	**epilogue**

Sound	Spelling	In These Sample Words
h (as in hat)	wh	who
	g	Gila monster
	j	Jerez
i (as in pit)	a	village, climate, certificate
	e	enough
	ee	been
	ia	carriage
	ie	sieve
	o	women
	u	busy
	ui	built
	y	nymph
i (as in pie)	ai	aisle
	ay	aye, bayou
	ei	height
	ey	eye
	ie	lie

Sound	Spelling	In These Sample Words
	cu	biscuit
	lk	talk
	q	Aqaba
	qu	quay
kw (as in quick)	que	claque, plaque
	ch	choir
	cqu	acquire
l (as in lid)	ll	tall, llama, Lloyd
	lh	Lhasa
m (as in mum)	chm	drachm
	gm	paradigm
	lm	balm
	mb	plumb
	mm	hammer
	mn	solemn
n (as in no)	gn	gnat
	kn	knife

Spelling	Sound	Example
igh	i (as in pier)	sigh, right
is		island
uy		buy
y		sky
ye		rye
e		here
ea		ear
ee		beer
ei		weird
d	j (as in jar)	gradual
dg		lodging, dodge
di		soldier
dj		adjective
g		register, gem
ge		vengeance
gg		exaggerate
c	k (as in kick)	call, ecstasy
cc		account
ch		chaos, schedule
ck		crack
cqu		lacquer

Spelling	Sound	Example
mm		mnemonic
mn		canny, inn
pn		pneumonia
n	ng (as in thing)	ink, anchor, congress, uncle
ngue		tongue
a	ɔ (as in pot)	waffle, watch, water, what
ho		honest
ou		trough
au	o (as in no)	hautboy, mauve
eau		bureau, beau
eo		yeoman
ew		sew
oa		foam, foal
oe		Joe
oh		oh
oo		brooch
ou		shoulder
ough		dough, borough
ow		low, row
owe		owe, Marlowe

Sound	Spelling	In These Sample Words
o (as in paw or for)	a	all, water
	al	talk
	ah	Utah
	ar	warm
	as	Arkansas
	au	caught, gaunt, automobile
	aw	awful, awe, Choctaw
	oa	oar, broad
	ough	bought, thought
oi (as in noise)	oy	boy
ou (as in out)	au	sauerkraut
	aue	sauerbraten
	hou	hour
	ough	bough
	ow	sow, scowl

Sound	Spelling	In These Sample Words
sh (as in ship)	sch	schism
	ss	pass
	ce	oceanic
	ch	chandelier
	ci	special, deficient, gracious, magician
	psh	pshaw
	s	sugar
	sc	conscience
	sch	schist
	se	nauseous
	si	pension
	ss	tissue, mission
	ti	election, nation
t (as in tie)	ed	stopped
	ght	caught
	pt	ptisan
	th	Thomas
	tt	letter
	tw	two

Sound			Sound		
oo (as in took)	o	woman, wolf	u (as in cut)	o	son, income
	ou	should		oe	does
	u	full, cushion		oo	blood
				ou	couple, trouble
oo (as in boot)	eu	maneuver	yoo (as in use)	eau	beautiful
	ew	shrew		eu	feud
	ieu	lieutenant		eue	queue
	o	do, move, two		ew	pew
	oe	canoe		ieu	adieu
	ou	soup, group		iew	view
	ough	through		ue	cue
	u	rude		ui	suit
	ue	blue, flue		you	you
	ui	fruit, bruise		yu	yule
p (as in pop)	pp	happy			
r (as in roar)	rh	rhythm	u (as in fur)	ear	earn, learn
	rr	cherry		er	herd, fern, term
	wr	write		eur	restaurateur
				ir	bird, first
				or	work, word
				our	journey, journal, scourge
s (as in say)	c	cellar, cent		yr	myrtle
	ce	sauce			
	ps	psalm			
	sc	scene, abscess,			

Sound	Spelling	In These Sample Words	*A, e, i, o,* or *u*
v (as in **valve**)	f	o**f**	These vowels are often represented in phonetic transcriptions by a symbol called the schwa (ə). The schwa is used to represent the indeterminate vowel sound in many unstressed syllables. It receives the weakest level of stress within a word and thus varies in sound from word to word. The **a** in **about**, the **e** in **item**, the **i** in **edible**, the **o** in **gallop**, and the **u** in **circus** are all pronounced with the schwa sound. Here are some frequently misspelled words that contain syllables with the schwa sound. If you look up such a word and fail to find it, try another vowel:
	ph	Ste**ph**en	
w (as in **with**)	o	**o**ne	
y (as in **yes**)	i	on**i**on	
	j	halle**lu**jah	
z (as in **zebra**)	cz	**cz**ar	absence definite exaggerate humorous privilege correspondence desperate grammar prejudice separate
	s	ri**s**e; her**s**	
	ss	de**ss**ert	
	x	**x**ylophone	
	zz	fu**zz**	
zh	ge	gara**ge**, mira**ge**	
	s	plea**s**ure, vi**s**ion	

Note: The letter **x** spells six sounds in English: ks, as in box, exit; gz, as in exact, exist; sh, as in anxious; gzh, as in luxurious; ksh (a variant of gzh), also as in luxurious, luxury; and z, as in anxiety, Xerox.

GUIDE TO SPELLING

The complexities and frustrating inconsistencies of Modern English spelling have been produced by a variety of causes. Three major factors have been: (1) The lack of consistency shown by older scribers, printers, and writers who did not always spell the same sound in the same way, or, for that matter, the same word in the same way. (2) The extensive sound shifts that took place since the spelling of English became fairly established about the year 1500, shortly after the introduction of printing. (3) The fact that the standard alphabet of twenty-six characters adopted by printers and writers did not provide one character, and one only, for each of the forty or more separate sounds of the English language.

Moreover, since the English vocabulary contains thousands of words borrowed from foreign languages, and in some cases these borrowings have retained their original spelling and pronunciation, it is difficult to formulate a set of rules that will cover the spelling of all English words. Many spelling difficulties arise in connection with suffixes, and the seven basic rules given here are intended as an aid in learning and understanding the correct spelling of a vast number of English words.

SEVEN BASIC RULES OF SPELLING

First rule: *Adding a suffix to a one-syllable word.* Words of one syllable that end in a single consonant preceded by a single vowel double the final consonant before a suffix beginning with a vowel:

bag	+	-age	=	baggage	red	+	-er	=	redder
hop	+	-er	=	hopper	run	+	-ing	=	running
hot	+	-est	=	hottest	stop	+	-ed	=	stopped

Exceptions: bus, buses or busses, busing or bussing; derivatives of the word gas (gasses or gases, gassing, gassy, but gasoline, gasiform, gasify).

Note: This rule does not apply if a word ends with two or more
consonants or if it ends with one consonant preceded by
two or more vowels instead of one:

debt	+ -or	= debtor	mail	+ -ed	= mailed
lick	+ -ing	= licking	sweet	+ -est	= sweetest

Second rule: *Adding a suffix to a word with two or more syllables.*
Words of two or more syllables that have the accent on the last
syllable and end in a single consonant preceded by a single vowel
double the final consonant before a suffix beginning with a vowel:

admit	+ -ed	= admitted	control	+ -er	= controller
confer	+ -ing	= conferring	regret	+ -able	= regrettable

> *Exceptions:* (a) *chagrin, chagrined; transfer, transferable,
> transference,* but *transferred, transferring.*
> (b) When the accent shifts to the first syllable of the
> word after the suffix is added, the final consonant is
> not doubled: *prefer + -ence = preference; refer +
> -ence = reference*

Note: This rule does not apply:
(1) If the word ends with two consonants or if the final consonant
is preceded by more than one vowel:

perform	+ -ance	= performance
repeal	+ -ing	= repealing

(2) If the word is accented on any syllable except the last:

benefit	+ -ed	= benefited	kidnap + -er	= kidnaper

> *Exceptions:* Some words like *cobweb, handicap, outfit,* follow
> the models of *web, cap, fit,* even though these
> words may not be true compounds. A few others
> ending in **g** double the final **g** so that it will not be
> pronounced like **j**: *humbug, humbugged; zigzag,
> zigzagged.*

Third rule: *Adding a suffix beginning with a vowel to a word ending in a silent e.* Words ending with a silent **e** usually drop the **e** before a suffix beginning with a vowel:

agitate	+ -ion	= agitation		glide	+ -ing	= gliding
force	+ -ible	= forcible		operate	+ -or	= operator

Exceptions: Here the exceptions are many:

(a) When the suffix being added begins with **-e,** the final **e** is not doubled:

route	+ -ed	= routed		trifle	+ -er	= trifler

(b) Many words of this type have alternative forms. In *The Word Book* the preferred form is always shown first.

blue	+ -ish	= bluish or blueish
move	+ -able	= movable or moveable

Note: In certain cases, alternative forms have different meanings. Thus: line + *-age* = linage or *lineage* (number of lines), but *lineage* (the only form for "ancestry").

(c) Words ending in **-ce** or **-ge** keep the **e** before the suffixes **-able** and **-ous.**

advantage	+ -ous	= advantageous
change	+ -able	= changeable
trace	+ -able	= traceable

(d) Words ending in a silent **e** keep the **e** if the word could be mistaken for another word:

dye	+ -ing	= dyeing		singe	+ -ing	= singeing

(e) If the word ends in **-ie,** the **e** is dropped and the **i** changed to **y** before the suffix **-ing.** (This is done to prevent two *i*'s from coming together):

die	+ -ing	= dying		lie	+ -ing	= lying

(f) *Mile* and *acre* do not drop the **e** before the suffix **-age.** Thus, *mileage* and *acreage. Enforce* retains the **e** before the suffix **-able:** *enforceable.*

Fourth rule: *Adding a suffix with a consonant to a word ending in a silent e.* Words ending with a silent **e** generally retain the **e** before a suffix that begins with a consonant, such as **-ful, -less, -ment, -some, -ty,** etc.:

plate	+ -ful	=	plateful
shoe	+ -less	=	shoeless
arrange	+ -ment	=	arrangement
awe	+ -some	=	awesome
nice	+ -ty	=	nicety

Exceptions: There are many exceptions to this rule. Some of the most common are: *abridge, abridgment; acknowledge, acknowledgment; argue, argument; awe, awful; due, duly; judge, judgment; nine, ninth; true, truly; whole, wholly; wise, wisdom.*

Fifth rule: *Adding a suffix to a word ending in y.*
1. Words ending in **y** preceded by a consonant generally change the **y** to **i** before the addition of a suffix, except a suffix that begins with an **i:**

accompany	+ -ment	=	accompaniment
beauty	+ -ful	=	beautiful

Note: (1) Adjectives of one syllable ending in **y** usually retain the **y** when a suffix is added: *sly, slyly; shy, shyness, wry, wryly.* But, *dry, drier, driest, dryly* or *drily, dryness.*
(2) The **y** is retained in derivatives of *baby, city,* and *lady* and before the suffixes **-ship** and **-like:** *babyhood, citylike, cityward, ladyship, ladylike.*

(3) Some words drop the final **y** before the addition of the suffix **-eous**: *beauty* + *-eous* = *beauteous*.

2. Words ending in **y** preceded by a vowel usually retain the **y** before a suffix:

buy   + -er   = buyer   key   + -less = keyless

Exceptions: day, daily; gay, gaily, gaiety.

Sixth rule: *Adding a suffix to a word ending in c.* Words ending in **c** almost always have the letter **k** inserted after the **c** when a suffix beginning with **e, i,** or **y** is added. This is done so that the letter **c** will not be pronounced like **s**.

panic   + -y   = panicky
picnic   + -er   = picnicker

Seventh rule: *The "ie" or "ei" syndrome.*
1. (a) **I** comes before **e** when the two letters have a long **e** sound (as in *feet*), except after **c**: *believe, grieve, niece, siege, shield, mischievous.*
   Exceptions: either, leisure, neither, plebeian, seize, sheik.
   (b) After **c**, **e** comes before **i**: *ceiling, conceit, deceive, perceive, receive, receipt.*
   Exceptions: ancient, financier, specie.
2. **E** comes before **i** when **ei** has the sound **a** (as in *cake*), **e** (as in *pet*), **i** (as in *fit*), or **i** (as in *mine*): *Fahrenheit, foreign, forfeit, height, neighbor, sleight, sovereign, surfeit.*
   Exceptions: friend, handkerchief, mischief, sieve.
   Note: Many words spelled with **ie** or **ei** present no difficulties because the vowels are pronounced separately: *deity, piety, science.* Others, however, do not follow the rules outlined above: *soldier, view, weir, weird.* In such cases, *The Word Book* (see, in particular, the sound map starting on page 342) or *The American Heritage Dictionary* will help you spell the word correctly.

PROOFREADERS' MARKS

Instruction	Mark in Margin	Mark in Type	Instruction	Mark in Margin	Mark in Type
Delete	ℓ	the ~~good~~ word	colon	⊙	The following words∧
Insert indicated material	good	the∧word	semicolon	∧	Scan the words;skim the words.
Let it stand	stet	the good word	apostrophe	∜∜	John∧s words
Make capital	cap	the∧word	quotation marks	∜/∜	the word word
Make lower case	lc	the Word	parentheses	(/)	The word word is in parentheses.
Set in small capitals	sc	See word.	brackets	⊏/⊐/	He read from the Word the Bible.
Set in italic type	ital	The word is word.	en dash	N	1964 1972
Set in roman type	rom	the (word)	em dash	M	The dictionary,how often it is needed belongs in every home.
Set in boldface type	bf	the entry word	Start paragraph	¶	"Where is it?" "It's on the shelf."
Set in lightface type	lf	the entry (word)	Move left	⊏	⊏ the word
Transpose	tr	the word/good	Move right	⊐	⊐ the word
Close up space	⌢	the wo rd	Align	‖	‖ the word ‖ the word
Delete and close up space		the wo∂rd	Wrong font	wf	the word
Spell out	sp	(2) words	Broken type	X	the word
Insert: space	#	the∧word			
period	⊙	This is the word∧			
comma	∧	words∧words, words			
hyphen	=/=/=	word∧for∧word test			

A 1. ammeter. **2.** Also **a., A.** acre. **3.** ampere. **4.** area.

a. 1. acceleration. **2.** adjective. **3.** answer. **4.** Also **A.** are (measurement).

A. 1. alto. **2.** America; American.

A.A. Associate in Arts.

A.B. Bachelor of Arts.

abbr., abbrev. abbreviation.

abr. 1. abridge. **2.** abridgment.

acad. 1. academic. **2.** academy.

acct. account.

ack. 1. acknowledge. **2.** acknowledgment.

A.D. anno Domini (usually small capitals A.D.).

add. 1. addition. **2.** additional. **3.** address.

adj. 1. adjacent. **2.** adjective. **3.** adjourned. **4.** adjunct.

ad loc. to (or at) the place (Latin *ad locum*).

admin. administration.

adv. 1. adverb. **2.** adverbial.

adv., advt. advertisement.

A.F., AF 1. air force. **2.** Anglo-French. **3.** audio frequency.

AFL-CIO, A.F.L.-C.I.O. American Federation of Labor and Congress of Industrial Organizations.

agr. 1. agriculture. **2.** agricultural.

agt. 1. agent. **2.** agreement.

AK Alaska (with Zip Code).

AL Alabama (with Zip Code).

Alta. Alberta.

a.m. Also **A.M.** ante meridiem (usually small capitals A.M.)

Am., Amer. 1. America. **2.** American.

amt. amount.

anal. 1. analogy. **2.** analysis. **3.** analytic.

ans. answer.

appt. 1. appoint. **2.** appointed.

approx. 1. approximate. **2.** approximately.

Apr. April.

AR 1. account receivable. **2.** Arkansas (with Zip Code).

assoc. 1. associate. **2.** Also **assn.** association.

asst. assistant.

attn. attention.

atty., at., att. attorney.

Aug. August.

av., ave., avenue.

avg., av. average.

AZ Arizona (with Zip Code).

b., B. 1. base. **2.** bay. **3.** book.

B. 1. bachelor. **2.** Baume scale. **3.** British. **4.** Bible.

B.A. Bachelor of Arts.

bal. balance.

bar. 1. barometer. **2.** barometric. **3.** barrel.

B.B.A. Bachelor of Business Administration.

B.C. 1. before Christ (usually small capitals B.C.). **2.** British Columbia.

bd. 1. board. **2.** bond. **3.** bookbinding. **4.** bound.

B.D. 1. bank draft. **2.** bills discounted.

bdl. bundle.

B/E 1. bill of entry. **2.** bill of exchange.

bet. between.

bf, bf., b.f. boldface.

B/F *Accounting.* brought forward.

bg. bag.

Bib. 1. Bible **2.** Biblical.

bibliog. 1. bibliographer. **2.** bibliography.

biog. 1. biographer. **2.** biographical. **3.** biography.

biol. 1. biological. **2.** biologist. **3.** biology.

bk. 1. bank. **2.** book.

bkg. banking.

bkpg. bookkeeping.

bkpt. bankrupt.

bl. 1. barrel. **2.** black. **3.** blue.

B/L bill of lading.

bldg. building.

blk. 1. black. **2.** block. **3.** bulk.

blvd. boulevard.

b.o. 1. box office. **2.** branch office. **3.** buyer's option.

B/P bills payable.

br. 1. branch. **2.** brief. **3.** bronze. **4.** brother. **5.** brown.

B.S. 1. Bachelor of Science. **2.** balance sheet. **3.** bill of sale.

bu. 1. Also **Bur.** bureau. **2.** bushel.

bull. bulletin.

bus. business.

bx. box.

c 1. carat. **2.** centi-. **3.** cubic.

C 1. Celsius. **2.** centigrade.

c., C. 1. cape. **2.** cent. **3.** century. **4.** Also **chap.** chapter. **5.** Also **ca** circa. **6.** copy. **7.** copyright.

CA California (with Zip Code).

cal. 1. calendar. **2.** caliber.

canc. cancel.

C.B.D. cash before delivery.

cc cubic centimeter.

cc. chapters.

c.c., C.C. carbon copy.

c.d. cash discount.

C.D. civil defense.

Cdr., Cmdr., Comdr. commander.

cert. 1. certificate. **2.** certification. **3.** certified.

cf., cp. compare.

c.f.i., C.F.I. cost, freight, and insurance.

char. charter.

chg. charge.

cit. 1. citation. **2.** cited. **3.** citizen.

C.J. 1. chief justice. **2.** corpus juris.

ck. check.

cl. 1. class. **2.** classification. **3.** clause. **4.** clearance. **5.** Also **clk.** clerk.

cm. centimeter.

cml. commercial.

C/N credit note.

CO Colorado (with Zip Code).

co. 1. Also **Co.** company. **2.** county.

c.o. 1. Also **c/o** care of. **2.** *Accounting.* carried over. **3.** cash order.

COD, C.O.D. 1. cash on delivery. **2.** collect on delivery.

col. 1. collect. **2.** collected. **3.** collector. **4.** college. **5.** collegiate. **6.** column.

Com. 1. commission. **2.** commissioner.

comm. 1. commission. **2.** commissioner. **3.** commerce. **4.** communication.

con. 1. *Law:* conclusion. **2.** consolidate. **3.** consolidated.

cons. 1. consignment. **2.** construction. **3.** constitution.

Const. 1. constable. **2.** constitution.

cont. 1. contents. **2.** continue. **3.** continued. **4.** control.

contr. contract.

coop. cooperative.

corp. corporation.

cos, c.o.s. cash on shipment.

C.P.A. certified public accountant.

cpd. compound.

cr. credit.

CST, C.S.T. Central Standard Time.

CT Connecticut (with Zip Code).

CT, C.T. Central Time.

ct. 1. Also **c., C.,** cent. **2.** court.

ctn. carton.

ctr. center.

cu. Also **c** cubic.

cur. currency.

c.w.o. 1. cash with order. **2.** chief warrant officer.

cwt. hundredweight.

CZ Canal Zone (with Zip Code).

d. 1. day. **2.** deci-.

d. 1. date. **2.** daughter. **3.** died. **4.** Also **D.** dose.

D. 1. December. **2.** Also **D.** democrat; democratic. **3.** doctor (in academic degrees).

D.A. district attorney.

dB decibel.

D.B. daybook.

d.b.a. doing business as.

dbl. double.

DC District of Columbia (with Zip Code).

D.D.S. Doctor of Dental Science.

DE Delaware (with Zip Code).

deb. debenture.

dec. 1. deceased. **2.** decrease.

Dec. December.

def. 1. definite. **2.** definition.

deg, deg. degree (thermometric).

del. 1. delegate. **2.** delegation. **3.** delete.

Dem. Democrat.

dep. 1. depart. **2.** departure. **3.** deposit. **4.** deputy.

dept. department.

dia. diameter.

dim. dimension.

dir. director.

disc. discount.

div. 1. divided. 2. division. 3. dividend.

dlvy. delivery.

do. ditto.

dol. dollar.

doz. dozen.

dr. 1. debit. 2. debtor.

DST, D.S.T. daylight-saving time.

dup. duplicate.

e 1. electron. 2. Also **E, e., E.,** east; eastern.

E Earth.

E. 1. Also **e.,** engineer; engineering. 2. Also **E** English.

ea. each.

econ. 1. economics. 2. economist. 3. economy.

ed. 1. edition. 2. editor.

EDT, E.D.T. Eastern Daylight Time.

educ. 1. education. 2. educational.

e.g. for example (Latin *exempli gratia*).

elec. 1. electric. 2. electrical. 3. electricity.

enc., encl. 1. enclosed. 2. enclosure.

eng., engr. Also **e., E.,** engineer.

esp. especially.

Esq. Esquire (title).

est. 1. established. 2. *Law.* estate. 3. estimate.

EST, E.S.T. Eastern Standard Time.

ET, E.T. Eastern Time.

et al. and others (Latin *et alii*).

etc. and so forth (Latin *et cetera*).

Eur. 1. Europe. 2. European.

ex. 1. example. 2. Also **exch.** exchange. 3. Also **exam.** examination.

exec. 1. executive. 2. executor.

exp. 1. expenses. 2. export. 3. express.

f. 1. Also **f, F., F** female. 2. Also **F.** folio.

F Fahrenheit.

F.B. freight bill.

FBI, F.B.I. Federal Bureau of Investigation.

Feb. February.

fed. 1. federal. 2. federated. 3. federation.

FL Florida (with Zip Code).

fl oz fluid ounce.

fm frequency modulation.

F.O.B., f.o.b. free on board.

fol. 1. folio. 2. following.

fpm, f.p.m. feet per minute.

fr. 1. franc. 2. from. 3. Also **freq.** frequently.

Fri. Friday.

frt. freight.

ft foot.

fut. future.

fwd. forward.

g 1. gravity. 2. gram.

GA Georgia (with Zip Code).

gal. gallon.

GAW guaranteed annual wage.

gds. goods.

gen., genl. general.

geog. 1. geographer. 2. geographic. 3. geography.

geol. 1. geologic. 2. geologist. 3. geology.

geom. 1. geometric. 2. geometry.

gm gram.

GNP gross national product.

gov., Gov. governor.

govt. government.

G.P. general practitioner.

gr. 1. grade. 2. gross. 3. group.

grad. 1. graduate. 2. graduated.

GU Guam (with Zip Code).

guar., gtd. guaranteed.

h hour.

h. Also **H.,** height.

ha hectare.

hdqrs. headquarters.

hf high frequency.

HI Hawaii (with Zip Code).

ho. house.

Hon. 1. Honorable (title). 2. Also **hon.** honorary.

hor. horizontal.

hosp. hospital.

hp horsepower.

hr hour.

h.s., H.S. high school.

ht height.

hyp., hypoth. hypothesis.

i., I., 1. island. 2. isle.

Is., is. island.

IA Iowa (with Zip Code).

ib., ibid. in the same place (Latin *ibidem*).

ID Idaho (with Zip Code).

I.D. 1. identification. 2.

intelligence department.

i.e. that is (Latin *id est*).

IF, i.f. intermediate frequency.

IL Illinois (with Zip Code).

IN Indiana (with Zip Code).

in. inch.

inc. 1. income. **2.** Also **Inc.** incorporated. **3.** increase.

ins. inspector.

inst. 1. instant. **2.** institute. **3.** institution. **4.** instrument.

int. 1. interest. **2.** interior. **3.** interval. **4.** international.

intr. *Grammar.* intransitive.

inv. 1. invention. **2.** invoice.

IQ, I.Q. intelligence quotient.

IRS Internal Revenue Service.

ital. italic.

J joule.

J. 1. journal. **2.** judge. **3.** justice.

J.A. 1. joint account. **2.** judge advocate.

Jan. January.

jct., junc. junction.

J.D. Doctor of Laws.

jour. 1. journal. **2.** journalist. **3.** journeyman.

J.P. justice of the peace.

jr., Jr. junior.

k 1. karat. **2.** kilo.

K 1. Kelvin (temperature unit). **2.** Kelvin (temperature scale).

kc kilocycle.

kg kilogram.

km kilometer.

KS Kansas (with Zip Code).

kW kilowatt.

KY Kentucky (with Zip Code).

l liter.

l. 1. Also **L.** lake. **2.** left. **3.** length. **4.** line.

LA Louisiana (with Zip Code).

lab. laboratory.

lat. latitude.

Lat. Also **L.** Latin.

lb pound.

l.c. lower-case.

L/C letter of credit.

l.c.d. lowest common denominator.

leg., legis. 1. legislation. **2.** legislative. **3.** legislature.

lf 1. *Printing.* lightface. **2.** low frequency.

lg., lge. large.

lib. 1. liberal. **2.** librarian. **3.** library.

lit. 1. literary. **2.** literature.

LL.B. Bachelor of Laws.

LL.D. Doctor of Laws.

loc. cit. in the place cited (Latin *loco citato*).

log logarithm.

long. longitude.

ltd., Ltd. limited.

m 1. Also **M, m., M.** male; medium. **2.** meter.

m. mile.

MA Massachusetts (with Zip Code).

M.A. Master of Arts.

Man. Manitoba.

Mar. March.

masc. masculine.

math. 1. mathematical. **2.** mathematician. **3.** mathematics.

max. maximum.

M.B.A. Master of Business Administration.

Mc megacycle.

m.c. master of ceremonies.

MD Maryland (with Zip Code).

M.D. Doctor of Medicine.

mdse. merchandise.

ME Maine (with Zip Code).

M.E. 1. mechanical engineer. **2.** mechanical engineering. **3.** Middle English.

meas. 1. measurable. **2.** measure.

mech. 1. mechanical. **2.** mechanics. **3.** mechanism.

med. 1. medical. **2.** medieval. **3.** medium.

M.Ed. Master of Education.

mem. 1. member. **2.** memoir. **3.** memorandum. **4.** memorial.

Messrs. 1. Messieurs. **2.** Plural of **Mr.**

mfg. 1. manufacture. **2.** manufactured. **3.** manufacturing.

mfr. 1. manufacture. **2.** manufacturer.

MI Michigan (with Zip Code).

mi. 1. mile. **2.** mill (monetary unit).

min minute (unit of time).

min. minimum.

misc. miscellaneous.

mkt. market.

ml milliliter.

mm millimeter.

MN Minnesota (with Zip Code).

MO Missouri (with Zip Code).

mo. month.

m.o., M.O. 1. mail order. **2.** medical officer. **3.** money order.

mol. 1. molecular. **2.** molecule.

mon. monetary.

Mon. Monday.

mpg, m.p.g. miles per gallon.

mph, m.p.h. miles per hour.

Mr. Mister.

Mrs. mistress.

ms 1. manuscript. **2.** millisecond.

MS 1. manuscript. **2.** Mississippi (with Zip Code). **3.** multiple sclerosis.

Ms., Ms Title of courtesy for a woman.

msg. message.

MST, M.S.T. Mountain Standard Time.

MT Montana (with Zip Code).

mt., Mt. 1. mount. **2.** mountain.

m.t., M.T. metric ton.

MT, M.T. Mountain Time.

mtg. 1. meeting. **2.** Also **mtge.** mortgage.

mtn. mountain.

mun. 1. municipal. **2.** municipality.

mus. 1. museum. **2.** music. **3.** musical. **4.** musician.

N Also **n, n., n.** north; northern.

n. 1. net. **2.** noun. **3.** number.

N. 1. Norse. **2.** November.

N.A. North America.

nat. 1. Also **natl.** national. **2.** native. **3.** natural.

nav. 1. naval. **2.** navigation.

n.b. note carefully (Latin *nota bene*).

N.B. New Brunswick.

NC North Carolina (with Zip Code).

NCO noncommissioned officer.

ND North Dakota (with Zip Code).

NE 1. Nebraska (with Zip Code). **2.** northeast.

N.E. New England.

neg. negative.

Nfld. Newfoundland.

NH New Hampshire (with Zip Code).

NJ New Jersey (with Zip Code).

NM New Mexico (with Zip Code).

no., No. 1. north. **2.** northern. **3.** number.

nos., Nos. numbers.

Nov. November.

N.P. notary public.

N.S. Nova Scotia.

NV Nevada (with Zip Code).

NW northwest.

N.W.T. Northwest Territories.

NY New York (with Zip Code).

O 1. Also **O.** ocean. **2.** Also **O.** order.

obj. 1. *Grammar.* object; objective. **2.** objection.

obs. 1. obscure. **2.** observation. **3.** Also **Obs.** observatory. **4.** obsolete.

Oct. October.

O.D. 1. Doctor of Optometry. **2.** overdraft. **3.** overdrawn.

OH Ohio (with Zip Code).

OK Oklahoma (with Zip Code).

Ont. Ontario.

OR Oregon (with Zip Code).

org. 1. organic. **2.** organization. **3.** organized.

o.s., o/s out of stock.

oz ounce.

p. 1. page. **2.** participle. **3.** per. **4.** pint. **5.** population. **6.** Also **P.** president

PA 1. Pennsylvania (with Zip Code). **2.** public-address system.

P.A. 1. Also **P/A** power of attorney. **2.** press agent. **3.** prosecuting attorney.

Pac. Pacific.

par. 1. paragraph. **2.** parallel. **3.** parenthesis. **4.** parish.

pat. patent.

P.A.Y.E. 1. pay as you earn. **2.** pay as you enter.

payt. Also **p.t.** payment.

P.B. 1. passbook. **2.** prayer book.

p.c. Also **pct.** per cent.

p/c, P/C 1. Also **p.c.** petty cash. **2.** prices current.

pd. paid.

P.E.I. Prince Edward Island.

pf. preferred.

Pfc, Pfc. private first class.

phar., Phar., pharm., Pharm., 1. pharmaceutical. 2. pharmacist. 3. pharmacy.

phi., philos. 1. philosopher. 2. philosophical. 3. philosophy.

phr. phrase.

pk. 1. pack. 2. park. 3. peak. 4. Also **pk** peck.

pkg., pkge. package.

pl. 1. platform. 2. platoon.

plf. plaintiff.

pm., prem. premium.

p.m. 1. post mortem. 2. Also **P.M.** postmortem examination. 3. Also **P.M.** post meridiem (usually small capitals P.M.).

P.M. 1. past master. 2. Also **PM** postmaster. 3. prime minister. 4. provost marshal.

P.M.G. postmaster general.

p.n., P/N promissory note.

P.O. 1. Personnel Officer. 2. Also **p.o.** petty officer; post office. 3. postal order.

P.O.E. port of entry.

poet. 1. poetic. 2. poetical. 3. poetry.

pol. 1. Also **polit.** political. 2. politician. 3. Also **polit.** politics.

pos. 1. position. 2. positive.

poss. 1. possession. 2. possessive. 3. possible. 4. possibly.

pot. potential.

POW, P.O.W. prisoner of war.

pp. 1. pages. 2. past participle.

p.p., P.P. 1. parcel post. 2. parish priest. 3. past participle. 4. postpaid.

ppd. 1. postpaid. 2. prepaid.

pr. 1. pair. 2. present. 3. price. 4. printing. 5. pronoun.

PR 1. Also **P.R.** public relations. 2. Puerto Rico (with Zip Code).

Pr. 1. priest. 2. prince.

pref. 1. preface. 2. prefatory. 3. preference. 4. preferred. 5. prefix.

prep. 1. preparation. 2. preparatory. 3. prepare. 4. preposition.

pres. 1. present (time). 2. Also **Pres.** president.

prim. 1. primary. 2. primitive.

prin. 1. principal. 2. principle.

prob. 1. probable. 2. probably. 3. problem.

prof., Prof. professor.

pron. 1. pronominal. 2. pronoun. 3. pronounced. 4. pronunciation.

prop. 1. proper. 2. properly. 3. property. 4. proposition. 5. proprietary. 6. proprietor.

pro tem., p.t. for the time being; temporarily (Latin *pro tempore*).

P.S. 1. Police Sergeant.

2. postscript. 3. public school.

PST, P.S.T. Pacific Standard Time.

pt. 1. part. 2. pint. 3. point. 4. port.

PT, P.T. Pacific Time.

P.T. physical therapy.

PTA, P.T.A. Parent-Teachers Association.

ptg. printing.

pub. 1. public. 2. publication. 3. published. 4. publisher.

pvt. Also **Pvt.** private.

q. 1. Also **qt** quart. 2. Also **qu., ques.** question.

quad. 1. quadrangle. 2. quadrant. 3. quadrilateral.

Que. Quebec.

quot. quotation.

qr. 1. quarter. 2. quarterly.

qt. 1. quantity. 2. Also **qt.** quart.

r 1. Also **R** radius. 2. *Electricity.* Also **R** resistance.

r. 1. Also **R.** railroad; railway. 2. range. 3. rare. 4. retired. 5. Also **R.** right. 6. Also **R.** river. 7. Also **R.** road. 8. rod (unit of length). 9. Also **R.** rouble.

R. 1. rabbi. 2. rector. 3. Republican (party). 4. royal.

rd. 1. road. 2. round.

RD, R.D. rural delivery.

R.E. real estate.

re concerning; in reference to; in the case of.

rec. 1. receipt. 2. recipe. 3. record. 4. recording. 5. recreation.

recd. received.

ref. 1. reference. 2. referred. 3. refining. 4. reformation. 5. reformed. 6. refunding.

reg. 1. Also **Regt.** regent. 2. regiment. 3. region. 4. Also **regd.** register; registered. 5. registrar. 6. registry. 7. regular. 8. regularly. 9. regulation. 10. regulator.

rep. 1. repair. 2. Also **rpt.** report. 3. reporter. 4. Also **Rep.** representative. 5. reprint. 6. Also **Rep.** republic.

Rep. Republican (party).

req. 1. require. 2. required. 3. requisition.

rev. 1. revenue. 2. reverse. 3. reverend. 4. review. 6. revise. 7. revision. 8. revolution. 9. revolving.

RF radio frequency.

RFD, R.F.D. rural free delivery.

RI Rhode Island (with Zip Code).

rm. 1. ream. 2. room.

r.p.m. revolutions per minute.

R.R. 1. Also **RR** railroad. 2. Also **RT. Rev.** Right Reverend (title). 3. rural route.

r.s.v.p., R.S.V.P. please reply.

s 1. second. 2. Also **S, s., S.** south; southern. 3. stere.

s. 1. son. 2. substantive. 3. shilling.

S. 1. Saturday. 2. school. 3. sea. 4. September. 5. Sunday.

S.A. 1. South Africa. 2. South America.

S.B. Bachelor of Science.

Sask. Saskatchewan.

Sat. Saturday.

SC 1. Security Council (United Nations). 2. South Carolina (with Zip Code).

sc. 1. scene. 2. scruple (weight). 3. scilicet.

s.c. *Printing.* small capitals.

S.C. Supreme Court.

sch. school.

sci. 1. science. 2. scientific.

SD South Dakota (with Zip Code).

S.D. special delivery.

SE 1. southeast. 2. southeastern.

sec. 1. Also **secy.** secretary. 2. sector. 3. second.

sen., Sen. 1. senate. 2. senator. 3. Also **sr.** senior.

Sept. September.

seq. 1. sequel. 2. the following (Latin *sequens*).

ser. 1. serial. 2. series. 3. sermon.

serv. service.

sgd. signed.

sgt. sergeant.

sh. 1. Also **shr.** share (capital stock). 2. sheet. 3. shilling.

shpt. shipment.

shtg. shortage.

sic thus; so.

sig. 1. signal. 2. signature.

sing. singular.

sm. small.

soc. 1. socialist. 2. society.

so. 1. south. 2. southern.

s.o. 1. seller's option. 2. strikeout.

soln solution.

SOP standard operating procedure.

soph. sophomore.

SOS 1. international distress signal. 2. Any call or signal for help.

sp. 1. special. 2. species. 3. spelling.

Sr. 1. senior (after surname). 2. sister (religious).

S.R.O. standing room only.

st. 1. stanza. 2. state. 3. Also **St.** statute. 4. stet. 5. stitch. 6. stone. 7. Also **St.** street. 8. strophe.

St. 1. saint. 2. strait.

sta. 1. station. 2. stationary.

std. standard.

stk. stock.

sub. 1. Also **subs.** subscription. 2. Also **subst.** substitute. 3. suburb. 4. suburban.

subj. 1. subject. 2. subjective. 3. subjunctive.

suff. 1. sufficient. 2. Also **suf.** suffix.

Sun. Sunday.

sup. 1. above (Latin *supra*). 2. Also **super.** superior. 3. *Grammar.* Also **superl.** superlative. 4. supplement. **5.** supply.

supt., Supt. Also **super.** superintendent.

surg. 1. surgeon. **2.** surgery. **3.** surgical.

SW southwest.

sym. 1. symbol. **2.** symphony.

syn. 1. synonymous. **2.** synonym. **3.** synonymy.

t 1. ton. **2.** troy.

T temperature.

t. 1. teaspoon. **2.** *Grammar.* tense. **3.** Also **T.** time. **4.** *Grammar.* transitive.

T. 1. tablespoon. **2.** territory. **3.** Testament. **4.** transit.

t.b. trial balance.

tbs., tbsp. tablespoon.

tech. technical.

technol. 1. technological. **2.** technology.

tel. 1. telegram. **2.** telegraph. **3.** telephone.

temp. 1. in the time of (Latin *tempore*). **2.** temperature. **3.** temporary.

Thurs. Thursday.

tkt. ticket.

TN Tennessee (with Zip Code).

tn. 1. town. **2.** train.

tnpk. turnpike.

t.o. turnover.

trans. 1. transaction. **2.** *Grammar.* transitive. **3.** translated. **4.** translation. **5.** translator. **6.** Also **transp.** transportation.

treas. 1. treasurer. **2.** treasury.

Tues. Tuesday.

TV television.

TX Texas (with Zip Code).

U. 1. university. **2.** upper.

uhf ultra high frequency.

UN United Nations.

univ. 1. universal. **2.** Also **Univ.** university.

USA, U.S.A. 1. United States Army. **2.** United States of America.

UT Utah (with Zip Code).

V 1. *Physics.* velocity. **2.** *Electricity.* volt. **3.** volume.

v. 1. verb. **2.** verse. **3.** version. **4.** Also **vs.** versus. **5.** vide. **6.** voice. **7.** volume (book). **8.** vowel.

V. 1. Also **v.** vice (in titles.) **2.** village.

VA 1. Also **V.A.** Veterans' Administration. **2.** Virginia (with Zip Code).

var. 1. variable. **2.** variant. **3.** variation. **4.** variety. **5.** various.

vhf, VHF very high frequency.

VI Virgin Islands (with Zip Code).

VIP *Informal.* very important person.

vol. 1. volume. **2.** volunteer.

V.P. Vice President

VT Vermont (with Zip Code).

v.v. vice versa.

w 1. width. **2.** Also **W, w., W.** west; western.

W 1. *Electricity.* watt. **2.** *Physics.* Also **w** work.

w. 1. week. **2.** width. **3.** wife. **4.** with.

W. Wednesday.

WA Washington (with Zip Code).

Wed. Wednesday.

whse., whs. warehouse.

whsle. wholesale.

WI Wisconsin (with Zip Code).

w.i. when issued (financial stock).

wk. 1. weak. **2.** week. **3.** work.

wkly. weekly.

w.o.c. without compensation.

wt. weight.

WV West Virginia (with Zip Code).

WY Wyoming (with Zip Code).

x symbol for an unknown or unnamed factor, thing, or person.

XL extra large.

Xmas *Informal.* Christmas.

y ordinate.

y. year.

YMCA Young Men's Christian Association.

yr. 1. year. **2.** younger. **3.** your.

Y.T. Yukon Territory.

YWCA Young Women's Christian Association.

Z 1. atomic number. **2.** *Electricity.* impedance.

z. 1. zero. **2.** zone.

zool. 1. zoological. **2.** zoology.

WEIGHTS AND MEASURES

Length

U.S. Customary Unit	U.S. Equivalents	Metric Equivalents
inch	0.083 foot	2.54 centimeters
foot	1/3 yard. 12 inches	0.3048 meter
yard	3 feet. 36 inches	0.9144 meter
rod	5½ yards. 16½ feet	5.0292 meters
mile (statute, land)	1,760 yards. 5,280 feet	1.609 kilometers
mile (nautical international)	1.151 statute miles	1.852 kilometers

Area

U.S. Customary Unit	U.S. Equivalents	Metric Equivalents
square inch	0.007 square foot	6.4516 square centimeters
square foot	144 square inches	929.030 square centimeters
square yard	1,296 square inches. 9 square feet	0.836 square meter
acre	43,560 square feet. 4,840 square yards	4,047 square meters
square mile	640 acres	2.590 square kilometers

Volume or Capacity

U.S. Customary Unit	U.S. Equivalents	Metric Equivalents
cubic inch	0.00058 cubic foot	16.387 cubic centimeters
cubic foot	1,728 cubic inches	0.028 cubic meter
cubic yard	27 cubic feet	0.765 cubic meter

U.S. Customary Liquid Measure	U.S. Equivalents	Metric Equivalents
fluid ounce	8 fluid drams. 1.804 cubic inches	29.573 milliliters
pint	16 fluid ounces. 28.875 cubic inches	0.473 liter
quart	2 pints. 57.75 cubic inches	0.946 liter
gallon	4 quarts. 231 cubic inches	3.785 liters
barrel	varies from 31 to 42 gallons, established by law or usage	

U.S. Customary Dry Measure	U.S. Equivalents	Metric Equivalents
pint	½ quart. 33.6 cubic inches	0.551 liter
quart	2 pints. 67.2 cubic inches	1.101 liters
peck	8 quarts. 537.605 cubic inches	8.810 liters
bushel	4 pecks. 2,150.42 cubic inches	35.238 liters

British Imperial Liquid and Dry Measure	U.S. Customary Equivalents	Metric Equivalents
fluid ounce	0.961 U.S. fluid ounce. 1.734 cubic inches	28.412 milliliters
pint	1.032 U.S. dry pints. 1.201 U.S. liquid pints. 34.678 cubic inches	568.26 milliliters
quart	1.032 U.S. dry quarts. 1.201 U.S. liquid quarts. 69.354 cubic inches	1.136 liters

gallon	1.201 U.S. gallons. 277.420 cubic inches	4.546 liters
peck	554.84 cubic inches	0.009 cubic meter
bushel	1.032 U.S. bushels. 2,219 36 cubic inches	0.036 cubic meter

Weight

U.S. Customary Unit (Avoirdupois)	U.S. Equivalents	Metric Equivalents
grain	0.036 dram. 0.002285 ounce	64.79891 milligrams
dram	27.344 grains. 0.0625 ounce	1.772 grams
ounce	16 drams. 437.5 grains	28.350 grams
pound	16 ounces. 7,000 grains	453.59237 grams
ton (short)	2,000 pounds	0.907 metric ton (1,000 kilograms)
ton (long)	1.12 short tons. 2,240 pounds	1.016 metric tons

Apothecary Weight Unit	U.S. Customary Equivalents	Metric Equivalents
scruple	20 grains	1.296 grams
dram	60 grains	3.888 grams
ounce	480 grains. 1.097 avoirdupois ounces	31.103 grams
pound	5,760 grains. 0.823 avoirdupois pound	373.242 grams

GUIDE TO THE METRIC SYSTEM

Length

Unit	Number of Meters	Approximate U.S. Equivalent
myriameter	10,000	6.2 miles
kilometer	1,000	0.62 mile
hectometer	100	109.36 yards
dekameter	10	32.81 feet
meter	1	39.37 inches
decimeter	0.1	3.94 inches
centimeter	0.01	0.39 inch
millimeter	0.001	0.04 inch

Area

Unit	Number of Square Meters	Approximate U.S. Equivalent
square kilometer	1,000,000	0.3861 square mile
hectare	10,000	2.47 acres
are	100	119.60 square yards
centare	1	10.76 square feet
square centimeter	0.0001	0.155 square inch

Volume

Unit	Number of Cubic Meters	Approximate U.S. Equivalent
dekastere	10	13.10 cubic yards
stere	1	1.31 cubic yards
decistere	0.10	3.53 cubic feet
cubic centimeter	0.000001	0.061 cubic inch

Capacity

Unit	Number of Cubic Liters	Approximate U.S. Equivalents Dry	Liquid
kiloliter	1,000	1.31 cubic yards	
hectoliter	100	3.53 cubic feet	2.84 bushels

dekaliter	10	0.35 cubic foot	1.14 pecks	2.64 gallons
liter	1	61.02 cubic inches	0.908 quart	1.057 quarts
deciliter	0.10	6.1 cubic inches	0.18 pint	0.21 pint
centiliter	0.01	0.6 cubic inch		0.338 fluidounce
milliliter	0.001	0.06 cubic inch		0.27 fluidram

Mass and Weight

Unit	Number of Grams	Approximate U.S. Equivalent
metric ton	1,000,000	1.1 tons
quintal	100,000	220.46 pounds
kilogram	1,000	2.2046 pounds
hectogram	100	3.527 ounces
dekagram	10	0.353 ounce
gram	1	0.035 ounce
decigram	0.10	1.543 grains
centigram	0.01	0.154 grain
milligram	0.001	0.015 grain

METRIC CONVERSION CHART — APPROXIMATIONS

When You Know	Multiply By	To Find
Length		
millimeters	0.04	inches
centimeters	0.4	inches
meters	3.3	feet
meters	1.1	yards
kilometers	0.6	miles
Area		
square centimeters	0.16	square inches
square meters	1.2	square yards
square kilometers	0.4	square miles
hectares (10,000m²)	2.5	acres
Mass and Weight		
grams	0.035	ounce
kilograms	2.2	pounds
tons (1000kg)	1.1	short tons

When You Know	Multiply By	To Find
	Volume	
milliliters	0.03	fluid ounces
liters	2.1	pints
liters	1.06	quarts
liters	0.26	gallons
cubic meters	35	cubic feet
cubic meters	1.3	cubic yards
	Temperature (exact)	
Celsius temp.	9/5, +32	Fahrenheit temp.
Fahrenheit temp.	−32, 5/9 x remainder	Celsius temp.

When You Know	Multiply By	To Find
	Length	
inches	2.5	centimeters
feet	30	centimeters
yards	0.9	meters
miles	1.6	kilometers
	Area	
square inches	6.5	square centimeters
square feet	0.09	square meters
square yards	0.8	square meters
square miles	2.6	square kilometers
acres	0.4	hectares
	Mass and Weight	
ounces	28	grams
pounds	0.45	kilograms
short tons (2000 lb)	0.9	tons
	Volume	
fluid ounces	30	milliliters
pints	0.47	liters
quarts	0.95	liters
gallons	3.8	liters
cubic feet	0.03	cubic meters
cubic yards	0.76	cubic meters

. PERIOD

The period is used:
1. To mark the end of a sentence or sentence fragment that is neither exclamatory nor interrogatory: *Lobsters are crustaceans. Do not be late.*
2. After some abbreviations: *U.S.A.; Dr.*
3. Before a decimal and between dollars and cents in figures: *.90 pounds; 14.5 feet; $9.95.*

? QUESTION MARK

The question mark is used:
1. To mark the end of a direct query, even if not in the form of a question: *"Did she do it?" he asked. Can the money be raised? is the question.*
2. To express uncertainty or doubt: *Pocahontas (1595?-1617), American Indian princess; The mail clerk said the book weighed 50 (?) pounds.*

: COLON

The colon is used:
1. To introduce a series: *Four items were sold: a painting, two sculptures, and a rare book.*
2. To introduce a clause or phrase that extends, illustrates, or amplifies preceding matter: *Forestry is not an outdoor sport: it is a science.*
3. To introduce formally any material that forms a complete sentence, question, or quotation: *A topic came up for discussion: Which monetary policy should be pursued?*
4. After a salutation in formal correspondence: *Dear Sir:*
5. In expressing clock time: *2:40.*
6. In Biblical and bibliographic references: *Luke 4:3; Boston: Houghton Mifflin Company.*
7. To separate book titles and subtitles: *The Strong Brown God: The Story of the Niger River.*
8. In ratios: *Mix oil and vinegar in the ratio 3:1.*

" QUOTATION MARKS

Double quotation marks are used:
1. To enclose direct quotations: *"Karen," asked Kathy, "why are you singing?"*
2. To enclose titles of speeches or lectures, articles, short poems, short stories, chapters of books, songs, short musical compositions, radio and TV programs: *a lecture entitled "The Atomic Era"; The article "The Gypsies" appeared in the last issue. She read Shirley Jackson's "The Lottery" and Keats's "Ode to a Grecian Urn." Review the chapter "Money and Banking." The chorus sang "God Bless America." We watched ABC's "Happy Days."*
3. To enclose coined words, slang expressions, or ordinary words, etc., used ironically or in some other arbitrary way: *references to the "imperial Presidency" of Richard Nixon; George Herman "Babe" Ruth; His report was "bunk."*

, COMMA

The comma is used:

1. To separate independent clauses joined by a coordinate or correlative conjunction (as *and, but, for, nor,* and *or*): *It snowed yesterday, and today the road is closed.*

2. To separate independent clauses not joined by a conjunction when the clauses are short, closely related, and have no commas within: *I came, I saw, I conquered.*

3. After a dependent clause that precedes the main clause: *If there is any error, please let us know.*

4. To set off a nonrestrictive clause, phrase, or word: *Joan Smith, who lives next door, is ill.* (But *not* in the case of a restrictive clause as in: *The girl who lives next door is ill.*)

5. To set off parenthetical expressions, whether words, phrases, or clauses: *Our host, Bill Martin, is an excellent cook.*

6. To set off words or phrases expressing contrast: *Mr. Smith, not Mr. Jones, was elected.*

7. To set off transitional words and expressions (as *in short, of course*) or conjunctive adverbs (as *however, consequently, therefore*): *We found, in short, many errors in his work. Your question, however, remained unanswered.*

8. After expressions that introduce an example or illustration (as *namely, i.e., for example*): *Some of the presidential candidates, i.e., Jackson, Church, Bayh, are also senators.*

9. To separate words, phrases, or clauses in a series: *Mary, Louise, and Rachel are sisters. He stalked out of the room, turned around, came back, and resumed the argument.*

10. To separate two words or figures that might otherwise be misunderstood: *To Mary, Louise was very kind. Instead of hundreds, thousands came.*

11. To separate two adjectives that modify the same noun and can be interchanged in position: *an eager, restless young man.* (But *not* in: *three silver spoons; a rare second chance.*)

12. To set off a short direct quotation: *He said, "Now or never."*

13. To set off a word or phrase in direct address: *Please go, Mary, I'm tired.*

14. To indicate the omission of a word or words: *Then we had much, now nothing.*

15. After a statement followed by a direct question: *You are sure, are you not?*

16. To set off items in dates, addresses, names of places: *She was born on June 5, 1936, at 64 Chestnut Street, Boston, Massachusetts.*

17. To separate a proper name from a title: *Philip Smith, Esq.*

18. After the salutation in informal correspondence: *Dear Mary,*

19. After the complimentary close of a letter: *Very truly yours,*

20. To separate an inverted name or phrase: *Jones, Edith.*

21. To separate thousands, millions, etc., in numbers of four or more digits: *5,256; 1,000,000.*